THE
UNIVERSITY COLLEGE
OF WALES
ABERYSTWYTH
1872–1972

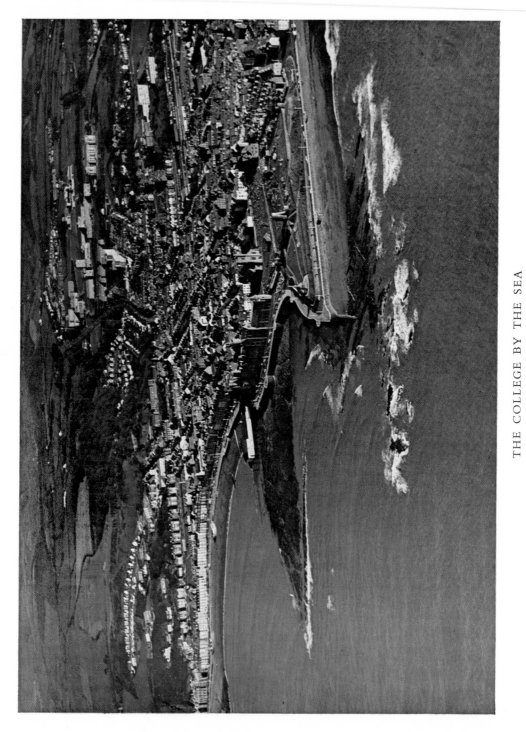

THE COLLEGE BY THE SEA

A general view of Aberystwyth: the old College building in the foreground, and the new campus on Penglais in the background

THE
UNIVERSITY COLLEGE
OF WALES
ABERYSTWYTH
1872–1972

BY

E. L. ELLIS

NID BYD BYD HEB WYBODAETH

CARDIFF
UNIVERSITY OF WALES PRESS
1972

ISBN 0 7083 0507 5

Printed in Great Britain
at the University Press, Oxford
by Vivian Ridler
Printer to the University

TO ALL
MEMBERS OF THE COLLEGE
PAST, PRESENT, AND
FUTURE

So many universities have been established by far-sighted benefactors, or by enlightened authority, but few can claim, with Aberystwyth, that they were founded in response to popular pressure.

From the earliest times, the people of Wales have had a deep respect for learning and scholarship and the sense of personal association with the University has persisted throughout the 100 years since the University College of Wales was founded at Aberystwyth.

I am naturally delighted that The Prince of Wales himself was able to spend some time at Aberystwyth and so to gain a better understanding of the feeling and life of Wales.

I am sure that this full-scale history of the College, which it has commissioned to mark the Centenary Year, will give much pleasure to a wide circle of readers, particularly in Wales, but also well beyond the boundaries of the Principality.

I find, somewhat to my surprise, that in the Centenary Year I complete a quarter of that time as Chancellor of the University of Wales. Even in that relatively short time there have been many changes and developments, but I can truthfully say that the University has never lost sight of its prime purpose to maintain the very highest standards of teaching and scholarship.

Philip

Introduction

AKNOWLEDGEABLE and skilled writer can describe the life of a single individual in a way that illuminates the history and character of a whole nation. The individual himself need not be of importance and could indeed be imaginary—but by describing the relationship between him and his environment the writer can shed new light on the political, social, and economic life of the time.

Since the life-story of an individual can be told in this way, how much richer a subject is provided by the history of a university college!

The foundation of a college calls for the investment of considerable resources of men and materials, and so requires significant discussion and decision-taking. Its teaching and research activities reflect the growth of knowledge in a large number of fields. The gifted men who make up its staff and governing bodies contribute not only to learning but to the general life of their time, while their personal lives are inevitably of great human interest. Then there are the successive generations of students—the ablest young people of their time—who spend their most formative years in the College before going on to play leading roles in society.

It was with such considerations in mind that the College decided that one of the most constructive ways in which it could celebrate its centenary would be to arrange for a suitably qualified member of its staff to write its history. The aim would be to do much more than bring together material likely to be of personal interest to those who knew the College, though they would surely find it absorbing. It would present a serious study of the foundation and development of the University College of Wales in relation to the general history of our times. It would, therefore, be of value not only to those who have been, or are, themselves connected with the College, but to all who are interested in the history of Wales or of education.

The choice of writer fell on Dr. E. L. Ellis, an old student of the College, who is a Senior Lecturer in the Department of History, and has specialized in modern British History. That the choice was a good one will be at once apparent to the reader.

Ben Bowen Thomas,

B. B. THOMAS

Goronwy Daniel

G. H. DANIEL

Preface

'**M**OST centenaries', according to A. J. P. Taylor in an encyclical dressed up as a book-review (*The Observer*, 30 May 1971), 'are drab affairs. Forgotten episodes are piously exhumed and then reburied after a few speeches.' He concedes that there are exceptions; some anniversaries retain their 'glory'. One such, at least for those on the Left in politics, was the centenary of the Paris Commune of 1871, which was the occasion for his typically acute gloss. The Commune, in the short-run anyway, was a failure; it soon became 'a shattered Utopia'.

The year 1972 is the centenary of another event, no doubt of more modest significance, which may also justly claim to have retained its glory: the foundation of the University College of Wales at Aberystwyth. The men who aspired to found a college of university status in Wales in the middle of the nineteenth century also seemed to most of their contemporaries to be hopeless visionaries, doomed to ludicrous failure. But limitless faith and great courage brought success as they could not to the Communards. In October 1872 the dream was partly realized when the College at Aberystwyth first opened its doors. Perhaps even the courage of the founders would have failed had they known the years of struggle that lay ahead. The history of the College is a romantic story of a slowly successful fight against the odds: against deep-seated prejudice and the indifference or hostility of the powerful; against the crushing burden of penury and the demoralizing intervention even of natural disaster. It is a tale well worth the telling, and the occasion of the Centenary is an appropriate time when it should be told at length.

The story has been recounted, in part, once before. *The College by the Sea*, which appeared in 1928, is, in the main, a fascinating anthology of reminiscences; a suitably unorthodox method of presenting a picture of a College which, in many respects, has always been unique. This present work lays no claim to supplant that book, which so marvellously encapsulated the ethos of the College in the first half-century of its existence. The only complaint the present writer has against *The College by the Sea* is that it pre-empted the obvious natural title for this Centenary history.

Among the many thousands who know and love the College there are those who sense some weakening of its particular pride, 'the Aber. spirit'. Perhaps this is no more than a settled conviction, fairly general among those of us whose student days are over, that things cannot possibly be as good as they were in our time. However this may be, it remains the duty of all friends of the College to nourish its best traditions. Aberystwyth has a great and colourful past: to understand whence we came may offer some small help to the charting of the future. At the very least it may be claimed, as *The Dragon* (xxxxiii. 166) asserted long ago, that 'to know the history of the College is to go far in the formation of a proper College sentiment'. It is with the strong conviction that this is indeed so that this particular version of the history of the College is offered for consideration.

I have many obligations to acknowledge. I am grateful to those former students of the College who wrote short accounts of their days at Aberystwyth for my benefit. Most of these contributions are acknowledged separately in the footnotes; I am no less grateful for the help of others whose observations are not directly cited. Many members of the different departments of the College allowed themselves to be badgered time and again with questions which must have tried their patience sorely on occasion. I am particularly indebted to Miss D. S. Meyler, Dr. R. F. Walker, and Dr. W. M. Jones and his colleagues in the Physics department for their help. Professor E. G. Bowen supplied the map of College property in the town and the graph which is included as Appendix F. I derived great profit from discussions with Mr. Arthur Pinsent, Mr. J. Morgan Jones, and Sir Ben Bowen Thomas, who also allowed me to see the draft of his short history of the College, which is to accompany this volume. I am grateful to Professor Harold Perkin for allowing me to see R. D. Laurie's manuscript 'History of the A.U.T.'. Mrs. T. I. Ellis gave me permission to use some manuscript letters in her possession; and Mrs. Ifor L. Evans provided information about her husband's upbringing and education, and allowed me to test the validity of my notions about Principal Evans against her unique knowledge.

I am deeply indebted to Mr. David Jenkins (who made some letters and the interesting manuscript Diary of T. Gwynn Jones available to me) and his staff at the National Library of Wales, especially Mr. Walter Morgan and Mr. R. W. MacDonald, for their generous assistance and limitless patience. I received help of a similar kind from the staff of the General Library of the College, where Mr. R. Brinkley responded unfailingly to my frequent pleas for assistance. My obligations to Dr. Huw Owen for his arrangement of the material in the College archives are spelt out elsewhere in this book.

Mr. Gwyn Jenkins rendered valuable assistance during the short periods when he acted as my research assistant, and, subsequently, Mr. David Egan, at a time of particular difficulty, came to my aid unofficially in the same capacity. Mr. R. S. Thomas helped to arrange the mountain of material that I had collected, and I received a great deal of assistance from several members of the staff at Pantycelyn. I have relied heavily on the infinite patience of Mr. D. H. Jenkins (formerly Secretary, now Personal Assistant to the Principal), whose rare quality has been fully appreciated by the last four Principals of the College. I have the greatest admiration for the skill of Miss Christine Chapman who typed a manuscript which, more often than not, had to be deciphered rather than read. I have derived great benefit from the encouragement and criticism of Mr. David Steeds, Mr. J. H. Morris, and Professor S. H. F. Johnston, who read the whole of my typescript. I wish to thank members of my family and certain friends whose support sustained me during a period of illness when I was engaged on this book.

Finally, my greatest obligations are to Principal Thomas Parry and the late Mr. Maelgwyn Davies, who first suggested that I should be invited to write this history, and to the members of the Council of the College for endorsing their recommendation. It is an honour of which I am duly sensible.

Pantycelyn, Aberystwyth
January 1972

Contents

List of Illustrations

Abbreviations

Add. MSS.	Additional Manuscripts.
B.M.	British Museum.
Bodl.	Bodleian Library.
C.A.	College Archives, University College of Wales, Aberystwyth.
D.N.B.	The Dictionary of National Biography.
D.W.B.	The Dictionary of Welsh Biography.
Iwan Morgan	*The College by the Sea* (ed. Iwan Morgan, Aberystwyth, 1928).
N.L.W.	National Library of Wales, Aberystwyth.
O.S.A.	Aberystwyth Old Students' Association.
Parl. Debates	Hansard's *Parliamentary Debates* (3rd series).
P.R.O.	Public Record Office.
S.R.C.	Students' Representative Council.
Trans. Cymm.	Transactions of the Honourable Society of Cymmrodorion.
U.C.N.W. Bangor	Library of the University College of North Wales, Bangor.
G. Lib.	Library of the University College of Wales, Aberystwyth.
U.G.C.	University Grants Committee.

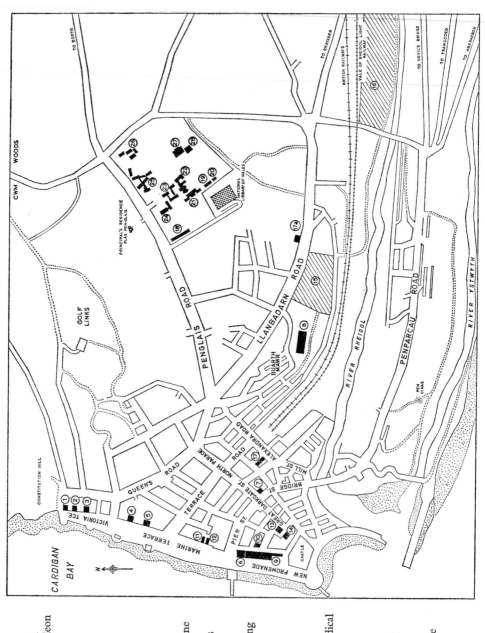

1. Alexandra Hall
2. Alexandra Hall Annexe, Hafodunos and Clarendon
3. Plynlymon Hall and Caerleon
4. Ceredigion Hall
5. Carpenter Hall
6. Theological College
7. Padarn Hall
8. Chemistry Department
9. Main College Buildings, English and Music Departments
10. History Department
11. German and Extra-Mural Departments, and 12 Marine Terrace
12. Careers and Dental Offices
13. Students' Union
14. Students' Union Annexe
15. Main Sports Field (including Old Gymnasium)
16. Blaendolau Playing Fields
17. Faculty of Education
17a. Dairy Building

Penglais Campus

18. Pantycelyn (including Medical Centre)
19. Sports Hall
20. Swimming Pool
21. Biology Building
22. Physical Sciences Building
23. Llandinam Building
24. Rural Sciences Building
25. Penbryn Halls of Residence
26. Neuadd Cwrt Mawr
27. Great Hall
28. New Students' Union

I

'The Day of Small Beginnings'[1]

THE struggle for Welsh national identity and the striving for educational opportunity have almost always gone hand in hand. It is not an accident that the first seemingly serious attempt to establish universities in the Principality occurred during the brief period in the early fifteenth century when, under the leadership of Owain Glyndŵr, the last self-styled Prince of Wales, numbers of the Welsh fought a war of liberation from English rule. For a time Glyndŵr's rebellion had its successes, and he quickly showed that he was very much more than a momentarily successful but limited chieftain-guerrilla with his eye set merely on loot and quick returns. He attracted to his side men of ability and standing; he sought alliances with the French, the Scots, and the Irish, and he had plans for consolidating his independent Principality on sound foundations. By the so-called 'Pennal policy' of 1406, Glyndŵr and his entourage aimed at a bargain with the French-sponsored Pope (or perhaps rather anti-Pope) at Avignon. In return for Welsh recognition the anti-Pope was expected to make several concessions: among other things, the Welsh Church was to have a separate metropolitan identity under Welsh not English secular control; and, of chief interest for this present purpose, two universities were to be established, one in North and one in South Wales, at centres to be decided subsequently.[2]

Glyndŵr recognized that an independent Welsh state would need a trained political, ecclesiastical, and administrative élite which universities alone could supply. Practical necessity, not a mere vainglorious desire for the trappings of independence, prompted his sponsorship of Welsh universities. But, unfortunately for the future of Welsh higher education, it was not to be; Glyndŵr was defeated and later mysteriously disappeared, and with him went all hope of the early establishment of a Welsh university.[3]

Thereafter Wales was made to feel to the full the rigour of defeat and subjugation: formal political annexation to England followed in due course; the Welsh

---

[1] H. J. Fleure, 'An Old Student Looks at the College', *Trans. Cymm.* (1955), p. 63.

[2] It is evident that even Glyndŵr, who showed an exceptional military awareness of the difficulties of Welsh geography, had no snap-answer to the problem of location.

[3] J. E. Lloyd, *Owen Glendower* (1931), pp. 119–22, and Glanmor Williams, *The Welsh Church from Conquest to Reformation* (1962), pp. 210–26.

Church became increasingly the Church in Wales, dominated and emasculated by alien influences; ambitious Welshmen with an eye to the main chance quickly learned the lesson of the times that, if they were to prosper and grow modestly great, they had better set up as *ersatz* Englishmen and serve, or at any rate not openly oppose, the English crown. Nor was this merely a matter of individual enterprise. The emerging Welsh squirearchy, and especially their more successful members who achieved noble rank, became more and more assimilated to their English equivalents in manners, religion, and language. The Welsh had begun to lose most of their natural leaders, and were increasingly left to endure as best they could the legal marks of inferiority and contempt, and the neglect that was the inevitable lot of an economically backward and remote part of the kingdom.[4]

For two centuries or more, in these circumstances, there was no hope that Glyndŵr's early initiative would be followed up. Until recent times, colleges and universities customarily owed their foundation to the largesse of kings, bishops, or inordinately wealthy peers and commoners who looked to posterity for some sort of fame. But no British monarch, not even the partly Welsh Tudors (other, perhaps, than Queen Elizabeth who incorporated Jesus College, Oxford), had any concern for the higher education of their Welsh subjects; and such rich Welshmen with a taste for educational patronage as there were, looked beyond Offa's Dyke for the objects of their benefaction. As for the Church, it never before the nineteenth century conceded that Wales and the Welsh language posed special educational or other problems.

Only in exceptional circumstances, therefore, would a further possibility of a Welsh university arise. These were provided by the Cromwellian rebellion and the consequent temporary supplanting of traditional authorities. In the 1650s, three men of varying degrees of Puritan commitment raised again the suggestion of a Welsh college. Dr. John Ellis, one-time Fellow of Jesus College, Oxford, currently the moderate Puritan rector of Dolgellau, and John Lewis, Cardiganshire squireen and Presbyterian pamphleteer, responded warmly to a proposal in favour of 'a college with academical privileges for Wales' made by Richard Baxter, the celebrated Presbyterian divine.[5] Despite the relatively modest status of some of its sponsors, the proposal was, in the short run at any rate, not entirely a forlorn hope. The Puritans were enthusiastic for education: Cromwell's Privy Council in 1656 endorsed the founding of a college for the North at Durham endowed from Church revenues; in Wales, between 1649 and 1653, the Parliamentary Commissioners, led by the regicide Major-General Harrison, established a con-

---

[4] All this was, of course, a long, slow, often confused and contradictory process extending over several centuries. It may most easily be followed in the short specialist essays in *Wales Through the Ages* (ed. A. J. Roderick, 2 vols., 1959).

[5] This interesting correspondence has been published by G. F. Nuttall in Merionethshire Hist. and Rec. Soc. *Journal*, II, ii (1954).

siderable number of schools.[6] During the 1640s Baxter had vainly tried to interest Humphrey Mackworth, Governor of Shrewsbury, in the idea of a Welsh college; subsequently he sought to enlist the support of James Berry, Major-General for Wales, who, of course, had direct access to high places.

Berry appears to have promised Baxter 'his best assistance', but there is no surviving evidence of an actual approach to the Lord Protector. Meanwhile, Baxter and his friends were open-eyed about the chief difficulties, and their appraisal of prospects anticipates some of the problems which had to be solved later by the successful founders of a university in Wales. 'The want is money', wrote Baxter at the outset; and, undismayed by the refusal of assistance from a wealthy Shrewsbury man with no direct heirs and reputedly worth £40,000, he optimistically believed that a capital sum of £1,000 and an annual income of £200–300 would serve to establish a college for a hundred students. Once started, such a college could not fail for lack of support, 'for many will give to such a work when they see it in a hopeful way, that will not begin it'. Baxter thus confidently pinned his hopes on private endowment and he did not doubt that Cromwell and Parliament would license such a foundation. For all his goodwill towards the Welsh ('his love to our nation', as Ellis put it), Baxter's purpose in all this was to enable some of the benighted Welsh to learn English. Naturally enough, therefore, he proposed that the college should be set up 'a little within the verge of England', at Shrewsbury, where there was already a considerable school which would be a useful preparatory academy for the college.

John Ellis, a Merionethshire Welshman, was prepared to accept the arguments in favour of Shrewsbury, though in fact he would have preferred to establish the college in 'some equidistant town' between North and South Wales, such as Machynlleth, Cardigan, or, anticipating the nineteenth century, Aberystwyth. Ellis looked to the tithe moneys of Wales for financial support and he raised thus early the possibility of a 'contribution' from the Welsh people at large which, as he wrote to Lewis, 'would not be much upon the thirteen counties'. His former Oxford experience persuaded Ellis that the two ancient universities would certainly resist the proposed foundation, but he was confident that the Almighty could 'make way through all difficulties'; and, perhaps in case the mysterious ways of Providence were unduly slow, he relied on the more immediate summary power of Cromwell, whose ancestors came 'as they say, from Wales'.[7]

John Lewis had already anticipated the expected opposition of Oxbridge with the argument (which is to be heard again later) that a new Welsh college involved not 'the least entrenchment' on the privileges of the ancient universities to which

[6] C. E. Whiting, *The University of Durham, 1832–1932* (1932), pp. 16–29. H. P. Roberts, 'Nonconformist Academies in Wales, 1662–1862', *Trans. Cymm.* (1928–9), pp. 3–4.

[7] All these quotations are from letters by Baxter and Ellis to Lewis printed in Nuttall, loc. cit., pp. 130–3.

it would necessarily be 'subordinate' and 'derivative'.[8] Ten years before, in an earlier plea for a college in Wales, Lewis had countered Oxbridge opposition with the argument (which, also, is to be used many times again later) that for every one Welsh student able to afford 'the charge and distance' of the ancient universities, there were three whose means were sufficient only to meet the expense of a much more modest college education nearer home.[9]

In fact, nothing came of all this. If the Commonwealth, or some such similar unorthodox regime, had survived for a longer period of years, a college might well have been established in Wales in the seventeenth century. As it was, Cromwell's death ended the existence of the Durham college, and Baxter's maltreatment after 1660 indicates that, had his college ever in fact been set up, it would certainly have received short shrift from the restored traditional authorities.

With the proprieties thus restored, Wales, on the surface at least, fell back into quietude. The processes of social and economic change already briefly outlined continued steadily. The Welsh aristocracy and greater gentry prospered, looked ever more naturally to London, or at any rate England, and became more and more divorced from the mass of the people. The lesser gentry (for centuries their pedigrees had been more impressive than their rent-rolls) fell on harder times and often sank from ownership into embittered tenancy; or, if this ultimate in social and economic failure were avoided, they aped the attitudes of their more successful fellows in order to maintain at least the semblance of their former status.

The eighteenth-century Church in Wales was in a sorry case. Sir Thomas Phillips, himself a strong Churchman, catalogued in scholarly detail the besetting weaknesses that devitalized the Welsh Church: extreme poverty, alienation of revenues, neglect, pluralism, absenteeism, nepotism, an inability to respond to relatively rapid population changes, and, perhaps least easily remediable quickly, a body of clergy all too many of whom could not speak fluently the preferred language of the majority of their parishioners.[10]

For those with eyes to see, there were plenty of warning signs for the Church in Wales before 1800. The older nonconformity had made no great impact on Wales. But, during the eighteenth century, the Church failed to come effectively to terms with the spiritual, emotional, and educational forces represented by men such as Griffith Jones, Howell Harris, Daniel Rowlands, William Williams, and, later, Thomas Charles; and the result of this, early in the nineteenth century, was the reluctant separation from the Church of the Welsh or Calvinistic Methodists, and their astonishingly rapid growth in numbers, coupled with a very considerable increase in the membership of the other Welsh Nonconformist bodies.

[8] *Some seasonable and moderate thoughts in order to the . . . promoting the affaires of Religion, and the Gospel, especially in Wales* (1656), p. 30.

[9] *Contemplations upon these Times, or, The Parliament explained to Wales* (1646), p. 33.

[10] Sir Thomas Phillips, *Wales: the language, social conditions, moral character, and religious opinions of the people* (1849), passim.

By the middle of the nineteenth century, the Church, for all its established position, claimed the allegiance of only a minority—perhaps a quarter or a fifth—of the Welsh people, though it still retained overwhelmingly the allegiance of the aristocracy, gentry, and the well-to-do generally.

Of course, some of the leaders of the Church tried to counter these alarming tendencies. In particular, Thomas Burgess, Bishop of St. David's, initiated long-overdue reforms in his diocese almost as soon as he had been enthroned in 1803. He licensed four grammar schools to train ordinands and, in 1812, began to collect money to found a college. Burgess recognized that it was vitally important to improve the quality of his clergy and, thereby, in the longer run perhaps, begin the missionary reclamation of the people lost to nonconformity. Burgess had verve, great energy, and a highly persuasive tongue: he coaxed a good site and a donation of £1,000 out of J. S. Harford, a local Anglican squire; Burgess himself contributed—annually—a tenth of his income and, thus encouraged, many of his clergy followed suit from their meagre stipends. The Bishop even managed to talk down the customary Oxbridge 'dog in the manger' objection to new educational foundations and some money was forthcoming even from that source. In 1822 the foundation stone was laid of the new college, St. David's, at Lampeter. Unfortunately, Bishop Burgess was translated in 1825 to Salisbury and his successor lacked the same driving purpose. However, as an Anglican foundation, St. David's had powerful friends in high places. Lord Liverpool's government made a grant of £6,000; King George IV gave £1,000 from his Privy Purse and made over to the College the income from six livings in the diocese; and this combined sum was supplemented by an annual Treasury grant of £400 until it amounted to £950 a year. By 1827 new buildings at a cost of £20,000 were completed and, in the following year, the College was incorporated by royal charter 'for the reception and education of persons destined for Holy Orders'; as an earnest of intentions, it is to be noticed that in the first public advertisement of the College, the Welsh language headed the list of subjects to be studied.[11]

Despite this promising beginning, St. David's College did not at first realize the hopes of its friends, especially Bishop Burgess. Certainly the number of students (an average of about sixty) in the opening years was encouraging and their calibre, surprisingly enough, was reasonably good; moreover, several useful scholarships were annexed to the College and in a very short time a valuable library was built up. The teaching staff was small but not initially inadequate. But from the outset the College had to be run on a shoe-string; fees for the typically poor student had to be kept as low as possible; the initial endowment was barely adequate and, within a few years, the College was in serious financial difficulties. Perhaps even more important was the inertia of the first Principal (whose careful

---

[11] Sir Thomas Phillips, op. cit., pp. 315–17. H. K. Archdale, *St. David's College, Lampeter: its past, present, and future* (Lampeter, 1952), pp. 10–12.

conservation of his energies enabled him to survive as head of the College for half a century), and the absence of interest and support from the next two bishops of St. David's, whose vigorous exercise of authority as Visitors of the College was crucial to its success.

The Charity Commissioners in their *Report* in 1836 frankly recognized that the College was in difficulties and stressed that the inability to award a degree was one especially crippling weakness. However, gradually things improved. In 1847 the Vice-Chancellors of Oxford and Cambridge agreed to appoint external examiners, a step which considerably enhanced the College's status and prefaced a certain amount of off-handed Oxbridge sponsorship of the new foundation. Encouraged by the successful Church foundation of the University of Durham in the 1830s, Lampeter's friends began to petition the crown for similar degree-granting powers. For years these efforts were unavailing; not least, perhaps, because Bishop Thirlwall of St. David's inexplicably refused to support the plea. However, in 1852, a second royal charter awarded the right to grant a bachelor's degree in divinity and, in the following year, enabling legislation was passed which sought to strengthen the secular side of the College and thereby to attract numbers of lay students to the College. Finally, in 1865, there was a third charter which empowered it to grant bachelor's degrees in arts and an additional endowment of £1,500 was arranged. It is evident that, for all its poverty and unfashionable Welsh location, St. David's College enjoyed powerful advantages from its Establishment respectability. The political climate of the times was not unfavourable and there seems little reason to doubt that, had its case been presented with the pioneering energy shown by Bishop Burgess, St. David's College would have had the chance to develop in those years into a small Welsh utility-model Oxbridge; indeed, the enabling legislation of 1853 had specifically suggested that Lampeter and the Church establishments at Brecon should be united to form a university.[12]

Lampeter, of course, was not the only theological college in Wales. Dissenters were debarred from Oxford and Cambridge and were often reluctant to attend such grammar schools as Wales possessed, mainly because they, too, were largely in the grip of the Church. In these circumstances, enterprising nonconformist teachers set up private-venture academies which often flourished during the working life of the founding tutors, who were sometimes men with a real gift for teaching. The nonconformist sects also had to make provision for the higher training of their ministerial candidates and, to answer this need, the Independents established a college at Brecon, while the Baptists, with notable economy, built

---

[12] Sir Thomas Phillips, op. cit., pp. 318–29. Archdale, op. cit., pp. 10–29. For Thirlwall's dissociation, see Iwan Morgan, 'A Preliminary Investigation into the Origins and Development of the University Movement in Wales . . . in the period 1804–89' (unpublished M.A. thesis, University of Wales, June 1929), p. 17.

one college at Pontypool in 1836 for less than £2,000 and, later on, added another at Haverfordwest for a slightly higher sum. The Calvinistic Methodists, after some wrangling over sites, in which Aberystwyth again rated consideration, eventually took over a preparatory school opened at Bala in 1837 by Dr. Lewis Edwards and transformed it into a college. A few years later, a smaller Welsh Methodist College was also opened at Trefecca. In some respects the most interesting of these denominational foundations was the so-called Presbyterian College at Carmarthen. Neither its small staff nor its student body was restricted to any particular denomination and, for a time at any rate in the nineteenth century, it achieved a higher standard than the other colleges.[13]

Every one of these institutions lived precariously on the margin of penury.[14] Their teaching staffs were ill-paid and pitifully few in number: two tutors apiece for the Baptist colleges, only three at the more ambitious Carmarthen institution, while at Trefecca David Charles laboured heroically alone for twenty years. Academic standards were inevitably low with the handful of tutors ranging over an impossibly large number of subjects; moreover, many of the students were raw, ill-prepared country lads who were badly handicapped by their initial limited knowledge of English, the medium, curiously, of most instruction. Despite these crippling disadvantages the dissenting colleges did at least supply the sects with a steady stream of ministers and afforded a modest form of higher education to numbers of Welsh students. Some of the tutors were outstanding scholars (the name of Lewis Edwards inevitably springs to mind) who effectively set the stamp of their learning on their abler pupils who often subsequently achieved considerable eminence. Of course, there were not lacking suggestions that the dissenting colleges should unite together to overcome their individual weakness.[15] But this was a forlorn hope, for the Welsh denominations were divided by at best wary, at worst bitter, suspicion of each other that all too often erupted into open hostility.

However, the nonconformist denominations in Wales were occasionally driven to unite in defence against attacks made indiscriminately upon dissent as a whole. One such striking instance occurred in the 1840s. An apparent attempt by the government to increase Church control of the education of the poor, clearly for missionary purposes, provoked a flurry of nonconformist activity in establishing British (that is, non-Church) schools in North Wales, making use of state grants that were available on certain conditions for this purpose.[16] In South Wales the nonconformists, scorning aid from the State, which was regarded by many of them

---

[13] H. P. Roberts, loc. cit., pp. 60–92.

[14] Lewis Edwards at one point had to threaten resignation to shame the connection into a more generous support of the Bala College.

[15] B. T. Williams, *The Desirableness of a University for Wales* (1853), p. 13.

[16] For Welsh nonconformist suspicions of the government's purpose, see Hugh Owen to the Revd. Roger Edwards, 7 September 1846, Bangor (Yale) MSS. 41, No. 54, and the evidence of nonconformist ministers in *Aberdare Report, Minutes*, pp. 564, 680.

simply as the secular arm of the Church of England, set up many voluntary schools. In reply, the National Society, the educational agency of the Church, stepped up its activities in Wales, and the rivalry of the two Societies, British and National, led to a government inquiry into the state of education in the Principality.[17]

The Instructions (written by the great Kay-Shuttleworth) issued to the Commissioners drew their attention to the need for courtesy and discretion in their handling of witnesses and for a scrupulous regard for the susceptibilities of the religious communities.[18] Unfortunately, the Commissioners, three young barristers marking time in their profession, were astonishingly ill-equipped for the task before them: they were hostile to dissent, knew little of schools and teaching, and did not understand a word of Welsh, though it is fair to say that they had the proxy assistance of some ill-chosen Welsh-speaking aides. Not surprisingly, the Commissioners leaned heavily on Church witnesses (for every dissenter consulted, there were three Anglicans) and in their final *Report*, these cocksure young men exceeded their brief by adding gratuitously a variety of moral strictures on the Welsh, which provoked an outraged reaction, especially from the nonconformists who joined together in regarding the *Report* as a Church-inspired malevolent libel on the Welsh people—*Brad y Llyfrau Gleision*, 'The Treason of the Blue Books'.[19]

But interested calumnies aside, the 1847 *Report* did catalogue in undeniable detail the appalling contemporary state of Welsh education generally, and stimulated a considerably increased interest in the subject at all levels among Welshmen of all religious persuasions. William Williams, Welsh-born former M.P. for Coventry, whose almost single-handed promptings in the House had led to the appointment of the 1847 Commission, followed up the publication of the *Report* in 1848 with two pamphlets by way of commentary upon it.[20] In the second of these tracts, he took up again a theme which he had already developed at length in the Commons—the disparity between the generous financial provision made by the government for education in Scotland and Ireland, and the niggardliness of similar expenditure in England and especially in Wales. Moreover, he went on to argue that it could be an 'inestimable . . . blessing' to Wales if a college (including provision for teacher training) similar to the Queen's Colleges recently set up in Ireland were established in Wales.[21]

[17] David Williams, *A History of Modern Wales* (1950), pp. 253–5.

[18] Instructions, pp. i–iv. *Reports of the Commissioners of Inquiry into the State of Education in Wales* (1848).

[19] There is an excellent examination of the *Report* and the subsequent controversy by D. Salmon, 'The Story of a Welsh Educational Commission, 1846–7', *Trans. Cymm.* (1913). Sir Thomas Phillips, whose vigorous Churchmanship has already been instanced, was provoked by the *Report* into writing the book on Wales cited above.

[20] Williams, an engaging and interesting character, is noticed more fully below, pp. 14–15.

[21] *A Second Letter on the present defective state of Education in Wales* (1848), p. 8.

Williams was not the only Welsh Churchman living in England who advocated such a course. Indeed, there is some evidence suggesting that he had been anticipated by that curious body, the Association of Welsh Clergy in the West Riding of Yorkshire. This was a society of expatriate clerics, some of them of considerable ability, who left Wales in disgust at the inveterate preference for Englishmen shown in nominations to higher offices in the Church there. They met annually on, appropriately enough, St. David's Day to discuss matters concerning the Church in Wales and the general welfare of the Principality. They published pamphlets and regularly sent petitions to the government on the subjects which engaged their attention; and it would appear that, from at least the early 1840s, they had regularly petitioned for the setting up of a university in Wales. They did not envisage an Anglican monopoly for they recognized that Wales was predominantly nonconformist and they looked to a broadly based institution to answer the needs of Churchmen and chapel-goers alike.[22]

Much the same motif runs through an interesting pamphlet, *The Desirableness of a University for Wales*, written in 1853 by Benjamin Thomas Williams, a young Welshman who graduated in that year from Glasgow University. Williams had been educated initially at the Presbyterian College at Carmarthen where he became a Unitarian. Not prepared to bend his principles to circumvent the Oxbridge religious tests, and with no great opinion of the London degree, he, therefore, made the long trek north to Scotland. Williams pleaded strongly for Welsh national unity. 'Animosity and party strife', he wrote, must be put aside, otherwise the Principality would soon fall entirely under the 'predominance and sway of the Saxon race'. He took it for granted that any university in the Principality must be unsectarian, for 'any sectarian Institution in Wales is necessarily not a Welsh institution'. This at one blow disposed of any claim St. David's College might have to form the core of a new university; in any case, St. David's (and the individual dissenting colleges for that matter) 'was not catholic enough' in its teaching to partake of 'the universality of a university'.

On the other hand, Williams believed that a merely secular institution along the lines of University College, London, would not suit the Welsh, who were too profoundly religious to accept a Godless institution. His formula for answering these difficulties was ingenious: he suggested that each of the sects, as well as the Church, should maintain a Divinity hall at the seat of the university; students would separate for their work in theology, but otherwise would study together the full range of subjects, including law and medicine, appropriate to a university. Despite the apparent uncompromising quality of his dissent, Williams was prepared to make large concessions to the Church in order to engage the 'patronage of liberal and enlightened bishops and clergy', without whose support a Welsh

---

[22] There is a useful discussion (somewhat vitiated by overstatement) of the work of this Association in Iwan Morgan's thesis, pp. 31–43.

university, in his opinion, could not possibly succeed. He would concede a certain precedence to the Anglican Divinity hall and, by inference, it would seem that he argued for an Anglican Principal who, if a layman, would be at least 'an honorary Professor of Divinity'.[23]

It is evident, therefore, that, notwithstanding the seemingly paralysing discord of religious divisions in Wales, there were men drawn from different sides who were prepared to accept the logic of the Welsh situation and to go to considerable lengths to bring about an effective national unity on the university question.[24] But this was more easily done on paper than in practice; and when at long last Welshmen did go beyond words, they found themselves faced with unexpected difficulties great enough to make the stoutest heart quail.

The new departure came in 1854. In April of that year a conference was held in London of some few distinguished London Welshmen and certain eminent Welsh dissenting ministers who came up for this purpose. It was an interesting gathering of the new type of leader which the Welsh people, shorn as has been seen of the natural leadership of their largely Anglicized peers and gentry, had discovered for themselves. Many of these men were of comparatively humble origin, but had made their way in the world by one route and another; the London Welshmen usually through success in business, medicine, the law, and politics. The immense authority of the great dissenting ministers was based on the respect, amounting to little short of veneration, in which they were held by their congregations: 'the Welsh people', wrote Henry Richard, 'know that they owe much—almost everything—to their preachers'.[25] Present at the conference in the house of Thomas Charles, a distinguished London surgeon, son of a great Calvinistic Methodist family, were three future Welsh Liberal M.P.s: E. G. Salisbury, Richard Davies, and George Osborne Morgan. Pre-eminent among the nonconformist leaders present were Dr. Lewis Edwards of Bala, his brother-in-law, David Charles of Trefecca College, the Revd. Henry Rees, and Samuel Roberts (S.R.), the well-known Independent minister.

But the most important figure at the meeting was the man who had called it

[23] B. T. Williams, op. cit., pp. 33, 15–16, 18–23. After flying this early kite, Williams applied himself for thirty years to nourishing a distinguished legal and political career; however, years later, he reappears prominently in the story of Aberystwyth College. Hugh Owen said later (*Aberdare Report, Minutes of Evidence*, p. 12) that for sixteen years he was wholly ignorant 'of the existence of Williams' pamphlet and was thus deprived of the valuable co-operation of its learned author'.

[24] For other nonconformist statements of willingness to co-operate at this time, see *Y Traethodydd* (1848), p. 62, *Yr Haul* (1849), pp. 127–9 and *Y Drysorfa Gunnulleidfaol* (1849), p. 61, which called for '*chwareu teg i bawb o blant Gwalia*' ('fair play for all the children of Wales'). I am indebted to Mr. B. L. Davies for drawing my attention to these references.

[25] C. S. Miall, *The Life of Henry Richard* (1889), pp. 153–4. The aggressively Anglican Dean H. T. Edwards told Gladstone that Henry Rees the great Calvinistic Methodist minister, who was present at the meeting in 1854, 'wore no mitre and enjoyed no revenue, but he was, for all that, in his day the successor of St. David in his authority over the religious mind of his country'. H. T. Edwards, *Wales and the Welsh Church* (1889), p. 160.

PLATE 1

Sir Hugh Owen (1804–81)

into being and whose paper on the Welsh university question provided the basis of discussion by the conference. This was, of course, Hugh Owen, the man who more than anyone else was to be responsible for translating the hope of a Welsh college into reality. Hugh Owen was an Anglesey man of little formal education who had come up to London in his early twenties and made a considerable career in the Civil Service; he more than measured up to Edwin Chadwick's taxing administrative standards and ultimately became Clerk to the Poor Law Commissioners. Owen clearly had ability, but, perhaps more important, he had a fixity of purpose that was proof against almost any discouragement. He was not a particularly original thinker, but he had a strongly practical cast to his mind that enabled him to give effect to other men's notions; moreover, he had a demoniacal energy almost the equal of that of Gladstone, and an unflagging interest in philanthropic and educational works that leap-frogged from one good cause to another, especially those of benefit to Wales.

It was Hugh Owen who had taken the lead by public exhortation and organizing flair in stimulating the flurry of school-building by the British and Foreign Schools Society in North Wales in the 1840s. In the same period he was active in educational work on behalf of the deaf and dumb children in Wales. Now, in the 1850s, he turned his attention to the question of Welsh higher education. Unlike many nonconformists in Wales (and at least one, Samuel Roberts, at the 1854 meeting), Hugh Owen had no inhibitions about utilizing public funds for educational purposes. And it was to Ireland, where the Queen's Colleges and Queen's University had recently been established on the firm foundation of public money and continuing Treasury support, that he turned for his model for Wales.[26] The hope was (vain as it turned out) that the Queen's Colleges scheme would mask the destructive religious animosities of Ireland. Hugh Owen believed that a similar set of institutions would overcome, or at least allay, the bitter sectarian rivalries that all too often divided Wales.

The 1854 conference accepted Owen's ideas at least to the extent of appointing a subcommittee of three (Osborne Morgan, Salisbury, and, inevitably, Hugh Owen himself) to draw up a general scheme for a Welsh university on the Irish model. Subsequently, the subcommittee produced a plan called 'The Outline of the Constitution of Proposed Welsh Queen's Colleges', but, at that point, the movement came to a halt.[27] Unfortunately, there is no detailed record of this private meeting, and the reasons for what looks like a false start have to be inferred. Clearly, Owen's plan rested crucially upon government money, and it may be that more than one of those present at the meeting had continuing scruples about accepting such suspect patronage, as they regarded it. Possibly, as one of the

[26] T. W. Moody, 'The Irish University Question of the 19th Century', *History*, vol. xliii, no. 148, 95–100, succinctly explains these Irish arrangements.
[27] See Appendix no. 1, *Aberdare Report*, p. 865.

participants subsequently admitted, the plan was premature and too ambitious.[28] At any rate, later experience with niggardly governments was to show that the problems posed by Ireland exerted a leverage on the attention of British cabinets that Wales could never equal in the nineteenth century, or, for that matter, ever subsequently. In any case, the outbreak of the Crimean War in 1854, and the onset soon afterwards of serious difficulties in India, killed off whatever slight hope there was of immediate government assistance. It is probable, too, that another order of priority was suggested at the conference; in particular, the need for more and better trained teachers for the existing primary schools in Wales. At all events, for several years the Welsh university question lay fallow, and Hugh Owen (who was never the man to remain long inactive) and several of his friends turned their attention to other possibilities.[29]

In July 1856 a meeting was held at Rhyl (following up a preliminary session at Bangor in April) of about thirty men known to be interested in 'the cause of education on liberal principles' in North Wales. The circular of invitation to attend was signed by the Revd. John Phillips, Hugh Owen's energetic aide in the British and Foreign Society's school-building drive in North Wales some years before, and among those present at the meeting were Richard Davies, the Revd. Henry Rees, E. G. Salisbury, and, predictably, Hugh Owen, all of whom had participated in the 1854 conference. At a later date other names, already or soon to be familiar in the story of the establishment of the first Welsh University College, appear on the list of members of the committee whose activity led finally to the founding of Bangor Normal College. The early minutes of this committee record the activity on its behalf of Dr. Lewis Edwards, Morgan Lloyd, Thomas Gee, Hugh Pugh, John Jenkins of Llanidloes, and J. Foulkes Roberts of Manchester, all of whom are to be important later in the history of Aberystwyth College.

These manuscript minutes show clearly Hugh Owen's central importance (not far short of dominance) in the committee's work. Inevitably, he was elected honorary secretary and, of all the people involved, he alone was ever-present in London and in the various towns in North Wales where committee meetings were held. He wrote the Welsh and English versions of the appeal for funds; he negotiated on behalf of the committee with the Education Department; he was the link with Welsh M.P.s, and he took rather more than his share of the public speaking necessary to drum up support throughout North Wales. Finally, it is to be noticed that most of the crucial decisions (including the choice of Bangor for the site of the College) were made on Hugh Owen's proposition. He was clearly a first-rate man of business: adroit, assiduous, painstaking, with a good eye for essentials and a remarkable talent for button-holing the half-interested and

[28] Osborne Morgan, M.P., in his speech (*Cambrian News*, 18 October 1872) at the opening of the College at Aberystwyth.
[29] See Hugh Owen's evidence to the Aberdare Committee, *Minutes of Evidence*, p. 12.

engaging their enthusiasm. He was to need all these talents and more in the much greater task that lay ahead of him.[30]

For some years the greater part of Hugh Owen's attention was absorbed by the affairs of the new Normal College and a scheme which he worked out to set up a Social Science Section of the National Eisteddfod.[31] The university question was brought to life again late in 1862, not perhaps as one would expect, by Hugh Owen, but by Dr. Thomas Nicholas, then a tutor at the Carmarthen Presbyterian College. The year 1862 was the bi-centenary of the high-principled withdrawal from the Church of England of nearly 1,000 Presbyterian and Congregationalist divines who could not accept the post-Restoration definitions of the Act of Uniformity. Dr. David Thomas, a Congregational minister at Stockwell, had the idea that the best way to celebrate the bi-centenary would be to establish a college in Wales. He suggested this in a letter to the *Cambria Daily Leader*, a newspaper owned by his son; soon afterwards, Thomas, if his own testimony is to be believed, met Dr. Nicholas and set him 'ablaze' with enthusiasm for the idea. At any rate, Nicholas wrote six long letters to the *Cambria Daily Leader* which were later published (at the expense of William Williams, M.P.) as a pamphlet entitled 'Middle and High Schools and a University for Wales.'[32]

Nicholas believed that for far too long the Welsh had looked to their past, 'its glories and its humiliations', and it was high time they rid themselves of their 'crestfallen spirit', which was the 'sure mark of a subjugated, enervated race'. Despite this trumpet call to national action, Nicholas's exclusive concern at this stage was for the education of the small middle class in Wales; he held that recent advances in popular education sufficiently catered for the needs of the poor. He advocated two colleges, one in the north and one in the south, which would combine to form a university for Wales; he was prepared to take either London University or the Irish Queen's Colleges as his model and he was quite certain that, whatever the voluntaryist objections about accepting government financial aid, 'university education without it is totally impossible'. In actual fact, Nicholas gave the highest priority to the establishment of secondary schools, but it was his university proposals which attracted attention, not least that of Hugh Owen.[33] At Owen's suggestion, Nicholas read a paper on his proposals to the Social Science Section of the Swansea National Eisteddfod in the summer of 1863, and in October

[30] U.C.W. G. Lib. Hugh Owen MSS.

[31] The Aberdare Eisteddfod in 1861 approved his proposals and the Social Science Section instituted provided useful opportunities for the discussion of questions of national interest. W. E. Davies, *Sir Hugh Owen: his Life and Life-work* (1885), p. 43.

[32] David Thomas, *The University College of Aberystwyth: an authoritative account of its origins and establishment* (1886), pp. 1–3. Thomas wrote this tract, which is heavily laced with self-pity, because he felt that he had not been given public credit for his pioneer services. He was one of the founding members, but soon withdrew because his patience was exhausted by the 'creeping processes' by which 'committees . . . reach their conclusions'.

[33] *Middle and High Schools and a University for Wales*, pp. 5–10, 20–30.

of that year Nicholas went up to London to meet Owen and a handful of his
friends in the capital who had similar interests.[34] It is at this point that the Welsh
university movement develops an effective purpose.

As a result of these informal discussions Nicholas was commissioned to draft
an Address to the friends of education in Wales. He produced a first-rate document: dignified, persuasive, reasonable, superbly expressed. 'Wales [said Nicholas],
with nearly a million and a quarter inhabitants, remains to this day without
a single High Class College', the only province of the United Kingdom left thus
'destitute', for Scotland had four universities supported by £20,000 annually out
of public funds, and in Ireland the government had spent over £100,000 in
establishing three Queen's Colleges, federated into the Queen's University, even
though Ireland had anciently possessed Trinity College, Dublin. It is evident that
Nicholas had one eye on the government's reaction and for this reason his Address
disclaimed 'all fanciful ideas of nationality', and, as a strong selling point, maintained that a Welsh university would 'spread a knowledge of the English language
and literature among the people of Wales'. At the same time, it was firmly asserted
that the Welsh were an authentic nation and that 'a truly national provision' must
be made to answer their wants.

Technically, of course, the Address was directed to the Welsh people, particularly its middle-class members, and Nicholas was at pains to draw their
attention to the recent rapid increase in the 'demand for educated talent, for
scientific acquirements, for engineering skill', which resulted from the pheno-
menal growth of the industries of Wales—her mines, manufactures, railways, and
shipping interests. As it was, the chief posts in the country's large undertakings
were 'monopolized by foreigners'. The Address took it for granted that it was now
crystal clear to all that any Welsh university must necessarily be unsectarian.[35] In
December 1863 two meetings of those who had responded to Nicholas's Address
were held at the Freemasons' Tavern in London. Officers were appointed, a provisional committee formed, and an appeal for public subscription was launched
with the promise of a magnificent initial donation of £1,000 by William Williams,
now the Radical M.P. for Lambeth, who had taken the chair at these meetings
and had agreed to become treasurer of the new undertaking.

So far as Williams was concerned, it was thoroughly unfortunate that there had
been the long hiatus in the university movement between 1854 and 1863. He
had been interested in educational questions for many years (it will be remembered
that he had prompted the Inquiry into Welsh education in 1847) and there is
plenty of other evidence of his concern to promote the interests of his homeland.
Williams was a thoroughly engaging character: a self-made man who amassed

[34] Hugh Owen's testimony to the Aberdare Committee (*Report, Minutes of Evidence*), pp. 12–13.
[35] 26 October 1863. 'A University for Wales'. U.C.W. G. Lib. History File. The draft was closely
vetted to eliminate provocative language.

a very large fortune in the cotton trade, he became and remained a maverick, highly individualistic, radical member of the Commons '*the* Williams', as his old enemy *The Times* (26 March 1857) called him. He had great courage and spoke his mind freely: he moved in the House that a statue of Cromwell should be erected at public expense, and had no hesitation in calling Charles I a 'tyrant'; when the Marxist Chartist Ernest Jones was in prison, Williams paid him a visit. Williams was a Churchman who, again untypically and indeed not far short of uniquely, believed that Church and State should be separated. More to the point, he was unmarried and had already promised a considerable sum to the university movement. It is probable that had it been further advanced and its future less uncertain than it was at the time of his death in 1865, Williams might well have made over a very much larger sum than £1,000.[36]

At any rate, Williams did at least prime the pump. In February 1864 an enlarged and modified Address, also written by Nicholas, was issued to the public. The revised Address played down any suggestion of Welsh separatism. The belief was strongly asserted that the hope of Wales lay in 'nearer approximation to England in general culture and in commercial enterprise', and again the aim of 'fostering a merely Welsh nationality' was specifically disclaimed as a 'great evil', which was no part of their purpose, for it was taken for granted that Wales must 'become an integral part of the United Kingdom'. All this no doubt, at least partly, was designed to disarm possible English objections. But it was not mere politic tergiversation; Nicholas, Owen, and most of the rest of their friends genuinely believed that this was the right prescription for Wales. There was a strong general conviction that only in this way could Wales get her fair share of the material advancements being brought about by the industrial revolution.[37] 'Without depreciating or wishing to extinguish the vernacular language', the Address insisted that what was required by Wales was 'the diffusion of English'. They were, in fact, prepared to leave 'the perpetuation of the vernacular, and other peculiarities' of the Welsh nation, to 'the free choice and sympathies of the people'.[38]

It is not surprising that a group of men, most of whom had found success by a voluntary expatriation and an early mastering of English, should think in these terms. With hindsight, it is easy to see that with supreme over-confidence they were eagerly grasping a tiger by the tail. But, in fairness to the committee, it must

---

[36] Daniel Evans, *The Life and Work of William Williams* (Llandyssul, 1940), p. 239, asserts as much. On Williams, see, in addition, the *D.W.B.* article by David Williams.

[37] David Davies of Llandinam, already well on his way to amassing a very large fortune, told his countrymen at the Aberystwyth Eisteddfod in September 1865: 'the best medium to make the money by was the English . . . if they were content with brown bread, then let them, of course, remain where they were. But if they wished to enjoy the luxuries of life, with white bread to boot, the way to do so was by the acquisition of English. He knew what it was to eat both' (*Aberystwyth Observer*, 30 September 1865).

[38] 'A University for Wales', 22 February 1864. U.C.W. G. Lib. History File.

be pointed out that they repeatedly insisted that they wanted a bi-lingual Wales: 'the Welshman', Nicholas wrote in his pamphlet in 1862, anticipating modern thinking on the subject, 'would be no loser but a gainer by the knowledge of two languages instead of one. A bi-lingualist, all other things being equal, is a more accomplished man than a monoglot.'[39] As we know, all other things did not remain equal. But in 1864 the Welsh language was in an extremely flourishing way: this was the period when there was an enormous growth in the number of Welsh language newspapers and periodicals; Welsh was the first (and, as the committee saw, in many instances, the only) language of a majority of the people. Moreover, the large mass-migration of English-speaking immigrants into North-east and South-east Wales, which permanently tipped the balance in these areas against the Welsh language, came after this time with the completion of the railway network and the much more extensive working of the coal-fields. Meantime, the rural people of Wales in search of work, 'were colonizing their own country' by a mass-movement to the south; they took their language with them and its hold was reinforced by the remarkable spurt of Welsh nonconformist chapel-building in the industrial towns.[40]

Any indictment, therefore, of the early promoters of a Welsh university as witless, myopic Anglophiles prepared heedlessly to throw away the ancient and valuable heritage of their nation, must take account of the circumstances in which they worked and the quite reasonable conclusions they drew from the facts around them.

In their revised Address the committee found it necessary once more to insist that the projected university must 'avoid fettering itself with ecclesiastical or denominational peculiarities'. In self-defence, this required re-stating because, at this time, there were not lacking voices suggesting that St. David's College, Lampeter, which was angling for its third charter giving it the power to award a B.A. degree, should take an important, perhaps the leading, place in a Welsh university.[41] Indeed, during the spring and summer of 1864, there were protracted negotiations between Hugh Owen and his associates and a small team of representatives of St. David's College, led by Professor Perowne, aiming at joint action in securing a government grant and founding a Welsh university.

[39] T. Nicholas, op. cit., p. 30.

[40] All these points are worked out in a first-rate article, 'Language, Literacy and Nationality in Wales', by Glanmor Williams in *History*, vol. 56, no. 186, February 1971, pp. 11–15. See also R. T. Jenkins, 'The Development of Nationalism in Wales', *Sociological Review*, xxvii. 178, and *The Aberdare Report*, Summary of General Results, pp. xlvii–xlviii, where the key observations, which refer to 1881, are: 'To those who are resident in Wales, the prevalence of the Welsh language is a matter of daily experience. . . . There is every appearance that the Welsh language will long be cherished by the large majority of the Welsh people.'

[41] Revd. Owen D. Thomas, *A University for Wales* (Dowlais and London, December 1863), p. 14, writes that 'it would be the most advisable plan for all Wales to unite at once to support Lampeter as a university . . . it would cost Wales less . . . it would surely succeed'.

The early meetings were cordial enough and there is no reason to doubt the goodwill expressed on either side. But in no time at all the negotiations ran into difficulties. Hugh Owen and company envisaged a close union of the two sides, a joint approach to the government for assistance, and the expenditure of the greater part of the money raised thus, and by public subscription, on the erection of one or more colleges which would combine with St. David's College to form the university. The Lampeter representatives favoured a much more limited alliance in which the two sides would retain a very large independence of action, something like an equal sharing of whatever government aid was forthcoming, entirely separate appeals for public support, and not much more than the necessary minimum of co-operation thereafter in founding, and presumably operating, the university. In May the two sides were firing off sharply-worded commentaries to each other on the various misunderstandings that had arisen between them. In June, with each side insisting stiffly on adhering to its position, the negotiations had reached deadlock and were broken off, with common-form emollient expressions of mutual regard and a reiteration of the thin hope that, in time, effective co-operation could be resumed.[42]

In fact, the negotiations never got to grips with the nub of the differences between the participants; and it is difficult to see how the most consummate diplomacy could have reconciled aims that were diametrically opposed. The university committee had been clear from the beginning that any national college or university in Wales would have to be unsectarian in character, if it were not to collapse hopelessly at the outset because of the religious divisions of the Welsh. For this reason the committee excluded the study of theology in order to avoid a Babel of contention. As for St. David's College, despite its recent attempt to strengthen its lay appeal, it remained overwhelmingly a Church college and had a vital need to retain theology which, after all, was an indispensable requirement in the training of its students. The only possibilities of union here were: firstly, a rush marriage before the incompatibilities became really stark; or, secondly, a shot-gun wedding imposed by the State, perhaps as the condition of support and university status. Neither of these, of course, occurred. Lampeter went its own way; in 1865, profiting from its official affiliations, it won its third charter and an increased annual endowment. But, despite these considerable encouragements, the small minority allegiance to the Church in Wales set a prohibitive limit to Lampeter's chances of growth into an authentic Welsh university.

Meanwhile, the committee for the University of Wales, or the London committee as it may be called in short-hand terms, was driven back on its own

---

[42] There is a full record of these negotiations in the 'University for Wales Minutes and Memoranda' (ff. 6–18), the handwritten formal record of the committee's activity for the years 1863–74. This large (281 ff.) volume (cited hereafter as Committee Minutes) in the U.C.W. Archive is indispensable for the early history of the College. See also, Archdale, op. cit., pp. 14–15.

resources. Why, it may reasonably be asked, was London rather than Wales itself the focus of this early struggle for the Welsh university? The answers are obvious enough: the Principality had no capital and no natural geographical centre; despite the improvements brought by the railways, communications remained appallingly difficult; there was the historic division of, and alleged lack of sympathy between, North and South Wales, as well as, always and ever, the divisive jealousies of the sects, and their common hostility to the Church. The personal leadership of the Welsh peers and gentry could, by now, be discounted entirely and, as yet, county councils had not appeared to provide alternative machinery for consultation and unity. Moreover, it should be remembered that the substitute leaders of the Welsh at home, the great dissenting ministers, were, to a man almost, involved in leading and precariously maintaining their own denominational colleges which, at rock bottom, were rival claimants with the would-be university for the interest and support of the Welsh people. In December 1863, for example, the London committee anxiously assured Dr. Lewis Edwards that the university would not 'interfere' with any existing Welsh college and held out the hope, in particular, that his college, Bala, somehow or other could be affiliated to the new foundation.[43] There is evidence that Lewis Edwards, despite the tentative support for the university proposal suggested by his presence at the 1854 conference, remained guardedly doubtful about the university scheme; indeed, in 1868, he expressed the opinion that good schools of various grades were a more important need.[44] There was a good deal of sense in the argument that considerable numbers of the Welsh should be taught to walk before some few of them were encouraged to run at the whim of a handful of sophisticated, rather suspect expatriates in London who were demonstrably out of touch with real conditions in Wales. An adroit devil's advocate could reasonably argue that, with the best will in the world, Wales at this time simply did not have an adequate number of good secondary schools to support a genuine university.[45] At any rate, in all these circumstances, London alone could provide the energizing initiative that Wales could not, or would not, give.

By 1865 the inner core of this group of London Welshmen is clearly identifiable. First and foremost, scarcely ever absent from meetings, was Hugh Owen, in fact, if not in name, effective chairman of the undertaking. The salaried secretary was Dr. Thomas Nicholas who had now moved to the capital. In that year, William Williams, treasurer, had died (by his will, keeping his promise to contribute

---

[43] T. C. Edwards, *Bywyd a Llythyrau Lewis Edwards* (Liverpool, 1901), pp. 445–6.

[44] 'Yr Hen Brifysgolian a'r Brifysgol i Gymru', *Y Traethodydd* (1868), pp. 133–43. See similar arguments in correspondence in *The Times* (24–8 December 1864).

[45] This opinion is endorsed by one of the best modern commentators, J. R. Webster, 'The Place of Secondary Education in Welsh Society, 1810–1918' (unpublished Ph.D. thesis, University of Wales, 1959), p. 170. See a letter in *The Times* (28 December 1864) where the sponsors of the university are described by a London Welshman as 'would-be patriotic nobodies'.

£1,000, but not, unfortunately, supplementing it) and been replaced by the sub-treasurer, Morgan Lloyd.[46] He was a farmer's son from Trawsfynydd who was educated at Edinburgh University, read for the Bar, and made a considerable career as a particularly gifted defence counsel; he later became a Liberal M.P., but failed to display the same deft touch at Westminster. More often than not, the committee met at his chambers in the Temple. The honorary secretaryship (held jointly with Hugh Owen) was filled for a time by George Osborne Morgan, a North Wales vicar's son, who had been a Fellow of University College, Oxford, became a barrister, and later a prominent Welsh Liberal M.P. who served Aberystwyth College well in the Commons. In November 1864 the Revd. Robert Jones accepted an invitation to join the committee. He was a Llanfyllin man who went up to Oxford and afterwards was Vicar of Rotherhithe for more than thirty years: a most eloquent man, 'a host in himself' in the words of a contemporary, and a decided acquisition to the committee which he attended regularly.[47] The Revd. Dr. David Thomas of Stockwell attended more often than not until 1868, when, presumably, his patience with interminable committee work was exhausted.[48] Finally, there was John Griffith of Barmouth, former grocer, one-time clerk, who finally discovered his real niche as a publicist and journalist, London correspondent of *Baner ac Amserau Cymru*, who is better known by his pseudonym, *Y Gohebydd*, 'the Correspondent'. His weekly London Letter to the *Baner*, among many other things, did a great deal to keep the case for Aberystwyth College before the attention of his influential readership.[49] Gohebydd's genial good nature was often used as an emollient to soothe the irritations of ruffled supporters of the movement. There were others, of course, but this was the regular inner circle: able, devoted, dedicated men who did not stint their time and energies in the service of what the *Westminster Review* conceded to be 'a splendid cause to plead'.[50] Why, then, did it take them so long to succeed?

The short answer to that question may be given in a word—money, or, rather, the lack of it. Initially it had confidently been expected that a national fund of £50,000 could be raised by public subscription from Wales, London, Manchester, and elsewhere. The committee spent many long hours discussing how best they could 'agitate Wales' on the question, and did their best to compile 'a Directory of Influential Welshmen' throughout the United Kingdom to whom approaches could be made.[51] Circulars appealing for support were fired off repeatedly like

[46] Williams' old enemy *The Times* (8 and 9 December 1864), the wish being father to the thought perhaps, had reported his death several months before the event.

[47] *T. C. Edwards Letters* (ed. T. I. Ellis, Aberystwyth, 1952), p. 68. *Trans. Cymm.* (1880), iii. 126–9. *U.C.W. Magazine*, i. 255–6.

[48] See p. 13 n. 32, above.

[49] Even the *Western Mail* (5 February 1870), in a particularly snide attack on *Gohebydd*, reluctantly conceded his great influence with his readers.

[50] Vol. xli. 358.   [51] Committee Minutes, ff. 11–12, 22–3.

clouds of arrows; committee members held meetings all over Wales, in London, and in the great English provincial centres where Welsh exiles were thick on the ground; agents for collection were appointed and given the inducement of commission payments on the sums they collected.[52]

The public meetings were initially encouraging, and the committee was heartened by reports of the considerable interest aroused; but, unfortunately, this enthusiasm proved all too evanescent and, as was later admitted, this was a poor method of raising funds on a large scale. There was almost always a disheartening disparity between the promises made in the flush of patriotic enthusiasm generated at the meeting and the moneys actually handed over later in the more cautious light of day.[53] It was a constant ebb and flow of disappointment and encouraging response: a great canvass of London Welsh merchants in March 1865 was a dismal failure; occasionally, and often unexpectedly, a small Welsh town would respond handsomely. More often than not, though, the regular reports to the committee in London were discouraging enough to make the stoutest heart quail; indeed, in January 1865, the committee admitted that the 'tardiness' of response was threatening the whole venture. To meet immediate necessities a few gentlemen had to be approached, cap in hand, for something (anything almost) on account of the promises they had made; and in desperation it was wistfully suggested that an approach should be made to the Prince of Wales to accept the Presidency of the movement.[54] By mid 1865, something like a sum of £5,000 was in hand, and a slightly larger nominal amount lay exasperatingly in unfulfilled promises.[55] It looked as though the opening of a Welsh university would be postponed to the Greek Kalends.

However, later in 1865, things picked up. In July the committee was offered, by Dr. Nicholl Carne of St. Donat's Castle, six acres of land at Llantwit Major as the site of the South Wales college. This was immensely encouraging, but the committee's capital resources were, of course, far too slender for it to seize this opportunity and start immediately on a building programme: Carne's offer was gratefully acknowledged, but left for the moment dangling. All the same, it had given a push in the direction of starting operations, and in the autumn of 1865 the committee seriously investigated the idea of opening a temporary makeshift college at Chester. This madcap notion was no more than an earnest of the committee's desperation and, mercifully, was quickly forgotten.[56]

[52] Committee Minutes, ff. 29–46. Mercifully, this scheme was soon abandoned, for the balance accruing to the committee after commission (10 per cent) and the expenses of agents had been paid, was perilously small.

[53] Nicholas reported in December 1865, for example, that a canvass of Liverpool elicited promises of £2,481, of which £353 only was immediately forthcoming; Brecon promised £156, but paid in only £36.

[54] Committee Minutes, ff. 28, 31, 42–6.   [55] U.C.W. Reports (1863–91), p. 17.

[56] Committee Minutes, ff. 49–50.

By now, however, things were stirring. In December 1865 the committee received the offer of a site of seven acres, apparently free of charge, at Menai Bridge near Bangor, where the Britannia Park Company had plans (which had hung fire for years) for building a hotel, and ambitious paper schemes for residential development. This project was the outcome of the railway mania of the 1840s and never realized the hopes based on it. In 1865 the scheme was not far short of collapse and the approach to the university committee was evidently designed to give it renewed life.[57] Soon afterwards a Captain John Jones of Liverpool came forward with an offer to make over his valuable private museum if the committee would promise to build their college in the vicinity of Bangor and give assurances that its teaching would be 'equally favourable to all classes, Church of England and sectarian alike'.[58]

The committee responded to this double offer with considerable enthusiasm and further negotiations (carried on by Hugh Owen) ensued. The position is not entirely clear, but there is rather more than the suggestion that the Britannia Park Company had a fly-by-night touch to it. At any rate, it speedily appeared that the offer of a free site was not quite what it seemed. The proposal was that the committee, in the first instance, should pay £1,400 for the 7-acre site; if within three years they had built this college, their purchase money would be refunded. If, however, the college had not been built within that time, Mr. Barnett, chief proprietor of the Britannia, engaged to buy back the land at the original price.[59] There was clearly a strong element of risk and, in the end, the committee shied off because of its doubtfulness.

In January 1867 Dr. Nicholl Carne came forward with another proposal: he offered St. Donat's Castle, as he said, 'as a temporary hospice' for a college, if the committee would definitely commit itself to building eventually on the site he had offered at Llantwit Major. But the committee, still dominated by the shortage of funds (despite continuing efforts, especially by the ceaselessly itinerant Nicholas, the total amount collected in 1866 was only £700), replied that it 'hardly felt justified in finally deciding upon the permanent site of the South Wales College, or, without further consideration and a large increase of funds, venturing upon commencing Collegiate operation'.[60]

There is an oddly curt tone to this answer to a generous offer; the irritated reaction, perhaps, of men who, for the moment, are sunk in despair. Perhaps the Britannia Park negotiation had made them doubly wary. It must be remembered, also, that the most active members of the London committee hailed originally from North Wales and this possibly explains their curiously limp response to Dr. Carne. It may well be that the committee missed a good opportunity here. The first Address had pointed to the great industrial developments then taking place

---

[57] M. L. Clarke, 'Britannia Park'. *Trans. Caerns. Hist. Soc.*, xix. 54–60.
[58] Committee Minutes, ff. 36–40.   [59] Ibid., ff. 47–8.   [60] Ibid., f. 52.

in South Wales, where enormous private fortunes were being made, and where the bulk of the population of the Principality was soon to be overwhelmingly concentrated. A pioneer college at Llantwit Major would have had large advantages not available in other parts of Wales. A reasonably successful start there might well have meant, in time, that Wales had one large unitary university, not the federal dispersed university that was ultimately established.[61]

Indeed, in the light of the later history of the University of Wales, it is ironic that the committee came as close as these two proposals suggest to establishing its pioneer college at either Bangor or Llantwit Major, a few miles from Cardiff. These were really close calls for Aberystwyth. It is clear that had either of these proposals been taken up, there would never have been a College by the Sea, with immense consequent loss to the Welsh people. It is equally clear, as the later experience of Aberystwyth College in the early 1880s showed, that had Aberystwyth's claims ever had to be submitted to a free conference, the town would never have been chosen as the site of the first Welsh university college.

Sheerest accident, not human wisdom, gave Aberystwyth its chance. It came, early in 1867, as a result of the personal misfortune of an interesting man, Thomas Savin, of Llwyn-y-Maen, Oswestry. Savin was a flamboyant character, a typical Victorian entrepreneur with a tremendous personal drive fired by limitless ambition. A former Mayor of Oswestry, he was a draper who became a great railway contractor, a one-time partner of David Davies of Llandinam.[62] Savin had ambitious plans for developing some of the Cardigan Bay towns into a string of seaside resorts, equipped with ample hotel accommodation, linked to the great centres of population by his own railways. He had especially grandiose schemes for Aberystwyth, which he planned to make, of all things, 'the Brighton of Wales'.[63] Savin was no mere Victorian money-grubber: he had a largeness of view, a consciousness of amenity, and a really strongly developed sense of public-spiritedness.[64]

Savin's hustling, headlong methods are exemplified by the incredible story of the building of his vast Castle hotel at Aberystwyth. J. P. Seddon, the distinguished London architect, was summoned hastily in 1864 from Towyn, where he was engaged on other work for Savin, to Aberystwyth and, at not much more than a moment's notice, commissioned to erect a hotel around the nucleus of an existing small mansion (called the Castle House) built in the early nineteenth

---

[61] It is not suggested, of course, that all the advantages lay one way. For an account of the curious, quickly abortive, attempt in 1857 to found a technical university or college at the Gnoll, Neath, see Iolo Wyn Williams, 'Coleg y Gnoll, 1857', Y Gwyddonydd, iv. 152–7.

[62] For Savin and David Davies, see Ivor Thomas, Top Sawyer (1938), pp. 40–70, and R. Christiansen and R. W. Miller, The Cambrian Railways (Newton Abbott, 1967), i. 14–71.

[63] The Aberystwyth Guide (p. v) for 1874 is so prefaced.

[64] Even the Railway Times (February 1866), a fierce critic of his hustling business methods, conceded that Savin had great claims 'upon everyone . . . who regards the public welfare'.

century by the great John Nash. Seddon had to work with Savin at his elbow constantly changing his instructions as his imagination took flight. First, a southern wing only was to be attached to Nash's house; later, a much larger northern wing, originally three floors high, subsequently raised to six, was ordered, and there was to be a great tower ten storeys high topped by an observatory. Poor Seddon, driven from pillar to post, never had time to make complete drawings; a rough wooden model and working diagrams hastily sketched as required were the most he could manage, not least because Savin insisted on instant work being available for a labour force amounting to 500 men.[65] Despite this impossible rush, Seddon managed to provide some magnificent features for this great building; in particular, a bowed seafront section (designed as the hotel-bar, subsequently the College Chapel), a fine stair-tower, and a most impressive arched entrance, all of which outmatched anything built at Oxford and Cambridge at that time.[66]

No doubt Savin's imagination far outran common prudence, and his ambitious schemes were founded on too many false propositions to succeed.[67] In any case, soon after his Aberystwyth ventures were launched, there was a sharp commercial recession amounting to a national-scale financial crisis, sparked off by a Stock Exchange panic following the spectacular failure of Overend and Gurney, the great London discount house. For three months in 1866, bank rate stood at 10 per cent; railway interests were especially hard-hit and Savin, who was hopelessly overstretched, came crashing down into the hands of liquidators. He had spent £80,000 on his still unfinished Castle hotel at Aberystwyth; now, in February 1867, it came on the market at a fraction of its cost.

Curiously enough, Savin had a connection with the Welsh university committee going back to 1863; he intermittently attended their meetings, which were occasionally held in his London offices. It is ironic, in the light of later events, that the first time Savin took the chair (members did so on a casual *ad hoc* basis) was the first time the committee discussed possible sites for a college.[68] In February 1867 the Castle hotel was offered to the university committee for, initially, £15,000.

This time, spurred on by provincial grumblings over the endless delays, the committee acted decisively and resolved that 'it was the unanimous opinion that the securing of the Castle hotel for a sole and central college for Wales was desirable'.[69] This was superb opportunism: hitherto, they had talked and planned for years of two colleges, one in North Wales, and one in the South, federated into a university. Now, all too painfully aware of their penury, they spoke blandly of 'a central and sole college'.

[65] J. P. Seddon, 'On the University College of Wales and other buildings at or near Aberystwyth', *Trans. Royal Inst. British Architects* (1871–2), pp. 148–52. See also *Bye-Gones* (August 1882), pp. 100–1.
[66] H. R. Hitchcock, *Architecture: 19th and 20th Centuries* (vol. xv of the Pelican History of Art, ed. N. Pevsner, 1958), p. 187.
[67] David Davies had cannily dissolved their partnership earlier.
[68] Committee Minutes, ff. 3–36. [69] Ibid., ff. 52–3.

Detailed negotiations (including a considerable haggle over fittings and furniture) followed, but eventually the committee secured the building for £10,000, only a portion of which was paid over immediately. Savin, magnificently philosophical in the midst of personal ruin, still had the magnanimity to write to congratulate the committee on their 'advantageous purchase'.[70] At long last, the movement had a site and a building with great possibilities. There was every hope that now the country would rally round in earnest and enable the college shortly to open its doors. At first the signs were encouraging; during 1867 subscriptions increased handsomely to a total for that year of over £5,000, with the town of Aberystwyth alone contributing £1,032 as a result of a month's intensive canvass.[71] But public subscription alone did not seem likely to prove enough.

Of course, the committee had never expected to be able to finance a university or a college by private enterprise alone. The preliminary literature had endlessly emphasized Wales' relative poverty and repeatedly pointed to the generosity governments had shown in the past to Scottish and Irish universities. The committee had always been buoyed up with the hope that, given a reasonable effort by the Welsh themselves, government aid would be forthcoming. With the Castle hotel in their possession, the time seemed ripe for an approach to the government. In January 1868 an encouragingly friendly letter was received from the veteran Earl Russell (Lord John Russell of old), a former Prime Minister, now, however, on the eve of retirement. But later in the year the incumbent Prime Minister, Disraeli, brusquely refused even to meet a Welsh deputation.[72]

With the return of a Liberal government later in 1868, however, prospects seemed to brighten. Twenty-three Welsh Liberal M.P.s were returned and several of them had succeeded in breaking the hitherto unshakeable monopoly of traditional Tory landlords. To many in Wales, it seemed the dawn of a new and better age: 'Wales', wrote an exultant Cardiganshire Liberal, 'has now found its tongue'.[73] Prominent in the ranks of the new Welsh members was George Osborne Morgan, honorary secretary of the university committee, and he, together with Henry Richard, newly returned for Merthyr Tydfil, who had by now long overcome his scruples about state aid, was commissioned to see Gladstone informally on the

[70] Committee Minutes, ff. 61–2. Happily, although his career as a railway and property tycoon was now over, Savin subsequently enjoyed a modest prosperity based on his lime business at Llanymynech, and remained prominent in Oswestry public life until his death in 1889 (*Oswestry Advertizer*, 23 July 1889). Ivor Thomas, op. cit., p. 61.

[71] *U.C.W. Reports (1863–91)*, p. 17. Committee Minutes, ff. 68–71.

[72] Ibid., ff. 92–3, 100–1. In March 1868 Disraeli readily agreed to meet a large and influential deputation from Owens College, Manchester. He received them 'courteously' and behaved 'in his grandest manner': in the end, despite the practised blandishments, they went away empty-handed. J. Thompson, *The Owen's College: its foundation and growth* (Manchester, 1886), pp. 326–31.

[73] 15 April 1869. N.L.W. MSS. 5505B. K. O. Morgan, *Wales in British Politics, 1868–1922* (Cardiff, 1963), pp. 22–7, makes it clear, however, that the social and political significance of the change in Welsh parliamentary personnel has been exaggerated.

committee's behalf. The interview on 28 May 1870 was vastly encouraging: Gladstone listened with great interest to Richard's short formal statement of the committee's case. In reply, the Prime Minister readily admitted that Wales had been 'badly used'; he was prepared to concede that the government grants to Ireland 'were clearly in point as precedents', and even went so far as to say that Wales, 'with its clearly marked nationality, divided from England by a strong line of demarcation, both of race and language', had claims which could not be placed on the same level as those of 'any English town or district, however populous and important'. This latter comment seemed especially important, because it suggested that the reasons for rejecting a recent strong claim from Owens College did not, in his opinion, apply to the Welsh case. Gladstone was careful to insist, of course, that he could not be expected to commit his Chancellor of the Exchequer, but it seemed clear that the Prime Minister, already responding constructively to Irish nationalism, was privately strongly sympathetic to Wales and might reasonably be expected to respond in the same generous way. Gladstone heartily endorsed the unsectarian idea and, meantime, he urged the committee to mobilize as broad a front of Welsh support as possible. Henry Richard drew from the interview the 'general inference', as he told the committee, that 'if we could only bring a sufficiently strong pressure to bear upon the Government, they were not indisposed to yield'.[74]

The committee, much heartened, was anxious to follow up this encouraging preliminary as soon as possible, but nearly a year elapsed (a frustrating delay occasioned by the many exigencies engaging the attention of the Ministry) before a deputation was able to see Gladstone again. Confident hopes were quickly dashed: the Prime Minister, who had evidently had second, more cautious, thoughts (inspired almost certainly by a hostile Treasury caveat), did not entirely go back on his earlier expressions of sympathy, but, in his own peculiarly labyrinthine way, he now disputed the relevance to Wales of the Irish Queen's Colleges' precedents, and seemed afraid that a grant to Wales would provoke a great clamour of protest from Owens College, Manchester. Gladstone's final comment 'I see . . . no likelihood of . . . the Government as a whole, or of Parliament, providing financial aid', seemed to the deputation, and the anxious committee behind them, like the knell of doom.[75]

This final rejection was all the more demoralizing because public subscription, after rising sharply as a result of the fillip given by the Castle hotel purchase in 1867, had not continued quite at that level in subsequent years. There were good reasons for this. With some notable exceptions, the landlord class, long accustomed

[74] This account of the interview is collated from Osborne Morgan's statement (30 June 1870, N.L.W. MSS. 5509C) and Richard's report to the committee. Committee Minutes, ff. 124–7. Rather surprisingly, Gladstone placed no embargo on public knowledge of his opinion.
[75] Ibid., ff. 124–7, 158–60. Gladstone to Richard, 14 April 1871, U.C.W.G. Lib. History File.

to look to Oxbridge, especially Jesus College, Oxford, for the education of their sons, did not respond. Some of them were scornfully hostile to Aberystwyth's pretentions: 'my real opinion about a Welsh college at Aberystwyth', wrote Sir John Hanmer (of Eton and Christ Church, but not encumbered with an Oxford degree), 'is, that it would be a little provincial South Welsh concern . . . of no advantage to Wales'.[76] The committee, of course, had looked especially to the middle class for support of their venture; after all, the early literature of the movement had specifically stated that the proposed college was designed almost exclusively to meet the needs of that section of Welsh society. And down to 1869, at least, the greater part of the money received had been drawn from 'persons in respectable circumstances', as the secretary put it in genteel Victorian terms.[77] Unfortunately, the Welsh middle class, however broadly defined, was relatively small and, as the committee's balance sheets gloomily indicated, not wealthy enough, nor apparently sufficiently enthusiastic, to support the foundation of a Welsh college without wider help.

Moreover, these people had to meet many other calls upon their generosity; in particular, the continuing requirements of the nonconformist chapels and colleges. Between 1856 and 1865, for example, the Calvinistic Methodists raised £26,000 for the support and rebuilding of their Bala College.[78] There is no doubt that this sort of competition queered the pitch for the canvassers on behalf of the university movement. A college or university for Wales had no choice but to be unsectarian, but a heavy price had to be paid for this; it meant a certain uninspiring, innocuous vagueness and the movement could not, as a matter of course, count on the instinctive loyalty and support of any large existing corporate body in Wales.[79] Not that everybody accepted its claim to be genuinely unsectarian. Dean H. T. Edwards, for one, flatly rejected an early invitation to join the Welsh university movement on the ground that its claim to be 'a national and unsectarian institution' was spurious, despite the reassuring presence on the committee, along with the dissenters, of several Anglican clergy and laymen.[80] And there is some suggestion that certain members of the other nonconformist sects felt that there was an all-too-strong Calvinistic Methodist touch to the whole movement, and that the College would be dominated by *yr hen Gorph*.

In these circumstances, certain members of the committee came to understand

---

[76] 29 March 1871. Bangor (Yale) MSS. no. 42, Letter 36. Hugh Owen, however, managed later to soften Hanmer's asperities and persuaded him to sign a Memorial in favour of Aberystwyth College. Hanmer to Revd. R. Edwards, 3 April 1871. Ibid.

[77] 1869. U.C.W. G. Lib. History File (Dr. Charles' statement).

[78] H. P. Roberts, loc. cit., p. 73. The Welsh Independents were similarly engaged (Committee Minutes, ff. 116–17) in fund-raising.

[79] Nicholas (*Y Faner*, 20 January 1869) spelt out in detail these reasons for relative failure in collecting money.

[80] H. T. Edwards, op. cit., p. 82. See also his letter in the *Western Mail* (25 November 1870).

that the basis of support would have to be widened and began to see the merits of a democracy that, hitherto, had not been strongly evident in their calculations. In 1869 Osborne Morgan was insisting that Wales must be taught that the university was 'a people's question', and the secretary claimed that for some time he had 'been laying the foundations of operations with regard to the masses of people [who] . . . would be their great strength'. Already the generous response of the quarrymen of North Wales to appeals for support was being cited as a reproach to well-to-do Welshmen who refused their assistance.[81] From this point onwards, the Aberystwyth College movement becomes more and more genuinely the concern of the Welsh commonalty, and, in the longer run, the aggregated pittances of humble people (thousands of contributions of half-a-crown or less) helped just to tip the financial scale in its favour and gave the most convincing evidence that the College had established for itself an especial, indeed unique, place in the affections of the Welsh people.

But this lay mainly in the future; in the 1860s, the fact was that the committee lacked the proper paraphernalia for an effective canvass of the Welsh nation at large, and until the machinery of the chapels, quarterly meetings, Sunday collections among the congregations and the like could be fully harnessed, subscription by the mass of the people could, at best, only limp along, however heroic the efforts of individual collectors.[82]

Meantime, the committee was hemmed in by one financial crisis after another: the 'commercial depression' of the mid 1860s raised considerably the interest that had to be paid on the £6,000 borrowed for the down-payment on the Castle hotel; several times the bank had to be asked to postpone the payment of subsequent instalments on the purchase price. Seddon (kept on a very tight rein) had to dun the committee repeatedly for payment for his work in adapting the hotel to college purposes, and efforts to obtain mortgages on the property failed dismally.[83] And although there was never at any time the slightest whiff of a suggestion of malversation, essential expenses swallowed up a disconcerting proportion (about one-third) of the money actually collected. Contradictory statements about the movement's financial circumstances led to misunderstandings and newspaper attacks alleging incompetence; Seren Cymru, for example, in one edition strongly advised Welshmen to stop contributing to the cause.[84]

Moreover, even the committee, hitherto united, was riven by differences. Not

[81] Osborne Morgan and D. Charles at the Westminster Palace Hotel, 25 February 1869. U.C.W. G. Lib. History File. Committee Minutes, ff. 109–11.

[82] In 1865 Nicholas suggested the appointment of four full-time paid canvassing agents for Wales who were 'to be College educated men', but the committee lacked the means to finance the scheme. Efforts to recruit the aid of the chapels were made in the 1860s, but the response then was not very considerable because the sects were preoccupied with answering their own needs. Committee Minutes, ff. 30, 42–6.   [83] Ibid., ff. 63–111.

[84] 22 October 1869. See also critical articles in the Daily Leader in October 1869.

surprisingly, Dr. Nicholas had been worn down by his endless journeys with the begging-bowl and he resented what he regarded as untoward nagging for frequent detailed reports from men who did not have to face the daily grind of embarrassing solicitation that he had to endure. He was thoroughly irritated by the committee's rejection of his proposal to move the headquarters of the movement to Aberystwyth. But the decisive factor was that Nicholas and Hugh Owen grated on each other: 'both good men in their way, they seemed to have a mutual repugnance', as one member of the committee put it.[85] In time, Nicholas's dislike for Owen turned to violent hatred; he accused him later of keeping everything jealously 'under his own thumb', and rounded off a violent denunciation thus: 'I have not met such depth of scheming and duplicity in my short course of life as I have seen in the noble Hugh Owen.'[86] There is no doubt that Hugh Owen was not quite the plaster saint that appears in W. E. Davies' Victorian *Life*, and his bureaucratic methods were not to everybody's taste. But Nicholas' denunciation defeats itself by the absurd exaggeration of the charges he makes.

At any rate, in November 1867 Nicholas tendered his resignation which was to become effective at the end of the year.[87] It was unfortunate that he should go on such a sour note, for Nicholas had made a great contribution to the cause in its difficult early years. The new salaried secretary was Dr. David Charles, brother-in-law of Dr. Lewis Edwards of Bala; Charles' terms, especially his expense allowance, were rather less generous than those of Nicholas. The new secretary set to work energetically and in the first flush of enthusiasm he managed to increase slightly the rate of subscriptions. But the old difficulties remained, and Charles discovered that many people would give no money until a grant from the government had been obtained. From Wales there were ominous rumblings of discontent with the arrogant dominance of a London clique, which did not even have the saving merit of success to bless its operations.

The committee sensibly took heed of these warnings. In May 1868, at a general meeting of subscribers at the Freemasons' Tavern in London, a Representative General Committee of one hundred was nominated. On this list, excluding eleven M.P.s, an esoteric group best left aside, fifteen are identifiable as prominent London Welshmen, thirteen are from Merseyside, four from Manchester and its environs, four from other English towns, three from Aberystwyth (reflecting its new significance), twenty-seven from South, and seventeen from North Wales. Additionally, a new Executive Committee of thirty members was appointed

---

[85] Dr. D. Thomas, op. cit., p. 2.

[86] Nicholas to Henry Richard, 21 and 24 October 1872. N.L.W. MSS. 5505B. See also Nicholas' letters to the *Aberystwyth Observer* in August-September 1868.

[87] Committee Minutes, ff. 88–9. Soon afterwards, his friend, Dr. David Thomas of Stockwell, left the committee, along with his son, D. Morgan Thomas. However, the committee had been considerably strengthened before this by the adhesion of Stephen Evans, a Cardiganshire man who did well in business in London, who rendered yeoman service to the College over several decades.

which included three M.P.s and seventeen provincial members. This was clearly an attempt to give the committee a much wider, less London-dominated base, and it was agreed to hold half-yearly meetings of subscribers alternately in London and Aberystwyth.[88] From this time onwards, the provincial members took a much more sustained and active part in the committee's affairs, and began to press steadily for a start to be made at Aberystwyth. Gradually, the patient attempts to form effective local committees in Manchester (where J. Foulkes Roberts was a tower of strength), Liverpool, Aberystwyth (where Johnathen Pell of the Belle Vue hotel was the most vigorous member of an energetic committee), and other places begin to make some headway.

It was just as well that the committee received this infusion of new blood. There is no question of the enormous debt owed to the London Welshmen. But, despite their vital contribution hitherto, there is no doubt that in the late 1860s, face to face as they had been for years with the demoralizing fact of sheer lack of money, some of them were flagging badly. At a rather desperate meeting of subscribers at the Westminster Palace hotel on 25 February 1869, Osborne Morgan admitted that 'the boat seemed to have got upon a little reef', and the London committee pleaded for help in 'getting it fairly afloat again'.[89]

But the signs remained unpromising: for the half-year ending in June 1870 money received in subscriptions totalled in round figures £883, and payments (including the secretary's salary) amounted to £841. Perhaps, inevitably, there was constant bickering between the officers in London and its fund-raising secretary, David Charles, now based in Aberystwyth. The repair and maintenance of the Castle hotel was a constant drain on their meagre resources. So much so that, in September 1871, there was a proposal to lease the building, at a rent of £150 *per annum*, to the British Schools Society for use as a college for women teachers; and this negotiation was broken off only because there was a possibility that the whole building might be offered for sale. From London, the Castle hotel began ominously to look like a gigantic white elephant.[90]

But this London defeatism (or so it seemed to those at a distance, less familiar with the grim facts of penury) provoked what may be called the Provincial Revolt. In September 1871 the London committee received a sharply worded Protest, that did not shrink from allegations of incompetence, from members 'in the country', the spokesmen for the provincial local committees, insisting that an immediate start should be made.[91] As a result, a special meeting was convened in London on 26 October 1871, at which provincial interests were strongly

---

[88] Ibid., ff. 96–9, 109–11. *U.C.W. Reports (1863–91)*, pp. 5–6.

[89] Committee Minutes, ff. 109–11. Thomas Gee of *Y Faner* made a powerful speech promising support. *T. C. Edwards Letters*, p. 25, for Foulkes Roberts' opinion that the London committee 'require to be pushed on'.

[90] Ibid., ff. 142–3, 178–9.   [91] Committee Minutes, ff. 179–82.

represented. Here a Manchester member, William Rowland, made an eloquent plea that 'a pull altogether' would accomplish the desired end. It should be said that Hugh Owen, whose determination, unlike that of some of his London colleagues, had not been emasculated by disappointment, had sent off a circular earlier in the year to members of the Executive Committee proposing an early opening of the College. At the London meeting, and at a supplementary conference at Liverpool addressed by Owen and Foulkes Roberts, it was decided to reorganize the wilting Guarantee Fund machinery and to establish five regional committees (London, Manchester, Liverpool, North, and South Wales), each of which would accept responsibility for raising for a three-year period an annual quota of £400 for running expenses. Soon afterwards, in November, it was finally agreed to open the College not later than 1 October 1872.[92]

The die was cast: provincial impatience, combined with a surge of local enthusiasm, had overcome a London caution induced by the weary burden of financial worries long sustained. There is no doubt that the provincials were right: if this decision had not been taken (or, perhaps, rather, if this act of faith had not been made), the chances were strongly, as was said in an Aberystwyth newspaper, that 'the undertaking must speedily collapse'.[93]

Much remained to be done: as cheeseparingly as possible, the College had to be adapted for use; some sort of interim constitution had to be worked out; a Principal and a small handful of professors had to be appointed and students recruited from somewhere. In December 1871 there was a johnny-come-lately overture from St. David's College, Lampeter, proposing a resumption of the negotiations for union broken off in 1863. In February 1872 the Bishop of St. Asaph met Hugh Owen, Osborne Morgan, Foulkes Roberts, and Morgan Lloyd, and certain suggestions for association in a proposed Welsh university were adopted. Nothing came of this eleventh-hour irrelevance; negotiations broke down, as before, on the issue of theological teaching.[94] In May, in the middle of all these preparations, David Charles, secretary since 1867, announced, with evident dudgeon, his resignation, effective in October 1872.

There was a substantial application for the Principalship, but the committee, Hugh Owen in particular, preferred a private approach to Thomas Charles Edwards, son of Dr. Lewis Edwards of Bala. T. C. Edwards, who was then nearly thirty-five years old, was a leading Calvinistic Methodist minister in Liverpool. He was a scholar of great distinction. After taking a bachelor's degree and an M.A.

[92] Committee Minutes, ff. 186–7 (Pell of Aberystwyth, restlessly impatient, pressed in vain for opening in January 1872). Hugh Owen's letter of 27 February 1871, and the report of the Liverpool conference (prompted by a Manchester initiative) are in U.C.W. G. Lib. History File.

[93] *Observer* (18 November 1871).

[94] Papers entitled, 'University College of Wales, Special', 12 January 1872, and 'University for Wales', 12 February 1872, in U.C.W. G. Lib. History File. See also Committee Minutes, ff. 194–214, and the *Cambrian News* (1, 8, and 14 March 1872).

(where he was topped on the list only by Stanley Jevons) at London, Edwards had had a brilliant career at Oxford where he took a First in Classics and became the protégé of Benjamin Jowett and Mark Pattison, and impressed T. H. Green with the quality of his mind.

The negotiation over the Principalship at Aberystwyth was a curious, long-drawn-out affair. At first, Edwards himself was unenthusiastic: his father agreed with him that the new College rested on such frail foundations that there was a strong probability of 'the whole thing collapsing' in a year or two. Moreover, there were family complications, for Edwards' uncle, David Charles, seems for a time to have nurtured hopes of the appointment himself. Charles, ruled out on grounds of age, was never, in fact, in the hunt; he realized this and, on the face of it, welcomed his nephew's probable appointment, but in such lukewarm terms as positively to discourage. Subsequently, Charles kept up a carping criticism (not wholly without point) of the London committee and all its works, laced with a venomous hostility towards Hugh Owen: 'I pity any man', wrote Charles, 'that will have to work under his rule. He is the most unpleasant man I ever tried to work with.'[95]

However, Jowett and Pattison were strongly in favour of Edwards going to Aberystwyth and, ultimately, Dr. Lewis Edwards, after havering for some time, eventually counselled acceptance. He had come to see that his brother-in-law's 'dog in the manger' attitude, as he put it, to the Principalship was prompted by disappointment, and after over forty years' experience in the connection tartly observed to his son that 'the shabbiest members of the Committee cannot be more shabby than some Calvinistic Methodists that I have had to deal with'. From all this contradictory advice, T. C. Edwards sensibly drew the conclusion that he would be wise to insist on certain written conditions: in particular, he asserted his right to continue some preaching after he had taken up the appointment, insisted that he must not be saddled with fund-raising duties and that he must have a completely free hand on the academic side. The committee was a little doubtful of the wisdom of the Principal of an avowedly non-sectarian college preaching, but finally reluctantly agreed and left the frequency to T. C. Edwards' 'sense of duty', reserving the right to submit disputed cases to the judgement of two men, one of whom was to be Lewis Edwards. Finally, the tortuous negotiations were completed; T. C. Edwards accepted the appointment. Soon afterwards, two professors, one of Classics and one of Natural Science, and a Registrar-cum-Librarian were appointed. This pathetically small Senate is just one more illustration of the founders' need to watch every penny.[96]

---

[95] T. C. Edwards, op. cit., p. 405. Letters to and from Lewis Edwards, Hugh Owen, David Charles, and T. C. Edwards in *T. C. Edwards Letters*, pp. 2–28.

[96] Ibid., pp. 4–32. Committee Minutes, ff. 204–32. T. C. Edwards to Hugh Owen, 10 July 1872. U.C.W. G. Lib. History File.

And so, the great day eventually came. On 9 October 1872 operations began when eighteen candidates appeared to sit for a handful of Exhibitions and Scholarships that the College had scraped together as bait.[97] On 15 October there was a public celebration: Aberystwyth observed a general holiday, all shops were closed and the town, including the recently opened great pier, was festooned with decorations. In the morning, there was a public breakfast in the splendid dining hall at the College; a crowded public meeting, with the proceedings almost entirely in Welsh, was held at five o'clock in the large Temperance Hall in the town; and, at seven in the evening, a *conversazione* which lasted several hours was held at the College. Most of the great promoters of the movement were present, there were many eloquent speeches, much music and happy singing: all was joy and marvellous triumph.[98]

It will be remembered that, initially, it had been hoped to set up a university, with two or more constituent colleges. That had proved to be an undertaking far beyond the capacity of the committee and it had had to settle for something less, though never at any time abandoning the original great dream. There was now, at least, as the *Cambrian News* proudly reported: 'a *bona fide* national College belonging to the country irrespective of creed, religious or political'.

The College by the Sea, which was to make so great a contribution to Wales, and evoke in her sons an exceptional, perhaps unique, affection, had been born. However, as the *Cambrian News* with sober realism also rightly said: 'In many respects, the real difficulties of this immense undertaking have only just commenced.'[99]

---

[97] This useful idea stemmed from Jowett's suggestion, and T. C. Edwards had made its adoption by the committee one of his conditions in accepting the Principalship.

[98] The best and fullest account is to be found in 'Report of the Proceedings in connection with the opening of the U.C.W.' (reprinted from the *Welshman*, 18 October 1872).

[99] *Cambrian News* (11 October 1872).

2

'Let the College be Wales Writ Small'[1]

ON 16 October 1872 the College at Aberystwyth opened its doors for the formal start of its first session. It had, at any rate, been given a heartening send-off: the public breakfast the day before had been enlivened by the unexpected receipt of a telegram from the Prime Minister. Gladstone, perhaps seeing the need now to keep his Welsh political options more open, sent a message that he had written 'a letter to say how much honour . . . this undertaking does to its promoters'. This at least was some improvement on his blank refusal of a parliamentary grant the year before. More immediately comforting to the promoters was the generous response of several of the more wealthy supporters present at the College that day.

Pride of place inevitably goes to David Davies of Llandinam. The meeting, full of expectation, gave him a tremendous reception, and there followed from him a typical teasing speech, punctuated with his own special brand of humour. He said that he had watched the College from the outset, and, at first, concluded that it was 'a sick child, perhaps consumptive'. He was not the man to throw good money away lightly, so at first he had given only £100. Of course, he realized that it was born at an unfortunate time, 'the great panic' of the late 1860s; however, it had survived and when he found that 'some small idle dogs began to bark at it', he gave another £300 by way of encouragement. They had heard many good speakers that day, but, as he observed drily, 'this young child of ours cannot live on speeches'. A self-made man himself, he put no great faith in the hope of government assistance, at least not until Wales had made a better effort than hitherto; nor would he agree that Wales was poor: 'We have in Wales one-third of the coal in the United Kingdom, therefore Wales is rich.' What was needed was an endowment fund of £50,000. He did not like to see the uncompleted building 'showing its bare ribs' to all and sundry, so, feeling as he confessed a 'little elevated' that day, he was prepared to give £1,000 towards the building fund, and later on, given the fulfilment of certain conditions, another £2,000 towards

---

[1] T. C. Edwards, Introduction to U.C.W. *Magazine*, i. 3.

scholarships. In fact, despite his businessman's eye for essentials, subsequent events were to show that, at this stage at least, David Davies had no very clear idea of the educational purposes for which the College had been established.[2]

Nevertheless, this magnificent contribution in October 1872 was the first of a number of large benefactions to the College over the years from the Llandinam family. Indeed, to anticipate, it is not too much to say that without the steady support, especially at times of crisis, of David Davies, the one very rich Welshman whose generosity put the others to shame, it is difficult to see how the College could have avoided closure by bankruptcy.

In the happy euphoria of that public breakfast, other well-to-do supporters of the College similarly responded as far as their purses would allow. Foulkes Roberts gave £500, as did another unnamed Manchester Welshman, and several other friends in that notably sympathetic area each promised £100. Stephen Evans of London added £500 to the £150 he had already donated, and it was announced that Samuel Morley, Liberal M.P. for Bristol, a generous English benefactor of a whole range of good causes and an employer with an exceptionally advanced view of industrial relations, had promised a second contribution of £500.[3] Other lesser sums were forthcoming and, at the end of that day, over £5,000 in cash or promises for one College purpose or another had been obtained.[4]

Every penny of this money was desperately needed. The College endowment at the outset amounted to no more than £1,200; that is, William Williams' original contribution of £1,000, improved over the years by interest and dividends. Almost £5,000 had been paid over on the College building, but the downpayment had been so small and the rate of interest on the purchase money outstanding so high, that little reduction of the debt had been possible; it remained, forbiddingly, at over £7,000. And now that the College had opened there were, of course, all sorts of other day-to-day needs for money that had to be met.[5]

But at least the large drain on resources (which had aroused so much criticism in the past) occasioned by the need for a salaried secretary had been mercifully sealed off. Dr. Charles had attended the official opening and had regaled the audience with a ruefully humorous account of the difficulties he had encountered in fund-raising. But Charles' responsibilities were now ended and he was not to

---

[2] See below, p. 50. Later in the morning, David Davies withdrew the conditions he had laid down for his £2,000 contribution to scholarships.

[3] According to the *D.N.B.*, Morley, a magnificent builder of chapels, pensioned off his retiring employees at an annual cost of £2,000.

[4] 'Report of the Proceedings at . . . the Opening of the University College of Wales', reprinted from the *Welshman* (18 October 1872). There is a good account in the *Cambrian News* of the same date, and a full description, in Welsh, by Gohebydd in *Baner ac Amserau Cymru* (30 October 1872). *U.C.W. Reports (1863–91)*, pp. 8–9.

[5] 'Statement of Receipts and Expenditure' (9 December 1863–30 June 1873). *U.C.W. Reports (1863–91)*; see also, pp. 15–16.

be replaced. Certainly the local area committees had accepted the responsibility of filling annual quotas for running expenses, and the Manchester committee, especially, was hearteningly active. But in October 1872 no one could say with certainty that this money would be forthcoming, or would, for that matter, be enough; moreover, there was still the need for co-ordination, for drumming up additional support anywhere and everywhere inside and outside Wales, and, inevitably, there would be a mountain of humdrum clerical work to be done. Predictably, in this emergency, Hugh Owen, the one man who, as Henry Richard said, like an ancient Roman 'had never despaired of the Republic', came forward.[6] Owen was then sixty-eight years old; a lesser man would have reasonably concluded that with the College at least opened, enough was enough: but not Hugh Owen. At the end of the year he retired from the Local Government Board and devoted his whole time to the service of the College. There now began that magnificent saga whereby Hugh Owen, with his familiar little black bag, crossed and criss-crossed on the railway routes of Wales, largely at his own expense, in search of money for the College.[7] It is difficult to see how the necessary money would have been forthcoming without this herculean personal effort over several years by a man soon to be in his seventies.

In all these activities, Hugh Owen's singleness of purpose was indispensable: elsewhere it had made him enemies. Dr. Nicholas, the former secretary, had been infuriated by the praise lavished on Owen at the opening ceremonies and wrote in bitter complaint to Henry Richard, and subsequently to the press.[8] Dr. Charles, in his letters to his nephew, kept up a battery of criticism of Owen and, late in October, a long letter appeared in the *Western Mail* posing eleven questions, laden with malevolent innuendo, to Hugh Owen. Much play was made with the fact that the College building had not been handed over to responsible trustees and was still technically in the name of Hugh Pugh, Owen's son-in-law, who could sell the premises if he chose, and was alleged to have 'threatened so to do'.[9]

Owen does not seem to have been at all ruffled by these public criticisms. For the moment everything was in flux: the ambitious title 'the University College of Wales' was self-given and did not obscure the fact that, as yet, it was no more than a private-venture College which had made a frail beginning. In these circumstances, it had not been possible to work out an effective constitution and, meantime, a 'Tentative Scheme' for the temporary government of the College had been drafted. In effect, this placed the management in the hands of the Executive

[6] *The Welshman* (18 October 1872).

[7] W. E. Davies, op. cit., pp. 112–13. I have also been allowed to see Mr. B. L. Davies' thesis, 'Sir Hugh Owen and Welsh Education', shortly to be submitted for the Ph.D. degree of the University of Wales.

[8] 21 and 24 October 1872. N.L.W. MSS. 5505B. See also the *Cambrian News* (1 November 1872).

[9] *Western Mail* (26 October 1872). 'Is it not evident', continued the letter darkly, 'that there is something rotten in the state of Denmark?' *T. C. Edwards Letters*, pp. 8–9, 15–16.

committee; critics, David Charles in particular, insisted that this meant in practice Hugh Owen, who was '*de facto* the Executive committee'.[10]

There was some substance in these charges, and there were certainly unresolved ambiguities in the proposed relationship between the Executive committee and the tiny Senate, led by the new Principal. At the inaugural ceremonies, T. C. Edwards had made a moving declaration of patriotic faith which indicates the high seriousness with which he approached his task:

> I am almost unable to believe it [he said], yet it seems to me that the dream of my boyhood is about to become true, in a very extraordinary way. . . . Ever since I can remember anything, I remember that the most ardent desire of my boyish days was to serve Wales . . . and when I was asked to preside over this College, I began to think, 'Surely this is my boyish dream beginning to come true'. For that reason, I determined . . . to devote the best energies of my whole life to the great work of bringing up young men in this place.[11]

Edwards' professorial assistants had also spoken (sensibly, and in a lower key) at the opening celebrations. The Revd. W. Hoskyns-Abrahall, professor of Classics, was a Herefordshire man, a former Fellow of Lincoln College, Oxford. His colleague, the Revd. H. N. Grimley, professor of Mathematics and Natural Philosophy, was a Cambridge man, 12th Wrangler in 1865. The Registrar, who doubled up as Librarian, was E. Penllyn Jones, a thirty-two-year-old bachelor who had been educated at Bala and at Glasgow University, and was then a master at Towyn School. His name had been suggested by the Principal; Hugh Owen had interviewed Jones at Towyn station and engaged him at £80 per annum, with the further stipulation that he would spend the vacations raising money for the College.[12] Abrahall was not to last long and Grimley was to have his share of troubles: but Penllyn Jones took root and became a much-loved favourite of many generations of students.[13]

The College opened with twenty-six students; during the course of the session numbers rose to sixty-two and, additionally, there were thirty-one others who attended, at least intermittently, an evening preparatory class, which was all that remained of an earlier more ambitious scheme to establish a substantial preparatory school in association with the College.[14] Their average age was between nineteen and twenty, but the range was considerable, boys of fourteen or fifteen appearing side by side with men in their middle twenties. It had been evident from their entrance applications that many of the students would be raw youths deficient in

---

[10] *T. C. Edwards Letters*, p. 10. Committee Minutes, ff. 206–7.

[11] *The Welshman* (18 October 1872).   [12] Committee Minutes, ff. 229–32.

[13] 'Servant of all, beloved by all', as one early student put it. T. T. Lucius Morgan, *Rupert of Glamorgan* (Dolgellau, no date), p. 60.

[14] *U.C.W. Reports* (*1863–91*), p. 7. Owens College had no more than thirty-three students at the outset in 1856.

previous training: however, there was the cheering news that some of the older entrants, ministerial candidates largely, included some of the best students from the Bala College, 'the muffs' there, according to Lewis Edwards, 'having decided to go elsewhere'.[15] It had been hoped to board all the students in the College; after all, it had been designed as a hotel, and had dozens of suitable small rooms, but the plain fact was that there was no money available for even the simplest furnishing and therefore, regretfully, students had to be lodged separately in the town. This at least had the great merit of cheapness: according to the testimony of one of the first students, board and lodging cost no more than 15*s*.–16*s*. a week. All lodgings were to be 'approved' and the authorities issued a stern injunction that 'no public houses or beer shops shall be approved of'. At any rate, town–gown relations began encouragingly; the people of Aberystwyth went out of their way to be kind to the novitiate students and, at the end of the session, the Principal reported that he had received no complaints of bad behaviour.[16]

It was unfortunate that students had to be dispersed into lodgings because the great disparities in age did not make for easy contact; and in this first session there were no debates and numbers were too small for effectively organized games. Moreover, students very rarely met all their fellows even in classes. As had been expected, in the main they 'were a scratch lot', ill-prepared and not especially able.[17] Inevitably, therefore, classes were very small and the teaching had to be conducted at several different levels; Latin and Mathematics students, for example, were divided into four groups: higher senior, lower senior, higher junior, and lower junior.

However, an attempt had been made to give the College some sort of academic semblance: in October the committee decided that, from the start of the second term (called Lent, a description which was to cause trouble), students attending lectures were 'to wear a suitable academical dress', and it was recommended that the Principal and staff should do so too.[18] Early in the second term, T. C. Edwards went up to Oxford and took the opportunity to consult his old mentor, Jowett. Naturally enough, an Oxford man was in favour of residential education, and Jowett strongly urged the Principal to get as many students as possible, 'the scholars, at least, lodged in College'. Jowett was evidently much interested in Aberystwyth; he insisted that Edwards' chief purpose should be 'to inspire the students with enthusiasm', by personal contact as far as possible, and for that reason he should not undertake too much teaching. Jowett also thought it wise

[15] *T. C. Edwards Letters*, pp. 28, 33.

[16] W. R. Evans, 'The First Students' Reminiscences', in Iwan Morgan, pp. 53–6. Committee Minutes, ff. 232–4. *U.C.W. Reports (1863–91)*, p. 12.

[17] W. R. Evans, loc. cit., pp. 54–5. Because of poor standards of performance, not all the scholarships on offer in October 1872 had been awarded.

[18] Committee Minutes, ff. 232–4.

'to encourage athletics', for it seemed to him that dissenting students were much 'too bookish', which tended 'to enfeeble the mind'.[19]

Internally then, in view of the very considerable difficulties, the College had made a fair start. And the Guarantee Fund and sundry other items of income, including students' fees, produced enough money in that first year to meet essential expenses and leave a small balance in hand of just over £300.[20] But otherwise, the external relations of the College during the first session soon ran into heavy weather. From the beginning, the promoters of the College had been all too aware of the need not to arouse the disrupting jealousies of the religious sects in Wales. At the same time, despite the repeated stress on the unsectarian character of the College, the committee were all, at least formally, strongly Christian (Foulkes Roberts, for example, insisted in 1873 that it was 'essential to get Christian men as professors so as to influence the young men') and, naturally enough, the committee at the outset expressed a wish that there should be voluntary daily Prayers at the College; students with 'conscientious scruples' could simply stay away. The form of Prayer to be used was left to the discretion of the Principal.[21] The two professors were, of course, Anglicans, and T. C. Edwards was an exceptionally liberal-minded Calvinistic Methodist, with a taste for beautiful language; no such curiosity as an unsectarian manual of prayers existed, and in these circumstances it seemed quite natural to read daily the matchless prose of the Book of Common Prayer.

Among the small batch of students that first year was T. W. O. Pughe, son of John Pughe of Aberdovey, physician and *littérateur*, friend and biographer of the Welsh poet, *Eben Fardd*. Pughe was the leader in the Aberdovey district of a small group of Plymouth Brethren. Dr. Pughe's first letter of protest to the Principal about the daily Prayers was written more in sorrow than in anger. Despite all the talk of an unsectarian college, Aberystwyth, he insisted, was simply 'a denominational College with a conscience clause':

> Instead of the promised gold, we are put off with aluminium [he said, and, quickly switching his metaphors]. . . . The noble ship, from which we have expected so much, is now on a rock we little thought of. Helm about without a moment of childish delay, or her destruction is certain.[22]

In fact, as Pughe pointed out, the matter had already been taken up by the press, especially the denominational newspapers. Immediately a tremendous hubbub developed in the correspondence columns and leader pages of the press of Wales,

---

[19] *T. C. Edwards Letters*, pp. 39–40.

[20] 'Statement of Receipts and Expenditure', 21 October 1873. *U.C.W. Reports (1863–91)*.

[21] *T. C. Edwards Letters*, pp. 56–7. Committee Minutes, ff. 232–4. Christian beliefs apart, it is possible that the Prayers were designed to counter the charge of critics (*Western Mail*, 30 December 1872, for example) that unsectarian Aberystwyth was, *ipso facto*, a 'Godless institution'.

[22] *T. C. Edwards Letters*, p. 36.

especially Thomas Gee's heavyweight, the *Baner ac Amserau Cymru* of Denbigh. Of course, this was a subject dear to the hearts and minds of almost all Welshmen, ministerial and otherwise. A debate of Byzantine tortuousness and increasing stridency now followed over the next year and more. Gohebydd, a staunch Independent, did his best to defend the College in the columns of the paper for which he wrote, and for his pains was attacked as an Anglican in disguise.[23]

The affair did bring out one important feature: the unclear division of responsibility between the Executive committee and the Senate; and there is evidence of an attempt by some members of the committee (including, it would seem, Hugh Owen), at least in public, perhaps for general political reasons, to shuffle off their responsibility on to the shoulders of the staff.[24] No doubt the whole controversy was a storm in a teacup, but the College rested on such weak foundations that it could not afford to alienate any of its supporters; not surprisingly, Welsh nonconformists were acutely sensitive to any suggestion of an extension of Church privileges which were already, by the legacy of the past, intolerable in their eyes. At any rate, on the Principal's initiative, the College authorities tried to answer criticism with the production of their own Manual of Prayers and Hymns 'from various sources', a *mélange* designed to satisfy the most carping sectarian. This new publication was prefaced by a round-robin endorsement signed by the Principal of the Baptist College, Pontypool, by the Chairman of the Congregational Union of Wales, by Dr. Lewis Edwards for the Calvinistic Methodists, and by the Revd. John Griffiths, Rector of Neath, representing the Church.[25]

The Rector had tried to play a useful emollient part in the controversy. In May 1873 he had written at length to Thomas Gee, in terms of sensitive understanding of nonconformist fears, appealing to their common Protestantism, and pointing to Rome (then making converts in England in droves) as the real enemy. Griffiths was now emerging as a strong supporter of the College at Aberystwyth. 'It is of the greatest importance to Wales [he wrote to Gee], that this College succeed. . . . Are we in Wales doomed to everlasting contention and strife?'[26]

Griffiths received more kicks than plaudits from his fellow Churchmen for this and other sensible attempts (including his support for the Aberystwyth College) that he made to come to terms with nonconformity. But it is to be noticed, as an indication of the almost impossibly difficult position of the College authorities in matters bearing on religion, that Griffiths, for all his conciliatory temper, threatened that, 'if the present effort to eliminate all recognition of religion within

---

[23] E. Pan Jones in *Y Faner* (22 October 1873). One correspondent earlier (16 July 1873) had taken the Aberystwyth transgression a considerable stage further and had attacked the 'poisonous Catholic teachings' at the College.

[24] Compare, for example, Owen's public statement reported in *Y Faner* (24 September 1873), with his letters to T. C. Edwards at that time in *T. C. Edwards Letters*, pp. 58–9.

[25] *U.C.W. Reports* (*1863–91*), pp. 19–20. There is a copy of the Manual in the College archives.

[26] 13 May 1873. N.L.W. MSS. 8306D, f. 98 a and b.

the walls of the College' should succeed, in conscience, he would have to with-draw his support.[27]

Of course, nonconformist suspicions of the College were sharpened by the fact that, concurrently with the storm over daily Prayers, there was yet one more attempt to come to terms with St. David's College, Lampeter. It appeared to have been given some new life by Hugh Owen. In January 1873, Owen was on a fund-raising sweep through North Wales. He called on Lord Penrhyn and found him 'brimful of prejudice' against the College; later Owen saw Joshua Hughes, the Bishop of St. Asaph, the first authentic Welsh bishop of the see since the early eighteenth century. Bishop Hughes and Owen enjoyed cordial relations; both had the interests of Welsh higher education very much at heart, and the two of them were genuinely anxious, if possible, to unite the Aberystwyth and Lampeter Colleges in a university of Wales. Despite the mutual goodwill, and a lengthy and interesting correspondence on the merits of a teaching as opposed to a merely examining Welsh university (an important question with a future), once more the fundamental incompatibilities between the needs and ambitions of the two Colleges became evident and the negotiation petered out.[28]

This negative result was no great disappointment to the Executive committee, most of whom had expected little else. Nor were they unduly disturbed by con-tinued rumblings of discontent from intransigents over College Prayers. Lewis Edwards, for one, thought that the best course was to take no notice of 'howling dogs'.[29] The staff, however, had borne most of the brunt of public criticism and there were signs that their morale had suffered. There is the suggestion in August 1873 that T. C. Edwards had at least momentarily considered leaving the College, and earlier the Principal and his two professorial colleagues had bitterly resented the 'grave injustice' of the malicious attacks on them which had 'greatly hindered' their work.[30] However, all was not unrelieved gloom at the College. In February 1873 a College debating society was instituted with an Inaugural Lecture, finely phrased as were most of his Addresses, by the Principal. The society, which met every Friday at 7.30 p.m., aimed at providing 'a medium for the interchange of thought and feeling amongst the students of the day and evening classes'. During the year the routine grind of ordinary classes was enlivened by occasional lectures by distinguished outside friends of the College; and the Executive committee, hemmed in as usual by shortage of money, voted an appropriation of £100 a year for the formation of a College library and, boldly lifting their eyes to the future, set up a committee for the collection of rare books and manuscripts in the Welsh

---

[27] *T. C. Edwards Letters*, p. 46. Griffiths had told Principal Edwards earlier (ibid., p. 37) that his advocacy of the claims of the College did 'not please many of my brethren'.

[28] Ibid., pp. 41–60. J. Gibson, *Higher Education in Wales: The University College, Aberystwyth, in relation to existing institutions* (1878), pp. 28–9.

[29] *T. C. Edwards Letters*, p. 55.

[30] Ibid., pp. 54–5. Revd. J. Griffiths to Thomas Gee. N.L.W. MSS. 8306D, f. 98 a and b.

language, which, it was hoped, in time, would form the nucleus for the establishment of 'a National Library of Wales'.[31]

Indeed, there were other signs that, for all the difficulties, the College authorities were growing in confidence. From the beginning, some of those associated with the College had argued that an intense love of music was an important ingredient of the Welsh genius, and any national Welsh College ought naturally to foster its study. In September 1872 Gohebydd had suggested that, as soon as possible, a professor of Music should be added to the staff, and he proposed that the obvious man for the job was his protégé, Joseph Parry, then living in America.[32] Parry's career hitherto had been romantic: born in Merthyr Tydfil in 1841, he had worked as a pit-boy at the tender age of nine; when he was thirteen the family emigrated to Dannville, Pennsylvania. Joseph Parry grew up in a musical environment, and in America he studied harmony in his spare time when work in the Dannville rolling-mills was over. Compositions which he sent to the Welsh National Eisteddfod in 1863–4 aroused a good deal of enthusiasm, and a public fund was raised in Wales which enabled him (having successfully evaded two attempts to press-gang him into the Yankee army during the American Civil War) to come over to study at the Royal Academy of Music and later to take a bachelor's degree in Music at Cambridge. In June 1873 the Executive committee empowered Gohebydd to engage Parry as professor of Music at the College. His functions were, according to his patron, 'to lift the standard of music in the nation generally', and to act as 'a stepping-stone' for Welsh musicians, 'from the village choir to the Royal Academy of Music'.[33]

At the end of the first year Hoskyns-Abrahall resigned his Classics chair. The ostensible reason was that his leave of absence from the English benefice that he still held could not be extended.[34] Abrahall was popular with the students, but T. C. Edwards was evidently dissatisfied with him, and Jowett had advised the Principal not to re-engage Abrahall for a second year.[35] He was replaced by J. Mortimer Angus, then twenty-three years old, who now began an exceptionally long association with the College and, later, the University of Wales. Angus became professor of Latin and was prepared, with no great confidence, to double up as professor of History.[36] Six months later, Grimley's duties were divided and Leonard Lyell, nephew of the great geologist, Sir Charles Lyell, became professor

---

[31] *U.C.W. Reports (1863–91)*, pp. 19, 21–2, 56. It was not inappropriate, for a College attempting to lift itself by its bootstraps, that in the following year a parcel of books bought at half-price for the Library should include several of the works of Samuel Smiles, including *Self-Help* and *Character*.

[32] *T. C. Edwards Letters*, p. 31.

[33] For Parry see E. Keri Evans, *Cofiant Joseph Parry* (Cardiff, 1921); Owain T. Edwards, *Joseph Parry, 1841–1903* (Cardiff, 1970); Parry's almost indecipherable manuscript autobiography, N.L.W. MSS. 9661D; and *Baner ac Amserau Cymru* (13 and 24 September 1873).

[34] *U.C.W. Reports (1863–91)*, pp. 17–18. [35] *T. C. Edwards Letters*, pp. 39–40.

[36] *T. C. Edwards Letters*, pp. 52–8. *U.C.W. Reports (1863–91)*, p. 9. J. M. Angus, 'Reminiscences of the Early Days', in Iwan Morgan, pp. 57–60.

of Natural Philosophy. Some short time before that, Dr. George Thibaut, who had studied at Heidelberg, was made professor of Hebrew and Modern Languages. Thibaut replaced a Mr. Nichols who had been engaged at the outset as part-time tutor in languages at £5 a term. Once in the job, Nichols tried to raise his payment to £35 a term, and the committee (with Hugh Owen for once prepared not to stint a few pounds) decided that, if they were going to pay more, they might as well have the real professorial article.[37]

Gradually, as funds allowed, the tiny staff was being built up, and in October 1874 the Principal was calling for a doubling of the size of the Senate and pointing, in particular, to the need for a professorship of Law and, more especially still, pleading for the establishment of a chair of Celtic Literature.[38] Gohebydd was moved to hyperbole by these signs of progress: 'Aberystwyth', he wrote in *Y Faner*, 'is the Athens of Wales, the centre of learning and knowledge.'[39]

Dispensing with rose-coloured spectacles, it is fair to say that at this time the Executive committee was acting with sense and energy. T. C. Edwards, who had not hitherto (individuals like Foulkes Roberts aside) thought too highly of them, admitted as much. And he was delighted when, by the start of the third session, it had been possible to furnish rooms for one professor and ten students to live in the College. The Principal had no doubt at all that, although lodgings were a little cheaper, residence was infinitely better: a young man was brought into close contact with others who were 'confessedly superior to him'; his teachers could exert a more direct and powerful influence on him. On the other hand, living in College, he had the privacy of his own room, a matter of vital importance for a young man who wished 'to be something better than a wave driven by the wind and tossed by the caprice of public opinion'. The residential system incorporated the two 'strongest influences in forming character, ...: solitariness and society'. Fees, fixed as low as possible, were £10 a term (with a supplementary terminal charge of £1 for coal); a matron, Mrs. Edwards, 'of great respectability and experience', had been appointed, and it was confidently expected that her care and concern for the students would 'invest College residence with the comfort and cheerfulness of home'.[40] Gradually, as money allowed, it was hoped to increase the number living in College. In this modest way began a system which was to exert a profound influence during the next eleven years, particularly on the small but brilliant second generation of students who came to Aberystwyth in the middle 1870s.

There was one other striking illustration of the Executive committee's resourcefulness at this time. In June 1873 the debt on the building stood at £7,360: the

37 *T. C. Edwards Letters*, pp. 38–9. *U.C.W. Reports* (1863–91), pp. 7–9.
38 Principal's Report, 21 October 1874. *U.C.W. Reports* (1863–91), pp. 9–13.
39 6 May 1874.
40 Principal's Report, 21 October 1874. *U.C.W. Reports* (1863–91), pp. 9–12, 17–18.

committee resolved to make a major effort to rid themselves of this crushing burden which was constricting development. Ten members of the committee contributed, in all, £5,100 towards the redemption: David Davies gave lead again with £1,000, and he was followed by two other coal-owners, the brothers, David and Lewis Davis of Aberdare and Ferndale, who each gave a similar amount: Manchester friends contributed £1,800, with Foulkes Roberts and Thomas Jones heading the list with £500, and with William Rowland, whose eloquent plea had triggered the decision in October 1871 to open the College, following with £100. Hugh Owen's son-in-law, the publicly maligned Hugh Pugh, gave the same amount, and Samuel Morley, M.P., ever-generous, though not then officially connected with the College, gave yet another £500. By October 1874, with the addition of smaller sums, enough money had been collected to clear the debt; and the committee, for once able to answer their critics convincingly with deeds, pointed out proudly that 'the entire work of getting in this money was undertaken by members of their own body, who defrayed their own expenses'.

The way was now clear for vesting the freehold College building in public trustees, and replacing the makeshift interim management arrangements with a proper constitution. The time had come, according to the Executive committee in its dignified swan-song, 'when the permanent may take the place of the provisional'. It had been the Executive committee's privilege to bring the College into existence, 'it will be no less the privilege of the Court of Governors to place it on a lasting foundation'.[41]

On 21 October 1874, on the proposition of Hugh Owen appropriately enough, since he had been publicly vilified for allegedly delaying the transfer previously, control of the College premises was put in the hands of Trustees, twenty-one men all of whom had contributed at least £100 in a lump sum to the College funds.[42] At that same meeting of subscribers a new constitution was formally adopted and, at an adjourned meeting on 1 January 1875, elections were held bringing the new machinery into operation.

The government of the College henceforth was vested in three bodies: a Court of Governors (not less than thirty, not more than a hundred in number) constituted 'the supreme governing body'; the direct management of the financial and other ordinary business of the College was remitted to a committee, to be known as the Council, of thirty members elected by the Court, together with the officers of the College; the Senate, consisting of the Principal (who was a member, *ex officio*, of all three bodies) and the professors, which was to meet at least once a month and, 'subject to the control of the Council', have charge of the academic work and discipline of the College.

Apart from the changed nomenclature, this machinery did not differ strikingly from the old informal arrangements which had been superseded. But the principle

[41] *U.C.W. Reports (1863–91)*, pp. 16–17, 19.   [42] Ibid., p. 5.

of ultimate lay control of the College was re-emphasized and spelt out in unambiguous language. Of course there had never been any question of any other disposition: a would-be national College, owing its foundation to the forces which established Aberystwyth College, could not be anything but popular in its governmental arrangements: the representatives of those who paid the piper were in a position to call the ultimate tune.[43] Principal Edwards accepted this position without hesitation:

Our aim will be to form such a College as the educational wants of Wales from time to time may demand. . . . We ask only to be judged by this simple test: is this the sort of thing Wales at present wants? We heartily desire, above all things, to be in entire sympathy with the great mass of our countrymen. . . . The height of our ambition is to make it the representative of the highest type of intellect and culture among the Cymry.[44]

All the same, there would be the need for considerable lay tact on Court and Council to avoid entrenching upon the legitimate academic interests of the Senate.

The new President of the College was H. A. Bruce, recently ennobled as first Baron Aberdare. Bruce was a moderate Liberal who had been Vice-President of the Committee of the Council on Education in the early 1860s. In 1868 Gladstone invited him to join the Cabinet and was delighted to have discovered 'a heaven-born Home Secretary'.[45] Gladstone's government, busily active in several reforming directions, soon ran into difficulties and Bruce had had a hard time at the Home Office. His licensing legislation infuriated the liquor trade, and did not answer the expectations of the temperance interests. In 1873 his political stock was low and he went upstairs to the House of Lords and became Lord President of the Council in the dying months of Gladstone's first ministry.[46]

In some respects, Aberdare's election as President of the College was natural, even ideal. He had the status appropriate to the position; his adhesion might well encourage other potentates to come to the aid of the College. Of course, he was a Churchman (this, too, might soften the considerable asperity felt by many Anglicans towards the College), but an exceptionally liberal one. He favoured the disestablishment of the Church in Wales; he lamented 'the unfortunate alienation' of the great majority of Welsh people from the Church, but recognized the logical consequences, especially in education, of that fact. He thought it particularly unfortunate that the clergy did not join 'in promoting objects of general

---

[43] The constitution is set out in full in *Minutes of the Court of Governors* (1875), pp. 5–14. Article 14 reflected the old stubborn determination to be genuinely unsectarian: 'No student, professor, teacher, or other officer connected with the College shall be required to make any declaration as to, or to submit to any test whatever of, his religious opinions.'

[44] Principal's Report, 21 October 1874. *U.C.W. Reports* (1863–91), p. 13.

[45] *The Letters of the Rt. Hon. Lord Aberdare* (Oxford, 1902), i. 5.

[46] R. C. K. Ensor, *England 1870–1914* (Oxford, 1944), pp. 20–1. M. E. Chamberlain, 'Lord Aberdare and the Royal Niger Company', *Welsh Hist. Rev.*, iii. 62.

Welsh interest', and he was sharply critical of the 'undisguised hostility' shown by so many Churchmen to the Aberystwyth College which, in his opinion, was 'necessarily of unsectarian character'.[47] Aberdare had been interested in education for a long time and, indeed, in future was to make it the chief work of his life; moreover, he had charm, a conciliatory temper and considerable tact. All in all, it seemed, in the circumstances of the time, he would be the very model of the perfect President. There was one flaw, not then generally evident, which was to appear later, with drastic consequences for a time for Aberystwyth: Aberdare thought the College had been wrongly sited.

What say you to the University of Wales? [he wrote in 1863 to his Merthyr agent]. I do not think it would do for Wales what the Scotch and Irish colleges have done for their countries, unless it were attached to some considerable town, such as Swansea or Cardiff. *It might* then become a common intellectual centre, and do much for us.[48]

However, to Hugh Owen's delight, Aberdare accepted the invitation to become President, modestly disclaiming any particular understanding of the academic world as he had not himself had a university education.[49] At the same time, David Davies of Llandinam (who better to manage money?) was elected Treasurer, and in addition became one of the fifteen Vice-Presidents elected. Hugh Owen, of course, continued as honorary Secretary.

The Governors still hoped to build up an endowment fund of £50,000, and were now sufficiently confident to believe that this could be achieved in the course of three or four years; they were encouraged in this, no doubt, by the generous gift at that time of £2,500 for the capital endowment of the chair of Natural Science by Henry Parnall, a London businessman, who, along with his brother, Robert, had been elected a Vice-President of the College. In the interim something new was required as the old Guarantee Fund, with its area quotas, though it had served its purpose well enough, was now showing diminishing returns and was, in any case, due to be wound up in October 1875. 'I fear that the difficulty of getting money is making me hard [wrote Hugh Owen in May 1875], and leading me to grudge to part with a shilling more than I am obliged to.'[50]

By this time, student fees could be expected to produce just under £1,000 and annual subscriptions a slightly larger sum: but, in the absence of a government grant, another £2,000 a year would be required. It was decided to launch a 'Temporary Sustentation Fund' for that annual amount with a general appeal to the people of Wales. Gohebydd, enthusiasm undiminished and fertile as ever in suggestion, proposed a house-to-house canvass of Wales, and Hugh Owen, well-versed by now in fund-raising, looked to the assistance of the chapels. For the

---

[47] *Letters of . . . Lord Aberdare*, ii. 30–2.   [48] Ibid. i. 203–4.
[49] *T. C. Edwards Letters*, p. 70. *Minutes of the Court of Governors* (1875), p. 10.
[50] *T. C. Edwards Letters*, p. 77.

canvass, committees were formed in all important towns in the Principality; circulars were sent to all ministers and clergymen soliciting congregational collections, and the denominations, Baptist, Congregational, Wesleyan, and Calvinistic Methodist, adopted resolutions in their respective assemblies recommending their constituent chapels to make the proposed collections. At long last, the College had discovered proper machinery for engaging the interest and appealing for the support of the mass of the Welsh people. There were stray criticisms: one correspondent in *Y Faner*, for example, thought that it was unfair to ask for help from ordinary people who were poor and had their own problems.[51] But the general response was astonishingly good: nearly all the nonconformist chapels and some of the parish churches made the collection on the last Sunday in October, designated *Sul y Brifysgol* or University Sunday. It was believed that over 70,000 people had contributed, mostly small amounts, which was all they could afford. In all, during the year, over £3,100 was raised in this way.[52]

The College authorities, of course, had by no means abandoned the hope of obtaining a grant from parliament. In the summer of 1875 the time seemed ripe for another approach to the government: the debt on the College building had been wiped out; the teaching staff had been increased and there were now a hundred students in attendance; regular constitutional machinery for the government of the College had been adopted; and there was a distinguished President to head a delegation asking for aid. On 15 June 1875 an impressive deputation, led by Aberdare, waited upon the Duke of Richmond, Lord President of the Council, the minister with primary responsibility for education in Disraeli's Tory government. Aberdare was supported by ten Welsh M.P.s and a representative group of College Governors. Hugh Owen ('My friend, Mr. Hugh Owen, whom I have known for many years now', as the Duke called him) had briefed the Lord President the day before on the detail in the Memorial, so there was no need for a protracted discussion.

Aberdare understood that, in addition to the government's doctrinaire objection (common to both parties) to voting money for higher education, he would have to meet the argument that as Wales, since the sixteenth century anyway, was simply an extension of, indeed politically an integral part of, England, there was no case for special treatment. Aberdare combated these twin objections with the usual arguments: 'the fostering care of England had not been extended to Wales', and this neglect contrasted sharply with the generous treatment of Scotland and Ireland; Wales was poor and her educational endowments were pitifully few and small; moreover, political union or not, the Welsh, overwhelmingly different in language and religion, were a separate people and could not be treated in the same

---

51 W. Rowlands in the edition of 27 October 1875.

52 *U.C.W. Reports (1863–91)*, 20 October 1876, pp. 10–12. *Minutes of the Court of Governors*, 13 April and 20 October 1875, pp. 22, 49.

way as the inhabitants of an agglomeration of any dozen English counties. The only successful college in England outside Oxbridge was Owens, Manchester, but that was situated in a great centre of population: Aberystwyth's central position linked North and South Wales, but the sparse population of the hinterland added to the difficulties of maintenance. However, poor as they were, the Welsh had made a magnificent effort in self-help, and upwards of £30,000 over the years had been collected for the College. Modest assistance from the government was all that was asked: 'an annual subsidy of £2,500, and a grant of £5,000' towards the completion of the magnificent but still uncompleted building was the limit of their request.

Some few others in the delegation spoke briefly in support, including, unwisely perhaps, David Davies. Richmond, in reply, was all practised disarming ducal charm: he well understood the importance of institutions such as the Aberystwyth College; of course the deputation would realize that the government faced similar requests from other colleges in the kingdom (the special plea for Wales apparently thus blandly pushed aside); moreover, he himself had 'no power to grant the money', that was a matter for the Treasury. No doubt there was a case for educational advance: on the other hand, there was a case against, best represented by that gentleman (David Davies) who, 'from being a working man has raised himself . . . to represent his native country in Parliament', and whose untutored eloquence that day indicated that formal education was not everything. 'If I had been Lord Aberdare', said the duke slyly, 'I should have kept that gentleman in the background.' However, the Memorial would receive the Cabinet's 'best attention' and, for his part, he hoped that some assistance would be forthcoming.[53]

Curiously, Principal Edwards had not accompanied the delegation: incredible as it may seem, it may well be that the money to pay his travelling expenses was simply not available. The Principal had not attended the meeting in London when Mortimer Angus was appointed; Foulkes Roberts was scandalized at his inability to be present: 'I think it should be a standing rule of the Committee [he wrote] that the Principal should attend *every* meeting of the Executive held in London, and of course his expenses paid.'

Possibly the Principal's absence was sheer tactless oversight on the part of the Governors; as Foulkes Roberts said later, 'We have all so much to do with our own businesses that we often forget all about you.'[54] In any case, there was more than enough to occupy T. C. Edwards at the College. Despite Jowett's cautionary advice against too much teaching, of necessity the Principal undertook a great deal: he taught Greek, Logic, and Moral Philosophy, and also delivered 'splendid lectures on English', in the opinion of one bright new student. In all, his teaching

---

[53] 'Report of the Deputation', 27 July 1875. *Minutes of the Court of Governors*, pp. 35–8.
[54] *T. C. Edwards Letters*, pp. 57–8, 76.

programme was fourteen or fifteen hours a week.[55] He and his professorial colleagues had a hard row to hoe: because of generally inadequate preparation and
great variations in the age and previous training of students, classes had to be sub-
divided and instruction was a mixture of formal lecturing and 'catechetical' teaching; that is, the tutorial question and answer methods better suited to individual
requirements. Laboratory equipment for science teaching was hopelessly rudi-
mentary, although occasionally panache could overcome deficiencies. 'We had
a good lecture on Wednesday night,' said one student of a Chemistry class conducted by Grimley, 'the experiments being performed in a grand style.'[56] But
perhaps this was more an indication of an inexperienced student's impressionable
response to new mysteries than of Grimley's teaching skill. The Principal certainly
had no good opinion of Grimley's ability as a teacher: 'if Mr. Grimley is not
a satisfactory teacher, he ought to be got rid of at any cost', Mark Pattison replied
to the Principal's complaints of Grimley's inadequacies.[57]

In fairness, Grimley was simply filling in as Chemistry teacher and soon handed
this responsibility over to Leonard Lyell, whose range of teaching was wide
enough to daunt the most confident: he was responsible for classes in Chemistry,
Physiology and Zoology, Botany, Physical Geography and Geology. As the
Principal well said, in Wales one man must undertake almost alone 'to train
completely the human intellect', and, not surprisingly, 'he is in danger of being
despised unless he resembles Hippias the Sophist whose foible was omni-
science'.[58] Despite the relatively easy entrance requirements, attendance at classes
was closely watched and students were driven hard all the time.

> It is not very hard to enter the College [young Tom Ellis wrote to his friend, D. R.
> Daniel]. I believe you could pass easily if you study Mathematics and English Grammar. . . .
> You must study here, they are not home lessons; you may escape some of them some-
> times, but that will not do. It will be your own loss.[59]

And away from College in the town, there was no escape into anonymity:

> I do wear the University cap and gown . . . We must wear them all the while and
> everywhere [said the same correspondent], except in chapel and at our lodgings. They
> cost 23s. . . . I am grand in them, man; the gown something like a parson's surplice only
> it is black.[60]

---

[55] 'Classes', 1875. *U.C.W. Reports (1863–91)*, p. 43. T. E. Ellis, January 1875. N.L.W. D. R. Daniel
MSS. no. 186.

[56] T. E. Ellis to D. R. Daniel, 26 April 1875. N.L.W. D. R. Daniel MSS. no. 180.

[57] *T. C. Edwards Letters*, p. 90. David Samuel, a former student who went on to Cambridge, said
that lectures at Clare and Caius were worse than those at Aberystwyth, 'so that, after all, old Grim-
[ley] should not be blown up'. N.L.W. T. E. Ellis MSS. no. 1921.

[58] 'Classes', 1875. Principal's Report, 20 January 1875. *U.C.W. Reports (1863–91)*, pp. 51–4, 13–15.

[59] Principal's Report, 21 October 1874. Ibid., p. 9. N.L.W. D. R. Daniel MSS. no. 188.

[60] Ibid., no. 188.

Happily, it was not all dull grind: new students, as the world over, quickly found it wise to watch their tongues in the presence of their seniors and, for a time at least, to 'do like a mouse'. But the probationary period was soon over, and new men quickly picked up the lingo ('I am stewing [studying] like old boots now'), which established that one had arrived and helped somehow to make difficult academic work seem less awesome. Once accepted, 'everyone is kind in the College', and as Tom Ellis reported to his envious friend, Daniel: 'We have plenty of University songs here, you would laugh for ever.' After a Latin class at noon, there was time for a quick game of 'Rounders on the Castle' before a 'Geology (Rocks)' class at 2 p.m.; later in the day (in March 1875, between games' seasons), there was time for scratch cricket and football before an evening's work on Virgil and English, the day ending with 'supper, prayers, bed'. Organized matches had already begun: on Saturday, 20 February 1875, the College football team took on the St. David's College, Lampeter, eleven and a pattern (inevitable in view of the religious edge between the two) that was to become traditional was already established: 'Fierce game for one hour and half. One goal to Lampeter.' In spring or early summer, when Cardigan Bay put on its occasional marvellous placid face, there was rowing, even a 'boat race between College and town', which the skilled local boatmen naturally 'won easily'.[61]

Despite the naïve, schoolboy tone of Tom Ellis' first-year accounts, there was nothing namby-pamby about the small student body. Indeed, the Principal's early Reports show his evident anxiety about the quality of College discipline: in fact, in January 1875, he admitted to the Governors that 'from the beginning discipline had been one of our difficulties'. Principal Edwards was no narrow-minded martinet determined to apply indiscriminately a rigorous set of regulations: effective discipline, in his opinion, meant self-discipline, and he insisted that 'the rules laid down appeal for their sanction to the enlightened reason and good sense of the students'. He was, as he said, 'extremely anxious' to treat his students 'as men who can respect themselves, and as gentlemen who know how to respect others'. Therein, however, lay the rub; all too many of the students were boys in their middle teens, not men. Accordingly, in 1875, a Dean of Residence had been appointed to supervise the students living in College.[62] Two years later, the Senate resolved that the professors should 'act as Proctors, everyone for a week in turn', presumably to exercise some supervision over students in lodgings, and

[61] Ibid., nos. 186, 188a, and 188b. In June the town also won a cricket match by an innings and eleven runs.

[62] Principal's Report, 20 January 1875. *U.C.W. Reports* (1863–91), pp. 9–10. 'Regulations with respect to discipline', *U.C.W. Calendar* (1877), pp. 34–6. Regulation 5 sternly forbade entry 'into a public house without the special permission of the Dean'. Not all students obeyed: on 26 February 1875, F. W. Jones was reported (C.A. S/MN/1) to have been the 'worse for drink' and, evidently deciding to go the whole hog, 'in that state had disturbed a public meeting' (carrying the war to the enemy) 'at the Temperance Hall'.

the Proctors were to be assisted in these duties by the College porter, Mr. Joseph Jones, who was evidently cast as a modest bulldog.[63]

One great cause for disquiet, so far as students were concerned, in those early years, was the fact that so many of them came for so short a time: 'their short-lived careers of three, six or nine months do the students great wrong and the College some injustice', as the Principal said. In some cases early departure occurred simply because, despite the low fees, money had run out; in others, it was the result of an inability to keep up with their work. Not surprisingly with an institution novel in Wales, many came who had no clear idea of the difference between a school and a college. Perhaps they should not be blamed for this, for some of the Governors harboured serious misconceptions about the real purposes of the College.

My object in assisting the College [said David Davies, M.P., in March 1876] was to give the Welsh poor or lower middle class a higher standard of education than they could get elsewhere on account of its cheapness; to fit the young men of Wales for better stations in the mercantile world . . . I understood it to be pure and simple a mercantile college, or school purely elementary. . . . If there is [sic] not sufficient young men seeking the advantage offered by the College for elementary education, it only proves that it is not required.[64]

The Principal, with his day-to-day experience in the classroom, was under no illusions that, very probably for years, the College could do no better than occupy some indeterminate mezzanine status, rather more than a school, not quite an authentic college; at least, not a genuine university college. In April 1875 he had asked the Governors to decide whether they would be content with 'a high class school' preparing youths for the matriculation examinations of Oxbridge and London, or whether they aimed at making the College 'the intellectual centre of Wales'. If the more ambitious purpose prevailed, the teaching staff would have to be increased.[65]

The Governors had done their best and the Senate had gradually grown: when Thibaut left, he was replaced by Dr. Hermann Ethé, polyhistor, multi-linguist, a magnificently idiosyncratic German scholar of European reputation who now began forty years of service to the College. Lyell, perhaps worn down by a too heavy demand on his energy and experience, had gone, but his endowed Natural Philosophy chair had been more than adequately filled by the gifted F. G. Rudler, whose quality quickly won high praise from the Principal. In the summer of 1875, to the delight of all those who cared about the Welsh language, the Revd. D.

---

[63] 14 February 1877. C.A. S/MN/1. Who better to see that students were home betimes than Joseph Jones, whose punctuality was summed up in his nickname 'the Clock'.

[64] Principal's Report, 21 October 1874. *U.C.W. Reports (1863–91)*, p. 12. *T. C. Edwards Letters*, p. 97.

[65] *Minutes of the Court of Governors*, 13 April 1875, p. 19. Unable, of course, to award degrees, the College had worked out an advanced course leading to an 'Associateship'. This modest attempt at lifting students' sights was 'greatly laughed at' by the College's many enemies. J. Gibson, op. cit., p. 28.

Silvan Evans, a prolific writer and, in time, distinguished lexicographer, accepted an appointment to a new chair of Welsh.[66] There was also a new professor of English, the Revd. J. R. Buckley, and when he left after a short stay, he was quickly replaced by W. J. Craig from Trinity College, Dublin. Temporary part-time assistance was also forthcoming from C. J. Cooper, on a year's secondment from the Cambridge University extension scheme to teach History, Political Science, and Law; and R. D. Roberts, an Aberystwyth man, a future great pioneer of adult education in England and for many years a power on the Aberystwyth College Council, rallied round in difficult temporary circumstances and lectured with considerable aplomb in Chemistry, a subject outside his recent experience.[67]

Almost as soon as he joined the Senate, R. D. Roberts proposed that the College should put on special Saturday classes for schoolmasters, and in 1877 these were arranged, the part-time schoolmaster-students paying a fee of 10s. for two terms' instruction. Roberts had dynamic energy and great vision; he did his best to interest his fellow townsmen in classes in physical geography; and at a public lecture in October 1876, the first university extension lecture ever given in Wales, he looked forward to the day when it would be considered 'as necessary to have in every town and district educated teachers of the people as it is now to have pastors to look after their religious education'. He believed strongly that 'one of the functions of the University College of Wales . . . [was] to stand forth as a witness ever before the people, that they must not rest until the means of obtaining higher education [were] within the reach of all'.[68]

Very many years were to pass before Roberts' dream of large-scale provision for extra-mural work in Wales was to begin to come true. However, in 1876, through the further generosity of Henry Parnall, there was an attempt to make the College immediately serviceable to one important section of the Welsh people; Professor H. Tanner of the South Kensington Science and Art Department was engaged to give courses of lectures in Agriculture at the College. In fact, this pioneer venture in a field in which the College, ultimately, was to achieve an international reputation, was not a success, as the potentially large farmer-audience was frightened off by the need to master a little elementary Chemistry. However, Tanner's book, *The First Principles of Agriculture*, was translated into Welsh and 20,000 copies were distributed free, Parnall generously defraying the cost.[69]

---

[66] Principal's Report, 20 January 1875. *U.C.W. Reports (1863–91)*, pp. 8–9. T. C. Edwards to Silvan Evans, 21 July 1875. N.L.W. Cwrt Mawr MSS. 898B.

[67] *U.C.W. Reports (1863–91)* for 1875, p. 4. R. D. Roberts to F. G. Rudler, 27 October 1876. C.A. (MSS., not numbered). N.L.W. D. R. Daniel MSS. no. 6.

[68] C.A. S/MN/1, for 17 November 1876. B. B. Thomas, 'R. D. Roberts and Adult Education', in *Harlech Studies* (ed. B. B. Thomas, Cardiff, 1938), p. 2.

[69] *Cambrian News* (24 August 1877) for an account of the relative failure of the classes and a leader seeking to persuade the bashful to attend. *U.C.W. Reports (1863–91)* for 1877–8, pp. 22–3, for Parnall's

Praiseworthy as these attempts by the Governors to build up the staff were, they were probably trying to do too much too soon, and in no time at all the College's financial situation was again causing serious concern. During the session 1875–6 subscriptions had brought in £4,717 but, with increased numbers, staff salaries had risen to £2,580, and over £1,250 had had to be spent on adaptation of the College building and such minimum furnishing of rooms as could be afforded. Furthermore, the increase in the number of students at the College created additional difficulties; for, as Hugh Owen admitted later, with fees as low as £10, every student had to be subsidized to the extent of £43 a year.[70] At his wits' end for money, Hugh Owen watched the administration of the College lynx-eyed. When poor Penllyn Jones (who had done yeoman service in setting up local cadres for house-to-house canvassing for money) rashly bought a dozen bottles of gum at 1s. each and six gross of paper clips at 1s. 6d. a gross, Hugh Owen pursued him hotly with a reiterated 'Why so many?' Jones had compounded his crime in the Secretary's eyes by paying £4. 13s. 0d. for 500 quill pens for students' use in examinations; an absurd extravagance, according to Owen, for these quills were more expensive than those used in the House of Lords.[71]

There seemed little likelihood of assistance from the government. Lord Aberdare had not been surprised that the Duke of Richmond had been 'guarded' in his reply to the deputation asking for a grant in June 1875. It was quite evident that the Tory cabinet was in no hurry to give its final answer; whistling in the dark to keep up their courage, the Governors decided that the long delay did not imply rejection. As the government lay stubbornly doggo for nearly two years, in April 1877 the College tried to bring public pressure to bear; town councils, school boards, and other public bodies in Wales, 256 authorities representing over a million people in all, were persuaded to send in resolutions in support of a further Memorial from the College, praying for a grant, which was submitted to the Duke of Richmond on 18 July.[72] The government remained unhurried and unimpressed, and it was not until June 1878 that a decision was given: Richmond wrote curtly to say that he and his cabinet colleagues 'do not see our way to making any such grant as you suggest'. Bravelys wallowing their bitter disappointment, the Governors of the College asserted their confidence that, ultimately, a grant would be obtained and, meantime, the College, somehow or other, would 'not fail to be sufficiently provided for'.[73]

endowment. When he died in 1878, Henry Parnall generously remembered the College with a legacy of £5,000.

[70] U.C.W. Reports (1863–91), pp. 9–10. Aberdare Report, Minutes of Evidence, p. 14.

[71] T. C. Edwards Letters, p. 95.

[72] Richmond's reply (The Times, 19 July 1877) this time to the deputation's assertion was much more vigorously challenging, and he sharply rebuked those of the deputation who seemed to him to want 'the power of granting cheap degrees'.

[73] Ibid., p. 81. U.C.W. Reports (1863–91), 20 October 1876, p. 13, 10 October 1877, p. 13, 16 October

This was more easily said than done and, disquietingly, while expenses con-
tinually rose, there was an alarming downward trend in the amounts produced
by the congregational collections each October, despite a manful effort by Hugh
Owen and his small army of helpers. In 1875, £3,572 had been collected; the next
year, with the onset of economic depression in South Wales, the figure had
dropped to £2,752, and it fell again by £200 in 1877.[74] There were signs that
some members of the Court and Council were losing heart and Foulkes Roberts,
not the man to mince matters, came to the conclusion in the summer of 1877 that
'new blood' was 'wanted in the Council *badly*'; the October meeting of the
Governors was poorly attended and proceedings were so limp and unenthusiastic
that one keen local observer concluded that 'the interest of the promoters was
falling off'.[75]

Matters were not helped by repeated hostile sniping by the critical press: the
Western Mail, hotly Tory and Anglican in its partisan bias, had never looked with
favour on the College. The South Wales newspaper's disparagement, which soon
became automatic, began at the outset: in August 1872 Savin's fine building was
described as 'a disused or unfinished hostelry' and, with the journal's regional
patriotism showing strongly, Aberystwyth was 'the most absurd spot that could
by any possibility have been chosen'; Merthyr Tydfil, of all places, appeared to
the leader-writer to be much more suitable. Later that year a correspondent
viciously assailed the College as a 'Godless institution', the haunt of radicalism,
sensibly ignored by the 'aristocracy of blood, wealth and intellect, and the educated classes' in Wales, 'almost to a man'. When Professor Buckley resigned in
1876, the *Western Mail*, blithely ignoring Buckley's express disclaimer, insisted
that he had left because he found the College 'uncongenial', and followed up with
further sneers at the nonconformists' 'new toy at Aberystwyth'.[76] Possibly, the
Western Mail's predictable malevolence partly answered itself, but repeated
criticism by warm friends of the College was much more damaging.

In September 1873 young John Gibson, already at thirty-two a formidable
newspaper polemic, had been brought from Oswestry to Aberystwyth to edit
the *Cambrian News*. In no time at all, Gibson, fearless, hard-hitting (the crusading
editor of legend, almost), not always fair to those he attacked, had built up the
newspaper into one of the most influential weeklies in Wales. Gibson was keenly
and genuinely interested in the College and reported its affairs at great length: but

---

1878, pp. 20–1. As a pointer to their real future hopes, perhaps, College Reports from 1877 were
prefaced by some laudatory remarks on the College and Welsh willingness to make sacrifices for
education by Gladstone, more forthcoming out of office than in, in a speech at Nottingham.

[74] *Aberdare Report, Minutes of Evidence*, p. 13. *U.C.W. Reports (1863–91)*, 10 October 1877, pp. 11–12.
Baner ac Amserau Cymru (24 October 1877).
[75] *T. C. Edwards Letters*, p. 124. J. Gibson, op. cit., p. 30.
[76] *Western Mail* (4 August, 30 December 1872, 9 March 1876).

he was convinced that the higher management was defective and that far too much power was engrossed jealously by Hugh Owen.

> The assistance rendered to this Institution by Mr. Hugh Owen is simply beyond computation [Gibson wrote in 1876], but the price paid for services such as his may be too high. . . . The danger is of there being an Owen's College, Wales, as well as an Owen's College, Manchester.[77]

These and other criticisms, malicious or well-intentioned, gradually built up 'in the minds of thousands who are unacquainted with the real state of the College', as Tom Ellis noted with anxiety in 1878, 'an impression . . . that there is something weak in the system, and insufficient in the training'.[78]

In all these circumstances, it was not surprising that raising money from the public to keep the institution alive was becoming desperately more difficult year by year. The refusal of a government grant seemed the last straw; even the normally unruffled, mild-mannered Hugh Owen recalled in exasperation the opinion years before of Henry Lingen, one of the notorious Commissioners of the Educational Inquiry of 1847: 'You Welsh', Lingen had told Hugh Owen, 'deserve all the kicks that you get, because you do not assert your rights.' Owen thought that things had not altered much since then: 'Ireland is petted by the government, while peaceable Wales received their kicks.'[79] In the summer of 1878 financial difficulties were at crisis point and the Principal was asked to suggest economies. As a result, professorial salaries, already abysmally low, were reduced still further and three members of the Senate were given notice: Grimley and Craig, whose teaching ability was suspect, and Walter Keeping, who had replaced Rudler, not altogether effectively, were the three who were jettisoned to lighten the boat. Some time later, three new appointments at a cheaper rate were made: T. S. Humpidge, who drove himself by overwork to an early death, became professor of Natural Science, M. W. MacCallum, starting a distinguished academic career, became professor of English, and R. W. Genese, a slave-driver with no time for idlers, and not much patience with dullards, was appointed to the chair of Mathematics which he was to occupy for over forty years.[80]

---

[77] *Cambrian News* (13 October 1876).

[78] T. E. Ellis' Diary, October 1878. N.L.W. D. R. Daniel MSS. no. 6.

[79] Hugh Owen to Henry Richard, 19 November 1878. N.L.W. MSS. 5505B. One favourite argument supporting an educational grant for Wales was that, as the Principality was much more law-abiding, less public money had to be spent on police and prisons. The actual figures seem to show that Taffy, whatever the English might say, was not a thief: on the other hand (see W. R. Lambert, 'Drink and Sobriety in Wales, 1835–95', unpublished Ph.D. thesis, University of Wales, 1969), he was quite likely to be drunken and prone to violence.

[80] *Council Minutes* (1878), pp. 151–61. *The Dragon*, vol. 50, pp. 9–11. T. R. Dawes, 'Aberystwyth in "85"', in Iwan Morgan, p. 82. Of Craig, it was said (T. T. Lucius Morgan, op. cit., p. 62): 'No man knew more or could teach less.'

Soon afterwards, there was one other important departure. In the opinion of several of the Governors, Joseph Parry had proved a disappointment. He had quickly attracted a score or more students to the College and, needing female voices for his College choir, had persuaded the authorities to allow women students of Music to be registered. The professor was a prolific composer and he used the choir in concerts in Aberystwyth and elsewhere to try out his choral works; moreover, bounding with restless energy, and with a good American eye for money, he travelled all over Wales adjudicating at *eisteddfodau* and conducting *cymanfaoedd canu*, the great Welsh chapel singing festivals. The Governors began to look askance at these frequent absences and tried to control Parry's extra-mural activities; it was felt by some that, musical talents aside, many of Parry's students were of poor quality and their presence in disproportionate numbers did not enhance the College's reputation. Nor was Parry a good disciplinarian; several of his Aberystwyth concerts were disrupted by rumbustious behaviour by students from other departments in the College.[81]

In July 1878 the Council got rid of the Music department's specialist students (thus effectively killing off Parry's choir); the professor's terms were re-negotiated and his music teaching, for the future, was to be confined to the ordinary students of the College. In practice, this meant the end of the Music department.[82] In August 1879 R. D. Roberts, already fanatical in his championship of extra-mural work, harangued a crowded town meeting in favour of Parry and his moribund department. But at the October meeting of the Council the professor's position was blandly glossed over, and Gibson of the *Cambrian News* sarcastically observed that there ought at least to have been some mention of Parry, if only as 'the first holder of a sinecure at the University College of Wales'.[83]

Joseph Parry's position was humiliating; moreover, his income had dropped considerably. In 1878 he had taken a doctorate in Music at Cambridge and it had cost him £300 to take a South Wales choir up to Cambridge to perform the composition which won him his higher degree, and the publication of his opera, *Blodwen*, had also been expensive. He opened a private music school in the town where he was wildly popular. But it was not enough; Parry was a proud man and, ultimately, at the end of the session in 1880, he resigned and left Aberystwyth, the townspeople turning out *en masse* to see him off.

There is no doubt that Joseph Parry, an authentic, impulsive, wayward artist, was a difficult man to fit easily into the work of a small struggling College, and certain aspects of the showman ballyhoo with which he was surrounded were open

[81] C.A. S/MN/1 (27 March 1878). N.L.W. D. R. Daniel MSS. no. 25 (1 April 1878). Owain T. Edwards, op. cit., pp. 37–41.

[82] *Council Minutes*, 20 July and 15 October 1878, pp. 151–61. *U.C.W. Reports (1863–91)*, 1878–9, pp. 12–13.

[83] *T. C. Edwards Letters*, p. 170. *Cambrian News* (24 October 1879). See also, *Baner ac Amserau Cymru* (August–September 1879).

to legitimate criticism. Nevertheless, it is impossible to avoid the conclusion that the Council acted unwisely; he did a great deal to keep the College in the public eye; his great hymn-tune, 'Aberystwyth', written during these years, certainly drew the attention of the Welsh all over the world in the best possible way. It is possible that if Parry's old patron, Gohebydd, had not died in 1878, he might have acted successfully as a sympathetic intermediary between a bewildered Parry and an exasperated Council. At any rate, he was now a national (in some respects, an international) figure and went off to South Wales to live the life of a great musical celebrity, *Y Doctor Mawr*, the Great Doctor, where the English does not quite convey the respectful awe suggested by the Welsh version.[84] Despite his wounded pride, Joseph Parry bore no malice towards the Aberystwyth College authorities; indeed, in September 1885, when the College ultimately received an effective government grant, Parry wrote to Stephen Evans to ask if the Council would now 'entertain the resuscitation' of the chair and department of Music at Aberystwyth, adding that he would be 'glad to resume' his 'happy connection with that College'. But it was not to be; Aberystwyth's loss was to be Cardiff's gain.[85]

The Council's criticisms of Joseph Parry's work at the College overlooked the fact that, in his own unorthodox way, he was an effective teacher, and, in consequence, was popular with the general body of students.[86] The truth was that the lay authorities of the College were so dominated by money difficulties that they failed to see and understand that, in the late 1870s, Aberystwyth was beginning to get into its stride and starting to fulfil the hopes that had been centred on its foundation. In the continued absence of a sufficient number of good grammar schools in Wales, students still came up to the College badly prepared. But Principal Edwards had noted and reported, as early as October 1874, that the quality was 'improving'. There was some ground for disappointment, even disquiet, that far too high a proportion of the entrants came from Cardiganshire (seventy-six out of one hundred and forty-nine students at the College between 1872 and 1874). In December 1874 Hugh Owen, ever concerned about adverse public reaction, suggested to the Principal that it might be 'expedient' to omit from his annual Report the customary listing of the county origins of students, because the local dominance of Cardiganshire showed 'that the benefits of the College were very restricted'.[87] Even so, Cardiganshire could produce some students of high quality, as witness David Adams from Talybont, who went on to a distinguished ministerial career, and David Samuel of Aberystwyth, who won

[84] Owain T. Edwards, op. cit., pp. 36–42. Parry's photograph, facing p. 48, is subtitled, *Y Doctor Mawr. The Welsh Outlook*, February 1924, pp. 48–9.

[85] 4 September 1885. C.A. (C), MSS., not numbered.

[86] J. E. Lloyd, 'A Retrospect, 1877–81', in Iwan Morgan, p. 72. T. T. Lucius Morgan, op. cit., p. 60. U.C.W. *Magazine*, iii. 95.

[87] Principal's Report, 21 October 1874. *U.C.W. Reports (1863–91)*, p. 8. *T. C. Edwards Letters*, pp. 69–70.

a scholarship to Cambridge, picked up several prizes against fierce competition, and was placed 12th Wrangler in 1879.[88]

Cardiganshire students continued their numerical dominance down to 1880 (one hundred and seventeen out of three hundred and thirteen students in all), but, in the later 1870s, several brilliantly gifted young men from other Welsh counties and elsewhere arrived at the College. Tom Ellis (accompanied by a testimonial from his headmaster ominously citing 'delicate health' as his 'great drawback') came from Bala; S. T. Evans, a future Solicitor General, President of one of the divisions of the High Court, and great international jurist, from Skewen; E. J. Ellis-Griffith, born in Birmingham, brought up in Anglesey, came to the College as a prelude to a brilliant career in law and politics; and there was J. E. Lloyd from Liverpool, future doyen of Welsh historians, and T. F. Roberts a prodigy from Aberdovey, who was to become the second Principal of the College. In 1880 the entrance examination list was headed by O. M. Edwards, from Merioneth, who came up with enough money to stay for two years and hoped that something would turn up to take him on later to Oxford.[89] These were, of course, only the very exceptionally gifted, and there were several others only slightly less talented, and indeed some equally able who, for one reason and another, did not quite fulfil subsequently their undoubted promise at this time.[90]

Nearly all these young men went on subsequently to Oxbridge, recording *en route* an astonishing array of open scholarship successes which testified not only to their natural ability but also to the quality of their preparation at Aberystwyth. The College, for all its publicized frailties, had drawn them like a magnet; almost every one of them was filled with a high patriotic purpose and, living in the College itself, as most of them did at one time or another, their ambition to serve Wales was strengthened and deepened, and their loyalty to the institution established for all time.[91] Nor did the teaching staff focus their energies on these obvious high-fliers. Tom Ellis noted in his Diary that 'poor and unpromising students are taken care of, quite as much, to say the least, as those who intend entering the Universities and thus bring[ing] some favour to the College'.[92] But the main point was that T. C. Edwards was no longer being asked to make bricks without straw. There is no doubt that the Principal was a complex man, curiously

[88] For an interesting account of Samuel's difficulties and his level-headed appraisal of Cambridge virtues and vices, see Samuel to Ellis, 20 February 1876. N.L.W. T. E. Ellis MSS. 1921.

[89] N.L.W. T. E. Ellis MSS. 2978. W. J. Gruffydd, *Cofiant O. M. Edwards* (Aberystwyth, 1937), vol. i, 164–6. O. M. Edwards thought that the examination was 'very hard'; he was delighted with his landlady who was exceptionally kind and motherly, and spoke fluently what he thought 'very odd Welsh, like all the people of the South here'.

[90] T. T. Lucius Morgan, 'The Days of Old in the U.C.W.', in Iwan Morgan, pp. 61–6, discusses their qualities with engaging candour.

[91] 'To all old students, "Aber." is one of the dearest recollections of the past', as one of T. F. Roberts' contemporaries put it. C.A. PC (7).

[92] 20 September 1878. N.L.W. D. R. Daniel MSS. no. 6.

withdrawn, perhaps because he had grown up in the shadow of a famous father and lived, himself, from an early age in the fierce light of public life. For all that, he had a striking personality that impressed itself unforgettably on his students; his nickname, 'the Prince', suitably expressed their unbounded admiration for him; they readily forgave him his quick temper, and realized that they were in the presence of something uncommonly like greatness.[93] T. C. Edwards was not just interested in brilliant examination successes, invaluable as they might be in convincing waverers of the value of his College. 'Beyond all University examinations lies the future work of life', and, meantime, as he told his students in November 1879, 'let the College be Wales writ small.'[94] This is what he achieved to an astonishing extent during his tenure, and perhaps most of all, at least in terms of tangible results, in the years when Tom Ellis and his friends were at the College.

They were a spirited group, pouring out their energy in work and play: Tom Ellis' record of work (more often than not, ten hours a day, aside from classes) is enough to daunt all but the utterly dedicated; and according to the testimony of Mortimer Angus, this was not untypical.[95] Despite the smallness of numbers, debates were lively, with a blend of wit and serious argument; and as the natural inclination of most was liberal, even radical, and anti-Establishment, it was customary for each in turn to be given a brief to champion a cause he utterly abhorred. In 1878 the first volume of the College *Magazine* (later, the *Dragon*) appeared. It was embellished with the College motto *Nid byd, byd heb wybodaeth* ('No world, world without knowledge'), which the Governors had chosen in October 1875.[96] A considerable (perhaps an excessive) proportion of the material in the early magazines was contributed by the staff. Inevitably, clandestine unofficial rivals, edited by students and not quite so respectful in tone, quickly appeared. Tom Ellis produced the *Cap* (S. T. Evans providing the cartoons), 'intended for the Insiders', that is, those living in College. It included skits on the staff and, predictably, food complaints: 'all sheep-rearers thoughout Cardiganshire and the adjoining counties speak highly of the U.C.W. and its domestic officials', says the edition of May 1877. The *Cap* soon had its rival, the *Gown*, edited by Lucius Morgan, who was quickly arraigned for libel in a 'case' in which the opposing counsel were S. T. Evans and E. J. Ellis-Griffith.[97]

For those not mesmerized by figures, there were plenty of signs of vigour in the College in the late 1870s. But the Governors thought otherwise; when Grimley and Craig had been given notice on veiled charges of incompetence in 1878, not unnaturally they had appealed to the Council which had suspended the

[93] See, for example, T. F. Roberts in U.C.W. *Magazine*, xxii. 321–3; T. E. Ellis in ibid. xxi. 298; and T. T. Lucius Morgan, 'Principal Edwards and the U.C.W.', in Iwan Morgan, pp. 66–9.

[94] Introduction to U.C.W. *Magazine*, i. 3–4.

[95] 'Reminiscences of Early Days', in Iwan Morgan, pp. 58–9.

[96] *Minutes of the Court of Governors*, 20 October 1875, pp. 49–50.

[97] 1 April 1878. N.L.W. D. R. Daniel MSS. nos. 12, 25. T. T. Lucius Morgan, op. cit., p. 62.

PLATE 2

The original College building—uncompleted, and before the fire of 1885

The old College—Main Entrance with (left) the Principal's House

PLATE 3

The Great Fire of 1885

The old Assembly Rooms, later the Students' Union

dismissals temporarily and decided to submit the work of the College to the objective test of experienced external examiners. These examinations were to be held at the end of the 1878–9 session. A considerable three-cornered contretemps, which did the College no good, quickly developed. The Senate, which obviously resented the implied slur on its professional competence, submitted on 4 June 1879 a Protest which asserted that the proposed examinations ought not to be held: the students were at so many different stages of progress that a very large number of examination papers would be required; insufficient notice had been given; and, moreover, most of the brighter students would be engaged on entrance examinations for the universities and could not, therefore, reasonably be expected to participate.[98]

At a meeting in London on 16 June the Council considered the Protest: the sequence of discussions which had brought the Council to decide on external examinations was set out, and particular play was made with the fact that the Principal had been present at all the earlier meetings, but had made no protest. So far as the Council was concerned, the examinations would be held. At this stage, the students intervened; they had held a general meeting on 7 June and came unanimously to certain resolutions. They insisted that insufficient time for revision had been allowed, that the additional tests were notably unfair to those already committed to important examinations elsewhere, and, in particular, they protested against the whole arrangement which seemed to them to show 'a want of confidence in the Principal and professors'. At any rate, they flatly and unanimously refused to attend the examinations. This spirited objection was signed on behalf of the student body by E. J. Ellis-Griffith.[99] The student Protest had originally been submitted to the Senate, which had declined to receive it; accordingly, it was forwarded to the Council. This Protest was not well received: the Council passed several heavy-footed resolutions denouncing 'the insubordinate conduct of the students', pointedly alleged collusion between Senate and students, and demanded to know what steps were being taken by the Senate to restore discipline.

On 16 June Dr. Leonard Schmitz, the veteran external examiner appointed, arrived in Aberystwyth: he met a deputation of students in the Library; they accorded him the utmost courtesy, but adamantly adhered to their decision not to sit the examinations, despite a plea from the Principal. Irresistible force had this time been outmatched by a number of immovable objects. To a further special meeting of the Council in London on 19 June, the Senate sent a reply which

[98] Unfortunately, discretion perhaps being the better part of valour, the pages of Senate Minutes for 7 March 1879–23 February 1880 have been torn out.

[99] When Ellis-Griffith had thought in 1878 to leave Aberystwyth and take his degree directly from London, the Principal successfully begged him to return. 'It will, I am sure', he said, 'be a cause of regret to you in after years to think that you had not done all you could to help to establish the College.' N.L.W. Ellis-Griffith MSS. f. 336.

denied collusion with the students and asserted that discipline was not unsatisfactory. The Principal was present at this meeting and he expressed the Senate's formal regret that there had been a conflict of opinion between Council and Senate and their desire to prevent a recurrence. The matter was concluded with a similar face-saving resolution passed by the Council.[100]

The enemies of the College were quick to make hay. The *Western Mail* gleefully ran the headline: 'The Unconditional Surrender of the Senate. Apology by the Principal.' T. C. Edwards was infuriated at the suggestion that he had caved in ignominiously in defence of a cause he thought vitally important.

I made no apology whatever [he wrote to Silvan Evans], and I had no authority whatever, even if I had wished it, to 'surrender' on behalf of the Senate. We all regret that a conflict should have arisen. But I do not regret the course which I myself took in the matter, and should be sorry if the Senate were to 'surrender'. I have always held that the actual administration should be in the hands of the Senate, but that we are responsible to the Council, whose ultimate authority none of us wished to deny.[101]

And his father, Lewis Edwards, who felt very strongly, erupted into the press with a powerful attack on the Council.[102] Mark Pattison (also a member of the Council), however, to whom the Principal turned for consolation, and who might have been expected to stand up for academic freedom, thought that T. C. Edwards had got his wires crossed. For Pattison, the issue was whether the College should be 'managed by those who find the money, or by those who receive it'—a curiously unexpected balance-sheet reading by a distinguished academic.[103]

It was evident that the constitutional arrangements had not, as yet, overcome entirely their early teething troubles. No doubt the Council had the authority to make the decisions they had arrived at; but, thereafter, the detailed arrangements should have been remitted into the hands of the Principal, not left to an eleventh-hour organization by an honorary secretary in London who did not arrange for examination papers in some of the most important subjects studied at the College, and appointed only two examiners who were not equipped to judge the whole range of the work to be covered. Lord Aberdare, for all his celebrated tact, had been sharply irritated over this course of events, and then and shortly afterwards took a very lordly line in his dealings with the Principal. Foulkes Roberts, the

---

[100] Council Minutes, 16 and 19 June 1878. C.A. BC/MN/1. *U.C.W. Reports (1863–91)*, 1879, p. 11. Foulkes Roberts thought, sensibly, that the Council would be wise 'to shut their eyes'. *T. C. Edwards Letters*, p. 163. Hugh Owen (3 July, C.A. MSS., not numbered) called it 'the Rebellion of the students'.

[101] *Western Mail* (2 July 1879). N.L.W. Cwrt Mawr MSS. 898B. The Principal's version of events is endorsed by a letter in *Baner ac Amserau Cymru* (30 July 1879), by John James of Aberystwyth, a member of the Council present at the meeting.

[102] *Y Goleuad* (July 1879) *et. seq.* T. C. Edwards, op. cit., pp. 477–8. Lewis Edwards believed that, if they could have managed it, certain members would have called for his son's resignation 'so that they might put in someone more pliable'.

[103] *T. C. Edwards Letters*, pp. 166–7.

last man to knuckle his forehead to any personage, thought the President's conduct 'most unacceptable' and tried to call up David Davies' financial power as a bridle on lordly arrogance: 'are we', Foulkes Roberts wrote to Davies, 'to be treated like children by the President?' Foulkes Roberts, who never wavered in his support of T. C. Edwards, blamed Hugh Owen for the recent affair and insisted again that what was badly needed was 'new names on the Council'.[104]

In fact, some new blood had been introduced in recent years. B. T. Williams, whose pamphlet in 1853 had made some important early running in the cause of a Welsh university, had become the London secretary of the College committee working for a Welsh National Library, and later joined the Council. So, too, in 1875, had A. C. Humphreys-Owen, a Cambridge-educated barrister who inherited substantial estates in Montgomeryshire; and Hugh Owen had recruited the assistance on the Council of Lewis Morris (of famous Welsh name), Oxford-educated poet, whose ambitious, but not especially inspired, *Epic of Hades* had appeared in 1877. In 1878 Hugh Owen had relinquished his post of honorary Secretary which was now shared by Morris and Dr. E. J. Evans, the hapless organizer of the abortive examinations in the summer of 1879.

This attempt to recruit more Council members with academic experience did not satisfy some, least of all certain lively spirits among the student body.

The truth is [wrote W. M. Williams before he left to go up to Oxford] the Council is not composed of suitable men. As you know, the leading spirits are commercial men who cannot help looking upon the College as they would upon a flannel warehouse or something of that kind; whereas the governing body of such an institution should be composed of experienced university men for the most part. But of course there is a serious obstacle to this in the fact that the nonconformists could not produce a sufficient number of this class to represent them on the board. . . . Between the *Cambrian News* and the Council, I hope the old Coll. won't be crushed.[105]

Whichever way one looked in 1879, outside the College itself, things were in a 'very critical condition'; and not least because closure by bankruptcy seemed, once again, a real possibility. To avoid taking the pitcher to the well once too often, it was decided for the time being to discontinue the congregational collections for that year. The ambitious endowment fund scheme still limped along, and an extensive appeal to Welsh landowners and the wealthy generally fell discouragingly flat. Necessary building works at the College were cut to the minimum, some relief accrued from the earlier staff salary cuts, and the fortunate

[104] Ibid., pp. 171–3.
[105] 27 May 1879. N.L.W. T. E. Ellis MSS. 2144. In his Diary, a short time before, Tom Ellis had denounced certain Council members who had 'even left their work in the ship' and assumed 'an attitude of pity and sorrow at the present state of the College', because they were 'men disappointed in their aspirations', or 'slighted by having pet productions of their originality neglected'. 14 October 1878. N.L.W. D. R. Daniel MSS. no. 6.

windfall of Henry Parnall's handsome legacy, together with private subscriptions (which had dropped to £1,335) and a small sum from the profits of the Mold National Eisteddfod, just about met the need. Even so, to balance the books, over £400 of the College's tiny investment stock had to be realized.[106] It was time for more desperate measures.

Several members of the College had come to the conclusion that, without a government grant, it would be impossible to continue the College for very much longer. The small sums voted annually from the profits of the National *eisteddfodau*, and the scholarship money provided by the South Wales Commercial Travellers' Association, showed hearteningly, as the Council claimed, the favour in which the College was held by the people of Wales, but these drops in the bucket would not suffice. Needs were too pressing to wait for the return of a Liberal ministry; on Hugh Owen's initiative, it was agreed to mobilize the support of as many Welsh M.P.s as possible in order to move the Tory government.[107]

On 1 July 1879 Hussey Vivian, M.P. for Glamorgan, introduced in a thin House of Commons the motion: 'That, in the opinion of this House, it is the duty of the Government to consider the best means of assisting any local effort which may be made for supplying the deficiency of Higher Education in Wales.'

An interesting, eventually a highly charged, debate ensued. Vivian had done his homework well (or perhaps been fully briefed by Hugh Owen); his speech was long and detailed setting out the usual Welsh complaints of inequitable treatment compared with Scotland and Ireland, and making elaborate play with the popular support for the Aberystwyth College shown by the hundred thousand contributions made to it by mainly humble people. He had no wish to raise the cry of 'Wales for the Welsh', and the gallantry of Welsh soldiers recently at Rorke's Drift indicated the imperial loyalty of the Principality. J. H. Puleston, Welsh Tory M.P. for Devonport, seconded the motion; he dilated on Welsh efforts at self-help and insisted that 'the barrier' of a 'distinctive nationality' could not be broken down and 'the grand old language' of Wales wiped out. Lord Emlyn, Tory M.P. for Carmarthenshire, broadly supported the motion but called for 'a full, searching, impartial inquiry' and, by amendment, sought to delete any special reference to the claims of Aberystwyth College.

There was an important intervention by Gladstone: he said that this was not a party question; Wales was not 'a mere geographical expression', and it was deplorable that 'nothing Welsh had received Parliamentary encouragement since the Revolution of 1688'; the attempt to proscribe the Welsh language was an 'unhappy circumstance', and, as for the argument that Jesus College, Oxford, answered the needs of the Principality, 'it had done nothing for Wales as Wales'.

---

[106] *T. C. Edwards Letters*, p. 169. *U.C.W. Reports* (1863–91), 1877–8, pp. 17–21, 1878–9, pp. 14–17.
[107] Hugh Owen to Henry Richard, 19 November 1878. N.L.W. MSS. 5505B.

Gladstone 'earnestly commended' the whole subject to the 'favourable consideration of the Government'.

B. T. Williams, a member of the Aberystwyth Council, came more directly
to the point: what was required was a subsidy for the Aberystwyth College; 'what
the Welsh people really wanted' was that it should be made 'a safe and permanent
institution'. Hitherto, the debate had been calm and not unreasonable. Lord George
Hamilton, however, replying for the government, soon made the sparks fly: he
agreeably diverted himself with some logic-chopping remarks on the vagueness
of the motion, followed up with a contrived and patronizing comment on the
Welsh language which evoked a laugh, and seemed to couple the claims of Welsh
nationality with a similar possible plea from the Cornish: 'Where', asked his lordship, 'were they to stop?' Nor did Hamilton forget to drag in a reference to the
recent quarrel between the Aberystwyth Council and Senate; any government
money granted 'to such a College' might well be spent 'not upon education but
litigation'. It was dangerous to cheapen university degrees, the Victoria University
might well answer the needs of Wales; meantime, let Aberystwyth prove itself.
The government could hold out no hope of help and its spokesman was disposed
to move the previous question. This concatenation of cheap sneers and Establishment insensitivity roused the Welsh members.

Osborne Morgan weighed in with a powerful counter-attack: 'They did not
ask much from the Government, not more than they were in the habit of shooting
away on a single morning over the heads of a couple of hundred Zulus.'

And as for his lordship's reference to Owen's College and its supporters, 'what
comparison was there between Lancashire cotton lords and the poor colliers and
quarrymen of Wales?' Morgan Lloyd, obviously angry, but with a weather eye on
a general election that could not be far off, pushed for a division so that the people
of Wales could see 'who were their friends'. The Chancellor of the Exchequer,
who did not seem to have followed the debate too clearly, spoke finally, less
insensitively than Hamilton but no more encouragingly. On a division, the
motion was lost by one hundred and five votes to fifty-four. The *Western Mail*,
its Welsh patriotism suspended, asked the next day how could a government be
asked to give a grant to Aberystwyth which 'it refuses to the infinitely more
important undertaking at Manchester'. In any case, as the next day's leader asserted,
the idea of a subsidy for Aberystwyth was 'simply absurd'.[108]

There was nothing for it but to wait for the return of a Liberal government.
Happily, this was not long delayed; Disraeli's miscalculation of the auguries
suggested by the favourable by-elections led to a dissolution in March 1880. In
Wales almost every candidate referred in his election address to higher and inter-
mediate education and pledged support for state grants for these purposes. The
Liberals won the general election handsomely and almost swept the board in

[108] *Parl. Debates*, 3rd Series, vol. 247, 1153–82. *Western Mail* (2 and 3 July 1879).

Wales, winning twenty-nine out of thirty-three seats. Early in May, Lord Aberdare wrote to Gladstone, again Prime Minister, suggesting that a Royal Commission should be appointed to consider the defective state of higher and intermediate education in Wales. Hugh Owen apparently was in favour of the same course. Hussey Vivian (supported by Stuart Rendel, M.P. for Montgomeryshire) preferred less elaborate machinery, perhaps a departmental inquiry, which would offer 'a better and speedier prospect of action'.[109] This latter course was chosen and it was soon agreed that Lord Aberdare, the obvious choice, would lead the inquiry. Thereafter, there followed a considerable negotiation over the choice of the other members of the committee. Hugh Owen, perhaps now feeling his age, refused to allow his name to be considered, but said that he attached special importance to the nomination of Henry Richard, M.P., and Lewis Morris.[110] Other names canvassed were those of Hussey Vivian himself, Humphreys-Owen (pushed by Rendel), Professor John Rhys of Oxford, Canon H. J. Robinson, Principal of York Diocesan Training College, an acknowledged authority on intermediate education, and Professor James Bryce, who seemed to prefer to give evidence to joining the inquiry.

Aberdare would have preferred Bryce to John Rhys, but ultimately he accepted the latter's nomination. The prospective chairman was also happy to have the assistance of Lord Emlyn, 'a sensible man', who would be 'of service in checking nonconformist ambition'. Henry Richard, the only dissenter appointed, thought the committee scarcely representative, but his attempts to redress the balance (among others, he suggested the nomination of Lewis Edwards) failed, as did the efforts of Morgan Lloyd to get a stronger representation for North Wales on the committee.[111]

From the point of view of the Aberystwyth College, the committee, prima facie, as finally constituted, could hardly have been bettered. Indeed, reputations for high-minded, disinterested public service apart, an enemy of the College could not unreasonably have claimed that the jury was packed. The chairman of the inquiry was Lord Aberdare, President of the College; of the other members, Henry Richard was a Vice-President and Lewis Morris honorary Secretary of the College; Professor John Rhys had been a Governor for some years. There was no special reason to be wary of Canon Robinson, though it was enough ('Sais ydyw') for Thomas Gee that he was English.[112] Only Lord Emlyn, in the parliamentary debate of July 1879, had shown any detached coolness towards the College.

[109] Rendel to Humphreys-Owen, 19 July 1880. N.L.W. Glansevern MSS. 51.

[110] 19 July 1880. N.L.W. Vivian MSS.

[111] The whole question of the committee's membership is exhaustively examined in B. B. Thomas, 'The Establishment of the Aberdare Departmental Committee, 1880: Some Letters and Notes', in Bull. Board of Celtic Studies, xix. 318–34. See also, Parl. Debates, 3rd Series, vol. 254, 1089, 1569; ibid., vol. 256, 93.

[112] Baner ac Amserau Cymru (25 August 1880).

It was a time of great expectations: at long last, educational justice would be done to Wales and, not least, the College at Aberystwyth would be saved from foreclosure; or, at least, so it seemed.[113]

[113] Current stringencies at the College are indicated by the fact that students were allowed to take books out of the library only on special professorial permit.

3

'The Ishmael of Colleges'[1]

THE result of the inquiry (popularly known, after its chairman, as the *Aberdare Report*) by the Departmental Committee into higher and intermediate education in Wales in 1880–1 has received high praise from most modern commentators. According to one scholar, for example, the *Report* provided modern Wales with its 'educational Charter'.[2] There is, no doubt, a good deal in this: certainly the Committee's recommendations led quickly to the establishment of two new university colleges in Wales, at Cardiff and Bangor; and the *Report* made proposals concerning secondary schools which, when implemented a few years later, put Wales for a time ahead of England in intermediate education. So far as the University College of Wales at Aberystwyth is concerned, however, the *Aberdare Report* is open to serious challenge. Indeed, it is not too much to say that the passages in the *Report* which deal with Aberystwyth amounted almost to a requiem, the Committee members evidently having decided beforehand that the institution was moribund, and there was, therefore, little point in delaying the post-mortem.

The evidence of five, perhaps six, of the Aberystwyth witnesses merits consideration. Hugh Owen and Stephen Evans confined themselves largely to the financial difficulties which the College had had to face. Owen pointed out that, over the years, more than £50,000 had been raised by public subscription, and he made particularly effective play with the fact that this support was uniquely broad-based; over 100,000 people from all parts of Wales and from all the religious denominations, as well as the Church, had contributed. There were some few large donations, but overwhelmingly and not surprisingly in a poor country, most contributions were of the order of half-a-crown or less. The Guarantee and Temporary Sustentation Funds (in which the 'University Sunday' collections were vital) had enabled the College to limp along without adequate endowment, but his unrivalled experience in fund-raising forced him inescapably to the conclusion that it would not be 'practicable to maintain the institution permanently without the assistance of the State'. Stephen Evans, Vice-President and member of the

---

[1] Revd. John Griffith, Rector of Merthyr. *Cambrian News* (17 August 1883).
[2] T. I. Ellis, *The Development of Higher Education in Wales* (Wrexham, 1935), p. 54.

College finance committee, endorsed Owen's opinion: 'A Government grant is indispensable', said Evans, 'without it the College in its present form must collapse.'[3]

The examination of Principal T. C. Edwards, who ought surely to have been the most important single witness, was curiously perfunctory; and several of the explanatory arguments advanced by the Principal were not probed further, as they should have been, and his mitigations, which were not without point, were largely ignored by the Committee in their final recommendations. Principal Edwards' testimony pointed to a slow but encouraging improvement in the quality of the work at the College: latterly, students came up better prepared, not least because people were 'beginning to understand what a college means'; admittedly a high proportion of the students came from Cardiganshire, but currently there were students 'from nearly all the counties of North and South Wales'. As for the drop in numbers that session, this was partly the result of a refusal to accept youths under fifteen years of age, and partly the consequence of economic depression, which had apparently caused a similar decrease in the number of students at Owen's College, Manchester.[4]

On the other hand, it is fair to say that Principal Edwards was much less spirited in his defence of the College than might have been expected; all too often he contented himself with a yea or nay, and his few supplementary glosses were not as convincingly informative or challenging as they might have been. It is possible that he felt he was appearing before a court which was not particularly well disposed towards him; within months, he was writing wearily to his father that, 'personally, it would be a positive relief to me to have my connection with the College severed'.[5]

But there is another possible explanation: T. C. Edwards was an exceptionally proud man who kept publicly silent for some time after the publication of the Report with its ominous implications for the future of his College. 'I have abstained from speaking [he told Lewis Morris in December 1883] because I thought my motives would be misrepresented, and people might think I was fighting for my own bread and cheese.'[6]

T. C. Edwards was too proud to appear to persuade, much less to plead, and it may well be that, mistakenly, he took refuge in dignified brevity. But a sympathetic Committee would have encouraged fuller answers, or even pressed so obviously important a witness to be more communicative. In contrast, Principal Jayne of St. David's College, Lampeter, was encouraged to dilate on a variety of subjects, and his testimony included some incredibly patronizing comments on

[3] *Aberdare Report*, Minutes of Evidence, pp. 14, 835.
[4] Ibid., pp. 402–11. For a warm encomium on Cardiganshire's exceptional regard for higher education, reflected in the number of students from the county at the College, see the evidence of Professor T. McKenny Hughes of Cambridge (ibid., p. 63).
[5] *T. C. Edwards Letters*, p. 188.   [6] C.A. (JI), not numbered.

the inhabitants of the Principality: 'accuracy is not a characteristic of the Welsh mind', said Jayne after two or three years' experience at Lampeter.[7] This and similar red-herrings including, for one who presumably prided himself on his trained precision, some curious juggling with the statistics of students at other colleges, prompted the Committee members to considerable supplementary questioning of Jayne. But one of the most important of T. C. Edwards' observations, that his College represented 'the national idea', that it was the 'College that we want in Wales', was brushed aside unconsidered with a half-snide rhetorical question.[8]

The evidence of two professors at Aberystwyth, Angus speaking for Arts and S. T. Humpidge for Science, buttressed the testimony of the Principal. Angus believed that although some students still came up badly prepared, there had been a decrease in the number of backward students in recent years; Humpidge said that although most of his students at entrance knew little science, many showed considerable aptitude for these new disciplines and attained a 'very fair' proficiency before they left. Angus and Humpidge emphatically insisted that the charge that the College was no better than a grammar school was completely wrong: 'that is nonsense, of course', as Humpidge put it. The Committee did not seize the opportunity to cross-examine closely these two witnesses who had up-to-date detailed knowledge of the work of the College and neither was long detained.[9]

The opinions of T. Marchant Williams, currently an inspector of schools for the London School Board, seemed to have registered particularly favourably with Lord Aberdare, not least, perhaps, because Williams spoke 'excellent English, without accent or provincialisms'. Williams was a former Aberystwyth student who left the College after five months, taking with him an unexplained but exceptionally rancorous hostility towards his *Alma Mater*. Williams, who remained excessively opinionated to the end of his life, gave Aberystwyth short shrift. The College building was 'still very ill-adapted' to the purposes (taking it for granted that it had no valid pretensions to be anything better) of 'a high grade school'; and, without further ado, Williams would transfer the College to Bangor where, along with another similar institution which he recommended should be established at Swansea, it would certainly become 'a much larger' college than the one at present at Aberystwyth. This was only one of the cock sure predictions of Marchant Williams that went subsequently astray, but in the opinion of Lord Aberdare at any rate, he was the 'best witness' who testified on that particular day,

[7] *Aberdare Report*, Minutes of Evidence, p. 454. Lord Aberdare told Gladstone (B.M. Add. MSS. 44087, f. 129) that 'it was the impression of all of us that Jayne's evidence was the best and weightiest we received'.

[8] *Aberdare Report*, Minutes of Evidence, p. 410.

[9] Ibid., Minutes of Evidence, pp. 413–18.

despite a jaundiced, dismissive attitude towards the College of which the chairman himself was President.[10]

The fact is that most, if not all, of the members of the Committee came to a consideration of the Aberystwyth College with closed minds; several of them had clearly written it off beforehand as a failure. In his original letter to Gladstone asking for an inquiry into Welsh education, Lord Aberdare had damned the College with faint praise, insisted that its 'situation' was 'unfortunate', and would 'forever' prevent it from attracting endowments or 'students in sufficient numbers to enable it to fulfil adequately the purposes for which it was designed'.[11] As for Lewis Morris, honorary Secretary of the College, he had other fish to fry. It is evident from the number of times he faced witnesses with the same question, that Morris had privately decided that the answer for Aberystwyth was to turn it into a high school or college for girls. For some time after 1881, as will appear, he pursued this not unimaginative aim with some persistence. Henry Richard, although born in Cardiganshire, had by now switched his main allegiance to South Wales, and maintained subsequently a far more sustained interest in the College at Cardiff than he had ever shown in Aberystwyth; moreover, there is the weighty testimony of Stuart Rendel that Richard, for some time at any rate after 1881, was unhelpful in his attitude to the Aberystwyth College. Lord Emlyn, Tory landlord and Churchman, 'pledged' to St. David's College, Lampeter, was said in 1884 never to have 'been favourable to Aberystwyth'.[12]

It is not suggested of course that the members of the Committee were wilfully malevolent towards Aberystwyth. At worst, they were misguided, perhaps overly hasty and superficial in some of their judgements about the College. They were too quick to accept as a law of Welsh life that North and South Wales would ever pull asunder, and with no real knowledge of the internal life of the College failed to understand that already young men from North and South Wales were mixing there to mutual advantage.[13] In their *Report*, they recommended government financial support for Welsh higher education, and proposed a considerable advance in the provision of secondary education in Wales. They did not appear to realize that if these two important suggestions were followed up energetically,

[10] *Aberdare Letters*, ii. 106–7. *Aberdare Report*, Minutes of Evidence, pp. 843–50. On Marchant Williams' continuing hostility to Aberystwyth, see the *Cambrian News* (16 March 1883).

[11] B. B. Thomas, 'The Establishment of the Aberdare Departmental Committee, 1880', loc. cit., pp. 318–19. According to R. D. Roberts (to Mundella, 23 October 1882. P.R.O. Ed. 119/68), 'The President, from the outset, expressed his opinion that the College was no better than a school, and that his own district in South Wales was the proper site for the College'.

[12] Rendel to Humphreys-Owen, 15 December 1883, and 14 March 1884. N.L.W. Glansevern MSS. nos. 132 and 140. Humphreys-Owen to his wife, 29 October 1884. N.L.W. Glansevern MSS. (not numbered). See also, Mundella to Richard in N.L.W. MSS. 5505B.

[13] T. T. Lucius Morgan, *The Rev. J. Gwynoro Davies, Barmouth* (Llandyssul, 1941), p. 10. 'For the first time in history, in the new-born . . . University College of Wales, North and South Wales met unarmed.'

most of the problems besetting Aberystwyth would disappear, or at least substantially diminish. It would have helped if the Committee had taken more time
to digest the mass of material before it, and especially if it had made some serious
study of the similar teething troubles undergone by, for example, Owen's College,
Manchester, the Queen's Colleges in Ireland, and, perhaps even more illuminating,
Newman's Catholic University in Dublin.[14]

The Committee, looking backwards instead of forwards, was too ready to rate
too heavily the supposed inaccessibility of Aberystwyth, and much too confident
in the belief (unfounded as events proved) that colleges located in centres of
greater population would automatically attract considerably larger numbers of
students. Most important of all, despite the fact that five out of six of the Committee were at least nominally Welsh, they failed utterly to see that the Aberystwyth College, for all its alleged weaknesses, had already established a place for
itself in the minds and hearts of the mass of the Welsh people. Over the next few
years, one by one, the members of the Committee were forced reluctantly to eat
their words by an outraged Welsh opinion that they had overlooked or discounted.[15]

For all these heavy strictures on the work of the Aberdare Committee, it is fair
to say that they did not directly recommend the extinction of the College at
Aberystwyth. But the implications of the *Report*'s proposals at least half-pointed
in that direction. 'The experience of the University College at Aberystwyth,
where various adverse causes have operated, must not be taken to be conclusive
against the success of such colleges in Wales', as the *Report* put it, strongly suggested the case for a fresh start elsewhere. The Committee unanimously recommended the establishment of a college in Glamorgan, either at Cardiff or Swansea;
and, as for the rest, 'the College at Aberystwyth, whether retained on its present
site or removed to Caernarvon or Bangor, must be accepted as the College for
North Wales'. There was one final thrust at the existing Aberystwyth arrangements: in these new or removed institutions, 'the Principal should, in every case,
be a layman'.[16]

Nor did this end the catalogue of blows that the Aberystwyth College had to
endure at this time. Before the *Aberdare Report* had appeared, Gladstone, anticipating the advocacy of Lord Aberdare and Lewis Morris, had recommended the
Queen to confer a knighthood on Hugh Owen; rarely has the case for recognition
of public service been so overwhelming.[17] During that summer, Owen had been

---

[14] For the early difficulties of Owen's College, see J. Thompson, op. cit.; for the Queen's Colleges,
T. W. Moody, 'The Irish University Question of the Nineteenth Century', loc. cit., 95–100. There is a
good study of the Catholic University in F. McGrath, *Newman's University: Idea and Reality* (1951).

[15] J. R. Webster, op. cit., p. 331, for further illustration that the Committee members were out of
touch with the main springs of Welsh life.

[16] *Aberdare Report*, Conclusion and Recommendations, pp. lxvi–lxvii.

[17] W. E. Davies, op. cit., pp. 60–1.

unwell, and his doctors had sent him off to the South of France to recuperate; at Mentone, on 20 November 1881, Hugh Owen died, aged seventy-seven. The twentieth century, with its unremitting passion for seeking out clay-feet in heroes, has seen a decline in Hugh Owen's reputation. Some have found his almost exclusive stress on middle-class needs repugnant; others have pointed to the virulent dislike he inspired in several of those who worked with and under him. Modern Welsh patriots look askance at Welsh émigrés such as Hugh Owen, who accept, too uncritically as they think, English values and seek to impose them on their homeland. Finally, his air and appearance of saintliness are not perhaps to modern taste, and, undeniably, there was an unctuous touch to his personality that covered an occasional remorseless ruthlessness in certain of his public and private dealings.

But nothing can gainsay the fact that for 'well-nigh forty years he had been the one great central figure and moving spirit of the Welsh educational movement'.[18] Others came and went, but Owen was ever-present, unremitting, undeterred by difficulty or disappointment, 'behind all, moulding all', the indispensable anchor-man who held fast when others around him lost their foothold.[19] The foregoing account has made it clear that without Hugh Owen the University College of Wales at Aberystwyth would never have opened its doors; it is equally certain that without his incredible labours in the years of nominal retirement, the College would never have survived its early crippling difficulties. Now, at the time of even greater peril, the College lost his matchless service.

However, before the danger became really urgent, there was a short period of delay. The Queen's Speech in February 1882, included a statement of the government's intention to legislate on Welsh education, but by July, A. J. Mundella, Vice-President of the Council, had come to the conclusion that endless Irish difficulties blocked the way.[20] Indeed, before this, there had been other obstacles to overcome. In 1881 Lord Spencer, Lord President, the minister responsible for education, had written a Cabinet paper arguing that there was no point in establishing additional Welsh colleges as there were not enough young men qualified to fill them; subsequently, Spencer had changed his mind. A more junior colleague, Leonard Courtenay, continued to object on the old ground that it would be much better for young Welshmen to go to universities in England.[21] Finally, the government decided that an intermediate education bill would have to be postponed, but, meantime, an annual grant of £4,000 could be allocated to a college for North Wales, 'at Aberystwyth, or elsewhere', and a similar sum to a college for

[18] High testimony indeed from the waspish iconoclast, T. Marchant Williams ('The Romance of Welsh Education', *Trans. Cymm.* (1901–2), pp. 37–8).
[19] T. T. Lucius Morgan, *The Rev. Gwynoro Davies, Barmouth*, p. 10.
[20] 6 July. B.M. Add. MSS. 44258, ff. 192–3.
[21] Carlingford and Mundella to Gladstone, 26 June 1882. Ibid., ff. 188–9.

South Wales, 'at Cardiff, or Swansea, or elsewhere'.[22] The scene was set for a furious double battle of the sites.

T. C. Edwards had no illusions about the difficulties ahead: he thought that the Aberdare Committee's treatment of Aberystwyth had been 'unjust', and he was quite clear that the best, perhaps only, hope for his College lay with the people. 'I do wish', he told his father in September 1881, 'the country would let its voice be heard.'[23] But that would take time and, perhaps, some organization; in any case, for the moment, Aberystwyth still had a chance on paper of acceptance as the College for North Wales.

At a considerably lower level, the Principal had other difficulties. In 1881 a deputation of students asked if a College athletics meeting could be arranged. 'This is a matter for prayer, I will give you my answer in a few days time', said the Principal. Shortly afterwards, he gave his permission, adding, 'I myself will be present'.[24] On Saturday, 9 April 1881, the first athletic sports meeting at the College was held on the Vicarage field, hired for a nominal fee. The sun shone, the Cardiganshire Militia band paraded the town and later entertained on the field; there was a very large turn-out of spectators, but a great crowd of locals (authentic 'Cardis' to a man, with inherited scruples about spending money) watched the proceedings free from the vantage point of the Buarth hill.[25]

Some of the students, ministerial candidates mainly, 'the unco' guid', as the College Magazine called them, objected strongly to the athletics meeting; and many Welsh nonconformists were scandalized that the Principal had endorsed these very doubtful activities by his presence. There was some talk of summoning him to face a vote of censure at the Cardiganshire Methodist Monthly meeting, and one deacon seemed to think it was not far short of a hanging offence.[26] Principal Edwards remained completely unruffled. 'I believe in the education of the body no less than the education of the mind', he told an audience of students and townsfolk. And earlier he had peremptorily asked the dedicated bookworms why they did 'not run and play football and maintain the honour of the College in the field as well as in the schools'.[27]

The Principal had good cause for satisfaction at the improvement in the academic work of the College at this time. The reports of the external examiners in June and October 1881 on the work of the students were studded with compli-

---

[22] Memorandum by Spencer and Mundella, 5 May 1882. B.M. Add. MSS. 44258, f. 191.

[23] *T. C. Edwards Letters*, p. 188.

[24] I am indebted to Miss Eira Johnson for this agreeable tale. One of Miss Johnson's forbears was a member of the student deputation.

[25] In 1882, when the Buarth was closed to spectators on Sports' Day, a diehard rump of locals, who knew their geography, as well as the value of money, simply moved to the hill overlooking Llanbadarn road.

[26] *T. C. Edwards Letters*, p. 187. See also the *Goleuad* and *Y Faner* during May–July 1881, and *U.C.W. Magazine*, iii. 224–30, and iv. 178–82.

[27] Ibid., iv. 139, 186.

mentary remarks. A mathematics don from Trinity College, Cambridge, 'was agreeably surprised by some of the work of the best students'; in Latin, most students did well, 'some very well', and results in Natural Science were considered 'highly creditable' to the students and their teachers.[28] And on 12 October 1882 the Principal was able to say that 'in no previous year' had he had 'the pleasure of presenting a more satisfactory Report on the state of the College'; moreover, the Senate felt that 'less teaching' went 'to waste than was formerly the case'.[29] Equally encouraging was the fact that some Aberystwyth students were distinguishing themselves in London University examinations; several were placed in the first division of the matriculation and preliminary B.A. examinations, and E. J. Ellis Griffith completed his London bachelor's degree with first class honours. Within the next two years, the list of external successes was considerably larger, with star performances from Ellis Griffith, who took first place in the first class division of the Cambridge Law Tripos, and T. F. Roberts, who walked away with a First in Classics at Oxford.

In his evidence to the Aberdare Committee, Principal Edwards had called for a doubling of the Aberystwyth professoriate. Despite the improved financial position of the College (for the present, at least, the government grant was paid to Aberystwyth), this was hardly possible as yet. However, one important recruit to the teaching staff was the brilliantly gifted Henry Jones, a shoe-maker's son who, against all the odds, had carved out for himself an outstanding academic career at Glasgow and Oxford.[30] In the first instance, he was temporarily engaged as an assistant at £150 a year, but in February 1883 the Principal gave notice to the Council of his intention to propose Jones' permanent appointment as professor of philosophy.[31]

All in all, the College was flourishing as never before: Owen M. Edwards, who had started to write regular articles for a new Welsh periodical, noted in October 1882 that there was 'more enthusiasm about everything in College than we have seen for many a long term; . . . every College Club is prosperous, every class is full of life'.

During that session, the Debating Society, easily the most important College club, which formed 'the strongest bond' between all the students, was in particularly good fettle: there was much good speaking, on well-chosen subjects, before large and enthusiastic audiences. The rugby team had been undefeated for some time, and the association eleven, after some early defeats, was improving

---

[28] Reports, June and October 1881. C.A. S/MN/1. There were, of course, some geese among all these swans: 'some of the students write an English style which is scarcely intelligible', reported Dr. Schmitz, external examiner now as in 1878.

[29] *U.C.W. Reports* (1863–91), p. 7.

[30] For Jones, see his intersting autobiography *Old Memories* (1924) and H. J. W. Hetherington's biography, *The Life and Letters of Sir Henry Jones* (1924).

[31] 28 February 1883. *Council Minutes*, p. 266.

steadily. For those who lived in College, there were special opportunities for close contact with fellow students from all over Wales; in these informal discussions around the fireside late at night, there was, as he said, 'a peculiar charm', and they were of immense educational value.[32]

But all these encouragements could not alter the fact that a gigantic question mark lay alongside the future of the College. The government grant of £4,000 a year to each of the two proposed Welsh colleges had been conditional on their being established within two years. In November 1882 a meeting of prominent Welshmen, under the chairmanship of Lord Aberdare, was held in London 'to determine "What next?"' The immediate question was that of sites. So far as South Wales was concerned, there were only two serious claimants: Swansea and Cardiff. A. J. Mundella met deputations from the two towns and tried to get them to work together and come to amicable agreement. In practice, he found 'much jealousy and more bitterness' than he had expected among the South Walians; ultimately, the question was submitted to government arbitrators whose final choice was in Cardiff's favour.[33] In October 1883 the South Wales College at Cardiff, equipped from the start with an annual government grant and with considerable private contributions (Lord Bute gave £10,000) towards its endowment, first opened its doors. The new Principal was Viriamu Jones, formerly Principal of Firth College, Sheffield, who disregarded the advice of a close friend, who offered the opinion that it would be foolish to apply for the Cardiff post because inevitably in the early years there would be uncertainty, confusion, and crisis, and the new Principal would end up as the natural 'scapegoat'. Jones, who had taken a triple First at Oxford, was then twenty-seven years old; before he died (at forty-five, having 'burnt himself out'), he was to show exceptional qualities, brushed with a touch of genius, as an educational leader.[34] A year later, the Cardiff College received its Charter and the first President was, predictably and perhaps inevitably, Lord Aberdare.

But the vital question for Aberystwyth was the location of the North Wales college. The initiative was taken by certain London Welshmen, with Marchant Williams especially prominent. At a meeting at Lord Aberdare's house, it was agreed to summon what purported to be a conference representative of North Wales at Chester on 23 January 1883. David Davies had done his best to short-circuit the Chester conference by summoning a meeting at Newtown which

---

[32] 'Gossip from the Welsh Colleges', *Red Dragon*, ii. 461, iii. 75–7. There were still, however, plenty of students living desperately from hand to mouth who could not afford these residential amenities. In the following year, the Principal sympathetically suggested that the College should dispense with caps and gowns, because 'the expense is great and a serious consideration to many of our men'. To J. B. Rogers, 26 September 1884. C.A. (JL), not numbered.

[33] *Aberdare Letters*, ii. 158. *Baner ac Amserau Cymru* (4 and 8 November 1882). Mundella to Henry Richard, 13 March 1883. N.L.W. MSS. 5505B.

[34] K. V. Jones, *Viriamu Jones* (1915), p. 81. N. Masterman, *J. Viriamu Jones* (Cardiff, 1957), p. 26.

passed unanimously a resolution that it was 'a monstrous absurdity' to move the College from Aberystwyth.[35] At the Chester conference, Aberdare took the chair: beforehand, he had drafted a resolution asking the conference to accept Aberystwyth as the North Wales College, but he did not put that motion to the meeting; instead, he recommended the appointment of a small committee to consider the claims of the various towns which had applied for the College. Thereafter, the meeting ran away with the chairman: Dean H. T. Edwards of Bangor, a declared and bitter enemy of Aberystwyth, proposed that the college must 'stand in one of the six counties' of North Wales and he was seconded by Thomas Gee of Y Faner. David Davies (supported by Lewis Edwards) moved an amendment in favour of Aberystwyth, but in a meeting overwhelmingly of North Walians, most of them with local axes to grind, he was crushingly voted down, and the Aberystwyth case summarily, and contemptuously almost, excluded from consideration.[36]

Aberystwyth, it seemed, was now doomed: it was already clear beyond all doubt that the College could not continue much longer without government support. The Chester decision seemed to ensure, as Principal Edwards wrote, sadly, that the University College of Wales, which had begun so bravely as the sole and central college for the Principality, an embryo university, would now 'languish and die slowly'.[37] Others were affected in the same way. The Revd. John Griffith, Rector of Merthyr, expressed his feelings in a letter to the press: 'Poor Aberystwyth College. It seems to me at the present moment the Ishmael of Colleges. Everybody's hand is against it . . . and yet there is no College in the Kingdom that has less of the "Ishmael" about it.'[38]

There was the real danger of a complete and ignominious collapse: in June 1883 Silvan Evans, part-time professor of Welsh at Aberystwyth, resigned, and despite Principal Edwards' strong plea that the chair should be filled quickly to indicate the intention to continue, nothing was done. Some students, fearing for their careers, talked of going immediately to Liverpool or Manchester; and in October, ten Aberystwyth students won scholarships at Cardiff and moved to the new College.[39] Nor was this all: Henry Jones accepted a part-time commission to work for the North Wales Sites committee, and seemed surprised that the Aberystwyth authorities objected to what seemed to them to be a disloyal hedging of personal bets. In July 1883 Henry Jones left Aberystwyth after a disappointingly short stay

[35] The Times (4 January 1883).

[36] Ibid. (24 January 1883). A very full report. The next day The Times had a strong leader in favour of Aberystwyth, which argued that the Chester meeting had 'pushed a purely geographical principle to an almost ridiculous extent'.

[37] June 1883. 'Extracts from College Correspondence.' N.L.W. J. H. Davies (U.C.W.) MSS.

[38] Cambrian News (17 August 1883).

[39] T. C. Edwards to Lewis Morris, June 1883. N.L.W. J. H. Davies (U.C.W.) MSS. U.C.W. Reports (1863–91), 16 October 1883, pp. 9–10.

during which his 'lively style of teaching' (as Lord Aberdare described it) had impressed everybody.[40]

Some ineffectual efforts to stave off disaster were made: an attempt in March 1883 to come to terms with the North Wales committee came quickly to nothing; in June some Aberystwyth emissaries saw Lord Carlingford, but subsequently, although the government accepted a written argument, Lord Spencer and Mundella refused to meet a stronger deputation in favour of Aberystwyth, as had been hoped. In August the same three arbitrators who had pitched upon Cardiff, chose Bangor as the site of the North Wales College. In October of that year the Aberystwyth Council resolved to continue the College for one more session, but evidently expected thereafter to be forced to summon a general meeting of constituents formally to wind up the institution.[41]

The story of the fight at the eleventh hour to save Aberystwyth College from extinction is one of the most heroic and moving in modern Welsh history. It is also incredibly confused; it became a protracted mêlée, with many of the combatants often found on the wrong side of the scrum, and a referee, Mundella, with some suggestion of a personal interest in the result. It is first of all necessary to distinguish the participants.

The nominal leaders for Aberystwyth were, of course, the Court and Council of the College, especially its President and Secretary, Lord Aberdare, and Lewis Morris; Osborne Morgan, an Aberystwyth champion for so long, had now switched his allegiance to Bangor. Aberdare and Morris, however, were in a hopelessly compromised position. Lewis Morris publicly admitted in a letter to *The Times* (3 February 1883) that if all those present at Chester had voted in favour of Aberystwyth as the site of the North Wales college, he would have 'held up' his 'hand against it'. Subsequently, in private correspondence with Mundella, Morris pushed strongly his pet nostrum: transforming Aberystwyth into a school or college for women.[42] Lewis Morris was a volatile man, lacking stability and patience; at the National Eisteddfod at Cardiff in August, he had begun to change his tune and was publicly demanding a temporary grant for Aberystwyth.[43] Lord Aberdare's interest was now focused almost exclusively on the Cardiff College, which engaged his enthusiasm in a way that Aberystwyth never did.[44] Within

[40] Henry Jones later ascribed his failure to get the Principalship at Bangor, in part at least, to the malevolence of Principal Edwards. This is not borne out by the facts (*T. C. Edwards Letters*, pp. 198–212). Lord Aberdare (to Lord Powis, 24 February 1884. U.C.N.W. Bangor MSS. 4374) thought Jones 'in the wrong' in his dispute with Principal Edwards.

[41] *Council Minutes*, 28 February 1883. N.L.W. Glansevern MSS. no. 103. Lewis Morris to Mundella, 25 August 1883. Mundella (Sheffield) MSS. *U.C.W. Reports (1863–91)*, 16 October 1883, pp. 14–15.

[42] 30 August and 14 November 1883. Mundella (Sheffield) MSS. According to Morris, there was currently a strong rumour that the Aberystwyth College would be sold to the Jesuits!

[43] Mundella to Henry Richard, 13 August 1883. N.L.W. MSS. 5505B. Mundella's disgust is evident; he had already begun to discount Morris' opinions, as (N.L.W. MSS. 19440E, f. 3) had others.

[44] Aberdare to Powis, 24 February 1884. U.C.N.W. Bangor MSS. 4579. *Aberdare Letters*, ii. 174–5.

months, he was talking of resigning his Aberystwyth Presidency. At any rate, the position of Aberdare and Morris was too equivocal for them to be able to lead a rescue operation with any conviction or hope of success.

The inertia of Aberdare and his supporters on the Court and Council let in an unofficial Aberystwyth town committee: *franc tireurs* disgusted with what they regarded as the cowardly incompetence of the regular troops. They, at any rate, believed wholeheartedly in Aberystwyth's cause, had little patience with careful manœuvring and, to a man almost, had no reservations about the virtues of head-long, frontal assault. The chief leaders of these Aberystwyth men were John James, a former mayor and an important tradesman in the town, Evan Evans, a local solicitor, John Gibson, editor and proprietor of the *Cambrian News*, and D. C. Roberts, a young member of an important Aberystwyth family which owned a large timber yard. Additionally, D. C. Roberts' brother, Dr. R. D. Roberts of Cambridge, worked in close collusion with them and enjoyed a roving commission as their spokesman in Whitehall. The opinions of this aggressive ginger group are fully documented in the *Cambrian News*.

Week by week, Gibson kept up a furious cannonade in the leader columns of his newspaper. It is fair to say that, however pugnaciously worded his comments were, Gibson made many valuable criticisms. He appreciated that the *Aberdare Report*'s picture of Aberystwyth was true of 1875–6, but manifestly unfair for 1880; that the government in its ignorance of Welsh conditions was willing to be guided, and 'a word' from the Departmental Committee would have sufficed to put the College on a sound foundation; that Aberystwyth was 'a people's college' to an extent hitherto undreamt of, and that the Aberdare Committee had given in weakly to Welsh parochial feelings, and thereby thrown away too hastily the chance of developing, in time, one large, unified Welsh university.[45] Unfortunately, Gibson was too quick to assume a conspiracy reading of affairs; he was convinced that Aberdare, Morris, Henry Richard, and even Hugh Owen formerly, while masquerading as friends, were the enemies of the College. Again and again, he called loudly for the resignation of the President and Lewis Morris, and, con-currently, as often as not, he would call for the Principal's head as well, because he spent too much time preaching. Gibson's huff and puff might have relieved a lot of frustrations, but it was unlikely to move a government, and, all too often, gave the impression that Aberystwyth's supporters were hopelessly riven by personal enmities. R. D. Roberts, whose opinions were the same as Gibson's, though rather less belligerently expressed, tried to argue the same case in private (and usually stormy) interviews with Mundella. Roberts got very little change out of Mundella, who refused to accept that the Aberystwyth town committee had any standing in the matter. Roberts thereupon tried to enlist the assistance of Joseph Chamberlain, whose popular posture in politics suggested that he, at least,

[45] The *Cambrian News* (1880–4), passim.

would appreciate the allegedly singular democratic virtues of the Aberystwyth College.[46]

Aberystwyth's champions faced a tremendous up-hill task: to save the College it was necessary to persuade a government with, for these years at any rate, a fairly substantial majority, to reverse completely its declared policy; and, in doing so, to throw over more or less entirely the unanimous *Report* of a committee commissioned by the Education department. No doubt there were plenty of recent instances of Irishmen forcing ministers to recant, but governments were accustomed to brushing off the habitual cap-in-hand supplications of the Welsh with patronizing indifference. Nor should it be forgotten that this was the government of Gladstone, the apostle of cheeseparing economy. The Prime Minister's letter to Mundella offering him the Vice-Presidency of the Council, the working headship of the department for Education, had drawn particular attention to the 'enormous' costs of public education, and the need for 'vigilant inquiry' into all 'augmentations', which, as like as not, were 'wasteful and . . . needless'. Mundella accepted this brief wholeheartedly and promised his 'utmost . . . vigilance to secure the highest educational results at the lowest possible charge to the country'.[47]

Not surprisingly, therefore, Mundella gave a dusty reply in August 1883 to a parliamentary plea for generous consideration of Aberystwyth's claims, and Lord Carlingford refused to reopen the question of the siting of the North Wales college after Bangor had been chosen.[48] The prospects were bleak, and a considerable campaign of attrition conducted with the utmost skill would be required to wear down government resistance. Happily for Aberystwyth, during 1883, new and much more effective official leadership was discovered. Four names are significant. As soon as the report of the Chester conference appeared in *The Times*, B. T. Williams, former M.P. and currently a county court judge, immediately wrote to the 'Thunderer' powerfully championing Aberystwyth. It will be remembered that Williams had been interested in the Welsh university question as far back as 1852.[49] In recent years, he had joined the Aberystwyth Council and when Dr. E. J. Evans resigned as joint honorary Secretary of the College, Williams willingly replaced him. Unlike Evans, Williams was prepared to fight for Aberystwyth.[50]

So, too, was A. C. Humphreys-Owen, who had joined the Aberystwyth Council as a result of Principal Edwards' persuasions in the 1870s. Humphreys-Owen was

[46] Roberts to Mundella, 23 October 1882. P.R.O. Ed. 119/68. R. D. Roberts to D. C. Roberts 16 July (2 letters) 1884. R. D. Roberts to J. Chamberlain, 16 July 1884. N.L.W. MSS. 16704D.

[47] Exchange of Letters, 27 April 1880. B.M. Add. MSS. 44258, ff. 163–6.

[48] *Parl. Debates*, 3rd Series, vol. 282, 1334. J. M. Pugh, M.P. (for Cardiganshire), to Carlingford, 23 August 1883. P.R.O. Ed. 119/68.   [49] See page 9–10, above.

[50] E. J. Evans to the Council, 6 February 1884. C.A. (JL), not numbered. Evans said that to maintain Aberystwyth and Bangor, 'institutions . . . with all the antagonism of two rival rural companies', would make 'serious mischief' for Wales.

a discreet, sensible man of affairs who was to play an increasingly important part in Welsh education during the next twenty-five years. David Davies, M.P., of course, had never wavered in his support for Aberystwyth. Davies, an instinctive fighter, did not take kindly to defeat, and the brusque treatment he had received at Chester had thoroughly 'soured' him; moreover, he was disgusted with Lord Aberdare and his Committee, and was convinced that their mischief had been 'done purposely' in collusion with the government.[51] In October 1883 David Davies once more came forward generously with the promise that if the Council would agree to continue the College, government grant or not, he would contribute £500 a year for six years. These men, with the backing of Stephen Evans and Foulkes Roberts (still, as even Gibson admitted, as 'true as steel'), provided the chief support for the man who led the fight to save Aberystwyth.[52]

Stuart Rendel was a wealthy Englishman, a product of Eton and Oxford, who became managing director of Armstrong-Whitworth. In 1880 he stood as Liberal candidate for Montgomeryshire and, to general surprise, broke the eighty-year-old dominance of the Wynnstay family. Until 1883 Rendel had no official connection with Aberystwyth College. He thought the Aberdare Committee's treatment of Aberystwyth 'cruel', and the Chester decision 'a blunder'; there was no point in trying to come to terms with the North Wales committee, for they would say, 'To Caesar thou hast appealed', and Aberystwyth would have to take the consequences. There was nothing for it, therefore, but to fight; Mid-Wales would rally round Aberystwyth, and Rendel was prepared to lead the struggle in Westminster and elsewhere.[53]

Rendel was ideally equipped for this exacting commission: he had a marvellous eye for essentials, great tact, unassailable integrity, a self-effacing manner, charm, tactical skill, a great and growing influence with Welsh M.P.s, and, last and not least, Gladstone's warm regard. But something more than this was required to turn the scale: the growing chorus of support of the Welsh people. In part, this was the spontaneous expression of national sympathy for the pioneer college which had struggled heroically for years against all the odds, and had been scurvily treated by the Departmental Committee and the Chester conference. Something was owed to the Welsh press which, almost unanimously, called for justice for Aberystwyth. And a great deal stemmed from the activity of friends of the College who held meetings up and down Wales prompting the passing of resolutions in favour of Aberystwyth, all carefully collated and forwarded to Downing Street. Principal Edwards, the embodiment of Aberystwyth's struggle, was

51 David Davies at Aberystwyth. *Cambrian News* (10 August and 27 December 1883). David Davies to J. B. Rogers, 1883. C.A. Loose, not numbered.

52 *Council Minutes*, 16 October 1883. *Cambrian News* (19 October 1883).

53 N.L.W. MSS. 19442E, f. 142. N.L.W. Glansevern MSS. 103, 119, 120, 128. N.L.W. MSS. 19440E, I, 26 December 1883. Rendel refused to join the Bangor Council, except in a purely nominal capacity as an M.P.

particularly effective at Carmarthen and Liverpool where, according to a former student, 'the "Prince" was in fine style' and the feeling in favour of Aberystwyth 'was more than unanimous, . . . it was overwhelming'.[54]

Moreover, certain North Walians were having second thoughts about the Bangor College. First of all, many of the spokesmen for the other towns which had claimed the North Wales college were thoroughly disgruntled with the choice of Bangor. Thomas Gee, for example, had pushed hard for Denbigh, and until the decision in favour of Bangor was made, his influential newspaper poured scorn on the idea of retaining Aberystwyth. Subsequently, however, Gee changed his tune. Quite apart from his disappointment over the rejection of Denbigh, Gee quickly came to the conclusion that a college in Bangor, in the shadow of the cathedral, would be overwhelmingly dominated by the Church. And the important influence exercised on the North Wales committee by Tory landlords and Churchmen, Lords Powis and Penrhyn in particular, and the energy displayed on Bangor's behalf by the combative Dean, H. T. Edwards, gave Gee and others pause for thought. William Rathbone, M.P., discovered that as soon as it became likely that Bangor would be chosen, he was 'treated as a traitor who has handed over the College to the Church and the Tories . . . the dreaded shade of the Palace and the Castle, and the personality of the Dean seem to have deprived of judgment some of my best friends'.[55]

On 29 August 1883 *Y Faner* changed its line almost overnight. From then on, its reiterated message was that Aberystwyth, the unsectarian College *par excellence*, where Welshmen of all religious persuasions were naturally at home, must be kept open at all costs and should be given a government grant: at all events, 'all Welsh nonconformists' should now rally to Aberystwyth's support.[56]

There were signs, too, that the counties of Merioneth and Montgomery much preferred Aberystwyth to Bangor; meetings at Bala, Dolgelley, and Newtown overwhelmingly passed resolutions in favour of the pioneer college.[57] This upsurge of opinion, which appeared also in Pembrokeshire, was not lost on Welsh M.P.s; moreover, as one of them noted, it was a 'growing feeling', and in response, prompted by Rendel, some of them wrote to Mundella urging a reconsideration of Aberystwyth's case.[58] The scene was now set for Rendel's campaign.

[54] J. E. Lloyd to T. E. Ellis, 8 February 1884. N.L.W. T. E. Ellis MSS. 1431. *T. C. Edwards Letters*, pp. 216–17.

[55] Rathbone to Lord Powis, 26 August 1883. U.C.N.W. Bangor MSS. 4288. See also, Dean Edwards to Powis, ibid. 4255, 4258, 4259, and 4261, Mundella to Gee, N.L.W. MSS. 8307D, f. 217. In October 1883 Sir Robert Cunliffe, M.P., an important Bangor supporter, was trying to take measures to 'stop the Dean of Bangor's mouth'. N.L.W. MSS. 19440E, f. 1.

[56] *Baner ac Amserau Cymru* (29 August 1883, *et seq.*, especially 12, 19 September and 7 November).

[57] Ibid. (5 September). *Cambrian News* (15 June 1883). *The Times* (4 September 1883). N.L.W. Llandinam MSS. 293. At Newtown, to draw the crowd, the name of David Davies' son, Edward, was put on placards advertising the meeting.

[58] Lord Kensington to Rendel, 23 December 1883. N.L.W. MSS. 19440E, f. 2.

In June 1883 Mundella and Carlingford, speaking for the government, had stated flatly that they would 'not recognize a third college under any circumstances'. Mundella, having Henry Richard, whom he took as his 'Welsh guide', on 'his side', believed that he could discount the growing Welsh opinion in favour of Aberystwyth; the most he was prepared to offer was a small temporary grant for three or five years to phase out the College, because he regarded its continuance permanently 'as a breach of faith' with Bangor and Cardiff. The first Aberystwyth counter-attack was an attempt to get around Mundella and Carlingford with an appeal to Gladstone to meet a deputation. This, however, was refused (not least because Aberdare was not associated with it) and, if anything, it had the effect of increasing the opposition of Carlingford and Mundella, whose *amour propre* had been upset by this attempt to by-pass them.[59]

There was nothing for it, therefore, but to mount a parliamentary campaign backed by as many Welsh M.P.s as could be mobilized, with the additional assistance of certain sympathetic English members, on whom Rendel was working assiduously in private. Moreover, Welsh public opinion was stirred up by a great series of meetings (especially at denominational assemblies) throughout the country. P. Mostyn Williams of Rhyl took charge of North Wales, and the southern counties were organized from Aberystwyth by the Revd. T. E. Williams. In this activity, the Aberystwyth local committee was especially energetic and they accepted wholeheartedly Stuart Rendel's leadership.[60]

On 14 March 1884 Rendel introduced in the Commons a motion asking for state support for Aberystwyth College. He was strongly supported (careful preparation paying dividends) by almost the whole body of Welsh M.P.s, as well as some sympathetic English members such as James Bryce, and a parcel of Tory members allegedly hoping to derive profit from a breach between the government and Welsh liberals. Sir Robert Cunliffe, a member of the Bangor Council, spoke up for Aberystwyth, and Osborne Morgan and Henry Richard, remembering earlier loyalties, did likewise; even Lord Emlyn, provoked by Mundella's attempt to buy time with a further inquiry into the College, recanted and added his support.[61] Mundella and Childers, Chancellor of the Exchequer, were boxed in: 'they could neither tunnel their way through, get round it, or climb over the top', as one newspaper put it.[62] This, however, was not achieved by the arguments (the traditional ones) advanced in the debate. Earlier in the day, Mundella, at a meeting with Rendel and some others, had been 'still savage', said that he

[59] Rendel to Humphreys-Owen, 25 June, 15 December 1883, 27 January 1884. N.L.W. Glansevern MSS. 94, 132, 137. Humphreys-Owen to Rendel, 23 January 1884. N.L.W. MSS. 19440E, f. 10.

[60] Letters to Rendel from Welsh and English M.P.s, B. T. Williams, Mostyn Williams, and Evan Evans in ibid., ff. 11–19; f. 108, for a tabulated list of meetings in North Wales.

[61] Rendel wrote ironically: 'Henry Richard, Osborne Morgan and Hussey Vivian and the Tories backing Aberystwyth was worth bringing about.' N.L.W. Glansevern MSS. 140.

[62] *South Wales Daily News* (17 March 1884).

disliked Rendel's motion, and would meet it with 'a direct "No"'. Before the evening's debate, however, Gladstone had intervened with a message to Mundella, who thereupon 'surrendered' with more or less good grace.[63]

At first the government was prepared to give no more than £2,000 a year, and that sum would be forthcoming only if Aberystwyth could supplement it with some considerable private subscriptions. David Davies immediately said that 'he would hold to his promise of £500 a year if the government would give £2,500'. Armed with this inducement, Rendel tried to persuade Mundella to concede the larger amount, but he remained 'firm' and would 'not recommend more than £2,000'. Mundella was convinced that the Aberystwyth Council would not 'declare war for the sake of £500'.[64] Mundella was a slippery customer; he preferred dealing with Henry Richard rather than with Rendel; indeed, at almost the same time that the Vice-President was refusing to accept Rendel's plea for £2,500, he was writing to Richard that if the government were to subsidize a third college, it must be 'on the same conditions as the other two'; that is, £4,000 a year, with no stipulations about private subscriptions.[65] At this point, Lord Aberdare was able to render Aberystwyth some useful service; he, too, had been forced to change his mind to some extent. Rendel noted in March that Aberdare 'quite eats his own declarations about a third college', and in April the President, at Rendel's instance, wrote to Mundella urging a grant of £2,500 for five years, conditionally on the raising of a private subscription of £1,000 a year for the same period. Ultimately, in June the Treasury, in a carefully worded face-saving communication written by the reluctant Leonard Courtenay, conceded the larger grant on the conditional terms.[66]

So far so good; but at this point the unity among Aberystwyth's friends, hitherto so impressive, began to break down. Rendel, Aberdare, David Davies, and B. T. Williams, all too aware of the tremendous efforts needed to move a government and a Treasury stocked with experts in foot-dragging, believed that, for the present at least, no more could be done. But others were furiously indignant that Aberystwyth had not been placed on exactly the same footing as Cardiff and Bangor with a £4,000 unconditional annual grant. The Aberystwyth local committee members were especially of this opinion. Early in July 1884, at a meeting of the College Council, the official spokesmen tried to explain that the £2,500

[63] N.L.W. Glansevern MSS., 140. *Parl. Debates*, 3rd Series, vol. 285, 1589–1631, for the debate.

[64] Rendel to Humphreys-Owen, 14 March 1884. N.L.W. Glansevern MSS. 140. Rendel to B. T. Williams, 9 April 1884. C.A. (C), not numbered.

[65] 17 March 1884. N.L.W. MSS. 5505B. Sir George Kekewich (*The Education Department and After* (1920), p. 289) for the following conversation immediately after Mundella's wilful hoodwinking of a deputation.

Cumin: 'How you did humbug them.'

Mundella: 'Yes, we are all humbugs, you know; that is part of our stock in trade.'

[66] N.L.W. Glansevern MSS. 141. Aberdare to Rendel, 2 and 17 April 1884. N.L.W. Rendel Letters and Papers, 119 and 120. 6 June 1884. P.R.O. Ed. 119/68.

grant had been achieved only by 'a common and harmonious' working of all the forces favourable to Aberystwyth. Later in the day, at a meeting in the College to distribute prizes for the session, proceedings were interrupted repeatedly by R. D. Roberts and Gibson, in defiance of a hapless chairman. The two local fire-brands attacked the negotiators for not demanding £4,000, and Gibson returned again and again to his pet notion that College officers who were less than whole-hoggers ought, in common decency, to resign. At various points, the meeting erupted in uproar with several unofficial chairmen usurping the functions of B. T. Williams, the accredited president.[67]

R. D. Roberts was not the man to be deflected; within days, he was badgering Mundella in London to commute the grant of £2,500 a year for five years into £4,000 for three years. From start to finish, it was a shouting match: Mundella, full of resentment at the way that he had been out-manœuvred earlier, insisted furiously that it was 'absurd' for a small country like Wales to have three colleges; Aberystwyth was lucky to have £2,500 when it 'ought to have none'. As for the suggested commutation: 'No', said Mundella, with great emphasis, 'it can't be done.' As he had run into a brick wall in the interview, Roberts wrote immediately to Mundella to say that it was clear that the Vice-President, along with Lord Aberdare and company, still 'misapprehended' the feeling in Wales about the College.[68]

Rendel and B. T. Williams were thoroughly disgusted at Roberts' headlong tactics, particularly the repeated allegation (which they wrote off as wisdom after the event) that £4,000 could have been extorted with a little more effort. For a time, Williams and Rendel seriously considered severing their connections with Aberystwyth.[69] And when, later in July, the College Council decided officially to ask the government to authorize the commutation, Rendel stood aside and the negotiation was entrusted to L. P. Pugh, M.P. for Cardiganshire. Pugh had far less skill and weight than Rendel and received a blank Treasury refusal to consider the question.[70]

During 1884, Lord Aberdare, not surprisingly considering the weight of public attack he had had to endure, was privately talking of resigning his Aberystwyth Presidency. Rendel had been powerfully impressed with Aberdare's refusal to bear 'malice' and, at the end, the 'generous and unself-regarding' way in which he had come round to accept a third college in Wales.[71] Humphreys-Owen had tried

[67] *Cambrian News* (4 July 1884). Thomas Davies of Bootle, a good friend to the College over many years, was infuriated at the virulence of the Aberystwyth men. 'The inaccessibility of Aberystwyth to the outside world', he wrote angrily to Principal Edwards, 'must be accepted as a dispensation of Providence. Such a town deserves to be isolated.' 11 July 1884. N.L.W. J. H. Davies (U.C.W.) MSS.

[68] R. D. Roberts to D. C. Roberts and to Mundella (copy), 16 July 1884. N.L.W. MSS. 16704D.

[69] Rendel to Humphreys-Owen, 2 August 1884. C.A. (C), not numbered. B. T. Williams to R. D. Roberts, 27 July 1884. N.L.W. J. H. Davies (U.C.W.) MSS.

[70] *Council Minutes*, 31 July 1884. *U.C.W. Reports* (1863–91), 22 October 1884, pp. 16–19.

[71] 19 March 1884. N.L.W. Glansevern MSS. 142.

hard to persuade Lord Sudeley, a wealthy Whig peer who lived in Montgomery-shire, to accept the Presidency, but Sudeley had been 'frightened by the way Lord Aberdare was bullied', and positively refused. Sudeley suggested Rendel, but Lord Aberdare thought that the President must be a Welshman. Other names canvassed were B. T. Williams, Humphreys-Owen, and Lord Londonderry who, it was thought, would be an acceptable figurehead who 'would do very much what he was told'; in despair, even Lord Emlyn was considered. Failing any of these, it looked as if the position would have to be given to 'some nonentity'. In the end, Aberdare was persuaded to continue.[72]

Despite these high-level difficulties, the College was in better fettle than ever at the start of the session 1884-5. Contrary to expectation, and despite the opening of Cardiff and Bangor, student numbers at Aberystwyth had crept up to 115 during the summer term of 1884, and gone up to 132 at the start of the new session. Moreover, five new lecturers, Ainsworth Davis (Biology), J. W. Brough (Philosophy), D. E. Jones, an old student (Physics), J. W. Marshall (Classics), and W. Scholle (French and German), had been added to the teaching staff. In November 1884 T. C. Edwards persuaded his brilliant former student, J. E. Lloyd, then completing a fine Oxford career, to return as lecturer in History; Lloyd would also double up as lecturer in Welsh, 'this strangely difficult post' to fill, as the Principal called it.[73]

At Oxford, J. E. Lloyd did his old College proud: as expected, he got a First in the History school and his papers were said to be the best of his year. The list of successes of old Aberystwyth students at Oxford, Cambridge, London, Owen's College, and elsewhere was bigger than ever. And close behind lay O. M. Edwards, who had had a thoroughly disappointing experience in the London University examinations ('you feel yourself in the grasp of a merciless life-crushing machine', as he described it), but had recovered his zest by a short period at Glasgow and was now on the threshold of an exceptionally brilliant career at Oxford.[74] In one area, however, the question of scholarship successes was a cause for concern. T. C. Edwards was strongly in favour of a healthy rivalry between Aberystwyth and its sister colleges, but there was currently a serious danger that this would degenerate into a competition for students with 'money bribes'. There were cases in Wales of students who capitalized on the advantage of a year or so at one college and gobbled up an undue share of major prizes at sister institutions. The Principal cited the instance of one man who had two years at Aberystwyth, two at Cardiff, and

[72] Rendel to Humphreys-Owen, 27 July 1884. N.L.W. Glansevern MSS. 155. Humphreys-Owen to his wife, 25 January and 29 October 1884. Ibid., not numbered.

[73] Principal's Report, 22 October 1884. U.C.W. Reports (1863–91), pp. 7–11. T. C. Edwards to J. B. Rogers, 12 November 1884. C.A. (JL), not numbered.

[74] Principal's Report, 16 October 1885. U.C.W. Reports (1863–91), pp. 11–12. O. M. Edwards to T. E. Ellis, 26 December 1883. N.L.W. D. R. Daniel MSS. 993. Edwards said that, despite these other attractions, he longed 'very much for the Aber. library and the sea'.

then blithely hopped off to Bangor equipped with a three-year scholarship he had won in supposedly open competition; a career reminiscent of the twelve-year apprenticeship of a medieval student. Aberystwyth had commissioned Humphreys-Owen to negotiate an agreement with Cardiff and Bangor to put a stop to such a possibility, but hitherto without success. The Principal, therefore, decided that Aberystwyth must join the free-for-all; he disliked it intensely but, as he said, 'necessity is the plea', and, to encourage the Council to action, he himself provided £50 for a new scholarship.[75]

In 1884 there was one other important innovation: women students entered the College for the first time. Of course, there had been women part-time students of Music in Joseph Parry's day, but they were scarcely regarded as authentic students. In October 1884 the first woman student studying a regular College course appeared; she caused quite a stir, half-enjoyed her unique status, but was rather relieved to be joined six months later by half-a-dozen more women. By the end of the session there were ten women students and, in the following October, the number had risen to nineteen. Soon afterwards, Abergeldie house on Victoria Terrace was taken over as a hostel for, in the first instance, three women students. There was evidently no question of lodging women in the College itself. When that had been mooted for women Music students in 1875, Hugh Owen had recoiled with horror; 'you would of course have partitions, locks, bolts, and all that sort of thing', he wrote, and he was sure that, in practice, 'no mischief might arise'. Nevertheless, he was certain it would 'surprise' the country and subject the College to 'damaging criticism'. Evidently, things had changed a little in less than ten years.[76]

At the start of the session 1884-5 then, things were going moderately well for Aberystwyth College. Lewis Morris even persuaded the old enemy Mundella to come on to Aberystwyth from Bangor, where he had attended the opening cere-monies of the new college. Mundella was evidently in high, good humour; he received a great welcome from the students and made a good speech with some nice light touches in return. Principal Edwards got the impression that Mundella was 'a converted man. His visit to Bangor converted him to side with Aberyst-wyth.' Even the belligerent local committee members, or at least some of them, were prepared to forgive and forget. But not Gibson of the *Cambrian News*; he pointedly asked why Aberystwyth should be required to find 300 students before it received £4,000 a year, when Cardiff had that sum with less than a hundred, and Bangor with no more than forty-seven. Gibson had no patience with recent talk (a useful crutch when Aberystwyth looked like being

[75] Principal's Report, 16 October 1885. *U.C.W. Reports (1863-91)*, pp. 15-17. T. C. Edwards to J. B. Rogers, 17 December 1884. C.A. (JL), not numbered.

[76] Miss L. Patrick, 'College Reminiscences 1884-6', in Iwan Morgan, pp. 77-9. Principal's Report, 16 October 1885. *U.C.W. Reports (1863-91)*, pp. 9-10. Humphreys-Owen to his wife, 8 November 1885. N.L.W. Glansevern MSS., not numbered. *T. C. Edwards Letters*, p. 93.

completely immobilized) of a college for central Wales. 'Depend upon it', said Gibson in his parting shot, the College always had been and always would be, 'the University College of Wales'.[77]

Converted or not Mundella still insisted in the Commons six months later that it was 'premature' for Aberystwyth's friends to raise again the question of the £4,000 grant; it was necessary to wait until there had been further experience of the College's success and progress.[78] In any case, Mundella's opinions on this question soon became idle, for in June 1885 the Liberal government resigned. But at least the negotiation for an increased grant had again been entrusted to the more adroit hands of Stuart Rendel. For reasons that are difficult to follow, Lord Aberdare thoroughly disapproved of this approach to the government; he had not 'the remotest expectation' that the Treasury would concede the larger amount; 'nor have I', he told Rendel, 'ever thought that the College had a right to expect it'. He refused to have anything to do with the proposal. It looks as if some of John Gibson's attacks on the President were not altogether unfair.[79]

Still, there was plenty of confidence at Aberystwyth in the future of the College; Mundella had encouraged the authorities to complete the building, and, in 1885, considerable private subscriptions were promised for this purpose, with David Davies, M.P., as ever, heading the list. Plans were far advanced though, mercifully, work had not begun when about midnight on 8/9 July, a fire, the source of which was never properly explained, broke out in the chemistry laboratory in the old College building. Luckily, only a handful of people were in the College, and they escaped unhurt. The alarm roused the town and hundreds of people came to help; unfortunately, water-hydrants were too few, hoses were inadequate and, at crucial moments, jets failed or played only feebly. Driven by a high wind, flames moved inexorably across the roof of the College, floors came crashing down, and thick smoke, falling masonry, and frightening explosions in the laboratories, imperilled the lives of the fire fighters, who were mainly willing amateurs. Others worked frantically to save the contents of the Library and, less successfully, the Museum; the fire continued for hours during darkness, and a change in the direction of the wind seemed at one time to doom the whole building. Luckily, the wind changed again to its usual direction from the south-west, and the Principal's house and the south wing were spared. When morning came, Savin's magnificently interesting old building presented a sorry spectacle: the whole north wing, where most of the teaching and laboratory work had been carried on, was gutted. Much of the remaining wood-work was charred and clouds of smoke rose from the ruins. The

[77] *Aberdare Letters*, ii. 188. *T. C. Edwards Letters*, pp. 229–30. *Cambrian News* (24 October 1884). A fortnight earlier, Joseph Chamberlain had thought it wise to refuse an invitation to come to Aberystwyth because it 'would not be approved' by his colleagues at the Education department. N.L.W. Rendel MSS. iii. 224.

[78] 23 April 1885. *Parl. Debates*, 3rd Series, vol. 297, 478.

[79] 30 January 1885. N.L.W. Rendel Letters and Papers, 122.

houses in Laura Place were crammed with salvaged material and a great overflow had to be left to the mercy of the open sky. Many had been injured and, later, the bodies of three local men were recovered from the ashes.[80]

It looked for all the world as if the elements had conspired together to achieve the end of Aberystwyth College, something that years of disappointment, grinding poverty, the contempt of the well-to-do, and the indifference of a succession of not especially helpful governments had failed to do. Some old enemies could scarcely conceal their elation. The *Western Mail* immediately concluded that the fire marked the 'end of Aberystwyth', and with an astonishing lack of taste advised the townspeople of Swansea that 'a long pull, a strong pull, and a pull altogether and the College is theirs. Aberystwyth's difficulty is their opportunity.'[81]

Not for the first or last time, the Cardiff newspaper completely misjudged the temper of the people of the Principality. If any doubt existed previously of the hold Aberystwyth College had on the imagination of the Welsh people, it was dispelled by the response to the destruction wrought by the fire. A great wave of sympathy swept the nation; meetings all over the country sent messages of support and condolence and the religious denominations, without exception, rallied to the side of the College. Principal Edwards was now quite sure of the future of his College: 'Wales', he said, 'will never now let it die.'[82]

Even Lord Salisbury's Tory government was not insensitive to the public mood of Wales. For months Stuart Rendel had been patiently at work trying to persuade the government to concede a £4,000 annual grant to Aberystwyth. Judged by his surviving correspondence on this question, Edward Stanhope, the Tory Vice-President of the Council, was a much less vain man than Mundella and did not deal in ambiguities to the same extent. Stanhope was prepared to dispense with a formal deputation, a Memorial setting out Aberystwyth's case signed by as many Welsh M.P.s as possible would do. For some short time, the issue trembled in the balance. Ultimately, late in August, the battle was won: almost every Welsh M.P. had signed the Memorial and 'all the surviving members' of Lord Aberdare's Committee of 1880 ate humble pie with good grace and signified their approval. After full consideration, the government had concluded that Aberystwyth could 'reasonably claim to be treated in the same manner as Cardiff and Bangor'. At last, something like justice had been done.[83]

---

[8] There is a graphic description of the fire by Professor J. Brough in Iwan Morgan, pp. 47–52. The *Cambrian News* (10 July 1885) adds a good deal of detail.

[81] 10 July 1885. *The South Wales Daily News* (13 July 1885) for a very different reaction and a magnificent rebuke to its rival.

[82] T. C. Edwards to the Mayor of Aberystwyth. *Cambrian News* (31 July 1885).

[83] Letters between Rendel and Stanhope, 29 July, 22 August, and 'August' 1885. N.L.W. Rendel Letters and Papers, 983–5. *T. C. Edwards Letters*, p. 251. *Council Minutes* (17 July 1888), p. 559, for Stanhope's goodwill towards Aberystwyth.

But there was still the need for large sums of money to rebuild the College. A meeting at the Mansion House in London elicited some good promises. Principal Edwards, who had long ago thrown overboard the condition that he had insisted upon in 1872 that he should not have to beg for money for the College, was especially active. He tried to enlist the aid of T. E. Ellis and other old students; almost all of these were willing missionaries for Aberystwyth. In Mold, an unnamed old student had kindled great enthusiasm for the College; H. B. Jones (*Garmonydd*) was eager to organize local committees in the area. His letter volunteering to do so is worth quotation at length, for it exemplifies the regard in which Aberystwyth was held.

I know hundreds of quarrymen, colliers, lead miners and agricultural labourers who have contributed out of their scanty earnings towards the funds of Aberystwyth College. . . . They, like all true-hearted and loyal Welshmen, sincerely rejoice at the good start made by the sister, or rather daughter, colleges at Bangor and Cardiff. But you shall find they cherish for Aberystwyth a kind of personal and proprietary attachment. When they heard the news of the fire, they went back in memory to those Sunday evenings ten or twelve years ago when in their little Bethels they contributed their crowns, half-crowns and shillings towards the *first* Welsh university college, and they felt as if some dire calamity had befallen themselves. . . . Facts like these unmistakably attest the depth and fervour of the national feeling on behalf of our national college *par excellence*.[84]

Principal Edwards was now prepared himself to stump the country in search of money. Every county in Wales had an agent for collection (sixteen out of the nineteen in 1885 were nonconformist ministers) who operated on the very minimum expense allowance. Of these unsung heroes, the Revd. D. E. Davies of Pwllheli was perhaps the most active; the effort he put into the venture over several years is almost incredible. In his spare time, he paraded around Anglesey, Denbighshire, and Caernarvonshire wheedling money for Aberystwyth; his surviving correspondence on the subject is massive, not surprisingly when every donation, no matter how small (a 3s. postal order, for example), was acknowledged laboriously by hand. By 1888 he had elicited promises worth £1,600 in his district, and it is evident that he had a short way with backsliders, 'sinners' as he called them appropriately enough. It is also clear that old prejudices died hard: even Davies' highly effective persuasions failed with the landed magnates (including Lord Penrhyn) and 'all the clergymen' he saw, 'except the Vicar of Caernarvon'. Nothing, however, deflected him: 'I feel for the "Mother College" so much', he wrote, 'that I shall not be discouraged by what people say or do.' Another of his functions was to arrange meetings that were usually addressed by the Principal. If T. C. Edwards came, there was never any trouble about the size of the audience: 'The name of the Principal is a guarantee of a good meeting.'

84 H. B. Jones to J. B. Rogers, 18 September 1885. N.L.W. J. H. Davies (U.C.W.) MSS.

But there was no effective substitute for T. C. Edwards' charisma: 'The people won't listen to any deputy you may send', D. E. Davies reported to the Principal in 1888.[85]

Gradually, in these and other ways, a sizeable amount of money was accumulated for the rebuilding of the College, and there was also, of course, £10,000 in insurance available. Immediately after the fire, there had been a debate on the question whether the College should be rebuilt on the old site or elsewhere in or around the town. An approach was made to the Powell (Nanteos) family to sell Laura Place but, ultimately, without success; Sir Pryse Pryse of Gogerddan would give no general indication of the valuation he placed on the many fields he owned near Aberystwyth, and insisted that the College should first choose its spot and he would then quote an appropriate sum. Naturally, sentiment argued strongly for the old site: the students voted overwhelmingly for it, and David Samuel, claiming validly to speak for the old students, pleaded eloquently (quoting Charles Lamb) that the College had already 'planted a terrible fixed root' in its original position. The decisive factor, as so often before, was money. Seddon had been called in to advise, and, in his opinion, the College could be restored (and considerably improved) on the old site for £25,670, whereas a completely new building elsewhere would cost £47,000.[86]

For some time, a special building sub-committee, led by Humphreys-Owen and David Davies, considered these questions in great detail. Meantime, *ad hoc* arrangements had to be made to enable the work of the College to continue. A new session was at hand, and for a time the schoolrooms of almost every chapel in the town were used for lectures and classes. The Queen's Hotel was hired for the session and all Arts teaching was centred there; a large room in the Principal's house was fitted up as a library, and the south wing of the old building was adapted to house the Science laboratories on a makeshift basis. The Principal had feared that the destruction by fire of a large part of the College would lead to a disastrous fall in the number of students, and he had written individually to them asking them, as a point of honour, to return. In fact, he need not have worried, for 132 students appeared for the new session, including twenty-four from England.[87]

The arrival at Aberystwyth of substantial and growing numbers of English students occasioned alarm in some quarters, especially as several of the new

[85] Revd. D. E. Davies' correspondence in U.C.N.W., Bangor MSS. 5540, especially his letters of May–July 1888, and April–July 1889. The list of agents is in 'Agents for collection for the Restoration Fund', 1885. C.A. (C), not numbered.

[86] J. James to Stephen Evans, 16 June 1886. C.A. (C), not numbered. G. Powell to the College Council, 9 August 1887 (copy) N.L.W. J. H. Davies (U.C.W.) MSS. *Cambrian News* (24 July 1885). *Aberystwyth Observer* (1 August 1885).

[87] Principal's Report, 16 October 1885. *U.C.W.Reports (1863–91)*, pp. 17–18. T. C. Edwards to J. B. Rogers, 23 July 1885. C.A. (JL), not numbered.

entrants had won College scholarships at the pre-sessional examinations. The cry 'Wales for the Welsh' was raised, and some people asserted that scholarships should be restricted to Welsh-born candidates. Principal Edwards would have none of it: such a policy would be 'unwise and ungenerous'; he thought that the influx of English students reflected great credit on the College and its teaching; English schoolmasters had taken note of the string of Aberystwyth examination successes at London and elsewhere, and drawn the right conclusions. One of the other Welsh colleges had already restricted its scholarships to prevent pre-emption by outsiders. T. C. Edwards wanted Aberystwyth to 'make the opposite experiment'; as he said, 'great colleges become what they are by opening their gates to all comers'. For the moment, Welsh students were handicapped in competition by the poor quality of the Principality's secondary schools, but this would soon be remedied when the long-promised Welsh Intermediate Education Bill was passed. The Principal also made some forthright criticisms of what he thought were his countrymen's weaker characteristics, and insisted that they needed 'to come out of their shell'. His comments were so severe that the College *Report* includes a footnote to the effect that the opinions expressed were his sole responsibility.[88]

At any rate, the College did not restrict its scholarships, and some of the English students who came were among the liveliest spirits at Aberystwyth. They provided a useful leavening of the student-body, and many of them developed a life-long affection for the College fully equal to that of any Welsh-born student.[89] The makeshift arrangements of the year or so following the fire do not seem in any way to have hampered social activities. In 1888 a College Dramatics Club was formally established (entertainments of one kind and another had been a strong feature from the beginning) under the leadership of Ainsworth Davis and Brough of the staff.[90] The College *Magazine* was now powerfully established, but as it still carried too strong an official imprimatur for some student tastes, the hand-written *College Critic* appeared in 1887 containing a commentary on the contents of the more sedate publication. Even in this anonymous, quasi-clandestine sheet, T. C. Edwards was above criticism: 'the King', said the first issue, 'can do no wrong'. Some other members of staff were treated rather less respectfully; the *Critic* was soon suppressed, and was immediately replaced by a less circumspect successor, which was even 'more objectionable'. Eventually, some plain speaking was necessary to show 'the men that they can go too far'.[91]

[88] Principal's Report, 19 October 1886. *U.C.W. Reports* (*1863–91*), pp. 13–16. For the contrary argument, warning against the Welsh colleges becoming mere replicas of those in England, see *Cymru Fydd* (1888), pp. 466–70.

[89] For example, T. R. Dawes, who has an interesting account of life at the Queen's Hotel in 1885 in Iwan Morgan, pp. 82–7.   [90] April–May 1888. C.A. S/MN/1.

[91] *College Critic* (December 1887). J. W. Marshall to J. E. Lloyd, no date (1888), U.C.N.W. Lloyd MSS. 314, f. 304.

This was a storm in a teacup compared with a row that had erupted at a higher level the year before. As a result of the Franchise Reform Act of 1884 and the Redistribution Act of the following year, there was now only one parliamentary constituency in Cardiganshire and the number of voters had been more than doubled. The sitting member in 1885 was David Davies, who had been regarded for some time by certain Cardiganshire liberals as unacceptably wayward and whimsical in his voting behaviour. When Gladstone brought in his Irish Home Rule Bill in 1886, Davies voted against it, and, in the subsequent general election, the Liberal Association ran a Gladstonian candidate, Bowen Rowlands.[92] At first, David Davies ('crafty old dodger', as Humphreys-Owen called him), lay low, but ultimately, in July, he announced his candidature. It was a fierce contest: Gibson pulled no punches in his newspaper; David Davies was accused of 'inordinate vanity', and of treating the electors like 'children'. One of his meetings in Aberystwyth was disrupted by students egged on by Gibson; David Davies was manhandled in the resultant disorder and had to be given police protection. In the end, Bowen Rowlands won narrowly by nine votes.[93]

It has been convincingly shown that this result was the consequence of general causes that had been in train some time before.[94] But David Davies, not unnaturally, saw it in personal terms. He said that he did not care a straw for the loss of the seat; that was due to the machinations of the Revd. Thomas Levi, 'King of the Methodists'. But Aberystwyth was 'responsible for the rough treatment' he had received, and he was particularly incensed that Principal Edwards (who allegedly agreed with him on Ireland) had not troubled to return home to vote, whereas Principal Jayne of St. David's College, Lampeter, had travelled all the way from Leeds to do so. David Davies had had enough: 'never another shilling will leave my pocket for anything at Aberystwyth', he said, 'I shall now . . . take no further interest in the College'. Soon afterwards, he resigned the Treasurership and could not be induced to reconsider his decision.[95]

This was an infinitely sad way for the College to lose its 'most generous and steadfast friend'; the man who had saved it from extinction more than once.[96] And sentiment aside, the College still had desperate need of all the friends it possessed;

[92] There is a fine account of this election in K. O. Morgan, 'Cardiganshire Politics: the Liberal Ascendency, 1885–1923', *Ceredigion*, v. no. 4, 311–25.

[93] Humphreys-Owen to his wife, 19 May 1886. N.L.W. Glansevern MSS., not numbered. *Cambrian News* (July 1886). David Davies to Stephen Evans, 29 July 1886. C.A. (Loose), not numbered.

[94] K. O. Morgan, loc. cit.

[95] David Davies to Stephen Evans, 21 June, 29 July, 9 August 1886. C.A. (Loose), not numbered. 'Eat, drink and be merry before the radical Gladstonites will take what we have and give it to others that will support their rotten policy', he wrote bitterly later (ibid. 23 May 1887).

[96] 19 October 1886. *U.C.W. Reports (1863–91)*, p. 25. 'I am afraid', a correspondent wrote to the Principal, 'Cardiganshire people love the Irish more than themselves, and are willing to alienate Mr. Davies and destroy the College for the sake of . . . a Parliament beyond the seas.' 29 June 1886. N.L.W. J. H. Davies (U.C.W.) MSS.

for the £4,000 annual government grant was still conditional on a yearly private subscription of £1,000, and had been conceded only for a three-year period. David Davies did not, in fact, summarily cut off his contributions entirely, much to the relief of the Council, for, had he done so, the College would have found it extremely difficult to meet the government's stipulations. It was obvious that these anxieties would continue until the College had been conceded its charter and the grant was made permanent.

Lewis Morris had been pressing the government for a charter ever since 1884. It was obvious that there was little hope of success until the constitution of the College had been given a more representative character in line with those of Cardiff and Bangor. In December 1884 the Council set up a small committee to revise the constitution, and Morris tried to win the backing of the Education Office in Whitehall for the proposals that he, Lord Aberdare, and Stephen Evans wished to see implemented. As things were, ultimate power lay with the Court of Governors, 'the constituents', subscribers to College funds, and the constitution could be amended only by that body. Morris did not expect the Court to eliminate itself wholesale at one stroke, and he proposed that its powers should continue until the number of 'constituents' had dropped from 406 to 250. He was, however, especially concerned to break the power of his old enemies, the Aberystwyth committee, a 'mischievous local clique of tradesmen and others', as he called them. Gibson and his friends would certainly turn up at any meeting in Aberystwyth, and Morris believed they were quite capable of creating votes overnight (with minimum guinea subscriptions) to dominate a forthcoming meeting to consider the revision of the constitution. Morris asked for the strong support of the Education Office to prevent this and other difficulties which he instanced, notably the need to place some prohibitions on the Principal's 'preaching tours'.[97]

In the event, the decisive meeting for the adoption of the revised constitution was held in January 1885 in London, in the hope, perhaps, of reducing the strength of the Aberystwyth contingent. The arrangements arrived at were a mixture of old and new. There were now to be three categories of Governors: sixty members of the former Court continued; there were *ex officio* Governors comprising the Lords-Lieutenant and M.P.s of seven Welsh counties, and the Principals of the three colleges; and a new class of 'representative Governors' was added. This latter category was made up of representatives of municipal corporations and local and school boards, the nominees of the Lord President of the Council, of the other Welsh Colleges and the Universities of Oxford, Cambridge, and London, together with three members representing old Aberystwyth students who had graduated, two nominees of the College Senate, and, an interesting touch, three women nominated by the new Court of Governors itself. A Council, forty-eight strong,

[97] Morris to Patrick Cumin, 2 October 1884. P.R.O. Ed. 119/68.

would be elected from the new Court. The proposals were endorsed by the Education department in March, and came into operation at the start of the session 1885–6.[98]

Thus equipped, Lewis Morris returned once more to his attempt to win a charter. In March 1886 he wrote a long and impressive letter to the Lord President of the Council, Lord Cranbrook. Morris was able to show that Aberystwyth's student numbers compared well with Cardiff's, and were double those of Bangor; a new constitution, approved by Whitehall, was in force, and the College building would be rebuilt without delay. Aberystwyth's continuing inequality was 'deeply . . . deplored through the length and breadth of Wales'. The reply, almost by return of post, was that it was 'premature' to reopen the question.[99] It is difficult to understand why, at this late stage, the granting of a charter should still have been resisted so resolutely; possibly officials at the Education Office resented the way in which they had been forced, very much against the grain, to reverse their policy on Aberystwyth. In defence of the officials and their political masters, it could be argued that it was reasonable to withhold the charter until the College building had been completed. Continuing shortage of money hampered the work of reconstruction, and, ultimately, a loan of £6,000 had to be wheedled out of a bank. Humphreys-Owen worked assiduously, watched every penny closely, and used a restraining hand on Seddon, who, nevertheless, did a fine job. By 1888 the south wing had been adapted to house all the Science departments, and although the north wing was not finally completed, a new library and examination hall had been erected, and the seaward frontage of the College had been improved.[100]

In July 1888 a strong Deputation, led by Aberdare (whose remarks indicated how utterly defensive he now was about his *Report* of 1881), waited on the Lord President. One interesting touch, indicating that the most bitter jealousies were now over, was that the Principals of Cardiff and Bangor were present in support. Lord Cranbrook was cordial, and even encouraging; it was clear that the back of official resistance had been broken. Some tidying up remained to be done: in 1889 the College constitution was again slightly amended, to take cognizance of the existence of County Councils, to increase slightly the representation of women and of the Senate, and to arrange for the lapsing by natural process of the old Governors who were 'constituents'. And a new nominated element joined the Council. A petition for a charter was sent in immediately.[101] There was one final,

---

[98] 16 October 1885. *U.C.W. Reports (1863–91)*, pp. 21–2.

[99] Morris to the Lord President, 26 March 1886. P.R.O. Ed. 119/68. 'Acknowledgment', 27 March 1886. Ibid., no. 6497.

[100] Principal's Report, 19 December 1888. *U.C.W. Reports (1863–91)*, pp. 23–4. Circular, 'Restoration Fund', 15 June 1888. U.C.W. G. Lib., LD 1155(1).

[101] 17 July 1888. *Council Minutes*, pp. 557–60. See also Appendix A of the accompanying Memorial (8 June 1888. N.L.W. J. H. Davies (U.C.W.) MSS.), for a most impressive list of the examination successes won since 1872 by Aberystwyth students.

important flurry. The College naturally wished to retain the old, national title which it had carried so proudly since 1872. The Education department suggested an alternative, 'the University College, Aberystwyth'. Cardiff immediately lodged an objection to the title 'the University College of Wales', and Viriamu Jones stirred up Principal Reichel of Bangor to protest that it was 'inconsistent with the titles of other state-aided Colleges in Wales', and would produce 'an erroneous impression' of the relationship of the three Colleges.[102]

But Aberystwyth was not prepared to throw away the symbol of its seniority, its magnificent pioneer struggle against the odds, and its claim to a national loyalty. For once, a matchless history could not be withstood. In 1889 Aberystwyth, styled 'the University College of Wales', received its charter, and the government grant was made permanent. Perhaps the most interesting and, in a curious way, glamorous decade in the history of the College was drawing to a close.

As 1880 had been the year that delivered the College into Egypt, so 1889 was the year that brought it into the Land of Promise.[103]

[102] U.C.W. Charter and Statutes, 10 September 1889. C.A. c/chc/bus/1. *Council Minutes*, 11 March 1889, pp. 588–9. Reichel to Lord Powis, 9 February 1889. U.C.N.W., Bangor MSS. 4521.

[103] J. O. Francis, *A Short History of the University College of Wales* (1920), p. 26. Francis, anticipating events, dates the deliverance in 1888.

4

'A Future Certain and Sure of . . . Great Success'[1]

THE worst years of storm and stress were now over for the College at Aberystwyth. The next decade was a time of steady, indeed rapid, expansion in which the predictions of those who had all along maintained that, given equal opportunity, Aberystwyth could more than hold its own with its sister colleges were fully vindicated. Moreover, in 1889 the basis of university work in all three colleges in Wales was to be substantially transformed by the passage of the Welsh Intermediate Education Act. Ever since 1872 all too many students had come up to the colleges hopelessly ill-prepared for advanced work; small wonder, therefore, that so much time and effort had to be spent in repairing these deficiencies, that the grandiloquent titles with which the colleges were equipped were more a matter of aspiration than of actual achievement. So long as Wales lacked an adequate number of efficient secondary schools, the colleges themselves must necessarily remain some considerable way short of genuine university standard.

The *Aberdare Report* had itemized in detail the weaknesses of Welsh grammar schools and had strongly recommended the reorganization in several cases of existing schools, and proposed some increase in the number of schools in Wales at the three different grades above the elementary. The educational endowments of the Principality were so meagre that public money, in the form of 'a local rate or a parliamentary grant, or . . . both', was essential, in the opinion of the Committee, if this great void in Welsh education were adequately to be filled.[2] Gladstone's government almost immediately accepted in principle the case for action on Welsh intermediate education, but in practice A. J. Mundella, Vice-President of the Council, who was eager to experiment, was faced with all sorts of clogging difficulties.[3] Inevitably, Mundella had to walk carefully around the entrenched

---

[1] A. H. D. Acland, Vice-President of the Council, at Aberystwyth. *Cambrian News* (18 November 1892).   [2] *Aberdare Report*, Conclusion and Recommendations, p. lvii.
[3] There is a good article on this important piece of legislation by J. R. Webster, 'The Welsh Intermediate Education Act of 1889', in *Welsh Hist. Rev.*, iv. 273–89.

interests of the Charity Commissioners, the School Boards, and the J.P.s, and at the same time make some concession to the insistent Welsh demand for popular control in education.[4] His first proposals were complicated and, as no mention was made of Treasury support, almost certainly they would have proved ineffective. Subsequently, Mundella had to fight a considerable battle against adamant Treasury resistance to a proposal to supplement rate-aid from Exchequer sources, and this struggle was won finally only by a direct intervention on Mundella's side by Gladstone himself.[5]

Mundella's subsequent permutations in his arrangements for the management of the schools evoked considerable criticism in Wales, and Hugh Owen's confident prediction to the Aberdare Committee that the Welsh would willingly consent to be rated for educational purposes was not entirely borne out by the initial public reaction.[6] In any case, endless Irish difficulties prevented a proper parliamentary consideration of Mundella's proposals, and the government resigned before the bill got very far. However, Mundella and the Welsh members kept up the pressure on Lord Salisbury's interim government of 1885 and on his stronger Ministry in the years after 1886. 'To keep the subject before parliament', year by year, Mundella introduced a slightly modified version of his bill of 1885, but to little effect. The establishment of county councils in 1888 provided a more reliable basis for the desired popular control of Welsh intermediate education, and in 1889 Mundella and the Welsh members agreed to make a major effort to get a bill through. All the Welsh members balloted for the right to introduce a private member's bill and, 'fortunately', as Mundella said, 'Stuart Rendel came out first', and the agreed measure was entrusted to his care.[7]

Thereafter there followed some hectic activity and a good deal of skilful manœuvring by the government and the opposition Welsh members and their allies.[8] Rendel's bill proposed that the local education authority should be the county council, which would submit its plans to the Charity Commissioners for transmission to the Education department and thence to Parliament. Schools would be financed by a half-penny rate, supported by an equivalent Treasury grant. There was to be a Board or Council of Education for Wales, made up of representatives of the Welsh counties. There was little chance that the government would accept Rendel's bill in all its popular glory: on the other hand, Sir William

---

[4] 'The people of Wales . . . insist with . . . unanimity on popular and representative management', as the *Aberdare Report*, Conclusion and Recommendations, p. liii, put it.

[5] Mundella to Gladstone, 22 October 1889. B.M. Add. MSS. 44258, ff. 264-5.

[6] J. R. Webster, loc. cit., pp. 281-2. *Aberdare Report*, Conclusion and Recommendations, p. lvii.

[7] Mundella to Gladstone, 22 October 1889. B.M. Add. MSS. 44258, ff. 264-5. In his speech on the Second Reading of the bill on 15 May 1889, Rendel made some flattering references to the Aberystwyth College. *Parl. Debates*, 3rd Series, vol. 336, pp. 126-31.

[8] K. O. Morgan, op. cit., pp. 99-102, for a short, clear account, and J. R. Webster, loc. cit., pp. 285-9, for some additional detail, and a different apportionment of the credit for the measure.

Hart-Dyke, the Tory Vice-President of the Council, was anxious that the bill should not be rejected out of hand, and he was sustained by strong backing in favour of a suitably modified bill from the Welsh Tory M.P.s and some Welsh bishops. Others played usefully constructive parts: Gladstone helped to get the bill into committee with a speech designed to lift the question above the ruck of party hostilities; Tom Ellis, Humphreys-Owen, Acland, and Mundella helped to allay Rendel's rooted suspicion of the Tories, and worked to persuade the Welsh Liberal members that half a loaf was better than none. Finally, a compromise was reached: Hart-Dyke took over the bill, which passed quickly through both Houses and received the Royal Assent early in August 1889. Joint education committees of five members (three nominated by the county councils, two by the Privy Council) were established in each Welsh county; the government insisted on striking out the proposed Welsh Council or Board of Education, and the authority of the Charity Commissioners was reinstated. Nevertheless, despite these disappointments to popular hopes, effective machinery for initiating schemes and for financing and managing the new schools was established. Within a decade or so, Wales had a network of ninety State-supported secondary schools; for a time, Wales was ahead of England in intermediate education and, gradually, the quality of entrants to the university colleges was enormously improved.

Principal T. C. Edwards, however, did not remain long enough at Aberystwyth to witness or profit from this important transformation. In the years of peril, he had fought manfully for his College, but he had received precious little thanks from some of the authorities for his efforts. The Aberdare Committee had pointedly insisted that, for the future at any rate, Principals of Welsh university colleges must be laymen. In 1884 Lewis Morris tried to get the backing of Whitehall for a proposal that the Principal should be 'peremptorily forbidden' from preaching, and insultingly insisted that 'only the wish not to disturb vested interests except where absolutely necessary', prevented his immediate removal.[9] Not long afterwards the Principal heard that only the earnest dissuasion of John Gibson, of all people, prevented R. D. Roberts (who rarely worried about rocking the boat) from proposing to the Council that T. C. Edwards should be asked to resign. Edwards was hardly the man to remain anywhere merely on sufferance but, in fact, he was also open-minded enough to believe that his critics were perhaps right. In August 1885 he wrote at length to his old pupil, J. E. Lloyd:

When I see you, I will explain to you my ideas about my resignation. Briefly, it comes to this: that I am afraid of being more of a hindrance than a help to the success of the College. If I were quite sure that the country wished me to remain, and that the staff

---

[9] Morris to Cumin, 2 October 1884. P.R.O. Ed. 119/68. Morris repeated these sentiments publicly in a 'Memorial' to the College Council. T. C. Edwards to Stephen Evans, 10 October 1884. C.A. (JL), not numbered.

would be loyal, I should certainly not leave the old ship. But I have an impression that the College would do better in the hands of a layman.

The resignation, enforced or otherwise, of the Principal in the months immediately after the great fire would have been a disaster. Happily, there were other members of the Council with rather more *nous* than Morris and R. D. Roberts, and Foulkes Roberts and Stephen Evans in particular persuaded T. C. Edwards to stay, though he subsequently regretted that he had not asked the Council formally to express its opinion.[10]

In the remaining years of his Principalship, T. C. Edwards spent a good deal of time in fund-raising, and in 1890 he made a great tour of the United States of America where he received a magnificent welcome from the vast army of Welsh-Americans, who handsomely contributed the sum of £1,050 for the equipment of the fine new library at the College. Lord Aberdare, who by now had come to appreciate T. C. Edwards' true quality, recognized that this money was not only the outcome of Welsh American *hiraeth*, but also a mark of the 'sympathy and admiration' felt for Principal Edwards by his countrymen overseas. In 1887 the University of Edinburgh had also signalized its regard by conferring an honorary doctorate of Divinity on him, as it had done previously on his father.[11]

When Lewis Edwards died in that same year, it was inevitable that sooner or later strong pressure would be exerted on T. C. Edwards to succeed to the Principalship of the Bala College. Almost every Monthly Meeting of the Calvinistic Methodists in Wales put forward his name.[12] Typically, Principal Edwards sought the opinion of his students. O. M. Edwards did his utmost to persuade the Principal to stay in Aberystwyth; Thomas Jones (the future 'T. J.' of cabinet fame and a later President of the College, then a young student) was commissioned to sound opinion among the students at the College. 'It is evident that the finger of Theology beckons you unmistakably to Bala', he wrote in reply, and he had to report that most of those he had consulted were 'reluctantly constrained to admit' that the call should be obeyed, provided an adequate successor for Aberystwyth was available.[13] J. H. Davies, a former student and future Principal, then up at Oxford, was mortally afraid that if T. C. Edwards left, 'the country' would 'lose all confidence in Aberystwyth'. Three months earlier J. H. Davies had written a lyrical account of a tremendous pulpit performance T. C. Edwards had given in a sermon preached at Mansfield College: 'Everybody without exception was

[10] T. C. Edwards to J. B. Rogers, 19 October 1885. C.A. (JL), not numbered. T. C. Edwards to J. E. Lloyd, 10 August 1885. U.C.N.W., Bangor. Lloyd MSS. C. no. 22.

[11] *T. C. Edwards Letters*, pp. 262–3, 274. Lord Aberdare at Aberystwyth. *Cambrian News* (18 November 1892).

[12] D. D. Williams, *Thomas Charles Edwards* (Liverpool, 1921), pp. 93–5. D. R. Daniel to T. E. Ellis, 7 March 1891. N.L.W. T. E. Ellis MSS. 392.

[13] J. H. Davies to his parents, 3 May 1891. N.L.W. Cwrt Mawr MSS. (T. I. Ellis donation 1958/63). *T. C. Edwards Letters*, p. 289.

enraptured, . . . everybody joined in praises, you will be able to understand what an effect the Principal's personality had upon these Oxford men.'[14]

Early in May 1891, after much heart-searching, T. C. Edwards resigned and took over the headship of the Bala College. The College Council had asked him to reconsider his decision, and the student body, when it came to the point, unanimously requested him to stay, but he felt that he could not resist 'the call of duty' to Bala, which he hoped to make a great theological college open to all the denominations.[15] There is no question that T. C. Edwards was a great Principal who did more than anyone else to set the tone of the Aberystwyth College. Administration, for which he had no great talent, did not much interest him, and there is a good deal of evidence that he was not particularly deft in personal relationships with his colleagues and the College dignitaries. He evoked strong reactions in those around him: 'he was either your hero or your enemy', as Jenkyn Jones, one of his students, put it.[16] T. C. Edwards was a considerable New Testament scholar whose published work brought prestige to the College; and he was undeniably a great teacher who had the gift, to an exceptional degree, of implanting in his students the belief that scholarship was one of man's noblest ends. During his hey-day he was acknowledged as one of the greatest living Welsh preachers whose name and fame extended wherever Welshmen were to be found. 'For many years', in the opinion of Tom Ellis, who had an unbounded admiration for him, 'he was the most striking personality in the life of Wales.' Despite an explosive temper and the withdrawn man's occasional caustic utterance, he was at his best addressing students: nobody 'could make a noble ideal glow and attract as he could', according to Jenkyn Jones, who was by no means blind to the Principal's weaknesses.[17] Not surprisingly, considering the tremendous difficulties he had to face, T. C. Edwards needed support and encouragement; these he got throughout his nineteen years at Aberystwyth above all from Foulkes Roberts of Manchester, who recognized a man of exceptionally high quality when he saw one. The measure of Principal Edwards' achievement is that under his leadership the College survived in incredibly difficult circumstances. When he left, it was, as he said, 'firmly established in the hearts of the nation', and several generations of students had gone out into the world imbued with an abiding loyalty to the College and inspired with a notion of service to the public that went far beyond mere career-making. In his published 'Farewell to the College', T. C. Edwards could legitimately say: 'I have done my very best, and leave the work to younger hands.'[18]

---

[14] J. H. Davies to his parents, 22 February and 9 May 1891. N.L.W. Cwrt Mawr MSS. (T. I. Ellis donations 1959/62 and 1959/67).

[15] U.C.W. *Magazine*, xiii. 286–7.   [16] 'Mainly about Persons', in Iwan Morgan, p. 89.

[17] T. E. Ellis, 11 March 1899. U.C.W. *Magazine*, xxi. 298. Jenkyn Jones, loc. cit., p. 89.

[18] U.C.W. *Magazine*, xiii. 287, xx. 66.

Wisely, he played no formal part in the appointment of his successor, though it is evident that he thoroughly approved of the choice that was made. There was, of course, a great deal of speculation about the appointment. In Welsh circles in Oxford, R. D. Roberts was 'freely mentioned' as a strong likely candidate. Had he applied and been appointed, it is highly probable that there would have been some change of policy, with a very much stronger emphasis on the extra-mural responsibilities of the College. Roberts, however, did not apply; nor did O. M. Edwards, who, it was thought, believed he would stand little chance against the more experienced Roberts.[19] One able young man, already on the staff at Aberystwyth, who did apply and did not think he was 'acting with any great presumption' in doing so, was J. E. Lloyd the historian. Lloyd argued that, as 'the feeling' was 'very strong that the new man should be a Welshman', all the likely candidates would be equally lacking in experience. Lloyd was not without support; the Welsh Congregationalists were working busily on his behalf. 'They are moving "earth", I do not know about "heaven", in his favour', as Stephen Evans reported.[20]

In all, eleven candidates, including J. M. Angus and Joseph Brough, professor of Philosophy at Aberystwyth, applied. Two candidates stood out in the opinion of those who made the appointment. The first was Thomas Darlington, Fellow of St. John's College, Cambridge, an Englishman with a remarkable facility for languages who had learnt Welsh when he was a boy. The other was T. F. Roberts, the boy prodigy from Aberdovey who had gone on from Aberystwyth to take a double First at Oxford, and had won golden opinions (not least that of Lord Aberdare) as professor of Greek at Cardiff. In addition to a battery of glowing testimonials, Roberts' application included a unique addendum, a round-robin plea for his appointment signed by twenty-two of the more distinguished of his old Aberystwyth fellow students. In the event, T. F. Roberts won handsomely: he received seventeen votes to seven for Darlington.[21]

The new Principal was thirty years of age; he was a deeply devout man (a pillar of the Baptist denomination), earnest, austere, grave in manner beyond his years with no great sense of humour, but kindly and invariably considerate. He was fired by an intense desire to serve Wales and was utterly devoted to the interests of the College. For years he had driven himself hard; at Cardiff, his colleagues had formed a 'Roberts Protection Society' to prevent his being worn out by overwork. His health was frail and he frequently suffered long bouts of illness during his Principalship. His appointment was generally warmly welcomed and

[19] J. H. Davies to his parents, 9 May 1891. N.L.W. Cwrt Mawr MSS. (T. I. Ellis donation 1959/62).

[20] J. E. Lloyd to T. E. Ellis, 11 June 1891. N.L.W. T. E. Ellis MSS. 1432. Stephen Evans to T.C. Edwards, 24 July 1891. *T. C. Edwards Letters*, p. 293.

[21] Humphreys-Owen to his wife, 23 June and 24 July 1891. N.L.W. Glansevern MSS., not numbered. T. F. Roberts to T. E. Ellis, 10 July 1891. N.L.W. T. E. Ellis MSS. 1835, and 'Letter of Application' U.C.W. G. Lib. History File, for the round-robin.

PLATE 4

Thomas Charles Edwards
(Principal, 1872–1891)

Lord Aberdare
(President, 1874–1895)

PLATE 5

Thomas Francis Roberts
(Principal, 1891–1919)

Lord Rendel
(President, 1895–1913)

he was saddled with perhaps impossibly great expectations of a brilliant tenure.[22]

Lord Aberdare had come to the conclusion that the retirement of T. C. Edwards was an opportune moment to resign the Presidency of the College; he had wished to do so for some time. Aberdare consulted Principal Edwards and Stuart Rendel. The latter argued strongly against resignation at that time: Rendel insisted that the President must be 'a man of station', that Lord Kensington, despite his rank, was 'hardly up to it' on personal grounds, and that Lord Sudeley, whose name was again suggested, was a Whig who would 'turn lukewarm' on important Welsh issues like Home Rule and Disestablishment, and was therefore an unsuitable nominee for the formal headship of the Aberystwyth College, the College which especially symbolized the loyalties and aspirations of Welsh Wales. Moreover, Rendel thought that if Aberdare resigned at that time, it would look for all the world like a snub to the new young Principal who should be handled carefully, not least because of his working-class antecedents and possible sensitivities. Rendel's advice to Humphreys-Owen about Aberdare was: 'Don't let him go 'till another suitable man is available.'[23]

Aberdare was persuaded to continue. The curious thing about these discussions is that no one seems to have thought of Rendel himself as a possible replacement. He was a rich man, a politician of standing, and his services to the College had been outstanding: it is perhaps a sign of the times that the fact that he was still a commoner seems to have ruled him out of consideration. However, in 1885 Rendel had become Treasurer of the College. There had also been one or two important changes in the teaching staff. During 1886 M. W. MacCallum, professor of English, had resigned, and it looked at first as though he would be replaced by O. M. Edwards. The Cardiff College had tried several times to tempt him away from Oxford, but he had flatly refused to go. His old College, Aberystwyth, was, however, a different matter: he wanted to return to Wales, he longed 'for the sea and bracing air', and, as he said, MacCallum had 'given the place prestige' by his scholarship. Most of the Oxford moguls consulted by Edwards advised him to stay, and the decisive influence appears to have been that of Benjamin Jowett, who persuaded Edwards that he was 'wanted in Oxford', and that he might well 'do more for Wales' there than in Aberystwyth.[24] In the end, much against the grain, O. M. Edwards did not apply for MacCallum's chair, which was filled soon afterwards by C. H. Herford, an outstandingly brilliant scholar who brought real distinction to the College.

[22] There is a good, short study (enlivened by characteristic tart asides) by David Williams, *Thomas Francis Roberts, 1860–1919* (Cardiff, 1961).

[23] *T. C. Edwards Letters*, pp. 292–3. Rendel to Humphreys-Owen, 24 September 1891. N.L.W. Glansevern MSS. 559.

[24] O. M. Edwards to J. E. Lloyd, no date (two letters), U.C.N.W. Bangor. Lloyd MSS. 314, ff. 90–1.

T. S. Humpidge, professor of Chemistry, in whose laboratory the great fire of 1885 had begun, died soon afterwards in tragic circumstances. He was a fanatical worker with a great passion for science which he could communicate to his novitiate students. Humpidge laboured heroically to maintain the work of his department in difficult makeshift circumstances; so much so, that his health collapsed and he died in 1887 at the age of thirty-four. For years a devoted band of his students regularly paid visits of homage to his grave at Clarach.[25] Humpidge was replaced by H. Lloyd Snape, who had studied extensively in Germany, a well-known Wesleyan lay-preacher whose strong religious convictions reassured one member of the Council who thought it vital in a post-Darwin world of doubt that the sciences at Aberystwyth should be taught by 'Christian men of character'. Snape quickly built up a considerable reputation and this, together with the exceptionally low fees at the College, attracted an outstandingly gifted band of Chemistry students to Aberystwyth, including F. D. Chattaway, W. H. Lewis, E. J. Russell, F. Soddy, and H. O. Jones, all of whom later achieved prominent positions in British science, several of them becoming Fellows of the Royal Society.[26]

One other important, not to say formidable, recruit to the College staff at this time requires notice. At the beginning of the session 1886–7, Miss E. A. Carpenter had been appointed (in the parlance of the time) 'Lady Principal' of the hall of residence for women students out of a strong field of over eighty applicants. Aberystwyth made a considerable early contribution to the higher education of women, and their numbers at the College steadily increased in the late eighties and nineties. The College, of course, was particularly careful that they should be effectively supervised, but it is fair to say also that Miss Carpenter was appointed to be a good deal more than an especially watchful Victorian chaperon. Indeed, T. C. Edwards asserted that 'the influence of our Lady Principal will be of more value to her students than even the professors' lectures'.[27] At first, women students lived in various converted houses, 'Ocean View', 'Abergeldie', and the like, but, as their numbers increased, the College began to think ambitiously in terms of a large, purpose-built hall for women. This, however, would require time and a good deal of money to establish. Meantime, Miss Carpenter, a dedicated servant of the College if ever there was one ('for me to live now is the College and its Hall', as she said simply in 1888), immediately assumed a large importance in the academic and social life of the College and its students. From the beginning,

[25] Jenkyn Jones, loc. cit., p. 91. 'The Humpidge Memorial Fund'. C.A. (C), not numbered. T. C. James and C. W. Davies, 'Schools of Chemistry in Gt. Britain and Ireland: the U.C.W., Aberystwyth', *Journal of R. Inst. of Chemistry* (October 1956), p. 569.

[26] R. Roberts to Stephen Evans, 9 January 1888. N.L.W. J. H. Davies (U.C.W.) MSS. T. C. James and C. W. Davies, loc. cit., pp. 569–70.

[27] Principal's Report, 21 October 1887. *U.C.W. Reports (1863–91)*, p. 14.

as Miss Carpenter was able proudly to report in 1888–9, students in residence achieved better academic results than those in lodgings.[28]

By this time, the College had a vigorous social life. Isolated as it was in a small town, with few ready-made diversions to hand, staff and students had to make their own entertainments. Dances (governed by a rigid protocol), 'At homes', 'Smokers', sing-songs, and dramatics, were enjoyed with tremendous gusto; and there were certain great occasions in the calendar which no one would willingly miss. A visiting team from Bangor or Cardiff would be met at the railway station by a great crowd; it was a point of honour to throng the touchline for the match, and in the evening there would be a concert which would end with a march down the promenade to the women's hall where the men (assuming victory in the match) would sing happily for half an hour or so, the proceedings ending usually with three hearty cheers for Miss Carpenter. Debates commanded almost universal support, and annually a mock election, which generated great excitement, would be held. The Liberal candidate (with a hundred or so votes) usually won, with the Conservatives, Welsh Nationalists, and Socialists following in varying orders with almost half as much support.

St. David's Day was always an especial occasion. Old students would come down in droves; fraternal delegates from the other colleges would be present; in the evening staff and students would assemble in academic dress for a soirée; the College would be elaborately decorated, and the hall perhaps hung with Chinese lamps, sometimes illuminated by electricity. A specially written play, performed by staff and students, would be the centrepiece of the evening. Occasionally, as in March 1891, townspeople complained of roisterous singing late at night; a mass of students was escorted into the police-station, followed unobserved by Principal Edwards. Still, it all ended happily enough: the offending students were allowed to go home, after signing their names and promising the Principal they 'would never do such a thing again'.[29]

In 1889–90 there was a relatively small structural alteration to the College building that was to have a profound social significance. W. T. Jones of Melbourne, Australia, provided enough money for an ornamental inner roof to be built on the 'College corridor', so called. Thus the indoor 'Quad' came into existence, and from this time onwards, certainly until the 1950s, it became the great focus of student life. At first movement was regulated strictly, women on one side, men on the other, separated for a time by a 'mid-wall of partition', a long line of museum cases. Here, daily, between lectures, an elaborate separate crocodile

---

[28] Miss Carpenter to J. B. Rogers, 22 March 1888. C.A. (C), not numbered. Report of the Lady Principal, 25 October 1889. *U.C.W. Reports (1863–91)*, p. 16.

[29] St. David's Day festivities are reported at length annually in the U.C.W. *Magazine*. This account of 1891 is drawn from Nansi Davies to J. H. Davies, March 1891. N.L.W. Cwrt Mawr MSS. (T. I. Ellis donation 1963/6).

perambulation of men and women circulated, and all sorts of tricks and stratagems had to be learned in order to circumvent the official near-segregation of the sexes. The Quad (and its surrounding balcony) was the place to see and be seen, and, over the years, it made every bit as important a contribution to the education of Aberystwyth students as any lecture-room or laboratory.[30]

The early years of T. F. Roberts' Principalship were marked by several important developments in the work of the College. Within months of taking up his appointment, he began energetically to work for the setting-up of a Day Training or Normal department for elementary-school teachers. In 1890 the regulations of the department of Education were revised to allow recognition of such departments at colleges of university rank.[31] This initiative was suggested by T. E. Ellis, M.P., who in this and other expansionist ventures at this time acted as the chief and most persistent advocate of Aberystwyth's claims in Whitehall's corridors of power. At first things looked unpromising: Hart-Dyke at the Education department wanted the experiment to prove itself before adding to the number of colleges participating; moreover, the Bangor College also put in an application and here, as elsewhere, the ambitions of the two Welsh colleges collided. William Williams, chief inspector of schools for Wales, who was asked to assist, was not hopeful of Aberystwyth's success. He pointed out that the Welsh Training colleges were currently complaining that the market for elementary-school teachers was glutted, and he gently hinted that Aberystwyth was already saddled with 'several burdens', such as a considerable debt on a building that was not yet completed, the requirements of a new department of Agriculture, and the need for an adequate hall of residence for women students. In his opinion, the cart was already overloaded and to add more would be 'unwise'.[32]

However, Roberts and Ellis, supported by Lord Aberdare and Rendel, persisted. T. F. Roberts insisted that it would be 'a calamity' if the application were rejected, and, artfully suspending for the moment Aberystwyth's oft-reiterated claim to be above all a national college, he resurrected once again the seven counties of Wales (the old successful crutch of 1884) for which, when it suited, Aberystwyth claimed to have an especial responsibility. As he pointed out, there was no Training college in the seven counties, apart from the Church establishment at Carmarthen. Hart-Dyke, not unreasonably, wanted to consider the claims of Aberystwyth and Bangor together, but he succumbed to Aberystwyth's demand of first come, first served, agreed to meet a deputation, and early in 1892 conceded the case for a Training department of fifteen men and fifteen women in the first instance. 'That

[30] Principal's Report, 15 October 1890. U.C.W. Reports (1863–91), p. 16. U.C.W. Magazine, xiv. 168–9.

[31] T. I. Ellis, op. cit., p. 67.

[32] T. F. Roberts to T. E. Ellis, 7 and 17 September, 29 October 1891. N.L.W. T. E. Ellis MSS. 1837, 1839, 1841. Hart-Dyke to Rendel, 28 November 1891. N.L.W. T. I. Ellis deposit (1969). W.Williams to T. E. Ellis, 31 August 1891. N.L.W. T. E. Ellis MSS. 2123.

will do, I think, to begin with', T. F. Roberts wrote with evident satisfaction, and immediately arranged to hire the Queen's Hotel as a temporary hostel for the women students. Soon afterwards Henry Holman, a Cambridge man recommended by R. D. Roberts, was appointed Master of Method and head of the new department.[33] Holman was a remarkably energetic man who insisted, 'almost to aggressiveness', upon proper respect for his department of pupil-teachers with four years' experience but no matriculation certificates. Holman left at the end of 1893–4 and his replacement, Foster Watson, came with an impressive reputation as a historian of education, a reputation he was to add to during his years at the College.[34]

Aberystwyth had beaten Bangor to the gun with the application for a Training department: in the matter of establishing a department of Agriculture, Bangor got in first. It was natural that these two colleges set in rural areas should stress the importance of the scientific study of agriculture, easily the most important industry in their hinterland areas. It will be remembered that years before in the 1870s Aberystwyth had made some tentative efforts in this direction. At any rate in June 1891, Tom Parry, who continued to work his own farm, was appointed lecturer in Agriculture. Later in the year an application for a grant-in-aid was submitted to the Board of Agriculture and, as the greater part of Parry's work would be 'out-College'—that is, extra-mural practical instruction among the farmers in their own localities—applications for support from the rates were sent in to the seven county councils of central Wales. Once again T. F. Roberts sought the assistance of T. E. Ellis, which, as usual, in anything relating to the well-being of the Aberystwyth College, was freely and vigorously given. The Board of Agriculture gave an initial grant of £250 and on 'the faith' of this, T. F. Roberts, who wanted to drive on quickly, persuaded the College to appoint additional lecturers in Agricultural Chemistry and Veterinary Science. Gradually, some of the counties were persuaded to give help: in 1891 Cardiganshire voted £140, Pembrokeshire £15, Radnorshire and Breconshire £100 each; Carmarthenshire insisted on 'hanging fire' for the moment, but Roberts was confident that that county, too, would soon fall into line.[35] The counties of Montgomery and Merioneth posed problems for Aberystwyth: during the battle of the sites in the 1880s, these two shires had strongly supported Aberystwyth's claim to survive. But Bangor had already established classes in Agriculture in certain parts of the

[33] Aberdare to T. F. Roberts, 8 December 1891, Hart-Dyke to Rendel, 23 January 1892. N.L.W. MSS. 19440E (Rendel, I, ff. 1, 25). T. F. Roberts to Rendel, 11 February 1892. N.L.W. MSS. 19441E (Rendel, II, ff. 1, 1a, and 1b). R. D. Roberts to T. F. Roberts, 21 March 1892. C.A. PC(b). T. F. Roberts to T. E. Ellis, 1 April 1892. N.L.W. T. E. Ellis MSS. 1844.

[34] C. R. Chapple, 'The Department of Education', in Iwan Morgan, pp. 175–7.

[35] Humphreys-Owen to his wife, 5 June 1891. N.L.W. Glansevern MSS., not numbered. T. F. Roberts to T. E. Ellis, 3 December 1891. N.L.W. T. E. Ellis MSS. 1842. In 1892 Carmarthenshire (where Lewis Morris was active) contributed £350 to the new department.

two counties, and, at the outset, at the instance of the Board of Agriculture, Aberystwyth, perhaps unwisely, had submitted to an agreement dividing the area between the two colleges.

T. F. Roberts very soon began to dispute the validity of this agreement which, he claimed, was purely an interim affair. Aberystwyth was not prepared, as Roberts flatly insisted in a tart letter to Principal Reichel of Bangor, to surrender 'two counties the whole, or almost the whole of which, it claims on the grounds of geographical convenience, quite apart from the intimate educational associations, which have existed between them and the College since its foundation'. An unseemly demarcation wrangle between the two colleges was in prospect. So far as Merionethshire was concerned, however, Aberystwyth had certain advantages. Most of the county council members were well disposed towards Aberystwyth, and Tom Ellis, who used his best persuasions in favour of the College, was M.P. for the county. In the autumn of 1892 Merionethshire invited Aberystwyth to assume responsibility for agricultural teaching throughout the county, and Tom Ellis effectively argued at Whitehall that, as the county had not been a party to the original agreement between the colleges, it should be free to choose between the contestants and dispose of moneys derived from its own rates as it thought fit. In Montgomeryshire, where Lord Powis, President of the Bangor College, had considerable influence, Aberystwyth appears to have agreed to a division of responsibility and a sharing of the county grant.[36]

Tom Ellis' advice and assistance had been invaluable in the establishment of the departments of Agriculture and Education at the College. In 1892 he was chiefly responsible for the foundation of the Old Students' Association. From the beginning Aberystwyth had been remarkably, perhaps uniquely, successful in attracting and retaining the loyalty and affection of its old students. The small size of the College, the intimacies of the residential system, the close proximities of lodgings in a small town, the romantic struggle for survival, and the scenic beauty of a remote location on the margin of sea and hills all intensified the feeling for the College. From the 1870s old students regularly returned for flying visits to Aberystwyth and immediately took their place, as a matter of course, in the social life of the College. Away from Aberystwyth, old students who came together were, if anything, even more clannish; and it seemed the most natural thing in the world in May 1880 that the Aberystwyth College Club should be formed in Oxford. They met regularly in each other's rooms, put the world to rights, or simply enjoyed whatever high-jinks developed.[37] The College *Magazine* served

[36] Correspondence 'relating to delimitation of spheres of operation in Merioneth and Montgomery', October 1891–December 1892. C.A. P/M/1. T. F. Roberts to T. E. Ellis, 20 July 1892. N.L.W. T. E. Ellis MSS. 1846.

[37] The minute books (for 1880–1900) of this Oxford society of old Aberystwyth students are in C.A. R/AC/St/1. Much supplementary information will be found in J. H. Davies' letters from Oxford in N.L.W. Cwrt Mawr MSS. (T. I. Ellis donation 1959/62).

as a useful link between old and current students, keeping alive the 'three habits which especially characterize all connected with the College—*esprit de corps*, loyalty, and love towards the institution'.[38]

In March 1892 Tom Ellis called a meeting of old students at Aberystwyth. There was a good response and it was enthusiastically agreed to form a 'University College of Wales Old Students' Association', with the avowed aims of enabling old students to keep in touch with each other and, more especially, together 'to further the interests of the College'. A committee was formed and empowered to draft a constitution on broadly agreed lines. Inevitably, Tom Ellis was elected President, and for several years he remained the chief driving force in the Association, despite the heavy demand on his energy made by the post of Deputy Whip, to which he was appointed when Gladstone took office again in August 1892. At the inaugural meeting of the Association, T. F. Roberts, who became a Vice-President, drew attention to the load of debt which encumbered the College, and from the outset the Association accepted fund-raising for one beneficent purpose and another as one of its chief obligations. The foundation meeting had also agreed to hold an annual reunion of old students at Aberystwyth in March, but after three years' experience of disappointing attendances it was decided that, for the future, reunions would be held at Easter, the already recognized 'season for old College folk'. Ever since 1892 the Old Students' Association (O.S.A. in common parlance) has been perhaps the most durable single support to the College, the most obvious exemplification of the old, proud tag 'once an Aber' man, always an Aber' man'.[39]

Despite the continued overwhelming dominance of this primary loyalty, there were now three colleges in Wales, all firmly established, all growing in size and confidence. Each one of them was entitled to call itself a university college, an 'uncouth designation', in T. C. Edwards' description, which he defined 'as an institution that ought to be a university, but is not'.[40] The old dream of one central Welsh university had been shattered by the Aberdare Committee, and there was no question of the three colleges independently achieving university rank. Lord Aberdare and his colleagues in 1881 had havered on the question of recommending the immediate establishment of a university in Wales. There was the complication of St. David's College, Lampeter, which already possessed the authority to award degrees in Arts and Divinity. With no great confidence that the suggestion would

[38] David Samuel, 'Looking Backward', U.C.W. *Magazine*, xiii. 280.

[39] O.S.A. Minute Book (1892–1907), pp. 1–7. O.S.A. Circular, 2 March 1892. U.C.W. *Magazine*, xiv. 191–6, xviii. 22–3. T. I. Ellis, op. cit., p. 69. In 1897 there was an unofficial branch of the O.S.A. established by old Aberystwyth men studying at the University of Berlin. A. J. Grieve, 10 June 1898. C.A. R/AC/St/1.

[40] 'Notes on American Colleges', U.C.W. *Magazine*, xiii. 167. This title he sardonically differentiated from 'the name which our friends at Lampeter sometimes affect: *quasi* University. This', he said, 'may be defined as an institution that is a University, but ought not to be one.'

be taken up, the Aberdare Committee half-heartedly recommended that Lampeter's second charter should be withdrawn, and that a new 'syndicate', made up of representatives in equal numbers of the governing bodies of Lampeter, Aberystwyth, and any other similar colleges subsequently established, should be conceded a new authority to grant degrees in Arts, leaving Lampeter undisturbed in its power to award degrees in Divinity. This curious proposal, neither fish nor fowl, would have satisfied nobody, least of all Welsh nonconformists, fully three-quarters of the population, who would have bitterly resented the Church's monopoly control of degrees in Divinity. The Aberdare Committee was, in effect, proposing a *quasi* University, as T. C. Edwards would have called it, as an interim measure until Wales was, as the *Report* said, 'ripe' for full university status.[41]

With a settled official resistance to proliferating degree-giving powers, the proposal stood no chance of acceptance, and it was simply ignored. And when in 1888 representatives of all three Welsh colleges attended the deputation to Whitehall in favour of a charter for Aberystwyth, a supplementary attempt to broach the question of a Welsh university was immediately ruled out of court by Lord Cranbrook.[42] However, the three colleges had at least set up machinery for consultation and joint action on the question. At one of the early meetings of representatives of the three colleges, T. C. Edwards 'startled' those present with the argument that, if Lampeter would surrender its exclusive degree-giving powers and enter into a Welsh university 'with an undenominational faculty of Historical Theology, Wales would accept the solution'. Humphreys-Owen considered that this was an imaginative suggestion which, if taken up, 'would remove nearly all bitterness'. Doubtless the more intelligent Church leaders would endorse it, but he was sure that 'the ruck of parsons' would stupidly defend to the death the 'little supremacy' their exclusive degree gave them. Humphreys-Owen was right; nothing came of this sensible attempt to allay the bitter hostilities of the past that still divided every Welsh locality.[43]

At another meeting of the committee of the three colleges a few weeks later, Lord Aberdare was voted to the chair (Lord Powis, President of Bangor, to avoid any embarrassing counter-nomination, 'discreetly' delayed his arrival until business was well under way), and R. A. Jones of the Bangor Council was made secretary. There was 'a great tug-of-war' over the question whether the proposed Welsh university should insist on residence at a college as an essential qualification for a degree. Viriamu Jones of Cardiff and Principal Reichel of Bangor, then and subsequently, 'vehemently' maintained that residence should be a necessary condition, and they were supported by the professorial members of the committee. Principal

[41] *Aberdare Report*, Conclusion and Recommendations, pp. lxvii–lxviii.

[42] *South Wales Daily News* (18 July 1888). Lord Aberdare, 19 December 1888, in *U.C.W. Reports* (1863–91), pp. 27–8.

[43] Humphreys-Owen to his wife, 9 June 1888. N.L.W. Glansevern MSS., not numbered.

T. C. Edwards, Rendel, Humphreys-Owen, Henry Richard, and one or two more argued against making residence an inflexible requirement because they were afraid that, 'to insist on it at present, would make the university so unpopular that we should lose half the support one ought to have'.[44] It was natural that the spokesmen for the Aberystwyth College, with their experience of the crucial importance of the support of the people, should be hypersensitive to the opinions, or supposed opinions, of the general public. These fears appear to have been exaggerated, and there is no doubt that Viriamu Jones and Reichel were right. T. F. Roberts certainly agreed with them, and T. C. Edwards (who was anxious to promote the interests of students at the Welsh nonconformist colleges) later changed his mind and fell into line on the same side.[45]

It was evident that there was little immediate prospect of persuading Lord Cranbrook and the Tory government to establish a university in Wales. Moreover, a Royal Commission was currently considering the reorganization of London University, and it was possible that an amended scheme would answer the needs of Wales. It was argued by some that it would be foolish to 'sacrifice the prestige which now attaches to the success of Welsh students in the London University'. The whole question evoked no great enthusiasm in the mass of the Welsh people, who, according to T. F. Roberts, were unable to appreciate the distinction between a university college and a university.[46]

But the leaders of the Welsh educational movement did not intend to be deflected. In T. F. Roberts' opinion the argument in favour of waiting for an amended London scheme was beside the point.

We ask for a Welsh university [he wrote in April 1891], and can accept no reorganized London University as sufficient for our needs, because we know that such an influence as a university can exert must, in order to be effective for us, be exerted from within Wales itself.[47]

Tom Ellis similarly believed that only with the establishment of a Welsh university would Wales get its 'deliverance from the grasp of London', and Viriamu Jones, the chief driving force of the movement, insisted forcefully that there was 'a sore need' for a university in Wales, not merely to 'complete the edifice', but to bring coherence to a 'disorderly' educational system that had grown up higgledy-piggledy.[48]

It is apparent that these men were looking to the return of a Liberal government

---

[44] Humphreys-Owen to his wife, 5 July 1888. Ibid.

[45] T. F. Roberts, 'The Proposed University for Wales', *Trans. Cymm.* (1891–2), p. 227. T. C. Edwards' speech at Aberystwyth, 15 November 1892, reported in the *Cambrian News* (18 November 1892).

[46] T. F. Roberts, loc. cit., pp. 224–5.

[47] Ibid., p. 242.

[48] T. E. Ellis to O. M. Edwards, 12 February 1890 ('*na chaiff Cymru ei gwared o afael Llundain hyd nes y cawn Brifysgol i Gymru*'). N.L.W. T. E. Ellis MSS. 2765. Viriamu Jones at Aberystwyth, 15 November 1892. *Cambrian News* (18 November 1892).

to achieve their aim. Meantime, there was a great deal to be done, and there were many meetings (usually at Shrewsbury, the Welsh 'Jerusalem') to work out a draft charter for the proposed university which, at one stage, was provisionally entitled the 'Albert University', presumably after the Prince Consort.[49] Most of these meetings were chaired by Lord Aberdare; on one occasion the Bangor members flatly refused to accept Lord Bute. Aberdare cheerfully 'slept like a top' for the first hour of one discussion, but roused himself later when some 'nice steering' was required to bring a 'good deal of lively talk', conducted in 'excellent tone and spirit', to effective conclusion.[50] However, the detailed direction of business was carried out by H. Isambard Owen, the London Welsh doctor, who was the main author of the draft proposals for a charter.[51] Before these detailed negotiations were completed, a Liberal government had been returned in August 1892. Tom Ellis believed that, if Asquith and A. H. D. Acland were given cabinet posts, Wales would speedily receive 'fair play' on the three great questions of disestablishment, land, and the university.[52]

Acland, who became Vice-President of the Council in Gladstone's fourth government, was an energetic man who immediately took up the Welsh university question. In October 1892 he wrote to the Prime Minister suggesting that the matter should be independently investigated on behalf of the government by O. M. Edwards.[53] Acland mercifully decided that there was no need for an elaborate 'deliberative commission'; O. M. Edwards was asked simply to summarize briefly for the convenience of the Cabinet 'the state of the work already done in the Shrewsbury conferences'.[54] Edwards, despite some waste of time in an itinerary of the Welsh colleges in which he asked the Principals perfunctory questions (T. F. Roberts was forewarned that he would be asked, for example, 'What subjects are taught?'), worked quickly and submitted his report early in 1893.[55]

By this time, of course, Gladstone was utterly obsessed with Irish Home Rule, and, in other circumstances, it is possible that the Prime Minister's preoccupation would have prevented speedy action on the Welsh university. As it happened, however, Gladstone had been staying at Stuart Rendel's London home when the Ministry of 1892 was being formed. On grounds of ability and his leadership of the Welsh Liberal M.P.s, Rendel had a strong claim to office, but for a variety of reasons it was not possible to include him in the government. However, in con-

49 16 June 1891. C.A. S/M/N1. *Western Mail* (27 February 1896) for the description of Shrewsbury.

50 *Aberdare Letters*, ii, pp. 286–8.

51 There is a very full study of Owen by Gwilym A. Jones, 'The Life and Work of Sir Isambard Owen (1850–1927)', unpublished M.A. thesis, University of Wales (1967).

52 T. E. Ellis to D. Rowland Jones, 17 August 1892. N.L.W. T. E. Ellis MSS. 2854.

53 20 October 1892. B.M. Add. MSS. 44516, ff. 192–5.

54 A. H. D. Acland at Aberystwyth, 15 November 1892. *Cambrian News* (18 November 1892).

55 O. M. Edwards to T. F. Roberts, 28 December 1892. C.A. PC (9). Penllyn Jones reported soon afterwards (5 January 1893, C.A. PC (Misc.)) that Edwards was 'very much in favour of making Aberystwyth the seat of the Welsh University'.

sultation with Rendel at that time, Gladstone settled the Welsh policy of his Cabinet. In return for his 'self-effacement', his loyal acceptance of his omission from the Cabinet, Rendel was asked what he wanted for Wales. He asked for three 'boons': an inquiry into the land problem in Wales, a Church Suspensory bill, and a university for Wales. According to Rendel's account, 'as to the university', he 'had no need to say a word beyond a request, at once granted', and Mr. Gladstone's pledge thus freely given, 'secured the whole policy'.[56]

But before the government could take action, the Welsh had first of all to decide exactly what sort of university they wanted. Majority opinion among those involved, led by Isambard Owen and the three college Principals, was determined that it should be a teaching university, not merely an examining body on the model of London. Isambard Owen's Memorandum on the proposed charter therefore laid it down that residence at a college was an essential requirement for a degree.[57] Predictably, the opposition to this was led by Dr. R. D. Roberts, the unyielding champion of the interests of extra-mural students. The word 'combative' might well have been invented to describe R. D. Roberts. It was already apparent that he would be defeated, but this did not prevent Roberts from writing a lengthy detailed criticism, clause by clause, of Owen's proposals, and submitting an alternative outline charter. Roberts believed that Owen's proposed university was much too narrowly drawn to 'meet the expanding higher educational requirements of Wales'. Roberts was a visionary who saw no reason why students outside the constituent colleges should not pursue degree courses at their own pace over a longer period of time than three years. His counter-memorandum did include one interesting suggestion that merited more consideration than it received. Roberts proposed that a special category of university (as opposed to college) professorships should be established; holders of these chairs would be paid considerably more and would have more time and money for advanced work. Inevitably, their departments (though duplicated in the other colleges) would achieve a primacy in the university and, wherever that occurred, 'the very highest teaching in the university would be provided at that particular college'.[58] Possibly this would have done no more than give the three colleges an endless succession of bones to fight over furiously for years, but at least it would have helped to concentrate resources that were in danger of being too widely dispersed in the University of Wales to be effective.

[56] Rendel to T. F. Roberts, 25 October (two letters, one a copy) and 27 October 1906. N.L.W. MSS. 19442E, ff. 140–1, 142, 143–4. Rendel was stung into writing this account by what he regarded as the 'shabby' suppression of his contributions to Welsh education in the book *The Welsh People* (1900) by John Rhys and D. Brynmor Jones. See also, Rendel to Roberts, 3 September 1903. N.L.W. MSS. 19441E, f. 68.

[57] 28 December 1892. There is a copy of the Memorandum in the College archives.

[58] 'Suggested outline of a charter to constitute the University of Wales', December 1892. N.L.W. J. H. Davies (Misc.) MSS.

At the final Shrewsbury conference on 6 January 1893, Isambard Owen and his supporters carried the day; by twenty-one votes to two Roberts' alternative suggestions were negatived.[59] When in August the question was considered in the House of Commons, Roberts' ideas were expounded by two Welsh members, Bryn Roberts and D. A. Thomas, but again in vain. In the House of Lords the Welsh bishops and some of their English brethren tried to block the granting of the charter until arrangements had been made for the inclusion in the University of St. David's College, Lampeter. This was a grievance largely manufactured by religious enmities, for Lampeter, despite the presence of its Principal at the Shrewsbury conferences, had shown practically no disposition to enter the fold of the University. The bishops carried the Lords with them in their motion by a small majority, but Gladstone had already decided to ignore that resolution. On 30 November 1893 the charter (which as a matter of fact included a clause which would have enabled St. David's College later to enter into the university) received the Royal Assent.[60]

The University thus constituted was a federal organization made up of the three colleges which entered 'on absolutely equal terms'. Isambard Owen pointed to the 'commendable delicacy' with which those who had drafted the charter had carefully not mentioned the colleges by name in order to avoid giving 'an unauthorized precedence among them'.[61] In 1898 Isambard Owen gave a somewhat disingenuous account of the drafting of the charter; according to this, all was for the best in the best of all possible worlds: the 'almost unreconcilable antagonisms' of early meetings had been smoothed away by the over-mastering logic of 'a consistent educational theory'.[62] Eighteen years later he rather more frankly admitted that 'the scheme was necessarily one that could be "got through" as an unofficial and, practically, unopposed measure'. It had therefore to take account of the fact that the teaching apparatus in the colleges pre-dated the charter, and it was necessary to accept the 'continued independence' of the colleges as 'axiomatic'. Owen admitted that this was so constricting that the creation of a University of Wales, 'in the full sense of the term', was not within the bounds of possibility. Accordingly, those who framed the draft charter necessarily lowered their sights: they sought to find a way of freeing teachers at the colleges from the domination of the examiners of London University, and they pursued the collateral purposes of 'securing the educational unity of Wales and its autonomy in

---

[59] The conference is reported in detail in the *Manchester Guardian* (7 January 1893). The considerable subsequent discussion in the press of the proposals is examined in Gwilym A. Jones, loc. cit., pp. 123–34.

[60] *Parl. Debates*, 4th series, xvi. 1316–35, 1442–56. K. O. Morgan, op. cit., pp. 129–32. For the continuing equivocations of Principal Owen of Lampeter, see his letter in *The Times* (23 September 1893).

[61] 'Memorandum on the Proposed Charter of the University of Wales', 28 December 1892.

[62] *The University of Wales and its Educational Theory*, pp. 1–2.

educational matters'.[63] In these circumstances, no great centripetal authority could be ascribed to the University, which was endowed with very little more than a power of co-ordination.

However, the formal machinery of the University was expected to exert a considerable influence for unity. The entire legislative and executive power was lodged in a University Court of 101 members. In 1898 Isambard Owen, with justifiable pride, had stated:

> Education is a matter of public business in Wales to an extent that may seem strange in England. . . . In the absence of a separate Departmental administration for Wales, education has in our country largely and frankly become a branch of local self-government.[64]

The colleges themselves were public corporations, subject to popular lay control, and it was perfectly natural therefore to extend the same principle to the government of the University. The Court was made up of twelve representatives of each of the three constituent colleges, twenty-six members named by the county councils of Wales, thirteen nominees of the Crown and thirteen representatives of graduates of the University; additionally, to maintain the connection of the University with the earlier grades of education, six members of the Court were nominated by the Central Board of Intermediate Education, and three each by the head teachers of Welsh elementary and secondary schools. The number was completed by the Chancellor, elected by the Court, who held office for life.

The charter recognized that, while ultimate legislative power must reside in popular hands, there was the obvious need for expert, academic assistance. This was provided by the 'second estate', the University Senate, an advisory body made up of the three Principals (who served in turn as Vice-Chancellor) and the heads of all departments in all the colleges. Article XVIII of the charter provided that no statute or regulation concerning schemes of study or examinations should be enacted or revoked unless first recommended or reported on by the Senate. Isambard Owen claimed that Court and Senate guaranteed a nice balance between popular control and professional guidance. Not surprisingly with the long and not altogether happy Welsh experience of the rigid requirements of London University examinations, those who drafted the charter were anxious to free teachers in the new University from this sort of tyranny. Accordingly, 'the liberty of divergent curricula', as Owen called it, was conceded to the colleges, which were given the right to propose schemes of study, which thereafter had to run the gauntlet of scrutiny by the Senate, before formal submission to the Court. In an attempt to guarantee uniformity of standards, the University ascribed rather more importance to external examiners than was customary.[65]

[63] Memorandum to the Royal Commission on University Education in Wales (Cd. 8991. Hereinafter referred to as the *Haldane Report*). Final Report, Minutes of Evidence, pp. 258–60.

[64] *The University of Wales and its Educational Theory*, p. 16.

[65] Ibid., pp. 17–21.

Finally, in an attempt to 'make the University an intellectual bond of union among all her children', and to emphasize the corporate fellowship of membership, the draft charter proposed the establishment of a general assembly or Guild of Graduates. Initially, the Guild had been vested with considerable powers: it could administer independent funds, and initiate, sponsor, or undertake learned work. These important powers, however, were elided by Whitehall caution, and the Guild was left with the truncated power of collecting funds, but not of administering them independently. The Guild, like the University Court, was required to visit each of the colleges in annual rotation.[66]

When the time came to elect a Chancellor for the University, it was evident that there was only one possible nomination: Lord Aberdare. Despite his detached, even occasionally insufferably patronizing, attitude to the Welsh and their supposed national deficiencies, and notwithstanding some grievous misjudgements, Aberdare's services to Welsh higher education over a period of many years were unmatched. Viriamu Jones called him 'the commander-in-chief of the Welsh educational army', and so long as it is realized that Aberdare depended heavily on the fighting generals beneath him, that is an apt description.[67] He had certain rare qualifications for leadership in the Welsh educational struggle: he was a Liberal, as were most of those he led; he was a politician of standing, wielding very great influence in Whitehall and Westminster, and all too frequently in those years Welsh education had to turn to official sources for assistance. Finally, in a rank-conscious world, he was a peer who possessed to perfection, as one of his admirers said, '*l'art d'etre grand père*'.[68] Uncertain Welsh democrats, almost all outsiders to the world of high politics, who lacked the will or power to behave like Parnell and his Irishmen, no doubt needed the reassuring touch of confidence that Aberdare's endorsement of their aims gave them.

In recent years Aberdare's health had been failing. For this reason he urged the election of a younger man to the Chancellorship, but he was overborne and was obviously highly delighted at the distinction conferred upon him. 'As I could not reasonably expect to be chosen Archbishop to disestablished Wales [he wrote to his daughter], nor to succeed Prince Llywelyn in his temporarily suspended dignity, I feel that Wales could bestow on me no greater honour.'[69]

Within weeks, however, Aberdare was dead. He had been the President of the Aberystwyth and Cardiff Colleges from their foundation. He had served Cardiff throughout with energy and genuine enthusiasm: Aberystwyth never engaged his

---

[66] *The University of Wales and its Educational Theory*, pp. 22–4. On the charter generally, see D. Emrys Evans, *The University of Wales: a historical sketch* (Cardiff, 1953), pp. 42–50, and for an exhaustive examination, based on twenty-five years' experience of its working, the *Haldane Report*, passim.

[67] *Aberdare Letters*, i. 13.

[68] Sir George Goldie, *Lectures and Addresses by the Rt. Hon. W. A. Bruce* (1895), p. x.

[69] 11 February 1895. *Aberdare Letters*, ii. 337.

full loyalty. This was not a matter of indifference or malevolence; with the best will in the world for years he simply could not see that a college so placed could prosper and, with a limited understanding of the spirit that moved the Welsh people, he underestimated the possibility of triumph over adversity. Stuart Rendel's judgement on him was severe but not unfair.

Lord Aberdare was a charming personage and a delightful companion, and he had a genuine enthusiasm for Welsh education. But in no capacity and in no part of his career did he exhibit any creative faculty. He could discuss: he could not act. His administration of Aberystwyth was feeble, and his betrayal of it in the Report most inexplicable and unpardonable. But though Scotch, he was part Welsh and born in Wales and is dead, and that is enough.[70]

At first it was hoped that Gladstone would replace Aberdare as Chancellor of the University, but the Prime Minister refused and eventually the Prince of Wales accepted the office.[71] Almost twelve months before, on 6 April 1894, the University Court met for the first time in the dingy Privy Council chamber at Whitehall. To O. M. Edwards, historian of Wales, 'the day was a prouder one than a day of victory'. It was the crowning triumph of a struggle rare in human experience. 'It was', he said, with not too much hyperbole, 'the day of the establishing of a peasants' University.' Without much help from the educated classes, those who ought to have led them, the Welsh people had risen out of ignorance and superstition and created a more or less complete system of education. Almost from the beginning the Welsh educational movement had engaged the enthusiasm, and depended to an astonishing degree on the support, of the mass of the people. Herein lay its rarity.[72]

It was this capacity for mass self-help which so much attracted Stuart Rendel to Welsh causes.[73] Rendel was the obvious replacement for Lord Aberdare as President of the Aberystwyth College. The year before, Gladstone had recommended Rendel for a peerage, and he was now semi-retired from politics. Moreover, Rendel's services to Aberystwyth in the 1880s entitled him to be considered, as his friend Humphreys-Owen said with justice, 'the preserver of the College'.[74] In 1895 Lord Rendel became the second President of the University College of Wales. Curiously enough, Rendel had formerly considered the Presidency a merely ceremonial post appropriate to an agreeable figurehead. In fact, during his tenure, apart from short periods when hypochondria drove him into

[70] Rendel to T. F. Roberts, 25 October 1906. N.L.W. MSS. 19442E, f. 142.
[71] W. Rathbone to Gladstone, 2 April 1895. B.M. Add. MSS. 44520, f. 113.
[72] 'The Court of the University of Wales', *Wales*, i. 39–40.
[73] 'I desire, as I have always declared, that Wales, like Italy, should *fara da se*', he wrote to T. F. Roberts, 25 October 1906. N.L.W. MSS. 19442E, ff. 143–4.
[74] Humphreys-Owen to Mortimer Green, 22 March 1895. C.A. (I. Owen packet). For Rendel's peerage, see Humphreys-Owen to his wife. N.L.W. Glansevern MSS., not numbered, and Rendel to T. F. Roberts, 27 October 1906. N.L.W. MSS. 19442E, f. 145.

quiescence, he took a vigorously active part in the direction of the College. Rendel and Principal T. F. Roberts quickly established a close and sympathetic relationship which remained unbroken to the end, and was of immense benefit to a College that had suffered all too often in the past from incompatibilities at the top.

It was well that this harmony should be so quickly established because the College was faced with considerable problems in which, as always, shortage of funds was the central difficulty. There was a large debt outstanding on the still uncompleted building, the accounts of the hall of residence for women, despite Miss Carpenter's adroit management, were a cause of constant concern, and the county councils saw to it that they got full value (and often rather more) for every penny they contributed to the agricultural instruction carried out on their behalf by the College.[75] However, the situation had its favourable side: there was still a Liberal government in office, Gladstone was Prime Minister and Rendel had his ear; Tom Ellis was soon to become Chief Whip, and he remained as industriously active as ever in promoting Aberystwyth's interests; A. H. D. Acland continued to be as sympathetically helpful as before. Beginning in 1893 the College mounted a campaign to persuade Sir William Harcourt, Chancellor of the Exchequer, to make a large grant towards the completion of the building. The detailed manage-ment was left to Humphreys-Owen: Rendel worked on Gladstone; Acland, from within the government, attacked the Treasury, and Tom Ellis added his weight wherever he could.[76]

Events followed their, by now, time-honoured sequence: a brusque Treasury refusal was gradually worn down to a grudging willingness to accept a Memorial and receive a deputation. Ultimately, a Treasury grant with the usual strings was elicited. In August 1894 Harcourt announced that he would give the sum of £10,000 towards the completion of the College building, provided that a volun-tary contribution of £5,000 was raised from private sources within two years.[77] Helped by £1,000 from William Jones, a Birmingham benefactor of the College, £500 anonymously from the Llandinam family, and a steady effort by the Old Students' Association, the £5,000 was finally collected, though with no great margin of time to spare.[78] Work began immediately on reconstructing and en-larging the central portion of the building, the area occupied formerly by Nash's Castle House, the nucleus around which Savin's hotel had been built. Additional

---

[75] On 8 December 1894, Tom Parry, itinerant lecturer in Agriculture, relayed his fears to the Prin-cipal: 'Long observation of the ways, little and big, of these county councils makes me very anxious of the future success of the Agricultural Department, unless we make it a *real power* amongst the people themselves.' C.A. PC (9).

[76] T. F. Roberts to T. E. Ellis, 3 November 1893, 30 July and 8 August 1894. N.L.W. T. E. Ellis MSS. 1854, 1857, 1858. Humphreys-Owen to his wife, 8 November 1893. N.L.W. Glansevern MSS., not numbered.

[77] T. F. Roberts to Rendel, 22 August 1894. N.L.W. MSS. 19441E, f. 4.

[78] T. F. Roberts to T. E. Ellis, 20 October 1894. N.L.W. T. E. Ellis MSS. 1859. T. F. Roberts to Rendel, 25 July 1894. N.L.W. MSS. 19441E, f. 3.

space was urgently needed for the Science departments, and for a projected dairy-school for butter and cheese-making.

Nor was this all. The steady increase in the number of women students, and the settled policy that they should all live in hall, or with relations, pushed the College into a bold scheme for the construction of a large purpose-built hall of residence. The pump had been primed by a grant of £2,000 wheedled out of the Pfeiffer Trust by Lewis Morris. Aberystwyth corporation had generously given a fine large site, free of charge, at the north end of the promenade. For the rest, it was hoped to raise perhaps £3,000 from the ever-generous friends of the College, and a bank-loan of £10,000 at 4 per cent was available on the security of the College building. Architects had been given strict instructions to keep the cost down to £15,000, including furnishings. With expected economies of scale in a large modern hall, and Miss Carpenter's prudent housekeeping, it was confidently expected that the debt would be extinguished by accrued profits in twenty years' time.[79]

Spurred on by Foulkes Roberts (who insisted that Aberystwyth 'should take the lead in Wales'), Principal T. F. Roberts was evidently keen to extend and diversify operations in as many directions as possible. In 1894 a Secondary school teachers' training section was added to the Education department; in order to counter another attempt by Bangor to get a stronger foothold in Merionethshire, Roberts proposed a considerable extension of Aberystwyth's technical instruction work in the county in Agriculture, Dairying, Cookery and Geology, once more using Tom Ellis' local influence on Aberystwyth's behalf.[80] Inevitably, there was a good deal of rivalry between the three Welsh colleges. Ever since the 1880s teachers at the colleges had annually compiled, gleefully or otherwise, league tables of comparative results in London University matriculation and degree examinations, and drawn whatever encouraging moral the results suggested.[81] This (as some thought) unhealthy emphasis on examination performance did not escape criticism.

It is the examination fiend that is the curse of the University Colleges [wrote R. E. Hughes, an old Aberystwyth man]; it is examinations, always examinations.

[79] Council Minutes (February–November 1894), pp. 244–317. C.A. BC/MN/a. T. F. Roberts to Rendel, 25 July 1894. N.L.W. MSS. 19441E, f. 3. The Registrar (to T. E. Ellis, 6 March 1894. N.L.W. T. E. Ellis MSS. 2024) hoped that 'red tape' would not prevent the Local Government Board from sanctioning the gift of a site, not least because Sir Hugh Owen, the old founder's son, an official at the Board, 'ought to feel a special interest in his father's child'.

[80] Foulkes Roberts to T. F. Roberts, 24 September 1894. C.A. PC (13). T. F. Roberts to T. E. Ellis, 8 August 1894. N.L.W. T. E. Ellis MSS. 1858. In November 1895 the Senate (C.A. S/MN/1) regret-fully reported that resources were insufficient to mount a proposed range of instruction in 'special Commercial subjects'.

[81] For example, J. W. Marshall to J. E. Lloyd, 9 September 1887. U.C.N. W. Bangor. Lloyd MSS. 314, f. 302, and K. V. Jones, op. cit., pp. 190–1.

They have carried it to its *reductio ad absurdum*. Some of the professors have made it a fine art.

And cheek by jowl in the same journal that carried Hughes' complaint, O. M. Edwards drew attention to the disproportionate number of students in Wales who intended to teach. He insisted that the Welsh University had not been called into existence merely 'to swell the number of would-be schoolmasters who are willing to work for starvation wages'.[82] Indeed, at this time, when the syllabus of the new University was published, there was some disgruntlement that, for all the brave talk of striking out in new directions, courses of study appeared all too traditionally humdrum. In particular there were critics who complained that the Welsh language, an alternative to Greek in the syllabus, was regarded as 'a foreign, . . . a dead language', and now, as before, the University Colleges 'shamefully neglected' their duty to the history and literature of Wales.[83]

So far as this latter obligation was concerned, the Guild of Graduates of the University had accepted a special responsibility. O. M. Edwards, who became the first Warden of the Guild, and Tom Ellis were particularly active in initiating scholarly work in Welsh studies. Indeed, Ellis, despite the calls of high office and failing health, produced in the 1890s (in conjunction with his brother-in-law, J. H. Davies) an edition of the works of Morgan Llwyd. O. M. Edwards believed that the foundation of the Guild offered 'a golden opportunity'. In time it would have one or more members in every locality in Wales where they could provide leadership and encouragement for their less well educated countrymen, and act as the link between the University and the people. In his opinion the choice was quite open. The Guild could become 'the greatest power in Wales', or it could neglect its opportunity and become a 'phantom and a sham'.[84]

Edwards was also aware of the danger that the Guild might be paralysed by the rival primary loyalties of its members. At the early meetings a competitive feeling was not too far below the surface, but, although the Guild scarcely realized O. M. Edwards'ambitious hopes for it, at least it was not riven by inter-college jealousies. On other issues, however, where definite decisions had to be taken, it was not possible to avoid a clash of interest between the constituents of the University. There was, for example, a sharp fight between Cardiff and Aberystwyth for the honour of staging the installation of the University's Chancellor, the Prince of Wales.

Brynmor Jones, M.P., a leading member of the Council of the Cardiff College, was confident that, once the University Court considered the immensely superior facilities for ceremonial and hospitality available at Cardiff, Aberystwyth would

---

[82] *Wales*, ii. 39, 182.

[83] 'Patriotism and Pedantry', ibid. ii. 53–5. See also, Llewelyn Williams, 'The Welsh University: its Opportunity', *Young Wales*, ii. 145–7.

[84] *Wales*, i. 176–7, ii. 481–3.

stand no chance. Cardiff corporation (Lord Windsor was the incumbent Mayor) had offered a large sum of money to defray costs, Lord Bute was equally eager to help, and Lord Tredegar had a big house available nearby where the Prince could stay. The large buildings in a great and growing city would provide an admirable back-cloth for the ceremonies. Jones itemized in detail Aberystwyth's limitations, not least the inadequacies of Crosswood, Gogerddan, Nanteos, and Plâs Machynlleth, all relatively small houses in which to entertain a royal party. At the meeting of the University Court at Shrewsbury in February 1896, all the supposed Cardiff advantages were listed in detail: it was a highly persuasive performance. Humphreys-Owen (supported by R. D. Roberts, for once not on the losing side, and Ellis Edwards of Bala) put the opposing case. Aberystwyth was 'essentially the national college, and the birthplace of the whole movement', sentiment and justice demanded its choice, no matter what the difficulties. There was, in fact, very little discussion; happily for Aberystwyth a Cardiff spokesman added that the Prince might well be asked also to open an Exhibition which was to be held in the city at the same time. This alienated some who felt it 'meant putting the University in the second place', and may well have just tipped the balance. Finally, the Court decided for Aberystwyth by thirty votes to twenty-six.[85]

T. F. Roberts regarded this as a great triumph for Aberystwyth, a due recognition of its seniority, and Tom Ellis was overjoyed. Brynmor Jones was thoroughly put out by his defeat. He tried later to reverse the decision, and, under pressure, admitted that he was afraid of being 'chaffed by the smart people' in London about the 'poverty and rusticity' of the Welsh University, a piece of snobbery for which he was rebuked by Humphreys-Owen. Rendel, a politician to his finger-tips, despite his semi-retirement, offered the opinion that the real leaders of Wales should see to it that 'the Tories did not take the whole thing' out of their hands and put them 'in the second place'; a point of view that was to have an interesting sequel.[86]

As the great day approached, there was a flurry of activity. After some skilled negotiation by Humphreys-Owen, it was agreed that the Princess of Wales would open the large new hall of residence for women at Aberystwyth. Sir Francis Knollys, who supervised the royal side of the arrangements for the Prince's visit, was 'disturbed' that the University was going to confer honorary degrees on three Liberals but not on any Conservatives. He suggested Joseph Chamberlain, bête noir of Gladstonians, and was told it was 'out of the question'; the suggestion of Lord Londonderry was 'still worse'. As Humphreys-Owen explained, these and other Tories had done nothing for Welsh education, and were honouring

[85] Humphreys-Owen to his wife, 23 February and 5 March 1896. N.L.W. Glansevern MSS., not numbered. T. F. Roberts to Rendel, 24 February 1896. N.L.W. MSS. 19441E, f. 5. Western Mail (22 and 27 February 1896) for Cardiff's disappointment.

[86] Humphreys-Owen to his wife, 5 March and 26 April 1896. N.L.W. Glansevern MSS., not numbered.

the Prince, not the University, by their presence. There were other problems at a less exalted level. There was a rush to hire houses in Aberystwyth for the event. Humphreys-Owen and Edward Davies of Llandinam were 'staggered' at the prices blithely quoted by townspeople who knew a sellers' market when they saw one. However, the town council had rallied round valiantly and rendered all possible assistance.[87]

The installation of the Chancellor on 26 June 1896 was a great day in the history of the University and the College at Aberystwyth. It was a brilliant scene: there were several naval units anchored off the town, the soldiers' uniforms and the mass of academic hoods added a fine dash of colour. Arrangements went off without a hitch. The ceremony itself took place in a large temporary marquee set up outside the Town Hall. Later there was a luncheon for five hundred guests in the Pier Pavilion and in the afternoon the Princess of Wales formally opened the new hall of residence to which she gave her own name, 'Alexandra'. Months later the *Western Mail* generously conceded that it was the 'most brilliant pageant witnessed in Wales in modern times'.[88]

Aside from the royal couple, the central figure at the proceedings had been Gladstone, upon whom an honorary degree had been conferred. The ex-Prime Minister, aged and infirm, had at first resisted all efforts to persuade him to attend. Finally, Rendel, exerting every ounce of leverage that their long and close friendship allowed, succeeded in his pleadings. Rendel's purpose was to use the majestic presence of the Grand Old Man, a venerated national hero to most people in Wales, to keep the Anglicized Tory peers in their place. Years later Rendel wrote that he had struggled to get Gladstone to Aberystwyth 'to save *Welsh* Wales from the humiliation of taking a wretchedly subaltern place on that occasion'.[89] Rendel's gambit evidently succeeded. One observer at any rate thought that the aristocracy and the dignitaries of the Church present looked 'abject'.[90] Gladstone made a short eloquent speech in which he offered a warning against the growing power of the spirit of plutocracy. 'This University', he said, 'represents the antagonism which is offered to wealth by mental cultivation.'[91]

The acceptance of the Chancellorship by the Prince of Wales created a certain difficulty. 'The Chancellor of the University', Isambard Owen had written in 1892, 'is not intended to be a *roi fainéant*, but the actual President of the Court.' It was not to be expected that the heir to the throne would be able to fulfil this duty quite in the way envisaged. The Vice-Chancellor, title to the contrary, was

[87] Humphreys-Owen to the Registrar, 16 April 1896. C.A. (I. Owen packet). Humphreys-Owen to his wife, 8 June 1896. N.L.W. Glansevern MSS., not numbered.

[88] *Cambrian News* (including an interesting illustrated special *Supplement*, 26 June 1896) gives a very full account. *Western Mail* (31 December 1896.)

[89] Rendel to T. F. Roberts, 25 October 1906. N.L.W. MSS. 19442E, f. 142. By 'Welsh Wales', Rendel meant predominantly Liberal and nonconformist bilingual Wales.

[90] Llywelyn Williams in *Young Wales*, ii. 172.   [91] *Cambrian News* (26 June 1896).

an academic officer, and not the Chancellor's deputy.[92] This problem was solved by the creation of the posts of Senior and Junior Deputy Chancellor, the first-named office inevitably, and justly in view of his services, being filled by Isambard Owen.

Not all the problems of the infant University were resolved quite so easily. In 1897 there was another bout of in-fighting on the question of the location of the office of the University. At one time it looked as though the furious heats of the battles of the sites in the 1880s would return. Matters never quite reached that pitch of intensity, but again some of the old arguments reappeared: Aberystwyth's centrality, Caernarvon's claim on historical grounds, Swansea's right as a great and growing centre hitherto denied a college. Cardiff, backed up by a generous offer of land and money from its corporation, put in a strong claim, and, according to T. F. Roberts, cleverly confused the issue with a collateral demand for recognition as the capital city of Wales. Some local authorities in South Wales responded to Cardiff's invitation to support its claim. T. F. Roberts strongly resisted the choice of Cardiff. He was convinced that such a decision would have 'substantially hampered' the Aberystwyth College, and he did his best to drum up support for Welshpool which he considered to be the 'only practicable point of co-operation for Wales regarded as one whole', because of its central position. Roberts evidently had persuaded himself (or perhaps feared that the unthinking would come to believe) that if the University office went to Cardiff it would confer some additional advantage or prestige on the South Wales College. The University Court heard deputations from the various towns which had put in a claim, and, as it was clear that there was no convincing majority in favour of any one place (even Lloyd George's matchless eloquence could not swing the vote for Caernarvon), pusillanimously postponed the decision for five years. T. F. Roberts thought this 'a thousandfold better' than a 'snatched' vote, and he reported with evident satisfaction that 'the grasping spirit' shown by Cardiff had created an unfavourable impression in Wales. In the meantime, the University office was set up, apparently at the suggestion of Isambard Owen, in the 'neutral point' of 'ancient Brecon'.[93]

Just before this tempest in a teapot began to rage, the Aberystwyth College had been faced with another, and rather more important, problem. As soon as the University was established it was taken for granted that students in the colleges would read for Welsh degrees. After all, there had been enough Welsh criticism of the constricting effect of the rigid curricula of London University. If students in Wales were not to take the Welsh degree, why else had the University been founded? Aberystwyth's position was not quite so simple as this suggested. In

[92] 'Memorandum on the proposed Charter of the University of Wales.' 28 December 1892.

[93] *The Times* (9 February 1897). T. F. Roberts to Rendel, 10 February and 26 May 1897. N.L.W. MSS. 19441E, ff. 6, 7. Isambard Owen to T. F. Roberts, 26 April 1897. C.A. PC (7). The debate is reported fully in U.C.W. *Magazine*, xix. 364–7.

1895–6 and 1896–7 just over a third of the students at Aberystwyth were English (about 10 per cent of them the offspring of Welsh parents living in England). And, a further point, a majority of the English students were women, nearly all of them working for a London degree, an option open to them when they entered the College.

In March 1896 the Treasury, in the course of announcing its financial provision for the Welsh University, included an addendum, minatory in tone, to the effect that the constituent colleges should prepare their students for the Welsh degree exclusively. Some people read into this the implication that, if the Treasury's wishes were not complied with forthwith, government grants might be cut or even withdrawn. Bangor and Cardiff fully agreed with the Treasury's argument, and Viriamu Jones hinted strongly that people who thought otherwise showed a deplorable lack of faith in the value of the new Welsh degree. This was less than fair to Aberystwyth. Ever since 1872 its teaching had been geared to London, and the striking series of successes by Aberystwyth students had gained a considerable reputation for the College reflected in the influx of students from England. To answer the needs of women entrants, Alexandra Hall had been built at very considerable expense and no small risk. Furthermore, the income derived from these students' fees was an important item in the accounts of the College which, if summarily cut off, would 'cripple the College' at a time when its responsibilities were being rapidly extended. In March 1896 the Council decided to resist the Treasury's pressure, and resolved that it was undesirable that any restriction should be placed upon the College during the period of 'change and reconstruction'. T. F. Roberts cleverly turned the tables on Viriamu Jones with the argument that 'any action having the appearance of a protective policy would produce the impression that the Welsh degrees' were unable 'to challenge comparison with those of other universities'. Aberystwyth's London connection was far stronger than those of Cardiff and Bangor, and the College, not unreasonably, wanted more time to phase out its work for the London degree. The ably written Memorandum in which Aberystwyth set out its case pointed out that the prohibition suggested by the Treasury was 'without precedent' in university history and added tartly that Aberystwyth needed 'no external or coercive stimulus' to do its duty towards the Principality, for the College had 'graven its name deeply on the history of Wales', and had been 'the principal motive power' in the achievement of a Welsh University.[94]

Lewis Morris, Vice-President of the College, was convinced that it was all part of a dastardly plot. 'I happen to know [he wrote to T. F. Roberts] that the enemy hath done this thing, and with the direct object of crippling and, if possible,

---

[94] Memorandum: 'To the Lords Commissioners of her Majesty's Treasury', 16 November 1896. C.A. PC (12). T. F. Roberts to Rendel, 7 October 1896. N.L.W. MSS. 19441E, f. 13. T. F. Roberts to T. E. Ellis, 11 August 1896. N.L.W. T. E. Ellis MSS. 1862. Young Wales, ii. 145.

ruining the College. It is an exceedingly clever move from their blinded and miserable point of view.'[95] It is not clear exactly who these unnamed malignant ones were. There were whispers that the leaders of the Bangor and Cardiff Colleges were behind the affair. But J. Young Evans, an old Aberystwyth student who always kept his ear close to the ground, firmly discounted this. He suggested that the Treasury's action had been prompted by the champions of the interests of three or four big Church schools in Wales who wanted a monopoly of preparation for Oxbridge and London; one latter-day sign perhaps that the old Anglican Adam was not dead so far as Aberystwyth was concerned.[96] In so obviously political a matter as this, T. F. Roberts sought the guidance of Rendel. The President thoroughly approved of the Council's resistance to the Treasury, which, in his opinion, had grossly exceeded its legitimate authority, and should be opposed lest it should be encouraged into greater entrenchments on academic freedom. 'A Treasury Clerk', he wrote, 'has no authority that I know of to dragoon Aberystwyth.' Rendel was confident that no government, in the ultimate, would seriously attempt to impose its will in this way. Rendel was right. Aberystwyth had made out its case, and the 'preposterous condition', as Young Evans called it, was quickly withdrawn by the Treasury.[97]

Principal Roberts had had his way in this instance, but elsewhere he, along with Viriamu Jones and Reichel of Bangor, had suffered a disappointment. All three Principals had hoped that the University of Wales would be vested with the power to inspect and conduct examinations in the secondary schools of Wales. At the conferences in Shrewsbury which preceded the establishment of the University, representatives of the Welsh schools had been present, and a motion in favour of conferring this jurisdiction on the University had been defeated. Subsequently, a scheme to establish an alternative authority, the Central Welsh Board, was in train, with A. C. Humphreys-Owen very much to the fore in the negotiations. In 1896, on the eve of the establishment of the Board, Viriamu Jones returned to the attack. Jones, Reichel, and T. F. Roberts believed that University supervision of the schools was essential to give coherence to the whole educational structure of Wales. Viriamu Jones had persuaded himself that the Unionist government would do whatever the body of Welsh M.P.s asked for in the matter. Humphreys-Owen, who was now Liberal M.P. for Montgomeryshire, quickly disabused him of this naïve notion. In 1889, said Humphreys-Owen, the 'Tories

---

[95] 10 November 1896. C.A. PC (8).

[96] 'Our Welsh University Forum', *Young Wales*, iii. 39–40. Evans wondered who advised the Unionist Government on Welsh matters.

[97] Rendel to T. F. Roberts, 14 October 1896. C.A. PC (12). Young Evans, loc. cit., p. 39. The U.C.W. *Magazine*, xix. 90–1, pointed out that, in 1896, Aberystwyth had a larger number of students entered for Welsh University examinations than Cardiff or Bangor, and claimed additionally that, over the years, more students had taken the London B.A. degree from Aberystwyth than from any other college in Britain.

were flirting with Wales', and this accounted for the government's relatively benign attitude to the Welsh Intermediate Education bill. In 1896 things had changed, 'the bishops had control of the whole Tory party'. Not that that mattered, anyway, in Humphreys-Owen's opinion, for three government departments had been involved in the detailed negotiation concerning the Central Board, and there was little likelihood that, at the eleventh hour, they would be prepared to 'tear up the scheme and begin afresh'. Undeterred, Viriamu Jones tried to get the backing of the University Court, but was 'hammered' in the debate and defeated. In May 1896 the Central Welsh Board came into existence with the proviso (apparently suggested by its first chairman, Humphreys-Owen, and by Tom Ellis) that the scheme should be reviewed, and perhaps amended, after some years' experience of its operation.[98]

Despite this setback—if such it was—Principal Roberts had good reasons for satisfaction at the way the College was developing under his leadership. By 1898 the reconstruction of the central portion of the building was nearing completion, and the architect, C. J. Ferguson, had succeeded pretty well in marrying his 'free Gothic' additions to Seddon's original structure. Considerably more space was now available for the Science departments, and Ferguson had also managed to repair the damage to the tower caused by the great fire of 1885 and to fit up additional rooms in that area for teaching purposes.[99] The College now had the appearance that it retains to this day.[100]

It was felt that these structural additions should be formally opened by some great public figure. For one reason and another the Duke of Devonshire and Lords Roseberry and Spencer could not come, and, ultimately, it was suggested that Sir William Harcourt, who as Chancellor of the Exchequer had sanctioned the grant of £10,000 that had made the addition possible, should be invited. Harcourt received a great welcome. He was met at the railway station by a crowd of students who drew his carriage through the streets in triumphant procession (this had now become the traditional Aberystwyth greeting for visiting dignitaries). At later ceremonies Harcourt was entertained by a student choir which included a rendering in Welsh and English of the College song (the outcome of a competition during the 1890s) in its programme. In his speech Harcourt said that Wales had 'given the lead' to England in secondary education, and in 'bringing all classes of the community up to the universities'. In his opinion, it was high time these examples were followed in the larger country, not least (the Great War of 1914–18

[98] Humphreys-Owen to his wife, 5, 15, and 23 February 1896. N.L.W. Glansevern MSS., not numbered.

[99] *Cambrian News* (28 October 1898) gives a full description of the changes.

[100] The curious mosaic on the castle end of the building had been presented by Seddon in his rebuilding of the south wing in 1888. There is no formal record of the mosaic's significance, but traditionally it is said to depict the wonders of modern science (steam locomotion and the like) being presented for the inspection of Archimedes.

casting a long shadow before it) because of the mounting challenge in the world of the much better educated German people.[101]

All in all, it was a great day for the College, and there was considerable resultant favourable publicity.[102] At least this helped to combat the effects of another episode soon afterwards in which the College appeared in a ludicrous light. A lively young woman student at Alexandra Hall had responded to some light-hearted whistling by a man student outside the building, and had had the temerity to talk to him from an open window. Miss Carpenter, who had had her eye on the young lady for some time, insisted that the student could not stay in the Hall. At first she was sent down from College, but later she was allowed to return and live in lodgings with the family of a member of the Senate. The man student was rusticated for two terms. Inevitably, the episode got into the press—London as well as Welsh. The *Western Mail* dubbed it the 'Romeo and Juliet' episode, and reported subsequent developments in detail. A great procession of men students marched to Alexandra Hall, removed their mortar-boards (customarily worn at that time), and sang several hymns. Later the man student was carried by a great cheering crowd to the station *en route* for home. There was some opposition in the Senate to the Draconian punishment handed out and, in all, the Senate held eight special meetings and deliberated for thirty-three hours on the matter. Considerable feeling was aroused in the town and, at one time, it seemed that a riot would develop outside Alexandra Hall. The police warned men students that they should be ready, if called upon, to help to keep the peace. Nothing came of this, but harsh words were spoken at a meeting of the Town Council (Alexandra Hall was called 'a barracks'), and a corporation grant of £400 towards the building fund was carried only with difficulty. Still, in the end, rough justice was done. Principal Roberts, on his way home from a late meeting of the Senate, was caught riding his bicycle without lights and fined 2s. 6d. by the magistrates' court.[103]

Everything seemed to go wrong at this time. Professor J. E. Lloyd, who had gone to Bangor in 1892, came down to address the College Celtic Society and, as he ruefully admitted, 'broke . . . a law of the Medes and Persians' by addressing it in English. When J. Ramsay McDonald arrived to lecture to the College Fabian Society, he was met by a snowstorm that thinned his audience to the point of embarrassment. Even Rendel, at a loose end, was fidgeting and, as his daughter

[101] Rendel to T. F. Roberts, 20 August 1898. C.A. PC (12). *Cambrian News* (28 October 1898). *Western Mail* (27 October 1898).

[102] Particular satisfaction was expressed also at the news, announced that day, that the University was going to confer an honorary doctorate of Divinity upon T. C. Edwards, a distinction 'most richly and heartily deserved' by this great 'moulder of men', as the *Western Mail* (27 October 1898) said.

[103] *Western Mail* (2–29 November 1895). *Cambrian News* (November 1898). C.A. S/MN/1, for 8 November 1898. It is fair to say that there is other evidence (the letters (cited hereafter as 'Marsh') of Olive Marsh, the future Lady Stamp) indicating a good deal of support among men and women students for Miss Carpenter.

said with alarm, when he had nothing to do, 'he buys new houses or else digs earth'.[104]

However, just before this time Rendel had put some of his money to a good College purpose. Ever since the foundation of the University College of Wales in 1872, its strongest friends had always hoped to make Aberystwyth a great centre of national studies. Even in the days of grim penury, some small sums of money had been set aside to buy books for a special Welsh library at the College.[105] On 30 September 1896, at the instance of Principal Roberts, the Council set up a committee to consider improving arrangements for the custody of books and manuscripts, and to examine proposals for the development of the Welsh side of the College library. The leading members of this committee were T. F. Roberts, Principal John Rhys of Jesus College, Oxford, and T. E. Ellis, M.P.[106] Others were co-opted or associated soon afterwards, notably J. Gwenogfryn Evans, the incredibly industrious Oxford-based Welsh palaeographer, Henry Owen, the London Welsh solicitor and antiquarian and, most important of all, Sir John Williams, the distinguished physician (medical adviser to royalty since 1886), who had already amassed a magnificent private collection of Welsh books and manuscripts.

In August 1897 Sir John offered his library to the College, provided that 'a suitable site for a building' was secured. The College committee acted with speed: serious consideration was given to the purchase of land on the *Buarth Mawr* overlooking the centre of the town, but soon afterwards four local members of the Council, acting privately, bought fourteen acres of land, part of the Grogythan estate on Penglais hill, for £2,000. This truly magnificent site, commanding a marvellous view of sea and countryside, was offered to the College Council at purchase price. Sir John Williams, Henry Owen, Tom Ellis, and T. F. Roberts were delighted with this brilliant coup.[107] Lord Rendel, however, was not impressed. He wrote sharply to Roberts warning him of the danger of 'megalomania' regarding ambitious building schemes. Rendel, however, had misunderstood the situation: he thought the College, already encumbered with more than enough outstanding debts, was proposing to burden itself with the obligation to erect a costly building. In fact, the proposal was that the College should buy only the land, part of which would be used for the erection, in due course, of a library building

[104] J. E. Lloyd to T. F. Roberts, 24 November 1898. C.A. PC (6). U.C.W. *Magazine*, xxi. 152. Humphreys-Owen to his wife, 19 December 1898. N.L.W. Glansevern MSS., not numbered.

[105] See above, pp. 40–1.

[106] Penllyn Jones to J. H. Davies, 26 October 1896. N.L.W. J. H. Davies MSS. (T. I. Ellis donation 1963/6). Davies was asked to join the committee. Council Minutes, 30 September 1896. BC/MN/2.

[107] J. H. Davies's note on Sir John Williams, no date, N.L.W. J. H. Davies MSS. (T. I. Ellis donation 1963/6). The Registrar to J. H. Davies, 21 July 1897. N.L.W. J. H. Davies MSS. (Corr.). Sir John Williams to Gwenogfryn Evans, 30 August 1897. N.L.W. Timothy Lewis MSS., f. 2. T. E. Ellis to Gwenogfryn Evans, 1 September 1897. N.L.W. Timothy Lewis MSS. (not numbered). T. F. Roberts to Rendel, 25 September 1897. N.L.W. MSS. 19441E, f. 12.

financed from other sources, private and perhaps public. T. F. Roberts, who was nothing if not an enthusiast, gently tried to get Rendel to look to the future. The College had no room to expand: some of these acres could be used for the work of the department of Agriculture (thereby qualifying for an extra government grant), there would be room for the Welsh theological colleges if some of them decided, as had been suggested, to move to Aberystwyth. Meantime, some land could be used for College athletics. Roberts was convinced that, if only Rendel could see the site for himself, he would soon forget his objections.[108]

Despite his uncharacteristically myopic initial response, Rendel was soon per-suaded, and, indeed, came round handsomely to the rescue of the Council which would have been hard put to it to find £2,000 at this time. Rendel bought the fourteen acres which he leased to the College at a peppercorn rent.[109] Within months, the Senate offered its provisional opinion that the Grogythan site could be used for a museum, art and music schools, new Agricultural buildings, a dairy, and a gymnasium. Henry Owen thought it was the obvious place to build hostels, 'without which Aberystwyth will never be what we wish to make it', as he told the Registrar. As an Oxford man, Owen confessed he had 'a prejudice in favour of a quadrangle'; a proposal to erect semi-detached villas (to house the staff?) aroused 'no enthusiasm' at all in his mind.[110]

The acquisition of the Grogythan land was to have a tremendously important effect on the future of the College, but some time elapsed before any striking developments occurred. Meantime, Principal Roberts was hotly in pursuit of other possibilities. Soon after the College had received its charter, the Court began to hold some of its meetings in the larger towns in the seven counties of Mid-Wales. These peripatetic sessions were designed to strengthen the con-nection of the College with the people, and especially to parade the College before the various local authorities of the area. On 24 March 1898, at a meeting at Welsh-pool, the Court of Governors resolved that the Council should be invited to consider the establishment of a department of Law at the College. T. F. Roberts, as usual, was eager to press on quickly. He believed that a start could be made with some help from the existing teaching staff and an additional annual expendi-ture of £250–300. Roberts admitted that this sum would not be achieved without a considerable effort: but, ever the blithe optimist, and accustomed to living dangerously where money was concerned, he was convinced that Law would be 'a popular department', and that within five years the income from students' fees would help considerably. The Principal's letter to Rendel, the hard-headed realist, announcing the launching of an appeal for subscriptions for five years, had a

---

[108] T. F. Roberts to Rendel, 25 September, 8 October 1897. N.L.W. MSS. 19441E, ff. 12, 14.
[109] Council Minutes, 18 February 1898. C.A. C/MN/2.
[110] Senate Minutes, 25 May 1898. C.A. S/MN/1. Henry Owen to the Registrar, 5 May 1898. C.A. (I. Owen packet).

strongly defensive note. But as Roberts reasonably pointed out, beggars could not be choosers, and, 'in our circumstances, the only way of launching a new venture is this tentative and not altogether satisfactory plan of a five year fund'. The College had a duty to develop as best it could in 'those directions in which we are likely to do good work'.[111] Subscriptions for this interesting scheme came in very slowly, so there was some delay before a start could be made. Moreover, in a relatively uncharted area the Council, determined to frame the curriculum of the new department 'on sound academic lines', had resolved to go carefully.[112]

Concurrently, T. F. Roberts had two other minor plans on foot. During the 1890s Training department students included some work in Music in their courses. Practical instruction on a part-time basis was given by David Jenkins, an old student who had studied under Joseph Parry and subsequently taken a bachelor's degree in Music at Cambridge. Roberts proposed that Jenkins should be paid £100 instead of £30 a year, and asked to raise the level of his teaching to include degree work. The additional expense here, too, was to be met by an appeal for subscriptions, but this would be directed to 'a different class of persons', and would not clash with the appeal for money for a Law department. The College should recognize its responsibilities, for 'Music is a subject which, on grounds of national taste and aptitude, ought to receive some attention from us'.[113]

This modest proposal to build up a Music department gradually succeeded. T. F. Roberts' other current hope of diversifying the work of the College quickly failed. He held strongly to the view that everything possible that was respectable on academic grounds should be done to assist the struggling small industries of rural Wales. In February 1899 the College petitioned the Worshipful Company of Clothworkers for a grant in support of a proposed school of Dyeing and Weaving at Aberystwyth, a smaller version of a development, substantially financed by the Clothworkers, at the Yorkshire College, Leeds. He made out a useful case which leaned heavily on the strength of the Chemistry department at Aberystwyth. His hopes, however, were quickly disappointed: the Clothworkers rejected the petition out of hand, and a similar application to the Drapers' Company immediately afterwards met the same fate.[114]

For all that, T. F. Roberts had good cause for satisfaction at the way his College had grown during the first nine years of his Principalship. By now there were over

111 Court Minutes, 25 March 1898. C.A. B/MN/1. T. F. Roberts to Rendel, 27 June 1898. N.L.W. MSS. 19441E, f. 19.

112 The Registrar to J. H. Davies, 29 June 1899. N.L.W. T. I. Ellis MSS.

113 T. F. Roberts to Rendel, 27 June 1898. N.L.W. MSS. 19441E, f. 19. In his Inaugural Address (October 1899) Professor T. McKenny Hughes, a former member of the Council, sharply criticized the 'injudicious management and weak administration' that had led to the over-hasty closing down of the Music department in Joseph Parry's time. U.C.W. *Magazine*, xxii. 10–11.

114 'Proposed School of Dyeing and Weaving' (January 1899). C.A. PC (4). Henry Owen to T. F. Roberts, 2 February 1899. C.A. PC (7). Humphreys-Owen to his wife, 10 February 1899. N.L.W. Glansevern MSS., not numbered.

four hundred and seventy students and, judged by the criterion of examination success in Wales and London, no falling off in quality. The teaching staff had grown in size, and most of the recruits exhibited that total commitment to the interests of the College and its students which had been evident in almost all members of the staff since 1872. These additional appointments were mainly to assistant lectureships, for by this time student numbers were too large to be dealt with exclusively by members of the Senate. There were one or two professorial changes of note. In 1892 when J. E. Lloyd went to Bangor, he was replaced by two men. Edward Anwyl of Oxford became professor of Welsh, and Edward Edwards was appointed lecturer in History and Political Economy, with the promise of a chair as soon as maybe. In time, Anwyl developed into a scholar of considerable distinction, and he became prominent in Welsh cultural life and was ultimately knighted.[115] Edward Edwards, then on the Bangor staff, had been encouraged to apply for the Aberystwyth post by his brother, O. M. Edwards, who conceded that the salary (£120 per annum) was abysmally small, but pointed to the virtues of Aberystwyth, 'a gentle place to live, a cheap place, a healthy place, a place not far from home'.[116] T. F. Roberts was ashamed that the salaries offered (despite his professorial title, Anwyl, too, was appointed at £120) were so small, but the Principal believed that, from the point of view of the College, it was better to appoint two men who could specialize rather than give one man a higher salary and ask him to shoulder an impossible load.[117] Edward Edwards made no great mark in the academic world, but he became a great College personality—Teddy Eddy as he was universally known—beloved of generations of Aberystwyth students.

There had been a professor of Physics since 1885 (D. E. Jones, a former student), and in 1891, when he resigned, D. Morgan Lewis succeeded. D. E. Jones had written several textbooks which rank among the earliest guides in a subject which was ignored in most schools at that time. Jones had hoped to establish a department of Electrical Engineering, and in 1890 a Crossley gas engine, bought half-price for £95, provided electric light for certain favoured parts of the College, one of the earliest electrical installations in Wales and, at the time, a source of great wonder. When Morgan Lewis took up his appointment, the College officers agreed that his predecessor had been underpaid, but it was still essential to 'walk warily' in money matters, and the new professor must be content with £200.[118] There was also a new Registrar. In 1891 the College offices, formerly in London, were removed to Aberystwyth. Ever since 1872, Penllyn Jones had acted as Registrar-cum-Librarian, but evidently he was not considered up to the increased responsibilities. Mortimer Green, 'a good man', in T. F. Roberts' opinion, became Registrar, and poor

[115] There is a good study of Anwyl's work by Brynley F. Roberts in *Trans. Cymm.* (1968).

[116] O. M. Edwards to E. Edwards (in Welsh), 13 June 1892. N.L.W. E. Edwards MSS. 9410B.

[117] T. F. Roberts to T. E. Ellis, 20 July and 18 August 1892. N.L.W. T. E. Ellis MSS. 1846, 1847.

[118] W. M. Jones (and others), 'Notes on the Department of Physics', pp. 4–5. Lewis Morris to T. F. Roberts, 3 September 1891. U.C.W. G. Lib. History File.

Penllyn Jones, who 'did not want to go if he could help it', devoted his time exclusively to the library.[119]

Throughout the 1890s, the College officers were constantly concerned at the low level of salaries (generally lower than in the other two Welsh colleges) that they were able to pay the staff.[120] Despite the government grant, Aberystwyth remained an exceptionally poverty-stricken College. With the best will in the world, it was difficult to see how any substantial improvement in staff conditions could be brought about. Once again, however, Lord Rendel came to the aid of the College. In 1899 Rendel had received a plea for assistance from Armstrong College, Newcastle. He turned it down flatly, indeed brusquely. 'Self help is the best help', he insisted, and went on to draw attention to Welsh education which was 'a stable and national possession' because it sprang 'from the spontaneous love of the Welsh people' and was 'essentially a voluntary and popular system'.[121] Prompted perhaps by the list of handsome endowments enjoyed by English colleges set out in the supplication from Newcastle, Rendel decided to help the Aberystwyth staff. Early in 1900 he announced a gift of £750 annually during his lifetime to supplement salaries.[122]

In 1900 Aberystwyth was well on the way to achieving a genuine university standard. There were still too many ill-prepared students for satisfaction, and there were idlers and incompetents on the staff as well as at a humbler level.[123] But there were men and women of outstanding distinction teaching at the College: Hermann Ethé, Snape, the brilliant.C. H. Herford, Foster Watson, and, pushing their way up from more junior status, G. A. Schott of the Physics department, and Miss Lilian Winstanley, assistant lecturer in English. Here and there among the students there were young men of outstanding promise: for example, H. J. Fleure, who was runner-up in the Entrance examination in 1897, and R. T. Jenkins, who arrived in 1898. The place was rich in character and characters at all levels: Ethé, as outsize a personality as a scholar, Miss Carpenter, utterly undeterred by the upsetting events of 1898, L. R. Roose, matchless in goal for College and (later) Wales, and Sergeant Wakeling, head porter, who arrived in 1896, provided his own uniform, and soon set up in business as lord and master of the Quad.

---

[119] 'Removal of the London Offices' (1891). G. Lib. LD 1155 (1). T. F. Roberts to T. E. Ellis, 3 and 5 December 1891, 1 April 1892, N.L.W. T. E. Ellis MSS. 1842, 1843, 1844.

[120] 'Schedule of present salaries . . . and past increments' (1900) C.A. PC (Misc.). As for students, T. F. Roberts pointed out that there was 'little danger of the student of a Welsh college . . . forgetting "what he was or where he is" ' . . . His student life is lived in the exercise of strict economy, and in the midst of his own people'. *The University of Wales and its relation to national life* (1894), p. 10.

[121] Rendel to Dr. T. Hodgkin, 1 July 1899. N.L.W. Rendel MSS., ii. 1309.

[122] T. Hodgkin to Rendel, 15 June 1898. N.L.W. Rendel MSS., ii. 1308. Foulkes Roberts to T. F. Roberts, 26 February 1900. U.C.W. G. Lib. History File. Humphreys-Owen to his wife, 23 February 1900. N.L.W. Glansevern MSS., not numbered.

[123] See the frank comments in R. T. Jenkins, *Edrych yn Ol* (Clwb Llyfrau Cymraig, London), pp. 102–30.

It was a genuine, closely knit academic community. Staff and students joined in everything together. The Principal customarily took the chair at general meetings, Miss Carpenter presided over assemblies of women students. Staff members took a leading part in all student activities, social, academic, athletic. Indeed, there was a growing feeling that the staff exercised too large and direct an influence on student concerns; a feeling that was to express itself shortly in a determined and successful attempt by the student body to establish a greater independence from official tutelage. That, too, was a sign of health.

In November 1900 the President, Lord Rendel, in a message to the Senate, could say with pride:

The College is fast becoming a true *Alma Mater* to staff and students. Everything that raises our feeling for it, and for one another, helps to build it up into solidarity as an enduring and invaluable national institution.[124]

[124] 23 November 1900. C.A. S/MN/1.

5

'I Hope to Advance all along the Line'[1]

I<small>N</small> the first decade of the twentieth century events at Aberystwyth followed
a pattern that had, by now, become almost classic for this small College that
had triumphed against all the odds on so many occasions in the past. Dogged
persistence again succeeded in situations which looked distinctly unpromising
at the outset. The new century, however, opened with a disappointing defeat.
The leaders of the College had always been concerned at the paucity of private
endowments; the considerable sums of money collected so painfully in the early
years were no sooner accumulated than spent in order to keep the College open.
T. F. Roberts had often asked himself why 'a College so devotedly loved by the
many, and so nobly aided by the few who have known it best' had failed to attract
large benefactions from the well-to-do. He had come to the conclusion that the
'pronounced democratic position' that the College had always taken up, although
to him 'its chief distinction and pride', unhappily was not 'calculated to attract the
kind of man' who was in a position to endow on any generous scale.[2]

Just after the turn of the century, Rendel, seeing little hope of a response from
British plutocrats, decided to ask for assistance for the College from his friend
Andrew Carnegie, the self-made Scots-American multi-millionaire. Rendel was
a masterly writer of begging letters and he was not above using the best butter
with a flattering reference to the unique 'virility and grit of the hardy Scot'. But
the real strength of Rendel's plea lay in the simple story he told of the magnificent
efforts of a poor people to help themselves, and the obviously genuine admiration
that Rendel himself felt for this mass exercise in national regeneration. Rendel's
performance was highly persuasive. 'You will wonder how we pay our way', he
wrote in his second letter, which included a detailed account of the penny-
pinching difficulties of the Aberystwyth College. 'I wonder at it also. We do, but
only Welsh thrift could accomplish such a miracle.'[3] Carnegie's first reply was that
universities were not on the list of institutions to which he was prepared to offer
assistance. When Rendel sought to get round this technical objection, Carnegie
showed, not surprisingly, that he was as skilled in answering begging letters as

[1] Principal T. F. Roberts to Rendel, 27 November 1908. N.L.W. MSS. 19443E, Rendel II, f. 194.
[2] T. F. Roberts to Rendel, 21 November 1907. N.L.W. Ibid., f. 185.
[3] January and November 1901. N.L.W. MSS. 19440E, ff. 52, 56a.

Rendel was in writing them. Carnegie's defence was the unexpectedly delicate suggestion that an American millionaire who usurped the public duty of British millionaires would be thought 'an officious, fussy, and, upon the whole, a bouncy fellow'.[4] Of course this was entirely beside the point, for the burden of Rendel's pleading had been precisely that British millionaires (with one honourable exception) had not come to the aid of the College. But Carnegie made it plain that, despite their friendship, he would not respond to Rendel's importunities.

For Aberystwyth, for the moment at least, there was to be no fairy godfather. The College had to fall back upon the old back-breaking business of a little by little aggregation of small contributions from its ever-faithful supporters, few of whom enjoyed more than relatively modest incomes. One of the objects for which Rendel had hoped to engage Carnegie's assistance was the projected Law department at Aberystwyth. On 24 February 1899 a meeting, with Lord Justice Sir R. Vaughan Williams in the chair, was held in London to promote the proposed new school. All those who spoke enthusiastically endorsed the idea and, from the beginning, it was clear that the study of Law at Aberystwyth was envisaged, as Isambard Owen said, 'as a branch of a liberal education'; the emphasis would be on teaching the general principles of law, providing a broad education, not merely a narrow professional training. At the meeting Principal Roberts recited the litany that was by now second nature to him. 'We are a poor College', he said, 'we are in need of outside help', and he had to admit that, up to that time, no more than £50 of the £400 per annum for five years required to make a start was in hand.[5] Also at this meeting, in addition to an Aberystwyth committee already in existence, two other committees were set up: one to enlist the support of members of the Bar on the North and South Wales circuits, and one in London to engage the support of Welshmen in the capital. Those present at the meeting expressed their confidence (how else could the pessimism induced by harsh reality be kept at bay?) that, in five years' time, the department would be self-supporting.[6]

Early in January 1901, despite the fact that the Sustentation Fund had not quite reached its target, the College Council resolved to establish a Faculty of Law forthwith. The original intention was to appoint a professor of English Law at an annual stipend of £300, and a lecturer in Roman Law and Jurisprudence at £200 a year.[7] There were six candidates for the chair, and, waiting in the wings, for special reasons unable formally to apply, another man whose qualifications were

[4] 14 February 1901 and 28 January 1902. N.L.W. Ibid., ff. 53, 56b.

[5] 'Preliminary List of Subscribers', 1899. T. I. Ellis MSS. (in private possession). Apart from ten guineas from Rendel and five pounds from Vaughan Williams, all other contributions were of one or two guineas.

[6] Report of the meeting, reprinted from the *Cambrian News* (3 March 1899), in C.A. P (VB) 5. S. T. Evans, M.P. and E. J. Ellis Griffith, M.P., two old students who were distinguished lawyers, were members of the London Committee.   [7] *Council Minutes* (11 January 1901), pp. 1–3.

outstanding. This was Dr. W. Jethro Brown, formerly professor of Law at the University of Tasmania, who had recently been appointed to a chair at University College, London. Brown had misunderstood the terms of the London appointment which carried a merely nominal stipend. He was a distinguished man whose ideas strongly impressed the members of the Council.[8] Head and shoulders above the other formal applicants was T. A. Levi, an old Aberystwyth student, son of the Revd. Thomas Levi, the so-called 'king' of the Cardiganshire Methodists.[9] T. A. Levi had taken a brilliant double First at Oxford, and the great A. V. Dicey had been so impressed with his quality that he had 'strongly advised' Levi not to apply for the Aberystwyth chair 'as his chances as a lawyer' were 'so good'. However, O. M. Edwards, ever watchful of Welsh national interests, had persuaded Levi of the truth of the maxim 'that every Welshman is bound to offer his services to Wales first, at whatever sacrifice'.[10]

Members of the Council were anxious to secure the services of Brown and Levi and, happily, they readily agreed to accept professorial appointments at the lower figure of £250 a year. Levi became professor of English Law, and Jethro Brown professor of Constitutional and Comparative Law. As the financial basis of the new venture was so rickety, the two appointments were made for a term of five years only. T. F. Roberts rightly believed that the College had been 'most fortunate' in recruiting the services of two men who made up a first-rate team in the early difficult days when the new department had to achieve instant success in order to survive.[11] In October 1901 the new Law school began operations. There was a curiously defensive note to the Inaugural lectures delivered by Levi and Brown; it is clear that they both felt that it was necessary to establish the validity of Law as a university discipline. 'The last function we would wish the present Faculty to fulfil is that of merely negotiating legal examinations', said Levi. And Jethro Brown complained that, all too often in the past, the education of lawyers had been 'looked upon as beneath the dignity of a University school'. At the same time, Levi, as befitted a man brought up in Cardiganshire, was quick to point out that, in America at least, a legal education was a thoroughly sound investment which paid off handsomely in time.[12]

The infant department needed all the propagandist support that it could get, and in the early years distinguished luminaries of the law were persuaded to come down to Aberystwyth to deliver Inaugural lectures at the start of each session.

[8] Brown's exceptional academic record at Cambridge and elsewhere, and his great qualities as a teacher, are set out in *The Dragon*, xxvii. 3–5.   [9] See above, p. 91.

[10] O. M. Edwards to T. F. Roberts, 28 January 1901. U.C.W. G. Lib. History File.

[11] *Council Minutes* (22 February 1901), pp. 20–1. T. F. Roberts to Rendel, 25 February 1901. N.L.W. MSS. 19441E, Rendel II, f. 35.

[12] T. A. Levi, 'The opportunity of a new Faculty of Law', pp. 5–6, 21–2, W. Jethro Brown, 'The Study of the Law', p. 12. U.C.W. Law department papers. See also T. A. Levi in U.C.W. *Magazine*, xxiv. 49–51.

Vaughan Williams lectured in 1901, Blake Odgers, Director of Legal Education for the Council of the Bar, in the following year; in 1903 Edward Jenks, Principal of the Law Society, gave an Address, and he was followed in 1904 by Paul Vinogradoff, who delivered a superb lecture on 'Welsh Law and Comparative Jurisprudence'.[13] But for all the ambitious talk of setting sights well above the mere coaching of students for professional examinations, the fact was that the Law department, somehow or other, had to find a way to make a direct contribution to its upkeep. During the first four years the Sustentation Fund, on average, failed by £200 to reach its annual target, and the mounting deficit was a constant source of worry to College officers who were already at their wits' end for money.[14] From the beginning, Levi and Brown had done their best to persuade the legal fraternity in Wales of the value of the department. They travelled regularly to Swansea and to other towns in Wales to deliver courses of extension lectures for articled clerks preparing for Law Society examinations. This bread-and-butter extra-mural work (only thus was there any hope of persuading the Law Society to make a grant to the department) was a sore trial to Jethro Brown, a regular contributor to learned journals, who resented the inroads made into the time available to him for scholarly activity. Indeed, in 1905 Brown told the Principal that he would rather resign than continue the wearisome trips to Swansea and elsewhere. Happily, Levi, who bore the brunt of this external work, was an exceptionally gifted popular lecturer who, as Brown noted with astonishment, 'likes rather than detests these flying visits'.[15]

The College could have had no better salesman of its wares than T. A. Levi. It is doubtful if any other man, week by week, could have persuaded the Swansea students that it was better for their local Society to pay over to the College the £100 received annually from the Law Society rather than spend it, as some of them were disposed to do, in drib and drab payments to local tutors prepared to cram students for examinations. However, even Levi's exceptional gifts occasionally caused trouble. In March 1905 a lecture he gave on law reform (Levi was a strong lifelong Liberal) offended his conservative-minded audience of future solicitors and barristers at Swansea, who promptly threatened to withdraw their donation to the Aberystwyth Law school.[16]

The year 1905 was, in fact, a time of severe crisis for the Law department. The

[13] T. F. Roberts to Rendel, 14 January 1905. N.L.W. MSS. 19442E, Rendel II, f. 90. *The Dragon*, xxvii. 14–15.

[14] T. F. Roberts to Rendel, 11 October 1905. N.L.W. MSS. 19442E, Rendel II, f. 115.

[15] T. A. Levi, 'The Faculty of Law'. U.C.W. Law department papers. Jethro Brown to T. F. Roberts, 'Friday' 1905. C.A. P (VB) 5. In 1904 Levi and Brown wrote to the Principal: 'In learning we can hold our own; as teachers we are nowhere', compared with American lawyers. 9 September 1904. C.A. P (VB) 5.

[16] R. T. B. Jenkins, 22 March 1905, and T. A. Levi, 6 April 1905, to T. F. Roberts. C.A. P (VB) 5. 'I expressly repudiated party politics in the lecture', said Levi. 'I do not think you will ask me as a University Law lecturer to abstain from advocating *any* law reform.'

Sustentation Fund was entering its final year, and there was still no alternative source of adequate funds; the number of Law students at Aberystwyth was slowly increasing, but their fees made only a small contribution to the real cost of maintaining the department. Moreover, there were some critics in Wales who were obviously bitterly jealous of the enterprise shown by the Aberystwyth authorities. In the late summer of 1905 the *Western Mail* published an unsigned attack on the Aberystwyth Law school 'as a manifest failure financially', which ought in any case to be located at Cardiff. T. F. Roberts was convinced that this assault was inspired by Aberystwyth's inveterate enemy, Sir Marchant Williams, the old student who had turned sourly renegade years before.[17] Curiously enough, Williams had been present at the London meeting in February 1899 in favour of the foundation of the department; indeed, perhaps unwisely, since he had rarely shown anything other than hostility to his old College, Williams had been put on one of the committees formed in 1899 to organize support. In 1905 Williams, a restless intriguer never short of prescriptions for setting the world to rights, was pushing for all he was worth a scheme to reorganize the University of Wales; and at a meeting of the University Court he openly stated that the 'new régime' he was proposing would, if established, immediately 'suppress' the Aberystwyth Law school.[18]

However, the new department also had its friends. In North Wales F. Llywelyn Jones, an old student, an influential solicitor with a wide acquaintance, worked hard to drum up support. Even more valuable was the assistance rendered by Daniel Lleufer Thomas, then a barrister on the South Wales circuit. Over a period of more than forty years Lleufer Thomas was one of the most resourceful and effective champions of the College. Despite frail health, he had an astonishing appetite for hard work, and he never spared himself in his efforts for Aberystwyth. He had been active on behalf of the Law school from the beginning. Thomas lived in Swansea at this time, and he was indefatigable in his efforts to persuade the Swansea Law Society to throw all its weight on the side of Aberystwyth.[19]

Principal Roberts was determined, despite present difficulties, to persevere; he was convinced, as he told Rendel, that, if only the Law department could surmount the current 'critical stage', it would 'become a source of strength not of weakness to the College'. And, as he insisted to a despairing meeting of the Court of Governors in October 1905:

The experience of the Law school only repeats that of several other departments of the

---

[17] See above, pp. 68–9.

[18] *Western Mail* (9 September 1905). T. F. Roberts to Rendel, 11 October 1905. N.L.W. MSS. 19442E, Rendel II, f. 115. Rendel advised Roberts not to lose heart: 'I would sow the seed again and again and abide in patience.' 14 October 1905. C.A. P (VB) 2. Marchant Williams' myopic opinion was that the Aberystwyth Law school was 'a foolish and expensive luxury'. Marchant Williams to J. Glyn Davies, 2 June 1905. N.L.W. J. Glyn Davies MSS. No. 7807.

[19] See his letters to T. F. Roberts, 10 July and 4 August 1905. C.A. P (VB) 5.

College, some of them now large and flourishing. By labour and patience in the initial stages . . . the way opens out step by step until a satisfactory solution is eventually attained.[20]

The worst, in fact, was now over. Lleufer Thomas and others had won over the Swansea Law Society which wholeheartedly backed an application from the College for a grant of £200 from the Law Society. Soon afterwards the Chester and North Wales Law Society also endorsed the application. The Council of the Law Society responded handsomely. On the initiative of Principal Edward Jenks, a grant of £250 (subsequently increased) was made to Aberystwyth which promised, in return, to extend its teaching work for articled clerks, and to continue to raise itself a sum of £250 a year for the support of the department.[21]

Not long afterwards, in December 1906, Jethro Brown, 'with great reluctance', as he wrote to T. F. Roberts, resigned his chair to take up an appointment in Australia, his homeland. He felt able to do so because he was convinced that 'the cause of legal education in Wales' was 'now assured'. The Principal regarded the loss of Brown, 'an able and gifted teacher' as a 'calamity', but his resignation did at least ease the financial difficulties of the department.[22] Despite obstructive tactics by Marchant Williams, who was infuriated by Aberystwyth's monopoly of university Law teaching in Wales, a few years later a Board of Legal Education for Wales was established and the Aberystwyth Law school was set on the high road to prosperity.[23] T. A. Levi, with the aid of a succession of talented young assistants, beginning in 1907 with Clement Davies, the future Leader of the Liberal party, built up a first-rate Law school which turned out an endless stream of able graduates who subsequently went on, many of them via Cambridge, to careers of great distinction in the legal profession. T. F. Roberts had been right: the Law department became and remained one of Aberystwyth's greatest strengths.

The struggle to establish the new Law department was, of course, only one of the College's major concerns at this time. Indeed, concurrently there was the great, and even more important, tug-of-war with Cardiff over the location of the proposed National Library of Wales. In this instance, however, despite a plausible Cardiff case, from the beginning Aberystwyth had certain advantages which, in the end, proved decisive. This is not the place for a full-scale account of the

[20] T. F. Roberts to Rendel, 11 October 1905. N.L.W. MSS. 19442E, Rendel II, f. 115. *Minutes of the Court of Governors*, 27 October 1905, p. 654.

[21] 'Application to the . . . Law Society', September 1905. C.A. P (VB) 5. Lleufer Thomas to T. F. Roberts, 27 September 1906. U.C.W. G. Lib. History File. T. A. Levi, 'The Faculty of Law'. U.C.W. Law department papers. 'The Law department', 1905–6. N.L.W. MSS. 19440E, Rendel I, f. 118.

[22] Jethro Brown to T. F. Roberts, 5 and 17 December 1906. C.A. P (VB) 5. T. F. Roberts to Rendel, 11 October 1905. N.L.W. MSS. 19442E, Rendel II, f. 115.

[23] Lleufer Thomas to T. F. Roberts, 7 November 1909. C.A. P (VB) 5. Marchant Williams to J. Glyn Davies, 10 February 1910. N.L.W. J. Glyn Davies MSS. No. 7886.

foundation of the National Library, but it is obvious that its ultimate establishment in Aberystwyth was an enormous accretion of strength to the College as a centre of higher learning. Moreover, it should not be forgotten that, as in the case of university education in Wales, nearly all the early running in favour of a Welsh national library had been made by the Aberystwyth College.

As far back as 30 June 1873 the College had set up a committee to promote 'a National Welsh Library', and over the years considerable numbers of books relating to Wales had been collected. At first they were simply added to the general book-store of the College. It will be remembered that, in September 1896, the College Council had reorganized and strengthened its Welsh Library committee and, in the following year, Sir John Williams had promised, in due course, to hand over his very large collection of books and manuscripts to the College, provided a suitable site for a building was made available. Lord Rendel's purchase of the Grogythan land on Penglais seemed to answer Sir John Williams' stipulation.[24] In 1897 Principal Roberts issued a national appeal and, in response, a very large number of Welsh books and manuscripts arrived at the College, notably a particularly large contribution from the library of Principal T. C. Edwards. In October 1899 all this material was hived off to form a separate 'Welsh Library' at the College. And in the next three years, as money became available from an appeal launched by J. H. Davies, several important manuscript collections (those of *Gwallter Mechain* and the Revd. Owen Lewis, for example) were added to this, by now, considerable accumulation of Welsh material which was arranged by J. Glyn Davies, the Welsh Librarian, and housed, ultimately, in the so-called Oval Room of the College.[25]

During the 1890s Welsh M.P.s began to demand in the House of Commons that Wales should receive its due share of money allocated for national museums. The lead was taken by J. Herbert Lewis, who was returned as Liberal M.P. for Flint in 1892. Lewis' interest in this subject, unremitting from first to last until final success was achieved, had been fired by a conversation with T. E. Ellis in 1891. It was this discussion, followed by a letter from Ellis detailing the handsome grants for museum and library purposes enjoyed by Scotland and Ireland, that made Herbert Lewis, as he said, 'resolve to agitate in and out of Parliament, for the acquisition by Wales of a due share of the Treasury grants to National Libraries and Museums in the United Kingdom'.[26] Undeterred by the opposition of certain English M.P.s, who ridiculed the notion that Wales had a separate identity any more than the regions or counties of England, Herbert Lewis returned to the

[24] See above, pp. 126–7.

[25] 'The Welsh Library at Aberystwyth', by 'Philip Sydney'. U.C.W. G. Lib. 1155 (1). Manuscripts were stored in a special strongroom in the basement of the College.

[26] T. E. Ellis to J. Herbert Lewis, 28 May (1891). N.L.W. T. E. Ellis MSS. 2886A. The quotation is taken from Lewis' endorsement of the letter.

charge time and time again.[27] In this, as in so many other Welsh causes since 1870 involving a demand for Treasury money, a 'Chinese-like perseverance' was required to wear down official resistance.[28]

Meantime, there were other difficulties to be faced. Naturally enough, Cardiff made a powerful claim for the projected Welsh library as well as the museum: a site in Cathays Park was available. There was a promise of money from the rates for maintenance, and Cardiff, too, had been collecting Welsh books and manuscripts for some time. Moreover, as T. F. Roberts noted with some alarm, several Welsh Liberal M.P.s were 'impressed with the idea of recognizing Cardiff as capital of Wales', and, 'on that ground', were 'disposed to accept without demur' a Treasury declaration that the government would insist that any money given for a museum and a library must go to one centre only.[29] By May 1903 Herbert Lewis thought it was 'almost inevitable' that the museum would go to Cardiff, but he was prepared to fight hard to get the library for Aberystwyth.[30]

Despite Cardiff's apparently overwhelming advantages, Aberystwyth, which made no claim for the museum, had powerful arguments in its favour as the home of the library. But some careful manœuvring was necessary to make the Aberystwyth case decisively apparent. One strong objection which had to be overcome was the argument, put forward forcefully and repeatedly by Cardiff's champions, that the so-called Welsh library movement 'was a device for the exploitation' of government grants in the narrow interest of Aberystwyth College. This was an all too plausible charge: Aberystwyth's claim rested, initially, upon the pioneer work of the College Welsh Library Committee, the existence of the College Welsh library, the promises made of important accessions to it, and an available site, owned by Lord Rendel, leased to the College. As early as March 1901 the more acute members of the College committee had come to see that it was vital to put Aberystwyth's claim 'on a national' rather than 'a sectional or local basis'. Sir John Williams, Gwenogfryn Evans, and J. H. Davies particularly urged this course. T. F. Roberts, in his report to Rendel, made it clear that there was 'no lack of zeal for the College in those who favour the broader basis', it was simply that, as a matter of tactics, this seemed the best, perhaps only, way of attaining the main object: 'a great Welsh Library at Aberystwyth'.[31]

Over the next three years or so, T. F. Roberts had to walk carefully on the thinnest ice. Aberystwyth's claim rested, in part, on the availability of a magnificent site for the proposed library. But that site was owned by Rendel, and, for some time, it was by no means clear that he would be prepared to hand over his

[27] Lewis' parliamentary crusade on this subject is detailed in Thomas Parry, 'Herbert Lewis a'r Llyfrgell Genedlaethol', in *Syr Herbert Lewis, 1858–1933* (ed. K. Idwal Jones, Cardiff, 1958) pp. 57–78.
[28] 'The Welsh National Library', *The Dragon*, xxvii. 223.
[29] T. F. Roberts to Rendel, no date (1904). N.L.W. MSS. 19443E, Rendel II, f. 206.
[30] J. Herbert Lewis to T. F. Roberts, 14 May 1903. U.C.W. G. Lib. History File.
[31] T. F. Roberts to Rendel, 6 March 1901. N.L.W. MSS. 19441E, Rendel II, f. 36a–e.

land if the Aberystwyth library project ceased to be exclusively a College concern, as it had been hitherto. The fact was that Rendel had now to endure periodic bouts of ill health, prolonged and sharpened by an inveterate hypochondria. His active political life had been marked by a remarkable self-effacement.[32] But now, in retirement, he became, as he himself admitted, 'captious, caustic', absurdly touchy about minor points of precedence, and ready to cavil at any proposal which involved a compromise (even necessary, sensible compromise) with political opponents. Rendel had evidently, quite wrongly, come to the conclusion that his political career had been a failure, and, brooding endlessly on the past, it was difficult to persuade him to rise above petulance.[33]

Principal Roberts had inexhaustible patience, and continued to handle the President delicately: 'Your touch is the gentlest I have ever experienced', Rendel wrote to him on one occasion, 'and a letter from you is always healing.'[34] Roberts continued the emollient treatment over a period of years. He agreed with Rendel that it was 'not . . . agreeable altogether to flesh and blood' for the College, after its pioneer efforts, to have to hand over the assets it had so painfully collected to a national body, which it would not be able to control. But, as he insisted time and time again, the important thing was 'to succeed in getting the Library at Aberystwyth', for this would give 'the substance', even if 'the name of possession' had to be forfeited.[35] Finally, Roberts' kid-glove methods paid off: Rendel made over his site (indeed, he allowed it to be said that, if necessary, all fourteen Grogythan acres were available for the Library), he agreed to buy some additional land at Cae'rgog giving a much more direct access to the site, and he made a handsome donation to the building fund.

The availability of a site for a library building at Aberystwyth had been vital, but this was, of course, matched by Cardiff. The decisive factor which tipped the balance was the immeasurably superior quantity and quality of the manuscript collections already in, or exclusively promised to, Aberystwyth. Here, Sir John Williams' attitude was the crucial consideration. Happily for Aberystwyth, Sir John's 'whole heart' was 'enlisted in the advancement of the College'; moreover, he was scornful of Cardiff's 'mongrel and non-Welsh population'.[36] Over a period of years he had continued to add to his enormous private library of books and manuscripts and, ultimately, after a long and exasperating negotiation, he had completed, at very great expense, the purchase of the great Peniarth manuscript

<hr>

[32] K. O. Morgan, op. cit., p. 142.

[33] Rendel to T. F. Roberts, 1 March, 17 April, 14 June 1905. N.L.W. MSS. 19442E, Rendel II, ff. 96–7, 98a, 107.

[34] Rendel to T. F. Roberts, 3 September 1903. N.L.W. MSS. Ibid., f. 68.

[35] T. F. Roberts to Rendel, 25 May 1904. N.L.W. MSS. Ibid., f. 77. T. F. Roberts to J. H. Davies, 11 May 1904. N.L.W. J. H. Davies MSS. (Corr.).

[36] T. F. Roberts to Rendel, no date (1904). N.L.W. MSS. 19443E, Rendel II, f. 206. Sir John Williams to J. H. Davies, 12 May 1904, and 28 February 1905. N.L.W. J. H. Davies MSS. (Corr.).

collection which, along with the rest, was promised exclusively to a library at Aberystwyth. And second only to Sir John Williams' library was that of J. H. Davies, also promised exclusively to Aberystwyth.[37]

Eventually, when a grudging government had been persuaded by Herbert Lewis and others to give Wales a museum and library grant, the question of location went to arbitration. Aberystwyth's case was written up by Lleufer Thomas, who refused to accept payment for a mountain of professional work.[38] The National Museum went to Cardiff, and the National Library to Aberystwyth. The Treasury had been brought to accept the logic of the situation. 'There appears [said a departmental memorandum for the Chancellor of the Exchequer] to be no inherent reason why the Museum and the Library should be on the same site and under the same management.'

The brief went on to argue that, while the Museum must be in a great centre of population, the National Library, which would be primarily a research library, need not be. In any case, 'whether it [the National Library] is established there or not, there is no doubt that Aberystwyth will have in the near future much the finest library in Wales'.[39] Further wrangles with the Treasury over maintenance and building grants lay ahead, and several years elapsed before the National Library of Wales at Aberystwyth was properly established in its ultimate magnificent home. However, in 1909 the Library came into temporary makeshift existence in the Assembly Rooms (later the Students' Union) in Aberystwyth. At any rate, as T. F. Roberts had written in anticipation, this success was a tremendous 'stride towards making Aberystwyth the great Welsh seat of learning, investigation and intellectual influence', that he and others had striven for years to achieve.[40]

The sharp rivalry between the Aberystwyth and Cardiff Colleges was perhaps inevitable in the circumstances of a federal university, and it was sometimes conducted in unedifying terms. Even Marchant Williams, who revelled in hard-hitting controversy and whose instincts were scarcely conciliatory ('I am more than a match for the whole crew', was a typical combative comment), could legitimately deplore,

the want of unity between Aberystwyth and Cardiff. Some people here are jealous and suspicious of any suggestion that comes from Aberystwyth, and some people at

[37] See the letters of Sir John Williams, J. H. Davies, and T. E. Ellis in N.L.W. Timothy Lewis MSS. Evan Evans to J. H. Davies, 10 May 1904. N.L.W. J. H. Davies MSS. (Corr.). Gwenogfryn Evans to J. H. Davies, 10 May 1904. N.L.W. Cwrt Mawr MSS. (T. I. Ellis donation 1958/62).

[38] Letters between Lleufer Thomas and J. H. Davies, 20 and 22 December 1905. N.L.W. Lleufer Thomas MSS. IA.

[39] Memorandum for Sir William Anson, for transmission to the Chancellor of the Exchequer, no date (1905). P.R.O. Ed 39/974, U 1903. 'Aberystwyth', added the Memorandum, 'has the greatest hold of any of the Welsh Colleges on the affections of the people.'

[40] T. F. Roberts to Rendel, 26 February 1905. N.L.W. MSS. 19442E, Rendel II, f. 95.

Aberystwyth distrust every Cardiffian. This is very foolish and very detrimental to the interests of the country.[41]

When in 1902 the question of the final location of the University office came up for decision, Aberystwyth and Cardiff were again, predictably, in open conflict. Unable to reach agreement in 1897, the University Court had postponed the final decision for five years and, in the meantime for that period, the office was placed at Brecon, for no better reason, as Viriamu Jones bitterly remarked, than the fact that 'it was equally inconvenient for all three Colleges'.[42] This time municipal money-bags turned the scale. Cardiff corporation offered a free site in Cathays Park and a gift of £6,000 towards building costs. At the end of May 1902, at a meeting at Shrewsbury, the University Court received deputations from Wrexham, Swansea, Machynlleth, Welshpool, and Llandrindod Wells (which based its case, mainly, on its 'very low death-rate') as well as from Cardiff. The ensuing debate became acrimonious, and the Aberystwyth representatives fought hard to defeat a proposal in favour of Cardiff. R. D. Roberts made a typical fighting speech, even the normally mild-mannered Humphreys-Owen referred sharply to the 'insensible aggrandisement' of the South Wales College, and insisted that the consequence would be that Aberystwyth and Bangor would inevitably become 'humble satellites in the company of Cardiff'. T. F. Roberts, who was currently Vice-Chancellor, spoke in similar exaggerated terms.[43]

Principal Reichel of Bangor had tried beforehand to persuade Roberts that the Aberystwyth suggestion that the University office should circulate with the Vice-Chancellorship was simply not feasible. Reichel argued that Aberystwyth's national title was one guarantee that the public would not confuse the Cardiff College with the University. The Bangor Principal was in favour of accepting Cardiff's generous offer mainly, as he said, on grounds of academic convenience. But he was also seriously alarmed that, if the offer were rejected, it would be taken by the Cardiff people (already 'sore' over previous disappointments in 1896 and 1897) as 'proof of a settled unfriendliness' towards them, and this would 'give a dangerous impetus to the secessionist forces' which were undoubtedly at work there. If Cardiff seceded, a federal University of Wales consisting merely of Aberystwyth and Bangor 'would be as unsatisfactory as a committee of two persons'. Reichel insisted that he was not proposing paying Danegeld: on the contrary, it would be 'wise and politic' to accept the Cardiff offer, and thereby to strengthen the existing higher academic unity of Wales.[44]

At the Shrewsbury meeting of the University Court, Reichel and the Bangor

---

[41] Marchant Williams to J. Glyn Davies, 15 April and 18 December 1905. N.L.W. J. Glyn Davies MSS. Nos. 7802, 7817.

[42] See above, pp. 120–1. H. R. Reichel to T. F. Roberts, 28 May 1902. U.C.W. G. Lib. History File.

[43] The debate is fully reported in the *Cambrian News* (5 June 1902).

[44] Reichel to Roberts, 28 May 1902. U.C.W. G. Lib. History File.

representatives 'went strongly for Cardiff' and, to T. F. Roberts' intense disgust, that 'settled the matter'. Roberts and his Aberystwyth colleagues had been absurdly wrong-headed about the whole affair. The Principal gloomily determined to 'redouble' his efforts to make sure that Aberystwyth did 'not suffer' as a consequence of the decision. In fact, this was quite unnecessary: the University office (or Registry, as it was called) was established separately in Cardiff and this in no way, then or subsequently, altered the status of any of the constituent colleges of the University.[45]

Soon after the new University Registry was opened, Ivor James, who had been University Registrar since the beginning, retired. T. F. Roberts strongly supported the candidature of J. M. Angus, who had been a professor at Aberystwyth for thirty years. Angus (a thorough gentleman, in the opinion of a succession of student generations at Aberystwyth) had executive gifts of a high order; he had been Secretary of the University Senate for years and commanded widespread trust and admiration. Reichel and the Bangor representatives were prepared to support Angus warmly, but Reichel pointed out that there might be some opposition because Angus was not Welsh and was already in his fifties. Reichel suggested that Aberystwyth and Bangor ought to agree on several candidates because Angus was an academic and Reichel feared the hostility on the University Court of certain laymen, 'a small knot of wire-pullers and anti-academical fanatics who would vote against the angel Gabriel if he had ever occupied a chair in a Welsh university college'.[46] In the event, however, Angus was elected without trouble and gave excellent service as University Registrar for the next seventeen years.[47]

T. F. Roberts was delighted with Angus' appointment, not least because it would lead to increased efficiency at the Registry and reduce considerably the load of routine business devolving on whichever Principal was currently serving as Vice-Chancellor of the University.[48] Moreover, there was another consideration. In 1904 Sir Isambard Owen, Senior Deputy Chancellor of the University, had become Principal of Armstrong College, Newcastle-upon-Tyne. Sir Marchant Williams soon afterwards launched a campaign to reform the machinery of the University of Wales. Williams argued that the system of a rotating Vice-Chancellorship was hopelessly inefficient and that an effective paid 'working head', variously described as Rector or Dean or Principal, was essential to prevent the

[45] T. F. Roberts to Rendel, 2 June 1902. N.L.W. MSS. 19441E, Rendel II, f. 52. The *Welsh Gazette* (5 June 1902), a relatively new Aberystwyth newspaper, sourly commented that the decision in favour of Cardiff was a victory for 'jumboism', the triumph of 'whatsoever things are big'.

[46] T. F. Roberts to Rendel, 15 August 1905. N.L.W. MSS. 19442E, Rendel II, f. 110. Reichel to T. F. Roberts, 16 October 1905. U.C.W. G. Lib. History File.

[47] Angus died in 1945 at the age of ninety-five. At Aberystwyth he was known as 'Daddy Angus'; he had been prominent in all social and athletic activities, and it was he who introduced the famous song 'Nicodemus' to Aberystwyth and sang it for years at College soirées.

[48] T. F. Roberts to Rendel, 11 October 1905. N.L.W. MSS. 19442E, Rendel II, f. 115.

University from breaking up. On the face of it, Marchant Williams' case was not without its point. He instanced the difficulties that could arise from a situation in which the Vice-Chancellor was, say, at Bangor or Aberystwyth, the Registrar at Cardiff, and the unpaid, part-time head of the University was marooned far away to the north in Newcastle, where he was saddled with full-time duties as Principal of another college.[49] Williams was also convinced that the secessionist ambition at Cardiff was dangerously powerful: 'If the Aberystwyth people did but know how they are plotted against here by [Principal E. H.] Griffiths and company [he wrote]. These people want a University for Cardiff at all costs.'[50] Williams claimed that his scheme for a powerful 'working head' would be 'a permanent obstacle' to the disruption of the University. There is little doubt, too, that Marchant Williams was moved by a strong personal hostility to Isambard Owen, 'the old fox', as he called him.[51]

Marchant Williams' scheme of reform would have involved, as he himself admitted, a fundamental change in the University of Wales. Ebullient and aggressive to the last, he was scarcely the man to direct so delicate an operation. He vitiated his case by absurd exaggeration, and seemed to go out of his way needlessly to make enemies; sooner or later everybody else, in his version, was out of step.[52]

In one respect he had achieved the impossible: he drove the three Principals, whose relations at this time rarely rose above polite hostility, to stand shoulder to shoulder.[53] T. F. Roberts was thoroughly alarmed by Williams' proposals, which, in the Principal's opinion, threatened the 'freedom, independence and equality' of the constituent colleges. Roberts also thought that a 'working head' of the University would almost certainly be based at Cardiff, and this would give the South Wales College 'a preponderance' which would be disastrous. Marchant Williams' scheme stood very little chance of acceptance. The three Colleges opposed it resolutely and, apart from a reorganization of the University Registrar's duties

[49] Marchant Williams, 'The University of Wales'. P.R.O. Ed 24/571. *Western Mail* (7 and 9 June 1905).

[50] Marchant Williams to J. Glyn Davies, 15 April 1905. N.L.W. J. Glyn Davies MSS. no. 7802.

[51] Marchant Williams to J. Glyn Davies, 2 May and 18 June 1905, 11 May 1908. N.L.W. Ibid., nos. 7803, 7808, and 7864. See also, G. A. Jones, op. cit., pp. 157–64.

[52] Each of the Colleges, in turn, came under his lash:
'These Bangor folk must be watched and, if necessary,
preyed upon. To pray *for* them is quite hopeless.'
'I have . . . decided upon having nothing whatever to
do with the Aberystwyth College, *qua* College, ever again.'
'The College at Cardiff, believe me, is in a rotten state,
and I sometimes wish I had nothing to do with it.'
Marchant Williams to J. Glyn Davies, 12 September and 17 October 1905, 30 September 1907, N.L.W. J. Glyn Davies MSS. nos. 7809, 7812, and 7850.

[53] 'In the presence of the common enemy', Williams wrote, 'the three have become chums.' 17 October 1905. N.L.W. Ibid., no. 7812.

(in which Angus' capacity to cope with an additional work load was a factor), nothing further was done.[54]

In 1905 there was also a change in the Registrarship of the College at Aberystwyth; Mortimer Green, who had been ill for some time, resigned. There was some talk that Lleufer Thomas was interested in the appointment, and D. R. Daniel, who had never held a post fully commensurate with his very considerable talents, was strongly urged by O. M. Edwards to apply.[55] In the end Daniel did not apply: he came to the conclusion that he stood no chance, not least because J. H. Davies was desperately keen to return to Aberystwyth to serve his old College. O. M. Edwards was delighted with this news; he thought that, if J. H. Davies were appointed, 'it would be the best thing that has happened to Aberystwyth for many a long year'.[56] Principal Roberts, although he recognized J. H. Davies' great qualities, especially his vigour and shrewdness, wondered whether Davies had a strong enough taste for routine executive duties. In this, as in so much else, the Principal sought Rendel's advice. The President thought that the new Registrar ought to be a Welsh-speaking Welshman, preferably one devoid of 'platform qualities' which he distrusted. 'If you can find a Saxon head with a Welsh heart', said Rendel, 'he is your man.' Ultimately, Rendel came to the conclusion that J. H. Davies' candidature was overwhelmingly strong; and the appointing committee was of the same opinion. Davies won a clear majority over his three rivals on the first vote.[57]

Hitherto at Aberystwyth the Registrar had never been much more than a more or less efficient chief clerk. J. H. Davies transformed the position. He had always been interested in a wide range of public activities; he continued and extended these extra-mural duties, acting as the accredited representative of the College. And within the College Davies' influence steadily increased until ultimately, when T. F. Roberts' health began seriously to fail, the Registrar operated virtually as the Principal's deputy.[58]

Just before J. H. Davies joined the staff, another great Aberystwyth personality resigned. For some time Miss Carpenter had wanted to retire; as she said, at

[54] T. F. Roberts to Rendel, 11 October 1905. N.L.W. MSS. 19442E, Rendel II, f. 115. In October Henry Jones, specially imported for the purpose, largely demolished the case for a 'working head' of the University in a lecture at Cardiff. *The University of Wales: the Line of its Growth*, especially pp. 14–33.

[55] Marchant Williams to J. Glyn Davies, 28 March 1905. N.L.W. J. Glyn Davies MSS. no. 7801. O. M. Edwards to D. R. Daniel, 13 and 25 March 1905. N.L.W. D. R. Daniel MSS. nos. 1036, 1037.

[56] O. M. Edwards to J. H. Davies, 10 April 1905. N.L.W. J. H. Davies MSS. (Corr.). J. H. Davies to Gwenogfryn Evans, 5 June 1905. N.L.W. Timothy Lewis MSS.

[57] T. F. Roberts to Rendel, no date (1905), and 30 May 1905. N.L.W. MSS. 19442E, Rendel II, ff. 101, 205. Rendel to T. F. Roberts, 12 and 23 May 1905. C.A. P (VB) 4.

[58] Mortimer Green's status is made clear in J. Glyn Davies' endorsement of a letter from Green, 3 March 1904. N.L.W. J. Glyn Davies MSS. no. 8146. For J. H. Davies' Registrarship, see T. I. Ellis, *John Humphreys Davies, 1871–1926* (Liverpool, 1963), pp. 88–131.

seventy years of age 'even the grasshopper is a burden'. She had come to the conclusion that a difference of nearly fifty years between students and Lady Principal was far too great to be bridged effectively. Things, so far as women students were concerned, had changed radically during Miss Carpenter's tenure of twenty years. Young women came up to College with a confidence and an assurance that would have shocked their grandparents: 'The flood has not carried me away', said Miss Carpenter, 'but I am getting rather breathless, and it is time I retired.'[59] It is evident that, for most of the time, Miss Carpenter managed her large hall with marvellous economy; her concern for the well-being of her students was endless. There is not much evidence that she was beloved by her students, but it is clear that, over a period of twenty years and more, she achieved something much more important: she won and retained the respect of men and women students. She had an unmistakable air of authority, but she was not overbearing and never devoid of humour. Lord Rendel, in a superb letter, expressing the gratitude of the College, recognized that Miss Carpenter could never be replaced; her resignation marked the passing of an age. Her successor would inevitably be different.[60]

It is clear that, without prejudice to the genuine admiration felt for Miss Carpenter, the senior authorities of the College believed that her resignation afforded the opportunity for changing and, as they thought, raising the tone of Alexandra Hall. There were two outstanding candidates for the post of Warden (as the Lady Principal now came to be known): Miss A. M. Dobell, an old student, and Miss H. M. Stephen, daughter of a distinguished Judge and niece of the celebrated Leslie Stephen. Rendel and Humphreys-Owen, products of Oxbridge, were immensely attracted by the potentialities represented by Miss Stephen. Highly educated and widely cultured, she would open up all sorts of intellectual possibilities for women students, especially the particularly able ones.

We need not be provincial because we are Welsh [said Rendel]. . . . We must, if we can, touch the level of the older universities. This is a great opportunity of raising the whole tone and level and standing of the women's side of the College.[61]

Professor C. H. Herford, formerly at Aberystwyth then at Manchester, where Miss Stephen was currently working, sounded a warning note. He thought that Miss Stephen, for all her undoubted qualities, was too unbendingly upper middle-class and not spontaneously forthcoming enough to succeed with Aberystwyth students, especially the Welsh girls.[62] Miss Stephen was appointed, but events soon suggested that Herford was not altogether wide of the mark.

[59] Miss Carpenter to T. F. Roberts, 28 December 1904. C.A. P (VB) 4. Miss Carpenter to Rendel, 1 February 1905. N.L.W. MSS. 19440E, Rendel I, f. 71.
[60] Marsh, passim. H. J. Fleure, 'An Old Student looks at the College', *Trans. Cymm.* (1955), p. 58. *Council Minutes* (24 February 1905), pp. 569–70. Rendel to Miss Carpenter, 11 May (1905). N.L.W. MSS. 19440E, Rendel I, f. 106.
[61] Humphreys-Owen to T. F. Roberts, 25 May 1905, Rendel to T. F. Roberts, 23 May 1905. C.A. P (VB) 4.   [62] C. H. Herford to T. F. Roberts, 3 and 24 May 1905. Ibid.

In 1906, in order to strengthen the academic side of Alexandra Hall, a tutor (Miss Lindsell of Newnham College, Cambridge) for first-year women students was appointed. The College was doing its modest best, as the Principal said later, to place the Warden, '*de facto* as well as *de jure*, in the position of a Head of a large women's [sic] College'. Miss Stephen faced the daunting task of getting to know, as quickly as possible, the two hundred women students in her care. She was confident that things were going well. Inevitably in so large an establishment, there were difficulties and rivalries not always easily contained: there was some hostility between 'two mutually exclusive camps, one Church the other Nonconformist'; professionally the Hall staff were excellent, but they were all English and occasionally there appeared to be a lack of sympathy between some of them and the large contingent of Welsh students.[63]

However, these or similar problems are perennially present in any large residential community, and no doubt patience and goodwill could in time in normal circumstances have reduced their divisive effects. Indeed, Alexandra Hall already possessed the machinery for regular joint ameliorative consultation between staff and students. Poor Miss Stephen, however, was decidedly unlucky: times had changed. During the greater part of her tenure Miss Carpenter had exercised unchallenged authority in the Hall; her decisions had never been seriously questioned by the students, and had always been ratified by the Senate, which 'acted as a steam-roller to enforce them'. There had been a Student Hall Council in Miss Carpenter's time and, after the turn of the century, there were signs that its members were becoming increasingly restive under the constraints of a traditional and rather old-fashioned code of discipline. It was this new spirit, as much as anything, that had persuaded Miss Carpenter that it was high time for her to go. There was during these years a general unrest in the British student world; one degree ceremony at Aberystwyth ended in a disorderly shambles. And at a time when Mrs. Pankhurst and her suffragist supporters were challenging the assumptions of former centuries in the most direct and provocative way, it is not surprising that the temper of women students, even in unsophisticated Aberystwyth, should be strongly militant.[64]

In 1906 Miss Stephen had insisted on limiting the right of male escort of women students to and from social events. There was an unfortunate minor scandal, involving allegations of theft (dismissed by the court) by a woman student, in which Miss Stephen took up a stiff-necked attitude that required all of Rendel's persuasive skill to overcome. During 1907 relations between staff and students in Alexandra Hall steadily deteriorated. The students, who were convinced that

[63] Miss Stephen to T. F. Roberts, 14 August 1906. T. F. Roberts to Rendel, 7 January 1908. C.A. P (VB) 4.

[64] T. F. Roberts to Rendel, 9 January 1908. Ibid., Miss A. Kimpster to J. H. Davies, 9 December 1907. N.L.W. J. H. Davies MSS. (Corr.).

they had legitimate grievances, had discovered a determined leader in Miss Olive Wheeler, a spirited young woman of marked ability. Ultimately, in December 1907, the students addressed to the Senate and the College Council a long catalogue of complaints regarding food and services in Hall, which included an assertion that the Warden was demonstrably out of sympathy with them. The Council instituted a detailed investigation which, in fact, dismissed most of the complaints as either trivial or the consequence of necessary economies (towards the end Miss Carpenter's housekeeping had been rather less successful).[65]

The so-called Alexandra Hall 'revolt' of 1907 has an interest that goes beyond questions of the number and quality of eggs provided for breakfast. The fact is that two different conceptions of the Hall were at issue. Miss Stephen had been imported to make it a collegiate hall where academic values were given considerably greater prominence than hitherto. The students seemed to prefer to have a Warden, as Rendel said, who was 'little more than a lodging house-keeper'. Principal Roberts admitted later that the College had made a mistake in not telling the students 'plainly' of the changes envisaged.[66] In any event, it would have taken some time (several years very likely) to achieve any significant alteration in the quality of Hall life. As it was, the attempt unluckily coincided with an upsurge in student militancy, itself engendered in part by traditionalist conservative official codes too long left unreformed.

Something was gained from the episode: the College Council re-stated, more clearly than ever before, the official version of the status and authority of a Warden, and certain new procedures for a more rapid consideration of grievances were instituted. The Principal also suggested the appointment of a committee to which the Warden could turn for consultation and advice when necessary; this was the first glimmer of the future Hostels' Sub-Committee of the College.[67] But there is little doubt that the 'revolt' slowed down the modestly ambitious attempt to strengthen the academic side of Hall life. This called for an exceptionally gifted Warden with a rare combination of qualities. Miss Stephen had considerable intellectual ability, but she was handicapped by a reserved manner that conveyed an impression of aloofness that did not beget sympathy. Given time, and drawing as she did the right lessons from the recent episode, she might very well have succeeded in the end. Unfortunately, her health, never robust, deteriorated sharply

[65] Miss Wheeler to the Senate, December 1907, and 'Report of the Committee on Alexandra Hall'. C.A. P (VB) 4. *Council Minutes* (7 February 1908), pp. 219–22. Subsequently, Miss Wheeler became a distinguished professor of Education at University College, Cardiff, and a Dame of the British Empire.

[66] Rendel to T. F. Roberts, 25 January 1908. T. F. Roberts, Memorandum on Alexandra Hall (1908). C.A. P (VB) 4.

[67] *Council Minutes* (7 February 1908), pp. 219–22. T. F. Roberts to Rendel, 7 January 1908. C.A. P (VB) 4.

during 1908; on medical advice she had to resign and, sadly, died soon after-wards.[68]

1907, the year of the 'revolt', was not a time of unrelieved gloom and wholly adverse publicity in the history of the College. On the contrary, it was the year when the Chemistry department, one of the largest and most successful in the College, was rehoused in a magnificent and, for the time, ultra-modern large new laboratory. The fact was that the College had discovered fairy godparents at last: the breach with the Llandinam family had been repaired. It will be remembered that in 1886 David Davies had severed his connection with the College as a result of the treatment he had received at Aberystwyth during the general election campaign.[69] In 1890 David Davies died and in the following year his only son, Edward, a shy, retiring man, accepted an invitation to become joint Treasurer of the College, an office he continued to hold until his death in 1898 at the age of forty-five. The very large Llandinam fortune was now inherited by Edward's three children, the Misses Gwen and Margaret Davies, and their elder brother, named David after his grandfather.[70] Luckily for the College, Edward Davies' three children had also inherited the strong family tradition of public beneficence, and soon after David Davies came down from Cambridge, Aberystwyth began to reap great advantage from the renewed Llandinam interest in its fortunes.

By 1901 it was evident that additional space would have to be found for the Chemistry department, which had grown steadily during Snape's tenure of the chair. The first suggestion was that an additional storey should be added to the old College building, but the estimated cost (£5,000, or more) was beyond the resources of a Council already struggling to support the Law department, and striving might and main to raise money for the projected National Library building. Rendel suggested erecting a temporary zinc building on some waste land to the south of the Castle, but instead the Assembly Rooms (then, as subsequently, invaluable as a temporary hospice) were rented and equipped as a laboratory for the time being.[71]

This was one more illustration of the unsatisfactory shifts to which the College, in the continuing penury of its private endowment, was reduced. Without generous help from outside, the Chemistry and Agricultural departments, two obvious growth points, in which great hopes had always been placed, would have been stunted for the foreseeable future. However, in March 1903 David Davies and his two sisters and their stepmother offered £2,000 to build a new Chemistry

---

[68] T. F. Roberts to Rendel, 7 January 1908. Miss Stephen to T. F. Roberts, no date (1908). C.A. P (VB) 4. Miss K. Stephen to Rendel, 20 August 1908. N.L.W. MSS. 19440E, Rendel I, f. 101. Happily, Miss Stephen's last term at Aberystwyth 'was an easy and pleasant one'.   [69] See above, pp. 91–2.

[70] Sir Charles Tennyson, 'D.D. The Life of David Davies, first Lord Davies of Llandinam' (unpublished manuscript), i. 13–15.

[71] T. F. Roberts to Rendel, 5 and 9 May 1902. N.L.W. MSS. 19441E, Rendel II, ff. 47, 48. *Council Minutes* (24 October 1902), p. 226.

laboratory in memory of Edward Davies, who had always been keenly interested in scientific research. T. F. Roberts was overjoyed at this 'noble action' which, at one stroke, removed seemingly insuperable difficulties.[72]

There was a protracted debate over the siting of this important new building: in the first instance, four possibilities were considered. Some people thought it essential that the laboratory should be in close proximity to the College; the Nanteos family was asked to name its price for the land on which the Assembly Rooms and two houses in Laura Place stood, but the £5,000 demanded effectively ruled out that possibility. Alternatively, it was suggested that the laboratory should be erected on the strip of land reclaimed from the sea by the recent extension of the promenade, which lay between the College and the Castle. Ultimately, this site was rejected as too constricted.[73] The third proposal was to build on a waste site of five acres in Queen's Road (later used for the College Hall) which was available for about £2,500. Finally, there was, of course, Rendel's land at Grogythan on Penglais. There was much anxious comparison of distances: Grogythan, sixteen minutes away (with more practice, people walked faster seventy years ago), was considered by a Senate committee to be too far away, as it would rupture 'the close inter-connection' between the Chemistry department and its sister disciplines on the Science side. Queen's Road was only six minutes away, but the site itself was flat and unimpressive. Sir John Williams and David Davies favoured a root and branch decision in principle to move everything by stages to Grogythan.[74]

Subsequently, however, a site of about eleven acres on the *Buarth Mawr* was offered to the College for £2,500 by W. H. Colby, a member of the College Council. This was nearer than Grogythan, and larger and much more attractive than the Queen's Road land; indeed, at one time it was suggested that the Buarth would provide a suitably majestic site for the National Library. David Davies, for whom one scheme was the natural prelude to another, once he had been assured that the smoke and noise from the railway station would be no worse a hindrance to study than 'the continual beating of the waves' at the old College building, went strongly for the Buarth, not least because he had his eye on the nearby Vicarage Field for College athletics.[75]

[72] T. F. Roberts to Rendel, 4 March 1903. N.L.W. MSS. 19441E, Rendel II, f. 64. Humphreys-Owen to his wife, 16 February 1903. N.L.W. Glansevern MSS., not numbered. David Davies' Cambridge tutor had suggested a large contribution to the College Library, but T. F. Roberts successfully argued for the laboratory.

[73] T. F. Roberts to Rendel, 11 August, 16 October, and 12 December 1903, 6 February 1904. N.L.W. MSS. 19441E, Rendel II, ff. 67, 69, 72.

[74] Ibid., no date (1904). N.L.W. MSS. 19443E, Rendel II, f. 74. Report of Senate Committee, 10 June 1903. C.A. S/MN/1. David Davies to J. H. Davies, 26 January 1904. N.L.W. J. H. Davies MSS. (Corr.).

[75] T. F. Roberts to Rendel, 6 February 1904. N.L.W. MSS. 19441E, Rendel II, f. 74. David Davies to J. H. Davies, 31 January 1904. N.L.W. J. H. Davies MSS. (Corr.).

In 1901 Lloyd Snape had resigned and the chair of Chemistry had been filled by J. J. Sudborough, who had served the term of years in Germany on advanced research that seemed obligatory at this time for ambitious British chemists. Sudborough, assisted by T. Campbell James, an old student, who joined him in 1904, rapidly built up a strong research school at Aberystwyth. Sudborough carefully planned the new building, after a tour of inspection of the most modern laboratories in the country. In all, accommodation for over one hundred and twenty students, as well as private laboratories for the staff and postgraduate students, was provided.[76] On 1 November 1907 the magnificent Edward Davies Chemistry laboratory (which ultimately cost £23,000 to build) was opened by H. H. Asquith, the Chancellor of the Exchequer. He had asked to be briefed on the College by Lord Rendel, and the President, writing from the heart, replied that it was 'the foremost expression of the emancipation of Wales. Do not think me merely dithyrambic', said Rendel, 'I *feel* this way about the Aberystwyth College and all that it stands for to Wales.'[77]

A fortnight or so before this great Llandinam gift was formally opened, David Davies came forward with another generous offer which eased the College out of a pressing difficulty. The professor of History had pleaded for teaching assistance, but there was little hope that it could be provided, as the Principal wearily admitted, out of the existing 'scanty purse'.[78] David Davies was ready to endow a chair of Colonial History and, until that scheme of study was properly formulated, there would be no objection to the new professor assisting in the History school. David Davies aspired to be an independent politician on the model of his grandfather: he was strongly for Disestablishment in Wales, but, according to his stepmother, he had 'been got at' while at Cambridge by 'a clever, young New Zealander', G. Gray Russell, who had convinced him that British national survival depended upon the introduction of colonial tariff preferences, the policy currently being advocated so powerfully by Joseph Chamberlain.[79] There is little doubt that David Davies saw the chair of Colonial History at Aberystwyth as one means of educating his countrymen in the realities, as he saw them, of the contemporary world.

There was, however, one awkward difficulty about the proposed endowment. David Davies made one 'substantial stipulation': that he was to have 'virtual nomination' of the person to be appointed to the chair. As it happened, the man he had in mind was his former tutor at King's College, Cambridge, T. Stanley

[76] T. C. James and C. W. Davies, 'Schools of Chemistry ... The U.C.W.', loc. cit., pp. 570–1, list the main research achievements of the school and name an impressive number of gifted postgraduate students.

[77] Rendel to Asquith, 7 October 1907. N.L.W. MSS. 19440E, Rendel I, 91 (1–5).

[78] T. F. Roberts to Rendel, 17 October 1907. N.L.W. MSS. 19443E, Rendel II, f. 182.

[79] Humphreys-Owen to his wife, 23 March and 6 June 1904. N.L.W. Glansevern MSS., not numbered. Sir Charles Tennyson, op. cit., i. 23–6.

Roberts, a staunch and known champion of Disestablishment who was in the embarrassing position of having to teach Church History at St. David's College, Lampeter: the squarest of pegs in the roundest of holes. Everybody agreed that Stanley Roberts was a thoroughly worthy candidate, but Principal Roberts was clearly uneasy at the proposed breach of standard academic practice in appointments. His letter to Rendel reporting the offer had a strongly defensive note and included a good deal of special pleading. As a way out of the dilemma, it had been suggested that a subcommittee consisting of David Davies, the Principal and the chairman of the Finance Committee should recommend a fit person for the chair to the next meeting of the Council.[80] Rendel's reply was all worldly wisdom: 'the case', he said, 'is quite simple. Mr. Davies happens to know the very man for the appointment. Why should he not know the very man?' All the same Rendel thought the stipulation 'very undesirable', and hoped it would not 'reach any ears but ours', because it would certainly lead to hostile criticism. David Davies accepted the uneasy compromise proposed and the subcommittee accepted Stanley Roberts, who was appointed to the new chair in October 1907.[81]

This appointment is of particular interest because, in some respects, it anticipates in miniature a much greater controversy later, in which David Davies was centrally concerned, involving a clash of diametrically opposed opinions on the basic purposes of academic appointments. However, these difficulties aside, the College again had cause to be grateful to Llandinam munificence. And in no time at all David Davies, this time in company with his sisters, made an even more generous proposal of assistance.

Some people connected with the College had never ceased to lament the fact that, as a result of the great fire of 1885, the residential system, which had played so important a part in the life of the College in the early years, had had to be abandoned. Women students had Alexandra Hall, but all the men lived in lodgings, to the considerable regret of those who aspired to see Aberystwyth become a modest Welsh version of Oxford. In the summer of 1901 a start was made when No. 1 Marine Terrace, a substantial house adjoining the College, was leased and converted into a small hostel for men students, with the immensely popular professor 'Jimmy' Marshall as Warden.[82] In the following year there was a strong possibility that a house next door to the existing hostel, as well as the large Cambria Hotel (now the Theological College) would come on the market. These properties, too, it was thought, could be converted into halls for men. T. F. Roberts began to think again of help from Carnegie, but Rendel was not hopeful of success. He pointed out that Carnegie had already rejected his pleas

[80] T. F. Roberts to Rendel, 17 October 1907. N.L.W. MSS. 19443E, Rendel II, f. 182.
[81] Rendel to T. F. Roberts, 18 October 1907. C.A. P (VB) 2. *Council Minutes* (31 October 1907), p. 193.
[82] Ibid. (24 May 1901), pp. 52-3. U.C.W. *Magazine*, xxiv. 52-3.

twice: 'I fear', said the President, 'he will respect his own verdict as a good Catholic a Vatican decree.' In Rendel's opinion Carnegie was a man who admired strength and prosperity far more than he pitied 'weakness or adversity', and he was obviously immune to flattery. However, Rendel himself was prepared to advance the purchase price as a loan to the College at 3 per cent.[83]

In fact, nothing came of this. Rendel's financial assistance was required for other purposes with a higher College priority; and some few years later David Davies bought the Cambria Hotel, which was converted into the Theological College, a project strongly supported by T. F. Roberts who hoped it would lead to a concentration of dissenting colleges at Aberystwyth. However, the possibility of making Aberystwyth substantially a residential college continued to attract: 'I long to see the men's Collegiate domestic life set going', Rendel wrote in 1908.[84]

In the following year it seemed as if these dreams would, in part at least, be translated into reality and, inevitably, the magic wand was waved by David Davies. He came up with an astonishingly generous proposal. The Board of Education required that hostel accommodation should be provided for men students in the Training department. David Davies suggested that this should be combined with an ambitious scheme to provide residential accommodation in stages for, eventually, all men students. He and his sisters were prepared to give £8,000 to build a College hall sufficiently large to accommodate a high table for 50 professors and dining space for 300 students, together with suitable staff and student common rooms. Certain conditions were attached to the offer: he required that ordinary and Training department students should live in the same building; that the College would, at the outset, provide residential accommodation for at least one-third of its ordinary students. If after three years the scheme had succeeded and no financial loss had been incurred, the College was to undertake to provide accommodation for two-thirds of its men students, and three years later again, assuming the same conditions of success obtained, complete the scheme: the College would then be completely residential.[85]

It was a magnificently imaginative scheme. There is little doubt that, if it had been put into operation, it would have transformed the quality of university life in Aberystwyth, and may well have given the College an indisputable primacy among the Welsh colleges.[86] The initial reaction to the offer was, naturally, enthusiastic, and a subcommittee was appointed to collect information on

---

[83] Rendel to T. F. Roberts, 20 May 1902. C.A. P (VB) 2.

[84] Rendel to T. F. Roberts, 24 March 1908. Ibid.

[85] David Davies to T. F. Roberts, 17 June 1909. C.A. PC (4) 2. *Council Minutes* (18 June 1909), pp. 401–5. David Davies had the Buarth in mind as a suitable site. David Davies to J. H. Davies, 1 December 1909. N.L.W. J. H. Davies MSS. (T. I. Ellis donation, October 1965).

[86] It is fair to say that a motion in October 1909 in favour of residential life at the 'Lit. and Deb.' was carried by only 175 votes to 161, the large minority speaking up strongly for the educative virtues of the rigour of life in lodgings. *The Dragon*, xxxii. 39–41.

residential accommodation elsewhere. Somehow or other, however, in ways that are not altogether clear, the scheme dribbled away into the sand. To a limited extent the proposal envisaged some financial assistance from the seven county councils affiliated to the College; it is possible that, discouragingly, this was not forthcoming. There are some few subsequent references to the scheme in the deliberations of the Court, but eventually these peter out. By inference it would seem that, ultimately, the authorities came to the conclusion that they would be unable to comply with David Davies' stipulations. At any rate, in February 1910, the offer was withdrawn.[87] It is curious that Principal Roberts who, as he said in 1908, hoped 'to advance all along the line', and who had never been afraid of chancing his arm in financially risky adventures of great potential benefit to the College, did not follow up this great possibility.[88]

There is one possible explanation for this uncharacteristic inertia. Ever since the 1880s the three Welsh colleges had received an annual government grant of £4,000. Since that time the number of students had more than tripled, but the grant had remained unchanged. Moreover, it should be remembered that fees in Wales had always been kept deliberately low in order to assist students from humble homes who made up an astonishingly high proportion of the student body in the University. Certainly no university in England had anything like as many working-class students as the Welsh colleges. Beginning in 1889 some English provincial colleges had received government grants, and in 1904 Austen Chamberlain, Chancellor of the Exchequer, announced that he proposed to double these subsidies. By this time the Welsh colleges, despite the most frugal management, were in serious financial difficulties. Indeed, they were able to continue operations on the current scale only at the cost of mounting debts and the long-suffering willingness of their teaching staffs to accept stipends that were considerably lower than those paid to their English equivalents.

In March 1904 a deputation from the Welsh colleges met the Chancellor of the Exchequer to urge an increase in grants. As usual, the relative poverty of Wales formed the nub of the case for separate and, it was hoped, more generous treatment. Austen Chamberlain's answer was that, in his opinion, Wales already received preferential treatment; he advised the deputation to look to increased local aid and, failing that, to tighten their belts. He held out no immediate hope of increased grants.[89]

When the Liberal party returned overwhelmingly to power in December 1905 prospects seemed brighter but, in fact, a considerable campaign of attrition was

---

[87] *Minutes of the Court of Governers* (22 October 1909 and 7 January 1910), pp. 435, 456–7. Rendel to T. F. Roberts, 23 February 1910. C.A. P (VB) 2.

[88] T. F. Roberts to Rendel, 27 November 1908. N.L.W. MSS. 19443E, Rendel II, f. 194.

[89] 'Interview between the Chancellor of the Exchequer and the Deputation for the Welsh University Colleges', 3 March 1904. P.R.O. Ed 24/570.

necessary to wear down a stubborn Treasury resistance. The lead, on behalf of the Welsh colleges, was taken by Principal Reichel of Bangor, currently Vice-Chancellor, and invaluable assistance was rendered from within the ministry by J. Herbert Lewis, who had been made a government whip.[90] An attempt was made, first of all, to mobilize the support of Welsh M.P.s, and an impressive document was drawn up which showed that many of the financial difficulties of the Welsh colleges stemmed from the 'abnormal success' that had blessed their work. This document was given a wide circulation in Wales in order, as Reichel said, to generate sufficient 'political steam' for a national campaign to ensure ultimate success.[91]

At that point there was an alarming diversion: the Cardiff College half-decided to go it alone, to opt out from the Welsh application, and to ask that its grant should be determined by the same criteria (in which population and local income were especially important considerations) as grants to English colleges. Reichel regarded this as a 'betrayal' which sundered the united front hitherto presented by Wales to the Treasury and imperilled the whole future of Aberystwyth and Bangor. Eventually, with great difficulty, the Cardiff College was persuaded to hold off its bid for separate consideration for one year.[92]

In 1906 a new joint application for an increased grant was submitted to the Treasury, and soon afterwards the three Welsh colleges agreed to submit to a quinquennial inspection. Officials at the Board of Education admitted that Welsh grants were inadequate, but the Treasury insisted on an inquiry.[93] In July 1907 a small committee, under the chairmanship of Sir Thomas Raleigh, for no apparent reason heavily overloaded with Scots, was appointed to consider the educational quality and the financial needs of the University of Wales and its constituent colleges.[94] It could not be said that this was a notably sympathetic commission of inquiry. And yet, when the *Report* appeared a year later, it made no damaging criticisms and included a fair meed of praise. There was a 'very creditable output' of work of a genuine university standard; considering their heavy teaching duties, the research output of the staffs of the colleges was 'somewhat

---

[90] There is a very considerable correspondence on this subject in the Penucha MSS., the papers of Herbert Lewis.

[91] T. F. Roberts to all Welsh M.P.s, 13 February 1906. 'Treasury Grants to the Welsh University Colleges', 16 March 1906. Reichel to Herbert Lewis, 12 April 1906. Penucha MSS.

[92] Reichel to Herbert Lewis, 21 and 24 April 1906. Reichel to E. H. Griffiths, 21 April 1906 (copy). Penucha MSS. David Davies to T. F. Roberts, 15 May 1906. G. Lib. U.C.W. History File. It is fair to say that Marchant Williams, for once on the side of the angels, argued forcefully that the Welsh colleges should 'sink or swim together'. *Manchester Guardian* (28 April 1906).

[93] F. G. Ogilvie to the Secretary of the Board of Education, 2 March 1907. G. H. Murray of the Treasury to R. S. Morant, 6 May 1907. P.R.O. Ed 24/573. Asquith to Herbert Lewis (March 1907). Penucha MSS.

[94] 'Dear old Sir Thomas Raleigh and his Mac this and Mac that' as Marchant Williams, typically, put it later. *Western Mail* (19 July 1910).

remarkable'. All the colleges had been exceptionally successful in adding to the number of departments, but these developments had been made 'at the expense of the teaching staff', who were inadequately paid. The committee did not recommend any precise increase in grants (an excess of Scots ca' canny, perhaps), but the unmistakable implication of the committee's conclusions was in this direction.[95]

Despite this favourable endorsement by its own committee of investigation, the Treasury was in no hurry to act.[96] Principal Roberts was buoyed up by the hope that Lloyd George, who was now Chancellor of the Exchequer and had publicly promised to make 'a very substantial' Treasury contribution, would solve the financial problems of the University once and for all.[97] But the difficulty was that, quite apart from Treasury expertise in stonewalling, the Chancellor was involved in the early months of 1909 in highly charged political battles over naval estimates. Herbert Lewis had tried in vain for months to get Lloyd George to turn his attention to the University of Wales. Ultimately, these persuasions succeeded: Lloyd George 'with great courage and determination', as Herbert Lewis thought, demolished the objections of his officials and in March 1909 the annual Treasury grants to the Welsh colleges were slightly more than doubled.[98]

Ever since the first approach to the Treasury in 1904, T. F. Roberts had been filled with anxiety by the delays over increased grants, and it is possible that, for the moment at least, his nerve had failed him. And it may be that this explains his unusually limp response to David Davies' suggestion about residential accommodation. Nor could it be argued that a doubled Treasury grant significantly improved the College's ability to finance its part of Davies' scheme. Every penny of the additional grant was urgently needed for existing requirements and, indeed, the terms of the award expressly forbade expenditure from it on new developments.[99]

One department which was not helped directly by the increased government grant was the school of Agriculture. On paper this was separately financed by grants from the Board of Agriculture and subventions from the county councils. In fact, in recent years the Agricultural work of the College had been carried on at a substantial loss which added to the mounting deficit on the general account.[100] But at least it could be said in 1909 that the department itself was in good fettle. It had not always been so. During the 1890s Tom Parry, the lecturer in Agri-

[95] *Report of the Committee on the University of Wales and the Welsh University Colleges*, 25 June 1908.

[96] The *Western Mail* (13 October 1908) attacked the Welsh M.P.s for pusillanimity; they were sheep in sheep's clothing put to shame by any 'suffragette in petticoats'.

[97] 'Mr. Lloyd George and the Future of the Welsh University.' Penucha MSS. T. F. Roberts to Rendel, 27 November 1908. N.L.W. MSS. 19443E, Rendel II, f. 194.

[98] *South Wales Daily News* (13 March 1909). Herbert Lewis' *Diary* (26 February and 11 March 1909). Penucha MSS.

[99] Treasury Minute (18 December 1909). *Council Minutes* (7 January 1910), p. 463.

[100] *Council Minutes* (22 April and 14 October 1910), pp. 489, 551.

culture, with assistance from his two junior colleagues in the department, had worked heroically to propagate the gospel of Agricultural Science among the intensely conservative-minded farmers of west and central Wales. A large part of the work was extra-mural and, additionally, much effort was put into a variety of short courses and vacation schools held at Aberystwyth. The College had always held firmly to the conviction that it had a special obligation directly to assist the main industry of the rural area in which it was situated. Accordingly, it was pre-pared to undertake a whole range of technical instruction (butter- and cheese-making and the like) which bore little relation to genuine university work. Only in this way could parsimonious county council committees be persuaded to give their grudging supplemental assistance.

Unfortunately in 1901 Tom Parry, who, as T. F. Roberts readily admitted, had served the College well for many years, left under a cloud as a result of allega-tions of improper conduct. In 'recognition of his services' in building up the department, he was given a golden handshake of one year's salary.[101] Although Parry's rank had been no higher than that of lecturer, he had been senior enough to keep a strong grip on his colleagues and, after his resignation, the department fell into disarray. The staff had gradually increased in size and, shorn of effective leadership, there was a good deal of bickering and a total lack of effective team-work in the department which, additionally, was 'crippled', especially in its work at the higher levels, by inadequate funds. This 'general muddle', as T. H. Middle-ton, an influential and sympathetic official at the Board of Agriculture, put it, was a bitter disappointment, especially to Principal Roberts who had always hoped that Agriculture would be 'the one great technological branch' which the Aberyst-wyth College would develop 'to the highest point'.[102]

Eventually, the College decided on drastic action. Early in January 1907 a chair of Agriculture was established, and C. Bryner Jones, a young Welshman then on the staff of Armstrong College, Newcastle upon Tyne, who, as Isambard Owen accurately predicted, was 'destined to take a high place among the teachers and organizers of agricultural education' in Britain, was elected.[103] Soon afterwards a special committee of the College Council reported that the department was 'in need of entire reorganization'. Bryner Jones' plenary authority was spelt out unequivocally; all other members of the staff of the department were given notice; and the number of lectureships was reduced. Those who had been dismissed were at liberty to apply for the new posts and, in fact, two of them were reappointed, but a clean sweep was made of the others. As a result of these changes in personnel, and aided considerably by the vastly improved facilities provided by the new

    [101] T. F. Roberts to Rendel, 27 March 1901. N.L.W. MSS. 19441E, f. 38.

    [102] Bryner Jones to T. F. Roberts, 4 May 1907. T. H. Middleton to J. A. Murray, 16 May 1907. T. F. Roberts to Rendel (1907). C.A. P (VB) 2.

    [103] T. F. Roberts to Rendel, 25 January 1907. N.L.W. MSS. 19443E, Rendel II, f. 155. In Isambard Owen's testimonial, 17 January 1907. C.A. P (VB) 6.

Chemistry laboratory, the department of Agriculture at Aberystwyth began increasingly to fulfil the high hopes that had always been vested in it.[104]

Not unnaturally, the teaching staff of the College were much disturbed by these summary dismissals, without given cause and with no right of appeal, from the department of Agriculture. Statute 43 of the constitution, whence the power of dismissal was derived, seemed to most members of the staff to be a sword of Damocles poised over their tenure. A deputation met the Principal and, with only one abstention, the staff signed a memorandum of protest which asked that the offending Statute should be amended. The staff pointed out that, legal or otherwise, these proceedings set a precedent that would certainly 'prejudice' the interests of the College. T. F. Roberts maintained that the Council had the power of dismissal, but pleaded that there had been 'an emergency' situation in the department of Agriculture which justified the exceptional action taken. The Principal hoped that Rendel, who was sincerely respected by the staff, would draft and move a resolution in Council reaffirming the legality of Statute 43 but also formally recognizing the College's utmost indebtedness to the 'unabated devotion' of the staff and the inestimable value of their services to the College. Rendel insisted that the Council could not divest itself of its responsibilities, but offered assurances that it would 'avoid all reasonable reproach of peremptory or arbitrary action' in the exercise of its powers. Soon afterwards, evidently as an emollient, it was resolved, on the motion of the Principal, to increase the Senate's representation on the Council to four.[105]

Conciliatory gestures apart, this was justified on the ground that the Senate and the non-professorial staff had grown in size in recent years. There were two particularly notable additions to the staff in this period; in 1901 two Aberystwyth students had graduated with first-class honours on the same day: H. J. Fleure and O. T. Jones, two future Fellows of the Royal Society. In 1904 Fleure had been given, as he put it, an 'odd job post' as assistant lecturer in Zoology, Botany, and Geology. Outstandingly able and astonishingly industrious, Fleure had undertaken a large-scale investigation, which attracted the favourable notice of the Raleigh committee, into the anthropology of the Welsh people.[106] In 1906 R. D. Roberts had persuaded the Royal Geographical Society to make a small grant to help Aberystwyth to establish a lectureship in Geography. When this appointment fell vacant in 1907, Fleure begged to be given a 'chance of concentrating on a definite

---

[104] 'Report of Special Agricultural Committee', *Council Minutes* (26 March, 31 May 1907), pp. 135-7, 139-41. There were now three men surnamed Jones in the department; to avoid 'confusion', J. Griffith Jones agreed henceforth to be known as J. Jones Griffith. Bryner Jones to J. H. Davies, 10 June 1907. N.L.W. J. H. Davies MSS. (Corr.).

[105] Letters between T. F. Roberts and Rendel, 28 May–20 June 1907. N.L.W. MSS. 19443E, Rendel II, ff. 165-7, 171. *Council Minutes* (28 June and 4 July 1907), pp. 156, 277.

[106] H. J. Fleure to J. H. Davies, 19 July [1907]. N.L.W. J. H. Davies MSS. (Corr.). *Report of the Committee on the University of Wales and the Welsh University Colleges*, p. xiv.

and congenial line' of work for which he felt far better equipped than he was for his work in Botany. His professor, Ainsworth Davis, strongly endorsed Fleure's request and pointed out that his qualifications were 'very unusual'; the full development of Geography at Aberystwyth would 'require time and funds', but, without doubt, given the opportunity Fleure was the man to carry it out.[107]

In 1907 Fleure's work was rearranged and he was appointed additionally to the lectureship in Geography. In 1910 he was promoted to the chair of Zoology and in the fullness of time, as will appear, completely justified the confidence felt in his ability to build up a great school of Geography. This side of the academic work of the College was enormously strengthened by the appointment of O. T. Jones to a chair of Geology in 1910. For some years Jones had been working on a massive study of the geological structure of the Plynlimon area, and in 1909 he had published his results in a paper, immediately recognized as a classic, which gained him the D.Sc. degree of the University of Wales.[108] Fleure and O. T. Jones were superb teachers and prolific scholars: as members of the staff, and in their subsequent careers elsewhere, they were to bring great lustre to the College.

Not the least item in the long catalogue of services rendered by Fleure to the College had been performed at the turn of the century when he was still a student. Fleure and another senior student, J. P. Millington, had been the most active members of a drafting committee whose labours led eventually to the establishment of the Students' Representative Council.[109] There is no question that this important innovation was, if anything, overdue. No doubt a great deal had been gained, not least by students, from the system which had obtained since the 1870s whereby all College societies enjoyed the active participation and assistance of members of the teaching staff, and general meetings of the student body were presided over by the Principal. But it was high time that these leading strings were cut.

For some years there had been a growing desire for a greater degree of student control over their own affairs. It was 'not a revolutionary feeling, nor one of insubordination': on the contrary, it was a perfectly legitimate ambition which reflected 'a healthy spirit of self-discipline and a desire for self-improvement', as a well-written independent student publication described it.[110] There was some resistance in the Senate where a few of the more conservative sages clung to the old ways, but there was sufficient support from men like 'Jimmy' Marshall who conceded that, 'with changing times, new wants had arisen', for the Senate

[107] R. D. Roberts to Sir John Williams, 13 December 1909. N.L.W. MSS. 16704D. H. J. Fleure to J. H. Davies, 19 July (1907). N.L.W. J. H. Davies MSS. (Corr.). Ainsworth Davies to T. F. Roberts, 9 December 1907. C.A. Misc. Letters (1905–15).

[108] Sir William Pugh, 'Owen Thomas Jones', *Biographical Notices of Fellows of the Royal Society*, xiii. 226.

[109] H. J. Fleure, 'The Students' Council', U.C.W. *Magazine*, xxii. 216–18. *The Dragon*, xxvii. 32.

[110] *The Arrow*, no. 1 (1 March 1904), pp. 3–5. C.A. R/OSA. One of the joint editors was Walter Ward, whose nickname at College was 'Father', an evident recognition of unusual maturity.

ultimately to accept the student proposals. In 1900 the Students' Representative Council, democratically elected, came into existence and to it was entrusted some degree of control over student affairs.[111] In the very early years the elected officers behaved with circumspection and, gradually, other concessions were won. During the first twenty-six years of its existence, the *Magazine* had maintained a high standard, not least because it had regularly included erudite articles by first-rate scholars like Ethé and Herford. Recognizing that there might well be some falling-off in quality as a consequence, the students, asserting that 'a man's reach must exceed his grasp', nevertheless asked that full control of the *Magazine* should be remitted to a committee of the Students' Representative Council. In 1904 this request was granted, and the *Magazine* became henceforth *The Dragon*. The first volume published under the new dispensation included a cartoon depicting a sprightly young dragon prancing away while an old lady in national costume (presumably the voice of Wales) reproached an anxious-looking member of the Senate with the words: 'Professor *bach*! Why didn't you let him walk before?' In the following year, the Senate offered no objection to a proposal that, for the future, the President of the Literary and Debating Society should be a student.[112]

It would be idle to pretend that these changes were made entirely without difficulty. In some respects the new machinery eased the Senate's disciplinary problems. And it could certainly be said that the willingness of the student body to vote overwhelmingly for the compulsory levying of an amalgamation fee for the financing of student societies, the achievement of 'a long-cherished dream' of the College, owed something to the new spirit of responsibility engendered by the reforms. But it quickly appeared that the original constitution of the S.R.C. conceded too much power to the less senior students, and in 1905 constituencies had to be redrawn in a more conservative direction. Moreover, some student appetites simply grew with every concession, and in no time a demand for S.R.C. representation on the Senate was being voiced.[113]

Of course when the Senate perforce had to take disciplinary action, the S.R.C. naturally organized resistance in those cases where there was a widespread feeling of injustice over a too severe punishment. This was unexceptional enough, no more than the normal exercise of the right of protest, 'without which the most elaborate constitution was a mere *Duma*', as *The Dragon*, with a keen eye for contemporary events in Russia, commented in 1907.[114] But unfortunately the S.R.C. did not always command sufficient authority to make its decisions binding on its constituents, some of whom, the younger more boisterous element, occasionally

---

[111] Senate Minutes (6 June 1900). C.A. S/MN/1. J. W. Marshall, 'The Old and the New', *The Dragon*, xxvii. 57. 'The Students' Council', *Students' Handbook* (1904), pp. 35–6.

[112] *The Arrow*, no. 1, p. 4. Senate Minutes (16 November 1904, 15 May 1905).C. A. S/MN/1. *The Dragon*, xxvii. 85.

[113] Ibid. xxvii. 251, xxviii. 32, xxx. 133. 'The Amalgamation Fee Scheme', *Students Handbook* (1909), pp. 50–2.   [114] *The Dragon*, xxx. 62.

followed freelance unaccredited leaders. This was the main explanation of the so-called 'eruption of 1907'. Rowdy behaviour in the Common Room (in the basement near the Main Entrance) at a time when the Raleigh committee, whose recommendations would be vital for the future of the College, was in session nearby had been punished, unduly severely as some thought. The S.R.C. decided on a restrained dignified protest which was insufficiently militant for some sparks. A spontaneous rag the evening before charged up feelings which erupted uncontrollably at the degree ceremony the next day. Insults, and rather more solid missiles, were hurled at the platform and proceedings, which approached riot proportions, had to be suspended with undignified haste.

Stern retribution followed immediately: the men's Common Room was closed until further notice, nearly all the major social and athletic events (including participation in Inter-College competitions) in the calendar were cancelled, and incumbent male officers of the S.R.C. were prohibited from holding office until further notice.[115] It is difficult to avoid the conclusion, student protestations to the contrary, that there was a touch of the revolutionary spirit about at this time. A month before, the annual parliamentary election at the Literary and Debating Society had been won handsomely (with over 150 votes) by the Socialist candidate, who usually at this time was at or near the bottom of the poll.[116] And 1907, of course, was also the year of the troubles at Alexandra Hall. To some extent, this militancy was the price that had to be paid for reforms that had been too long delayed and then, once started, pushed on perhaps too quickly. No permanent damage was done. The S.R.C. tendered an apology to the Senate and to the University of Wales. One old student suggested that, latterly, the S.R.C. had made the mistake of setting its sights too high: 'It is influence not power that it should aim at.'[117] Most people seemed to agree that that was the appropriate lesson to be drawn from recent experience.

Otherwise, the social life of the College remained as beguiling as ever, sometimes too much so: 'I found the social life of college so agreeable that work was apt to take a second place', wrote one young man who enjoyed a vigorous athletic career that lasted exactly one session.[118] Sport loomed large at Aberystwyth. There were some titanic struggles with Cardiff on the rugby field, and Bangor could always be relied upon to be strong at soccer. However, in this period both were beaten for the first time on their own grounds by Aberystwyth teams which rarely lost at home. There were two important improvements in games amenities at this time. For years College teams had played most of their matches on the

[115] Ibid. xxx. 133–6, 191–4. *Council Minutes* (6 December 1907), pp. 210–12. Sir John Williams to J. H. Davies, 28 November 1907. N.L.W. J. H. Davies MSS. (Corr.).

[116] *The Dragon*, xxx. 44–7. In 1906 the Labour candidate polled eighteen votes. The 'suffragette' candidate (who but Miss Olive Wheeler!) received fifty-two votes. Ibid. xxix. 46–8.

[117] Ibid. xxx. 192–3.

[118] Harold M. Watkins, *Life Has Kept me Young* (1951), p. 47.

unsatisfactory Barracks field or else deep in the mud at Smithfield, or 'Smith-swamp' as it was called in disgust. In 1906, however, the Vicarage Field was leased from David Davies and, with some financial assistance from the Old Students' Association, this large area was levelled and improved. At long last College athletic teams had been given a suitable, indeed a very fine, home.[119]

From the earliest days there had been a gymnasium of sorts in the College building. None of the rooms available was suitable; indeed, it was agreed doctrine that the risk of injury by accident outweighed any possible callisthenic benefit that could be gained in these dismal surroundings. Later on in 1901 Penry Vaughan Thomas, then a student at Aberystwyth, sought an interview with the Principal. Vaughan Thomas was keenly interested in gymnastics and he had collated a mass of information on the most advanced techniques employed in Sweden and the U.S.A. More to the point, he had started a fund (already amounting to almost £1,000) among members of his family to build a modern gymnasium at Aberystwyth, and to provide the nucleus of an endowment for an Instructorship. T. F. Roberts pointed out that the pressing needs of the Law school and the Chemistry department must have a higher priority, but he promised some assistance from College funds because, in his experience, students were 'wonderfully benefited in body and spirits by a course in gymnastics, even of the meagre and unsatisfactory kind' currently available. Others gave some help: the Old Students' Association arranged a bazaar which raised a useful sum of money; David Davies gave a free site. But the major contribution was made by Vaughan Thomas and his family. In 1908 a fine, well-equipped gymnasium was completed on a good site overlooking the Vicarage Field, and soon afterwards an Instructor, A. G. Noehren, was appointed at a modest stipend. Within a short time a very strong College gymnastic tradition had been built up, and Aberystwyth may legitimately claim to rank among the pioneers of physical education in British universities.[120]

Aberystwyth students in those days were certainly not devoid of a social conscience. In 1900 when Rendel was put out by what he regarded as excessively jingo rejoicing at the College over the relief of Mafeking, the Principal replied that

Welsh students detest beyond everything the grasping materialistic temper of some of the gunfire mongering of the day. Their interest in the British Empire is as different from this, and also from militarism, as the east is from the west. The Empire is to them an ideal—and as such it is exercising a wonderful fascination—which means broader standards, vaster brotherhood, purer democracy.[121]

---

[119] *Council Minutes* (26 October 1906), p. 63. A. Pinsent, 'The New College Building Fund, 1933–65' (MS. notes), p. 1. *Western Mail* (12 October 1908). In November 1909 the all-conquering Welsh international rugby team, led by the 'wonderful midget' half-back Dicky Owen, played an exhibition match on the Vicarage Field against the College XV.

[120] T. F. Roberts to Rendel, 28 January 1902. N.L.W. MSS. 19441E, Rendel II, f. 46. 'The New Gymnasium', *The Dragon*, xxxi. 26–7. *Council Minutes* (5 March 1909), p. 356.

[121] T. F. Roberts to Rendel, 23 May 1900. N.L.W. MSS. 19441E, Rendel II, f. 31.

And these generalized sympathies with the less fortunate could be particularized to useful effect. Unable to give money, a group of students offered time and service instead. A Working Men's Institute was opened in temporary premises, hired by the month as funds were scarce, in Mill Street, where there was a reading room, a games room and where concerts were regularly organized by teams of students. Subsequently, larger premises in Chalybeate Street were acquired, and in 1905 a branch Mission Room was opened in Trefechan.[122]

As one would expect, former students played some part in this social work. The Old Students' Association went from strength to strength in this period. The Oxford, Cambridge, and London branches had been in a flourishing condition well before 1900; in 1899 three new local branches, at Swansea, Cardiff, and in the North of England, were established. Reunions at Aberystwyth were strongly supported; more often than not, over 200 old students returned to enjoy the 'Aber. air, a draught of genuine *eau de vie*', as well as a packed programme of social events.[123] In 1905 an enjoyable trip to Rome was arranged, and in 1909 a miniature Reunion was held in Paris, where cries of 'Aber. *am byth*' during dinner led to loud whispers of 'Americans, Americans' from the other astonished diners.[124]

Sadly, however, the man who had founded the Old Students' Association, its President and the main driving force behind it in the first seven years of its existence, was no more. In 1899 Tom Ellis, the embodiment of resurgent Wales, had died in the prime of life. It was at Aberystwyth, as T. F. Roberts said, that Ellis 'got his first glimpses into that new vision of a regenerated and united Wales, which became the governing passion of his life'.[125] No old student loved the College more than Ellis did, and none of them more amply repaid his debt to it. Three years later J. Foulkes Roberts, Senior Vice-President, who had supported the College through thick and thin with thirty-eight years of 'ungrudging labour' on its behalf, also died.[126] Nor did this end the catalogue of losses among the senior lay officers of the College at this time. In 1905 A. C. Humphreys-Owen, Junior Vice-President, died. Full justice has never been done to his immense services, unobtrusively performed, to Welsh education and to the Aberystwyth College in particular. Two years later Sir Lewis Morris, Senior Vice-President, died. Morris had soon retrieved his early errors so far as Aberystwyth was concerned, and in the last twenty or so years of his life he worked unstintingly for its advancement.

The old guard leaders on the Council were passing away. But, happily, they were replaced by new men of like quality and similar dedication to the interests

[122] *The Dragon*, xxiii. 40–1, xxviii. 35–6.

[123] 'The Old Students' Association', *Students Handbook* (1909), pp. 64–7. *The Dragon*, xxx. 243. In 1910 an Old Students' Association branch was established in Switzerland.

[124] T. K. Brighouse to J. H. Davies, 30 December 1904. N.L.W. Cwrt Mawr MSS. 854D. *The Dragon*, xxxi. 222.

[125] U.C.W. *Magazine*, xxi. 334.

[126] Senate Minutes (5 November 1902). C.A. S/MN/1.

of the College. The new Vice-Presidents were Sir John Williams and young David Davies, who had already given ample indication, in the most tangible way, of their deep interest in Aberystwyth. And alongside them on the Council, ceaselessly active in good works, was Daniel Lleufer Thomas. Short as it was of endowments, the College had cause for great pride in its ability to inspire such loyalties.

6

'Let Us See to it that the Right Seed is Sown'[1]

IN 1911 T. F. Roberts completed twenty years as Principal of the University College of Wales. Moreover, in that year the King and Queen visited Aberystwyth to lay the foundation stone of the National Library building. It was confidently expected that, during the course of the royal visit, Roberts would be knighted in recognition of his long and devoted services to Welsh higher education. There were good precedents: Reichel of Bangor had been honoured thus in 1907 when King Edward VII went to North Wales to perform a similar duty. Indeed, six of the eleven heads of provincial universities and university colleges in England and Wales in 1911 were knights, and of the remaining five, three were of very recent appointment and the fourth, E. H. Griffiths of Cardiff, was ten years junior to Roberts. The King and Queen came to Aberystwyth, but Roberts did not receive the anticipated accolade. This was all the more surprising, indeed even embarrassing, because Edward Anwyl, professor of Welsh at Aberystwyth, had been knighted earlier that year. Rendel, Sir John Williams, who felt 'very strongly on the subject', and David Davies wrote jointly to the Prime Minister in August 1911 asking him to advise the King to confer the desired honour on Principal Roberts. Asquith, however, refused. It is difficult to understand why he did so.[2]

The case for public recognition of Roberts was a strong one and, as a matter of fact, when Asquith had visited Aberystwyth in 1907 he had said that he had been particularly impressed with the Principal's qualities.[3] And there is the even more curious fact that only shortly before, when Asquith was face to face with a recalcitrant House of Lords which might have to be coerced into passing the Parliament bill, T. F. Roberts' name was on the list of 250 Liberal peers the King had agreed,

[1] Miss Gwendoline Davies, Llandinam, to J. H. Davies, 25 June 1916. N.L.W. J. H. Davies MSS. (Corr.).

[2] Rendel, Sir John Williams, and David Davies to the Prime Minister (August 1911). C. Hobhouse, David Davies, and Sir John Williams to Rendel, 8 August, 21 August, and 9 September 1911. N.L.W. MSS. 19440E, Rendel I, ff. 55, 55a, 102, 103.

[3] Rendel to T. F. Roberts, 3 November 1907. C.A. P (VB) 2.

if necessary, to create to convince the Lords that the government meant business.[4] The Lords, of course, ultimately gave way to avoid a swingeing mass addition to their number. Evidently, a peerage for Roberts to help the Liberal government out of its political difficulties was one thing, a knighthood for a lifetime's service to education was another. Lloyd George was not the only Liberal leader with a cynical attitude to the honours system. In this instance, Lloyd George, although he does not appear to have had any great opinion of T. F. Roberts, had supported the proposal to confer a knighthood upon him.[5]

But it was not to be; Principal Roberts had to rest content with the honorary LL.D. degree given him in 1902 by the Victoria University, a run-of-the-mill celebration gesture of goodwill to the incumbent Vice-Chancellors of other British universities. Soon after the disappointment in 1911, Roberts lost one of the great supports to his Principalship in the removal by death of his friend and great confidant Lord Rendel, President of the College. As far back as the summer of 1901 Rendel, who was then in his late sixties and feeling his years, had suggested that, in the interest of the College, he ought to resign. T. F. Roberts bent all his best energies to persuading the President to continue; the Principal suggested that Rendel should retain his office but should limit 'its scope to such guidance and inspiration on the broad questions of educational policy' as his 'ripe wisdom and experience pre-eminently' fitted him to provide. He was Aberystwyth's chief link with the Establishment and, as the Principal said, Rendel's Presidency meant 'more to a College like ours than to similar institutions which are in the great highways of the world'.[6] Rendel agreed to continue as President on the less active basis suggested. But he remained concerned at his inability, for reasons of growing infirmity, to attend formal College occasions and in subsequent years at various times he suggested resignation. Each time the Court, Council, and Senate of the College, and particularly Sir John Williams, who was by now clearly the logical successor as President, pleaded with Rendel to continue.[7] In fact, despite his protestations, Rendel retained a most active, indeed detailed, interest in the College to the end. And towards the close of his life Rendel, if anything, became even more lyrical in his attachment to the Welsh people.

The quality in Wales that secured my love and respect [he wrote in 1912] was Welsh superiority to merely material objects. In England the 'Drum and Trumpet' or the

---

[4] David Williams, *T. F. Roberts*, p. 43.

[5] C. Hobhouse to Rendel, 8 August 1911. N.L.W. MSS. 19440E, Rendel I, f. 102. A few years later Sir John Williams, recounting Lloyd George's hostility towards Principals Reichel and E. H. Griffiths, excepted T. F. Roberts because, as Lloyd George said, 'there was not very much to be said about him'. Sir John Williams to Thomas Jones, 14 January 1916. N.L.W. Thomas Jones MSS., Class J, II, f. 1.

[6] T. F. Roberts to Rendel, 15 August 1901. N.L.W. MSS. 19441E, Rendel II, f. 45.

[7] Rendel to T. F. Roberts, 7 October 1907, 9 June 1909. C.A. P (VB) 2. Sir John Williams to Rendel, 10 October 1907, 17 April 1911. N.L.W. MSS. 19440E, Rendel II, ff. 97, 98. David Davies to T. F. Roberts, 30 May 1910. U.C.W. G. Lib. History File.

'Bread and Butter' policy furnish, as occasion offers, trump cards. But Wales has genuine idealism and lofty imagination and spiritual instincts permeating the whole people. There is not a 'clodhopper' or a 'chawbacon' in Wales.[8]

High praise indeed from a man of the world who had a sharp eye for human frailties and had endured his share of disappointments in political life, some of them relating to Welsh concerns. There is no question at all of the genuineness of Rendel's commitment to Wales and, for him, the Aberystwyth College above all embodied the national virtues that commanded his regard. For almost thirty years he had served the College without stint: he had come forward as its brilliantly effective champion in the 1880s when it faced extinction; subsequently his very considerable abilities and sizeable amounts of his money were used to further the interests of the College. From the beginning, as T. F. Roberts said, Rendel insisted 'that the highest ground of all should be taken', or at least that the College should aspire to the heights.[9] No officer of the College was ever more concerned for the well-being of students and staff; from 1901 to 1913 Rendel subscribed £750 annually to supplement the abysmally low salaries paid to the staff. When he died, in June 1913, he left £5,000 to the College. In the course of one hundred years and more, the Aberystwyth College has never had a truer friend than Rendel.[10]

As expected, Sir John Williams succeeded to the Presidency. He had already made the first of his long list of benefactions to the College. In December 1909 Sir John offered to give £120 a year for three years to pay the salary of a lecturer in Welsh History, provided that the College undertook to find a similar sum for the same period to defray the salary of an assistant lecturer in Welsh Literature. Early in 1910 Timothy Lewis was appointed to the latter post and, the same day, E. A. Lewis, an old student who had gone on to do distinguished research work at London University, was appointed assistant lecturer in Welsh History at a slightly higher salary than was originally intended.[11] These appointments were timely. For years it had been a legitimate reproach to the University of Wales that it had neglected to promote the study of the language, literature, and history of Wales itself. Indeed, in 1912 Hubert Hall of the Public Record Office offered the opinion that, in recent years, the 'bulk and quality' of research on Welsh subjects seemed

---

[8] Rendel to T. F. Roberts, 2 September 1912. N.L.W. MSS. 19443E, Rendel II, f. 201. It is doubtful if, in some respects, this eulogy on Welsh public opinion was as fully deserved in 1912 as it had been earlier in the 1880s and 1890s. There is some evidence, for example, that the idealism of the Welsh in educational matters was wearing a little thin; certainly there was very little disposition in Welsh local authorities at this time to vote money from the rates for the support of higher education.

[9] 'The Late Lord Rendel', *The Dragon*, xxvi. 73.

[10] In 1914 Rendel's Grogythan land on Penglais was conveyed to the College and the income from this, combined with the interest on his legacy, was used to endow a Rendel chair of English Language and Literature.

[11] *Council Minutes* (15 December 1909, 4 March 1910), pp. 442, 469–70.

to be 'dwindling rather than rapidly expanding' as had been hoped.[12] At any rate Aberystwyth, operating as usual on a shoe-string, was doing its best to make up for past neglects. Three years later the position was further improved when T. Gwynn Jones was appointed to a new Readership in Welsh Literature. And in 1914 T. H. Parry-Williams, another old student with an outstanding research record in Celtic studies, joined the staff as a temporary assistant lecturer.[13]

There had been other changes of note in the teaching staff in recent years. In 1901, when C. H. Herford was ultimately lost to Manchester, the chair of English had been filled by G. C. Macaulay who, although not in Herford's class, was a scholar of distinction and an exceptionally energetic and inspiring teacher.[14] In 1906 Macaulay returned to Cambridge and he was replaced by Herford's protégé, J. W. H. Atkins, another old Aberystwyth student, who achieved international recognition as a scholar late on in life when in retirement after thirty-four years as a member of the Senate. When J. M. Angus became Registrar of the University in 1905, the chair of Latin went to E. Bensly who remained at Aberystwyth until 1919. From 1903 to 1909 L. E. Kastner, a prolific scholar who earned the admiration of his students, a notable chastiser of the indolent, was professor of French.[15] Ultimately, he, too, was lost to Manchester, but his successor, J. L. A. Barbier, a Frenchman, stayed at Aberystwyth until his death in 1944.

In 1911 J. W. Brough, professor of Philosophy, who had been at Aberystwyth in one capacity or another since 1883, retired. He had always been prominent in the social life of the College (he was a consummate actor and an accomplished musician), but had no great talents as a teacher (a hopeless disciplinarian, his lecture-room, more often than not, was as noisy as a fairground) and fewer as a scholar.[16] It was necessary to give Brough a pension, and this was almost a straw that broke the camel's back: for a time it looked as if, for reasons of economy, the chair of Philosophy would have to be discontinued. Ultimately, W. Jenkyn Jones, a gifted teacher who could hold an audience even for classes at 7 a.m., was appointed, though at a reduced salary. And the same depressing expedient was necessary when, at the same time, Alexander Findlay succeeded J. J. Sudborough as professor of Chemistry.[17] The College suffered a serious loss in 1913 when Foster

[12] Hubert Hall to J. H. Davies, 31 July 1912. N.L.W. J. H. Davies MSS. (Corr.). Hall, who had sent his daughter to the College, said he had 'come to regard Aberystwyth as the intellectual centre of Wales'.

[13] *Council Minutes* (24 October 1913, 26 June 1914), pp. 290, 295–6, 402. H. J. Fleure to Thomas Jones, 1 May 1914. N.L.W. Thomas Jones MSS., Class J, vol. i, f. 14.

[14] *The Dragon*, xxviii. 163–4.

[15] Ibid. xxxii. 54–6, lists Kastner's very considerable research output.

[16] R. T. Jenkins, op. cit., pp. 112–13. See also the careful euphemistic account in *The Dragon*, xxxxviii. 93–5. Whatever his deficiencies as a teacher, Brough fought a heroic battle against blindness in the last years of his life.

[17] T. F. Roberts to W. P. Ker, to A. S. Pringle Pattison, and to T. D. Roberts, 20, 27 May, and 5 July 1911. C.A. P/Cr/B/1. *Council Minutes* (15 September 1911), p. 72. *The Dragon*, cvi. 17.

Watson, who had built up a considerable reputation in recent years with several important books on the history of education, gave up his chair to begin a career as a freelance writer.[18] The new professor of Education was C. R. Chapple, an old Aberystwyth student.

In 1909 the department of Mathematics was divided into two: Genese, who remained a stormy petrel to the end of his long career at Aberystwyth, continued as professor now of Pure Mathematics. The Applied Mathematics department was headed by G. A. Schott who was promoted to a chair in 1910. Schott, who had an exceptional 'mastery of the classical theory of electromagnetism', was an Adams Prizeman who became a Fellow of the Royal Society in 1922, and remained, universally respected for his ability and his integrity, at Aberystwyth until 1933.[19] In 1903 R. H. Yapp became professor of Botany and, during his tenure, which lasted until 1914, he made a detailed study of the vegetation of the Dyfi estuary, 'a classical investigation which has never been excelled'.[20] Yapp was succeeded by J. Lloyd Williams, a leadminer's son who had achieved academic distinction in the face of considerable difficulties. Lloyd Williams, who was also a gifted musician, did important work on marine plants; he was one of those on the staff at this time who, as H. J. Fleure said, were consciously trying by means of ambitious research schemes 'to make the U.C.W. a real university'.[21]

Aberystwyth had always claimed to be a college of the people to an exceptional degree, but because of endless financial stringencies for years it had not been possible for the College to take an effective initiative in extra-mural work, other than the specialized out-College teaching in Agriculture and Law which was partly self-supporting. However, in 1909, at the instance, predictably enough, of Dr. R. D. Roberts, the University of Wales was persuaded formally to recognize its obligation to make some contribution to the higher education of working people.[22]

Roberts, who was by this time 'the foremost figure in the university extension world' in Britain, set to work immediately.[23] A committee (inevitably under his chairmanship) was formed to examine existing facilities and probable demand. Spurred on by Roberts, who never let the grass grow under his feet, work went ahead energetically. But in November 1911 R. D. Roberts died and, shorn of his

[18] T. F. Roberts to P. A. Barnett, 25 April 1914. P/Cr/B/3.

[19] D. S. Meyler, 'Notes on the Department of Mathematics'. A. A. Conway, 'George Augustus Schott', *Biographical Notices of Fellows of the Royal Society*, ii. 451–4.

[20] P. W. Carter, 'A Short History of the Department of Botany at U.C.W., Aberystwyth'. U.C.W. G. Lib. LD 1155 (1).

[21] H. J. Fleure to J. H. Davies, 9 May (1915). N.L.W. J. H. Davies MSS. (Corr.). Fleure specifically mentioned Lloyd Williams and O. T. Jones as members of this group.

[22] D. Lleufer Thomas, 'University Tutorial Classes for Working People', *Trans. Cymm.* (1914–15), pp. 100–1.

[23] The judgement on Roberts is that of the historian, J. A. R. Marriott, quoted in B. B. Thomas, 'R. D. Roberts', loc. cit., p. 30.

crusading enthusiasm, the University committee lapsed and no report was ever made. It may well be true, as has been suggested, that R. D. Roberts was ill-equipped to win the confidence of working-class organizations, which was vital to the success of the movement, especially in the industrial areas.[24] Nevertheless, of the university people in Wales involved in the movement at that time, Roberts alone had the overmastering sense of mission that swept difficulties aside. With his death, university-sponsored adult education lost its most uncompromising champion, and the Aberystwyth College a staunch if excessively combative friend.

However, Aberystwyth did respond to Roberts' initiative so far as it could. Principal Roberts, J. H. Davies, and Lleufer Thomas believed whole-heartedly in the possibility of an educated populace in Wales; money, not lack of interest, was the problem. In 1911 a modest start was made in Aberystwyth itself: Stanley Roberts taught a class in constitutional history, and T. Gwynn Jones one in Welsh literature. For two years the cost was borne by a local committee, but in the third year it devolved on the College. In 1913 four classes (later six) were organized in Merionethshire, and in 1914 several more in Carmarthenshire, all in Economics. Some assistance from central and local government sources was forthcoming, but here, too, a part of the cost had to be met from College funds.[25] T. F. Roberts believed that this extra-mural activity was to be ranked with 'the most valuable work' of the College and, if the early difficulties could be surmounted, it would grow into a most effective means of educating the mass of the people. But rising costs and the exigencies of war brought this particular venture to an end in 1915.[26]

The outbreak of war in 1914 made a large immediate impact on Aberystwyth. By December 1914 there were almost 9,000 troops in and around the town; additionally, there was a substantial number of Belgian refugees, including an exotic group of artists and musicians. The refugees, who were brought over at the expense of the Llandinam family, were conducted to Aberystwyth early in October by Fleure; they received a public reception that 'beat the royal visit' of 1911 'to fits'. A great crowd of students welcomed the Belgians with renderings of the Welsh national anthem, the hymn-tune 'Aberystwyth', and 'Men of Harlech'; packets of Algerian and Brazilian cigarettes were rustled up from somewhere for the newcomers, and women students produced a 'bag of small change for shopping'.[27] The unfortunate Belgians quickly settled down and some of them, the artistically gifted, were soon found congenial work, as will appear.

[24] B. B. Thomas, 'R. D. Roberts', loc. cit., pp. 21–2.

[25] Lleufer Thomas, 'University Tutorial Classes', loc. cit., pp. 103–4.

[26] T. F. Roberts to E. Jones, 5 November 1914, and to the *Morning Post*, 11 October 1915. C.A. P/Cr/B/3 and 4.

[27] H. J. Fleure to Thomas Jones, 4 October 1914. N.L.W. Thomas Jones MSS., Class J, vol. i, f. 19.

A very different reception awaited the arrival of another foreigner in Aberystwyth soon afterwards. Hermann Ethé had joined the College staff in 1875 and, during the intervening forty years and more, he had been the one scholar at Aberystwyth with, indisputably, an international reputation. His learning was prodigious; he customarily taught half a dozen languages (and their attendant literatures), and College *Reports* in the nineteenth century always included a laconic footnote to the effect that Dr. Ethé would 'be happy to read with students in other Oriental languages'; that is, in addition to Hebrew, Arabic, and Sanskrit, which he taught along with German, French, and Italian. And this, as R. T. Jenkins, whose regard for Ethé was not far short of idolatrous, said, was not mere 'window-dressing'. Short, thick-set, a man who marched rather than walked, Ethé was altogether larger than life. To the end of his days he retained a thick German accent; he 'drank like an ox' (when asked whether he wanted beer or brandy, his immediate answer was 'both'); he had a quick wit that verged, occasionally, on the blasphemous, and a great uproarious laugh that reverberated like thunder.[28] For all his idiosyncracies, which were occasionally embarrassing in strait-laced nonconformist Wales, Ethé was properly valued by the authorities.

No one has had more reason than I have [T. F. Roberts wrote in 1908] to recognize the great services he has rendered the College by his vast learning and his power and enthusiasm as a teacher, or to know the goodness and kindness of heart that he carries along with his many gifts.[29]

Ethé was a political exile who was too liberal to live easily in Bismarck's new Germany. At the same time, as he himself said, he was 'and always would be a German', though the Germany he stood for was that of Goethe, Schiller, and Beethoven.[30]

When war broke out in August 1914, Ethé and his English-born wife were in Germany. After some short delay, at the request of the College authorities, he was allowed to return to Britain.[31] The Ethés came back to Aberystwyth where they were met at the station by the Principal and the Registrar who informed them of the dangerous, indeed hysterical, temper of public opinion in Aberystwyth. Spy mania, whipped up by rumours, true and false, of German barbarities during the advance through Belgium, was rampant all over Britain, and enemy nationals in this country, Germans and Austrians especially, were regarded with fear and hatred.[32]

[28] R. T. Jenkins, op. cit., pp. 104, 113–16. Despite his facility for picking up languages, Ethé did not learn Welsh. According to one of his colleagues, he used to say that the only Welsh word one need know in Wales is '*cwrw*' [beer]. N.L.W. 'The Diary of T. Gwynn Jones', p. 12.

[29] T. F. Roberts to J. H. Davies, 19 April 1908. N.L.W. J. H. Davies MSS. (Corr.).

[30] Ethé's reply to a toast at a dinner celebrating his hundredth term at Aberystwyth. *The Dragon*, xxx. 244.

[31] Formal request for permission signed by T. F. Roberts, 5 October 1914. C.A. P/Cr/B/3.

[32] C. Hazlehurst, *Politicians at War* (1971), pp. 143–8, discusses the national mood at this time.

The next day a large crowd, estimated to be two thousand strong, assembled (instead of a tocsin, slips of paper had been handed about summoning the meeting) in the square in front of Siloh chapel. The people were harangued by two prominent local men, T. J. Samuel, solicitor and town councillor, and Dr. T. D. Harries, medical man and magistrate, who demanded that all enemy aliens should be driven out of the town. Some of the mob (for such, on the most generous interpretation, it was) called out 'Shoot them', and one of the speakers suggested a 'rope and a lamp-post as a remedy'. Subsequently, a long procession, headed by a Union Jack mounted on a long pole, marched up to Caradoc Road where there were angry scenes outside Ethé's house. Professors Marshall and O. T. Jones, who tried to remonstrate with the mob, were roughly handled and, eventually, the police, who were clearly in sympathy with the crowd, had to intervene. Mercifully, Ethé himself was not at home at the time. Later the mob went off to the house of Professor Schott who, despite his name, was in fact English, though his wife was German. He, too, was given twenty-four hours to leave the town.[33]

That evening the Ethés left Aberystwyth, and took refuge in Reading with Mrs. Ethé's family. Despite the receipt of telegrams from elsewhere bearing the message, 'Bravo Aberystwyth', the Ethé affair was a disgraceful episode that brought Aberystwyth into deserved disrepute.[34] With all due allowance for the disturbed temper of the times, the picture of a brute mass of townspeople, spurred on by public men, hounding out a harmless old scholar in his seventies is utterly shameful. Nor did the vindictiveness stop there. A public meeting soon afterwards denounced the College authorities for according Ethé 'a welcome' and demanded his dismissal from the staff.[35]

On the whole, the College came out of the affair much better than the town. Ethé's private savings were locked up in German and Hungarian government stocks and, without his salary, he was 'pennilessly adrift'.[36] Until the position was clarified, the Principal, the Registrar, H. J. Fleure, and one other unidentified colleague paid Ethé £200 from their own pockets.[37] T. F. Roberts tried to enlist the assistance of two former students, E. J. Ellis Griffith, who was then a junior Minister at the Home Office, and S. T. Evans, M.P., in support of Ethé's application for naturalization. This did not succeed, but at least these efforts saved him

---

[33] *Cambrian News* (16 October 1914). N.L.W. 'The Diary of T. Gwynn Jones', pp. 11–16. Other aliens in the town were similarly driven out. Schott stood his ground and was left unmolested.

[34] See the magnificent rebuke, 'Hooliganism in High Places', by H. Idris Bell in the *Cambrian News* (30 October 1914).

[35] Ibid. (23 October 1914). The Principal later received an anonymous letter warning him that, if Ethé returned after the war, 'his life' would be in danger if he had 'the face to come here and take our English [sic] money'. C.A. P (VB) 3.

[36] H. Ethé to J. H. Davies, 22 October 1914. N.L.W. MSS. T. I. Ellis donation (October 1965). For student opinion, see *The Dragon*, xxxviii. 209–11.

[37] T. F. Roberts to Col. Dunn, 14 June 1915. C.A. P (VB) 3.

from repatriation and an anguished separation from his wife, whose courage was his chief support at this time.[38]

At first the College Council simply ignored the letter from the Aberystwyth town public meeting demanding Ethé's dismissal, and remitted the question of the payment of his salary to the Finance Committee.[39] Eventually, however, it became apparent that at least one member of the Council shared the sentiments of the Aberystwyth vigilantes, if their unheroic belligerence can be so dignified. In June 1915 F. Llewelyn Jones, the old student who had done so much to help to establish the Law department, threatened to move in the Council to deprive Ethé of his chair. Llewelyn Jones (whose nickname at College, 'Cromwell', suggests a self-righteous certitude) had been outraged by the German sinking of the *Lusitania* and their use of poison-gas. 'We are dealing with a nation of savage barbarians who will stop at nothing in their attempt to crush Britain', he wrote to T. F. Roberts. The Principal made a great effort to head off this attack, apparently successfully, but only at the price of Ethé's willingness to resign, and accept a small pension, which the Finance Committee unanimously recommended should be paid.[40]

For Ethé this was 'a bitter blow, the bitterest' that had ever befallen him. For the next two years he lived in Reading, eating his heart out for his work and his life at the College he had served with such distinction for nearly half a century.[41] The ludicrousness of the whole situation is exemplified in the fact that, all this time, Ethé continued his important work for the India Office and the British Museum. To the end he buoyed himself up with the hope that some day ('when we return (when?)', he wrote pathetically) he would be able to come back to Aberystwyth.[42] But even that consolation was denied him: in June 1917 he died. Despite his age, he was a casualty of war just as certainly as any young soldier killed at the Front.[43]

T. F. Roberts' attitude to the Ethé affair was governed by simple humanity. On the wider question of the war itself, he believed that British resistance to Germany was just and necessary, and he was anxious that the College should

---

[38] Ellis Griffith to T. F. Roberts, 12 November 1914. C.A. (C), not numbered. T. F. Roberts to Ethé, 22 March 1915. S. T. Evans to T. F. Roberts, 1 July 1915. C.A. P (VB) 3. Ethé to J. H. Davies, 4 July 1915. T. I. Ellis MSS. It is evident that the College officially would not support the naturalization application. The Home Office to T. F. Roberts, 30 December 1914. C.A. PC (6).

[39] *Council Minutes* (23 October 1914), pp. 454–5.

[40] Llewelyn Jones to T. F. Roberts, 4 June 1915. T. F. Roberts to Llewelyn Jones, 7 and 9 June 1915. C.A. P (VB) 3 and 4. *Council Minutes* (24 September 1915), pp. 577–8.

[41] H. Ethé to J. H. Davies, 18 September 1915. T. I. Ellis MSS. There is a considerable heart-rending correspondence in this collection.

[42] H. Ethé to J. H. Davies, 2 May 1915. Ibid.

[43] The Aberystwyth municipal authority pursued him into the grave. In October 1917 the Mayor resigned from Court and Council because the College had ignored the protests of the Town Council over the payment of a pension to Ethé.

play its full part in the war effort.[44] At the time of the Boer War a company of Volunteers had been formed at Aberystwyth under the command of Professor Ainsworth Davis (who sported a fierce, waxed moustache), seconded by 'Jimmy' Marshall. In 1908, as a result of Haldane's army reforms, the Volunteers were transformed into the Officers' Training Corps. By 1914 about 250 students had passed through, or were currently members of, the contingent.[45] Within weeks of the outbreak of the war there was a rush to the colours. Principal Roberts was infuriated by the fact that many of these student-recruits, who had received some military training, were refused commissions; and he was all the more angry because commissions were being 'freely given', not only to Oxbridge men, 'but also to public school cadets without the knowledge of life possessed' by Welsh university students.[46] The exceptionally high casualty rate among subalterns soon overcame this Establishment snobbery, if such it was and not the inevitable confusion of a civilian nation painfully gearing itself for war. At the College 'Intensive Training Classes' were instituted for a flood of student volunteers, and by the spring of 1916 the Aberystwyth O.T.C. was 'represented on every front and in almost every arm of the service'.[47] The contingent's record books list the name of every member who passed through and on into the services; the names of those killed are written in red ink, and almost every page has its sombre reminder of the toll exacted by this most terrible of British wars.[48]

As there were so many troops in the Aberystwyth area, the College organized classes for officers and men in map-reading, French conversation, and gymnastics, and there were general lectures on the background of the conflict. As these courses were purely voluntary, not surprisingly to those who know the instinctive reaction of British servicemen, there were not many takers, except when, in response to Principal Roberts' complaints of poor attendances, commanding officers called for 'volunteers'.[49]

A considerably more successful wartime College venture, at least initially, was an ambitious 'Music scheme' generously financed by Miss Gwendoline Davies of Llandinam. In the years before the war, Music had flourished in a small way at Aberystwyth under the leadership of David Jenkins, who had been promoted to a

[44] T. F. Roberts, 'Changing Standards', *The Welsh Outlook*, ii. 260–1. In 1915 he put himself for the long vacation at Lloyd George's disposal for war work. 26 May 1915. C.A. (C), not numbered.

[45] 'Recruiting in Cardiganshire', *Cambrian News* (11 September 1914). T. C. James, 'Our O.T.C. and the War', *The Dragon*, xxxviii. 191–3.

[46] T. F. Roberts to Lt.-Col. David Davies, 23 November 1914. T. F. Roberts to Lord Haldane, 9 November 1914. C.A. P/Cr/B/3.

[47] T. C. James, 'Our O.T.C.', loc. cit., pp. 192–3.

[48] For a pacifist's view of the war and an interesting account of the growth of disillusionment, see N.L.W. MSS. 'The Diary of T. Gwynn Jones.'

[49] T. F. Roberts to the Board of Education, 22 December 1914, and to military commanders, 3, 11, 22 February, 3 March 1915. C.A. P/Cr/B/3. In July 1915 the Chemistry laboratories were put at the disposal of Lloyd George, who had just become Minister of Munitions.

chair in 1910. For years at various times during the session choral concerts (which often included Jenkins' own compositions) were performed to the great pleasure of the College community. Unfortunately, Jenkins' health began to fail and, for some time, he was unable to continue his work. Happily, Madame Barbier, wife of the professor of French, was an accomplished musician and she was able to fill the breach. But it had always been felt that instrumental music had been sadly neglected in Wales, and in April 1914 it was arranged that Monsieur Gaston Le Feuve, a distinguished French violinist, should give part-time instruction to students in string instruments. Additionally, Le Feuve and three French assistants were to form a string quartet which, under the general direction of Madame Barbier, was to give some concerts at centres in various parts of Wales. The amount of money available was so small that it is doubtful if much would have come of this scheme.[50]

However, in June 1914 Miss Davies of Llandinam came forward with the magnificent offer of £3,000 a year for five years to finance a more ambitious scheme, which was designed particularly to 'encourage and educate the taste for good classical music' throughout Wales.[51] The war came before a start had actually been made but, after some hesitation, Miss Davies decided in October 1914 that the plan should go ahead, and it was hoped that some of the musicians among the Belgian refugees would be recruited to enlarge the small ensemble.[52] During 1915 several additional classes in Music were organized at the College (a successful mixed choir had to be dropped because of the overriding demands of O.T.C. training), and small orchestral concerts were given in various parts of Wales. All, however, was not plain sailing: there were some student grumblings at the not always tactful dominance of foreigners; 'could there not be found one English or Welsh ewe-lamb capable of teaching Welsh lambs how to baa?', asked a petulant correspondent to *The Dragon*.[53]

Gradually, the scheme broke down: Le Feuve was called away and, later, two of his French assistants drifted off; the work at the College continued but with a diminishing number of students. By early 1916 Miss Davies had come to the conclusion that, in current circumstances, the whole arrangement was 'extravagant'. For her, the major object had been a significant raising of the level of public taste for orchestral music by concerts, lectures, and extra-mural courses of instruction in the towns and villages of Mid-Wales. When Le Feuve had gone she rather reluctantly agreed to continue her support. Unfortunately, Madame Barbier, a powerful, indeed formidable, personality bursting with energy and

---

[50] *Council Minutes* (24 April 1914), pp. 383–4.

[51] Ibid. (26 June 1914), pp. 405–7.

[52] Miss G. Davies to J. H. Davies, 4 October 1914. N.L.W. J. H. Davies MSS. (Corr.).

[53] Madame Barbier, 'The Department of Instrumental Music', 28 May 1915. N.L.W. Thomas Jones MSS. Class J, vol. i, f. 71. *The Dragon*, xxxvii. 191–5. Ibid., pp. 249–50, for a spirited student defence of Madame Barbier.

enthusiasm but notably short of tact and discretion, had ruffled Miss Davies by her domineering ways. In mid 1916 the scheme, which had enjoyed encouraging early success, was for the moment at least wound up. Miss Davies had not abandoned her public-spirited ambitions; a trial run had simply gone amiss. But there would be other schemes: as she wrote to the Registrar, 'let us see to it that the right seed is sown in the furrows, and that the right sowers are there to cast the seed'.[54]

Inevitably, as the war went into its grim second and third years, the character of student life at Aberystwyth became more and more attenuated. Student numbers fell drastically; by October 1916 there were only 250 students in all, and 172 of these were women.[55] The vigorous social life of pre-war days was largely gone. There were entertainments of a sort, but they were conducted *sotto voce* and the old name, 'soirée', lay under 'a ban' because it was too frivolous for the gravity of the times. With a dearth of senior students the quality of leadership fell and standards (especially those governed largely by convention) declined. In the Literary and Debating Society the 'gods', whose more or less witty interjections had always been able to make or mar a debate, got completely out of hand and destroyed the authority of the chairman. By the end of December 1917 relations between men and women students were openly hostile; the women were accused of using their numerical superiority to set up 'petticoat government' by engrossing too many official positions on student committees.[56]

However, all was not gloom: there was always Sergeant Wakeling, head porter and part-time proctor, to lighten student spirits. Wakeling was a great character, the 'universal information bureau' of the College. His maxims, generously laced with malapropisms, were treasured and related with delight by generations of students.[57] He knew his Aberystwyth: 'They call this a mixed College—but, by gad, if they catch you mixing', he said with justice. The war, of course, was made to measure for the old soldier's *ex cathedra* pronouncements: according to him, 'fifty per cent of every man who joins the British army is chucked out of the cavalry'. Wakeling was no mere figure of fun: he was awesome in his way and could be a stickler about the observance of regulations, particularly in the Quad, his especial domain. For all his occasional clashes with students, he remained much-loved and respected and some of the ablest men in College were proud to make use of Wakeling's testimonials to their personal qualities. When

[54] Miss G. Davies to J. H. Davies, 6 January and 25 June 1916. N.L.W. J. H. Davies MSS. (Corr.). Miss G. Davies to T. F. Roberts, 3 April (copy), Lleufer Thomas to Thomas Jones, 10 April 1916. N.L.W. Thomas Jones MSS. Class J, vol. ii, ff. 4, 6.

[55] Principal's Report, 27 October 1916. *U.C.W. Reports* (1916), p. 26.

[56] *The Dragon*, xxxviii. 13, 86–7, xl. 62.

[57] 'Night rain', said the Sergeant, 'is better than day rain, being less evaporating and more percolating.' Almost every volume of *The Dragon* in these years has its quota of 'Sergeant's Sayings'.

he died, in 1924, the College O.T.C. contingent travelled up to Shropshire *en masse* to fire a farewell salute over the old warrior's grave.

Despite the inevitable reduction in the amount of the academic work of the College during wartime, the general temper of things at Aberystwyth was more promising than ever before. The staff included some exceptionally able men who were bursting with enthusiasm for new developments. There is some evidence that Aberystwyth was in better fettle at this time than its sister-Colleges. 'They tell me [Fleure wrote in 1915] Cardiff is "middle-aged" and does not want to stir, that Bangor is a lot of old men . . . I don't know, but I do know that Aberystwyth is seething with life.'[58]

There was, however, the danger that this enthusiasm might be turned by the constraints of wartime into bitter frustration. And, additionally, there was the real possibility that Aberystwyth's control over its own destiny might be sharply reduced by a large-scale reform, then under preliminary consideration, of the machinery of the University of Wales.

Although the additional Treasury grants conceded in 1911 had improved matters considerably, the financial position of the Welsh colleges remained unsatisfactory. By 1914 each of the three colleges was burdened with a deficit on capital account of about £20,000. Aberystwyth's annual bank charges amounted to £800; Rendel's death had meant the loss of £750 a year in income; and the maintenance of the Edward Davies laboratory building, for which no provision had been made in the original benefaction, was a considerable drain on College funds. In February 1914 the Advisory Committee on University Grants (under the chairmanship of Sir William McCormick) recommended to the Chancellor of the Exchequer that sinking funds should be created to eliminate the accumulated debts of the Welsh colleges. McCormick and his colleagues also recommended that the annual Treasury grants should be further increased, on condition that the Welsh local authorities agreed to provide an additional pooled sum from their rates for the University and the colleges.

But McCormick and company also pointed out that the power of the University was so weak in comparison with that of the colleges that it could not co-ordinate their activity effectively and, meantime, there was a 'real danger of wasteful over-lapping of work'. Shortly afterwards, a Departmental Committee of the Board of Education argued strongly that no Treasury aid should be given to the proposed National Medical School for Wales until the structure of the University had been subjected to rigorous examination. Thus armed, in February 1915 the Treasury issued a Minute which postponed the consideration of an increase in grants to

---

[58] Fleure to Thomas Jones, 19 May 1915. N.L.W. Thomas Jones MSS. Class J, vol. i, f. 53. Miss Mary Rathbone, a leading member of the Bangor Council, conceded Aberystwyth's current advantage. 'Our Senate', she said, 'is a singularly lethargic body as a whole . . . almost all the brighter spirits have gone.' To Thomas Jones, 3 October 1915. Ibid., Class J, vol. i, f. 72.

Wales until the University had been reformed. In the first instance, the University and the colleges were invited to consult and to make suggestions for a constitutional revision.[59]

Accordingly, meetings of a Welsh University Conference were held in London during mid 1915. It was speedily evident that the old guard, Isambard Owen and Principal T. F. Roberts in particular, were 'intent upon proving that *their* university' had been 'a very great success', and for many of the College representatives the general watchword was 'maintain our Charters'.[60] It was apparent, too, that some of the Cardiff people still dreamed of a unilateral declaration of independence. Principal E. H. Griffiths especially was believed to be 'determined to achieve Cardiff University' before he retired.[61] This seemed to some so likely to succeed that two friends of Aberystwyth and Bangor began tentatively to discuss plans to combine their two colleges more closely 'to create a *real* University for Wales', which might perhaps also include a new constituent in the technical college at Swansea.[62] Ultimately, the Welsh University Conference ended in stalemate. The Treasury thereupon refused an increase in grants unless the University and the colleges asked for the appointment of a Royal Commission, and agreed beforehand to accept whatever decision the government arrived at on the basis of the findings of the inquiry. By the end of 1915 these stiff terms had been accepted reluctantly.[63]

The conservative-minded officials of the University believed that they would be able to exert sufficient influence to get 'their own nominees' appointed to the Commission. Others, who thought of themselves as the 'Progressives' and did not fear radical changes, hoped that men sympathetic to 'Wales and her aspirations' and above the pull of 'local considerations' would be named. Sir Henry Jones, Gilbert Murray, Dr. Christopher Addison, and W. N. Bruce were mentioned as particularly suitable members.[64] Early in January 1916 Sir John Williams saw Lloyd George, whose influence with the government in anything relating to Wales would certainly be paramount, to urge the nomination of Brigadier-General Owen Thomas, the popular Welsh-speaking Director of military recruiting in North Wales, to the Commission. Lloyd George was highly critical of the Welsh colleges: in his opinion, they had failed to capture the genuine spirit of

[59] *Welsh University and Colleges (Grants In Aid)*, pp. 33–6. T. F. Roberts to Herbert Lewis, 19 February 1914. C.A. P/Cr/B/3.

[60] J. H. Davies and H. J. Fleure to Thomas Jones (two letters), 4 May 1915. Thomas Jones, 'Notes of the Conference', 20 March 1915. N.L.W. Thomas Jones MSS. Class J, vol. i, ff. 29, 45, 46.

[61] Thomas Jones to Fleure, 3 May 1915, Mary Rathbone to Thomas Jones, 3 October 1915. N.L.W. Thomas Jones MSS. Class J, vol. i, ff. 45, 72.

[62] Mary Rathbone to Thomas Jones, 3 and 4 October 1915. Ibid., Class J, vol. i, ff. 72, 73.

[63] Haldane *Report* (Final Report, Part I), pp. 22–3.

[64] Mary Rathbone to Thomas Jones, 4 October 1915. N.L.W. Thomas Jones MSS. Class J, vol. i, f. 73.

Wales, and were quite unable as a consequence to exert any great influence on the country. He said that he did not think that he could do much for the University while Reichel and E. H. Griffiths remained at the head of two of the colleges. Lloyd George made it clear that his influence would be exerted in favour of a Commission made up of 'independently-minded men of stature, not solely or even chiefly drawn from Wales'.[65]

It looks as if Lloyd George had his way. Only two members (Sir Henry Jones and O. M. Edwards, also recently knighted) of the Commission appointed on 12 April 1916 were authentically Welsh, while a third, W. N. Bruce (Lord Aberdare's second son), could be said to be partly Welsh by association. The other Commissioners were Sir William Osler, the distinguished Oxford professor of Medicine, W. H. Bragg, the physicist, W. H. Hadow, an authority on Music who was Principal of Armstrong College, A. D. Hall, an agricultural expert, and Miss Emily Penrose, Principal of Somerville College, Oxford. The chairman of the Commission, a great catch, was Lord Haldane, the philosopher-statesman who had been shunted out of high Cabinet office the year before by absurd politically-interested allegations that he had pro-German sympathies. The Commission's brief was a full-scale examination of the organization of University education in Wales. Over the best part of the next two years the Commission was hard at work.

In the meantime, however, there were private developments of tremendous significance for the Aberystwyth College. In October 1915, even before the appointment of the Royal Commission, it was being bruited about that Aberystwyth had been offered a large sum (£150,000 was mentioned) by unnamed benefactors 'to enable it to set up as an independent University'. Mary Rathbone of Bangor, already unnerved by rumours of Cardiff's separatist ambitions, was naturally thoroughly alarmed: 'what becomes of Bangor?', she asked in anguish.[66] Her fears, of course, were needless. Talk of a large private benefaction to Aberystwyth was premature, the sum mentioned was exaggerated, and there was no question then, or, for that matter, ever subsequently of Aberystwyth wanting to go it entirely alone.

In July 1916 Miss Gwendoline Davies of Llandinam wrote to the Registrar to say that she and her sister, Margaret, were 'very keen on helping Aberystwyth College'. At this stage, no precise sum of money was mentioned; indeed, Miss Davies believed that, until the Royal Commission had made its report, nothing would be done. As she was about to leave for France to do war work, Miss Davies said that she had already 'made provision' for the benefaction in case she did 'not return'. In her letter Miss Davies instanced the things that particularly appealed to her: the acquisition for the College of the land behind the National Library,

---

[65] Sir John Williams to Thomas Jones (in Welsh), 14 January 1916. Ibid., Class J, vol. ii, f. 1.
[66] Mary Rathbone to Thomas Jones, 15 October 1915. Ibid., Class J., vol. i, f. 75.

the building of a Hall in memory of students killed in the war, 'some kind of Music scheme', travelling scholarships for students, and some method of 'obtaining the finest men to fill the university chairs'.[67]

As a matter of fact, a much more elaborate blueprint of the purposes to which the proposed benefaction might, at least in part, be put had already been worked out by Thomas Jones, the close friend of the Llandinam family upon whose advice in philanthropic ventures the Misses Davies especially leaned heavily. Tom Jones (or 'TJ' as he was known to his multitudinous acquaintance) was an old Aberystwyth student who had gone on to a distinguished career at Glasgow University, become a professor of Economics in Belfast for a short time, and had then been called back to Wales in 1910 by David Davies to organize a great national campaign against tuberculosis. In 1916 he was Secretary of the Welsh Insurance Commission and, very shortly, he was to be summoned to London by the new Prime Minister, Lloyd George, to serve as assistant secretary of the Cabinet, and generally lend his energies to the policy of 'push and go' that was to win the war.

Tom Jones' commitment to the Aberystwyth College was total. He had a warm sympathy for Cardiff and Bangor, but this did not begin to approach the strength of his feeling for Aberystwyth. For him the College was, or ought to be, a great 'engine of social progress'; Aberystwyth's 'mission' was to strengthen all that was best in Welsh life, and the vital thing was to have at the College a battery of men in sympathy with 'national ideals' and blessed with great 'inspirational power'.[68]

Early in July 1916 Tom Jones produced a magnificent set of proposals for consideration. He was open-eyed about the current weaknesses of Welsh education: the Intermediate Schools had improved steadily in recent years, but the general level was still too low; students at the university colleges were 'over-lectured, under-tutored and over-examined', and, regrettably, 'degree hunting' tended to emasculate worthier educational ideals. History, perhaps unfortunately, had given Wales three university colleges, and the way to avoid a senseless and expensive duplication of work was for Aberystwyth, Bangor, and Cardiff to specialize in those subjects which were of especial importance to their hinterland areas, or in those disciplines for which each was particularly fitted.

Jones' chief concern, however, was for the future of Aberystwyth. He believed that the College enjoyed certain exceptional advantages: in a special sense the whole of Wales was 'its province', and its more famous old students in the past had made an unmatched contribution to 'nationalist ideals'. Moreover, experience had shown that it was possible to have 'a far intenser College life' at Aberystwyth than at either Bangor or Cardiff; and there was certainly 'no comparison' between

[67] Miss G. Davies to J. H. Davies, 16 July (1916). N.L.W. J. H. Davies MSS. (Corr.).
[68] Thomas Jones to J. H. Davies, 31 May 1916. N.L.W. J. H. Davies MSS. (Corr.).

the strength of the Old Students' Associations of the two other colleges and that of Aberystwyth. These were 'priceless' factors in any system of education. Currently at Aberystwyth there was a group of young teachers moved by the highest of ideals and committed particularly to an intensive study of every phase of the life and history of Wales. Finally, Aberystwyth had the National Library and 'all that it connotes'.

The prescription for Aberystwyth, therefore, seemed obvious: it should strive to become a great centre of humanist education. The training of 'character and personality', to which examination success would be subsidiary, should be openly avowed as the main object; a tutorial and seminar system should be introduced and, as quickly as possible, halls of residence, a students' union, and a large hall or theatre (with a stage, an organ, and facilities for art exhibitions) should be erected to provide the setting for a vigorous social and intellectual life.

Certain academic interests should be especially emphasized. Aberystwyth had a strong claim to be selected (it was on the cards that a choice would have to be made) by the Haldane Commissioners as the one place in Wales where advanced work in Agriculture was to be carried on. The College should make Celtic Studies a special feature with an ambitious programme of teaching and research (perhaps including endowed Readerships at the National Library) in Welsh, in cognate Celtic languages, in palaeography and in archaeology. Tom Jones believed that Welsh students were aesthetically underprivileged, and developments in Music and Art loomed large in his proposals. And his memorandum stressed the need for a school of Social Science at Aberystwyth. It was apparent that there would be a great post-war demand for the teaching of applied sciences and, convinced that 'the secularization of science' had been the 'curse' of Germany, something which Britain must avoid at all costs, he thought that studies in depth ('we must try at Aber. to think things together') of man in society provided the best countervailing influence. The College should make a determined effort in these four areas to offer teaching of a quality and range 'unsurpassed' in the United Kingdom; and it could all be done in a natural setting difficult to equal. Finally, he looked to a great surge in extra-mural work which could, in a generation or two, 'work a revolution' in the rural life of Wales.

TJ was convinced that all this was 'in no sense visionary or utopian'. Given adequate funds, ten or fifteen years of 'push and go', as he called it, would bring it about. As for the location, land was available at the Buarth, but he would much prefer to develop the College on Penglais where the 'genius' of Greenslade, architect of the National Library, could have free play. His estimate was that a sum of £250,000 would be adequate for all these needs. Once the war was over, 'industrial warfare' would be resumed ever more sharply: the University should stand for the public good against all class or sectional interests, it should be a 'great reconciling force'. Here, in all these great purposes, was Aberystwyth's 'fine destiny' and the Misses Davies could help the College to work it out, as TJ persuasively said, better than anyone else he knew.[69]

David Davies, at this time at any rate, seems to have been strongly of the opinion that there should be a central fund for the whole of the University and that all subscriptions should be pooled, a suggestion hotly resisted by Principal T. F. Roberts who saw it as a threat to College independence.[70] In the event, the Misses Davies decided to confine their benefaction to Aberystwyth, and on 20 October 1916 the Haldane Commissioners were told that anonymous donors had signified their intention to give £100,000 to the College in instalments of £20,000 spread over five years.[71]

There was one instance where immediate action was called for: there was a very real danger that Fleure and O. T. Jones, two of the College's brightest stars, might be lost. Neither of them wanted to go, but there was no doubt that they could command considerably higher salaries elsewhere, and the fact was that for years they had financed their extensive research schemes from their wholly inadequate salaries. For economic reasons, O. T. Jones had had to resign his seat on the Council of the Geological Society; and Fleure, who was personally against a policy of high initial salaries for professors because of the risk of 'a social cleavage' between the professoriate and 'the world to which the students belong', pleaded for research grants as a way out of the difficulty.[72] In October 1916 the Misses Davies, who understood that it would be a 'calamity' if Fleure and O. T. Jones moved elsewhere, agreed that an increase of £150 a year for five years in their salaries was a legitimate charge on the benefaction.[73]

Early in 1917 O. T. Jones was virtually offered an attractive post at Liverpool University at a considerably higher salary but, ultimately, on the 'high grounds of zeal and devotion' to Aberystwyth, as T. F. Roberts noted with pride, the overture was rejected.[74] O. T. Jones, of course, was already working in his chosen field, and his research interests would certainly help to keep him in Wales for some time. But Fleure, although he also held a lectureship in Geography, was professor of Zoology and the teaching duties of his chair deflected him from his primary interest in Geography and Anthropology. Geography was developing

---

[69] TJ (endorsed so), 8 July 1916. N.L.W. Thomas Jones MSS. Class J, vol. ii, f. 23 (1–18). Printed in Thomas Jones, *A Theme with Variations* (Gregynog Press, 1933), pp. 68–85.

[70] Miss G. Davies to J. H. Davies, 25 October 1916. N.L.W. J. H. Davies MSS. (Corr.). Lleufer Thomas to Thomas Jones, 28 November 1916. N.L.W. Thomas Jones MSS. Class J, vol. ii, f. 49.

[71] Haldane *Report* (Minutes of Evidence), p. 135.

[72] O. T. Jones to J. H. Davies, 31 August 1916. N.L.W. J. H. Davies MSS. (Corr.). H. J. Fleure, 'Memorandum *re* College Development', 1916. N.L.W. Thomas Jones MSS. Class J, vol. ii, f. 37.

[73] 'Statement *re* Fleure and O. T. Jones Salary Increase', October 1916, and John Owens to J. H. Davies, 26 October 1916. N.L.W. J. H. Davies MSS. (Corr.). *Council Minutes* (15 December 1916), p. 122.

[74] T. F. Roberts to Thomas Jones, 20 and 24 March 1917. N.L.W. Thomas Jones MSS. Class J, vol. iii, ff. 43, 44.

rapidly in the schools, but it had not yet achieved general recognition by British universities. Fleure believed, with a crusading passion, that Geography, especially 'if treated on humanistic lines', could make an immense contribution to the advancement of learning. The University of Wales had already agreed to accept Geography as an honours degree course, and Fleure was desperately anxious to exchange his chair in Zoology for a new one (endowed from the Llandinam gift to the College) in Geography and Anthropology.[75]

Inevitably, there were delays before the new chair could be established. The Principal, Tom Jones, Lleufer Thomas, and the Llandinam ladies wanted to endow the chair in perpetuity, but J. H. Davies, who feared that Fleure might be attracted elsewhere (Oxford had been mentioned as a strong possibility) when the war was over, argued for a five-year endowment only. Tom Jones conceded that, if Fleure were to go, 'we may not get another Fleure', but he insisted that this was a risk that had to be taken. In any case, as he said, 'there were great men before Agamemnon, and there will be great men after him'.[76] On 29 May 1918 the new chair of Geography and Anthropology (endowed in perpetuity) was established and Fleure was appointed to it.[77] The new honours degree course was the first one in Britain which enabled students to read for initial and higher degrees in Geography in both the Faculties of Arts and Science. Oxford, Cambridge, and London Universities had been anticipated, and even Liverpool, which had established a chair a few months before Aberystwyth, confined its work to the Faculty of Arts. A great new department, which was to make an immensely important contribution to the growth of an infant university discipline and bring considerable prestige to Aberystwyth as a consequence, had been established.[78]

There was, at the outset, some degree of misunderstanding about the Llandinam benefaction. J. H. Davies understood that it had been made unconditionally, and, indeed, had so described it to the Haldane Commission.[79] This was not strictly true. The donors wanted their gift applied broadly along the lines of Tom Jones' memorandum, although they were certainly prepared to discuss other possibilities. Principal T. F. Roberts had hoped that £20,000 could be used to rid the College once and for all of the crippling weight of debt that unbalanced its finances. He also hoped that some portion of the second instalment would be available to attract a supplemental £ for £ grant from the Board of Agriculture

---

[75] Haldane *Report* (Minutes of Evidence), pp. 150–1, Appendix VII, pp. 289–91.

[76] Thomas Jones to John Owens, 9 and 29 January 1918. N.L.W. Thomas Jones MSS. Class J, vol. viii, ff. 103, 106. Thomas Jones to J. H. Davies, 26 January 1918. N.L.W. J. H. Davies MSS. (Corr.). The analogy was apt: Fleure had mastered cognate subjects on something like the scale that Agamemnon conquered territories.

[77] *Council Minutes* (29 May 1918), pp. 277–8.

[78] *Geography at Aberystwyth* (ed. E. G. Bowen, H. Carter, and J. A. Taylor, Cardiff, 1968), pp. xix–xx, and passim.

[79] Haldane *Report* (Minutes of Evidence), p. 135.

to enable the College to erect a new building for the department of Agriculture. The Misses Davies were 'not keen' on either of these two proposals, although, reluctantly, they were prepared to make a loan (to be paid back as soon as possible) from the benefaction for the Agricultural building.[80]

It was certain that a considerable sum of money would be used to launch an ambitious Music scheme, which the Misses Davies had very much at heart. In 1915 David Jenkins, the professor of Music at the College, had died. Soon afterwards L. J. Roberts, a civil servant at the Board of Education, suggested to the Registrar that the very man for the vacancy ('Aberystwyth with him as its Music professor could hold up its head alongside Cardiff and Bangor') was D. Vaughan Thomas, known alternatively as 'Dai *bach* piano'.[81] Despite the patronizing nickname, this was a perfectly sensible suggestion. Vaughan Thomas, who had received his early training from Dr. Joseph Parry, had gone on subsequently to Oxford where he had taken a degree in Mathematics and, later, a doctorate in Music. He was a prolific composer of instrumental music whose work imaginatively expressed the distinctive qualities of Welsh culture; moreover, as a pioneer in the movement to lead his countrymen forward from their traditional 'limited choralism' to an appreciation of other musical forms, he seemed to be ideally equipped for the particular campaign that the Misses Davies had in mind.[82]

But the donors and their advisers had their eyes on a bigger, or at any rate a better-known, fish. Throughout 1917 the Music scheme remained under consideration and, at an early date, Henry Hadow of the Royal Commission, who thought that in a musical sense Wales was 'an unworked gold-mine', was consulted. Early in June it had been decided to make a tentative approach to Dr. Walford Davies who, despite his name, could not claim, according to his biographer, to be more than 'one-eighth Welsh'.[83] Walford Davies was then organist and director of the choir at the Temple in London, where his recitals drew 'enormous congregations'. Late in June 1917 Hadow reported that Davies was immensely attracted by the 'Welsh project', but that he would not accept a position that was less than 'authoritative'. Hadow sensibly offered an option: Davies could choose between 'a supreme directorship' of Music for Wales, a university appointment (endowed by the chair at Aberystwyth) conferring plenary power, or, less obtrusively, he could work through a 'general Musical Council' on which the three professors of Music in Wales would be technically equal but where Davies'

---

[80] T. F. Roberts to Thomas Jones, 26 April, Thomas Jones to T. F. Roberts, 4 September 1917. N.L.W. Thomas Jones MSS. Class J, vol. iii, ff. 48, 79.

[81] L. J. Roberts to J. H. Davies, 4 September 1916. N.L.W. J. H. Davies MSS. (Corr.).

[82] There is a very good notice of Vaughan Thomas in *D.W.B.*

[83] 'Notes of Dr. Hadow's conversations', 27 April 1917. Thomas Jones to Miss Daisy [Margaret] Davies, and to H. Hadow, 2 June 1917. N.L.W. Thomas Jones MSS. Class J, vol. iii, ff. 51, 57, 59. Oddly enough, at first, in Tom Jones' letters it is Walter, then Waldorf, and Walford only at the third attempt. H. C. Colles, *Walford Davies* (Oxford, 1942), p. 11.

personality and reputation would in practice ensure that he was at least *primus inter pares*. On reflection Walford Davies said he preferred the latter proposal, the other was 'a little too autocratic for Wales'.[84]

However, when in February 1918 the Royal Commission *Report* appeared, its recommendations on the organization of Music in the University, which were almost certainly written by Hadow, incorporated some features of both suggestions. The *Report* proposed that there should be a university post of Music Director which, 'preferably', would be combined with a chair at a constituent college. The Director would enjoy 'a certain primacy' over his professorial colleagues roughly analogous to that exercised by the Vice-Chancellor over the other Principals. The Director would be *ex officio* chairman of a Council of Music which should act as the supreme consultative body on all matters concerning musical education in Wales.[85]

John Owens, friend and one-time steward of the Llandinam family, freely admitted that the scheme would stand a much greater chance of success if the Director were based at Cardiff and had ready access to the great population of Glamorgan. But, as he said, 'Aber. is our College', and the offer that was made (as discreetly as possible to avoid hostile criticism) to the University ultimately was a sum of money sufficiently large to endow a chair in Music at Aberystwyth and a Musical Directorship for Wales. And it was made clear that the gift was 'definitely dependent' upon the appointment of Walford Davies, in the first instance, to the Directorship for a period of ten years. By April 1918, after a flying visit to Aberystwyth to see 'how it felt to be there', Walford Davies had agreed to accept the twin posts if they were offered to him. In November 1918 the University Court appointed him to the Directorship, and soon afterwards he was elected to the chair at Aberystwyth.[86] With the indispensable help of Llandinam money, another inspiring teacher of outstanding reputation had been secured for Aberystwyth.

There had been a danger shortly before that Aberystwyth would lose or at least for the future have only a share of the extremely valuable unofficial services of Tom Jones. In 1917 with no great enthusiasm because, as he said, his loyalties were 'much more closely interwoven' with Aberystwyth than Cardiff, TJ had allowed himself to be persuaded by Sir Henry Jones to apply for the Principalship of the Cardiff College which seemed likely soon to become vacant. Henry Jones was 'determined to leave no stone unturned' to get his friend and former pupil appointed, and he managed to persuade David Davies to endorse the candidature

[84] H. Hadow to Thomas Jones, 24 June 1917. N.L.W. Thomas Jones MSS. Class J, vol. iii, f. 62.

[85] Haldane *Report* (Recommendations), pp. 86–8.

[86] John Owens to Thomas Jones (June 1917), Thomas Jones to Miss Davies, 17 April, and to John Owens, 5 June 1918. N.L.W. Thomas Jones MSS. Class J, vol. iii, f. 61, vol. iv, f. 14, vol. viii, f. 111. Colles, op. cit., p. 117.

with the argument that Cardiff was 'a more important arena' than Aberystwyth and, if appointed, TJ could do a great deal to 'ease' the difficult labour problems besetting South Wales.[87]

David Davies' two sisters were aghast at the prospect of losing Tom Jones. They called him 'a broken reed' and prophesied that his going to Cardiff would mean the collapse of 'the Aberystwyth programme', or at least that part of it concerned with Music, Art, and the construction of aesthetically attractive buildings at the College. TJ admitted that for Principal Roberts and J. H. Davies these things were much less important than some other aims. One way out of the difficulty would be for the Llandinam ladies to establish a national fund for the University, 'the bulk' of which would be 'earmarked' for Aberystwyth. TJ, even if at Cardiff, could act as chairman of the fund and administer it along the agreed lines. This desperate and probably unworkable proposal indicates Tom Jones' extreme reluctance to sever his connection with Aberystwyth. The Misses Davies would not listen to any suggestion of diverting any part of the proposed benefaction from Aberystwyth; they felt that Cardiff had 'plenty of money' whereas Aberystwyth had 'none'.[88]

In the event, nothing came of TJ's Cardiff application. His friend Sir Percy Watkins, who took some early soundings, found 'people lukewarm', and TJ himself thought that he had no more than an outside chance. Fleure and John Owens tried to persuade him to stand down, and perhaps he would have been well advised to do so. He received ten votes at the Cardiff College Council meeting, but he was strongly opposed by the medical men (who had long memories of his work on the Insurance Commission), by certain Cardiff city councillors, and some Church and Tory members who disliked his socialism. Ultimately, Principal E. H. Griffiths was asked to continue for another year, and TJ concluded 'it was goodbye to Cardiff'.[89]

Almost immediately his friends began to formulate schemes to bring him to Aberystwyth. Henry Jones, whose excessively vigorous advocacy had hindered rather than helped TJ's candidature at Cardiff, continued to behave like a bull in a china shop. He suggested that Principal Roberts, whose health was visibly failing, should be invited to retire with a pension provided by the Misses Davies. In July 1918 the infinitely more tactful John Owens proposed that TJ should go to Aberystwyth as Director of Social Studies, a suggestion warmly welcomed by Principal Roberts. John Owens argued that at Aberystwyth TJ would be on the spot to carry through the various development schemes that were in train. Moreover, the Directorship of Social Studies could be a discreet soft-shoe shuffle

---

[87] *Whitehall Diary* (ed. K. Middlemass, 1969), i. 37. N.L.W. Thomas Jones Diary (1917), pp. 84, 93.
[88] N.L.W. Ibid. (1917), p. 99.
[89] Ibid., pp. 82–3, (1918), pp. 21–2, 43, 49–50, 56–7, 60–2. John Owens to Thomas Jones, 22 January 1918. N.L.W. Thomas Jones MSS. Class J, vol. viii, f. 104.

towards the ultimate target, for it would 'no doubt . . . lead to the Principalship in due course'.[90]

Despite his ardent desire to work officially for the College, Tom Jones had doubts about this scheme. His wife, Rene, who was also an old Aberystwyth student, riddled John Owens' proposal with her shrewd criticisms. She pointed out that the Directorship of Social Studies would not necessarily be a stepping-stone to the Principalship, and she thought that the Senate and Council might well 'resent' having TJ 'thrust on them by the Davies family', upon whom she did not think her husband should become personally dependent.[91] Ultimately, TJ came to the conclusion that he would feel 'too restricted' in the position suggested and that it would be foolish to give up an assistant secretaryship of the Cabinet for so limited an alternative. However, he was willing to consider 'any other suggestion' to bring him to Aberystwyth that J. H. Davies and other friends might propose.[92] T. F. Roberts' health steadily deteriorated, and in October it was apparent that he would be unable to return to duty for some considerable time. Lleufer Thomas thought that fairly soon the College Council, however reluctantly, would be forced to consider the appointment of a Deputy Principal and, if this were offered to TJ, it would be sufficiently important to 'justify' his resignation from the Cabinet secretariat. In fact, nothing came of this either.[93]

Meanwhile, Tom Jones continued his unofficial work for the College, and in one instance of the utmost significance for Aberystwyth at this time his influence was crucially important. Almost as soon as the war ended in 1918, David Davies offered, jointly with his sisters, to give £20,000 to establish a chair of International Politics at Aberystwyth. At that time, perhaps of necessity to keep their sanity, men almost everywhere hoped devoutly, indeed believed confidently, that the late conflict would be 'the war to end wars', a just compensation for the terrible carnage endured for four years. Idealists, of whom David Davies was certainly one, looked to 'a League of Free Peoples' to maintain justice in the world, and they did not doubt that a 'righteous' peace settlement was at hand. But there were limits to what even the most enlightened statesmanship alone could achieve; it must be sustained by a 'new spirit' in the world, and to bring that about 'consecrated energy, goodwill, knowledge, and enlightened public opinion in all countries' would be vitally necessary. It was now the day of the small nation as well as of the great, and by means of the new chair Wales could offer

---

[90] Thomas Jones to Sir Henry Jones (copy sent to J. H. Davies, who was thus early forewarned and perhaps forearmed), 24 July 1918. N.L.W. J. H. Davies Cwrt Mawr MSS. (T. I. Ellis donation 1958/62).

[91] Thomas Jones to Sir Henry Jones (copy to J. H. Davies), 25 July 1918. N.L.W. Ibid.

[92] Thomas Jones to J. H. Davies, 22 October 1918. N.L.W. Ibid.

[93] Lleufer Thomas to Thomas Jones, 25 October, 7 December 1918. N.L.W. Thomas Jones MSS. Class W, vol. xviii, ff. 191, 196. Thomas' idea was that TJ should be professor of Public Administration, Director of Social Studies, and Deputy Principal, but, as T. F. Roberts was too ill to be consulted, nothing could be done, any action taken 'might appear to be an attempt to bring about his resignation'.

'a comprehensive commission of scientific research into the world's most pressing problem of the immediate future'. With an endowment of £20,000, the College could attract 'the best international scholar the world possesses' to the chair, which was to be in memory of Welsh University students killed in the war and was to be associated with the 'illustrious name' of President Woodrow Wilson.[94]

Aberystwyth's friends were delighted with this marvellously generous and imaginative offer. Lleufer Thomas was convinced that the new endowment would 'do more than anything else to give international rank to the College'. He believed also that a chair in International Politics would provide a great fillip to Aberystwyth's efforts to introduce a new department (or rather Faculty) of Social Science and Public Administration. He hoped that it would soon be possible to establish a chair of Public Administration, and that Economics would be divided into two, Economic History and 'Economics proper', to which 'great prominence and attention' should be given, 'both from the national (or domestic) and international point of view'. Lleufer Thomas half assumed that Tom Jones, so endlessly fertile in suggestion, had prompted the Wilson chair foundation. In fact, as TJ said, 'The idea originated with David Davies himself and the only credit I can take is for having fought for Aberystwyth as against Oxford, and in this Miss Davies supported me heartily.'[95]

Once again Tom Jones, strategically placed, had done his old College a power of good. There is no question that the Wilson chair (the first ever established in International Politics in the world) did a great deal for scholarship generally, and for the Aberystwyth College in particular. Certainly over the years, as will appear, there were times when the chair and its occupants occasioned the stormiest of controversies, inside and outside the College. But the foundation enabled Aberystwyth to pioneer an entirely new university discipline, and it brought to the College (and from thence sent all over the world on high prestige lecture tours and missions of academic inquiry) a succession of eminent scholars whose published work redounded very much to the credit of the College.

At the end of the 1914–18 war, Aberystwyth was poised, as never before, to make a gigantic stride forward. It was sad that Principal T. F. Roberts, the man who had laboured so heroically in the sometimes impossibly difficult days of the past, should be unable to lead his College at this time when an exceptionally bright future was so close at hand. In September 1918 he was buoyed up by his doctor's promise that, with a further period of convalescence at Towyn, he would

---

[94] David Davies to Sir John Williams, 5 December 1918, and 'Memorandum on the establishment of a chair of International Politics in the University of Wales', 5 December 1918. N.L.W. Llandinam MSS. (Wilson chair, box 2).

[95] Exchange of letters, Lleufer Thomas and Thomas Jones, 7 and 10 December 1918. N.L.W. Thomas Jones MSS. Class W, vol. xviii, ff. 196, 197. Aberystwyth's proposal to establish a Faculty of Public Administration and Social Studies was presented to the Royal Commission, 23 March 1917. Haldane *Report* (Minutes of Evidence), pp. 44–57.

be fit to return to work after Christmas; in October, however, he was 'unable to see to anything', and thereafter there was never any question of his return.[96] In December Tom Jones, seconded by Herbert Lewis M.P. and Sir Evan D. Jones, tried hard to persuade Lloyd George to make amends for past neglects by recommending the Principal for a knighthood, but the Prime Minister, elsewhere so open-handed (perhaps in more than one sense) with honours, did not respond.[97] After lingering painfully for many months, T. F. Roberts died at Westcliff-on-Sea on 5 August 1919, a few weeks before his fifty-ninth birthday.

It cannot be said that T. F. Roberts was a great Principal, although, in detail, over the years he built up an impressive record of achievement. In 1891 in many respects the College still fell some way below a genuine university standard: by 1919 the obvious deficiencies had all been eliminated, and T. F. Roberts had made a very considerable contribution to the transformation. Yet an air of disappointment hangs over his career. Possibly he scaled too many ladders too quickly early on in life, and when he failed to realize his full exceptional promise, something less than justice was done thereafter to his reputation. Certainly it was true, as Fleure said, that Wales never accorded him the recognition that was his due.[98] Partly this stemmed from superficial impressions. Roberts did not have a commanding presence, and his lugubrious demeanour ('It is a pity', wrote Marchant Williams, the cruellest of lampooners, 'that he always wears the appearance of a monk who has broken his vows') masked whatever natural vivacity he possessed.[99] He was the least masterful of men: he allowed himself to be hectored by Reichel, and largely ignored by Isambard Owen; Lloyd George, overflowing with *brio*, evidently thought him of little account. All three underestimated him.

Despite recurrent ill health, T. F. Roberts had remarkable stamina; this was a matter of will and a sense of duty that never faltered. The characteristic note of his life was an intense earnestness, and the chief driving force was an utter devotion to the College. This was clearly recognized by those around him who, over the years, learned to ignore his anxious prolixity on paper, and to look beyond the unexciting manner. Rendel, especially, Lleufer Thomas, Tom Jones, and the rest of the Council recognized the Principal's solid if unspectacular qualities; the more able members of the staff, Herford, Fleure, Ethé, for example, all genuinely

[96] T. F. Roberts to the Registrar (copy), 10 September 1918. N.L.W. Lleufer Thomas MSS. IA. Mrs. T. F. Roberts to Thomas Jones, 12 October 1918. N.L.W. Thomas Jones MSS. Class J, vol. iv, f. 87.

[97] Exchange of letters, Thomas Jones and Lleufer Thomas, 12 and 13 December 1918. Ibid., Class W, vol. xviii, ff. 198, 199. It is difficult not to agree with Mrs. Roberts who wrote after her husband's death that the omission was 'a national scandal'. 13 August 1919. N.L.W. Lleufer Thomas MSS. IA.

[98] H. J. Fleure to Thomas Jones, 27 February 1915. N.L.W. Thomas Jones MSS. Class J, vol. i, f. 25. In Fleure's opinion, Roberts exemplified 'the best and broadest nationalism' of the Welsh.

[99] Marchant Williams to J. Glyn Davies, 23 August 1906. N.L.W. J. Glyn Davies MSS. 7835.

respected his scholarship. By and large the impact he made on his students, compared with that of T. C. Edwards, was not great. But for twenty-eight years, with an infinity of pains, T. F. Roberts had worked to make Aberystwyth a great centre of higher studies, especially those relating to Wales. Considering the difficulties he had to face, he had succeeded to a surprising extent.

7

'We are Face to Face with New Conditions'[1]

O
N 6 February 1918 the long-awaited (not altogether without trepidation in some quarters) Final *Report* of the Haldane Royal Commission
appeared. During the period of inquiry, especially at the outset,
rumours of one kind and another, perhaps inevitably, had caused
alarm in some circles. Professor John Morris Jones and several of his Bangor
colleagues had been thoroughly disturbed by a 'suspicion' that Aberystwyth, basing
its case on the possession of the National Library of Wales, was going to lodge
a claim that all advanced studies in Welsh should be concentrated exclusively at
that College. 'Welsh national sentiment', he warned J. H. Davies, 'will revolt
against a proposal to degrade that subject at any College.'[2] There was, of course,
nothing in this rumour, although the Aberystwyth authorities were certainly
planning a considerable expansion of Celtic Studies at the College. There was
rather more substance in some of the fears engendered by the attitude of Cardiff
on certain questions. A committee of the South Wales College Council, established
to draw up proposals for submission to the Royal Commission, suggested in May
1916 that Cardiff should get 50 per cent of whatever grants from the rates the
Welsh local authorities could be persuaded to vote to the University.[3] And a
month later, Herbert Lewis, M.P., picked up a 'hint', which caused him much
concern, that Cardiff's separatist ambitions were 'telling upon some of the
members of the Royal Commission'.[4]

In the event, the Haldane *Report*, when it appeared, gave a general satisfaction
which stemmed perhaps, at least partly, from a sense of relief that its tenor was
less radical than had been expected. The University Court, for example, congratulated the Commissioners on the 'thoroughness' of their labours and the

[1] J. H. Davies, 'Memorandum on the policy to be pursued by the authorities at Aberystwyth',
12 December 1918. N.L.W. Thomas Jones MSS. Class W, vol. iv, f. 94.

[2] J. Morris Jones to J. H. Davies, 26 March 1916. N.L.W. J. H. Davies MSS. (Corr.).

[3] Confidential Report of the Committee of the Council, 29 May 1916. N.L.W. Thomas Jones
MSS. Class J, vol. ii, f. 12.

[4] J. Herbert Lewis to J. H. Davies, 23 June 1916. N.L.W. J. H. Davies MSS. (Corr.).

'insight' shown in their recommendations.[5] It will be remembered that the Royal Commission owed its appointment to the desire of the government, perturbed by the critical comments of two committees, to strengthen the weak authority of the University. In these circumstances, there had been widespread fears in the Colleges that their much cherished autonomy would be sharply diminished. But the Commissioners resisted whatever temptation there was to recommend a root and branch alteration in the structure of the University and, as J. E. Lloyd, Registrar of Bangor, said, the Colleges had 'no reason to complain' of the changes that were suggested.[6]

The Commissioners had no hesitation in recommending the continuance of the national, federal University, despite a feeling evinced by several witnesses that, currently, it was not particularly in consonance with the needs of Welsh national life; and, in the end, the Cardiff Senate failed to persuade the Commissioners that the interests of Wales as a whole would best be served by allowing their secessionist ambitions free rein. Even the hostile observations of the Treasury were judged by the Commissioners to be more a timely warning of future dangers than a valid indictment of the practices of the past. The Commission accepted the arguments of the considerable majority of witnesses, with certain members of the Aberystwyth College Council cited as particularly forceful advocates, that Welsh sentiment, buttressed by strong practical considerations, demanded one national university rather than two, or possibly three, palpably weak ones.[7]

At the same time it was evident that the governing bodies of the University needed some considerable reorganization. One great problem was 'how to put life' into the University Court. Haldane and his colleagues wished to make it 'a Parliament of higher education', a thoroughly democratic body closely in touch with the mainsprings of national life. They proposed, therefore, that the Court should be considerably enlarged (rather more than doubled in size) and that the representation on it of the Welsh local authorities should be more than trebled. Sound democratic theory apart, there was another solid reason supporting this change. There was the strong hope that, if the local authorities were given a more powerful voice in the calling of the tune, they might be persuaded to make a considerable contribution to the paying of the piper by means of a special rate of a penny in the pound for University purposes. The Commission proposed that executive functions should be exercised by a small Council, representative of the Court, but vested with important independent powers in the allocation to the Colleges of the block grants received from government sources.[8]

It was overwhelmingly apparent that the University Senate had 'few friends'.

[5] Emrys Evans, op. cit., p. 82.
[6] J. E. Lloyd to J. H. Davies, 8 April 1918. N.L.W. J. H. Davies MSS. (Corr.).
[7] Haldane *Report* (The Present System and its Problems), pp. 24–32.
[8] Ibid., pp. 35, 37. Recommendations, pp. 60–7.

Principal E. H. Griffiths, without too much exaggeration, offered the opinion that it would take two years or, at best, nineteen months to get even the Ten Commandments through the cumbrous processes of the University Senate.[9] The Commission proposed that it should disappear and be replaced by an Academic Board of seventeen members, mainly elected by the Faculties of the Colleges, whose chief function was to provide advice on academic matters to the Council. The old offices of Senior and Junior Deputy Chancellor were also to disappear; instead, there was to be one officer, called the Pro-Chancellor. There were some other recommendations of particular interest: it was proposed that the University should be adequately represented on the specialist committees upon whose recommendation the Councils of the Colleges based their appointments to chairs; apart from its inherent reasonableness, this was a response to the insistent Treasury demand for a greater central University control. And, recognizing that there were certain fields of scholarship and culture of particular importance to Wales, the Commissioners proposed the establishment of a Board of Celtic Studies, a Council of Music, and, to co-ordinate the work of the Colleges in extra-mural work, a University Extension Board. Additionally, the setting up of a University Press was suggested.[10]

Apart from minor suggestions, left to the Colleges themselves to implement in detail, the Commission was prepared to leave the system of government of the constituent Colleges by Court, Council, and Senate unchanged. The system had worked well over the years and Haldane and his colleagues were content broadly to follow the advice of Lord Kenyon, Senior Deputy Chancellor of the University, to let 'sleeping dogs lie'.[11] There were, however, to be two new colleges in an enlarged University: despite Cardiff's strong claim to a straightforward annexation, the Commission recommended that the proposed National School of Medicine should become a separate constituent College, and, given the fulfilment of certain conditions, the Technical College at Swansea should be transformed into a University College constituent of the University.[12]

By and large the Haldane Commission had succeeded in striking a nice balance between the University and the Colleges; some old weaknesses had been overcome, others had been reduced if not eliminated, and no legitimate interest had received outrageous treatment of the kind suffered by the Aberystwyth College at the hands of the Aberdare Committee. Moreover, there were other grounds for general satisfaction. The University of Wales and the constituent Colleges had never been adequately financed and the Haldane Commissioners, who were not short of sympathetic understanding, clearly recognized that dominant fact. The

---

[9] Ibid. (The Present System and its Problems), p. 37. Minutes of Evidence, pp. 12–13.
[10] Ibid. (Recommendations), pp. 66, 83–8, 90, 92.
[11] Ibid. (Minutes of Evidence), p. 160.
[12] Ibid. (Recommendations), pp. 72–5.

Report admitted, without reservation, that the need for additional funds for university education in Wales was 'great and pressing'. The Commissioners earnestly called on the Welsh local authorities to face up to their obligations. The produce of a penny rate levied over all of Wales, matched by a Treasury contribution on a £ for £ basis (an equivalence that ought to apply to private benefactions, too), would enable university education in Wales, in the opinion of the Commissioners, 'to be at last established on a really worthy basis'. And the *Report* also suggested that the Treasury should be prepared to offer grants in aid of capital expenditure proportionate to local contributions made specifically for that purpose.[13]

On the face of it the times were propitious, as never before, for an adequate public financing of university education in Britain. It was common doctrine among thinking men that the country had fought the late war against a formidable adversary (which, for years, had given education a much higher national priority) with a dangerous insufficiency of trained brain power. This was certainly the considered opinion of the Prime Minister, Lloyd George. Indeed, his imaginative appointment of the distinguished academic, H. A. L. Fisher, to the Board of Education in December 1916 was publicly recognized as a long overdue attempt to make up for the criminal neglects of the past.[14] With Lloyd George in Downing Street and H. A. L. Fisher at the Board of Education, British universities had legitimate cause for optimism. Nor was this all: wonder of wonders, even English public opinion, that notoriously late developer in matters educational, seemed at last to have caught up. 'For the first time in national history', Fisher referring to England especially, wrote in 1918, 'education was a popular subject.'[15]

On 14 August 1918 a large deputation from the University of Wales, led by Lord Kenyon, had an interview at Downing Street with the Prime Minister and H. A. L. Fisher. The purpose of the meeting was to ask for considerably increased Treasury assistance to the University on the scale suggested by the Royal Commission. The deputation based its claim, as ever, on the relative poverty of Wales supported by the severely practical argument that, if Britain were to 'hold its place' in the world against its more formidable foreign rivals, considerably more

---

[13] Haldane *Report* (Recommendations), pp. 93–8. Curiously enough, at the very time when the Haldane Commission was exhorting Welsh local authorities to do their duty to the University, the Minister of Education was insisting that it was 'undesirable' that rate assistance to the English civic universities should be increased because 'one of the main dangers which confronted academic life in the civic universities was unintelligent municipal control, and any further increase in municipal influence would have to be very seriously and anxiously watched'. Memorandum of an interview with the Chancellor of the Exchequer by H. A. L. Fisher. 22 July 1918. P.R.O. Ed. 24/2027.

[14] For the general delight (especially among academics) at Fisher's appointment, see the congratulatory letters (December 1916) in Bodl. Fisher MSS. Box 3.

[15] H. A. L. Fisher, *An Unfinished Autobiography* (Oxford, 1940), p. 94. In January 1919 Lloyd George considered moving Fisher elsewhere but he received so many 'representations' against it that he decided it would be 'disastrous' to make the change. Lloyd George to Fisher, 9 January 1919. Bodl. Fisher MSS. Box 3.

Exchequer money would have to be spent on all British universities. Additionally, Vice-Chancellor Reichel and others pointed out that 75 to 80 per cent of the students of the University of Wales were working class, a proportion approached but not equalled even by Scotland, and one that was far greater than anything that obtained in England. Praiseworthy as this was, it was achieved only at the price of very low fees and a consequently reduced income. Lord Kenyon said that if a larger Treasury grant were conceded, on a conditional basis, it would give the University 'a great lever' to overcome any continuing reluctance on the part of Welsh local authorities to vote rate aid.

Two questions only prompted lengthy discussion. Principal Griffiths, basing his case substantially on the very real sacrifices the Cardiff College had made for the Medical School (other departments, as he said, had been 'starved' to assist it), argued strongly against its separation from his College. The deputation was told to submit a scheme for consideration. Griffiths had carefully said nothing about the national pooling of rate aid and he was taken to task for the omission by the Prime Minister. Lloyd George, perhaps with bitter memories of the death-blow given to *Cymru Fydd*'s national aspirations by the parochial tendencies of South Wales years before, weighed in with some downright remarks.[16]

This is a Welsh University, and not a sort of little local show [said the Prime Minister bluntly]. . . . You cannot earmark for local purposes when you are dealing with a great national problem. This is not the time when powerful and rich counties can say, 'We will not . . . pool our resources for little counties'. . . . We impose that condition . . . there must be a pooling of resources.[17]

Lloyd George also said that he wished that it had been possible at that time to co-ordinate properly the whole of Welsh education and break down the two or three 'water-tight compartments' into which it had been thrust in the past. This pious genuflection was the Prime Minister's only response to a determined attempt made a month earlier by Sir Alfred Davies to persuade Lloyd George to go well beyond the Haldane proposals. Davies, who was present at this meeting with the deputation, was an old Aberystwyth student who had become Permanent Secretary of the Welsh Department of the Board of Education, a subdivision established in 1907 with limited powers as a sop to a disappointed Welsh opinion that for years had yearned for a National Council of Education with full autonomy in educational matters. In a confidential memorandum to the Prime Minister, Davies argued that, because of the piecemeal consideration of Welsh education in the past, it was a thing of shreds and tatters marked by 'lack of co-ordination, duplication of machinery and effort, . . . rivalries and the friction and ineffectiveness

[16] On *Cymru Fydd* and Lloyd George, see K. O. Morgan, op. cit., pp. 160–3.
[17] Notes of Lloyd George's meeting with the deputation, 14 August 1918. N.L.W. Thomas Jones MSS. Class J, vol. iv, f. 76.

which they quickly engender'. He maintained that there was now a golden opportunity to bring elementary, technical, secondary, art, and university education in Wales under the control of one 'central authority, a thoroughly democratic national body' directly responsible to Parliament. Among other things, the Central Welsh Board, which for years had been engaged in a tug of war over school inspection with Davies' Welsh Department, would disappear.[18] Davies' scheme was not without its attractions, but, unfortunately for him, just before the University deputation appeared, H. A. L. Fisher nobbled the Prime Minister during a walk in the garden behind Downing Street, and persuaded him not to adopt Davies' proposals.[19]

The members of the deputation do not seem to have been aware of (or at least they made no overt reference to) Alfred Davies' enterprise behind the scenes. Indeed, there is some evidence, admittedly drawn from a slightly later period, that the enthusiasm in University circles for an all-embracing National Council of Education in Wales had waned considerably since the days of Viriamu Jones.[20] In any case the deputation was more interested in the prospect of immediate financial assistance for the hard-pressed University than in further constitutional changes, however desirable. On the whole Lloyd George had given satisfaction: it was evident that the £ for £ Treasury contribution to match rate aid and private benefactions would be forthcoming; the Prime Minister had effectively ensured that Glamorgan's wealth would not be used selfishly to succour only the Cardiff and Swansea Colleges. And although for the moment judgement was reserved on equivalent Treasury grants for capital expenditure, Lloyd George conceded that he was 'not altogether hostile' to this proposal, and indeed admitted that there was perhaps a case for special consideration under this heading for Aberystwyth and Bangor, 'the only highland universities' in the country.[21]

The final determination in detail of all these important questions proceeded at not much more than the pace of a bullock cart. Meantime, the Colleges had to brace themselves to meet the rapidly approaching post-war situation. Aberystwyth had been quick to respond to some of the special problems caused by the war. In November 1917 arrangements were made for the Education department to begin a free crash-course for the training of disabled, discharged soldiers as elementary school teachers.[22] In February 1918 two Serbians (joined later by several more)

[18] Memorandum by Sir Alfred Davies (copy), 19 July 1918. N.L.W. Thomas Jones MSS., Class J, vol. iv, f. 67.

[19] 14 August 1918. Bodl. Fisher MSS. Box 8a. Fisher's senior officials at the Board had denounced Davies' scheme as 'a kind of educational *coup d'état*' designed, by an empire-building Welsh Department, 'to suppress' its old enemy the Central Welsh Board. 1 August 1918. P.R.O. Ed. 24/2027.

[20] Emrys Evans, op. cit., pp. 87–9.   [21] N.L.W. Thomas Jones MSS. Class J., vol. iv, f. 76.

[22] *Council Minutes* (15 November 1917 and 18 October 1918), pp. 232, 318. According to *The Dragon* (xl. 1), Aberystwyth was the first university institution in the country to offer this opportunity to returning ex-servicemen.

were accepted as students; their fees were remitted and they were maintained throughout their stay at Aberystwyth by private subscriptions from friends of the College.[23] Soon afterwards a substantial group of American soldiers arrived to take short courses, and an inquiry about similar arrangements for South African veterans evoked from J. H. Davies, the Registrar, the comment, 'Let them all come'.[24]

But the problems posed by these exotic arrivals were minor compared with the difficulties of coping adequately with the great influx of students, especially ex-servicemen, after the war. The teaching staff had to be more than doubled in size, and there were frantic efforts to find additional teaching and laboratory space and hostel accommodation for the 971 students at the College at the opening of the session in October 1919. There was a considerable change in the professoriate at this time; as a result of resignations and appointments to additional chairs, there were ten new members of the Senate, and the list of newcomers included some outstanding names. The chair of International Politics was filled early in 1919 by the appointment of A. E. Zimmern. His name had been suggested by David Davies, and the Senate had no hesitation in endorsing his fitness for the post. Zimmern had had a distinguished career at Oxford where he had held a Fellowship at New College. During the war he had been at the Ministry of Reconstruction before being seconded to important work at the Foreign Office. Among other things he was the author of an outstanding book, *The Greek Commonwealth*, published in 1911. There were certain special conditions attached to Zimmern's chair: he was required to be in residence for only two terms in the session; at other times he was to be free to travel wherever in the world his researches in his new subject took him. It was also agreed that he was to have an assistant and Zimmern, self-confessedly 'a terrible man hunter', soon attracted to his side young Sydney Herbert, a first-rate teacher who, in one capacity and another, was to render the College outstanding service over the succeeding decades.[25]

Despite the short duration of his stay and the unfortunate circumstances of his departure, Zimmern made a great impact on Aberystwyth. Lively, ebullient, a scholar of distinction, his lectures, which were always followed by lengthy periods of open discussion, attracted great crowds of students who obviously hungered for the intellectual stimulation Zimmern provided. His 'newspaper class', a weekly commentary on the background of the great international issues of the day, attracted attendances of just under a hundred students, very few of whom had any examination commitment in Zimmern's subject.[26] He threw

[23] *Council Minutes* (18 October 1918), p. 319.   [24] T. I. Ellis, *J. H. Davies*, p. 126.

[25] *Council Minutes* (7 March and 25 April 1919), pp. 358, 366–7. Zimmern to Thomas Jones, 23 February 1919. N. L. W. Thomas Jones MSS. Class W, vol. xx, f. 211.

[26] Zimmern to Thomas Jones, 1 November 1919 and 26 August 1920. N.L.W. Thomas Jones MSS. Class W, vol. xx, ff. 220, 229.

himself with great zest into his work: he set about learning Welsh and, despite some difficulty ('the ancient tongue of Dafydd ap Gwilym is not easy for the strange Englishman', he admitted), in no time he was able to write passably well, earnestly proclaiming in the newly acquired language that his heart was wholly in Wales.[27] Zimmern was delighted with the response he evoked in the students, who were 'the easiest crowd to handle' that he had ever encountered. He had a high opinion of their natural abilities, but he thought that they matured later than their English equivalents, and he believed strongly that an unrelieved diet of lectures, to which most of them were subject, was pernicious. 'It deadens their faculties, so that the "freshers" are sometimes (I am horrified to discover) more intelligent and interested than the third year', he reported to J. H. Davies. The remedy, which alone would do full justice to the abilities of the students, was 'more individual attention' which he provided by letting it be known that he was freely available for tutorial consultation.[28]

No doubt Zimmern was quite right in all this, and a general lecture that he gave to the students, subsequently published in *The Dragon*, on the essential difference between a school and a university, was full of ripe wisdom and created a great deal of interest. But Zimmern was not the most tactful of men; some of his remarks seemed to reflect obliquely on certain of his colleagues who for years, with inadequate assistance, had answered as best they could the heavy teaching demands of large departments.[29] Zimmern was needlessly brash. 'Welsh education', he told Thomas Jones after little more than a year's limited experience of it, 'is a ghastly travesty.' Even earlier Zimmern had written that he intended to remain 'leech like' at Aberystwyth and make it 'a place of education and sound learning' so far as it lay within his power to do so.[30] Arrogant immodesty of this kind made enemies and this was not without its importance soon afterwards when Zimmern's position came under challenge.

On the same day that Zimmern's appointment was confirmed an even greater name, in many respects the most illustrious ever associated with the College, was added to the Senate. R. G. Stapledon had been on the staff, as Adviser in Agricultural Botany, since 1912. As a young student Stapledon had been unsure of the direction of his career (his mother nicknamed him 'Shilly-Shally'), but ultimately agriculture caught his interest and Wales fired his imagination. The war confirmed overwhelmingly his long-standing conviction, which he preached unheeded but with passion before 1914, that it was suicidal for Britain not to grow all the food

[27] Zimmern to Thomas Jones, 28 July and 26 August 1920. Ibid., ff. 227, 229. Zimmern to J. H. Davies, 29 July 1920. N.L.W. Cwrt Mawr MSS. 854D.

[28] Zimmern to J. H. Davies. 3 April (1920). N.L.W. J. H. Davies MSS. (Corr.).

[29] 'What it is to be a student', *The Dragon*, xliii. 12–17, and the succeeding student correspondence (ibid., pp. 77–175) which is not kind to the professoriate and the lecture system.

[30] Zimmern to Thomas Jones, 1 November 1919 and 26 August 1920. N.L.W. Thomas Jones MSS. Class W, vol. xx, ff. 220, 229.

possible.[31] The grim toll exacted by the German U-boats soon called Stapledon away to help the national food-growing campaign for survival, but in 1919 he returned to Aberystwyth in circumstances which gave full opportunity to his magnificent talents.

In January 1919 Bryner Jones, the professor of Agriculture, wrote to J. H. Davies to say that, at last, 'something definite' had emerged from his lengthy consultations with Laurence Philipps, the later Lord Milford.[32] Within days Laurence Philipps offered the College an endowment fund of £10,000 and an annual sum of £1,000 for ten years to establish at Aberystwyth (Bryner Jones' influence had been important in deciding the location) a Plant Breeding Station modelled on the highly successful Institute of Agricultural Botany at Cambridge, which had done so much to assist English agriculture. Wales, where there were so many hill farms, had particular need of specially bred hardy strains which could flourish in high-lying ground and, as Philipps said, there was an 'enormous field of work' open to such a research station which could be of incalculable benefit to the Principality.[33]

This generous offer, which at last enabled the College to make the great contribution to Welsh rural life that its more percipient leaders had always hoped it would do, was gratefully accepted, and it was immediately agreed that Stapledon was the obvious man for the Directorship. On 25 April 1919 he accepted the twin posts of Director of the Plant Breeding Station and professor of Agricultural Botany at the College.[34] Soon afterwards a substantial additional staff, headed by T. J. Jenkin, was appointed to assist Stapledon, and a large building in the town, formerly Green's Foundry, together with an adjoining slate works, was bought for £3,700 and hastily adapted for use of the new venture. The College was also able to put four acres of garden ground at Stapledon's disposal, and in October 1920 a ninety-two acre farm at Frongoch, a mile or so away, was purchased for the Station's large-scale trials and growings of selected strains. Stapledon was careful to damp down exaggerated hopes of swift and spectacular successes: he was engaged, as he said, in 'a long and tedious undertaking', and the community must exercise considerable 'patience'.[35] In make-shift if commodious surroundings the Welsh Plant Breeding Station thus came into existence under the leadership of a seer and prophet who may fairly be called a man of genius. Over the next decades, notwithstanding Stapledon's sensible initial caution, the Station made an

[31] R. Waller, *Prophet of the New Age: the Life and thought of Sir George Stapledon, F.R.S.* (1962), pp. 25-9.

[32] Bryner Jones to J. H. Davies, 24 January 1919. N.L.W. J. H. Davies MSS. (Misc. Letters.)

[33] Laurence Philipps to the Council, 26 January 1919. *Council Minutes* (6 March 1919), p. 359.

[34] Ibid. (25 April 1919), pp. 367-8.

[35] Ibid. (27 June 1919), pp. 388-9, 396. R. G. Stapledon, 'A Scientific Development in Wales', *Welsh Outlook*, viii. 306-8.

enormous contribution to land improvement the world over and, in doing so, made Aberystwyth's name internationally known.[36]

Quite apart from its intrinsic importance, the establishment of the Welsh Plant Breeding Station financed substantially by private sources, at least at first, had another beneficent effect on the fortunes of the College. Aberystwyth and Bangor had both, from a very early date, sought to develop agricultural studies to the uttermost and, for practical reasons, as has appeared, the two Colleges had also sponsored much other work, immediately serviceable to the farming community, which was not of university standard. It was common knowledge that the Haldane Commission would almost certainly recommend that, to avoid wasteful duplication, advanced work in Agriculture should be concentrated at one or other College. This inevitably sharpened the rivalry between the two and, with desperate bravado, Aberystwyth and Bangor, in their statements to the Royal Commission, put forward elaborate and expensive schemes (Bangor estimated that an income of £9,500 would be required, Aberystwyth called for £11,050) for developments in Agriculture. Most witnesses on behalf of the Colleges tried hard to persuade Haldane and his colleagues that local variations in soil and climate demanded full-scale departments, answering the special particularities of North and Mid-Wales, at the two Colleges, but the real nub of the difficulty was expressed by Bryner Jones. He conceded that, given a fresh start, 'a single agricultural department would be the best', but, for good or ill, there were two departments, each supported by 'an intense amount of local feeling'. The Royal Commission *Report* made some sharp criticisms of the existing degree course in Agriculture, demolished the special pleadings of interested parties, and recommended that advanced work (in effect, for technical reasons, this was taken to mean postgraduate study) in Agriculture should be concentrated at either Bangor or Aberystwyth, the actual decision on location being left to the University itself. At the same time the *Report* did not rule out advanced work at a second College provided that it was financially supported by private benefaction.[37]

Laurence Philipps' endowment of the Plant Breeding Station took a good deal of the heat out of the rivalry of the two Colleges (as Fleure, in a violent denunciation of the Haldane *Report*'s recommendations on Agriculture said, it 'has altered the situation'), and it guaranteed that, whatever the eventual official outcome, Aberystwyth would be a centre for advanced work, particularly research, in

[36] The best account of the pioneer work of the Station is R. G. Stapledon, *The Welsh Plant Breeding Station* (Aberystwyth, 1933). See also Waller, op. cit., where the full richness of Stapledon's personality is excellently conveyed.

[37] Haldane *Report* (Recommendations), pp. 78–82, (The Present System and its Problems), p. 51. W. N. Bruce rightly thought that the Commissioners had 'underestimated the demand, both in quantity and variety, for provision for higher Agricultural Science and research'. 30 May 1919. P.R.O. Ed. 24/2027.

Agriculture.[38] In June 1919 Bryner Jones, who had done so much to bring the department out of the morass into which it had fallen in 1907, and whose influence had been an important factor in securing the Philipps benefaction for Aberystwyth, resigned his chair of Agriculture to become Assistant Secretary to the Board of Agriculture. From a large field of applicants Abel E. Jones, who had been on the Aberystwyth staff for some years, was promoted to the chair. Not the least of Jones' qualifications, as one of his referees said, was that he impressed farmers as 'eminently practical, and those who know how critical farmers as a class are of what they term "a College man" will realise how important an asset this power will be to the professor of Agriculture in a Welsh College'.[39]

In addition to Abel Jones, five other elections to chairs were made by the Council on the same day. Edward Bensly, professor of Latin since 1905, resigned, largely because the exceptional teaching demands of his department had virtually put a stop to his original work (he was anxious to complete a commentary on Burton's *Anatomy of Melancholy*, which had been commissioned by the Oxford University Press).[40] At the time Intermediate Latin was a compulsory subject for almost all Arts students and, inevitably, small classes at many different levels had to be offered to students whose previous training in the subject varied considerably. The large post-war increase in the number of students made a difficult situation almost intolerable. Bensly was replaced by H. J. Rose, an Oxford-trained Canadian, who was unanimously recommended by the advisory committee.[41] Rose, an unconventional colonial who often appeared at College wearing, among other things, a flowing gown and carpet slippers, was the terror of his hapless captive students. He had the shortest of ways with backsliders. 'Mr. X', he told one student whose frailty in Latin had been exposed in the Easter terminal examination, 'you have as much chance of ever passing Intermediate Latin as I have of becoming President of the United States.'[42]

Two long-serving members of the Senate retired in 1919: R. W. Genese, who had been at Aberystwyth for forty years, latterly as professor of Pure Mathematics, and Morgan Lewis, professor of Physics since 1891. The chair of Pure Mathematics went to W. H. Young, F.R.S., a prolific scholar who had published over one hundred and fifty papers in the journals during a distinguished career; the selection committee added an addendum to their report, recommending

[38] A conference to reconcile the Aberystwyth and Bangor positions had ended in deadlock. H. J. Fleure to Thomas Jones, 3 November 1919. N.L.W. Thomas Jones MSS. Class X, vol. v, f. 115.

[39] *Council Minutes* (15 August 1919), p. 407. H. E. H. Jones' testimonial, July 1919. N.L.W. Thomas Jones MSS. Class J, vol. viii, f. 52.

[40] Bensly to the Registrar, 12 May 1919. *Council Minutes* (23 May 1919), pp. 380–1.

[41] 25 July 1919. N.L.W. Thomas Jones MSS. Class J, vol. viii, f. 95.

[42] E. G. Bowen, 'Notes on student life in the post-war years', p. 1.

additional teaching assistance in the department so that the flow of Young's researches would not be interrupted.[43] Gwilym Owen, then out in New Zealand, comfortably defeated H. H. Paine, a lecturer at Aberystwyth, for the chair of Physics.[44] Despite a considerable eleventh-hour attempt to keep him at Aberystwyth, O. T. Jones ultimately succumbed to Manchester's blandishments. The Council recorded its 'high appreciation' of the work of the man who was eventually to become the internationally known doyen of British geologists. There were nine applications for the chair including a late bid by telegram from Boulogne by Dudley Stamp. The successful candidate was O. T. Jones' protégé, W. J. Pugh, a former Aberystwyth student (a notable College full-back who was the robust scourge of opposing soccer forwards), a young, much-decorated ex-serviceman, who was thus early launched on a very distinguished career. H. J. Fleure was delighted with this appointment of a man whose co-operation in research would be 'very valuable'.[45]

The last appointment made on that day was one of special interest. It marked the partial ending of an old and bitter story. In 1913 Sir Edward Anwyl had resigned his chair in Welsh at Aberystwyth to become first Principal of Caerleon Training College; Anwyl died before he took up his new duties. When Anwyl resigned, there was some talk of W. J. Gruffydd as his likely successor, and, slightly later, it was rumoured that the College would try, by means of 'a big salary', to attract applications from other well-known Welsh and Celtic scholars, including possibly John Morris Jones of Bangor.[46] There were certain local difficulties, for already on the Aberystwyth College staff there were two, possibly three, men who also had their claims to the chair: T. Gwynn Jones, who specialized in Welsh literature, Timothy Lewis, philologist and palaeographer, and, at a more junior level, recently given a chance to show his paces, T. H. Parry-Williams, who was apparently Anwyl's choice as his successor. After some hesitation the Council decided in April 1914 to postpone the appointment for a year, 'with a view to a more thorough consideration', a holding operation that included arrangements to make sure that none of the three men already on the staff established a pre-emptive right to the chair.[47] In December 1914, for example, when Timothy Lewis was made internal examiner in Welsh, Principal Roberts carefully pointed out that it 'was not to be interpreted as implying any preferential treatment for any other purpose'.[48]

[43] 'U.C.W. Chair of Pure Mathematics', July 1919. N.L.W. Thomas Jones MSS. Class J, vol. viii, f. 75. *Council Minutes* (15 August 1919), p. 406.

[44] H. J. Fleure to Thomas Jones, 19 August 1919. N.L.W. Thomas Jones MSS. Class X, vol. v, f. 4. *Council Minutes* (15 August 1919), pp. 404–5.

[45] Ibid. (27 June and 15 August 1919), pp. 400, 407. N.L.W. Thomas Jones MSS. Class J, vol. viii, ff. 17, 62. H. J. Fleure to Thomas Jones, 19 August 1919. Ibid., Class X, vol. v, f. 4.

[46] T. I. Ellis, *J. H. Davies*, pp. 105–6. H. J. Fleure to Thomas Jones, 1 May 1914. N.L.W. Thomas Jones MSS. Class J, vol. i, f. 14.

[47] Anwyl to H. Parry-Williams, 2 December 1913 (copy), and Fleure to Thomas Jones, 1 May 1919. N.L.W. Thomas Jones MSS. Class J, vol. i, f. 14, vol. viii, f. 87.

[48] T. F. Roberts to Timothy Lewis, 14 December 1914. P/Cr/B/3.

Financial stringencies and the continuing exigencies of war kept the chair vacant for five years, not without bitter criticism by interested parties of the authorities at Aberystwyth for their apparent neglect of Welsh and Celtic Studies.[49]

In fact, during the war years there was a very lengthy consideration of the future of Welsh and Celtic Studies at Aberystwyth. In 1917 a Senate committee, anxious to get away from the 'narrowness' which had 'prevailed in the past', wanted to establish a chair of Celtic Studies rather than of Welsh, but some members felt that the suggested change would provoke strong opposition.[50] In some minds the question became confused with a desire to give T. Gwynn Jones proper recognition. Gwenogfryn Evans, for example, suggested that the chair should be in Comparative Literature and Lleufer Thomas, endorsing the suggestion, thought that Gwynn Jones would be 'admirable' in a professorship with such broad terms of reference.[51] There had been some expectation that Sir John Williams would make provision for the endowment of Celtic Studies, but Sir John's investments had taken some hard knocks during the war and, eventually, Tom Jones and Lleufer Thomas turned to the Misses Davies of Llandinam.[52] In March 1919 the Council invited the University to set up a committee to select a professor of Welsh. In May the committee, aware by now that funds from the Llandinam benefaction would probably be available, recommended that there should be two chairs: one in Welsh Language and one in Welsh Literature. This was subsequently amended to a chair in Welsh, for which specialists in Literature and Language were invited to apply.[53]

These seemingly endless confusions created bewilderment and no little bitterness. Gwynn Jones was convinced that 'a very determined effort' was being made to exclude him. He felt that he was at the cross-roads: he was forty-seven; it had taken him years of laborious private effort to overcome the handicap of a lack of formal academic training and a long period of ill-health which had driven him overseas to a warm climate to recuperate. He was determined to fight a 'desperate battle' for what he thought was his last opportunity. If he failed, he would go to South America (presumably Patagonia); 'forseeing a possible necessity' for this, he had already worked up a knowledge of Spanish.[54] This bitter exile was not

---

[49] Beriah Evans to E. T. John, 30 September 1919. N.L.W. E. T. John MSS. Evans was Timothy Lewis' father-in-law.

[50] O. T. Jones to Thomas Jones, 1917. N.L.W. Thomas Jones MSS. Class J, vol. viii, f. 14. J. H. Davies' memorandum on Celtic Studies, Haldane *Report* (Minutes of Evidence), pp. 169–80.

[51] Lleufer Thomas to Thomas Jones, 25 October 1918. N.L.W. Ibid., Class W, vol. xviii, f. 191. Lleufer Thomas to J. H. Davies, 11 December 1918. N.L.W. Cwrt Mawr MSS. (T. I. Ellis donation 1958/62).

[52] Thomas Jones to Lleufer Thomas, 12 April 1919. N.L.W. Thomas Jones MSS. Class W, vol. xviii, f. 211.

[53] *Council Minutes* (7 March, 25 April, 23 May, 27 June 1919), pp. 358, 363, 379, 397.

[54] T. Gwynn Jones to Thomas Jones, 9 July 1919. N.L.W. Thomas Jones MSS. Class J, vol. viii, f. 82.

necessary. On 15 August 1919 the advisory committee unanimously recommended that Gwynn Jones should be appointed professor of Welsh Literature and,
after the Council had endorsed the proposal, the Llandinam benefactors agreed
to endow the new chair. After a 'long discussion', unfortunately not minuted in
detail, the Council decided to consider soon afterwards the appointment also of
a professor of Welsh Language.[55]

In fact, on 18 August the advisory committee agreed unanimously to recommend T. H. Parry-Williams for this chair, and commissioned W. J. Gruffydd to
write a detailed report for the Council on the qualifications of candidates. The
affair aroused the strongest of feelings. Some of Timothy Lewis' supporters were
convinced that 'a dead set' against his candidature was being made by 'the official
clique' at Aberystwyth.[56] Nor did it stop there; other deeply emotional factors
affected a situation already more than sufficiently highly charged. Lewis was an
ex-serviceman; Parry-Williams had had conscientious objections to the war.
When the matter came up for decision on 26 September 1919 the Council was
faced with a barrage of letters of protest from many branches of the 'Comrades
of the Great War' (precursor of the British Legion) and a petition signed by some
Aberystwyth residents. Perhaps pusillanimously the Council decided to postpone
the appointment until 1920 when the chair would be re-advertised.[57]

There was little sign a year later that the strong emotions aroused had subsided.
This time two names, Professor J. Lloyd Jones and Dr. Parry-Williams, were
recommended for the Council's consideration. Again there were messages of protest from the local and national headquarters of the ex-servicemen's organization.
Timothy Lewis' supporters on the Council managed to bring him back into consideration. All three candidates were interviewed and, finally, there was a ballot.
T. H. Parry-Williams was elected to the chair, and it was agreed that a special post
(a Readership in Celtic Philology and Palaeography) would be created for Timothy
Lewis.[58] All had ended more or less well, if not entirely happily. There were now
two chairs of Welsh at Aberystwyth occupied by two exceptionally gifted and
prolific scholars who respected each other's different qualities and were resolved
to work together effectively.[59] There is evidence that Timothy Lewis and his

[55] *Council Minutes* (15 August 1919), pp. 408–9. Parry-Williams warmly congratulated Gwynn
Jones on his success; the latter, delighted, hoped that the other chair would go to his sporting rival for,
as Gwynn Jones said, Parry-Williams was a man with whom he 'could work'. T. Gwynn Jones to
J. H. Davies, 22 August 1919. N.L.W. J. H. Davies MSS. (Corr.).

[56] Beriah Evans to E. T. John, 16 September 1919. N.L.W. E. T. John MSS.

[57] *Council Minutes* (26 September 1919), pp. 415–16. Beriah Evans to E. T. John, 30 September
1919. N.L.W. E. T. John MSS. 'Chair of Welsh Committee', 22 September 1919. N.L.W. Thomas
Jones MSS. Class J, vol. viii, f. 89.

[58] *Council Minutes* (6 July 1920), p. 36. 'Report of Committee', 28 June 1920. N.L.W. Cwrt Mawr
MSS. 1384E.

[59] T. Gwynn Jones, 'The Literary Outlook in Wales', April 1920. *Welsh Outlook*, vii. 88.

strongest supporters were not dissatisfied with the opportunity that had been provided for him.[60] As the editor of *The Dragon* wrote with relief, an 'unpleasant episode', during which the College had suffered much sharp criticism in the press, was now mercifully ended.[61] Happily, when in August 1919 Professor Findlay resigned his Chemistry chair, the appointment of his successor, B. Mouatt Jones, occasioned no public controversy.[62]

In the post-war years the College needed additional buildings as well as an enlarged teaching staff. During 1919 there was a feverish search for extra accommodation. One suggestion was that the College should buy the large nearby Pier for use, in the first instance, as a Students' Union; it was hoped that, subsequently, it would be converted into a Fisheries Research Station, a project that the College had pressed vainly on the government for years. Nothing came of this. The College could not afford to buy the Pier from its own resources, and the Llandinam ladies refused to advance the money.[63] Mounting student numbers made the race for adequate accommodation increasingly desperate. An offer for a large building (the Baths, later a cinema, in Bath Street) which it was hoped to convert into laboratories for Science departments was rejected as inadequate; a bid for the 'Hydro' (now the site of a public shelter on the Promenade), which it was planned to convert into hostel accommodation for a hundred students was later withdrawn, and a proposal to buy the Waterloo Hotel also fell to the ground. However, three large houses on the Marine Terrace were bought and hastily adapted as a hostel for women students. Fittingly, this newly acquired property was called Carpenter Hall in honour of the former 'Lady Principal' (then still alive and keenly interested in the college) whose fine service over so many years had merited special recognition. The aggregation of houses known as Plynlymon continued to be leased as a hostel for men. The Parish Hall and part of the Theological College were hired for use as lecture rooms, and two fine-looking houses adjoining the College were bought outright. No. 1 Marine Terrace became the home of the departments of Geography and International Politics, and Walford Davies established the Music department next door in No. 2. Other houses on Marine Terrace (Nos. 9 and 11) were leased at this time and, over the years up to the present day, provided teaching accommodation for a succession of College departments.[64]

[60] Beriah Evans to E. T. John, 13 July 1920. N.L.W. E. T. John MSS. A. E. Zimmern to J. H. Davies (1920). N.L.W. J. H. Davies MSS. (Corr.).

[61] *The Dragon*, xliii. 7–9. See as an example of newspaper criticism, the *Western Mail* (22 August 1919).

[62] *Council Minutes* (26 September 1919), pp. 416–17.

[63] Thomas Jones to J. H. Davies, 8 February 1919. N.L.W. J. H. Davies MSS. (Corr.).

[64] Thomas Jones to J. H. Davies, 11 July 1918. N.L.W. J. H. Davies MSS. (Misc. Letters). *Council Minutes* (27 June 1919), pp. 388–9, 395–6. 'Memorandum to the Council', March 1919. N.L.W. Thomas Jones MSS. Class J, vol. viii, f. 11. J. H. Davies, 'A Letter from the Principal', *Old Students' Annual* (1920), pp. 7–9.

No doubt some of these purchases and long-running leases of old properties were ill-advised because, over the years, the College was saddled with a considerable expenditure on adaptations and maintenance. But the harsh fact was that the College had no choice: the need for additional accommodation was overwhelmingly urgent, and there was not the time, and certainly not the money, for a new building programme. For Aberystwyth then, as on so many occasions in the past, it remained true that beggars could not afford to be canny choosers. One man who was disturbed by these stop-gap arrangements was Thomas Jones. For years he had nurtured the dream of a new, aesthetically satisfying complex of College buildings on Penglais hill, and he was 'uneasy' about the expenditure of considerable sums (by Aberystwyth's modest financial standards) on old properties like Green's Foundry.[65] Tom Jones' concern was natural enough for, shortly, he hoped to become the Principal of Aberystwyth in succession to T. F. Roberts.

As the war drew to its close, it was expected that Tom Jones, a temporary recruit to government service, would soon leave the Cabinet secretariat, itself regarded by many as an emergency device (which mercifully would quickly disappear in peace-time) of an outsider Prime Minister whose ideas stirred the resentments of the orthodox. T. J.s' friends were anxious that his great gifts, sharply honed by his London experience, should be put to the service of the Welsh people. At one time it had been suggested that T. J. should become Secretary of the Council of the University of Wales, a position which Lord Haldane (curiously misunderstanding the distribution of power in a university which he was then examining in detail) thought 'stronger' than that of any Principal of a constituent college. When Fleure heard in 1918 that the University of Wales was to have a member in a reformed House of Commons, he thought immediately of T. J., who could do so well 'the work . . . of championing the Labour cause in a "Brain and Hand" way'.[66] However, when T. F. Roberts died the way was open for Tom Jones to apply for the job upon which, above all others, he had set his heart.

The election of T. F. Roberts' successor at Aberystwyth in 1919 was the *cause célèbre* of Welsh public life in the post-war years. It was a tangled web of move and counter-move that would have delighted the heart of C. P. Snow, except that the affair was conducted with a robust Welsh vigour more or less in open view rather than with the smooth urbanity covering the shifting allegiances of an imagined

65 Thomas Jones to J. H. Davies, 4 June 1919. N.L.W. J. H. Davies MSS. (Corr.). J. H. Davies, nearer to the immediate difficulties, believed there was no other choice. 'Memorandum on policy', 12 December 1918. N.L.W. Thomas Jones MSS. Class J, vol. iv, f. 94.

66 N.L.W. Thomas Jones Diary (1917), p. 93 (1918), pp. 21–2. Oddly enough, in view of their celebrated confrontation elsewhere, it had also been suggested to J. H. Davies that he should stand for the University seat. W. Llewelyn Williams to J. H. Davies, 16 February 1918. N.L.W. J. H. Davies MSS. (Corr.).

set of Oxbridge College Fellows. Early on it was believed that Bryner Jones would be a candidate; and Henry Stuart Jones, the great Oxford Classical scholar, who will reappear later, certainly declared a strong interest, naïvely enough to J. H. Davies whom he asked to keep him informed.[67] Other lesser men were also mentioned and, indeed, some of them put in formal applications, but as autumn wore on it became clear that there were only three serious candidates: Thomas Jones, J. E. Lloyd, the Bangor historian, a disappointed candidate in 1891, and, to the surprise of some, J. H. Davies, Registrar since 1905, whose interest in the appointment had been acutely divined by Lleufer Thomas during a fleeting visit to Aberystwyth in July. Indeed, Sir John Williams, President of the College, thought that J. H. Davies' claims to the Principalship were so overwhelming that all that was required was to invite his acceptance 'right away'. David Davies, Vice-President, immediately strongly 'demurred', and it was clear that there would be a contest.[68]

On 15 August 1919 the Council considered the Principalship at length; the discussion was high-toned and congenial in spirit; Fleure, for one, 'felt rather proud of Aber.' on this occasion. A committee (which soon lapsed into a curious inertia) was appointed to collate applications and recommendations, and it was agreed that a knowledge of Welsh was to be essential, a stipulation which provoked some outside criticism.[69] After these civilized preliminaries, the gloves were off. Tom Jones' candidature was managed with great energy by Lleufer Thomas, who was determined to leave no 'stone unturned'.[70] T. J.s' formal application was unquestionably a most impressive document; some thought it irresistible to all except those rendered myopic by prejudice. His referees included Lloyd George and Sir William McCormick, Chairman of the Treasury Committee on University Grants, and his application was supported by seventeen letters of recommendation, all pressing his claims eloquently, from H. A. L. Fisher, Haldane, Lord Esher, R. H. Tawney, Sidney Webb, the Master of Balliol, and three provincial university Vice-Chancellors among others. Perhaps wisely, because he could call up no similarly impressive array of formal support, J. H. Davies submitted no testimonials but simply referred the Council to Sir Owen M. Edwards and Sir (as he had now become) John Morris Jones. Davies rested his case on his services to the College, not least that he had always been rather more than simply Registrar and, in recent years, during T. F. Roberts' prolonged illness, Acting-Principal in

[67] W. J. Burdon Evans to Thomas Jones (1919). N.L.W. Thomas Jones MSS. Class X, vol. v, f. 11. H. Stuart Jones to J. H. Davies, 18 June 1919. N.L.W. J. H. Davies MSS. (Corr.).

[68] Lleufer Thomas to Thomas Jones, 17 July 1919. N.L.W. Thomas Jones MSS. Class W, vol. xviii, f. 215. N.L.W. Thomas Jones Diary (1919), pp. 68–71.

[69] H. J. Fleure to Thomas Jones, 19 August 1919. N.L.W. Thomas Jones MSS. Class X, vol. v, f. 4. *Council Minutes* (15 August 1919), p. 403. *Western Mail* (9 and 17 September 1919).

[70] Lleufer Thomas to Thomas Jones, 23 October 1919. N.L.W. Thomas Jones MSS. Class X, vol. v, f. 77.

all but name. J. E. Lloyd's application leaned heavily on his scholarly reputation and his administrative experience as Registrar at Bangor.

The campaign (no less martial word will suffice) unfortunately became increasingly scurrilous, and Tom Jones in particular had to endure some vicious attacks by innuendo. He was cast as the nominee, willing pawn even, of David Davies, a domineering plutocrat, whose money-bags, it was said, would undermine the puritan virtue of a poor but honest College. Additionally, it was strongly hinted that T. J., once an apprentice Methodist minister, had surrendered his religious faith in the sophisticated world in which he had lived for years.[71] In private, Tom Jones ruefully pointed out that David Davies had not latterly taken over-much interest in Aberystwyth and was 'rather inclined at times to despair of it'. As T. J. said, 'the real helpers of Aber.' were the Misses Davies, and they were 'the last people one would speak of as domineering'.[72] In a desperate effort to establish T. J.s fundamental religious orthodoxy, Bishop Gore and William Temple wrote to certain Anglican members of the Council, and T. J. himself privately met Archdeacon Williams of Llandeilo to offer reassurances of his soundness on the 'eternal verities'.[73]

Despite the glittering array of Tom Jones' supporters, J. H. Davies position was immensely strong. It was expected that the powerful Methodist vote would be his, as also that of the so-called 'nationalists'. What was certain was that the local members of the Council, those who lived in or near Aberystwyth, marshalled by Evan Evans and Professor Edward Edwards, were almost without exception for J. H. Davies. So, too, overwhelmingly was the College staff; those members of the Senate who supported Tom Jones thought it wise to walk softly at this time. It is evident that T. J.s' cause was not helped by the important part he had played in bringing to Aberystwyth Walford Davies and Zimmern, who were regarded with suspicion by some members of the staff as brash Uitlanders, smart-aleck showmen alien to the sober traditions of the College.[74]

As the day of decision approached, private efforts to win over doubtful voters

[71] *Western Mail* (4, 10, and 12 September, 13 October 1919). *Y Cymro* (8 October 1919). Lloyd George's influence was called into play in an effort to clamp down on what was believed to be a calculated press campaign organized by an enemy of T.J. Sir M. Hankey to C. Addison, 19 September 1919. N.L.W. Thomas Jones Diary (1919), pp. 86–7.

[72] Thomas Jones to Edgar Jones, 29 October 1919. N.L.W. Thomas Jones MSS. Class X, vol. v, f. 93.

[73] Thomas Jones to Lleufer Thomas, 9 October 1919. Archdeacon R. Williams to Thomas Jones, 27 October 1919. N.L.W. Ibid., Class W, vol. xviii, f. 216, Class X, vol. v, f. 84. In his Diary for 1917 (p. 84), T.J. ruefully tells the story that Lord Pontypridd, faced with an impressive list of Tom Jones' qualifications, for the Cardiff Principalship, said that if 'half the tale . . . were true', here was the right man, but characteristically added, 'Why isn't the fool religious?'.

[74] Miss Florence Williams to 'May' (1919), H. J. Fleure to Thomas Jones, 5 October 1919. N.L.W. Thomas Jones MSS. Class X, vol. v, ff. 41, 89. Fleure told T.J., 'if I worked too openly it would do your cause harm, I fear'. See also the *Cambrian News* (21 November 1919).

and persuade the committed to attend became even more feverish. Press coverage, in the main, continued to be unedifying, although the *Cambrian News* in October published a dignified leader denouncing the 'nauseating back-biting' of so much public comment on the appointment.[75] And it is worth recording that, in the middle of so much unrestrained bitterness, the two main rivals, Tom Jones and J. H. Davies, cordially reaffirmed their friendship and mutual regard.[76] Much less was said publicly about J. E. Lloyd, the third candidate, although it was admitted on all sides that he was the most distinguished scholar. One of Lloyd's supporters believed that if the other candidates' administrative and business capacities were allowed to outweigh Lloyd's scholarship, it would amount to 'a sort of Bolshevik revolution in Headships of Colleges'. Lloyd's friend on the spot was J. W. Marshall, Acting Principal at this time, while Ainsworth Davis, formerly on the Aberystwyth staff, worked hard in private canvassing support. Davis thought that Lloyd should bestir himself as he was much too 'diffident' about the affair.[77] It was apparent to Lloyd's friends that his best, indeed his only, hope was that the 'Llandinam and Cwrt Mawr factions' would be evenly balanced, that neither would give way to the other, and there would thus be 'an excellent chance' for Lloyd to 'chip in' as the acceptable compromise choice.[78]

Forty-three members of the Council were present on the day the appointment was made. Sir John Williams, whose health had been failing of late, took the chair for the first time in years. The three candidates were interviewed: Tom Jones was in the room for just over a quarter of an hour, poor J. E. Lloyd got short shrift in five minutes, and they both had the impression that the Chairman 'was obviously impatient' to get them out of the room. J. H. Davies was before the Council for nearly three-quarters of an hour, and in the subsequent ballot he got twenty-three votes to sixteen for Tom Jones and four only for J. E. Lloyd: Evan Evans had been able to predict the result to within one vote and, as expected, 'the local block was practically solid' for J. H. Davies. Three, possibly four, of Tom Jones' strong supporters were unavoidably absent and the ballot showed that 'several people had been telling lies' about their allegiances.[79]

J. E. Lloyd's young son defiantly comforted his father ('I know you don't care a brass farthing'), and Tom Jones, after sending a sporting word of congratulation to the victor, left immediately for Llandinam. He was bitterly disappointed;

[75] Ibid. (17 October 1919).

[76] J. H. Davies to Thomas Jones, 15 October 1919. N.L.W. Thomas Jones MSS. Class X, vol. v, f. 63.

[77] Gwenogfryn Evans to Ainsworth Davis, 22 October 1919, Ainsworth Davis to 'Tibby', 17 and 29 September 1919. U.C.N.W., Bangor, Lloyd MSS. U235.

[78] W. R. Owen to J. E. Lloyd, 10 and 13 October 1919. Ibid.

[79] Thomas Jones to his wife, 8 November 1919, Revd. Richard Jones to Thomas Jones, 13 November 1919. N.L.W. Thomas Jones MSS. Class X, vol. v, ff. 135, 179. *Y Cymro* (12 November 1919). *Council Minutes* (7 November 1919), p. 436.

defeat, as one of his friends said, meant 'giving up a dream'.[80] None the less he took it all well and there was no real danger, as Miss Margaret Davies of Llandinam feared, that T.J. would be utterly soured and 'turn Irish'. David Davies was furious at the result; he considered resigning from the Council and mounting a press campaign, but was subsequently persuaded that his long-term interest in the future of Welsh higher education outweighed his present disappointment. T. J.s' friends up and down the country were outraged by the decision which, almost without exception, they ascribed to the dominance at Aberystwyth of 'the Parish Pump' mentality. Some of the London big-wigs, who knew least about the College, were the most forthright in denunciation, some of them absurdly writing off its future.[81]

All the same it is difficult to avoid speculating about the likely consequences for Aberystwyth if Thomas Jones had won. There is no doubt that he had great vision and aspired to lift the College to the heights; he could certainly have counted on the financial backing of the Llandinam family, and his remarkable talent for persuading other rich men to put their money to good social purposes would, without question, have been of immense benefit to a College still woefully short of endowment. Under his leadership Aberystwyth would have been a place of exceptional stir and movement (not perhaps to everyone's liking) and more cosmopolitan influences would perhaps have been brought to bear on the College, although it is to be remembered that all his plans for Aberystwyth specifically aimed at encouraging the best and highest qualities (as he saw them) of the Welsh. He could have been a magnificent Principal: perhaps it would all have ended in frustration.

So much of the comment on the affair was exaggerated and perversely *ex parte* that it is worth noting that all three candidates were considerably more than perfectly respectable possibilities; indeed, there was an embarrassment of talents, hence in part the great public interest in the challenge and the ferocity of the loyalties that were engaged. And it should not be forgotten that all three men were old Aberystwyth students who yearned desperately for the chance to serve the College. Most people, whatever their disappointments, quickly came to agree with Lleufer Thomas who said 'Whoever is appointed we must support him.'[82]

In many circles J. H. Davies' appointment gave great satisfaction: according to the *Manchester Guardian* 'national sentiment was satisfied', and the *Cambrian News* said that it marked the 'exaltation of common sense'.[83] The choice was

[80] Edward Lloyd to J. E. Lloyd (November 1919). U.C.N.W., Bangor, Lloyd MSS. U235. J. H. Davies to Thomas Jones, 10 November 1919, R. W. Jones to Thomas Jones, 10 November 1919. N.L.W. Thomas Jones MSS. Class X, vol. v, ff. 154, 157.

[81] Miss M. Davies to Mrs. Thomas Jones, 8 November 1919, W. J. Burdon Evans to Thomas Jones, 10 November 1919, H. A. L. Fisher and A. H. Kidd to Thomas Jones, 12 November 1919. N.L.W. Ibid., ff. 139, 152, 168, 173.

[82] Mrs. T. F. Roberts to Lleufer Thomas, 11 November 1919. N.L.W. Lleufer Thomas MSS. IA.

[83] *Manchester Guardian* (8 November 1919). *Cambrian News* (21 November 1919).

John Humphreys Davies
(Principal, 1919–1926)

Sir John Williams, Bart.
(President, 1913–1926)

PLATE 7

The Quad

The old College Hall, burned down 1933

wildly popular among the students. On the night of his election the new Principal addressed the student body in the Parish Hall, and later he and his sister (Tom Ellis' widow) were taken in a carriage through the streets of the town accompanied by a great crowd of cheering students. The evident satisfaction of staff and students was no mean testimony to J. H. Davies' standing in the College. The new Principal needed all the goodwill possible, for the post-war student-body included hundreds of ex-servicemen who did not take kindly to an old-fashioned code of regulations more suitable for boys than for men whose lives had recently been daily at risk. Indeed, on the general question of College discipline there had been 'thunder in the air' since the end of the war.[84] A personal appeal by the Principal to ex-service students to stay away from public houses so that young students who had come up straight from school would not be tempted to follow a bad example was not well received and was simply ignored. There was a rumbustious tone to student life in these years which was likely to pose disciplinary problems that would not be effectively answered by the old method of summoning the culprit (in traditional College parlance) to 'a haul' before the Principal; and the existing Discipline committee (made up exclusively of members of the Senate) was scarcely likely to hold the confidence of ex-servicemen, many of whom had had more than their fill of authority that could not be challenged. Strong support for sensible change came from several of the new professors; a new Joint Committee made of three members of the Senate and three representatives of the Students' Representative Council (subject, of course, to the ultimate control of the Principal and Senate, as required by the Charter) was established to replace the old authoritarian disciplinary arrangements. As Zimmern (a member of the Committee, along with H. J. Rose and Edward Edwards) said, the students were 'in a much better frame of mind in consequence'.[85]

There was some feeling after the war that, with the rapid rise in student numbers to over a thousand, much of the old warmth and close intimacy, which had been such important ingredients of College life at Aberystwyth in former times, would be lost. It was gloomily reported to the Court of Governors that the Quad., 'a place sacred to many generations of students', was too small for the much larger number of students; and the relaxation of social regulations, welcome as it was, inevitably weakened that concentration of student life in the old College building which had been so marked a feature of pre-war Aberystwyth.[86] But the fears of traditionalists were exaggerated, and most of the old staples of student life,

[84] 'Anent the Regulations', *The Dragon*, xliii. 82.

[85] *Council Minutes* (5 March 1920), p. 3. A. E. Zimmern to Thomas Jones, 16 February 1920. N.L.W. Thomas Jones MSS. Class W, vol. xx, f. 210. In October 1919 the ex-service students organized themselves into an association. As *The Dragon* (xliii. 83) said: 'The history of the emancipation of our students is really the . . . history of this body.'

[86] T. Quayle, 'Far Away and Long Ago', and Gwilym James, 'Post-War Aberystwyth', in Iwan Morgan, pp. 101–8, 144–51. The Acting Principal's Report, *Cambrian News* (24 October 1919).

quadding, ragging, 'smokers', soirées, and the rest continued. Aberystwyth remained 'splendidly democratic', with a student body made up of the 'jolliest mixture' of all the social classes, as one returning student noted with relief. The reintroduction of academic dress in 1922 (a change apparently welcomed by student opinion) helped to restore the old traditions.[87] Moreover, after 1922 student numbers began to fall: in October 1923 there were 810 students at College, and a year later 743.

And if the larger post-war numbers did lead to some inevitable weakening of the general corporate feeling, there were also compensations for this. There was, for example, Plynlymon hostel where, under the wise guidance of the Warden, E. D. T. Jenkins of the Classics department, there was a notably successful, but unfortunately short-lived, experiment in hall life for fifty or so men each year. Evening meals were formal and academic dress was obligatory. But the tone of the Hall was strongly democratic, with very close co-operation between the Warden and an elected student committee. In no time, as one student resident during these years recalls with pride, 'a fine conception of self-government, co-operation and individual responsibility grew up in this hostel'. There was a vigorous social life and Plynlymon regularly fielded teams in most College sports; here, as in other halls of residence, the record of academic success was demonstrably higher on average than for students in lodgings. When during 1925 for reasons of increasing financial difficulty, largely the result of a reduction in supporting grants from the Board of Education, it was decided to close the Hall, the resident men students, not surprisingly, petitioned for its retention. But in vain; penury had again cramped Aberystwyth's style.[88]

But of even greater general importance was the acquisition of the fine-looking Assembly Rooms for use as a Students' Union. The old Common Room, a cellar in the College basement, time lending enchantment to the recollection no doubt, evoked many happy memories for generations of pre-war students, but it was hopelessly inadequate and resembled nothing so much 'as a third-rate railway waiting-room, dingy and comfortless'.[89] During the war the Old Students' Association had largely suspended its operations, but in 1918 it came to life again, and began to raise money to be applied to some suitable purpose to celebrate the forthcoming Jubilee of the College in 1922.[90] Over £5,000 was raised by one method and another and in September 1921 the O.S.A. announced that, as a joint Memorial to the Founders of the College and to students who had fallen during the war, it had decided to buy and equip the Assembly Rooms for use as a

[87] *The Dragon*, xliv. 172, xlv. 24.

[88] E. G. Bowen, 'Notes on student life in the post-war years', p. 5. *Council Minutes* (24 June, 23 September 1925), pp. 517, 556. 'Plyn', bemoaned another former resident, 'was essentially Aber., and I fear that with the loss of Plyn. . . . Aber. has lost much.' I. C. Peate, *The Dragon*, xlvii, 106.

[89] Ibid. xxxvii. 90. *Welsh Outlook*, i. 363.

[90] H. J. Fleure to J. H. Davies, 22 August 1918. N.L.W. J. H. Davies MSS. (Misc. Letters).

Students' Union. In October 1923 the new amenity, which henceforth became the great social centre of College life, was formally opened by the Prince of Wales, Chancellor of the University.[91]

The O.S.A. continued to flourish during the 1920s. In 1923 a new branch was established for old students in India, Burma, and Ceylon. The London branch, 'a notoriously unpunctual crowd' who cheerfully allowed themselves a quarter of an hour's grace, held regular, well-attended meetings, and the Society of Old Aberystwythians, 'the only Society of its kind in Cambridge', was reported in 1926 to be 'particularly robust' in numbers, with its meetings wholly governed by that spirit 'which sets those who have an experience of Aberystwyth behind them in a class apart'.[92] The strength and unique loyalty of the O.S.A. for Aberystwyth provoked admiration and rueful envy elsewhere. Principal Reichel conceded that the Bangor old students were 'somewhat behind their compeers of Aberystwyth', and Principal Sibley of the new University College of Swansea fervently hoped that, in time, his students would develop some equivalent to that 'strange thing' the 'Aber. feeling', a natural enough ambition which provoked the rejoinder from an ex-President of the O.S.A., 'they won't for we hold the Patent Rights'.[93]

There is no doubt, too, that students in the other Welsh colleges in this period felt at a disadvantage, at least in some respects, compared with their fellows at Aberystwyth. An account in a popular journal of student Societies at Aberystwyth in 1924–5 is justly entitled 'Multitudinous Activities', whereas the report from Cardiff records the depressing failure of most Societies there, largely because so few students actually lived in the city. Swansea, where similar conditions applied, conceded Aberystwyth's primacy in these matters but none the less gamely tried to follow its example. Bangor, too, had a proportion of commuter students who were thus largely lost to evening activities.[94] This acknowledged superiority was not without its dangers. Frank Smith, a lecturer in the Education department at Aberystwyth, in a farewell message to the students in 1925, risked, as he said, a charge of 'blasphemy' to point out that the 'Aber. spirit' seemed to become 'so intense at times that it becomes parochial, so flamboyant that it becomes uncritical', and he suggested that the College was so well established that its students needed no air of 'assumed superiority' to sustain their standing. Moreover, there were so many Societies at Aberystwyth that some students wasted much time in

[91] *Welsh Outlook*, vii. 5. *Council Minutes* (29 September 1921), p. 132. *The Dragon*, xliv. 27, 160, xlv. 49, xlvi. 40–3.

[92] *Welsh Outlook*, x. 112. *The Dragon*, xlviii. 42. (Sir) David Evans to J. H. Davies, 11 December 1923, I. C. Jones to J. H. Davies, 20 January 1926. N.L.W. J. H. Davies MSS. (Corr.).

[93] Sir Harry Reichel reported in the *North Wales Chronicle* (26 March 1926). H. Howard Humphreys to J. H. Davies, 20 February 1926. N.L.W. J. H. Davies MSS. (Corr.).

[94] 'University Intelligence', *Welsh Outlook*, xii. 186–90. 'Swansea Letter', *The Dragon*, xlv. 42–3.

an attempt to keep up a crowded week of meetings which it was considered 'the correct thing to attend'.[95]

One Society of especial importance at Aberystwyth in the early 1920s was the Political Union, which owed its formation to a feeling that the old Literary and Debating Society was dominated by a tradition of too frequent debates on frivolous catch-phrase subjects, in which proceedings, all too often, degenerated into 'crude horseplay'. Political Union meetings in the Examination Hall (arranged for the occasion as nearly as possible on the model of the House of Commons) were usually crowded and provided an appropriate setting for hard-hitting debates on the great issues of the day, the clash of Labour and Capital, Communism and Imperialism, and the like. One particularly memorable confrontation, 'the best educational exhibition these fellows could get', as one left-wing member of staff present described it, was a debate in 1925 between Sir Alfred Mond and Frank Hodges, the trade union leader, who was beaten by 370 votes to 250: 'these *women*', said the same staff member with disgust, 'are Conservatives'. Eventually it became apparent that, in the long run, the College was not large enough to sustain two major debating societies and the Political Union and 'Lit. and Deb.' were reunited in a new Debates Union.[96]

In the 1920s *Y Geltaidd*, the Welsh Society, was particularly strong; indeed, for the first time it seriously rivalled the Literary and Debating Society. Aberystwyth produced at this time a string of gifted young Welsh dramatists of whom Idwal Jones (a notable character whose occasionally hilarious career at College has been affectionately recorded by his friend Gwenallt Jones) was perhaps the best known.[97] This strength was reflected in Aberystwyth's dominance of the Inter-College *Eisteddfod*. In 1923, for example, Aberystwyth competitors recorded thirty-two outright victories and shared five successes out of the forty major awards. Two years later, competing away from home at Swansea, Aberystwyth carried off fifteen out of twenty-five prizes. 'Is it fair', asked the President of the Students' Representative Council, 'that Aber. should year after year be depended upon to make the *Eisteddfod*?'[98] One consequence of this increased vigour, strengthened further perhaps by a consciousness that in the wider world outside the College Welsh culture (and particularly the language) was steadily succumbing to English influences, was a more aggressive attitude by the leaders of Welsh-speaking students. Iorwerth Peate constantly demanded that Welsh should be accorded its proper status in the life of the College, and Waldo Williams called

[95] 'Vale', *The Dragon*, xlviii. 14.

[96] E. G. Bowen, 'Notes on student life in the post-war years', p. 1. J. Morgan Rees to J. H. Davies, 21 March 1925. N.L.W. J. H. Davies MSS. (Corr.). *The Dragon*, xlvi. 213–14, xlviii. 163–4. Two star student speakers at the Political Union were D. J. Llewelfryn Davies and D. Seaborne Davies, both future professors of Law.

[97] D. J. Gwenallt Jones, *Cofiant Idwal Jones* (Aberystwyth, 1958).

[98] *The Dragon*, xlv. 251–3, xlvii. 161.

on his fellow students to decide, once and for all, whether Aberystwyth was to be a genuine part of 'the national university of Wales' or a mere appendage to the English provincial university system. Predictably enough this led to allegations of a narrow chauvinism, and for some years there was, as *The Dragon* admitted in 1929, an unhappy if not always overt 'antagonism' between some Welsh and English students.[99]

There were no divisions, however, on the sports fields, where Aberystwyth enjoyed something of a golden age. Until the very late 1920s the College rugby team had not lost a match against its rivals in the University of Wales for twenty years, and in 1927-8 the British university rugby championship was won by a team which drew great advantage from the inspiration provided by C. W. Davies, later a professor of Chemistry at Aberystwyth. In 1922 the soccer team, with the redoubtable Ned Harries highly skilled and tireless in the then fulcrum position of centre-half, was unluckily beaten in a replayed Final of the Welsh Amateur Cup by a Llanidloes team which had been outplayed for long periods. The British universities soccer championship was also won soon afterwards. In 1927-8 Aberystwyth had its best results for fifty years: the over-all Welsh Inter-College championship was won as well as the British university rugby cup; the women's hockey and tennis teams reached the British championship Finals, and Aberystwyth made a powerful contribution (five out of seven runners, including the legendary D. J. P. Richards) to the Welsh harriers team which carried off the British championship. During these years the Vicarage Field was considerably improved: a new tennis pavilion and changing rooms for men and women were added, and a fine new grandstand was built. There had always been a strong interest in gymnastics at Aberystwyth, and after the war, during the long Directorship of H. F. Stimson, the College made an important contribution to the development of physical education in Britain. Advanced courses leading to a diploma qualification (one of the first to be instituted) were introduced, and one of the highlights of the social year was a gymnastic display in which an astonishing acrobatic versatility entertained unfailingly packed audiences.[100]

After the war Music achieved an importance in the life of the College (and, for that matter, the town) that it had never had before. Walford Davies, equipped by the Misses Davies with ample funds, and supported by a substantial staff of lecturers and instrumentalists, set to work with his usual bounding energy. In addition to the normal degree work (inevitably for a relatively small number of students) the department, or perhaps rather the School of Music, immediately

---

[99] I. C. Peate, '*Bywyd Myfyrwyr Aber.*', *The Dragon*, xlviii. 155-8, 'Aber. and the Welsh Tradition', ibid., 4, 16, Waldo Williams, 'The Choice before Us', M. F. J., 'A Wider Vision', ibid. xlix. 5-6, 15-16. Aberystwyth, along with Bangor, made an important contribution to the foundation of *Y Blaid Genedlaethol Gymreig* (The Welsh National Party) in this period.

[100] *Welsh Outlook*, xvi. 191. *The Dragon*, xliv. 191-3, xlix. 47, ll. 79-80.

became engaged in a host of other activities of benefit to the College as a whole. Walford Davies was soon busily buying instruments for a College Orchestra which was formed in 1919, along with a College Choral Union (with a large membership) which was trained by W. R. Allen. Weekly College concerts (which attracted packed audiences with many prepared to stand so long as they could hear) were instituted, and there were Chamber music concerts each Friday evening for smaller gatherings at the Music House. The professor and his colleagues regularly gave Open lectures on the works of the great masters, and annual Summer Schools for teachers were held at Aberystwyth and, later, at Coleg Harlech. But the high point of the year was the ambitious Musical Festival held usually during the Summer term when distinguished conductors (Boult, Elgar, Vaughan Williams, Edward German, Gustav Holst, Sir Henry Wood, and others) were brought to Aberystwyth. In 1920 the London Symphony Orchestra came to give three concerts; this venture was inevitably expensive and it was difficult to find a hall large enough to cover the cost. Moreover, as one enthusiastic old student who lived in the town noted, tickets were 'not being snatched' up as unexpected: they were 'only twelve bob', but 'Aber. is not up to twelve bob yet'. In addition to all this, a superb College trio (Charles Clements, Hubert Davies, and Arthur Williams) visited many schools and gave lecture-concerts in the towns of the College Extra-Mural area.[101]

Walford Davies threw himself into his work with tremendous zest; his out-pouring of energy was prodigious and he lived constantly near the edge of break-down. For him Wales was 'a trilingual country; she speaks Welsh, English and Music, and the greatest of these is Music'.[102] He had an exceptional gift for establishing a rapport with his audiences; 'his easy, happy, jolly handling of a hall chock-full of students', as one fervent admirer described it, had to be seen to be believed. Davies himself was delighted to find that the students quickly became 'boister-ously affectionate', and his concert audiences, led by 'the gods' at the back, took up a chant: 'We want ford: What ford? Walford.' He believed that this represented 'something of a concession to Chamber music and instrumental music generally'; the Welsh were being weaned away from their obsession with choral music.[103] Walford Davies (or Sir Walford as he became in 1922) was able to rely heavily on the strong support of David de Lloyd, lecturer in Music, and con-siderable assistance was rendered by Lloyd Williams, professor of Botany, who was also a gifted musician. This was just as well for, inevitably, as Director of Music for Wales Davies had to be away from College frequently; moreover, he

[101] Florence Williams to 'May' (1920). N.L.W. Thomas Jones MSS. Class X, vol. v, f. 89. *A Review of the Activities of the Council of Music, 1919–41* (Cardiff, 1941). *Welsh Outlook*, xii. 259–60.

[102] M. G. Matheson to J. H. Davies, 19 December 1919. N.L.W. J. H. Davies MSS. (Corr.). Walford Davies, 'A Musical Policy for Wales', *Trans. Cymm.* (1921–2), p. 1.

[103] Florence Williams to 'May' (1920), Walford Davies to Thomas Jones, 22 November 1919. N.L.W. Thomas Jones MSS. Class X, vol. v, ff. 89, 195.

was much in demand for musical ventures all over the country and in 1924 he began a career as a radio broadcaster which was to bring him enormous fame.[104] This frenetic activity exacted its toll and in 1925 he was worn out and 'longing for dry dock'. By the following year he had decided that, in fairness to Aberystwyth, he must resign. A genuine musical evangelist, he could not resist the opportunity radio broadcasting offered of giving 'systematic weekly lessons on school music to a thousand schools'; and, additionally, he had come to the 'overwhelming conviction' that the Council of Music in Wales would never function effectively while its Director was 'located at and publicly identified with one of the four Colleges'.[105]

Sir Walford Davies evoked strong feelings: he had a host of ardent admirers many of whom were prepared to canonize him; some others thought him a humbug, a flashy showman whose quality was grossly overrated. His private correspondence shows him to have been warm, intensely human, endearing even (sometimes he signed letters to J. H. Davies, 'Walford *bach*'). There is no question that his drive, his capacity to communicate with, and rivet the attention of, large audiences and create in them an excitement for great music made a tremendous impact on Aberystwyth and Wales generally. He was replaced as professor of Music by Dr. David de Lloyd, and the offices of the Council of Music were removed to Cardiff.[106]

Walford Davies' close friend and colleague A. E. Zimmern had not lasted as long at Aberystwyth. During 1920 Zimmern became involved in a delicate situation which made his position at the College untenable. Madame Barbier, wife of the professor of French, had asked for a divorce from her husband in order to marry Zimmern. Strong feelings and deep loyalties were aroused by the situation, which was not devoid of tragic implications for some of those involved. A deputation of senior students saw the Principal to express the 'great admiration' felt for Zimmern by the general body of students and to urge his retention. Some members of the Council were outraged by Zimmern's behaviour and advocated drastic action; the Senate privately counselled Zimmern to resign and all his closest friends, deeply disturbed, urged the same course. At first Zimmern was disposed to be combative and he insisted on addressing the Council in defiant terms on 3 June 1921. Ultimately, however, wiser counsels prevailed, and he resigned on 23 June 1921, a day before the Council met again. It was an unhappy end to a tenure that had promised so much and, indeed, had achieved a great deal during its short duration.[107] After a short interval C. K. Webster, the distinguished historian, was

[104] Colles, op. cit., p. 130.
[105] Walford Davies to J. H. Davies, 12 November 1925 and 5 October 1926. N.L.W. J. H. Davies MSS. (Corr.).
[106] H. I. Parrott, *The Spiritual Pilgrims* (1968), p. 45. *Welsh Outlook*, x. 202. Walford Davies to J. H. Davies (no date). N.L.W. Cwrt Mawr MSS.
[107] 'Memorandum on A. E. Z.' (1921). N.L.W. J. H. Davies MSS. (Misc. Letters). Walford Davies

invited to the Wilson chair, and in January 1923 he accepted on condition that his work on British foreign policy in the early nineteenth century (on which he had been engaged for fourteen years) should be 'the first charge' on the time available to him for research. Webster thought that 'it would be a mistake to make "International Politics" a separate subject of study', and he proposed instead in his teaching during the term when he was in residence 'to assist other departments in the international aspects of their work'. Webster was a first-rate choice for the Wilson chair, and during his ten years at Aberystwyth his reputation for great scholarship mounted steadily.[108]

The Haldane *Report* had foreshadowed important developments in Extra-Mural work after the war, and it was not surprising that Aberystwyth should be quickly off the mark because some of the most influential members, lay and academic, of the College believed unreservedly in the importance of this general missionary work. J. H. Davies thought that Aberystwyth in particular (which had grown 'from the people') had a special responsibility to make itself 'serviceable in the average world', and Lleufer Thomas, the most continuously active member of the Council, agreed: he insisted in 1918 that 'a large and generous provision' of extension work should be arranged as soon as possible.[109] In 1920 Aberystwyth was the first of the Welsh Colleges to appoint a Director of Extra-Mural Studies, and rapidly 'succeeded in outpacing its sister Colleges'. When the University Extension Board eventually came into existence and began to function in 1922–3, as the co-ordinator of Extra-Mural work by the constituent colleges, it resolved that a special effort should be made in South Wales, which had lagged behind, and this amounted to a directive to Aberystwyth and Bangor to 'mark time' until the other Colleges had caught up. But a Board of Education decision in 1924 to recognize adult education as an integral part of the national system put the finances of the department on a much sounder footing, and until crude temporary retrenchments were imposed by the National Government in the financial panic of 1931, Aberystwyth's Extra-Mural work flourished and steadily expanded. In 1919 there were 7 classes, 3 tutors, and 167 students; by 1929 there were 31 classes, 22 tutors (mainly part-timers), and the number of students had risen to 631. In 1920 there had been six formal applications for the post of Director, but a casual 'verbal' inquiry drew the attention of the selection committee to the 'superior attainments', not least as

to Thomas Jones, 21, 28, and 29 June 1921. N.L.W. Thomas Jones MSS. Class W, vol. xx, ff. 231, 233, 234. C.A. A. E. Zimmern File. *Council Minutes* (29 April, 3 and 24 June 1921), pp. 100–1, 111, 113.

[108] J. H. Davies to C. K. Webster, 1 August 1923. C. K. Webster, 'The Wilson Chair of International Politics' (1923). C.A. C. K. Webster File.

[109] J. H. Davies, 'Notes on University Education' (1919). Lleufer Thomas to J. H. Davies, 11 December 1918. N.L.W. J. H. Davies MSS. (T. I. Ellis donations 1958/62 and 1963/6).

a 'publicist', of the Reverend Herbert Morgan of Bristol who was unanimously appointed.[110]

On that same day a new head (with the rank of independent lecturer) had been appointed to the department of German. After Ethé's unceremonious eviction in 1914 the department had been carried on in difficult circumstances by Miss Mary Brebner. Indeed, for a time after the war the revulsion against all things German was so strong that there was a short-lived danger that, when Miss Brebner resigned in 1920, the department might founder. However, at the suggestion of a member of the Council, David Evans, an old Aberystwyth man (a notable student gymnast), lately a civilian prisoner of war, currently on the staff of Birmingham University, was encouraged to apply and was appointed in September 1920.[111] David Evans remained on the Aberystwyth staff (as professor of German after 1936), a living embodiment of the long-term dividend derived from physical exercise, until his retirement in 1952. Soon afterwards another old student, already on the staff, was added to the Senate. T. C. James had applied for the chair of Chemistry in 1919 and his non-selection had been 'exploited' by some local patriots to show 'how the Llandinam influence' was exerted in favour of outsiders. Fleure thought that T. C. James had been 'persistently undervalued' and that he had been unfairly saddled by David Davies with the 'sins and negligences' of Findlay, the former professor of Chemistry. Quite apart from his quality as a chemist, Fleure ardently wanted T. C. James on the Senate because he had a 'very unusual judgment in deciding the promise of a student, and the Senate now lacks that valuable power of estimation'.[112] In 1921 when Mouatt Jones resigned to become Principal of the Manchester College of Technology, T. C. James was unanimously appointed to the chair. His rare power of judgement in matters relating to students was put to particularly good use during a long tenure later on as Vice-Principal.

When H. J. Fleure became professor of Geography in 1918, R. D. Laurie, who came to Aberystwyth from Liverpool University, succeeded him as head of the department of Zoology, initially with the rank of independent lecturer. Laurie soon made his mark at Aberystwyth; indeed, within a year of his arrival, Fleure wrote glowingly of the ability of his new colleague, who was 'fast earning a professorship'.[113] College finances were still too straitened to admit of immediate promotion, no matter how well deserved, but in 1922 the Honourable Samuel Vestey offered an annual sum of £250 for three years and it was thus possible to

[110] *A Survey of the work of the Extra-Mural department* (Aberystwyth, 1935), pp. 1–3. *Council Minutes* (24 September 1920), p. 47.

[111] Canon R. Williams to J. H. Davies, 8 July 1920. N.L.W. J. H. Davies MSS. (Corr.). *Council Minutes* (24 September 1920), p. 47.

[112] Lleufer Thomas and H. J. Fleure to Thomas Jones, 5 and 23 October 1919. N.L.W. Thomas Jones MSS. Class X, vol. v, ff. 41, 77.

[113] H. J. Fleure to Thomas Jones, 5 October 1919. N.L.W. Ibid., f. 41.

create a chair in Zoology, to which Laurie justly succeeded. 'Professor Laurie', wrote a later Principal with rueful admiration, 'is a man who knows what he wants and usually gets it.' Laurie's determination is exemplified by his fight for better accommodation for his department. In 1919 Zoology was inadequately housed in the old College building, but when the old slate works in Cambrian Street was acquired in that same year, primarily for the departments of Agriculture, Laurie saw possibilities there for Zoology. There was no money available for structural alterations, so in 1924, aided by his staff and some of his students, Laurie decided that private enterprise would have to serve instead. He appealed for funds for raw materials and he and his assistants set to work to adapt the building to their needs. For the next few years the work of the department was carried on partly in the main College and partly in Laurie's privately built addendum. Ultimately, impressed by Laurie's enterprise and worn down by his advocacy, in season and out, the College authorities undertook to complete the work and by 1929 Zoology had an adequate home of its own. 'A thing of beauty it is not', said that same Principal, 'but as a triumph of enthusiasm over mere finance it merits great respect.'[114]

R. D. Laurie was obviously a notable fighter for unpromising (indeed, at first sight, hopeless) causes. In the years before 1914, when the non-professorial staff members of modern British universities were regarded as mere assistants to heads of departments, the notion of forming an effective association of university teachers seemed an unlikely possibility, least of all an association that included the professoriate. The story of the foundation and growth of the Association of University Teachers, 'the key profession', as its historian with legitimate pride calls it, has already been told.[115] R. D. Laurie's contribution to the initiation, formation and subsequent development of the A.U.T. was unique: he was Founder, first President, and honorary General Secretary of the Association for the first thirty-three years and, as its historian says, his 'creative ability, dedication, modesty and charm' shine through its records.[116] It was an uphill struggle but Laurie, who for years at Aberystwyth ran the administration of the Association on a shoestring, was exactly the bonny, good-humoured fighter needed to lead patiently a forlorn hope to something ultimately not far short of triumph.[117]

During 1926 the College suffered a double blow in the loss of its President and Principal. Sir John Williams, who was well on into his eighties, had been ailing for years and for some time had felt 'not equal' to his many responsibilities.[118]

[114] Ifor L. Evans, *Departmental Surveys* (1936), p. 74.

[115] Harold Perkin, *Key Profession: the History of the Association of University Teachers* (1969).

[116] Ibid., dedicatory note. The 'modesty' is particularly apparent in Laurie's own unpublished account ('A History giving the origin and work of the A.U.T.') of the Association.

[117] I am indebted to Miss Dorothy K. Davies, Professor Laurie's secretary for many years, for valuable information on this subject.

[118] Sir John Williams to Gwenogfryn Evans, 11 March 1921. N.L.W. Timothy Lewis MSS., f. 186.

It is difficult to determine exactly how much influence Sir John wielded in the day-to-day affairs of the College during his Presidency, because after 1909 he lived in Aberystwyth and there was, therefore, little need for him to spell out his views on paper. The evidence, such as it is, suggests that he played a much less active part than his predecessor, Lord Rendel. There is no doubt that the warm friendship and mutual confidence that existed between Sir John and Principal J. H. Davies lubricated the running of the College administration at the highest level. It had been known for some time that, sooner or later, Sir John Williams would make a handsome benefaction to the College for the purposes of endowing studies relating to Wales, and this expectation was fulfilled on his death. He bequeathed to the College investments and cash to a total value of over £50,000, as well as his Aberystwyth home, 'Blaenllynant' (including its magnificent and valuable furniture), for use as the residence of the Principal or any other designated officer of the College. Few Welshmen in modern times have a greater call on the gratitude of their countrymen than Sir John Williams. A fairy-tale career took him into the highest places in the land: his heart remained in Wales, for which he strove with might and main throughout his life.[119]

Sir John Williams' successor as President was, inevitably, David Davies of Llandinam, who was nominated independently by almost every member of the Council. After his bitter disappointment over the selection of the Principal in 1919, David Davies (or 'DD' as he was known to his friends) had largely withdrawn from any active share in College affairs. In 1921 there were evidently many members of the Council who were anxious 'to conciliate him', but at that time DD thought his position in relation to the College 'most unfortunate'. As he said, he had 'introduced' A. E. Zimmern to the College and 'practically nominated' him to the Wilson chair, and David Davies was thoroughly embarrassed by the consequences.[120] However, in time these difficulties had eased and in 1926 when he was unanimously nominated for the Presidency DD ultimately accepted, not least because Tom Jones 'urged him' strongly to do so, and 'to put his back into the job'.[121]

Curiously enough, considering the reason for DD's withdrawal from the College, his return to active interest coincided with the need to appoint another Principal. The first half at least of J. H. Davies' Principalship was a time of unprecedented growth and bustle in the history of the College; the pressures were such that J. H. Davies could reasonably have said, with Talleyrand, that his major achievement had been at least to survive. In fact, he did rather more than that. His

---

[119] *Funds and Trusts* (U.C.W., 1936), pp. 13–17. For Sir John's great benefactions to the other institution close to his heart, see W. Ll. Davies, *The National Library of Wales* (Aberystwyth, 1937), pp. 48–50.

[120] Thomas Jones to W. H. Young (February 1920), David Davies and Lleufer Thomas to Thomas Jones, 12 February and 6 March 1921. N.L.W. Thomas Jones MSS. Class J, vol. viii, f. 36, Class W, vol. xx, ff. 228, 241.

[121] Thomas Jones to H. J. Fleure, 1 September 1926. N.L.W. Ibid., Class J, vol. ix, f. 4.

business capacity stood him in good stead in complicated negotiations, where time was at a premium, for a variety of properties which enabled the College to cope with the accommodation of more than double the usual number of students. Old-fashioned as he was in many ways, he nevertheless was able to come to terms with a generation of students impatient of old forms and not overly diffident about expressing dissent. The Principal's concern for the welfare of his students is well attested: he inaugurated a student medical scheme well before it became common practice, and there is some evidence of his administering and secretly replenishing a loan fund for needy students.[122] What is certain is that J. H. Davies retained to the end the great goodwill of his staff.[123] And this was important at a time when the close unity of a formerly small team was in danger of disruption by a very rapid growth in numbers.

Almost at the very moment when the post-war emergency was subsiding into relative calm, the Principal was cruelly injured in an accident. In July 1922 he was in London making arrangements for the College Jubilee when, near Chalk Farm station, he was struck by a falling tree. It sounded an odd business; Stanley Roberts, professor of Colonial History, an irrepressible joker, said that he could not understand how J. H. Davies, who lived at Cwm (a small mansion he had bought near Clarach), 'surrounded by trees, . . . had to go to London to get knocked down by one'.[124] But this was no joke. The Principal sustained severe injuries to his head and spine from which he never fully recovered; in 1925, at the age of fifty-four, he had to learn to walk for the second time. He fought bravely against his painful afflictions and made a great effort to play his part in the life of the College: but his health steadily deteriorated, ultimately he was bed-ridden, and he died on 10 August 1926.[125]

The Jubilee celebration in July 1922 was a time of great rejoicing at Aberystwyth. On 19 July large crowds from all over Wales descended on the town; scarcely a building was without a flag or bunting of some sort. The Prime Minister, Lloyd George, came down and received a tremendous reception from his own people. The Founders of a College, which 'owed its existence to dreams' and had always been 'the embodiment of national aspirations', were duly honoured; and particular tribute was paid to T. C. Edwards, who, as Lloyd George said in typically felicitous terms, was 'responsible for erecting the bridge over the chasm between the Wales of one Book and the Wales of many books'. That same day the statue

---

[122] J. L. Newbon to T. I. Ellis, 16 August 1926. N.L.W. J. H. Davies MSS. (T. I. Ellis donation 1963/6).

[123] 'We are muddling along somehow, but we long to have the captain on the bridge again', is a not untypical sentiment expressed by one member of staff at a time when J. H. Davies was out of action with infirmity. J. Lloyd Williams to J. H. Davies, 27 April 1925. N.L.W. J. H. Davies MSS. (Corr.).

[124] J. W. Marshall to J. H. Davies, 10 July 1922. N.L.W. J. H. Davies MSS. (Corr.).

[125] Sir John Williams to J. H. Davies, 7 May 1925. N.L.W. Ibid. Lleufer Thomas to Thomas Jones, 30 October 1925. N.L.W. Thomas Jones MSS. Class W, vol. xviii, f. 250. *The Dragon*, xlviii. 7.

PLATE 8

Sir Henry Stuart-Jones
(Principal, 1927–1934)

Lord Davies
(President, 1926–1944)

PLATE 9

Ifor Leslie Evans
(Principal, 1934–1952)

Thomas Jones
(President, 1944–1954)

of T. C. Edwards (criticized at the time as a poor likeness, not least because the Principal's spectacles were missing), which still stands in front of the College, was unveiled.[126] Lloyd George spoke in the new so-called University Hall (locally, and more properly, it was never called anything but the College Hall), a massive structure, mainly of wood, which was set up on land adjoining Queen's Road. This Hall (which cost just under £5,000) had seating accommodation for 2,500 people and, despite its relative cheapness, excellent acoustic qualities. A week or so earlier, the London Symphony Orchestra had performed there before one of the largest audiences of young people ever assembled in Britain for a purely orchestral concert.[127] The College Hall was a most valuable acquisition which was of inestimable advantage to the College and the Aberystwyth area until some years later it was destroyed by another visitation from that old scourge of the College, fire.

The appointment of a new Principal in 1927 attracted far less public attention than in 1919. This time the Council was prepared to concede a substantial initiative to the selection committee which, led by David Davies, conducted its inquiries discreetly. Several formal applications were submitted, including one from Dr. Thomas Quayle, the old Aberystwyth student. Other names of particular interest included Gwilym Owen, professor of Physics, T. Gwynn Jones (who recoiled with horror and implored William George to withdraw the nomination), Edward Edwards, W. J. Gruffydd, and the brilliant young Oxford historian, Goronwy Edwards. Bryner Jones was prepared to consider the appointment if invited to accept.[128] Inevitably, many minds turned to thoughts of Thomas Jones (who had firmly rejected strong advances from Swansea in 1922). David Davies was asked to feel TJ's 'pulse', but had to report that there was 'no hope in that quarter'.[129] With wry memories of 1919, David Davies could not resist a playful touch: with his tongue in his cheek, he circulated a memorandum to members of the selection committee suggesting a quantitative analysis of the various qualities (so many points for personality, academic attainments, administrative ability, and so on) required in a successful candidate.[130] In the light of later events, it is of interest that inquiries were made about Ifor L. Evans of St. John's College, Cambridge, but ultimately it was felt that he was not yet ripe, and he was said (a curious comment on the value of a supposedly knowledgeable

[126] *Cambrian News* (21 July 1922). *Welsh Gazette* (20 July 1922). *Daily Chronicle* (20 July 1922). *Y Cymro* (20 July 1922).

[127] *Council Minutes* (3 March 1922), p. 169. *Welsh Outlook*, ix. 154–5.

[128] W. B. Foot to J. L. Newbon, 3 February 1927. N.L.W. Llandinam MSS. (U.C.W. (1)), Gen. Corr. T. Gwynn Jones to William George, 15 February 1927. N.L.W. T. Gwynn Jones MSS. David Davies to Bryner Jones, 18 November 1926. N.L.W. Llandinam MSS. (U.C.W. Principalship).

[129] Exchange of Letters, Gwilym Owen and David Davies, March 1927. N.L.W. Llandinam MSS. (U.C.W. (1)), Gen. Corr.

[130] David Davies to Thomas Jones, 6 February 1927 (enclosing a letter, Sir Evan D. Jones to David Davies, 8 February 1927). N.L.W. Ibid.

private testimony) to have 'no liking for administration'.[131] Tom Jones drew the committee's attention to David Hughes Parry, a young man in his thirties, one of the most brilliant products of the Aberystwyth Law department, who seemed, as a matter of course, to demonstrate an effortless superiority (well up to Balliol standards) in everything that he attempted professionally.[132] Many members of the Council put forward the name of Henry Stuart Jones, the Camden professor of Ancient History at Oxford, an outstanding scholar with a European reputation. It will be remembered that Stuart Jones had indicated an interest in the Principalship in 1919. Finally, the committee confined their consideration to three names: Stuart Jones, Hughes Parry, and J. F. Rees, later the Principal of University College, Cardiff. On 28 April Stuart Jones was interviewed by the committee (which had agreed beforehand that the crucial considerations, in order, were, 'academic distinction, administrative ability, nationality') in a private session at David Davies' home in Llandinam.[133] Seven members present were prepared immediately to recommend Stuart Jones and, after some discussion, the reservations of 'two Doubting Thomases' were overcome. The next day the Council endorsed the committee's unanimous recommendation of Stuart Jones, who addressed the meeting and quickly showed that he was 'no orator', and was not likely to 'pander to the gallery'.[134]

Stuart Jones' election marked a break with the Aberystwyth tradition: he was not Welsh-born, and he was the first Anglican Principal the College had ever had; there were those who regretted that, unlike all his predecessors, he was not a man of the people, and some of the nationalists criticized the selection of an Englishman. But others welcomed the new departure: the election of an Anglican seemed, once and for all, to answer the old sneers (in which George Bernard Shaw had joined) about a Methodist Academy. But the consideration which proved 'irresistible', as Lord Justice Atkin of the selection committee said, was Stuart Jones' massive reputation as a scholar: nothing could gainsay that.[135]

Soon after Stuart Jones became Principal, another distinguished man was added to the Senate at Aberystwyth. A. W. Ashby, son of the remarkable Joseph Ashby, who had been rescued by Ruskin College, Oxford, from the oblivion to which he would otherwise have been consigned by a poor village school, came to Aberystwyth in 1924 as the first Advisor in Agricultural Economics in Wales. Ashby,

[131] Harold Temperley to David Davies, 10 March 1927. N.L.W. Llandinam MSS. (U.C.W. Principalship).

[132] Thomas Jones to David Davies, 24 January 1927. N.L.W. Ibid.

[133] 'Minutes of the Selection Committee', 10 February 1927. N.L.W. Llandinam MSS. (U.C.W. Principalship).

[134] David Davies and H. J. Fleure to Thomas Jones, 30 April and 1 May 1927. N.L.W. Thomas Jones MSS. Class J, vol. ix, ff. 9, 10. *Council Minutes* (29 April 1927), pp. 96–9.

[135] *Western Mail* (30 April, 2 and 4 May 1927), *South Wales Daily News* (30 April 1927). *The Complete Works of G. B. Shaw* (1934), p. 352. Lord Justice Atkin to David Davies, 26 April 1927. N.L.W. Llandinam MSS. (U.C.W. (1)), Gen. Corr.

who looked 'at rural Wales as a priest looks at his parish', soon won the confidence of the Welsh farmers. Within three years he had established a network of extension classes in several counties and had made himself known and freely accepted in the rural organizations of the area. Ashby was a prodigious worker and his writings (there are four large volumes of privately collected works, most of them published when he was at Aberystwyth) are strongly practical in tone and purpose. When in 1929 it became possible to establish a chair in Agricultural Economics at Aberystwyth, it was overwhelmingly clear that Ashby, already well on the way to becoming the foremost British authority in the subject, was, as Stuart Jones said, 'the only possible candidate'. Sensibly, the College Council did not advertise the chair (the first ever to be established in the United Kingdom) but simply appointed Ashby to it.[136]

In the dozen years after 1918 the College at Aberystwyth, as H. J. Fleure, with no more than a touch of hyperbole, wrote later in a fine epitaph, 'definitively emerged from the local to the international level facing new challenges and new judgements'.[137]

---

[136] 'Arthur W. Ashby, 1886–1953', *The Countryman* (Winter, 1953), pp. 3–8. The Collected Works of A. W. Ashby. *Council Minutes* (22 July 1929), p. 441. Stuart Jones to C. K. Webster, 1 August 1929. C.A. C. K. Webster File.

[137] H. J. Fleure, 'An old student looks at the College', loc. cit., p. 63.

8

'The College is now Facing a most Critical Period'[1]

THE period between 1930 and the outbreak of war in 1939 was a diffi-cult time for the College at Aberystwyth, as indeed it was for most university institutions in the United Kingdom. These were the years of worldwide depression, of massive unemployment at home, when public men (with some few exceptions whose more radical ideas were generally scorned or disregarded), bewildered by events which they could scarcely com-prehend, much less control, fell back in desperation on what seemed like the common-sense prescription of strict economy in government spending. Outside the depressed areas, it was not a heroic age; caution not imagination was dominant. In these circumstances it is not surprising that the College could not sustain the momentum of advance that had been built up in the previous decade; the most that could reasonably be expected was a more or less successful holding operation until conditions more favourable to growth returned. Nevertheless, during these years ambitious plans were drawn up which, in due time, were to lead to the building of substantially a new College on a different site.

The basis of these projected developments was the purchase in November 1929 of eighty-seven acres of land (vested in Trustees for the benefit of the College) on Penglais adjacent to the National Library of Wales by an old Aberystwyth student. Joseph Davies Bryan had lived for almost half a century in Egypt where he built up a large and prosperous business; throughout his years overseas he had remained closely interested in the affairs of the College, to which he was deeply attached. He bought a house in Aberystwyth against the day of his retirement, and his magnificent gift to the College of the Penglais land followed in due course.[2]

Shortly before, it had appeared for a brief moment (at least to the President of

[1] J. Davies Bryan to Thomas Jones, 20 April 1934. N.L.W. Thomas Jones MSS. Class J, vol. ix, f. 100.

[2] 'The Penglais Trust', *Funds and Trusts* (U.C.W., 1936), pp. 31–9. Joseph Davies Bryan had been a student at Aberystwyth in the middle 1880s, which he believed was 'the golden age' of the College. 'I have cherished that fancy through forty-six years of exile in a foreign land', he said in 1932. *The University College of Wales, 1872–1932* (anniversary brochure), p. 7.

the College) as if the money for a large building programme would be forth-coming from another private source. For some time David Davies had been angling for a substantial contribution to College funds from Sir Howell Williams, the well-to-do London Welshman. Two of the other Welsh Colleges had similar ambitions: in April 1929 David Davies heard with relief that Sir Howell had been taken 'out of the way of any shots' that Cardiff might aim at his benevolence; and three months later, when Bangor apparently made a bid, David Davies fired off a warning telegram ('please keep off the grass; this is not your bird') to the Registrar of the North Wales College.³ Within a week or two, DD was all jubilant triumph: somehow or other he had got the impression that Sir Howell had made a 'princely donation' of £100,000 to the College, for which the President hastened to express his 'heartfelt appreciation'. Unfortunately, it was not to be. DD had jumped the gun: Sir Howell Williams had made no such promise; not unnaturally he was 'in a great state of trepidation', and it was highly probable that he would be frightened off by the over-large expectations that had been aroused. In fact, not long afterwards, Sir Howell Williams, patiently persuaded by his friend John Burrell, a member of the Council, did make a considerable contribution to the College, but the benefaction amounted to £10,000, not the very much larger sum that DD had persuaded himself had been promised.⁴

Although there was no immediate prospect of building on Penglais or else-where, the Davies Bryan benefaction did prompt the College to come to an important decision. Ever since Lord Rendel had bought a parcel of land on Pen-glais, some people, lay and academic, had hankered strongly after a purpose-built College on the new site. When land on the Buarth was acquired later, another possibility was added to the range of choice. Almost as soon as he accepted the Presidency, David Davies began to make an appraisal of the general position of the College; in March 1929 he submitted his reflections to the consideration of the Council. He was 'perturbed and alarmed' to discover that the College was encumbered with an enormous debt, of about £100,000 in all, which involved annual payments of £5,000 in bank interest and loan charges; so long as this situation remained, the College could do no more than continue to live from 'hand to mouth'. Further development was impossible and, inevitably, sooner or later, there would be a decline in status and a progressive inability to compete effectively for staff and students with sister institutions not similarly constrained. It was common doctrine that the existing accommodation of the College was hopelessly inadequate, but there was no agreed policy designed to bring about improvement. College opinion was divided into 'two camps': there was 'the

³ John Burrell to David Davies, 7 April 1929, David Davies to the Revd. Richard Jones, 3 April 1929, and to W. P. Wheldon, 6 July 1929. N.L.W. Llandinam MSS. (U.C.W. (1)), Gen. Corr.

⁴ David Davies to Sir Howell Williams, 15 July 1929, and to John Burrell, 18 July 1929. N.L.W. Llandinam MSS. (Wilson (1)).

tinkering school, whose vision was confined to Laura Place'; and there was 'the root and branch contingent', who favoured a new 'stately structure' built on Penglais. The President believed that a short visit to the converted agricultural building was all that was needed to eliminate the case for further tinkering. DD never forgot or easily forgave his defeats and his memorandum included some sharp criticism (which took no account of the pressing urgency of requirements in 1919) of J. H. Davies for spending substantial sums on the conversion of 'an old and disused structure'.

The President was convinced that there was little hope of extinguishing the debt by an appeal to the public unless the redemption proposal was linked with a scheme for new buildings. He therefore suggested that Aberystwyth should launch an appeal for £300,000, which he hoped would be collected over ten or fifteen years. Thereby, the debt could be wiped out and £200,000 (doubled possibly by a £ for £ contribution from the Treasury) would be available for new construction. DD proposed that the old College building should be left to the Science departments, a curious suggestion which perhaps reflected his own priorities for, with the exception of Chemistry, all the Science laboratories at Aberystwyth at this time were no better than makeshift (though sometimes cunningly contrived) adaptations. 'Let us say "Exodus" to the humanities', wrote the President, who proposed that new Arts and administration buildings as well as residential accommodation for men should be built on Penglais.

Naturally enough, David Davies looked to old students (of whom by now there were several thousands) for strong support, and he hoped that a well-organized appeal to Welsh-Americans would produce a handsome amount. When J. H. Davies became Principal in 1919 the Registrarship was allowed to lapse and the duties were shared by two Secretaries (General and Academic). David Davies thought that it was high time that the College had a Registrar, 'who corresponds to the Quartermaster-General of an Army', who would assume the general direction of the public appeal for funds which was to be pushed with great 'drive and energy'.[5]

There was, in fact, a considerable opposition (headed by the Principal) on the Council to the proposal to revive the Registrarship, chiefly on the grounds that it was administratively 'unnecessary' and, for financial reasons, 'impracticable'. David Davies was exasperated by this, as he thought, myopic obstruction ('some people think backward', as he tartly put it), but he was not easily deflected and, eventually, he persuaded the Council to endorse in principle the restoration of the Registrarship.[6] Almost immediately the President began to cast about for the right

---

[5] 'Memorandum on the present position of the College', March 1929. N.L.W. Llandinam MSS. (Gen. Corr.).

[6] *Council Minutes* (5 December 1928, 1 May 1929), pp. 342, 389. H. Stuart Jones to Thomas Jones, 27 February 1929. N.L.W. Thomas Jones MSS. Class J, vol. ix, f. 35. David Davies to Arthur Jones,

man for the job. In June 1929 he wrote an engagingly breezy letter to W. P. Wheldon, then Registrar at Bangor, setting out the whole scheme, including details of the Davies Bryan negotiation, then in train, for the Penglais land. There was 'a devil of a tug of war going on' with an exceptionally stubborn owner: 'the Cardis', said DD ruefully, 'are devils on the *arian* [money]'. David Davies had come to the conclusion that Wheldon was the man to organize the great campaign envisaged. And, apparently without consultation with others, the President offered the Registrarship (with a salary which he was prepared to supplement), the strong possibility of public recognition in the honours list (perhaps a K.C.B. or a Companionship of Honour) given success, and the firm promise of support ('I think I could make things pretty awkward this next time if there was any opposition') for the Principalship when Stuart Jones retired within a few years. 'Well, now, *cher garcon*', concluded the President, 'chew it over, and spit freely, and then come to talk it over.' Three months later Wheldon replied that Bangor had responded with a generous increase in his salary, and that he had decided to stay on there. David Davies was thoroughly put out and expressed his disappointment sharply.[7]

Six years elapsed before the office of Registrar was again restored (the University Grants Committee refused to make a special grant for the purpose), but at least David Davies' initiative in favour of a new buildings programme, together with the Davies Bryan benefaction, which included a prodding addendum, forced the College to a momentous decision. A subcommittee in October 1929 rejected the notion that future development should be concentrated on the area between Laura Place and Pier Street (it was calculated that the freeholds alone would cost £30–40,000), and recommended that all future new building should be on the Penglais site. It was agreed that nothing could be done until enough money had been collected to build a block that would accommodate completely one section of the College, but, meantime, it was proposed to prepare a preliminary scheme for the layout of buildings on the new site. These recommendations were accepted the next day by the Council.[8] In November Tom Jones, who always placed aesthetic considerations very high on his list of priorities, persuaded the subcommittee to invite Sidney Greenslade, the architect of the superb National Library building, to prepare a general scheme for the new site. Greenslade accepted with enthusiasm but, unfortunately, soon afterwards he suffered a nervous breakdown and was unable to complete the commission, an irreparable loss of a fine artist who was ideally equipped to do full justice to a truly magnificent site.[9]

10 March 1929, and to W. P. Wheldon, 16 June 1929 (copy). N.L.W. Llandinam MSS. (U.C.W. (1)), Gen. Corr.

[7] David Davies to W. P. Wheldon, 16 June and 23 October 1929 (copies), W. P. Wheldon to David Davies, 26 September 1929. N.L.W. Ibid.

[8] 'Minutes of the committee to investigate College buildings', 22 October 1929. N.L.W. Ibid. *Council Minutes* (23 October 1929), pp. 463–4. *Court Minutes* (23 October 1929), p. 433.

[9] 'Minutes of the committee to investigate College buildings', 14 November 1929. Letters from

Even David Davies' determination to press on with the campaign for new College buildings could not succeed in the face of the world economic depression which steadily deepened in the years after 1929. The launching of the public appeal for support had to be postponed again and again; in 1932 Stuart Jones wrote despairingly that it was idle to talk of 'a Five Years Plan' of development, in current circumstances 'a Fifty Years Plan' would be nearer the mark.[10] However, in April 1933 the Old Students' Association responded to the promptings of the President of the College by appointing a committee to inaugurate an appeal for funds to all old students.[11] But here, too, at first, there were disappointments: many former students, particularly the more senior ones, were bitterly hostile to the Penglais scheme, and regarded any proposal to remove the College from its old location (which enshrined their fondest memories) 'as something akin to sacrilege'.[12] However, despite this unpromising beginning the Old Students' Appeal Committee persevered and, slowly, the total began to mount; within a year a sum of the order of £2,500, mainly in the form of subscriptions covenanted over a period of years, had been promised.[13] Additionally, there was Sir Howell Williams's gift of £10,000, and when the College Hall was destroyed by fire in the summer of 1933 the insurance money, amounting to some £8,000, was added to the New Buildings Fund of the College which, at the end of 1934, totalled just over £21,000.[14] There was, for the moment at least, obviously no hope of making a start on Penglais, and the ardent desire of David Davies and others to make Aberystwyth 'a residential College after the fashion of Oxford and Cambridge, in order to produce the right type of man', remained a dream.[15]

It is evident, too, that, even in its ordinary run-of-the-mill operations, the College, despite the hopes inspired by the Haldane Commission *Report*, was still inadequately financed. Professorial stipends in the University of Wales were distinctly lower than elsewhere, and the salaries of the junior staff at Aberystwyth were conceded to be deplorably low, certainly worse than at the other constituent Colleges. When in 1924 the U.G.C., which so often seemed content piously to

S. K. Greenslade, Thomas Jones, Lloyd Parry, and Stuart Jones, 22 November 1929–16 February 1930. N.L.W. Thomas Jones MSS. Class J, vol. ix, ff. 45, 48, 53, 55, 56, 60.

[10] H. Stuart Jones to David Davies, 26 February 1932. N.L.W. Llandinam MSS. (U.C.W. (1)), Gen. Corr.

[11] David Davies to J. Davies. Bryan 27 July 1932. N.L.W. Ibid. O.S.A. Minute Book (1930–43), 17 April 1933. *Cambrian News* (22 April 1933).

[12] E. B. Hicks to H. Stuart Jones, 7 June 1933. C.A. R/P. O.S.A. New Buildings Committee Minutes (1 December 1934). A. Pinsent, 'Notes on the O.S.A.', p. 5.

[13] O.S.A. Minute Book (1930–43), 2 April 1934.

[14] *Report on the work and needs of the College* (U.C.W., March 1944), pp. 32–3.

[15] David Davies to W. P. Wheldon, 16 June 1929. N.L.W. Llandinam MSS. (U.C.W.(1)), Gen. Corr. 'I don't say that a residential College will turn out men of character like sausages out of a machine', said David Davies, 'but I think it may tend to enhance . . . the development of our Welsh student.'

point the way without being willing or able to provide the means, urged the University to improve the position of its lecturers and to establish incremental salaries, the College Council at Aberystwyth reluctantly decided that its financial position was such that 'it could not honestly face such commitments'. Instead, a system of bonus payments, which varied with the state of College funds, was introduced confessedly as little more than an earnest of good intention. Eventually, in 1931 even the Treasury conceded that the position was intolerable and a special earmarked grant enabled the College to improve the salaries of non-professorial staff and to introduce a modest incremental scale. Even so, in this matter the University of Wales still lagged some way behind its more fortunate sister institutions.[16]

It cannot be said that the general policy of the U.G.C. was especially helpful. As late as 1947 it expressed conscious pride in its traditional attachment to the principle of helping those who helped themselves.[17] No doubt this useful extension of the philosophy of Samuel Smiles was not devoid of merit as a spur to local endeavour, but the Committee all too rarely seems to have made any serious evaluation of the relative capacity of universities to help themselves. In practice U.G.C. policy meant little more than the application of the principle, to them that hath (no matter how) shall be given; a comfortable doctrine for the comfortably placed, enabling a Treasury still dominated by the shade of Gladstone to turn a deaf ear to the cries for help of the less well-placed universities. There is evidence, too, that the officials of the U.G.C., at any rate in its early days, in the exercise of their discretion in the allocation of money took it for granted that there was an immutable pecking order among universities. When J. Herbert Lewis became M.P. for the University of Wales he drew attention to the large disparity between university grants to Scotland and Wales. Sir William McCormick, Chairman of the U.G.C., when pressed for an explanation, testily replied, as Herbert Lewis said, with 'the extraordinary argument that the Scottish universities were five centuries old, whereas the Welsh Colleges were only about thirty years old, as if that made the least difference'. And, at the same time, another official (by inference W. B. Riddell, a later Chairman of the U.G.C.) privately stated that, in his opinion, there was 'no comparison between the Welsh and Scottish universities'. The latter were 'celebrated throughout the world'. Admittedly, 'Antiquity and dignity would not perhaps go much for themselves: but to maintain a great reputation, great expenditure is necessary, and the Committee must clearly bear this in mind in allocating the grants.' Riddell calculated that the 'existing commitments' of Scottish universities were 'in the ratio of 425 to 105' to

---

[16] Council meetings with the U.G.C. *Council Minutes* (16 May 1929, 17 May 1934), pp. 399–400, 514–17. 'Allocation of increased Treasury Grant', *Council Minutes* (13 March 1931), Appendix I, pp. 1–9.

[17] *U.G.C. Report, 1935–47*, p. 79.

those of the University of Wales. So much, it would seem, for the legitimate aspirations of late developers in higher education who wanted to catch up.[18]

One consequence of Aberystwyth's continuing relative financial weakness was the loss of some members of the Senate to other universities, although in one important instance money was not the most significant factor. In 1930 H. J. Fleure, who had been a member of staff since 1908, accepted an invitation to a new chair of Geography at Manchester. The decision to go caused Fleure, as he said, 'some distress of mind'; the direct financial inducement was 'small', though he hoped that a bigger departmental library grant would significantly cut his enormous private book bills. Fleure was one of the great pioneers of Geography as a university discipline; for years he had worked through the Geographical Association to get the subject established in all universities. Gradually these efforts had succeeded, but there had been a decided reluctance to establish chairs in the new discipline: the professorship at Liverpool was 'an unique thing so far as the civic universities' were concerned, and was often explained away as an exceptional 'personal tribute' to its distinguished occupant, P. M. Roxby. Fleure believed passionately that Geography would not be properly accredited until all universities, as a matter of course, established professorships in the subject; and so, when Manchester offered to create a chair if Fleure would occupy it, he felt that his missionary duty left him no choice but to accept.[19]

Despite his departure, Fleure's interest in Aberystwyth remained as strong as ever: 'we who have a permanent "concern" (as the Quakers say) for Aber. ought to keep in touch', he wrote to Tom Jones in 1936. Fleure was nominated to the College Court and Council and, almost to the end of his exceptionally long life, he was an active member of the O.S.A.[20] Fleure was a truly distinguished scholar (in due course, an inevitable F.R.S.); his interests ranged widely, and every Thursday evening he lectured to a vast audience, which included students of all years, many teachers from other departments and members of the general public, on 'The Lands of Ancient Civilization'. Humour was not Fleure's strong point, and his sole visual aid was a battered map: nevertheless, his quality was such that he easily held his popular following. In the course of a dozen years Fleure had 'built up at Aberystwyth probably the best school of Geography in the kingdom'.[21] Fleure had hoped that he would be replaced by R. U. Sayce, one of his former

---

[18] J. Herbert Lewis to H. A. L. Fisher, 4 March 1920.'Welsh University Grants', 1920. P.R.O. Ed. 24/2027. Lewis' charge that there were too many Scots and no Welshmen on the Committee was blandly countered with the answer that members were 'expressly elected to represent subjects, not countries or institutions'.

[19] H. J. Fleure to Lleufer Thomas, 11 December 1929. N.L.W. Lleufer Thomas MSS. IA. H. J. Fleure to J. Glyn Davies, 7 March 1930. N.L.W. J. Glyn Davies MSS. 10505.

[20] H. J. Fleure to Thomas Jones, 3 May 1936. N.L.W. Thomas Jones MSS. Class J, vol. ix, f. 117.

[21] E. G. Bowen, 'Notes on post-war student life', p. 2. Thomas Jones to Colin Smith, 13 June 1930. N.L.W. Thomas Jones MSS. Class J, vol. ix, f. 117.

students, but the chair went to C. Daryll Forde, a prolific scholar and multi-linguist who, as Fleure agreed, was excellently equipped to continue the particular lines of anthropological inquiry in which Aberystwyth had specialized.[22]

In 1930 there was also a new professor of History. Edward Edwards had joined the College staff in 1892, and had occupied the chair since 1895. Genial and popular to the last with students, 'Teddy Eddy' was a character with a particular brand of dry Welsh wit. He did a good deal to cement town–gown relations and was a member of the Aberystwyth Town Council for many years. His contribution to the College was social rather than academic, and on his retirement from the chair he continued as Vice-Principal for another two years.[23] From a very strong field of applicants for the chair three were short-listed. Sydney Herbert had gradually transferred his allegiance from International Politics to History; he had an unorthodox academic background but had first-rate published work to his credit. Moreover, by general consent he was a superb teacher; C. K. Webster, whose admiration for him was unbounded, thought that Sydney Herbert had 'done more than any other man to raise the teaching of under-graduates' at Aberystwyth in recent years.[24] Also under consideration was Norman Sykes, the historian of the eighteenth-century Church, later Regius professor at Cambridge. The chair, however, went to R. F. Treharne, a product of the Manchester school of Medieval History, a young man of twenty-eight whose exceptional promise was almost immediately fulfilled with the publication of an outstanding scholarly book, built to last, on the thirteenth-century constitution.[25] It is fair to say that, from this time onwards, the general work of the department of History assumed a new quality.

There were several other changes in the Senate at this time. In 1930 Wilfred Robinson, who had succeeded to the chair of Botany in 1926, died suddenly. The selection committee (which included Sir John Russell, F.R.S., a distinguished old student) strongly recommended the appointment of Dr. Lily Newton. During the next few years, under the guidance of the new professor, the department established a considerable reputation in Wales and beyond; the number of students increased strikingly, partly the consequence of a growing interest in the schools in Biology, and a vigorous research programme, closely related to local problems, was undertaken.[26] In 1931 Aberystwyth lost another outstanding head of department to Manchester. W. J. Pugh, professor of Geology, had earned golden

[22] *Council Minutes* (22 May 1930), pp. 533–4. H. J. Fleure to Lleufer Thomas, 11 June 1930. N.L.W. Lleufer Thomas MSS. IA.

[23] 'We have always regarded him as one of us, the greatest compliment a university student can ever pay his teacher.' *The Dragon*, lii. 6. See also the *Cambrian News* (1 September 1933).

[24] C. K. Webster to David Davies, 30 June 1930. N.L.W. Llandinam MSS. (Wilson (2)).

[25] *Council Minutes* (29 May 1930), p. 562. Ifor L. Evans, 'Departmental Surveys' (1936), pp. 35–8. R. F. Treharne, *The Baronial Plan of Reform, 1258–63* (Manchester, 1932).

[26] *Council Minutes* (29 May 1930), pp. 562–3. Ifor L. Evans, 'Departmental Surveys', pp. 80–4. P. W. Carter, op. cit., passim.

opinions and had admirably filled the large gap left by the departure of O. T. Jones. Indeed, Fleure thought that, 'of the people on the spot', W. J. Pugh was 'the only man . . . fit to succeed Stuart Jones as Principal'. The new professor of Geology was H. P. Lewis, a Cambridge man, then a lecturer at Sheffield, who remained at Aberystwyth until 1947.[27]

In 1931, too, after several delays that occasioned sharp public criticism, at long last Aberystwyth was able to establish a chair of Welsh History. It had been agreed in October 1927 that the chair would bear the name of Sir John Williams, whose benefaction to the College made the new professorship possible. However, some time would elapse before the full income from the benefaction became available; in the interim the money accruing was to be used partly for postgraduate scholarships and partly for additional appointments in departments (those relating to Welsh Studies) which came within the terms of the bequest. In the following year a readership in Welsh History was advertised, but none of the applicants sufficiently impressed the committee and the appointment was postponed.[28] Ultimately, in 1930 it was agreed to appoint a Sir John Williams professor of Welsh History. Stuart Jones began to take soundings: he discovered that William Rees 'was sitting tight at Cardiff and waiting for their chair' in Welsh History to be established. Strenuous efforts, apparently not far short of entreaty, had failed to persuade J. G. Edwards of Jesus College, Oxford, to allow his name to be considered. It was hoped that R. T. Jenkins, the old Aberystwyth student, then a schoolmaster, a man of letters with a notably fine style who had recently published a good book on eighteenth-century Wales, would be interested, but Stuart Jones was disconcerted to find that Jenkins had already applied for an independent lectureship at Bangor. There was some doubt whether the Aberystwyth committee would 'go the whole hog' for R. T. Jenkins because it could be objected that he was only incidentally a historian.[29] This soon became idle speculation: R. T. Jenkins thoroughly disliked the town of Aberystwyth, not least for its abominable treatment of Hermann Ethé in 1914; moreover, he had developed a settled aversion for his old College. 'Beware the Greeks bearing gifts', was his instinctive reaction (and that of others too, so he claimed) to any gambit by the Aberystwyth College authorities. At any rate, in the summer of 1930 Jenkins accepted the appointment at Bangor.[30]

[27] The Dragon, liii. 4, for student concern at the departure of W. J. Pugh. H. J. Fleure to Lleufer Thomas, 8 April 1930. N.L.W. Lleufer Thomas MSS. IA. Council Minutes (29 April 1931), pp. 730–1.

[28] Council Minutes (19 October 1927, 25 July 1928), pp. 164–5, 276–7.

[29] H. Stuart Jones to Thomas Jones, 22 May 1930. N.L.W. Thomas Jones MSS. Class J, vol. ix, f. 63.

[30] R. T. Jenkins, op. cit., pp. 115, 265–72. The Welsh Outlook (xvii), 205, heartily congratulated Bangor for thus declaring that 'historical research need not be confined to documents written in dog-Latin or Norman-French and that a fine style, a truly catholic interest and a gift of humour need not be a disqualification in a university teacher'.

All these difficulties were occasioned by the fact that another very strong candidate, the obvious man in so many ways, already occupied another chair at Aberystwyth and, despite much persuasion, was not disposed to exchange professorships. Ever since 1912, E. A. Lewis ('Doc Lewis', as he was called with great affection by generations of students) had been professor of Economics and Political Science at the College, and during that time he had also been responsible for the teaching of Palaeography and Diplomatics. It had always been hoped that, sooner or later, the College (which fully accepted its special responsibility to conserve and promote the national heritage) would find it possible to enable E. A. Lewis to concentrate his attention fully on Welsh History, which had been his first and strongest scholarly interest. Now, when a marvellous opportunity occurred, there were difficulties, chiefly relating to the terms of the appointment to the newly endowed chair, which had been offered to E. A. Lewis before overtures were made to others. The general conditions of appointment were not wisely drawn up, and Stuart Jones objected to higher stipends for endowed professorships because 'they created jealousy'. Ultimately, after some hard bargaining, and a strong intervention by the President, new conditions were agreed and in 1931 E. A. Lewis became the first Sir John Williams professor of Welsh History.[31]

In March 1931 a selection committee that included J. M. Keynes recommended T. S. Ashton and R. B. Forrester, readers at Manchester and London Universities respectively, to the consideration of the Council, and the latter was elected to the chair of Economics which he occupied for twenty years.[32] A year later J. F. Mountford, professor of Latin since 1927, resigned to go to Liverpool where he continued a career of very considerable distinction. He was replaced by E. J. Wood, who collaborated in the preparation of the Oxford Latin dictionary during his years at Aberystwyth. Teachers in the departments of Latin and Greek were still badly handicapped by the ill preparation that most of their first-year students had received at Welsh secondary schools, which had no long-established tradition of classical teaching. As a consequence, the junior members of staff had to endure hours of drudgery teaching a 'Preliminary' class, a desperate attempt to overcome the shortcomings of weak new students as quickly as possible. In recent years, too, attempts had been made to introduce a stronger cultural element into the curriculum in Classics—not, however, altogether successfully.[33]

Most departments in the College at this time were badly understaffed, and perhaps none more so than Philosophy, where the honours course extended over four years. During the 1930s there was some fall in the numbers of students

---

[31] H. Stuart Jones to Thomas Jones, 22 May 1930. N.L.W. Thomas Jones MSS. Class J, vol. ix, f. 63. R. T. Jenkins, op. cit., pp. 270–1. *Council Minutes* (2 May, 23 July, and 15 October 1930), pp. 565, 585, 615.

[32] Ibid. (13 March 1931), p. 685.

[33] Ifor L. Evans, 'Departmental Surveys' (1936), pp. 10–15.

reading Philosophy (a high proportion of whom intended later to enter the ministry or the priesthood), but the indispensable essay work laid an exceptionally heavy burden on a small staff of three. In 1932 there was a new professor of Philosophy. When Jenkyn Jones retired, R. I. Aaron, a young man with distinguished work on John Locke to his credit, was elected to the chair.[34]

In recent years the departments of Mathematics had had their vicissitudes. W. H. Young, professor of Pure Mathematics, was without question a brilliant scholar and teacher who communicated a rare intellectual excitement to his students; soon after his arrival he initiated a most ambitious honours course in Pure Mathematics and collected around him an exceptionally able band of students. Outside the classroom Young was equally impressive, indeed formidable, and he quickly made his mark in the Senate. But there were difficulties: indeed, during his tenure the department, according to one account, went through 'the stormiest period' in its history. Young pressed for the appointment of exotic foreigners and repeatedly demanded leave of absence to go abroad. Finally, relations became impossibly strained and in 1923 he resigned.[35] This was a time of acute financial difficulty and Young was not replaced; Pure and Applied Mathematics were placed under the general direction of G. A. Schott. However, in 1926 V. C. Morton was appointed independent lecturer and head of the department of Pure Mathematics, and was promoted to a chair in 1933 when Schott retired. At the same time, Thomas Lewis became independent lecturer in charge of Applied Mathematics. The twin departments worked closely together and, after 1925, offered, in addition to their separate honours courses, a combined scheme which provided a good all-round qualification for students with no aptitude or taste for research. V. C. Morton was an ideal head of department leading a well-balanced team that included, for a time, O. G. Sutton, who was to return later on as Vice-President of the College after a most distinguished career in government service. Thomas Lewis, an old student of the College, was a persistent researcher who pondered long and deeply over his problems, and his published papers 'showed great independence of outlook and fertility of invention'.[36]

But during these years perhaps the chief concern of the College was the struggle to ensure the survival of its particular pride and joy, the Plant Breeding Station. In 1919 R. G. Stapledon had set to work with characteristic energy and drive; in no time his research institute was 'a going concern' manned by a first-rate staff, obviously utterly devoted to their chief.[37] After its early hesitations the

---

[34] Ifor L. Evans, 'Departmental Surveys' (1936), pp. 31–4. *Council Minutes* (11 March 1932), pp. 1–2.

[35] H. J. Fleure to Thomas Jones, 5 October 1919. N.L.W. Thomas Jones MSS. Class X, vol. v, f. 41. D. S. Meyler, 'Notes on the Department of Mathematics'. *Biographical Notes of Fellows of the Royal Society*, iv. 311–22. Ifor L. Evans, 'Departmental Surveys' (1936), p. 62.

[36] D. S. Meyler, loc. cit. Ifor L. Evans, 'Departmental Surveys' (1936), p. 62. E. A. Milne, 'Thomas Lewis', *Nature*, clxvi. 296.

[37] R. G. Stapledon to J. H. Davies (1921). N.L.W. J. H. Davies MSS. (Corr.).

Ministry of Agriculture quickly accorded recognition to the Station, and it is fair to say that this government department was not, by the standard of the times, ungenerous in the capital and other grants that it made annually to support the institute.[38] On the other hand, of course, the Station's practical successes were so striking that its claims to support could not be gainsaid, no matter how rigorous a test of payment by results was applied. In 1927 when eight Bureaux were set up in various parts of the Empire to collate information and to promote investigations into agricultural problems, Aberystwyth was selected as the centre for the Imperial Bureau of Plant Genetics (Herbage Plants). And the significant contributions that the Aberystwyth institute made to the solution of the problems of pastoralists in many different parts of the world encouraged the Empire Marketing Board in 1928 to make grants to enable Stapledon and his colleagues to extend their work in certain directions.[39]

But the Station still depended heavily on the support of Laurence Philipps' annual contribution of £1,000, and the last of these ten subventions was due in 1929. Stuart Jones felt that Sir Laurence (as he had now become) had been so generous that he could scarcely be asked for further help. Urgent appeals were made to a number of people to contribute £100 a year for several (ideally ten) years towards the upkeep of the Station. Lords Lisburne and Melchett responded, as did David Davies, predictably, and some few others. But when the appeal failed to reach its full quota of ten guarantors, some of those who had responded 'backed out'. Moreover, the financial panic of 1929 and the ensuing economic depression made money altogether tighter and the prospects of a successful appeal to private generosity less and less promising.[40] Sir Laurence Philipps' annual contribution was not replaced in full from other sources; moreover, in 1932 Neville Chamberlain, who had not inherited his father's imaginative gifts, proposed, as one item in a long catalogue of Treasury retrenchments, to wind up the Empire Marketing Board and prune drastically the research grants it had formerly dispensed. Stapledon fought hard to retain these vital financial supports to his work, but did not succeed entirely. The dominions and colonies, whose pastoral economies had been so strikingly assisted by the Plant Breeding Station, offered no help, and were considered to have 'behaved very shabbily'. In 1934,

[38] 'Reports of the Agricultural Developments Committee', *Council Minutes* (1919–29), passim.

[39] R. G. Stapledon, *The Welsh Plant Breeding Station*, p. 1. H. Stuart Jones to David Davies, 2 August 1928. N.L.W. Llandinam MSS. (U.C.W. (1)), Gen. Corr. L. S. Amery, *My Political Life* (1953), ii. 349, for generous praise of the 'notable work' of the Welsh Plant Breeding Station, particularly its massive contribution to successful research on 'grass, . . . by far the most important of all Empire crops', by a dynamic Colonial Secretary well placed to know the quality and range of the work carried out.

[40] H. Stuart Jones to David Davies and to W. J. Burdon Evans, 2 August 1928, 25 April 1929, David Davies to Owen D. Jones, 20 July 1934. N.L.W. Llandinam MSS. (U.C.W. (1)), Gen. Corr. In 1927 David Davies wrote dispiritedly that there was as much hope of getting a subscription out of one well-known North Walian skinflint of distinguished ancestry as of getting blood from a stone.

for reasons outside its control, the great research institute, as the President of the College gloomily conceded, was in an 'unfortunate position'.[41]

The situation would have been very much worse, perhaps to the point of disaster, had unexpected assistance not been forthcoming from another private source two years before. In July 1932, acting on a strong hint from the Ministry of Agriculture, Stuart Jones and Stapledon wrote to *The Times* appealing for £20,000 for the Plant Breeding Station. The appeal was directed to private generosity, as it was conceded that 1932 was 'not a time when a research station can look towards government departments for increased assistance'. The letter, under the headline 'Good Grassland', persuasively set out Stapledon's life-long philosophy: 'livestock production is the pivot on which the agricultural progress of these islands must in the last resort turn'; grasslands were the nation's great 'undeveloped asset', and Aberystwyth's success in producing improved strains of grasses and clovers had already amply proved the relevance of its work to the problems of New Zealand, Australia, Natal, and elsewhere in the Empire, as well as of Britain. At 'so critical' a time for the agricultural progress of the Empire, it was vitally important that the work of the Station should be continued and extended.[42]

Within days the Principal received an offer from Sir Julien Cahn, whose interest in agriculture equalled his passion for cricket, of a contribution of £3,000 per annum for seven years to the Plant Breeding Station: 'The object for which you are appealing', Sir Julien wrote, 'is of an importance which it is scarcely possible to exaggerate.'[43] With this assistance, and smaller sums donated by other friends supplementing the reduced government grants, the work of Stapledon and his assistants was able to continue. The scale of the operation was astonishing: during 1929–33 no less than 848 acres on 231 different farms in Wales were used in experiments conducted by the Station; in 1933 alone, records had to be kept of almost half a million seeds and seedlings. Luckily, this magnificent enterprise required no elaborately expensive scientific equipment, the laboratories were of the simplest kind; most of the work at this time was done by a band of eleven 'essentially out-of-doors biologists' working under Stapledon's direction. Sir Julien Cahn's benefaction made possible a large-scale experiment (the Cahn Hill Improvement Scheme) designed to improve hill land at considerable elevations and thereby make it possible to winter large flocks of sheep on these upland areas. In all this Stapledon was supported by A. W. Ashby and the department of Agricultural Economics, and by T. W. Fagan, professor of Agricultural Chemistry after 1930. The Director also received the willing co-operation of a host of farmers and

[41] L. S. Amery, op. cit., iii. 88. Owen D. Jones to David Davies, David Davies to Owen D. Jones, 17 and 20 July 1934. N.L.W. Llandinam MSS. (U.C.W. (1)), Gen. Corr.

[42] H. Stuart Jones to David Davies, 15 July 1932. N.L.W. Ibid. *The Times* (11 July 1932).

[43] Sir Julien Cahn to H. Stuart Jones, 12 July 1932. *Council Minutes* (22 July 1932), pp. 75–6.

others who well understood the crucial importance of his purposes.[44] The Welsh Plant Breeding Station, headed by a man of genius, continued during the 1930s, at relatively paltry cost, to add to the worldwide reputation it had earned for Aberystwyth. After the end of the 1939–45 war a former Minister of Agriculture said that he was convinced that, without Stapledon's victories, 'we most certainly would have been starved of food and there would have been no military victories about which our generals now may argue'.[45]

It had also been hoped, certainly by the chief donor of the chair, that Aberystwyth, through the work of its Wilson professor of International Politics, would be able to make a contribution to the well-being of the world perhaps equal to that of the Plant Breeding Station. The events of the inter-war years showed that these hopes were extravagant: war was a less tractable problem than unproductive land. C. K. Webster had not expected that his work as Wilson professor would evangelize world opinion in favour of peace; he was a superb historian, a specialist in international relations in the post-Napoleonic period, not a publicist with any particular axe to grind on contemporary issues. Nevertheless, Webster's great books on the Congress of Vienna, the European Alliance after 1815, and the foreign policy of Castlereagh, all written while he was at Aberystwyth, were not without their relevance to the problems facing the international organizations of the inter-war years. Additionally, Webster had written several important articles on cognate subjects. Fittingly, in 1930, he had been elected a Fellow of the British Academy. Now, in 1932, he resigned his chair to go to London. David Davies paid Webster a deserved tribute:

You have added prestige to the chair; in fact, you have founded it in the sense of creating a tradition and demonstrating its usefulness in the study of Inter[national] relationships. You have set an example to holders of similar chairs in this and other countries. . . . You have laid the foundations and mapped out the territory; it is for them to build and to explore.

This letter was written in reply to one from Webster congratulating the President on the peerage that had recently been conferred upon him. Lord Davies, as he had now become, was not altogether happy with his new dignity: 'as you know, this sort of thing . . . isn't much in my line', he wrote to Webster. Still, he was glad to return to politics, though the House of Lords would be 'less congenial' to him than the Commons where the customary cut and thrust gave better scope for his combative instincts. In the Lords he thought that he would set up as 'recruiting sergeant for the International Police Force', which, in his

[44] R. G. Stapledon, *The Welsh Plant Breeding Station*, pp. 2–10, 155–8.
[45] Sir Reginald Dorman Smith quoted in Waller, op. cit., p. 239, who makes much the same point (p. 3) in the comment: 'The names Aber.–Stapledon should join in the public mind in the same way as El Alamein–Montgomery.'

opinion, it was essential to establish in order to make the authority of the League of Nations effective. Aside from that, as he said: 'If I can succeed in cracking a few reactionary pates, I shall feel I have not lived in vain.'[46]

The President thought that Webster's resignation from the Wilson chair afforded the opportunity for stock-taking. Perhaps the time had come when an attempt should be made to build up Aberystwyth as a centre of postgraduate studies to which continental students would be attracted by 'a network of Wilson scholarships'. He also believed that, henceforth, it would be better 'to concentrate on Europe rather than America'. With a prescient eye for future long-range possibilities in the world, he added: 'I should like to see Aber. becoming the centre of study and research for a united Europe, the federation of Europe, as opposed to the conceptions of Imperialism or an Anglo-Saxon alliance.'[47]

Yet curiously enough, in the light of all this, the man appointed to the Wilson chair soon afterwards was not particularly well qualified to build up and direct a school of postgraduate academic research, and his experience, admittedly considerable, of public affairs was trans-Atlantic rather than European. This was the American, Jerome Greene, formerly Secretary of the Rockefeller Foundation. Greene's name had been suggested by Lionel Curtis and the proposal was endorsed by C. K. Webster, Sir Arthur Salter, and, with some reservation because Greene had no teaching experience, Gilbert Murray.[48] At first, Greene was taken aback: 'if I were offered the position of First Violin in the Boston Symphony Orchestra it could hardly have puzzled me more', was his initial response. However, the more he thought about it the more attracted he became and, eventually, he accepted the appointment with enthusiasm.[49] After the offer had been made to Greene, Lord Davies discovered that the prospective Wilson professor had already written a pamphlet 'condemning the use of economic sanctions' by the League of Nations. The President was decidedly ruffled.

I am as anxious as you are [he wrote to Webster] that the chair shall not be regarded as a propagandist institution. At the same time, one has to face realities, and it is quite

[46] Lord Davies to C. K. Webster, 30 June 1932. C.A. C. K. Webster File. 'Please drop the damned lord business and call me "D" or "DD", . . . Damn the Baron business, a little less of the Lord please!', he wrote soon afterwards to his friend John Burrell, who was evidently a stickler for protocol. 9 July 1932. N.L.W. Llandinam MSS. (U.C.W. (1)), Gen. Corr.

[47] Lord Davies to C. K. Webster, 30 June 1932. C.A. C. K. Webster File. 'Being human', as he said, the President hoped that the new Wilson professor would be 'sympathetic . . . towards the League', though that did not 'mean that he is to be a propagandist.'

[48] Thomas Jones, *A Diary with Letters, 1931–1950* (Oxford, 1954), p. 64. C. K. Webster to J. Greene, Sir Arthur Salter and Gilbert Murray to C. K. Webster, 23 July and 1 August 1932. C.A. C. K. Webster File.

[49] J. Greene to C. K. Webster, 23 July 1932. C.A. Ibid. In a later letter (2 August) to Webster, Greene said: 'The historians' craft is badly in need of unionizing if its members like you . . . take so lightly the protection of your union against the intrusion of people like me.'

clear that the holder of the chair can throw in his influence and weight either for or against the principles which some of us are contending for.

This was a far distant flash of lightning, a flicker of warning of a great storm that was to break over a later appointment to the Wilson professorship. In this instance, Lord Davies did not oppose Greene's appointment.[50] The American professor had great charm and was engagingly honest. He stayed at Aberystwyth for two years, and then returned home quite genuinely for family reasons. But he also felt that such advantages as he had to offer, 'an American point of view and a background of practical experience in international affairs', had been fully exploited and well nigh exhausted by 1934. Moreover, as he frankly admitted, he was 'painfully conscious' of his 'lack of scholarly equipment and felt something like an impostor masquerading as a professor'.[51] It was agreed that there was 'no urgency' about filling the chair: the return on the stocks upon which the Wilson endowment was substantially based had declined sharply during the depression and there was the need to husband resources. And there was no obvious British candidate in sight. Hitler had come to power and was already malevolently at work: 'What about a displaced German Jew? Perhaps you know of some Einstein in the world of International Politics who has been turned out of his position', was one imaginative possibility that was suggested to Lord Davies. Nothing came of this and the Wilson chair remained vacant for two years.[52]

By the time Jerome Greene's successor was appointed, Aberystwyth had a new and very different Principal. Stuart Jones had been ailing for some time; he had been forced to take several long periods of sick-leave and, finally, in March 1934 he resigned. Soon after Stuart Jones had been elected in 1927, T. Gwynn Jones, who did not pull his punches and in any case had favoured the appointment of another candidate, met the new Principal for the first time. Gwynn Jones was not impressed, 'He may be learned. I don't think he has . . . personality. Most likely he will not leave a greater impression after his departure than does a stick when it is drawn through water.'[53] This unflattering forecast was not entirely wide of the mark; in public all too often Stuart Jones was diffident and the full range of his great gifts only occasionally became apparent. And recurrent illness and prolonged absences from Aberystwyth did not help him in a difficult and demanding job in which, no doubt, one blessed with the virtues of the Archangel Gabriel would be thought by some people to be remiss. As a matter of fact, for all his retiring

[50] Lord Davies to C. K. Webster, 14 September 1932. C.A. Ibid.

[51] J. Greene to Lord Davies, 17 February 1934. N.L.W. Llandinam MSS. (Wilson (1)). J. Greene to Thomas Jones, 17 May 1934. C.A. R/Des/IP/1.

[52] Lord Davies to Ifor L. Evans, 19 April 1934, and Acting Principal Gwilym Owen to Lord Davies, 7 May 1934. N.L.W. Llandinam MSS. (Wilson (2)).

[53] T. Gwynn Jones to E. M. Humphreys, 1927 (copy). N.L.W. T. Gwynn Jones MSS. Gilbert Murray expressed, somewhat more circumspectly, a similar opinion. Gilbert Murray to David Davies, 14 March 1927. N.L.W. Llandinam MSS. (U.C.W. (2)), Gen. Corr.

disposition, Stuart Jones did register with his students, Welsh and English, as a man of warm feeling, genuinely interested in their activities and deeply concerned for their welfare.[54] Certainly everybody connected with Aberystwyth felt immense pride in the fact that the College was headed by a scholar of world stature.[55] Stuart Jones' Principalship coincided with increasingly difficult times: he held the line well when it would have been so easy to lose heart.

One dispiriting event that occurred not long before Stuart Jones retired was the burning down of the College Hall in August 1933. The origin of this holocaust (the huge building was burned to the ground in half an hour) was never discovered, although it was plausibly suggested that exceptionally powerful sun-rays (a temperature of over 100° was recorded in the town that Sunday) playing on the windows and the tarpaulin-covered wooden roof could well have set the structure ablaze.[56] The total destruction of the College Hall was a disaster for the College and the town. It had been invaluable for meetings, conferences, and concerts attended by audiences of two thousand people and more: Walford Davies had filled it to capacity, as had Baldwin, Lloyd George, and others. Perhaps the construction of another large hall of the same type, cheap but evidently too easily combustible, was an experiment, like the ill-fated airships of that time, too hazardous to be repeated. Lord Davies pressed hard for a new College Hall to be built on Penglais with the £21,000 then available. But the College authorities were marooned between the old site and the hitherto undeveloped new, and most members of the Council opposed placing a central assembly hall in such distant isolation. Moreover, the Town Council pleaded for rebuilding, with an 'incombustible material', on the Queen's Road site, and half-promised to take over the structure if and when the College ever did move to Penglais.[57] This came to nothing. It is difficult to avoid the conclusion that a serious mistake was made here. No doubt the College Hall insurance money and the Sir Howell Williams' benefaction primed the pump for other building later on Penglais. But the price of this decision was that for almost forty years the College lacked a hall large enough to provide an appropriate setting for important academic, social, and cultural occasions.

Despite defeat on the College Hall issue and a discouragingly small flow of money into the Appeal Fund, Lord Davies remained hopeful that a new College, 'remoulding the social life of the institution on the lines of Cambridge and Oxford', would be built on Penglais. He believed, as did others, that it was important that Stuart Jones' successor should be of the same mind. In December

---

[54] *The Dragon*, liv. 38, '*Golygyddol*' [Editorial], ibid., lvi. 4.

[55] The magnificent quality of his scholarship (recognized in 1933 by the conferment of a knighthood) is set out in *The Times* (30 June 1939).

[56] There is a full account in the *Cambrian News* (18 August 1933).

[57] W. J. Burdon Evans to Lord Davies, 3 April 1934. N.L.W. Llandinam MSS. (U.C.W. (1)), Gen. Corr. *Council Minutes* (6 December 1933), pp. 394–5.

1933 the President made a strong attempt to persuade O. T. Jones, Woodwardian professor of Geology at Cambridge, to return to Aberystwyth as Principal. But the President's eloquent pleading failed to overcome the great geologist's dedication to research.[58] There were ten formal applications for the Principalship, and twelve other names were nominated for consideration by members of the Council. Four candidates (including W. J. Pugh, who accepted his disappointment with notable good grace) were interviewed, but the committee unanimously recommended the appointment of Ifor L. Evans, Fellow of St. John's College, Cambridge, who was clearly thought to have ripened nicely since he had been dismissed from consideration in 1927.[59]

The new Principal was born in 1897 in Aberdare; his grandfather had been a section leader in the great choir that Joseph Parry had taken up to Cambridge to perform his doctoral composition in 1878.[60] In 1914 Ifor Evans was in Germany learning the language; after some rough treatment (there were plenty of German counterparts to those who bullied Ethé) he was interned for the duration of the war. In the detention camp he met David Evans, later professor of German at Aberystwyth, who taught him Welsh, whereupon he discarded his Anglicized given name, Ivor, for Ifor.[61]

At Cambridge after the war he had taken a First in both parts of the Tripos in Economics and History. There followed a Fellowship, considerable experience in College administration, much travel abroad, a book on agriculture in Rumania, and several articles on British colonialism in Africa. It was, as the selection committee said, an outstanding career of 'exceptional . . . promise'. Lord Davies ('the President is so taken with him') was delighted with the appointment and was convinced that the new Principal would prove 'a brilliant success'.[62]

At first President and Principal worked in complete accord: Ifor Evans wholeheartedly agreed with Lord Davies' opinion that the Penglais site was 'the only one' which offered 'really attractive prospects for planning over a period of years'. They both believed that it was important to erect at least one College building on Penglais without delay so that there would be 'no question of going back to the old Laura Place idea'; and they soon came to terms about the order of priority of new buildings. Lord Davies conceded that a hostel for men (which he listed first) was beyond their current means and was prepared to support the Principal's alternative suggestion of a new Plant Breeding Station: Ifor Evans made it clear that he was as eager as the President was to build residential accommodation as

---

[58] Lord Davies to O. T. Jones, 30 December 1933. N.L.W. O. T. Jones MSS. 75.

[59] *Council Minutes* (4 April 1934), pp. 489–92. W. J. Pugh to Lord Davies, 29 March 1934. N.L.W. Llandinam MSS. (U.C.W. (1)), Gen. Corr. See above, pp. 223–4.

[60] Above, p. 55.   [61] Ifor L. Evans MSS. in private possession.

[62] *Council Minutes* (4 April 1934), p. 492. Lord Davies to P. Price, 6 April 1934. N.L.W. Llandinam MSS. (U.C.W. (1)), Gen. Corr. J. Davies Bryan to Thomas Jones, 20 April 1934. N.L.W. Thomas Jones MSS. Class J, vol. ix, f. 100.

soon as possible.[63] Moreover, the new Principal, unlike his predecessor, agreed with the President that the College ought to have a Registrar, and when E. B. Hicks, Secretary since 1929, resigned in 1935, J. Morgan Jones, who had won high praise as A. W. Ashby's assistant some years before, was elected to the restored office which he took up in 1936.[64]

In that same year there occurred a dispute which rocked the College to its foundations. So long as President and Principal were in accord, they made a fine team, dynamic in leadership, fertile in resource. But both were masterful men, and when they disagreed over an issue of importance, neither was likely easily to give way: it was very much a case of Greek meeting Greek. But the controversy went deeper and was much more important than any mere clash of personalities, colourful and interesting as the antagonists were without doubt. In fact, the dispute turned to a limited extent on the balance of influence (a difficult question never ultimately entirely resolvable) between the lay and professional authorities in the making of academic appointments in a university college which was not, and never had been, a closed corporation. And at an even more important level, the controversy threw up a challenge to the very foundations of academic freedom, and put a question mark against privately endowed chairs vested with Messianic possibilities by a donor whose convictions were never less than passionately held.

In 1934 Stanley Roberts, professor of Colonial History, had retired. It could not be said that, over the years, the possibilities of this chair had been fully developed. To some people it seemed, in the stringent financial circumstances of 1934, a luxury that the College could scarcely afford, a provision of cake when bread and butter were in short supply. Jerome Greene and R. F. Treharne, who were asked to prepare a memorandum on the subject, recommended that there should be a lectureship only in Colonial History, and that the balance of the money thus saved should be used to appoint two assistant lecturers in the department of History, where there were many students and a desperate need for additional staff.[65] At first Lord Davies was unwilling to vary the terms of the Colonial History endowment trust. He wanted to take into consideration the future of both the Wilson and Colonial History chairs, and to develop a new course embracing 'history, economics, political science, and other cognate subjects',

[63] Ifor L. Evans to Lord Davies, Lord Davies to Ifor L. Evans, 14, 15, and 23 November 1934. N.L.W. Llandinam MSS. (U.C.W. (1)), Gen. Corr. Ifor L. Evans to Thomas Jones, 13 March 1935. N.L.W. Thomas Jones MSS. Class J, vol. ix, f. 108. Ifor L. Evans, 'The Programme for New Buildings', October 1936. C.A. P/Bld.

[64] Council Minutes (17 July 1935, 21 October 1936), pp. 98–9, 6. Ifor L. Evans to Lord Davies, 23 October 1935. N.L.W. Llandinam MSS. (Wilson (2)). A.W. Ashby to J. H. Davies, 14 June 1925. N.L.W. J. H. Davies MSS. (Corr.).

[65] H. Stuart Jones to Lord Davies (enclosing the Greene–Treharne memorandum), 24 January and 19 March 1934. N.L.W. Llandinam MSS. (Wilson (2)).

comprising a new degree scheme that would be 'unique', and would therefore attract students 'from all over the world'.[66] This was not so very different from the proposal to establish a Faculty of Social Studies at Aberystwyth made to the Haldane Commission by Tom Jones and Lleufer Thomas in 1917.[67] The President's idea was imaginative (as indeed were so many of his notions), but it perhaps took insufficient account of the danger of extending the teaching commitments of small departments, whose staffs, to their enduring dissatisfaction, had always been obliged to make the lecture the staple of their teaching in order to cope with the numbers of their students. Moreover, the growth of knowledge was enforcing a need for specialization which the handful of teachers in each department found it increasingly difficult to answer. There was no prospect of money for additional assistance and so, eventually, Lord Davies reluctantly gave way: the chair in Colonial History was replaced by a lectureship, and an additional appointment was made in the department of history.[68]

Meantime, the Wilson chair remained unoccupied. During 1935 an approach was made to Kingsley Martin, who came to the conclusion that he was not quite what was required and withdrew his name from consideration. This left only W. Arnold Forster, who had no formal academic qualifications, a well-known publicist with quite a respectable list of publications to his name, an official of the League of Nations who believed passionately in its principles. Principal Evans did not regard Arnold Forster as a serious candidate. Gilbert Murray thought very much otherwise: he drew Lord Davies' attention to Arnold Forster's 'evangelizing spirit', and argued that the Wilson chair should be devoted to the purpose for which it had been 'founded: that is, the teaching of the League and of International Relations'. Such advice indicated how even a great scholar like Murray could be led astray by political opinions cherished with the force of religion.[69] Eventually, it was decided to advertise the chair: in all, by formal application and nomination, some fifty-seven names, including several future academic notables such as A. J. Toynbee, Alfred Cobban, D. W. Brogan, and Geoffrey Barraclough, were considered. A short-list of four was reduced to three by the elimination of Herbert Butterfield, and the committee members confined their attention to the historian C. A. Macartney, E. H. Carr, who was then working at the Foreign Office, and Arnold Forster. At that stage unanimity broke down.

---

[66] Lord Davies to Principal-Elect Ifor L. Evans, 19 April 1934. N.L.W. Ibid.

[67] Above, p. 188. If the Commission had given strong support to this suggestion (it paid no more than lip-service to it), Aberystwyth would have anticipated Oxford in its establishment of the immensely popular and successful P.P.E. honours school. In fact, the Aberystwyth scheme contained even wider possibilities, for Law and Geography were also included as ingredients in the suggested degree course.

[68] *Council Minutes* (16 October 1935, 20 October 1937), pp. 5, 5–6. Ifor L. Evans to Lord Davies, 8 May 1935. N.L.W. Llandinam MSS. (Wilson (2)).

[69] Ifor L. Evans to Lord Davies, 8 May 1935, Gilbert Murray to Lord Davies, 30 July 1935. N.L.W. Ibid.

The selection committee (which, near enough, was the Wilson Advisory Board in another guise) consisted of seven members: the Principal, who was chairman *ex officio*; Lord Davies and Professor E. A. Lewis, representing the College Council and Senate respectively; Lord Granville, nominated by the Foreign Secretary; Professor Gilbert Murray, who represented the League of Nations Union; General Sir Neill Malcolm, appointed by the Royal Institute of International Affairs, and W. G. S. Adams, Warden of All Souls, who was a member on behalf of the University of Oxford. The committee voted on the three candidates, assigning each a first, second, and third preference, and the result was a total (where a low figure was obviously best) of seventeen for Arnold Forster, thirteen for Carr, and twelve for Macartney. Four members of the committee were of the opinion, later confirmed in writing, that Arnold Forster, for all his gifts, was not academically qualified for the appointment. Lord Davies proposed that all three names should go forward for the Council's consideration, but his motion was not seconded. After considerable discussion it was agreed, without dissent, that the names of Macartney and Carr should be sent to the Council.[70]

Lord Davies would not accept this defeat. He decided to submit a separate report to the Council. At first it seemed possible that Gilbert Murray would add his name to this but, on reflection, he changed his mind: 'How many somersaults can a professor execute in a month?' was the President's exasperated response to this vacillation.[71] Lord Davies now persuaded himself that he was fighting for a principle: 'namely, that the appointment rests with the Council of the College, as the final authority, and not with the committee, whose function it is to recommend'.[72] This was hardly in dispute: as the committee could not agree, two names had been sent forward for the Council's decision; a motion to remit three names had fallen to the ground unseconded. Lord Davies ignored these unpalatable facts. He had now cast the Principal as the villain of the piece: Ifor L. Evans was said to have acted 'virtually' as 'a dictator'. Eight days later, pursuing the same analogy, the President wrote: 'There are lots of Mussolinis knocking around. The only way of dealing with them is to fight them in the open, not to knuckle under in the dark.'[73]

Having appealed to the Council, Lord Davies, beforehand, said that he would 'loyally accept' its decision. On 6 March 1936 the Council was faced with two

[70] Ifor L. Evans, 'Lord Davies, the Wilson chair and the Presidency of the College', February 1941. C.A. R/DES/IP/3.

[71] Gilbert Murray to Lord Davies, 14 February 1936, Lord Davies to Lord Atkin, 27 February 1936. N.L.W. Llandinam MSS. (Wilson (2)).

[72] Lord Davies to W. Arnold Forster, 27 February 1936. N.L.W. Ibid. In 1934 the President argued otherwise. In a letter to the Principal-Elect, Lord Davies said that appointments to the Wilson chair in the past had 'been made, in effect, by the Advisory Board, which is in close touch with the needs of the International Politics department'. 19 April 1934. N.L.W. Ibid.

[73] Lord Davies to Gilbert Murray, 16 and 24 February 1936. N.L.W. Ibid.

reports: the President, alone but undeterred, recommended that all three candidates should be interviewed; the majority report advised the consideration of two. The Council adopted the majority opinion and E. H. Carr was appointed to the Wilson chair.[74] The President promptly resigned: he claimed that he had 'forfeited the confidence of the Council in an attempt to restrain academic intolerance', and alleged that the Council had 'shirked its duty', and thereby possibly 'lost the services of an outstanding personality who for so many years has devoted his life to the cause of justice and peace in international relationships'.[75]

This, surely, was the nub of the whole affair. There was perhaps something in the point that Arnold Forster (whose conduct throughout in difficult circumstances was impeccable) made after his first private meeting with Ifor L. Evans. The Principal created the impression that 'local problems', the need to find someone academically qualified to cover the 'gap' between various departments in the College, constituted a most important consideration in his mind. If this were indeed so, it could be said that, in this respect, the Principal's opinion did not quite rise to the level appropriate to the consideration of this particular chair.[76] But on the central and vitally important academic question Ifor L. Evans was absolutely and indisputably right. The Wilson professor certainly ought not to be appointed because of his commitment to any particular body of doctrine. And, despite his no doubt sincere protestations to the contrary, this, in effect, was what Lord Davies was demanding. 'My whole object', he wrote to Arnold Forster, 'is to serve the cause of international relationships by securing a professor for the chair who is wholehearted in his devotion to the cause of international co-operation.'[77] Perhaps without realizing it, Lord Davies had come to believe that the end in this case did justify the means. It must be remembered that the horrors of the 1914–18 war had pushed many people, more often than not the most sensitive and humane, to pin their hopes for the future of the world on the League of Nations with a commitment never less than absolute and a sincerity that was not to be doubted. Those who held these articles of faith thus strongly did not admit that there was room for, much less validity in, any contrary opinion. To believe was to know; all else was heresy.

Several ardent supporters of the League bombarded Lord Davies with the suggestion that the Wilson chair should be removed elsewhere, perhaps, as one,

[74] Lord Davies to Gilbert Murray, 16 February 1936. N.L.W. Ibid. *Council Minutes* (6 March 1936), pp. 76–8.

[75] Lord Davies to D. C. Roberts, 11 March 1936, and 'Explanatory Statement' (annexed), p. 11. C.A. Six years later, the President wrote that he regretted that he had not 'taken the matter to the Court of Governors and fought the battle there in public'. And so on, presumably, *ad infinitum.* Lord Davies to G. A. Edwards, 20 August 1942. N.L.W. Llandinam MSS. (Wilson (2)).

[76] W. Arnold Forster to Lord Davies, 29 February 1936. N.L.W. Ibid.

[77] 27 February 1936. N.L.W. Ibid. In a later letter the President wrote: 'I also believe that in a sense one is fighting for the cause against people like the Principal, who has very little interest in the development of the ideas which you and I have so much at heart.' 9 April 1936. N.L.W. Ibid. (Wilson (1)).

who was also a member of the Aberystwyth Court of Governors, proposed disdainfully, to 'Oxford, Cambridge or Edinburgh, where it might be more appreciated'. Lord Davies thought this 'would hardly be practicable'.[78] However, the unhappy affair was not yet over. Members of the College Council deeply regretted the President's resignation: in view of the long and honourable relationship of the Llandinam family (quite apart from its unmatched magnificent generosity) to the College, it seemed 'contrary to the nature of things' that the connection should be severed. Lord Davies was asked to reconsider his decision to resign.[79] After a delay of three months he replied to the effect that he was prepared to resume the Presidency nominally, but would take no active part in College business. At a time when strenuous efforts were being made to raise money and there was some hope of opening the building programme on Penglais, it was obviously desirable that the President should be fully active. It was accordingly proposed that Lord Davies should become Honorary President, or President Emeritus, and in due course another President should be appointed in accordance with the terms of the Charter. It was evident that the College was doing its best to find 'the most dignified solution to an absurd problem'.[80] After it had been agreed to recommend the appointment to the active Presidency of Lord Merthyr, a young peer 'full of public spirit' who had been Treasurer of the College during recent years, Lord Davies, who by now had got the bit firmly between his teeth, intimated that he intended to stand in opposition. An unseemly brawl looked in prospect. Not surprisingly, Lord Merthyr withdrew his candidature. After some further negotiation, Lord Davies agreed 'to undertake unconditionally the office of President', and in April 1937 he was re-elected for a further term of five years.[81] For what it was worth, Lord Davies had his way in one respect: he remained President but did not, in fact, resume his active part in College affairs. But on the vital issue he was resoundingly defeated, and with all possible allowance for the genuine nobility of his ultimate aims it was well for academic freedom, and not least the status of the Wilson chair, that this was so.[82]

Although this great conflict dominated the high politics of the College for some time, and, inevitably, attracted some public attention in the press, it made little or no impact on the tenor of student life. Things had changed very little. There

[78] Mrs. M. Tenney to Lord Davies, 1 May 1936, Lord Davies to Mrs. Tenney, 14 May 1936. N.L.W. Ibid. (Wilson (2)).

[79] Revd. Richard Hughes to Lord Davies, 22 April 1936. N.L.W. Ibid. *Council Minutes* (29 April 1936), p. 112.

[80] Ifor L. Evans, 'Lord Davies, the Wilson chair and the Presidency of the College'. C.A. R/DES/IP/3. Ifor L. Evans to Thomas Jones, 5 October 1936. N.L.W. Thomas Jones MSS. Class J, vol. ix, f. 123.

[81] H. Stuart Jones to Lord Davies, 6 June 1932. N.L.W, Llandinam MSS. (U.C.W. (1)), Gen. Corr. Lord Lisburne and others to the Registrar, 7 April 1937 (copy). N.L.W. Thomas Jones MSS. Class J, vol. ix, f. 136. *Council Minutes* (28 April 1937), pp. 87–9.

[82] Throughout this painful controversy, Ifor L. Evans was in close touch with the Chairman of the U.G.C., the Pro-Chancellor of the University of Wales, and the Principals of the constituent Colleges.

was some fall in student numbers: there were 831 students at the College in October 1935, 770 a year later, and 701 at the opening of the session 1937–8.[83] The College therefore remained small, an intimate community with an intense social life of its own. The motor-car had no relevance to student life, and little to that of the staff; the railway timetable during the greater part of the year seemed positively designed to ensure that Aberystwyth, once reached, was not easily left. Indeed, J. O. Francis, an old student who became a playwright of quality, had denounced an attempt some years earlier to speed up the running of the old Cambrian railway as utterly 'foolish'. Francis had a lyrical attachment to Aberystwyth; for him it was 'the centre of a nation's soul' and, as such, 'should be approached' in its own peculiarly fitting way.

It is quite in order that we should go hurtling into Cardiff at a rate that lays stress on every separate second. Cardiff is that sort of place. But to approach Aberystwyth in that manner would violate the sweet seemliness that ought to mark all human processes. Who goes to Cardiff goes there as a passenger. Who goes to Aberystwyth should go there as a pilgrim and the Cambrian railway sees that he does![84]

Many others shared these sentiments, though not usually quite so rapturously. In the inter-war years the College retained very much of the character that it possessed before 1914. The old familiar social rituals were as enthusiastically observed as ever: quadding continued; there was impromptu community singing whenever and wherever students congregated. No social occasion was likely to lack its quota of 'topicals', more or less affectionate rhymed chants on the idiosyncrasies or behaviour of student worthies, among other things a thoroughly effective weapon (though sometimes the rapier became a bludgeon) against pretentiousness. The Promenade was virtually an extension of the College, and for most students few days went by without a walk from lodgings down 'to kick the bar' of the railing outside Alexandra Hall.[85] On Sunday mornings and evenings, particularly in spring and early summer, the social parade (something shared by town and gown) along the sea-front terrace was not to be missed; it had a special formality and even, in terms of the appropriate greeting of friends and acquaintances, a protocol of its own. The major College athletic teams at this time were usually well supported, especially at matches against other colleges and universities; and at the end of the game players and many supporters invariably

---

[83] Principal's Report, *Court Minutes* (20 October 1937), p. 13.

[84] 'A Meditation on the Cambrian Railway', *Welsh Outlook*, vi. 106. The line from South Wales to Aberystwyth, at least from Carmarthen onwards, to the end of its existence, gave the student pilgrim, if anything, even more time to create the appropriate mood for arrival!

[85] One student who came up in 1937 at first thought this was 'a footling practice'. However, 'within a few weeks', as she wrote to her parents, 'I was kicking the bar as often as the rest'. Diana Lawrence (neé Bowman), 'Aber. 1937–41', p. 3.

joined with gusto in 'the Red Indian mystery of the College Yell'.[86] After the war this practice continued for some time with increasing self-consciousness until, during the 1950s, it petered out.

It was in many ways an unsophisticated society much given to introspection; in particular there was an endless discussion of the current state (inevitably represented as in permanent decline) of the celebrated 'Aber. Spirit', a peculiarly intense camaraderie that bound together indissolubly all Aberystwyth students of all generations for all time.[87] Very few students at the College had more than the bare minimum of means on which to live. Most people were supported by scholarships or local authority grants, often meagre, eked out by such assistance as their parents (who themselves more often than not had little to spare but were moved to this self-sacrifice by the traditionally strong feeling of the Welsh people for education) could offer. Many students had no real choice of vocation: they either committed themselves to school-teaching, and thus qualified for useful Training department grants, or gave up all hope of a university education. But at least there was some compensation for this if they subsequently took up teaching in Wales. The cultural setting of the Principality was such that, quite often, the teacher attained a position which had been 'postulated over and over again as the ideal place of a teacher in a community—the leader of a democracy', or at least, of a social democracy of sorts.[88]

Some students existed on the margin of real poverty. There were still too many men like Jack Griffiths some years before, who 'saw more dinner-times than dinners' when he was at the College.[89] In these circumstances the small sums available as loans to the desperately needy were invaluable.[90] During the years of depression there was serious concern about the extent of malnutrition among men students at Aberystwyth. Eventually, in 1934, partly to ensure that an adequate meal at low cost was made available daily, and partly 'to increase opportunities for social intercourse', it was decided to form a men's dining club. At first the club met in the College Refectory; later, as numbers steadily grew, No. 1 Laura Place was taken over, and with assistance from the College equipped for the purpose. The club was administered by a committee elected by the student members, and received invaluable help from those members of the teaching staff who had

[86] The description is that of John Van Druten (*The Dragon*, l. 58), who wrote the well-known play *Young Woodley* when he was a member of the staff at Aberystwyth.

[87] 'It is a Freemasonry, a golden key, and a password anywhere.... A treasured possession which has a currency in any old corner of the globe', as one student found during war-time service overseas. E. Lloyd Jones in *The Dragon*, lxvi. 5.

[88] George Green, 'An Onlooker's Point of View', *N.U.T. Conference: Aberystwyth Souvenir Handbook* (1933), p. 8.

[89] 'Stormy Passage', *Welsh Review*, i. 329.

[90] 'Funds for loans to students.' In 1931 Tom Jones, ever mindful of his old College, used his influence to persuade the Pilgrim Trust to give £200, and smaller sums subsequently, to the Students' Loan Fund. Thomas Jones to H. Stuart Jones, 1 April 1931. C.A. P/Cr/D/11.

initiated the venture and continued to render service as senior officers of the club. This was a valuable contribution to student health, and by 1939 was recognized as having performed 'a splendid social' purpose for men students.[91]

Aberystwyth was one of the first university institutions to establish a comprehensive medical scheme for students. It began in 1923 on a voluntary basis for men students only. In 1931 it was made compulsory for all men, and at the same time women students were admitted to the scheme. For an annual fee of 10s., later increased to 12s. 6d., students during term time were entitled to medical attention, medicines, and all hospital services. Astonishingly, the scheme just about paid its way. It did so because, from the outset, it was administered almost wholly without cost as a labour of love by David Evans, the professor of German at the College; moreover, the Aberystwyth doctors who operated the scheme were prepared to accept minimal fees. In the days before the National Health Service, the medical scheme was of inestimable benefit to Aberystwyth students.[92]

In 1935 the administration of the medical scheme, of the Students' Union, and of the College athletic fields was remitted to a new committee established in that year. This was the College and Students' Joint Committee which consisted of sixteen members, including representatives of the College Council and Senate, the Old Students' Association (an imaginative suggestion linking the past with the present), the Students' Representative Council and certain of its subordinate bodies. The Principal and Vice-Principal were members *ex officio*. In addition to its administrative functions, the Committee was vested with 'the power to consider any matter relating to the general well-being of the student body', upon which it was entitled to tender advice to the Council.[93] In this respect, too, Aberystwyth was a pioneer. By present-day standards this was, no doubt, a very modest experiment in student participation in the government of the College: at that time it was relatively adventurous. Certainly over the years it proved a brilliantly successful illustration of the virtues of joint consultation, and provided an invaluable forum where the opinions and aims of all members of the College, lay, academic and student (past and present), on subjects of great importance could be aired and reconciled.

There were other features of student life in the 1930s which gave less cause for congratulation. There was some feeling, for example, that *The Dragon*, which began life, in aspiration at least, as a modest 'sort of *Hibbert Journal*', had steadily fallen from grace in recent years. Nor was it currently fulfilling adequately its secondary purpose of holding up a mirror to the life of the College; all too many contributions were trivial in content and deficient in wit. In 1938 the editor

[91] 'Dining Scheme for men students', 23 November 1936. C.A. P/Cr/D/6. *The Dragon*, lxi. 39. Professor R. I. Aaron and Mr. Percy George served as President and Treasurer respectively for several years.

[92] Principal's Report, *Court Minutes* (29 April 1936), p. 26.

[93] *Council Minutes* (4 December 1935), p. 63.

could do no other than plead guilty.[94] There is evidence, too, of a serious decline in the Debates Union. Traditionally, women students took little or no part in debates, but they attended meetings, all too many of them, so it was said, primarily 'to be amused'. The 'gods' responded to this encouragement, and a frivolous tone, regardless of subject, again became dominant. By 1938 it could be said, though this was partly disputed, that 'Friday nights are for slapstick entertainment, the floor a sawdust ring for the budding Grimaldi'.[95]

It is curious that this should be particularly so at that time. After all, these were years when Britain was dominated by grim social problems at home and menaced increasingly by the threat of war in Europe. It is odd that these great issues should have made so little impact on student thinking. Possibly the political balance was so overwhelmingly Socialist, or at least anti-Conservative, that vigorous public debate was unlikely to arise, although there was evidently no shortage of political discussion in private.[96] Y Gymdeithas Geltaidd (the Celtic Society) remained strong, and the College branch of the Welsh Nationalist party, though small, was vigorously active. But even this ardent group could not energize political debate in the College at large, perhaps because the students at that time were drawn overwhelmingly from Wales.[97] They were not deemed sufficiently Welsh in spirit for the satisfaction of the writer of an editorial in The Dragon in 1932; he confessed his fear that Aberystwyth would have become 'an English College in Wales' by the time its centenary arrived in 1972.[98]

It may be that the student generation of the immediate pre-war years, perhaps without fully realizing it, took refuge from the harsh political realities of the wider world in an escapist preoccupation with their own concerns. These were the years of recurrent European crises, and once the worthlessness of the Munich Agreement had been brutally spelt out by Hitler, many young men in Britain at that time felt in their bones that, official and newspaper reassurances to the contrary, sooner or later, they would have to go off to war. This was a far cry from student opinion some years earlier. In December 1930 a general meeting of students passed a resolution which asserted that the O.T.C. was 'an adjunct to militarism', and called on the College to abolish it. The Council refused to do so. Subsequently, an Anti-War Committee, an unofficial offshoot of the College branch of the League of Nations Union, was formed, and on Armistice Day,

[94] The Dragon, xlvi. 175–6, lxi. 7. There were occasional exceptions: in 1933, for example, Alun Lewis, the brilliantly promising young poet who was killed during the war, contributed an excellent short story. 'Tudor Witch', ibid. lvi. 19–21.

[95] Ibid. lvi. 46, lxi. 39, 41.

[96] In 1930 the Conservative Club admitted its numerical weakness. Ibid. lii. 37. A fresher who came up in 1937 noted that there were 'heaps of budding socialists, communists, etc., here, and they turn up everywhere and anywhere to argue'. Diana Lawrence, loc. cit., p. 3.

[97] In 1937–8 there were only eighty-six students from England in the University of Wales as a whole. Emrys Evans, op. cit., p. 126.

[98] 'Golygyddol', The Dragon, lv. 6.

1933, organized a demonstration, as the *Cambrian News* reported, to express 'the tremendous feeling there was in the College against the eventuality of war'. Demonstrators carried placards inscribed with the legend 'We will not fight for King and Country'.[99]

These pacifist sentiments evoked some response in the Court of Governors. In May 1934 the Court asked the Council to consider whether 'Aberystwyth College, with its noble record of work in the Cause of Peace, should not now definitely declare that preparing for war is not one of its functions'. Lord Davies, ardent supporter of the League of Nations as he was, had never believed that international rivalries could be answered thus simply. In a letter to the Court counselling caution, he insisted that Britain was 'still dependent upon [its] national forces to defend the country if it is attacked, "negative" disarmament carries us nowhere'.[100] The Principal, who was asked to submit a memorandum on the O.T.C. for the guidance of the Council, argued that, 'by its very nature, a University should be open to all opinions'; it would be just as wrong to prohibit the O.T.C. as to make membership of it compulsory for all men students.[101] Ultimately, the Council took no action, and the O.T.C., under the command of H. F. Stimson, continued up to the war to engage the allegiance (the annual training camp was invariably enjoyed) of a section of the student body.

Just before the war another attack on a much more widely popular student interest had to be repelled. The academic authorities at the Welsh Colleges had never been entirely happy about the annual Inter-College week activities: it was felt that they unduly disrupted the work of the term, and, all too frequently, were marked by an excessive boisterousness that occasioned a good deal of public criticism. In 1938 the Bangor Senate invited Aberystwyth to co-operate in getting rid of the 'annual plague', as Principal Emrys Evans described it. The Inter-College *Eisteddfod* came in for particular attack, and it was proposed that the Senates of all four Colleges should unite to kill it off.[102] The prohibition was fiercely and successfully resisted by all shades of student opinion in all four Colleges, and, perhaps put on their mettle by the attack, students made sure that the Inter-College week of 1939 was an outstanding success. At any rate it was a triumph for Aberystwyth, which easily topped the sports championship table and enjoyed a crushing victory in the *Eisteddfod*.[103] During the war years Inter-College week

---

[99] July 1934. N.L.W. Llandinam MSS. (U.C.W. (1)), Gen. Corr. *The Dragon*, lvi. 33–4. *Cambrian News* (17 November 1933). Predictably, some local members of the British Legion tried to break up the procession.

[100] *Council Minutes* (20 July 1934), p. 524. Lord Davies to D. C. Roberts, 18 July 1934. N.L.W. Llandinam MSS. (U.C.W. (1)), Gen. Corr.

[101] 'Memorandum to the Council', 20 July 1934 (copy). N.L.W. Ibid.

[102] Emrys Evans to Ifor L. Evans, 17 March 1938, Report of the Senate Executive Committee, 9 May 1938. C.A. P/Cr/D/6.

[103] *The Dragon*, lxi. 7, 38. By this time there existed a Central S.R.C. where the student officers of the four Colleges united for consultation.

was necessarily curtailed, but it survived some further suggestion of its abolition and was immediately revived in 1946.[104] No doubt behaviour in Inter-College week was occasionally tiresome, even absurdly childish.[105] But it should be remembered, as had been realized years before, that the sports matches formed 'the strongest tie' uniting students who, all too easily, could forget that they were, after all, members of a loosely-knit national university.[106]

The outbreak of the war posed a rather different problem in inter-college cooperation for Aberystwyth. The expected aerial bombardment had prompted plans to disperse the University of London, and Aberystwyth was designated as host to certain departments of the capital's University College. At first relations between the two student communities were no better than suspiciously wary and often openly hostile. When the student evacuees arrived at Aberystwyth they were greeted with the College yell and immediately assumed that their hosts were 'manifesting hostility'. But there were deeper reasons than mere unfamiliarity to explain the initial friction: there was, for example, a social cleavage between the London students, many of whom were middle-class in background, and those of Aberystwyth who were overwhelmingly from working-class homes. One curious consequence of this, according to one observer, was that the Aberystwyth student socialists, whose political affiliations had been dictated more by experience ('a fair number . . . had known not just the pinch but the grip of poverty in their childhood years') than theory, were highly critical of the extremist, often Communist, political convictions of 'obviously middle-class London students who had never known hardship in the material sense'. And, perhaps inevitably, students from the capital, who prided themselves on their city sophistication, were inclined to patronize their hosts. 'Nothing', concluded the same observer with truth, 'goes down worse with the Welsh, nothing.'[107]

One unfortunate consequence of the presence of the London students was that, despite impassioned pleas for its continuance, quadding virtually died out. The newcomers did not understand its time-honoured importance, and they, together with Aberystwyth freshers, whose initial self-consciousness had always had to be overcome by coaxing, formed so substantial a proportion of the joint student body that their reluctance to join in gradually killed off (to the intense disgust of traditionalist old students) a distinctive and agreeable social practice. Quadding never again recovered its former glory.[108] Happily, after the initial difficulties of adjust-

---

[104] Letters between Ifor L. Evans and Emrys Evans, 1940–3. C.A. P/Cr/D/4.

[105] Diana Lawrence, loc. cit., p. 7., gives some good illustrations best left undescribed, and, not untypically of tolerant student opinion, concludes: 'Still, Inter-Coll. is only once a year—an excuse sufficient for everything.' [106] *The Dragon*, xxxix. 148.

[107] Diana Lawrence, loc. cit., pp. 1, 15, 17. It says something for Aberystwyth's capacity to engage strong loyalties that Mrs. Lawrence, herself English with middle-class parents, could write: 'I've never been quite so glad to be "Aber.".' For the initial friction, see *The Dragon*, lxii. 12, lxiii. 28.

[108] 'No longer does one see two dignified groups perambulating round quad, all we have instead is a

ment, Aberystwyth and London students co-operated well together. A new joint student constitution was drawn up, and the societies and athletic teams of the two Colleges were united. Eventually, the fusion was so complete that, in 1944, not long before the Londoners returned home, *The Dragon*, without any exaggeration, could say that everybody had 'come to regard U.C.W.-L.', as the coalition was known, 'as a single unit'.[109] It was entirely fitting that Aberystwyth, which in its early days had been partly nurtured by London University, should have had this opportunity to render some assistance to its former protector in this time of trouble.

During the war Aberystwyth's first duty, as the Principal said, was simply 'to carry on', and to strive to 'preserve the University tradition under conditions of ever-increasing difficulty'.[110] Nor was this a matter only for the College authorities. Rigorous food rationing posed particularly great problems for the corps of Aberystwyth landladies, whose enormous contribution year by year to the well-being of the students ought not to pass unnoticed. Not all landladies were angels, any more than their student-lodgers. But, overwhelmingly, Aberystwyth students had good cause to be grateful for the quality of the care (not least the great interest taken in their careers) they received in their 'digs'. Many Aberystwyth households had taken in students for generations and formed an integral part of the College. In 1940 *The Dragon* fully recognized the importance of this contribution to the College in a toast which ran:

Principals and professors come, principals and professors go; only landladies remain, only they are immortal. They are, for us, an assurance that . . . Aber. will go on for a thousand years. God bless 'em.[111]

There was, in fact, a considerable coming and going of professors at this time. Several long-serving members of the Senate retired. T. Gwynn Jones, who remained prolific in scholarly output to the end, and whose presence on the staff was a notable adornment of the College, retired in 1937. There had been a 'personal character' about his chair in Welsh Literature and this, together with straitened financial circumstances, led the College to decide not to make another appointment.[112] In 1938, when E. J. Wood resigned, the Greek and Latin departments, neither of which had more than a handful of advanced students, were united

---

miserable series of gossiping conglomerations who persist in impeding the transit of the last few faithful devotees of the great art. . . . God forbid that there grow up a generation of freshers who know not the noble art.' *The Dragon*, lxiii. 13, lxiv. 7. In October 1939 there were 550 Aberystwyth students and 520 from University College, London, at the College.

[109] *The Dragon*, lxvi. 2.

[110] Principal's Report, *Court Minutes* (23 April 1941), p. 15.

[111] *The Dragon*, lxii. 10. In that year the magazine changed the language of its title: henceforth it became *Y Ddraig*. In 1940, too, M. J. Morgan, College bellringer for fifty-two years, retired; the O.S.A. appropriately recognized his exceptionally long service. O.S.A. Minute-book (25 March 1940).

[112] Ifor L. Evans, 'Departmental Surveys' (1936), p. 7.

under the professorship of E. D. T. Jenkins, who received, as the Principal said, 'a well deserved, but long delayed, promotion'.[113] In the next year C. R. Chapple, professor of Education since 1913, retired. He was replaced by Idwal Jones, a former Aberystwyth student who returned to his old College from Swansea.[114] In 1940 there were several changes: T. A. Levi, who since 1901 had built up a massive reputation as a teacher of Law and was still, in the face of appalling transport problems in wartime, prepared to go to North Wales to hold classes in order to keep the 'Law Society's grants . . . alive', retired.[115] The new professor was D. J. Llewelfryn Davies, one of the Aberystwyth Law department's most distinguished former students, who had had an outstanding career subsequently at Cambridge, and extensive teaching experience in England and abroad. For the next thirty years Llewelfryn Davies acted, as Levi had for so many years before, as the indispensable anchor-man in a department where the turnover in junior teachers (who had professional opportunities not open to other academics) was unusually rapid.[116]

J. W. H. Atkins was replaced in the Rendel chair of English by Gwyn Jones, an authority on the Icelandic Saga, author of three novels, and editor of the *Welsh Review*, an interesting journal which had given considerable encouragement to the so-called school of Anglo-Welsh writers.[117] There was a very close contest for Laurie's chair of Zoology. Eventually, T. A. Stephenson, an old Aberystwyth man, then professor at Cape Town, who had a long list of publications on marine ecology to his name, was elected, despite his inability to attend for interview.[118] Later that month B. B. Thomas, an old student and a future President of the College, was elected Director of Extra-Mural Studies in succession to the Revd. Herbert Morgan, whose 'rare capacity' to inspire his colleagues and students, as B. B. Thomas said, was not reflected in the 'mere statistics' of the department's record during his tenure.[119] The new Director had gone on from Aberystwyth to Jesus College, Oxford, whence he returned as a full-time tutor on the Aberystwyth Extra-Mural staff. Subsequently, he was for thirteen years Warden of Coleg

---

[113] *Court Minutes* (19 October 1938), p. 7.

[114] *The Dragon*, lxi. 8, for a fine student tribute to Chapple.

[115] T. A. Levi to Ifor L. Evans, 28 February 1940. C.A. P/Cr/D/11.

[116] *Council Minutes* (24 April 1940), pp. 73–4. Glanville Williams, another brilliant product of the Aberystwyth Law School, later professor at Cambridge, had also been interested in this appointment. W. Ll. Davies to Lord Davies, 10 April 1940. N.L.W. Llandinam MSS. (U.C.W., Principalship).

[117] *Council Minutes* (24 April 1940), pp. 72–3. The strong runner-up for this chair was D. Gwilym James, an old Aberystwyth man, later Vice-Chancellor of Southampton University. W. J. Burdon Evans to Thomas Jones, 1 June 1940. N.L.W. Thomas Jones MSS. Class J, vol. ix, f. 150.

[118] *Council Minutes* (24 April 1940), pp. 74–5. H. J. Fleure's strong support for Stephenson was an important consideration in this appointment. W. J. Burdon Evans to Thomas Jones, 1 June 1940. N.L.W. Thomas Jones MSS. Class J, vol. ix, f. 150.

[119] *Court Minutes* (24 April 1940), p. 22. For an earlier criticism that Aberystwyth's Extra-Mural work compared 'unfavourably with [that of] Bangor', in quantity at least, see Thomas Jones to A. S. Firth, 22 March 1934. N.L.W. Thomas Jones MSS. Class J, vol. ix, f. 98.

Harlech; the exceptional range of his experience of adult education in Wales was recognized as 'unique', and his relationship to his predecessor suggested that this was almost an 'apostolic succession'.[120]

Curiously enough, considering the tremendous advances in the subject that the impetus of war was to bring, Physics had attracted fewer and fewer students after 1924. By and large, practical instruction in the schools was not good, and Gwilym Owen, professor of Physics at Aberystwyth, found it necessary to invent a range of demonstration experiments and apparatus (of value to this day in the department) to illustrate the fundamentals of the subject. Owen, a first-rate teacher, eloquent in Welsh and English, was Vice-Principal of the College from 1932 to 1936, but was struck down by illness and had to resign in 1938.[121]

The new professor of Physics, E. J. Williams, was perhaps, in terms of sheer intellectual power, the most gifted scientist ever to join the staff at Aberystwyth. After attending Llandysul School, he had gone on from Swansea to work with W. L. Bragg at Manchester, with Rutherford at Cambridge, and with Niels Bohr at Copenhagen. Williams had established a great reputation with a series of brilliant papers which showed his distinction both as an experimental and theoretical physicist. He came to Aberystwyth in 1938, and was elected to the Royal Society a year later when he was thirty-six. His reputation was such that, in the year or two before the war, young research workers began to gather around him at Aberystwyth. In 1940 he carried out at the College 'the most striking of his experimental achievements': namely, 'the direct demonstration . . . by the cloud chamber method of the decay of cosmic ray meson into an electron'. Soon afterwards Williams was called away to help in the technical fight against the U-boat menace which, for a time, was so threatening that it looked as if Britain would be eliminated from the war without any need for a German military invasion. First at R.A.F. Coastal Command and later at the Admiralty, E. J. Williams made technical and tactical 'contributions of decisive importance to the winning of the campaign' against the U-boat, thus rendering possible the later Allied invasion of Europe from the sea.[122]

It was inevitable that a man of such rare quality, 'a decided "find" for this College', as Ifor L. Evans put it with perhaps deliberate understatement, should receive handsome offers to move elsewhere. In March 1943 Glasgow tried to tempt him away, but he ultimately rejected the overture. According to the Principal, E. J. Williams was a radical member of the Aberystwyth Senate who, by his 'constant probings', gave the administrative authorities a good run for their money on questions of College policy.[123] There is evidence that Williams, like

[120] *Council Minutes* (26 June 1940), p. 91. Principal's Report, *Court Minutes* (16 October 1940), p. 7.
[121] Ifor L. Evans, 'Departmental Surveys' (1936), p. 66.
[122] P. M. S. Blackett, 'Professor E. J. Williams, F.R.S.', *Nature*, clvi. 655.
[123] Ifor L. Evans to Sir Hector Hetherington, 6 March 1943, and to E. J. Williams, 27 April 1943. C.A. P/Cr/D/14.

so many others before and after him, had 'grown to love' Aberystwyth, possibly sufficiently strongly to bring him back to the College when the war was over.[124] But it was not to be: for the last eighteen months of his life E. J. Williams knew that he had terminal cancer; defying pain he worked to the end, and died in September 1945, aged forty-two, internationally recognized as 'one of the most brilliant physicists of [the] generation'.[125]

Another member of the Aberystwyth Senate who had an international reputation had also been given partial leave of absence to do war work. After his appointment to the Wilson chair in 1936, E. H. Carr had considerably recast the curriculum of the department of International Politics, and he had delivered his quota of public lectures (which were occasions not lightly to be missed) at the College. In addition he had published several books and articles on international relations, culminating in his widely acclaimed volume, *The Twenty Years Crisis, 1919–1939*, in 1939. This work, which reflected a decisive shift from idealism to realism in the academic appraisal of international problems, was to become a classic, profoundly influencing most post-war Western thinking (especially the work of influential American scholars such as Hans J. Morgenthau) on international questions. Soon after the outbreak of war E. H. Carr had gone to work for the Ministry of Information; later he joined the staff of *The Times*. During this time he continued to publish books and pamphlets, mainly on post-war problems. In April 1941 the Wilson Advisory Board agreed to release him for the duration of the war from the normal conditions of part-residence in Aberystwyth, and the College Council adopted that recommendation.[126]

Lord Davies did not object to the Wilson professor's secondment to wartime government service; the President conceded that this was 'work of national importance'. But he did object, in the strongest terms, to E. H. Carr's joining *The Times*, 'a private commercial enterprise', as the President put it in words that calmly dismissed any claim 'The Thunderer' had to unique status and authority. Lord Davies also looked askance at the fact that, although the Wilson professor's stipend had not been paid when he was at the Ministry of Information, it apparently had when he wrote for *The Times*.[127] E. H. Carr's answer to this was the not unreasonable one that all professors were allowed to be paid for outside work; initially he had received very little for his articles in *The Times*, but latterly the sum had increased considerably. Moreover, he had continued his other serious writing and, in his opinion, 'except perhaps for a great national orator, who can sway

124 *Court Minutes* (23 October 1946), pp. 57–8. E. J. Williams to Ifor L. Evans, 22 February 1943. C.A. P/Cr/D/14.

125 P. M. S. Blackett, loc. cit., p. 655. There is an excellent bilingual anthology of articles, including some interesting detail of his war work, in *Professor E. J. Williams, F.R.S., 1903–1945*, ed. J. Tysul Jones (Llandysul, 1970).

126 *Council Minutes* (23 April 1941), p. 50.

127 Lord Davies to Ifor L. Evans, 24 December 1942 (copy). N.L.W. Llandinam MSS. (Wilson (2)).

large audiences, . . . the most effective way of instructing and moulding public opinion on international affairs and thus exercising an influence on them, is through the printed word'.[128]

Lord Davies was determined to ask the Council to institute an inquiry: beforehand he wrote to many members soliciting support; most replies were guarded, and a large number of members clearly had no intention of attending the meeting on 3 March 1943.[129] One who was unable to be present but who did not burk the issue was Thomas Jones. T.J. sent a telegram which he asked the Principal to read to the Council: it suggested referring the matter 'without discussion' to the Advisory Board; offered the hope that the President, 'after many years absence from duty', would attend the meeting of the Board; and ended with the downright opinion that 'Professor Carr on *The Times* is worth several generals in the field, and the brilliant strategist who put him there should be promoted Field-Marshal of the Home Guard'.[130]

As a matter of fact, the Principal decided that it was not necessary to throw down the gauntlet in this way. A simple motion to refer the question to the Advisory Board was carried by those who were firmly of the opinion that E. H. Carr was 'a great man' and that he was 'doing very good work'. The Advisory Board later reaffirmed its decision to allow the Wilson professor partial leave of absence.[131]

Lord Davies was furiously angry: he privately castigated the Advisory Board, the Council, and the Principal, and added a passage that expressed the bitter disappointment that he felt at the failure, as he saw it, of the hopes that had inspired the foundation of the Wilson chair.

I wish to God [he wrote to Burdon Evans] I had never initiated this proposal. Almost since the inception of this department it has worked consistently against the programme I have spent most of my time and money in advocating; namely, the development of the League with a real international authority. All the professors from Zimmern onwards opposed these ideas, with the result that we have been landed in another . . . war.[132]

Hell hath no fury like an idealist disillusioned. There is no question at all that Lord Davies was moved by the highest and noblest of public purposes; and it is impossible to disagree with the judgement of his friend, Gwilym Davies, who

[128] 'Report to the Advisory Board', *Council Minutes* (6 April 1943), pp. 48–54.

[129] Letters to Lord Davies, February 1943. N.L.W. Ibid. Ifor L. Evans, too, tried to ensure the attendance of those he thought sympathetic. Letters, February 1943. C.A. P/Cr/D/6 and 10.

[130] 3 March 1943. C.A. P/Cr/D/10.

[131] Ifor L. Evans to Thomas Jones, 8 March 1943. C.A. Ibid. Revd. Gwilym Davies to Lord Davies, 29 June (1943). N.L.W. Llandinam MSS. (Wilson (2)). *Council Minutes* (3 March and 23 June 1943), pp. 26, 48–54. E. H. Carr had been uneasy for some time about the financial arrangements during wartime. He had put aside £1,000 of his professorial stipend and, slightly later, this sum was transferred to a special account for use in connection with the chair when the war was over. It was also agreed, at his request, that he should receive a token salary of £10 per annum for the duration of hostilities.

[132] 5 March 1943. N.L.W. Llandinam MSS. (Wilson (2)).

wrote: 'No one in the history of the Principality has excelled Lord Davies's record for benefactions to Welsh institutions and organisations.'[133] No Welsh institution benefited more from this open-handedness than the University College of Wales. Unfortunately, Lord Davies did not fully appreciate the principles of democratic lay control (which left no place for government by Presidential fiat) on which the administration of the College had always ultimately rested. And it is evident that, at rock bottom, he misunderstood the nature and purpose of academic aims and invested them with possibilities that could scarcely be realized. For all that, he was a warm, intensely human personality, one of the most interesting characters ever associated with the College. He died in 1944 and did not live to see the United Nations begin falteringly to build up the international system that he had striven for so worthily.

The succession to the Presidency of the College presented no problem. There was 'an unanimous feeling in favour of nominating' Thomas Jones. He filled the bill on every possible count: he was an eminent man, with immense experience and influence; he was a determined commoner (an important consideration in the democratic mood of 1944) and, in all probability, the most distinguished old student still alive. It was an honour that had been richly deserved by more than half a century of magnificent service to the College. Old wounds still occasionally ached: T.J. insisted that, at the first sign of any opposition, his name was to be 'wiped out . . . quite ruthlessly'. He need not have worried. He was unanimously elected to the Presidency.[134]

[133] 'Some notes on the career of Lord Davies', N.L.W. Gwilym Davies MSS. I/3, f. 34.
[134] Ifor L. Evans to Ernest Evans, 24 August 1944, Thomas Jones to Ifor L. Evans, 9 September 1944. C.A. P/Cr/D/18.

9

'The Ultimate Home of the University College of Wales Must be on the Penglais Site'[1]

INCE 1945 two major developments have dominated the history of the College: the massive increase (to date not far short of fourfold) in the number of students; and the construction of many new College buildings (a programme not yet completed and likely, for the foreseeable future at least, to remain open-ended) on Penglais hill. These great changes did not proceed at an even rate over the period, nor did the provision of new buildings at first keep pace with the growth in numbers. There were 755 students at Aberystwyth at the beginning of the first session after the war; a year later, when the ex-servicemen began to return in strength, numbers topped the thousand mark. Subsequently, there was a gradual increase (with some fluctuation upwards and downwards from year to year) to 1,258 in October 1956. Since that time the number of students at the College has risen steadily and more than doubled to 2,629 in October 1971, with an average increase of just under a hundred students each year.[2]

The building programme on Penglais had, in fact, begun before the outbreak of war in 1939, but, despite much official enthusiasm for, or at any rate talk of, a large and rapid expansion of British universities, post-war economic and other difficulties reduced the resources available to more modest proportions than had been expected in the high noon of optimism at the end of the war in 1945.[3] Moreover, continuing balance of payments problems, involving a devaluation of the currency in 1949, and the additional economic strains resulting from the outbreak of the Korean war in the summer of 1950 forced the government in the

---

[1] *Report on the work and needs of the Agricultural Departments* (October 1947), p. 29.

[2] *College Reports* (1945–71). See Appendix F.

[3] Sir Ernest Simon, 'The Case for a Universities Development Council', 1 January 1944. C.A. P/Cr/D/4. In May 1946 the U.G.C. called for 'the doubling of the pre-war student population within the next ten years'. Ifor L. Evans to the U.G.C., 21 June 1946. C.A. P/Cr/D/17.

following year to curtail drastically the building programmes of all British universities. Some building on Penglais continued during the 1950s, but the programme did not get fully into its stride until the early 1960s, and it is only in the last decade that the College on the Hill has come to displace the old College by the Sea as the main centre of activities. These rapid alterations of size and, substantially, of location have exerted profound effects (inevitably a curate's egg of good and bad) on the character of the College.

After S. K. Greenslade had been forced by illness in 1929 to resign his commission to plan the proposed new College buildings on Penglais, H. V. Lanchester had been appointed architectural adviser.[4] He acted in this capacity for some years and, in fact, produced sketch plans for the layout of various buildings on the new site. In March 1935, for reasons which are not entirely clear, Lanchester's commission was withdrawn.[5] A suggestion that the College should sponsor an open competition to find the right man to do justice to the site was eventually rejected, and it was agreed that the only way to proceed was 'by appointing an architect and trusting him'. Soon afterwards Percy Thomas (who in due course became Sir Percy) was invited to prepare a new layout of the site and he was appointed successively as architect for a number of the first buildings constructed on Penglais. The relationship was defined thus by the Principal in 1946: 'We have regarded Sir Percy Thomas as our architect, though we have limited our legal commitments towards him to specific contracts.' It is fair to say that Sir Percy had been 'happy to accept these conditions', and to show by his willingness to provide advice without charge that he was prepared 'to interpret them in a most generous fashion'.[6] In March 1935 the Council had agreed that first priority on Penglais should be given to an Agricultural Research block, which would provide a new home for the Welsh Plant Breeding Station and the department of Agricultural Economics. In the following year the Ministry of Agriculture promised a substantial grant for this purpose, and in the autumn of 1937 work began on the new site.

Second priority had been accorded to a new building on Penglais for a Social Sciences block to house the allied departments of History, Economics, Geography, and International Politics, not least because the latter three for years had been forced to make do with inadequate temporary accommodation. But there were insufficient funds currently available for this purpose and, when in 1937 the Ministry of Agriculture again offered considerable assistance towards a new building for the College Dairy and the department of Dairy Bacteriology, it was agreed to go ahead immediately with this project.[7] It will be recalled that for many years the

[4] *Council Minutes* (23 July 1930), pp. 612–13.   [5] Ibid. (8 March 1935), pp. 61–2.

[6] Ifor L. Evans, 'A Note to the President on New College Buildings', pp. 1, 4. No date [November 1946]. C.A. P/Cr/D/17.

[7] *Report on the work and needs of the College* (March 1944), pp. 34–5.

Dairy department had occupied a basement area adjoining the men's cloakroom in the old College building. The result was that when the Dairy department began to function in April, 'the central heating of the College' promptly had to be 'discontinued'. For, as the Principal explained, 'if we keep the students warm in a cold April or May, we melt the cheeses'.[8] The technical nature of much of the work of the Dairy department called for a small self-contained factory with direct access to a main road rather than an orthodox collegiate building. And it was felt that this structure would not marry well with the other buildings proposed for Penglais. Fortunately a suitable site was available on Llanbadarn Road, just beyond the Vicarage Field, and in September 1937 work began on a new Dairy building there.[9]

These two successful ventures pointed the moral for a College still woefully short of adequate funds: the building programme could be continued only if substantial financial assistance were forthcoming from some external source. Intelligent opportunism might produce results: a strict adherence to the building priorities already agreed would get nowhere in the circumstances of that time. During 1937 the College and Students' Joint Committee, with its special concern for welfare, had carried out a survey of student participation in sports activities and drew the conclusion that the provision of a swimming bath merited the first place in any future developments on this side of College activities.[10] In the following year, the approaching war casting a shadow before it, there was much earnest discussion of the importance of physical fitness, and an application was made through the U.G.C. to the National Fitness Council for a special grant to build a swimming bath at an estimated cost of £17,000. In April 1938 it was announced that the National Fitness Council was prepared to offer a maximum grant of £10,000 for this purpose. By this time it was clear that very shortly the College would have other moneys, which it had already been agreed should be earmarked for additional welfare amenities for students, at its disposal.[11] Accordingly, the College accepted the offer of assistance from the National Fitness Council, and in January 1939 a contract was placed for the construction of a new swimming bath on Penglais. Moreover, as at that time a considerable amount of excavation (involving the use of special machinery) of the site was already in hand, it was decided to make further use of this equipment to excavate and level a site adjoining the swimming bath for use as a hockey pitch and running track. These schemes had not been completed when the war began and, in consequence of a rise in prices, their ultimate cost was somewhat higher than the original

[8] 'A Note to Lord Davies on priority of buildings on Penglais', 14 November 1934. N.L.W. Llandinam MSS. (U.C.W. (1)), Gen. Corr.

[9] *Report on the work and needs of the College* (March 1944), pp. 35–6.

[10] *Council Minutes* (1 December 1937), p. 29.

[11] Derived from the settlement of the College's claims under the Welsh Church Acts. See below, p. 269–70.

estimates. In the end, for an outlay of £96,000, the College had a fine new home for the Plant Breeding Station, an efficient Dairy Building, a first-rate Swimming Bath and an ideal athletic unit adjacent to it. Grants from one government body or another provided 36 per cent of this capital expenditure, the amenity money from the Welsh Church Acts 20 per cent, and the remaining 44 per cent had come from the all too slender resources of the College itself.[12]

All three buildings had been designed by Sir Percy Thomas; the two on Penglais were faced with Forest of Dean stonework, and it is commonly assumed that, if the astronomical rise in costs after the war had not ruled it out, all later building on the site would have been finished in the same material, with rather greater visual harmony than has been achieved. Whether this is so or not, it appears that the choice of the material for the Agricultural Research block was made at the instance of 'a lay member of the New Buildings Committee', who was said to have exercised 'undue influence' over a decision that was taken, apparently, 'against the advice of the architect'.[13] At any rate, at long last a start had been made on Penglais, and the 'dream of the College which started life in 1872 in a converted hotel' was on the way to fulfilment.[14]

Soon after the war began the Welsh Plant Breeding Station and the department of Agricultural Economics moved into their new home on Penglais. Sir George Stapledon (he had been knighted and elected a Fellow of the Royal Society in 1939) did not long remain to enjoy the improved accommodation: in February 1942 he resigned his appointments as Director of the Station and professor of Agricultural Botany at Aberystwyth and left Wales where his greatest work had been done.[15] He had created 'a national respect for grass', and the great Grassland Congress held at Aberystwyth in 1937 had 'spread that outlook internationally'. In addition to his matchless renown as a plant breeder, Stapledon was a superb teacher: he had no patience with avid student note-takers; he 'aimed at firing the imagination', and thereafter his disciples must follow wherever their investigations led them, for, as he insisted, 'there are no subjects, only problems'. He was evidently not altogether happy with the rigmarole of university examinations: as he admitted later, 'the alpha-plus and beta-minus caper always defeated me utterly'.[16] It is almost impossible to exaggerate the contribution Stapledon made to

[12] *Report on the work and needs of the College* (1944), p. 35.

[13] Ifor L. Evans, 'A Note to the President on New College Buildings', pp. 4–5. (November 1946). C.A. P/Cr/D/17.   [14] *U.C.W. Appeal for £300,000.* G. Lib. LD. 1158. Pam.

[15] 'My best work and the happiest of my memories have been bound up with Wales.' Sir G. Stapledon to Ifor L. Evans, January 1946. C.A. P/D/SRS.

[16] *Council Minutes* (6 March 1942), p. 44. Waller, op. cit., pp. 20, 35, 145, 226–34. Golf played an important part in Stapledon's social life at Aberystwyth. 'My golf experiences at Aber. with my colleagues in Science were comparable to nothing in my previous golfing career', he wrote. 'We carry our own clubs and do duty in turn at the flag, . . . lost balls are looked for here and found, especially when you know there is no more golf till the ball is found, and there are no caddies to swear at.' R. G. Stapledon, 'Notebook'.

the academic standing of the College: it will always be a matter of pride that the outstanding agricultural scientist of that generation, whose work in the cause of human betterment was of truly international significance, was a member of the staff at Aberystwyth for so long.

He was replaced in his twin appointments by T. J. Jenkin, an old Aberystwyth student, who had been Stapledon's senior assistant from the outset and latterly had been Deputy Director of the Plant Breeding Station.[17] There were several other changes in the allied department of Agriculture at this time. J. Jones Griffith, who had been professor of Agriculture since 1924, retired in June 1942. After a close contest, which went finally to a vote, E. J. Roberts, a senior member of the rival department of Agriculture at Bangor, was elected to the chair, which he occupied until 1945 when he returned to Bangor.[18] Agriculture was one of Aberystwyth's specialities ('the sacred cause of Agricultural education', as Ifor L. Evans once described it) and the war had heavily underlined its vital national importance.[19] When, therefore, in April 1946 the Council was faced with two particularly strong candidates with rather different specialist interests for the vacant headship of the department of Agriculture, it was decided to add a second chair and make a double appointment. J. E. Nichols, who was then Deputy Director of the Imperial Bureau of Animal Breeding and Genetics at Edinburgh, became professor of Agriculture (Animal Husbandry), and W. Ellison, a member of the department who had made an outstanding contribution to the work of the Agricultural Executive Committee in Montgomeryshire during the war, became professor of Agriculture (Crop Husbandry).[20] When T. W. Fagan retired from the chair of Agricultural Chemistry in 1939, the College, because of financial difficulties, was unable to make a professorial appointment, and R. O. Davies, an old Aberystwyth student, then a lecturer, who for years had worked in close co-operation with the Plant Breeding Station, was appointed to the headship of the department with the status of independent lecturer. And not until 1954 was it possible to restore the chair in Agricultural Chemistry, to which R. O. Davies, in belated recognition, was then elected unanimously.[21]

There was a change, too, at this time in the headship of another cognate department. In January 1946 A. W. Ashby returned to Oxford as Director of the Agricultural Economics Research Institute. Thereby Aberystwyth lost another outstanding teacher: during his years at the College, Ashby had done perhaps more than

[17] *Council Minutes* (6 May 1942), p. 47.
[18] Ibid. (6 March 1942), pp. 35–6. In July 1944 the Principals of Bangor and Aberystwyth, cousins and close friends as they were, exchanged sharp letters (indicating that the old jealousy was still very much alive) over the rival merits of their departments of Agriculture. C.A. P/Cr/D/4.
[19] Ifor L. Evans to B. B. Thomas, 3 September 1942. C.A. P/Cr/D/14.
[20] *Council Minutes* (26 April 1946), pp. 47–8.
[21] Ifor L. Evans, 'Agricultural Chemistry', pp. 1–3, Principal Goronwy Rees to R. O. Davies, 22 March 1954. C.A. P/Cr/E/1.

anyone else in Britain to establish Agricultural Economics as a legitimate university discipline; he insisted that his students must face the rigour of a sound training in Economics but he was also able to impart to them something of his own deep love of the countryside, and to persuade them to see the importance of understanding the sociology of rural communities. It is doubtful if the teaching of any other Agricultural Economist has quite so effectively straddled the sometimes conflicting demands of theory and practice.[22] Ashby's successor was E. F. Nash, an Oxford Classicist turned Economist, with a vast experience at home and abroad of the government agricultural services. His principal interest was to determine the role which agriculture ought to play in the national economy: rigorous in analysis and hard-hitting in debate, he was prepared to challenge many of the assumptions on which agricultural policy was based in the post-war years. Inevitably, he ruffled some feelings and was regarded as a controversial, even heretical, figure. Many of his ideas have been subsequently widely accepted.[23]

Finally, there was one other important addition to the agricultural work of the College. In February 1944 Lord Milford (formerly Sir Laurence Philipps) added one more item to the list of his benefactions to Aberystwyth: he offered the sum of £800 per annum for ten years to enable the College to establish a chair of Animal Health, a research professorship which was to be associated with the Welsh Plant Breeding Station.[24] There was a substantial application for the chair, and in February 1945 A. N. Worden of the Cambridge Institute of Animal Pathology, who had an exceptional range of experience in this and related fields, was unanimously elected.[25]

During the war years there were several other changes in the Senate. In 1944 two veteran members retired: J. L. A. Barbier, professor of French since 1909, and T. C. James, who had occupied the chair of Chemistry since 1921. They were replaced by E. R. Briggs, a Cambridge man who had been a member of the Bangor staff for some years before returning to teach at his old university, and C. W. Davies, the old Aberystwyth student who had been deputy head of department at the Battersea Polytechnic and honorary secretary of the Chemical Society for some years.[26] During the war, when several members of staff (D. A. Richards, for example, who designed a notably successful bomb-sight) were away on important secret work of military significance, I. C. Jones took charge of the Physics department. Increasingly, as the number of students dwindled, the formal

[22] The Countryman (Winter, 1953), p. 8.

[23] Agricultural Policy in Britain: Selected Papers by E. F. Nash (ed. G. McCrone and E. A. Attwood, University of Wales Press, 1965), pp. 9–12.

[24] Council Minutes (18 February 1944), p. 32.

[25] Ibid. (9 February 1945), pp. 24–5. Here, too, Aberystwyth was a pioneer: the Milford chair of Animal Health was the first of its kind to be established in a British university. A. N. Worden, 'Some Problems of Animal Health', Welsh Review, v, no. 1, 59.

[26] Council Minutes (10 March 1944), pp. 42–3.

academic work of the department came to be superseded by government-sponsored special courses in radio, radar, and electronics. After E. J. Williams' untimely death, R. M. Davies acted as head of the Physics department for a year with the rank of senior lecturer: in April 1946 he was promoted to the chair. He, too, was an old Aberystwyth student; genial and rotund, he had engaging traits: he invariably rolled his own cigarettes which he wrapped in liquorice paper, and as a built-in counter to the niggardliness of College equipment grants he coined the maxim, *'well i ni gael dau'* ('we had better have two'). Under his leadership in the post-war years an enlarged staff (partly reflecting the enhanced interest in a subject which made great strides during wartime) conducted a vigorous programme of research.[27]

In 1945 C. Daryll Forde, who had inspired some interesting postgraduate work by his students, resigned the Gregynog chair of Geography and Anthropology, as it was now called in honour of its founders. Before the appointment was advertised the Senate was asked to consider the duties of the new professor: the report asserted that, as the title of the chair suggested, Geography took precedence over Anthropology, and in making the appointment due account should be taken of the traditional emphasis at Aberystwyth on human geography rather than on Anthropology in the more specialist sense. In March 1946 E. G. Bowen, an old student and a member of staff since 1929, was elected to the chair. Trained by Fleure, he was ideally equipped to re-emphasize 'the older traditions of the department', and this he promptly attempted to do. However, during a long tenure, marked by a very considerable output of published work on a wide selection of subjects, E. G. Bowen also presided over a department which in recent years has had to adjust rapidly to the many new specialist developments (posing increasing difficulties of integration) in a discipline which, from its inception, was notably broad in its range. The success with which these difficult problems have been answered is best indicated by Aberystwyth's continued retention of the great reputation that it has always enjoyed as a centre of geographical studies.[28]

In 1942 E. A. Lewis, Sir John Williams professor of Welsh History, died suddenly. Quite apart from his distinction as a scholar and teacher, 'Doc' Lewis made an important contribution to the athletic side of College life. For almost thirty years he was chairman of the Central Athletic Board, the governing agency of all College sports activities. He was notably liberal in his attitudes, and always insisted, as *The Dragon* said, on 'the divine right of students to develop their own activities in their own way, subject to reasonable safeguards'.[29] E. A. Lewis exemplified a type which Aberystwyth in its hundred-year history has never lacked:

---

[27] Ibid. (26 April 1946), p. 48. W. M. Jones (and others), 'The Department of Physics', pp. 13–19.
[28] *Council Minutes* (7 December 1945, 6 March 1946), pp. 23, 37–8. *Geography at Aberystwyth*, pp. xxiii–xxix. Several of the articles in this volume indicate the nature of some of the new specialisms in Geography.   [29] Vol. lxiv. 4.

the long-serving member of staff who enjoys the respect as well as the affection of his students. The chair was not filled until 1945, but there was more than ample compensation for the delay in the appointment that was eventually made. For in June of that year David Williams became the second Sir John Williams professor. During the next twenty-two years he demonstrated again and again in a long list of publications what was already apparent in his earlier work: a superb meticulous scholarship and an unfailing capacity to write 'like an angel'. Before long, as the College student newspaper in a notable 'profile' which captured much of the essence of a tart and witty personality said, David Williams had 'wrested the leadership in Welsh historical scholarship' from the other Colleges in the University.[30] The committee which recommended David Williams' appointment suggested that T. Jones Pierce, who was the impressive runner-up for the chair, should be offered a senior appointment in the department. By an arrangement between the College and the National Library of Wales, a special lectureship in Welsh History was created for Jones Pierce; and in March 1948 he was elected to a newly created research chair in medieval Welsh History.[31]

There was also a new Registrar. In 1941 J. Morgan Jones had been seconded to war work in the Ministry of Agriculture, and he resigned his College appointment in January 1944 when he became Welsh Secretary of the Ministry.[32] There were over fifty applications for the Registrarship to which T. Maelgwyn Davies, an old student of the College who was then head of the Commerce department at the Oxford Technical College, was elected.[33] Thus began a long tenure of more than twenty years during which the authority and influence of the new Registrar grew steadily, not least because of his unflagging close interest in the College and all its concerns.

There is no doubt that the re-establishment of the office of Registrar in 1936 had been wise; it had certainly considerably improved the quality of College administration.[34] And this in turn made a contribution to the patient attempt to reduce the indebtedness of the College. In the five years before the war nearly £20,000 of a total debt of almost £70,000 was liquidated. The financial position was improved still further when in 1939, in response to earlier prodding by the U.G.C., all the Welsh Colleges introduced a higher scale of fees for new student entrants. Moreover, during the war years there was a substantial annual excess of income over expenditure: the basic grant received via the University from the

[30] *Council Minutes* (22 June 1945), pp. 45–6. H. A. Marquand, 'David Williams', *Welsh Hist. Rev.*, iii. 337–43. *Courier* (19 May 1956). The retirement of this acknowledged doyen of Welsh historians in 1967 was marked by a *festschrift* (*Welsh Hist. Rev.*, iii), to which some of his former pupils, several of whom had gone on to distinguished careers, contributed.

[31] *Council Minutes* (22 June 1945, 19 March 1948), pp. 46, 45–6.

[32] Ifor L. Evans to P. Scott, 20 February 1941. C.A. P/Cr/D/15. *Council Minutes* (18 February 1944), p. 31.

[33] Ibid. (14 April 1944), p. 45.   [34] *Report on the work and needs of the College* (1944), p. 3.

Treasury and the Welsh local authorities remained at its immediate pre-war level, despite the reduction in the work of the College and some enforced wartime economies. There was also a substantial increase in receipts from vacation lettings in the halls of residence: for once Aberystwyth's small size and supposed isolation (moderately safe from enemy bombing) became decided advantages. Between 1939 and 1943 another £28,000 of liability was extinguished. There was also an annual surplus in the first years after the war, and it was thus possible to continue, though more modestly, the policy of liquidating debts. It had taken the College 'many long and painful years' substantially to recover from the incubus of very heavy liabilities incurred in the emergency after the 1914–18 war.[35]

There were other encouraging signs of an improvement in the general financial position of the College. At long last, after seemingly endless delays caused by complex political, legal, and financial difficulties, the distribution to the secular beneficiaries of a substantial portion of the assets of the disestablished Church in Wales was in sight. A meeting of beneficiaries in January 1940 was not edifying. Some of the local authorities, Cardiff in particular, still resisted a national pooling of resources: 'Lord, how I hate the village pump', Burdon Evans wrote in disgust. Ifor L. Evans said that the meeting made him 'think of a crowd of vultures waiting to descend upon their prey', and three months later he wrote gloomily of 'the hopeless problem' posed by the remaining difficulties of the settlement.[36] These fears were unnecessarily pessimistic: during the war years the College began to receive its considerable share of the available assets, partly in capital payments, partly in the form of an annual income derived from the former Capitular estates which were transferred to the University by the Welsh Church Commissioners in July 1940, and administered subsequently by the University Estates Committee. For many years Ifor L. Evans was chairman of this Committee (a duty for which by inclination and experience he was well equipped), and his prudent stewardship of the assets committed to his care was not the least of his services to the University and the College. In due course very considerable sums in cash, stocks, income from land and from investments accrued to the College: in all, by July 1950, over £140,000 had been received.[37] The Colleges and the University had already

[35] *Report on the work and needs of the College* (1944), pp. 3–6. *Interim Report to the U.G.C.* (June 1950), pp. 8–11. By 1940 Alexandra Hall was free of debt, but Plynlymon, 'the most embarrassing' entry in 'the College balance sheet', accounted for almost £18,000 of liability. *The capital indebtedness of the U.C.W., 30 June 1940*, p. 5. Between 1939 and 1947 the debt of the Agriculture departments was reduced from £19,621 to £2,867. *Report on the work and needs of the Agricultural Departments* (October 1947), p. 33.

[36] Exchange of letters, W. J. Burdon Evans and Ifor L. Evans, 26, 29 January, and 3 April 1940. C.A. P/Cr/D/7.

[37] *Report on Trust Funds* (August 1944), pp. 20–3. D. Emrys Evans, op. cit., pp. 102, 127. 'Tithe and Capitular Monies: statement of Income and Expenditure to 31 July 1950'. C.A. There is a good short study of the long struggle over Disestablishment in K. O. Morgan, *Freedom or Sacrilege?: a history of the campaign for Welsh Disestablishment* (Church in Wales publications, 1965).

agreed that these additional resources should be devoted to objects bearing directly upon student welfare, particularly hostels for men and the provision of additional general amenities.[38]

Soon after the war the College also received two private benefactions of very great value. Ifor L. Evans had succeeded in engaging the interest in the College of Sir D. Owen Evans, Liberal M.P. for Cardiganshire for several years, who became Treasurer in 1938. When Sir David died in 1945, the College, which was nominated as residuary legatee of his estate, benefited to the extent of £35,000, and this large sum was unencumbered with any conditions whatsoever. It was decided to apply the income derived from the benefaction to purposes (a special lectureship fund, for example) for which financial provision could not otherwise be made.[39] And in 1946 another generous benefactor rescued the College from a difficult situation which was thought to pose a serious threat to the whole future of the Penglais site.

During the inter-war years Aberystwyth corporation had built a small council housing estate at Penparcau, which had not by any means answered the needs of the town. Additional land at Penparcau was available for further council building after the war, but, reasonably enough, the corporation wished to avoid concentrating its large housing programme in one part of the borough. Accordingly, it had taken steps compulsorily to acquire land opposite the entrance to the National Library on Penglais, where it was intended to build fifty council houses. The authorities of the College and the National Library were aghast: an agglomeration of small dwellings of this type threatened the whole basis of the planned future development of the hill site, which called for 'a small number of relatively large buildings', not 'a large number of small buildings' anywhere in the vicinity, as was urged in a strong plea to the corporation to reconsider. At first it seemed unlikely that the corporation would rescind its decision: some members were evidently moved by social resentments, and it is ironic that a College that had always justly prided itself on its very close identification with the mass of ordinary Welsh people should be accused of hostility to the interests of the working class.

In this dire emergency Ifor L. Evans appealed to D. Alban Davies, a member of the College Council, a retired London milk merchant who had promised to do something substantial for the College at some future date. The response was immediate and nothing short of magnificent.

It would be nothing less than a tragedy to the College, the National Library and the town of Aberystwyth, if the Penglais estate were to be spoiled by building developments unworthy of this magnificent national site [Alban Davies wrote to the Principal].

The value of Penglais cannot be measured in £.s.d., and it would be an everlasting

---

[38] *Council Minutes* (18 February 1938), pp. 59–61.
[39] Ibid. (28 March, 18 July 1947), pp. 36, 54. *Interim Report to the U.G.C.* (June 1950), p. 12.

shame to everyone concerned in its welfare if this unexpected opportunity to purchase the estate were lost. . . . All I want to say is: buy as best you can and I will foot the bill. I make no conditions or restrictions whatsoever, as these might hamper future developments.

Within forty-eight hours, 205 acres of the Penglais estate had been bought (the corporation's compulsory purchase had not as yet been completed) for £34,000. A deputation (led by Dr. Thomas Jones) from the College and the National Library returned to plead with the corporation. The President took up the charge that the College was hostile to working-class housing in close proximity to the new site; as he said, the College was opposed to any house building in the vicinity. He regretted the introduction of class issues; he himself was 'working class, and proud of it', and so overwhelmingly were the students and staff of the College. If the corporation would forgo its building programme on Penglais, the College offered to make over on perpetual lease at a nominal rent twenty-three acres of the land recently purchased for use as a public park for the town. After a sharp debate lasting three hours, the Council's Public Works Committee agreed by eleven votes to seven to recommend acceptance of the conditional offer, a proposal subsequently endorsed by the full Council. 'The splendid site is saved', exulted the President of the College whose interest in its proper development went back to the days of Lord Rendel's pioneer purchase.[40]

Ever since these early days the College and the National Library had a coequal interest in the Penglais site, although, in the first instance, the land had been provided by friends of the College, and it was always clear that much the greater part of it would be required for new teaching and other university buildings. Nevertheless, it was agreed doctrine that the needs of the National Library must be fully met. Indeed, the Penglais Trustees, who were vested with charge of the eighty-seven acres of the Davies Bryan benefaction, were empowered to allot to the National Library of Wales any part of the property which was considered 'necessary for the extension and benefit of the Library and the preservation of its amenities'. Eventually, by a series of agreements, the Library came to own, in all, eighteen acres of land on Penglais.[41]

The first College building constructed on the site after the war was placed alongside the National Library. This was the realization of a scheme that had a long premeditation. There had always been an overwhelmingly strong case for making Aberystwyth a more or less completely residential college, and certainly the most ardent friends of the College had worked for this for many long years.

[40] *Council Minutes* (23 October 1946), p. 2. *Cambrian News* (21 June 1946). Thomas Jones, *A Diary with Letters, 1931–1950*, pp. 542–3. At the same time D. Alban Davies also bought fifteen acres of land at Plas Hendre for the College, and made an unconditional gift of £10,000 to the Agricultural Development Fund. It can scarcely be said that the public park has been developed as well as it might have been.

[41] *Report on the Quinquennial period 1934–1939* (October 1939), pp. 45–6, Sir William Davies to Ifor L. Evans, 10 June 1938. C.A. P/Cr/D/5.

Apart from Oxford and Cambridge, the proportion of Aberystwyth students coming from outside a thirty-mile radius was higher than at any other British university. As far as the University of Wales was concerned, Aberystwyth far outstripped its sister Colleges in this respect: in 1938-9, for example, the figure for the senior College was 89 per cent, against Bangor's 56 per cent, Cardiff's 11 per cent, and 7 per cent only for Swansea.[42] A hall of residence for men students was accorded fourth place in the list of priorities drawn up by the College in 1935. On social and academic grounds, the U.G.C. had always been strongly in favour of residential accommodation, although before the war it was unable to provide capital grants, other than token payments, for this purpose.[43] In 1938, when there was some prospect that the amenity money from the Welsh Church disestablishment would be forthcoming, the College decided to go ahead with its plan for halls of residence for men.

The plan provided for two ideally-sized halls, each containing seventy-two single study bedrooms (designed as a compromise between the Oxbridge 'staircase' arrangement and the 'corridor' pattern customary in Redbrick universities), appropriate common-rooms, a refectory, some staff accommodation, and between the twin halls there was to be a house for a married Warden. By way of encouragement, the U.G.C. offered a non-recurrent grant of £8,000.[44] Excavation and levelling of the site was completed by 1939. After the war, the government and the U.G.C., having willed the end of a considerable expansion of universities, had no choice but to provide the means: capital grants for university building, including halls of residence, now became available. In the post-war years utility models of necessity retained their currency; the original plan for halls of residence had to be modified. A much larger single unit (to be built in stages) replaced the better-sized twin halls, and the detached house for the Warden disappeared from the plan, a change which, on balance, was no great loss.

Early in 1948 work began, but within months serious difficulties arose: it was discovered that a belt of soft clay underlay the foundations (a good deal of the time of Alan Wood, the recently appointed professor of Geology, had to be spent in taking anxious soundings), and eventually the problem had to be solved by an elaborate process of piling, which added substantially to the cost of construction. Mercifully, after some delay, the mounting concern of the College authorities was allayed when the University Grants Committee agreed to contribute £140,000 towards the £158,000 which had been expended. By 1951 the first stage of the new hall was completed and opened. Faced with Forest of Dean stone, it possessed a dignity which owed something to its subdued, even sombre, exterior; there were several superb rooms, notably a senior common room of particularly fine pro-

[42] Report on the work and needs of the College (1944), p. 37.

[43] University Development from 1935 to 1947 (U.G.C.), p. 54.

[44] Council Minutes (29 June 1938), pp. 94–6. Report on the work and needs of the College (1944), pp. 37–8.

portions. Appropriately enough, the new hall was named Pantycelyn, in honour of William Williams, the greatest of Welsh hymnodists.[45]

Meantime, there had been other developments in residential accommodation for men students. In October 1946 Plynlymon was reopened as a hall for men, and continued so until 1961, when it again became a hostel for women students for a short period. In 1948 Pantyfedwen, a large building at Borth, formerly a hotel, was leased from *Urdd Gobaith Cymru* (The Welsh League of Youth) for use as a hostel for men. The fact that accommodation thus far away in a small village poorly served by public transport had to be taken up is an indication of the shifts to which the College had to resort at this time. This rather desperate expedient was abandoned as soon as possible: nevertheless, despite its location, badly cut off from the mainstream of College life, a succession of lively young Wardens managed to create a strong sense of community in this small outpost at Borth. In 1950, with the aid of a grant of £23,000 from the University Grants Committee, other hotel property on the seafront at Aberystwyth was taken over and turned into a hall for men under the name Ceredigion.[46] These converted hostels could not in any way match the facilities and quality of accommodation at Pantycelyn. But as the number of students in each of them was not large, it was quickly possible, given a good Warden, for a fine hall spirit to be developed and carefully nourished thereafter.

Alexandra Hall remained the home of most women students. In an attempt to counter the danger of anonymity and impersonality, the bane of very large hostels, which all too easily can nullify the valuable social and academic experience residential life is designed to provide, a 'family' system had been developed within the hall. Seating arrangements for the formal evening meal ensured that students of all years were brought into regular contact. In many instances these small groups at separate tables developed an identity, and often acted as a countervailing influence to the natural tendency of like to cleave to like. It was immensely helpful for new members of the hall to be brought thus naturally into touch with their seniors, who were able to offer useful advice and initiate the newcomers into the traditions of the community. Ever since 1925 Alexandra Hall had been in the charge of Mrs. K. Guthkelch, who was entitled Senior Warden and vested with a special responsibility for the discipline of women students. At the time of her appointment, one influential old student was thoroughly alarmed at the embarrassing possibilities contained in the Senior Warden's surname.

Can't you get Mrs. Guthkelch to change her name [H. Howard Humphries wrote to J. H. Davies]? Heaven only knows what ribald youth will invent in substitution for such a . . . name. I fancy you would have made hay with it in your time![47]

---

[45] *Interim Report to the U.G.C.* (June 1950), p. 13. *Council Minutes* (31 October, 7 December 1951), pp. 8, 27.
[46] *Interim Report to the U.G.C.* (June 1950), p. 13. *Council Minutes* (28 October 1949), p. 8.
[47] 29 June 1925. N.L.W. J. H. Davies MSS. (Corr.).

As a matter of fact, nothing of the sort occurred: the Senior Warden, a powerful, indeed formidable, personality, who remained at Alexandra Hall for over twenty years, was known to succeeding generations of students usually as 'Mrs. G', sometimes, the mark of personage, as 'The G'.[48]

But, of course, despite the increase in residential accommodation, most men students at Aberystwyth continued to live in lodgings. From 1946 onwards for some years the ex-servicemen dominated student life, as they had done after the 1914–18 war. Yet there were some differences between the two post-war generations: indeed, the mood in which student-soldiers had gone off to the two wars had been quite different. In 1914, and subsequently for a time, they were moved by strong feelings of patriotic, even romantic, emotion: in 1939 and the following years they enlisted (or more probably were called up as required) soberly, under no illusions about what lay ahead. In fact, although there were exceptions (notably for those taken prisoner by the Japanese), in most cases in the later war reality was not quite as bad as had been feared: the First World War, with its apparently senseless trench-warfare slaughter, was a traumatic experience *en masse* for British troops for which, in scale and sustained savagery, there was no equivalent between 1939 and 1945 for the armies of the United Kingdom. After 1918 the men who returned to College knew that they were lucky to be alive; their relief was expressed in a boisterous, devil-may-care attitude to life and sometimes to work which left the staid College authorities puzzled and occasionally aghast. 'They drink, swear and break all the College rules', the professor of Education wrote to E. T. Davis, one of his former students. 'We don't understand them. Come and help us.'[49] For a time the hapless authorities could do little other than turn a diplomatic blind eye and hope for the best. Eventually, the ex-servicemen of the early twenties, so many of whom had undergone experiences that marked them as men apart with little in common with boys straight from school, left College and in time the old disciplinary code was substantially restored.

The ex-servicemen who returned, or first came up, to College in 1945 and subsequently were much less rumbustious. College regulations were still strait-laced in many respects: women students were not allowed to entertain men in their rooms in hall; there was an early curfew at night for women hostel residents, and all students were forbidden to enter licensed premises. Some of these restrictions had little effect on the behaviour of ex-servicemen after 1946: 'the pubs

[48] Idris C. Bell, 'Notes on Aber. in the late Thirties', p. 10. In January 1938 Mrs. Guthkelch and her students had to evacuate Alexandra Hall for a time when a great storm swept away several hundred yards of the Promenade and the foundations of the building were exposed to the sea.

[49] E. T. Davis, who had served for three years with the army in Greece, replied, 'Oh, I understand them alright. If they start swearing in my presence, I'll soon show them they are amateurs, for I know all that vocabulary.' This interesting illustration of fighting fire with fire is contained in a letter from E. T. Davis, who had a distinguished career later as Director of Education in Pembrokeshire and elsewhere, to Principal Thomas Parry, 3 February 1962. C.A. P/Cr/F/3.

were packed with ex-servicemen swinging the lamp', quite often in the presence
of members of staff, a conjunction unthinkable before 1945. Certainly the College
was 'full of ex-officers' greatcoats with the badges and epaulettes removed', and
young freshers up from school were no doubt 'hopelessly overshadowed' by men
who were anything up to five or eight years older, some of them married with
children.[50] But the returning servicemen quickly submerged their 'memories of
the immediate past', there was no inclination to form an aggressive ex-servicemen's
society (as in 1919), and many 'strove to re-create the kind of College society that
they had once known, or believed that they remembered'. There was, in fact,
almost no unseemly conduct in the post-war years, and no disposition to challenge
authority in any downright way: the general reaction to the petty restrictions of
College regulations was one of 'amused indifference', not the 'animated hostility'
expressed by ex-service students after the earlier war. Possibly the College authorities, too, had become a little more supple with the passage of the years. Certainly
many members of staff were impressed with the serious purpose with which most
ex-service students returned to academic work. The result of all this was that, in
the years after the 1939–45 war, despite a larger, much more heterogeneous student
body, the College remained a cohesive community with an immensely strong
corporate loyalty.[51]

Of course the fact that academic work and social activity were still mainly
centred on the old College building helped enormously in this respect. During the
mid-morning break between classes, Quad was always packed with students; the
old formalized perambulation had gone, but this was the time for announcements
of matters of general interest. From the 'grid' the student President talked directly
to his constituents, as had all his predecessors, and there is no doubt that this
immediacy of communication with virtually a daily general assembly kept the
officers in close touch with those they represented, accustomed the student body
to the leadership of their accredited spokesmen, and emphasized repeatedly,
as perhaps no other arrangement possibly could, the unity of the whole.

It was a boom time for College societies. Debates were generally well attended
and conducted with reasonable decorum; *Y Geltaidd* continued to meet on Mon-
day evenings, and its tone was then less political than it was to become subsequently.
There was a considerable interest in politics, but this expressed itself through the
political clubs (of which the Socialist Society was numerically the strongest and
perhaps the most vigorous, at least for a time) rather than in any more generalized
fashion. Despite post-war shortages, social life became more sophisticated: grants,
particularly for ex-servicemen, were not ungenerous, and the type of Aberystwyth

---

[50] J. L. Brace, 'U.C.W., 1946–52', p. 2. Of course a visit to the Black Lion inn during the 1930s
would have shown that the ex-servicemen had been anticipated, though moderately discreetly. Idris
C. Bell, loc. cit., pp. 2–3.

[51] W. J. Anthony-Jones, 'Aberystwyth, 1946–1948', pp. 2–4. *The Dragon*, lxix. 1.

student (of whom since 1872 there had always been some) who existed close to the breadline disappeared. The town's fish and chip shops were as popular as ever, but numbers of students were now seen eating in restaurants and hotels at times other than the grand occasions as in the past. There was no Friday exodus from Aberystwyth; indeed, the weekend, with its sequence of Debates Union meeting on Friday, College matches on the Vicarage Field on Saturday afternoon and a packed-out dance at the Pier in the evening, followed on Sunday afternoon perhaps by Choral Union, was 'a peak period in the social life of the College'.[52]

In the immediate post-war years College athletic teams were much stronger than usual. 'The rugby team now consisted of men not boys', and the tough mining-valley teams from South Wales, which had always provided the staple opposition of the College XV, soon learned the difference.[53] There was a very strong soccer team which in 1946–7 had a series of runaway victories *en route* to the U.A.U. Final where, sapped by influenza, it had to swallow some of its own medicine at the hands of Manchester University. Earlier in 1947 the Rag festivities had been revived: the culmination was a massive mile-long procession through the town in which young students and ex-service seniors combined in a great attempt to recapture some of the light-hearted pageantry of the past. A sum of £1,200 was raised for local charities, and a tradition of fund-raising for worthy purposes was established which, in later years, was to produce astonishingly large amounts of money.[54] And a month or two later the College Dramatics club set 'a new standard' of performance with a memorable presentation of Sean O'Casey's 'Juno and the Paycock', in which Rachel Roberts, who later became an internationally known film star, was the outstanding player.[55]

The relations of staff and students in these years remained friendly, in accordance with the Aberystwyth tradition. In 1951 the Principal, with legitimate pride, could write: 'For a number of years, we have maintained in this College a *modus vivendi* between staff and students which I believe to be unique . . . if it went, much of me would go with it.'[56] There is no doubt that Ifor L. Evans was speaking genuinely from the heart here. But for most students at this time the Principal, engrossed in the higher business of the College, was a remote figure rarely to be seen. More often than not, for students, the College was embodied in the Vice-Principal, and here, too, down the years Aberystwyth had been fortunate. Beginning with J. W. Marshall, the College had discovered a succession of Vice-Principals (usually reappointed annually for several years) who combined geniality with the necessary touch of authority, and brought a large reserve of downright common sense to bear on the awkward situations with which they were sometimes confronted. At one time it seemed quite likely that this office would be developed

[52] W. J. Anthony-Jones, loc. cit., p. 3. J. L. Brace, loc. cit., p. 2.   [53] Ibid., p. 2.
[54] *Western Mail* (24 February 1947).   [55] *The Dragon*, lxix. 17.
[56] Ifor L. Evans to the President of S.R.C., 3 December 1951. C.A. P/Cr/E/4.

PLATE 10

Morgan Goronwy Rees
(Principal, 1953–1957)

Sir David Hughes Parry
(President, 1955–1964)

PLATE 11

Thomas Parry
(Principal, 1958–1969)

Sir Ben Bowen Thomas
(President, 1964–   )

into an effective Deputy Principalship. In 1934, when Ifor L. Evans was first appointed and when the office of Registrar was still in abeyance, Lord Davies in an interesting paper on the future of the College had insisted that the maintenance of 'close personal relationships' between staff and students ought to be a primary concern of the Principal. In the President's opinion the 'curse of the present system' was that it divorced the Principal from the social life of the College; 'his administrative duties . . . swamped his responsibilities as a leader'. Lord Davies argued powerfully for a substantial devolution of administrative duties; if this were not done, the new Principal, with the best will in the world, could do no more than 'beat against the bars of the cage', constricted by the routine of business. The answer was to revive the office of Registrar, 'which should never have been abolished', and to develop the Vice-Principalship.[57]

In his reply to Lord Davies' paper, Ifor L. Evans agreed substantially with the line of argument put forward by the President, not least because for two years out of every eight the Principal was saddled additionally with the Vice-Chancellorship of the University. He already felt 'a very real need' for a Deputy, 'who would stand to him in much the same relationship as does the Chief Secretary to the Governor of a Colony'. Ifor L. Evans was quite clear that a 'Vice-Principal, who is also a head of a department', could not be 'expected to play this role', because the demands of his chair made it impossible. There should, therefore, be a 'Deputy-Principal-cum-Registrar', a person of high academic standing, a good committee man, who should be 'imbued with the belief that [the] College is a national institution, and be able to prove as much to a Welsh audience'.[58]

Financial stringencies ruled out this imaginative suggestion which, at least to some extent, would have enabled Principals once again to make something like the important direct impact on their students that T. C. Edwards had done in the early years of the College. As it was, a Registrar was appointed, and the Vice-Principalship remained undeveloped, a part-time additional appointment held by a busy senior professor who fulfilled his disciplinary functions, answered the many social demands on his time, and on occasion deputized uneasily for the Principal as best he could after he had coped with the needs of his department.[59] Nevertheless, despite these difficulties, a succession of Vice-Principals at the College managed to wear their different hats with considerable aplomb. When Gwilym Owen, who had succeeded Edward Edwards, had to retire in 1937, T. C. James became Vice-Principal and continued so until he vacated his Chemistry chair in 1944. Despite his physical slightness, he had an obvious air of authority that registered effectively with students. But he was no mere martinet and, in fact, it was in 1943, during his Vice-Principalship, that a Students' Disciplinary Committee

---

[57] 'The College and its Future', 3 April 1934. N.L.W. Llandinam MSS. (U.C.W. (1)), Gen. Corr.
[58] 'Devolution of Duties' [April 1934]. N.L.W. Ibid.
[59] 'Office of Vice-Principal', *Council Minutes* (16 October 1935), p. 26.

was instituted to act as a court of first instance in all breaches of discipline. This useful exercise in student self-government worked quite well; at any rate, in 1954, when the machinery of College discipline was subjected to review and simplification, there was then no question of its discontinuance.[60]

T. C. James was succeeded by R. B. Forrester, who quite obviously thoroughly enjoyed his long tenure as Vice-Principal. Unfailingly affable, he was a great social success, immensely popular with students, and there is no doubt that his relaxed geniality nicely lubricated the dealings of the College establishment with the mass of students in the years after the war.[61] He was the last of the old-style Vice-Principals who were reappointed to office for years on end. When he retired in 1951, the Senate recommended that, for the future, the office should be held by its members in rotation, normally for a period of two years.[62] There was, no doubt, much to be said for the change. It was more than likely that a department would be at some disadvantage if its academic head served as Vice-Principal for a lengthy period: on the other hand, whatever the qualities of the individuals appointed in succession to the position, a two-year period was scarcely long enough in which to build up that wide variety of personal relationships, based on mutual confidence, with other College personnel which is so vital to the exercise of the office. It ought, perhaps, to be a case of horses for courses: a notably successful Vice-Principal might well be given the option of an extended run beyond two years, particularly if he has a strong experienced second in his academic department who can deputize effectively for him.

R. B. Forrester was succeeded in the chair of Economics by Arthur Beacham, an old Aberystwyth student who had been professor of Industrial Relations at Cardiff since 1947. Energetic and exceptionally businesslike, the new member of Senate soon made his presence felt. Since 1945 there had been some few other changes in the professoriate. E. D. T. Jenkins had retired in June 1947, and the chair of Classics went to W. H. Davies, an old Cardiff student latterly a lecturer at University College, London. In January 1947 H. P. Lewis, who had been professor of Geology since 1931, died. He was replaced by Alan Wood, who was then an assistant professor at London and whose contributions to research in palaeontology, stratigraphy, and geomorphology had been recognized by an award from the Geological Society of London.[63]

In 1948 David de Lloyd, professor of Music since 1927, died. Temperamentally he and Walford Davies, the man he followed in the chair, were antithetical. Walford Davies was a brilliant extrovert showman: David de Lloyd was shy and habitually reserved outside the circle of family and friends. He had a more than

[60] Subcommittee Report, 26 January 1954. C.A. P/Cr/E/3.
[61] *The Dragon*, lxxiii. 19, and *Courier* (19 May 1951), for student regard for R. B. Forrester.
[62] *Council Minutes* (14 March 1951), p. 44.
[63] Ibid. (14 March 1951, 13 June, and 18 July 1947), pp. 31, 49, 51.

sufficient mastery of instrumental music, but, Welsh to the core, 'music was to him essentially something to be sung'. In collaboration with his close friend, Ifor L. Evans, he had published a selection of Welsh hymn tunes and lyrics, but 'a monumental collection' of over 400 Welsh melodies which he had arranged over the years had not been published at the time of his death. During David de Lloyd's long tenure the Music department had continued in its weekly and other concerts to give immense pleasure to many members of the College and some of the people of the town and district.[64] The chair remained vacant for two years. During the interregnum the department was headed by Charles Clements, lecturer in Music, the outstandingly gifted pianist. In 1950 H. I. Parrott, an Oxford man then on the staff of Birmingham University, was appointed to the Gregynog chair of Music, which he has continued to occupy down to the present time.[65]

The Music department, of course, made an important contribution to the adult education extension work undertaken by the College. During the late 1930s, there had been a gradual expansion of the work of the Extra-Mural department: three resident tutors had been appointed to organize classes and pioneer adult education generally in Carmarthenshire, Pembrokeshire, and the combined area of Montgomeryshire and Radnorshire; between 1934 and 1939 the activity of the department, measured by the number of classes organized and the students attending them, had gone up by almost 30 per cent. After a short period of uncertainty at the outbreak of war in 1939, there was a very rapid further expansion during the next four years; many part-time tutors were recruited to assist, new and difficult ground was broken with the aid of short courses (sometimes using the *Aelwydydd* (branches) of *Urdd Gobaith Cymru* (The Welsh League of Youth) as cadres for expansion), and the Extra-Mural work of the College generally was considerably more than doubled. Within the range of subjects taught, Welsh Studies, Economics and Politics, International Relations, Biblical Studies, Philosophy, and Music, in that order, were most in demand. In 1935 just over half the classes were conducted in Welsh, rather more than a third in English, and the rest bilingually: by 1944, however, the pattern had changed, and over three-quarters of the classes organized were carried on through the medium of Welsh. This substantial change partly reflected the stronger response which, for a variety of traditional reasons, was to be expected in the Welsh-speaking districts; more particularly, it was the result of a concentrated effort, which owed a good deal to the assistance provided by *Urdd Gobaith Cymru*. Inevitably, some of these classes were of a very modest standard. They were largely discontinued after the war: nevertheless, they helped considerably to establish a tradition of adult education work in areas which often hitherto had remained undeveloped. Since the

---

[64] Ifor L. Evans, 'David de Lloyd, 1883–1948', C.A. P/D/Arts. *Mawl yr Oesoedd* (ed. Ifor L. Evans and David de Lloyd, Cardiff, 1951).   [65] *Council Minutes* (10 July 1950), pp. 53–4.

war there has been a considerable expansion of classes conducted in English and the balance of the two languages is now more even.[66]

These encouraging advances aside, the department was not without its difficulties during the war years. In December 1941 B. B. Thomas, who had succeeded Herbert Morgan as Director of Extra-Mural Studies the year before, was seconded to war work of national importance with the Ministry of Labour. The leadership of the department thereupon devolved upon Ifan ab Owen Edwards, founder of *Urdd Gobaith Cymru*, who was appointed Vice-Chairman of the Extra-Mural Classes committee.[67] There was also a sharp bout of in-fighting with sister organizations in which rival ambitions for a time outweighed the familial relationship. In 1943 a fierce struggle developed between Cardiff and Aberystwyth over the control of an extension class at Builth Wells, which lay on the blurred border between the extra-mural areas of the two Colleges. The Builth class members evidently preferred Aberystwyth, but Cardiff would not give way: a running fight, in which the two Principals were involved, developed and continued for some time. An attempt had been made not long before to demarcate the respective areas of the four constituent Colleges, but a good deal of ground remained in dispute. Aberystwyth had especial difficulties in this respect because, centrally placed, it was the one College which shared a border (and, therefore, sooner or later, would very likely be involved in demarcation wrangles) with all three sister departments.

In this matter of delimitation of areas [Ifan ab Owen Edwards wrote to Principal J. F. Rees of Cardiff in 1943] I feel very much like the Germans, with the Russians pressing from the north, and the British and Americans attacking the 'under-belly'. It is high time that extra-mural areas should be settled.[68]

It was easier to call for a sensible settlement than to bring it about, for the four Colleges seem to have held to their claims to disputed territory with remarkable tenacity, and several more years elapsed before this problem, an endless source of bad feeling, was finally removed.[69]

There were similar difficulties within the Aberystwyth extra-mural area itself, for the department's relations with the Workers' Educational Association were not always of the best. The College territory, 'the most completely rural of all the Extra-Mural areas of England and Wales', was not promising ground for the W.E.A. There was no vigorous, strongly organized working-class movement

[66] 'Report on the work and needs of the department of Extra-Mural Studies' (September 1944), pp. 1–8. C.A. P/Cr/D/6. *University Extension Board: Survey of Adult Education in Wales* (Cardiff, 1940), pp. 7–47. 'Report on Adult Education in Wales' (The Co-ordinating Committee for Adult Education in Wales, 1970), pp. 1–20.

[67] *Council Minutes* (6 March 1942), p. 42.   [68] June 1943. C.A. P/Cr/D/6.

[69] As late as 1953 the guerrilla-style warfare with Cardiff over the border in Breconshire was still on, and at the same time there was a dispute with Bangor over jurisdiction at Bala. 'College Boundary in Breconshire', December 1953. C.A. P/Cr/E/5.

in these rural counties which would look to the W.E.A. rather than the College for a lead in adult education, and the W.E.A. district offices at Bangor and Cardiff were too far away to exert any effective influence. Indeed, for many years adult education in the Aberystwyth area had not been organized, as elsewhere, by a joint committee of the University institution and the W.E.A., but by a College committee on which the local education committees and the W.E.A. had some representation.[70] In 1934 Thomas Jones had registered a vigorous but ineffective protest on behalf of the W.E.A. against the small representation accorded to it on the College committee.[71] There may have been a case for an increased representation on grounds of general principle, but the fact was that the W.E.A., as its official spokesman admitted, had no more than a token organization in the rural areas.[72] Accordingly, in 1941 the College Extra-Mural department had itself begun the preliminary spade-work which in other areas was often carried out by the W.E.A. In these circumstances there was very little scope for the voluntary organization in the Aberystwyth area, even if it had suddenly developed the capacity to begin operations.

It is evident that at this time Aberystwyth was not looked upon with favour by the Welsh W.E.A. At a stormy meeting of the University Extension Board at Shrewsbury in February 1944, Ifan ab Owen Edwards had to fight hard to defeat a W.E.A. motion calling for an embargo on short courses organized by the Aberystwyth Extra-Mural department. This was his only success. 'I failed to get a seconder for anything [else]', he reported to the Principal. 'If I moved my lips, I was a marked man by all the legions of the W.E.A. I used extreme moderation, but felt like blowing the lot up.'[73] However, there is evidence that relations had improved considerably by the middle 1950s, helped perhaps by the substitution in 1951 of a new Joint committee (with a different balance of representation of the interested parties) for the old College committee which had made the running for so long.[74]

It was unfortunate that the University Extension Board, which might have been expected to have resolved these rivalries, lacked effective authority. The Haldane Commissioners, whose recommendation had brought it into existence, had not made sufficient provision for answering the problems that arose from conflicting claims to jurisdiction. Indeed, for many years at any rate, it was true, as Thomas Jones said in 1941: 'No one would mistake the University Extension Board for a power-house; for the source of heat and light of a national movement it has a

---

[70] 'Draft Memorandum prepared at the request of the University Extension Board' (October 1953), pp. 1–3. C.A. P/Cr/E/5.

[71] Thomas Jones to Herbert Morgan, and to A. S. Firth, 14 and 22 March 1934. N.L.W. Thomas Jones MSS. Class J, ff. 88, 98.

[72] A. S. Firth to Thomas Jones, 15 March 1934. N.L.W. Ibid., f. 92.

[73] 19 February 1944. C.A. P/Cr/D/6.

[74] 'Memorandum prepared by the Director of Extra-Mural Studies', March 1955. C.A. P/Cr/E/5.

low candlepower.'[75] But despite these irritating distractions, the fact is that the department of Extra-Mural Studies at Aberystwyth went on from strength to strength. Successive Directors gave a strong lead: in 1945 B. B. Thomas resigned to become Secretary of the Welsh Department of the Board of Education; he was replaced in 1946 by Ifan ab Owen Edwards, who was followed in 1949 by A. D. Rees, a social anthropologist who has published interesting work and whose tenure has continued to the present day. The record of the department is impressive: in 1955 it could be said (and this remains true today) with legitimate pride that 'the area as a whole has a fuller provision of adult education classes in relation to population than any other extra-mural area in the British Isles'.[76]

In the 1950s, too, there were important developments concerning another department of the College which, through the years, had steadily maintained the great reputation that it had established soon after its foundation. By 1950 the Welsh Plant Breeding Station urgently needed additional land for its operations. It already had a fine headquarters on Penglais, but it was also important that its field laboratories should be in close proximity to the main building, and it was by then apparent that an acreage sufficient for this purpose would not be available on the hill site. Moreover, the Station required not only more land but better land than was currently available to it. Just at that juncture the Gogerddan estate, a mile or two away from Penglais, came on the market, and in September 1950 the College bought 3,800 acres of Gogerddan land for £96,000. To some extent this transaction in real estate was designed (particularly by Principal Ifor L. Evans, who pushed the venture with some enthusiasm and, considering the run-down state of much of the property, some willingness to take risks) as a hedge against inflation for College funds.[77] But there was also the fact that the historic mansion, with the inner ring of the estate, formerly the home farm, could be adapted to provide an ideal permanent headquarters, with ample land nearby for extended field operations, for the Plant Breeding Station. With the aid of a grant from the University Grants Committee, the old mansion was handsomely converted (and, appropriately, inscribed with the name of Lord Milford, the chief original benefactor), and by 1953 the Plant Breeding Station was established in its ultimate home.

In 1950 T. J. Jenkin, who had combined the Directorship of the Plant Breeding Station with the professorship of Agricultural Botany (as had his predecessor, Sir George Stapledon) retired. The twin posts were now separated: P. T. Thomas,

---

[75] *Adult Education after Thirty Years: an Address* (Bangor, 1941).

[76] 'Memorandum prepared by the Director of Extra-Mural Studies', March 1955. C.A. P/Cr/E/5. *Report on Adult Education in Wales* (1970), p. 18.

[77] *Council Minutes* (25 October 1950), p. 4. Principal's Report, *Court Minutes* (25 October 1950), pp. 6–7. Subsequently this aspect of the purchase was strongly challenged, and, not long afterwards, on the advice of Principal Goronwy Rees, some outlying portions of the estate were sold off. 'Gogerddan Estate' (no date). C.A. P/Cr/E/5. In the long run, the investment appears to have worked out well.

a member of the staff of the department whose 'exceptional' qualifications strongly impressed the selection committee, was promoted to the chair of Agricultural Botany; and E. T. Jones, a senior member of the Plant Breeding Station staff, was appointed to the Directorship, to which professorial status was attached by the College. These two new members of the Senate were former Aberystwyth students.[78] When the Plant Breeding Station moved out to Gogerddan, an elaborate game of musical chairs, with improved accommodation as prizes, looked in prospect for several departments. It had been hoped that the departments of Geography and Geology, which were both inadequately housed, could be re-settled in the vacated building on Penglais, but the cost of conversion to these different purposes (estimated at a round £30,000) ruled this out.[79] Instead, the Rural Science departments moved up to the Penglais building, and Geography and Geology had to be content with the extra space thus available to them at the old Foundry premises in Alexandra Road, which now became their new home. Agricultural Economics came out none too well in the general post: over the vigorous protest of E. F. Nash, the department had to surrender its accommodation on Penglais and settle in rather less attractive quarters in Cambrian Chambers.[80]

The research professorship in Animal Health had by this time disappeared. During the short period of its existence, the department had done some very good work and, indeed, by 1948, as a senior member of the staff said, Aberystwyth was 'becoming well recognized throughout the country' for the quality of its contribution to the relatively new science of Biochemistry.[81] But there were difficulties of a personal and an administrative nature that led to the resignation of A. N. Worden from the Milford professorship in October 1948. Thereafter, on the recommendation of the College Agricultural Committee, the chair was united with the existing professorship in Animal Husbandry held by J. E. Nichols, who thenceforward became Milford professor of Agriculture (Animal Husbandry).[82]

[78] *Council Minutes* (25 September, 8 December 1950), pp. 17, 78. The very important contributions made by T. J. Jenkin, E. T. Jones, P. T. Thomas, R. D. Williams, and many others to the work of the Plant Breeding Station are detailed in the *Jubilee Report of the Welsh Plant Breeding Station, 1919–69* (Aberystwyth, 1969).

[79] College property at Nos. 1, 11, and 12 Marine Terrace, the Dairy Building in Llanbadarn Road, the Alexandra Road establishment and the recently acquired Cambrian Chambers in Terrace Road all came into consideration. 'Alternative Use of the Agricultural Research Building, Penglais.' C.A. P/Cr/E/1. Henceforward, the building was known as the Institute of Rural Science.

[80] E. F. Nash to the New Buildings Subcommittee, 10 March 1953. C.A. Ibid.

[81] Charles Evans to Ifor L. Evans, 30 November 1948. C.A. P/Cr/E/2.

[82] *Council Minutes* (27 October 1948, 23 March 1949), pp. 2, 57–8. During these years there was some buying and selling of College farms with, ultimately, a concentration on the Penglais farm together with some additions. In 1946 the specialist Advisory Officers, who had been attached to the Rural Science departments of the College for nearly half a century, were transferred to the National Agricultural Advisory Service at Trawscoed. In the course of their work they had helped considerably to keep the Rural Science departments in close touch with the farming community and had also rendered valuable part-time teaching assistance to the College.

For a short period the Wilson chair in International Politics (envisaged by its chief founder as an agency to promote peace among nations but, ironically, in the past, the source of several great storms in the history of the College) remained vacant. During the war years E. H. Carr had continued to deliver his public lectures at the College and, in addition to his work for *The Times*, he had published a number of important books. In 1945 the world was dangerously confronted with the new, immensely formidable power of the Soviet Union and, fittingly, E. H. Carr had decided to develop his already evident interest in Russian history: he now began a massive study which, in time, was to produce a series of brilliant books on Soviet Russia that enhanced to the point of illustriousness a reputation as a historian that was already very great. But this work had hardly begun when, impelled by personal reasons, he resigned the Wilson chair in December 1946.[83] The vacancy was not immediately filled: the fact was that, with the passage of time and the gradual improvement in professorial stipends, the original endowment no longer sufficed, without substantial supplementation from general College revenue, to meet the costs of the chair and the department. For some time the College was unable to provide this additional aid; the chair remained vacant, and the work of the department was carried on by I. G. John, lecturer in International Politics. In December 1949, however, Thomas Jones, President of the College, who had been closely connected with the Wilson chair since its foundation, pressed strongly for a new appointment, and his powerful advocacy was seconded by Sir Charles Webster, the distinguished former occupant of the chair. Moreover, the financial difficulty was largely answered by the Misses Davies of Llandinam who, bountiful as ever where the College was concerned, made an additional gift of stock to the value of £21,750; this, together with accumulated balances from recent years and E. H. Carr's gift of £1,000 in 1943, more than doubled the original endowment.[84]

The Misses Davies also expressed their wish that the Wilson chair 'might be assimilated, more closely than heretofore, to other chairs in the College': that is, that the Wilson professor should normally be in residence during all three terms of the session; that there should be a greater emphasis on undergraduate teaching than there had been in the past; and, presumably, that, in due course, it should be possible for students to read for a bachelor's degree in International Politics. In July 1950 D. A. Routh, formerly E. H. Carr's assistant in the department, and P. A. Reynolds, a young Oxford historian then on the staff of the London School of Economics, were interviewed by the Council: P. A. Reynolds was elected to the chair.[85] He remained at Aberystwyth for fourteen years. A special subcommittee

[83] *Council Minutes* (22 October 1947), p. 10.
[84] Ibid. (9 December 1949), pp. 28–9. *Report on the Wilson Chair of International Politics* (March 1950), pp. 5–16.
[85] Ibid., p. 16. *Council Minutes* (10 July 1950), pp. 54–5.

on the future of the department had, in fact, recommended that there should be very little change in the range of teaching undertaken.[86] Gradually this overly cautious attitude, which stemmed from a settled conviction in some quarters that International Politics was a discipline scarcely suitable for undergraduates, was worn down. During P. A. Reynolds' tenure, International Politics grew into an authentic, full-scale College department; the range of teaching was very largely extended to keep pace with the rapid development in recent years of new specialist additions to the subject; and it became possible, first of all, for students to read for an honours degree in which International Politics was one of two major ingredients and, later still, for a single honours in the subject. When in 1965 a new Faculty of Economic and Social Studies came into existence (thus at last realizing an ambition that reached back to 1917), the department of International Politics was fully equipped to become one of its chief supports.

No great progress was made with the building programme on Penglais during the 1950s, although the U.G.C. did sanction the completion of the second stage (providing accommodation, rather less spaciously laid out than in the first stage, for another fifty men students) of Pantycelyn, despite the sharp reduction in university building schemes imposed by the government at the time of the Korean war. This addition was opened in October 1953, and a year later J. N. Ball was appointed to a new full-time Wardenship (an innovation so far as men's hostels were concerned) of the hall.[87] During these years, too, Plâs Penglais, the large house formerly occupied by the owners of the estate on the hill, was renovated and transformed into an official residence for the Principal. It will be remembered that years before, Sir John Williams had bequeathed his home, Blaenllynant (together with its magnificent furniture), on the seafront for this purpose. In fact, Sir John's house was never occupied by the Principals: Sir Henry Stuart Jones lived in a hotel, and Principal Ifor L. Evans' home for many years was a house (now the Staff House) in Laura Place, in which Sir John Williams' furniture, rescued from storage, had been installed. It had been thought at one time that Plâs Penglais could be converted into a small hall of residence, but this proved impossible. Eventually, it was decided to adapt it to its present purpose. The house was badly run-down and the grounds were a wilderness. The interesting, occasionally hilarious, story of the conversion has been well told by Mrs. Ruth Evans. The grounds were transformed into a fine botanical garden, and the house, with an addition, became a fine official residence, a fitting setting for Sir John Williams' furniture.[88]

[86] Ibid. (22 March 1950), pp. 46–7.

[87] Principal's Reports and Acting Principal's Report, *Council Minutes* (31 October 1951, 28 October 1953, 27 October 1954), pp. 6, 6–7, 6. A curious feature, quickly noticed by *Courier* (4 February 1954), was that the fire-alarm was 'a nightingale' compared with 'the rising bell', which was apparently designed to rouse the dead.

[88] 'The Story of Penglais' (1951).

Principal Ifor L. Evans, however, did not long survive to enjoy his new home, for he died suddenly at the end of May 1952, aged fifty-five. He had been at Aberystwyth since 1934, and in many, indeed perhaps most respects, he had been an outstandingly successful Principal. Appointed at the age of thirty-eight, he was superbly equipped for this most exacting office: his academic credentials were impeccable, he had a well-developed talent for administration (which he exercised with relish), a wide experience of the ways of the world, a cultivated understanding of other peoples and other languages, to which he united a passionate interest in, and concern for, the culture of Wales. If anything, his interest in the Welsh heritage steadily deepened over the years; but it did not become narrow or turn in on itself, for 'he never surrendered his citizenship of Europe and the world'.[89] He had large ambitions for his College. Aberystwyth had natural advantages which must be developed to the uttermost: small, set in the heartland of rural, Welsh-speaking Wales, cheek by jowl with the National Library, with careful nurturing it could become indisputably what it had always aspired to be: the cultural capital of Wales. The title of the College was national, and it recruited its students from the whole of the Principality; it was residential to an exceptional extent, and in time, perhaps, with luck, hostels on a magnificent new site would give it a collegiate social character. Here was a marvellous opportunity to introduce a strong Oxbridge element into Welsh higher education.

It was an inspiring programme. But the harsh fact was that in 1934 the College was weighed down with debt. However, by prudent management and careful budgeting (in which every penny was closely watched), this crippling encumbrance was substantially eliminated in a surprisingly short time. This was Ifor L. Evans' first, and perhaps his greatest, contribution to the well-being of the College. Thereafter he worked steadily in discouraging circumstances to realize his ambition to build a new, largely residential College on the hill site. For years very little help was to be looked for from the U.G.C., and public appeals for money evoked no great response. Ifor L. Evans, however, was quick to snap up whatever limited offers of outside assistance were made, and a start at least had been made with the building programme by 1939.

The war was a thoroughly frustrating time for the Principal: development was at a standstill, there was some inevitable run-down in the work of the College; a mere holding operation held no great attraction for so dynamic a personality. Moreover, he was thoroughly disappointed that, in this acute national emergency, he was not called upon to help his country in some appropriate way. He became restless and to some extent oppressed by a feeling that his career had been a failure. The post-war period, with its great promise of rapid university development, would seem to be exactly suited to Ifor L. Evans' taste and talents. In a way, it was, and with the prospect of renewed action he recovered much of his old drive.

[89] A. D. Rees, 'Ifor Leslie Evans, 1897–1952', *The Anvil*, iv. 11.

But there were still frustrating delays, and he had strong reservations about the post-war emphasis by the U.G.C. on size and numbers. His concern had always been with quality, and, indeed, Aberystwyth's smallness had seemed to him to be one of its greatest virtues. He had striven not so much for a bigger College as a better one. By 1950, when student numbers at Aberystwyth had gone well above the thousand mark, in anticipation of Kingsley Amis' maxim that 'more means worse' (the rallying cry of an élite on the run), Ifor L. Evans 'devoutly hoped' that, in order 'to maintain academic standards', there would soon be some reduction in the size of the student body.[90]

He had always been particularly interested in Agriculture, especially that of Wales. Indeed, some of his critics (Lord Davies, for one) maintained that too much of his attention was concentrated in that direction.[91] There was, perhaps, some truth in this. On the other hand, Agriculture and its cognate disciplines did constitute one of Aberystwyth's chief specialisms. And certainly the work of these departments, quite apart from its very great success in fulfilling the orthodox university duty to advance the frontiers of knowledge, was of great immediate benefit to rural Wales, where a whole way of life, in an area to which the College had always owned an especial obligation, was under severe strain.[92] In partnership with A. W. Ashby, the Principal wrote a book on Agriculture in Wales which was well received, although he himself suggested that its only value was 'as a soporific'.[93] All his other publications during his Principalship were in Welsh: an anthology of readings from the Scriptures, a collection of hymns, a translation of the Fables of La Fontaine. Ifor L. Evans confessedly hated writing letters; but he was at his best drafting reports and memoranda which reduced complex problems to essentials. Administration interested him to the end. He was a great university statesman (almost certainly the foremost in Wales in his time), and his leadership in the affairs of the University, in the Estates Committee and on the Press Board in particular, was acknowledged by his colleagues to be outstanding. He played an important part in founding the Royal University of Malta, and rendered considerable assistance to the University College of Ibadan.[94]

Ifor L. Evans provoked strong feelings in those with whom he worked. Masterful, courageous, sometimes plainly obstinate, ruthless on occasion (no broken eggs, no omelettes, might well have been his answer), he had many ardent

---

[90] *Interim Report to the U.G.C.* (1950), p. 11.

[91] Lord Davies to W. J. Burdon Evans, 5 March 1943. N.L.W. Llandinam MSS. (Wilson (2)).

[92] In a script written in 1951 for a talk (not delivered) on the radio, Principal Evans explained, and perhaps sought to justify, his attitude thus: 'There are two topics upon which it is extremely difficult for a Welsh-speaking Welshman to speak impartially. One is the Welsh Language . . . and the other is the progressive depopulation of rural Wales. On both . . . I confess to feeling very deeply.' 12 June 1951. C.A. P/Cr/E/2.

[93] Ifor L. Evans to R. S. Hudson (Minister of Agriculture), 29 May 1944. C.A. P/Cr/D/9.

[94] A. D. Rees, 'Ifor L. Evans, 1897–1952', loc. cit., pp. 10–12.

admirers and, inevitably, a fair number of enemies, too. He had no time for popular gatherings and students generally complained that they saw little or nothing of him. But many individual students had cause to be grateful for his generosity, material and spiritual, and he certainly was concerned for the welfare of students *en masse*, as witness his interest in the dining and medical schemes and the provision of residential accommodation. He died (in the last few years his life was shadowed) before the College on the Hill had been substantially achieved, but he was one of its main progenitors.

10

The College on the Hill

THE later 1950s were a curious period in the history of the College. To outward view things had not changed greatly: by 1960 the number of students had not risen much beyond 1,500, and over 66 per cent of them were Welsh, or at any rate came from homes in Wales. The old College building remained the chief focus of academic activity, the pattern of student social life continued substantially unchanged, and the President of the Students' Representative Council could still maintain some direct contact with his constituents from 'the grid'. But the burgeoning signs of change were unmistakable: the student body was larger than ever before (it had already become 'an animal without a spine', in the opinion of one old student on the staff); it would almost certainly continue to grow steadily; every year there were additional appointments to the teaching staff, and the building programme on Penglais was at last about to begin in earnest.[1] Twilight was fast approaching for the old College by the Sea: tomorrow would belong to Penglais and the College on the Hill.

Year by year, the overcrowding in the existing buildings got worse. The provision of adequate living accommodation was a constant headache. When the second stage of Pantycelyn was opened, Ceredigion became a hall for women again for a time, and a modernization programme at Alexandra Hall was pushed ahead as quickly as possible. But even so, eventually, and not without misgiving in some quarters, the old rule that all women students must live in hostels had to be given up in 1956, when some postgraduate women were allowed to live out of hall. The problem of accommodation for men was, if anything, even worse, and J. I. Platt, a senior member of the Geology department who acted additionally as Supervisor of men's lodgings, worked heroically to add to the list of approved 'digs' in the town. Eventually, the University Grants Committee was forced to approve the construction of the final stage of Pantycelyn, which was completed by 1960 and then accommodated 250 men students in all. And in the same year, at a cost to the Treasury of just under £64,000, the Lion Royal Hotel in the centre of the town was bought and converted into a hostel (which was given the name

---

[1] 'The Opinions of Gwyn A. Williams', *Courier* (25 January 1958). Between 1955 and 1966 the teaching staff grew from 184 to 272.

Padarn) for sixty or so men. At that point, in 1961, Plynlymon once more became
a hostel for women.[2]

Overcrowding at social events was equally a problem. The loss of the old
College Hall was more grievously felt now than ever. Student officials were driven
from pillar to post and back again in their efforts to find a home for popular
functions: the Parish Hall, the Pier, the Coliseum and, of course, the King's Hall
were all variously pressed into service at one time or another. The Union, the
hub of so much student life, became hopelessly inadequate, and in 1957 a large
house nearby was bought and adapted as an Annexe. The Vicarage Field could
no longer answer all the demands made on it, and in 1957 six acres of land at
Llanbadarn were rented for use as additional playing-fields.[3] Despite the increase
in student numbers, according to the purists at least, there had been no corre-
sponding improvement in the quality of performance by College teams. In rugby
it appeared that the College XV, traditionally exciting and unorthodox in
approach, was no more capable of answering the destructive tactics of maraud-
ing wing-forwards than the international sides of the time. 'Our rugby team
seems to be about as unorthodox as the Patriarch of the Greek Church', wrote one
disgruntled observer. 'Our enjoyment of the game is being diagonally kicked out
of existence.'[4] The soccer team was in far worse case apparently. By 1955 it was
said to be 'a laughing stock', and its results so consistently poor that, in despair,
it was suggested that the club should withdraw from the Mid-Wales League.[5]
As for cricket, it remained 'the Cinderella' of major College sports, played
defiantly in the shadow of June examinations.[6]

Perhaps these individual lamentations should not be taken too seriously.
Unattractive to watch or not, the rugby team won the Welsh championship three
times out of four between 1950 and 1954, and in 1958 reached the U.A.U. Final
where, shorn at the last moment of two star players, it was defeated 14–0 by an
inevitably 'stronger, fitter side' from Loughborough College. In 1954 Aberystwyth
won five out of eight Welsh Inter-college championships, and even the supposedly weak soccer team finished as runners-up. The Inter-college *Eisteddfod*
continued to be dominated by the two northern colleges. '*Bangor ar y blaen ym
Mangor, ac Aber. ymbob man arall*' ('Bangor to the fore at Bangor, and Aber.
everywhere else'). In 1955 Aberystwyth 'swept the board', and in 1958 the *Eisteddy-*

---

[2] Reports of Acting Principals and Principals, *Court Minutes* (1953–1961), passim. In 1959 many
students were in lodgings in Borth. *Courier* (17 October 1959).

[3] *Courier* (15 October 1953, 29 January 1955). Acting Principal's Report, *Court Minutes* (20 October
1957), p. 10.

[4] 'Rugger Requiem or Variations on a Theme of Woe', *The Dragon*, lxxiii. 40.

[5] 'Decline and Fall', *Courier* (26 November 1955).

[6] 'College Cricket', *The Dragon*, lxxiii. 32. 'We are not without our martyrs', says this same article.
'There have been men who have died academic deaths for College cricket. . . . They are to be found
today among the purveyors of insurance and among the more civil of public servants.'

fod shield was won for the fifth time in six years. At the tail-end of 1957, Aberystwyth came second to Cardiff in the third N.U.S. Drama Festival at Bristol with Aneurin Rhys Hughes' production of 'The Crucible', and one of the players, Peter Knowles, was awarded the title of best individual performer of the week.[7]

Uncomfortably overcrowded as they were during these years, Aberystwyth students understood very well that, along with their fellows in other universities, they were a highly privileged group. They continued to show a steady concern for the less fortunate. No doubt the annual Rag festivities provided a fine opportunity for many simply to blow off steam. Nevertheless, year by year very substantial sums were raised for worthy causes: £1,700 for the Save the Children Fund in 1955, £2,260 for the National Fund for Polio Research in 1956, and an even larger sum for the Dr. Barnado's Homes two years later.[8] And the Rags, especially the mass Saturday afternoon processions, helped to remind all students powerfully of their ultimate unity. Sometimes a caution against disunity was necessary. In 1956, for example, the residents of Pantycelyn, overly concerned with their own social affairs, mounted a 'well-organized commando assault' to persuade a General Meeting of students to abandon the rule that certain nights in the week should be reserved exclusively for functions of interest to the College as a whole. The proposal was ultimately defeated, and those who had moved and supported it were sternly rebuked ('There is no room in Aber. for sectional clashes and faction feuds') for their separatist tendencies.[9]

Perhaps this growing emphasis on narrower loyalties was a natural consequence of the enlargement of the College. The reproof to the Pantycelyn dissidents had been administered by the *Courier*, the student newspaper, which itself owed its existence to the growth in size of the student body. *Courier* first appeared in 1948, appropriately enough perhaps in the light of its editorial tone in recent years, on Guy Fawkes Day. The declared aim was 'the awakening and stimulation of student opinion' on all aspects of College life, and the first number formally disclaimed any desire 'to blow up Coll.'.[10] *The Dragon*, the College magazine that had had a distinguished history, was now in advanced decline. Latterly it had become almost entirely literary in content and exasperatingly esoteric. The initiated were evidently very few, for in recent years it had been reduced from three numbers to one a year. In 1958, however, it briefly recovered some of its former glory. The editorial board was reconstituted and distinguished members of staff and some former students with literary reputations contributed articles to a

[7] *Courier* (9 March, 22 October 1954, 27 October 1956, 25 January, 1 March 1958). Professor Thomas Jones to Principal Goronwy Rees, 12 February 1955. C.A. P/Cr/E/9.

[8] *Courier* (28 May 1955, 19 May 1956, 1 March 1958).

[9] Ibid. (4 February 1956). Two years earlier the whole Aberystwyth student body had been publicly rebuked for its patronizing attitude (a long-standing complaint) towards the students in the other Welsh Colleges. 'Open Letter from Bangor', *Courier* (*Llais y Lli*, 20 May 1954).

[10] Ibid. (5 November 1948).

special Festival edition. It was a return to the practice of the earliest days: the magazine was vastly better, but it was not a student enterprise.[11]

Courier and *The Dragon* existed side by side. In 1957 it was suggested that the proper division of labour was that the newspaper's function was 'to tell us what we do', whereas 'an ideal College magazine should tell us what we are'.[12] *The Dragon* could scarcely be said to have fulfilled that duty in recent time. *Courier* soon extended its range beyond mere reportage. For many years its editorial comment was restrained, even notably high-minded quite often, and usually endorsed the official policy of the Students' Representative Council. This was so partly perhaps because, by custom, copy was seen by the President of the S.R.C. before it appeared in print.[13] That is not to say that the editor of *Courier* was simply the President's poodle.[14] Indeed, there were occasional disagreements. But the fact is that, at that time, the S.R.C. was not itself directly involved (and therefore saddled willy-nilly with responsibility for decisions) in the government of the College to the extent that it was to be later. In those circumstances the angle of observation of President and editor was much the same, and their broad agreement on most issues was perfectly natural.

It is fair to say that the quality of the student officers in these years remained high.[15] With the increase in size of the student body, the office of President of the S.R.C. was becoming more and more onerous, and in 1956 it was suggested that the time had come to recognize that it was now a full-time job. Nothing came of this for the moment. Meantime, the administration of Union affairs went on, helped by 'the annual miracle' whereby 'relatively inexperienced student officials take over from the old lags, who were themselves only just getting into their stride'.[16]

The administration of the College at the highest level, however, did not proceed quite so smoothly. When Ifor L. Evans died suddenly in 1952, Dr. Lily Newton, who was currently Vice-Principal, became Acting-Principal. Dr. Newton was admirably equipped to lead the College during the interregnum: she was the senior professor and already had a detailed knowledge of the administration of the College; direct in manner, unfailingly courteous, completely devoted to the College, the Acting-Principal possessed the confidence of the staff, the students, and the lay authorities.[17] Professor Newton was powerfully assisted by the two College officials with whom she worked most closely: the Vice-Principal and the Registrar. R. F. Treharne, professor of History since 1930 and a most experienced

---

[11] *The Dragon*, xc.   [12] Ibid. lxxxix. 3.   [13] *Courier* (24 May 1952).

[14] In 1953 the President of the S.R.C. said that he 'saw no reason why the editor should not make or print any reasonable criticism of either S.R.C. or its officials'. Ibid. (15 October 1953).

[15] In 1962 Aneurin Rhys Hughes was elected President of the N.U.S. in succession to Gwyn Morgan, another Aberystwyth man, an astonishing achievement for a relatively small College.

[16] *Courier* (27 October 1956).

[17] See the President's fine tribute, *Court Minutes* (28 October 1953), p. 8.

and influential member of the Senate, became Vice-Principal. The Registrar, T. Maelgwyn Davies, by now had an encyclopedic knowledge of the running of the College, and a sense of duty which a later Principal described as 'infectious', even a trifle 'intimidating' to relative newcomers.[18] These three officials (two of whom retained their additional responsibilities as the heads of large academic departments) worked in the closest accord, and the interests of the College were fully safeguarded during the interval between Principals.[19]

Wales remained one of the few countries where appointments to the headships of University Colleges excited a good deal of general public interest. There was the usual speculation in the columns of the press of Wales about the appointment of a successor to Ifor L. Evans. Although this time, mercifully, prominent Welshmen were spared the acute embarrassment that had often resulted on similar occasions in the past when individuals had been named (often with little or no warrant, other than well-intentioned personal preferences on the part of the commentators) as likely or actual candidates for the Principalship. This time public comment was concerned mainly with the general qualifications appropriate to the position: there was, however, mounting criticism by some of the avidly interested of what was said to be an unreasonably long delay in making the appointment.[20]

The selection committee had not been dilatory: it had met on eight occasions and had given the most detailed consideration to the claims of fourteen candidates. There were eleven formal applications, and three other people, nominated by members of the Council or the selection committee, agreed to allow their names to be considered. Five of the fourteen were interviewed and, ultimately, the selection committee, which was empowered to recommend one, two, or three names for the Council's consideration, unanimously agreed to recommend the appointment of M. Goronwy Rees, who was then a Fellow and the Estates Bursar of All Souls College, Oxford. After a motion to accept the selection committee's recommendation was proposed and seconded, an amendment seeking to defer the decision so as to give the selection committee 'further opportunity to consider the position' was put forward. The amendment was defeated, and it was resolved to interview the candidate, who gave assurances that 'he would take every step to become fluent again in the Welsh language as soon as he possibly could'. Thereupon, on 26 June 1953, M. Goronwy Rees was appointed to the Principalship.[21]

This was a case of the return of the native. The new Principal had been born in

[18] Principal Thomas Parry, *Court Minutes* (29 October 1958), p. 8.
[19] Ibid. (28 October 1953), p. 6.
[20] *Western Mail* (21 and 29 April, 6 and 7 May 1953). *Liverpool Daily Post* (22 May 1953).
[21] Report of the selection committee, *Council Minutes* (26 June 1953), pp. 64–6. The new Principal could read and understand Welsh, but his oral command of the language had decayed during the years he had lived outside Wales.

Aberystwyth. He was the son of the Revd. R. J. Rees, an old Aberystwyth student, a well-known Welsh Presbyterian minister who had been the pastor of the large Tabernacle chapel in the town for several years.[22] The Principal had attended the local elementary and secondary schools; later the family moved to Cardiff, and in 1927 he won an open scholarship to New College, Oxford. In 1930 he took a first-class degree in the P.P.E. honours school, and carried off a Fellowship at All Souls. Subsequently he had been a leader-writer on the *Manchester Guardian* and Assistant Editor of the *Spectator*.[23] He had joined the army in 1939, risen rapidly in rank, taken part in the raid on Dieppe (a harrowing experience), and served with distinction on Montgomery's staff. After the war he joined the Control Commission in Germany for a time, before going into business and later on returning to All Souls as Estates Bursar. He had written three novels, and published translations of works by Buchner and Janouch, the former in association with Stephen Spender.

It is apparent that the new Principal, who had travelled extensively, had an exceptionally wide range of experience. Apart from *Y Faner*, which questioned his knowledge of the traditions and problems of Wales, disputed his claim to understand Welsh, and was not prepared to accept the novels and translations as serious contributions to scholarship, the appointment was received with general satisfaction. The two Aberystwyth newspapers expressed particular pride in the success of a local boy.[24] Outstandingly able, distinguished in appearance, impressively sophisticated, blessed with a winning charm, and brilliantly articulate, Principal Rees seemed to be marvellously equipped for his new responsibilities. He made an instant appeal to the students, and many people were impressed, even captivated, by his Inaugural Address. The lecture, which was beautifully expressed in his usual limpid style, made it plain that the Principal's academic credo was one which would be endorsed heartily by those who cared deeply about universities. He viewed the State, 'which does not belong to those who believe that it is more blessed to give than to receive', with a healthy suspicion. And he was prepared to fight to the death 'the dangerous implication that the duty of universities is to produce the kind of men in sufficient quantities, and in the right proportions, which a modern state needs if it is to survive'; a heresy which seemed to him to be implicit in the government's latter-day open-handedness to universities.[25] Everything looked set for a brilliant Principalship.

[22] There is an interesting short autobiographical account of the Principal's upbringing in the town in *A Bundle of Sensations* (1960), pp. 19–32.

[23] Thomas Jones thought that, politically, the young Goronwy Rees of 1937 would have been 'more at home on the *New Statesman*'. *Diary with Letters, 1931–1950*, p. 347.

[24] *Baner ac Amserau Cymru* (1 July 1953). *Western Mail* (27 June 1953). *Cambrian News* (3 July 1953). *Welsh Gazette* (2 July 1953).

[25] Goronwy Rees, *On The Use and Misuse of Universities* (Aberystwyth, 1953), p. 4. *Courier* (15 October 1953).

Just over a year later, the aged and distinguished President of the College decided that the time had come for him to retire. Thomas Jones was now eighty-four years of age, two years older than the College of which he was such an adornment. He had come up to Aberystwyth as a raw young man thirsting for education in 1890. There followed a richly varied career that brought him honours, influence, and renown. But perhaps more important than the formal career was the incredible record of public service, unpaid, unself-seeking, unconcerned with personal reward or recognition, to almost every good cause in sight, especially those of benefit to Wales and the Welsh people. Examine the records and minute-books of those private and public societies concerned to improve the quality of life for ordinary people in Wales and there, inevitably as day follows night, will be found Thomas Jones, ceaselessly active, matchless in persuasiveness, endlessly fertile in resource. In comparison, even Hugh Owen seems the merest tiro.[26]

Ever since 1890, the College at Aberystwyth had been very close to Thomas Jones' heart. His interest in its affairs had never wavered; not even the cruel disappointment of 1919 could pierce and destroy his abiding concern to promote its welfare, as, doubtless, it would have done for many a lesser man. None of the many honours he received gave him greater delight than the Presidency of his old College. He graced the office for ten years, living for most of the time in Aberystwyth and bringing to the service of the College that 'particular combination of profound wisdom with the gift of eternal youth' that enabled him to be, as near as human fallibility would allow, 'the perfect President'.[27]

T.J. had hoped that his election to the Presidency would be followed, in due course, by that of other old students of the College.[28] The precedent has since been followed twice in succession. In 1954 four names were suggested, three of them those of distinguished former Aberystwyth students. The committee unanimously recommended one of the three, Sir David Hughes Parry (he had been knighted in 1951), for the Presidency.[29] 'No one', as the Principal said, 'could come to the office . . . better equipped than Sir David.' He, too, had maintained the closest interest in the College since his student days there. He had a magnificent record of service to Wales, and his experience of the university world was difficult to equal. He was a former Vice-Chancellor of the University of London; he had served as Chairman of the Committee of Vice-Chancellors and Principals, and for three years he had been Vice-Chairman of the University Grants Committee.[30] Moreover, he, too, like his predecessor in the Presidency, had sprung from the people and had never forgotten that fact.

[26] For an account of the astonishing range of T.J.'s public services to Wales, see Sir Ben B. Thomas, *Thomas Jones 1870–1955: a centenary address* (Coleg Harlech, 1971).

[27] Principal Goronwy Rees, *Court Minutes* (27 October 1954), p. 8.

[28] Thomas Jones, *Old and Young* (Cardiff, 1945), p. 3.

[29] Principal Goronwy Rees to Lord Lisburne, 27 September 1954. C.A. P/Cr/E/7. *Council Minutes* (27 October 1954), p. 21.   [30] *Court Minutes* (27 October 1954), pp. 8–9.

Soon after he took up his new appointment, Principal Goronwy Rees offered to the Court of Governors some account of his first impressions of the College. Like many others before him, he was struck by Aberystwyth's unique advantages: in addition to a beautiful natural setting, the relatively small size and detached location of the College made it possible 'to establish an academic society which is closer and more intimate than is feasible elsewhere'. He had been impressed with the quality, or at any rate the raw natural ability, of the students, but he believed that, all too often, because of defective early schooling, 'a narrow social environment', or insufficient exposure to the stimulus of completely free inquiry, young Welshmen failed to realize their full potential. Opportunity and necessity, therefore, persuaded him that what the College needed, above all, was some form of tutorial system based on 'close personal relations between the teacher and the taught'.[31]

This was to remain high on his list of academic priorities. Elsewhere he had little scope for striking initiatives. During the years of his Principalship, the University Grants Committee, constrained in turn by a niggardly Treasury, kept the universities on a tight financial rein. Some money in the form of capital grants was forthcoming, and this was used to convert existing College premises to new purposes; to acquire another house on the Promenade for extra teaching rooms, and a small private hotel (Cleeve Hill) for additional hostel accommodation. Alexandra Hall was improved, and a small extension was added to the Edward Davies Chemical Laboratory. With the aid of a grant from the Tithe and Capitular Estates (a permanently valuable crutch for a College that had to limp along without adequate private endowment), the Examination Hall was improved, and a brave attempt was made, with the use of bright paint, to overcome the dowdy appearance of the Union and the Quad.[32]

During 1955 the College authorities were hard at work on a programme of development to be submitted to the University Grants Committee. It was common doctrine, as Principal Rees said later, that most of the science laboratories at Aberystwyth were 'quite definitely sub-standard', and accordingly the highest priority in the programme was given to a new building for the Zoology and Botany departments, which it was hoped would be followed soon afterwards by another for Physics and Mathematics. It was also suggested that a new College Hall and additional hostel accommodation were urgently required. By this time Principal Rees was even more strongly of the opinion that a tutorial teaching system was necessary, and this requirement was put forward with especial emphasis, together with a demand for larger funds for equipment and research.[33]

[31] Address to the Court. Ibid. (28 October 1953), pp. 9–10.

[32] Ibid. (26 October 1955), pp. 6–7. *Council Minutes* (29 June 1956), pp. 75–6. *Courier* (29 January 1955). The redecoration of the Quad. provoked a lively controversy among the students: some of them thought that the colour schemes were outrageously daring.

[33] Report of a Special Meeting of the Senate, 12 December 1955. Senate Minutes (1955). *Council Minutes* (9 December 1955), p. 42. Principal's Report, *Court Minutes* (31 October 1956), pp. 6–12.

Considering the desperate needs of the College, it was a modest enough programme. In June 1956 the University Grants Committee visited Aberystwyth. The Committee had already given its sanction for the proposed Biology building on Penglais, but it also insisted that the College should make a substantial contribution from its slender resources towards the cost (estimated at £354,000) of the new block. The University Grants Committee made it plain that there was no hope of money for a new Physics and Mathematics building or a new Chemistry laboratory (which had also been suggested) before 1959. Members of the Council were thoroughly disappointed to hear that the University Grants Committee, although expressing 'interest' (which unbalanced no budgets), was unable to accept the provision of a College Hall 'as one of the highest priorities'. For the rest, in lieu of money, the visitors were lavish with praise for what they had seen at Aberystwyth. The College authorities were congratulated on the enterprise they had shown in answering, without benefit of costly new buildings, the problems of teaching and residential accommodation. The Freshers' Conference (introduced for the first time in October 1954) was warmly commended as a valuable means of bridging the awkward gap between school and university; and the College was congratulated on its 'foresight' in conceding some representation on the Senate and on the Council to the non-professorial staff, a thoroughly sensible arrangement not matched in most other universities at that time. The extension of tutorial teaching, that admittedly was financed by additional grants from the University Grants Committee, was warmly welcomed, but here, too, the official viewpoint seemed curiously one-eyed. The chief merit of tutorial teaching, according to the visitors (for whom numbers appeared to be the major consideration), was that it would reduce the failure rate among weaker students in the first year and at pass degree level. The more important possibility, that tutorial teaching might well raise significantly the quality of education provided at the College as a whole, appeared to escape notice. Finally, the College was complimented on the 'very happy relationships' that existed between staff and students.[34]

Elsewhere in the College at this time, relationships were far from happy. In May 1951 public confidence in the loyalty of senior officials at the Foreign Office, and in the competence of the nation's security services, was all but shattered when Guy Burgess and Donald Maclean, to outward appearances at least model scions of the Establishment whose patriotic loyalty was beyond suspicion, disappeared in mysterious circumstances that overwhelmingly suggested political defection to the East. On 11 February 1956 Burgess dramatically reappeared in public in Moscow, and early in March *The People*, the mass-circulation Sunday newspaper that specialized in lurid exposé feature articles, announced that it would shortly

[34] *Council Minutes* (16 March, 14 June 1956), pp. 57–8, 69–72. Principal's Report, *Court Minutes* (31 October 1956), pp. 6–12.

publish a series of articles on Burgess, 'the greatest traitor in all British history', based on disclosures (which 'would strip Burgess bare') made by 'his most intimate friend—a man in a high academic position'.[35]

Over the next weeks, five articles appeared. Burgess was described as utterly depraved: spy, blackmailer, sexual aberrant, permanent drunk. From start to finish it was a sordid story written up in sensational terms; and it was made clear that the friendship between Burgess and the man who had made the disclosures had continued right up until the hurried departure for Moscow.[36] It was not long before, from internal evidence, the source of the information from which the articles were written was identified. On 29 March 1956 a national newspaper named Principal Goronwy Rees of Aberystwyth.[37] The whole affair occasioned some stir in the country generally and particularly, of course, in Aberystwyth after the identification had been made. Inevitably, there was much speculation about the outcome and a spate of rumour-mongering. Many members, past and present, lay and academic, of the College were profoundly disturbed, some of them deeply outraged, by the course of events. Some of the officers and many of the senior academic members of the College believed strongly that the affair should not simply be ignored. It looked at one time as if the matter would be quickly resolved by the Principal's resignation, but this did not come about. On 20 June the students at Aberystwyth took a hand: a motion sponsored at a General Meeting by the executive of the Students' Representative Council, 'that the student body . . . would view with extreme concern and alarm any action that would result in the dismissal or resignation of the Principal', was passed by three hundred and ninety-nine votes to eight, with forty-nine abstentions. A detailed account of the General Meeting was published, accompanied by an editorial gloss expressing full support for the Principal.[38]

On 29 June 1956 the matter came before the College Council. The President made a statement, and a motion to appoint a Committee to consider 'the publication of the articles in *The People* and matters relevant thereto' was moved and seconded by two of the officers but not, apparently, put to the vote. The Principal made a statement, and 'a frank exchange of views' followed. Ultimately, the Council narrowly decided that 'no action was required and the matter was now closed': the Council unanimously expressed its confidence in the President.[39] But there were further developments. A special meeting of the Council was summoned in July. In the meantime the Treasurer, J. Alban Davies, and another prominent member of the Council had tendered their resignations, and several others signified their intention to do so unless a Committee of Inquiry were appointed.

[35] *The People* (4 March 1956).   [36] Ibid. (11 March–8 April 1956).

[37] *Daily Telegraph* (29 March 1956).

[38] *Courier* (22 June 1956). Most of the national press, quality and tabloid, carried accounts of the General Meeting of students in their editions of 21 June 1956.

[39] *Council Minutes* (29 June 1956), p. 96.

It was announced that a letter signed by eighteen members of the Senate asking for an independent inquiry had been received. There was a long discussion on a motion to appoint a Committee of Inquiry, and ultimately the Principal said that 'he would welcome the setting-up of such a Committee'. The motion was then carried, whereupon the Principal announced his intention to resign. The Council refused to accept the resignation and asked the Principal to reconsider his decision. Finally, it was decided to ask Sir Keith Murray, Chairman of the University Grants Committee, and Sir Emrys Evans, Vice-Chancellor of the University of Wales, to nominate three persons to serve on the Committee of Inquiry.[40]

The Committee, headed by the Rt. Hon. Henry Willink, Master of Magdalene College, Cambridge, opened its inquiry in October and presented its findings early in 1957. The Report was 'received' by the Council at its meeting on 15 March 1957, together with a Statement from the Principal indicating that he had been unable to accept the Committee's findings. Beforehand, on 11 February, the Principal had tendered his resignation. After a 'considerable discussion', the resignation was accepted by the Council, and it was agreed to accede to the Principal's request that he should cease forthwith to carry out his duties.[41]

So ended unhappily a Principalship that had started with such bright promise. Fourteen years later, in the course of answering questions put to him in an interview televised by the B.B.C., Principal Rees said that the nub of the difficulty that led to his resignation had been that he and his critics held fundamentally different ideas of the proper role of a university. He believed that a university's purpose was simply to pursue truth: his opponents, according to his version, thought that 'the University should serve Wales first'.[42] Later still (unfortunately when this book had been in the hands of the printer for some time), Principal Rees amplified his account of the circumstances that led to his resignation.[43] Perhaps not unnaturally, it is a highly subjective version: some of the criticisms that he makes of the College are not without their point, but the picture he presents can scarcely be described as balanced; indeed, here and there, it falls away to caricature. Certainly the charitableness that governed his attitude to Guy Burgess over so many years is conspicuously absent from his (and even more so his wife's) comments on Aberystwyth and, more especially, on the supposed frailties and limitations of the Welsh people. In this account, too, Principal Rees insisted that he and those at Aberystwyth who opposed him were irreconcilably at odds as to the true purpose of a university. It is open to conjecture whether anything more than a very small minority of the Principal's critics would accept this apparently antithetical

[40] Ibid. (27 July 1956), pp. 97–9.
[41] Ibid. (14 December 1956, 15 March 1957), pp. 55–6, 57–61. Official student opinion adhered to the Principal's side and pleaded that he should be 'forgiven' for the 'one possible indiscretion' of the articles. *Courier* (16 March 1957).
[42] *Cambrian News* (10 September 1971).
[43] *A Chapter of Accidents* (February 1972), pp. 235–70.

definition of the affair. What is certain is that, once the articles had appeared in print, a serious challenge to his position would be mounted. In the vivid account he has written of his boyhood in Aberystwyth, Principal Rees described the town (and the College can only partly be divorced from it) as 'a theocratic society, ruled by priests and elders' who formed 'a sort of unofficial Sanhedrin which exercised an absolute dictatorship over the morals and behaviour of the town'.[44] This is perhaps too much a view from the manse to be completely accurate, even for the years he had under consideration. But it has its validity, and even after the lapse of thirty years it was evident that the life-style of the Principal's close friend, Burgess, was utterly unacceptable to many members of the College. Given all the circumstances, it is difficult to see any other outcome to this painful episode, which occasioned so much distress in so many quarters.

Once again the College was fortunate in having immediately to hand a Vice-Principal who was very well qualified to assume the chief responsibility in the temporary absence of a Principal. V. C. Morton first came to Aberystwyth in 1926, and he had been a member of the Senate since 1933 when he became professor of Pure Mathematics. He knew and understood the College (which had engaged his loyalty and affection strongly) perhaps as well as anyone. Calm, widely respected by his colleagues for 'his integrity and magnanimity', he was a first-rate head of department. He now carried out his duties as Acting Principal with assurance and efficiency.[45] Once more, as in the similar emergency of 1952, the College called upon R. F. Treharne to fill the vacant Vice-Principalship for a time.[46]

By March 1957 the selection committee for the appointment of a new Principal was ready with its report. The customary procedure had been followed: the Principalship had been advertised, and, in addition to those who applied formally, other names suggested by members of the Council and by the members of the selection committee itself were taken into consideration. The committee soon came unanimously to the conclusion that the ideal candidate was already near at hand. Since 1953 Dr. Thomas Parry had been Librarian of the National Library of Wales at Aberystwyth, and during that time he had served on the College Council and had been a member of the centrally-important Finance and General Purposes Committee. Dr. Parry knew the College, and very many members of the College knew Dr. Parry. The Council had no hesitation in endorsing the recommendation of the selection committee, and on 21 March 1958 Thomas Parry was appointed Principal.[47]

Once again the College had turned to high scholarship for its leader: it was to prove a wise choice. Dr. Parry had been born in Carmel, a small village in

[44] Goronwy Rees, *A Bundle of Sensations* (1960), pp. 19–20.

[45] D. S. Meyler, loc. cit. Principal's Report, *Court Minutes* (29 October 1958), pp. 7–8.

[46] *Council Minutes* (22 March 1957), p. 82. Since October 1954 the Vice-Principal had been assisted in the performance of his duties by a new officer called the Senior Tutor.

[47] Ibid. (21 March 1958), pp. 68–9.

Caernarvonshire, of working-class parentage fifty-three years before. From Pen-y-groes secondary school he had won a scholarship to the University College of North Wales at Bangor (as a matter of fact, the merest flick to the wheel of fate would have brought him to Aberystwyth instead), and in 1926 he had taken a brilliant first-class honours degree in Welsh Language and Literature. The year of the General Strike was not a promising time for a young man with his career to make, but Thomas Parry's quality was such that, luckily for Welsh scholarship, he was appointed to an assistant-lectureship in Welsh and Latin at University College, Cardiff. Three years later, he returned to Bangor to a lectureship in Welsh. There was no rapid promotion for young men in those days, no matter how impressively gifted they were. Senior lectureships had not then been invented; the number of chairs was strictly limited, and for obvious reasons professorships in Welsh were rarer than gold. Death or retirement were the only means whereby chairs became vacant. A young lecturer counted his blessings and, if he had strong scholarly instincts, applied himself with relish to the opportunity (which was open to so very few) before him. So it was with Thomas Parry. Every year almost, a substantial volume and a cluster of articles came from his pen. And he was no narrow specialist: he edited manuscripts, wrote poetry and plays, translated T. S. Eliot's *Murder in the Cathedral* into Welsh, published a positively monumental study of the work of Dafydd ap Gwilym, and published several general studies of Welsh literature in different periods, culminating in his great *Hanes Llenyddiaeth Gymraeg* (*The History of Welsh Literature*), which appeared in 1945 and was immediately recognized as 'the indispensable basis on which all future historians of Welsh literature will build'.[48] In sum, it was a magnificent achievement, and earned for the future Principal a commensurate scholarly reputation. In 1947 he was elected to the chair of Welsh at Bangor, and six years later he became the National Librarian of Wales. In 1959 his scholarship was accorded the ultimate seal of recognition when he became a Fellow of the British Academy.[49]

Despite the vicissitudes at the highest level in recent years, the ordinary work of the College had continued unimpaired through all the changes. Nor had recent events caused any serious rift in the unity of the staff. Certainly in March 1957 the non-professorial staff had registered a protest that expressed 'strong dissatisfaction' at the 'paucity' of information they had received regarding the situation in the College during the previous year, and their regret that the Council had not thought fit to take them 'more fully into its confidence'.[50] But this was simply one more shot in the steady campaign waged at this time by those members of

---

[48] H. Idris Bell, *Welsh Review*, iv, no. 3, 220.

[49] In 1955 R. I. Aaron, professor of Philosophy at Aberystwyth since 1932, had been similarly honoured.

[50] *Council Minutes* (22 March 1957), p. 63. It should be said that, in 1961, spokesmen for the non-professorial staff assured the Chairman of the University Grants Committee that 'they knew what was going on and had an opportunity to express their views'. Ibid. (18 May 1961), p. 99.

staff who were not professors to improve their status and increase their influence. It was a plea for the right to participate, not a protest against the outcome of recent events. Internally, the College remained in good fettle. All the same, there was some feeling that what the College now required was a period of settled calm, undisturbed by sensation, in which it could reaffirm its old proud claim to stand first in Wales, not only in seniority but also in repute. Not the least of Principal Parry's contributions to the well-being of the College was that in the years after his appointment he set a tone which made this possible.[51]

But in other respects his Principalship was marked by greater and more rapid changes in the life of the College than had ever occurred before in any period of comparable duration since 1872. For these were the years when the tempo of university expansion in Britain steadily quickened. In September 1963 the Committee which had been appointed in 1961 under the chairmanship of Lord Robbins to consider Higher Education in Britain presented its report. Lord Robbins and his colleagues found that, seemingly ambitious as Britain's existing plans for university expansion were, they fell far short of those of some other advanced countries. The Committee believed that a highly educated population was essential to enable Britain 'to meet competitive pressures in the world', and a 'much greater effort' to expand higher education would be necessary if the nation were simply to hold its own. Gloomy prophesies to the contrary, the Robbins Committee's investigations provided convincing evidence of 'the existence of large reservoirs of untapped ability in the population, especially among girls'. The Committee called for the provision of 390,000 places for full-time students in all branches of higher education by 1973/4 (the existing number was 216,000), and 560,000 by 1980/1, of which 350,000 were to be in institutions of university status.[52] The Robbins Committee's recommendations were immediately adopted by the government, and thenceforth all existing universities were exhorted officially to grow as rapidly as possible. So far as Aberystwyth was concerned, it meant that in 1970 there were just over a thousand more students at the College than there were in 1960.

It also meant that, at long last, capital grants on a more generous scale would be forthcoming from the University Grants Committee for the programme of new building on Penglais. In fact, some considerable progress had been made even before the Robbins proposals prodded the government into speedier action. The Biology building had been completed and occupied by the departments of Botany and Zoology in September 1959, although the formal opening was delayed until the following April. In 1960 work began on a large new building on Penglais

---

[51] In May 1961 the Chairman of the University Grants Committee publicly congratulated the College 'on the appointment of a Principal, under whose leadership there was a growing feeling of solidarity'. *Council Minutes* (15 May 1961), p. 100.

[52] *Report of the Committee on Higher Education* (1963), pp. 268–72.

PLATE 12

The Physical Sciences Building, with (left) the Llandinam Building

The Swimming Bath, and (right) the Sports Hall

PLATE 13

Pantycelyn men's hall of residence

The Great Hall, Bell Tower, and (right) the new Students' Union designed to accommodate the departments of Physics, Mathematics, and the newly established department of Statistics.[53] This new accommodation, the result of very successful collaboration in planning between the architects and its future academic occupants, was completed and occupied in October 1962, and formally opened in May 1963 by Sir Graham Sutton (as he now was), a former Aberystwyth student and member of staff, head of the Meteorological Office and a Fellow of the Royal Society.[54] The Physical Sciences Building, as the new block was called, was a fine addition to the site. It provided excellent facilities, not least for research, and, by general consent, the building made a very strong aesthetic appeal. In 1971, when the General Post Office decided to issue a range of postage stamps bearing representations of some of the more attractive new university buildings in Britain, the Physical Sciences Building at Aberystwyth was chosen to decorate the particular postage stamp in greatest demand by the public.[55]

In October 1962, too, a large new laboratory (built at a cost of £209,000) was completed on the Buarth for the Chemistry department. Appropriately, this building was formally opened in January 1963 by Lord Davies, whose family had so generously answered the needs of the Chemistry department in 1907. It could not be said that the new laboratory, a box-like construction of steel and glass, was pleasing to the eye. Moreover, while sheer practical necessity dictated that, regardless of the contrast in building styles, the new building should be juxta-positioned with the original Edward Davies Laboratory, it must be conceded that the garish colours of some of the facings on the new building did little to help to produce a visual harmony. Nevertheless, attractive to look at or not, the new laboratory was an invaluable accession: near enough it doubled the accommodation available; enabled the department, one of the largest in the College, to make far better teaching arrangements; and made it possible to instal a 'wide range of modern analytical and physico-chemical apparatus'.[56]

Aberystwyth had always prided itself on its exceptionally strong residential character. In 1962 it could still be said that, Oxbridge aside, only Durham University had a smaller proportion of students who lived at home than Aberystwyth. And in that year 43·2 per cent of students at the College lived in halls of residence.[57] There was, naturally, a strong desire to see to it that, as numbers grew, the proportion of students in hall was at least maintained, and, if possible, increased. In any case, it could not be gainsaid, even by the University Grants Committee, that if the College were to play its part in the national expansion of student numbers, additional hostels would have to be provided. For, with the best will in

[53] *Court Minutes* (11 November 1959), pp. 8–9. *College Reports* (1960), p. 6.

[54] Ibid. (1962), p. 8. *Court Minutes* (30 October 1963), pp. 5–6. W. M. Jones (and others), 'The Department of Physics', p. 19.

[55] The Physical Sciences Building cost, in round figures, £460,000.

[56] Principal's Report, *Court Minutes* (31 October 1962), p. 8. *College Reports* (1963), p. 52.

[57] Principal's Report, *Court Minutes* (31 October 1962), p. 9.

the world and the utmost co-operation (which was, in fact, always forthcoming, particularly in times of especial difficulty) of local landladies, there was an obvious limit to the lodging accommodation available in the town and the sparsely inhabited immediate hinterland. Early in 1961 work began on a large new hostel for women students: in all, there were to be four halls, each with a separate identity, linked together for communal and administrative purposes, providing accommodation, ultimately, for nearly four hundred students. In October 1963, after a delay that posed some difficult problems, the first two halls in the new complex were occupied, and in succeeding years the other two components of the hostel were completed.

The four units were given names which honoured the memory of men whose work or generous benefactions had made the College on the Hill possible. *Neuadd* Rendel was named after the former President of the College whose far-sighted acquisition of land on Penglais soon after the turn of the century had first set the whole development in train. *Neuadd* Davies Bryan honoured the benefactor who in notably hard times had so largely extended the acreage owned by the College on Penglais. *Neuadd* Alban Davies commemorated the generosity of a man who, at short notice, offered the College a blank cheque in order to round off the estate and save it from a possibly unsuitable encroachment. *Neuadd* Ifor L. Evans was a fitting tribute to the Principal who had worked without stint for nearly twenty years to bring the College on the Hill into existence. Geography supplied a name (*Penbryn*: that is, top or head of the hill) that expressed the ultimate unity of the four halls.[58]

Gradually, the College on the Hill was taking shape. But it should not be thought that these new buildings were paid for exclusively by capital grants from the University Grants Committee. On the contrary, in 1961 the University Grants Committee still insisted that 5 per cent of the capital costs of building programmes should be contributed by universities from their own resources. At first sight, this percentage seemed a modest enough requirement: but in that year the cost of buildings planned, or in course of construction, at Aberystwyth was £1,105,000. So that the College had to find £55,000 to make up its contribution to the immediate programme, which was, of course, the lesser part of the building developments envisaged.[59] It will be remembered that, ever since 1933, the Old Students' Association had been working might and main to raise money to assist the College.[60] The Association had been encouraged in its efforts by Lord Davies, the President of the College, who, standing in generously as substitute for a

---

[58] *College Reports* (1963–6), *passim*. *Council Minutes* (18 December 1964), p. 93. *Neuadd*, of course, is the Welsh word for Hall. The name *Penbryn* has another Welsh association which partly accounted for its choice: Lewis Morris, the eighteenth-century Welsh polymath, had a house at Goginan with that title.

[59] Principal Thomas Parry to the Glamorgan County Council, 11 December 1961. C.A. P/Cr/F/1.

[60] Above, p. 230.

government that steadily refused to play its part, offered in 1935 a £ for £ contribution to the Appeal Fund, if the Old Students' Association succeeded in raising £10,000 within ten years. By December 1944 this target had been reached, the matching subvention had been paid, and, in all with accrued interest, the total amounted to £23,718. Over £13,000 of this had been made over to the College to assist in meeting the cost of preparing the site on Penglais for building work.[61]

In the post-war world of rapid if not galloping inflation where, year by year, the pound has steadily lost its value, the sum collected by the Old Students' Association may not appear to be all that impressive. Considered in the context of its time, however, it represented a very substantial achievement. Most Aberystwyth students entered the less well-paid professions, and few of them were in a position to make large contributions. It is fair to say that, by and large, the student generations of the years between the wars (like their predecessors in former times) had a feeling of loyalty and a sense of obligation to the College that their successors, for a variety of reasons, can scarcely claim to equal.[62] Edgar Jones of Barry exemplified superbly the total commitment of so many old students to the College. He was one of those Aberystwyth students who did so much to raise the quality of the work of the new county secondary schools ('the ideal Headmaster', as he was described in 1954) in Wales. His connection with the College remained unbroken for over sixty-five years, and he had the unique distinction of being elected President of the Old Students' Association (of which he was a founder member) for the second time, fifty years after he had first graced the office in 1901. His explanation of the hold the College exerted on him was expressed in his Presidential Message in 1951: 'I owe to Aber.', he said simply, 'everything that is most precious in life.'[63]

For many years Edgar Jones was Director of the Old Students' Appeal Fund, and he and his devoted committee members (the same staunch names appear again and again in the key positions) had worked manfully for almost twenty years in the cause. In 1952 a Renewed Appeal was launched, and it was hoped that enough money would be raised to equip and furnish a new Students' Union building on Penglais. The response, however, was not especially encouraging, and in 1954 Principal Goronwy Rees suggested that the Old Students' Association should concentrate its efforts on raising funds towards the cost of a new College Hall, as it was apparent that public money would not be forthcoming for that purpose without a very substantial contribution from private sources.[64] This Appeal, too,

[61] 'Abstract of statement on the O.S.A. Appeal Fund', O.S.A. New Buildings Committee Minutes (18 April 1960). *O.S.A. Renewed Appeal* (February 1952), p. 3.

[62] T. I. Ellis, *The Old Students' Association 1892–1942*, p. 7, summons the later generations to a due recognition of their obligations.

[63] *O.S.A. Annuals* (1951 and 1954), pp. 3, 14. O.S.A. New Buildings Committee Minutes (20 April 1954).

[64] *O.S.A. Renewed Appeal*, p. 4. O.S.A. New Buildings Committee Minutes (20 April 1954).

made very little headway. Some members of the Old Students' Association complained in 1957 that 'no clear lead' had been given by the College Council, which was evidently distracted by the troubles besetting the College at that time. This discord was soon allayed. In 1958 the Old Students' Association decided that its Appeal Fund was unlikely to be able to realize anything more than a minute fraction of the very large amount that would be required for a College Hall. The Association sensibly lowered its sights and decided to try to raise another £5,000 which, together with the sums already contributed to the College, would cover near enough the anticipated cost of a new Sports Hall.[65] The steep rise in prices frustrated even that hope and, eventually, some aid had to be sought from the University Grants Committee. However, in April 1964 a fine Sports Hall, the first of its kind in Wales, which provided excellent facilities for a wide range of activities was opened, appropriately, by Sir William Pugh, F.R.S., the distinguished former student and son-in-law of J. Davies Bryan, whose benefaction years before had given the College the land on which the Sports Hall stood. However, the Old Students' Association could claim, with legitimate pride, that its efforts over many years had at least met the greater part of the cost of the new building.[66]

In April 1960 the College itself launched an appeal for funds: it was hoped to raise £300,000. The University Grants Committee had demanded half that amount as the College contribution to the future building programme, and any additional money that came in would be used to finance developments that the Treasury would not underwrite.[67] Compared with most other universities and university colleges (many of which were also appealing at that time for public support), Aberystwyth lay under some disadvantages. There were no large, rich industrial corporations in proximity to the College that could be expected, as an expression of their local goodwill, to respond with sizeable contributions. Nor could the College approach 'industry on a practical or utilitarian basis', for Aberystwyth, as Principal Parry conceded, had 'none of those applied science subjects which appeal so strongly to industry, and from which industrial firms derive immediate and practical benefits'.[68] Some commercial concerns did respond quite generously, as did several of the local authorities in Wales; Aberystwyth Borough Council, for example, voted £5,000, which matched the contributions of Glamorgan and Cardiganshire. But, as so often before in its history, the College discovered that it had particular cause to bless the generosity of its tried friends (members of the Llandinam family, J. Alban Davies, Lord Milford's daughter and some others predictably, not all of whom could be described as wealthy people),

---

[65] O.S.A. New Buildings Committee Minutes (20 April 1957, 5 April 1958).
[66] Ibid. (18 April 1960). *Council Minutes* (16 March 1964), p. 112. *College Reports* (1964), p. 98.
[67] Report of the Council to the Court of Governors, October 1960. Ibid. (1960), p. 4.
[68] Principal Parry to R. W. Burgess, 14 November 1960. C.A. P/Cr/F/1.

and again a considerable sum was raised by the aggregated small contributions of a relatively large number of people. The students of the College, too, made several handsome donations.[69] By 1970, from one source and another and without any strikingly generous assistance from the big battalions, £277,000 had been received in response to the Appeal.

Much of this money has been disbursed in support of the building programme of the last decade. In October 1965 the largest teaching building hitherto constructed on Penglais was completed and opened. Built at a cost of £500,000, the Llandinam building (justly named in honour of the family to which the College has owed so much during its century of existence) provided a home for the new Faculty of Economic and Social Studies, the Faculty of Law, and the departments of Geography and Geology.[70] This building, too, has its critics, although complaint here has centred on the internal arrangements rather than on the external appearance. Indeed, it must be said that the sheer size of the building gives it an imposing quality, and its dominating nine-storey tower compels a certain attention.

Much of the criticism of building developments on Penglais has failed to identify the real villain of the piece. It must be remembered that, in recent years, the pressure for expansion has been such that most plans, no matter how carefully thought out, have been overtaken by events and unpredictable new developments before they have been put into effect. As a consequence, buildings have hardly been completed before work on much-needed extensions to the original design has had to be started. The Institute of Rural Science, the Llandinam Building, and the Biology block have all had to be extended either immediately or after an interval. Moreover, the College on the Hill has now been in course of construction for over thirty years, and during that time there have been changes in the textures and colours of building materials. So that the lapse of time and the hectic pace of recent growth account for much. But, even so, it should also be said that a great deal of the responsibility for the higgledy-piggledy development of university building must be put to the account of successive governments. 'Too little too late' might well be engraved on the hearts of several of the Ministers responsible for allocating money to the universities. No doubt higher education has to take its place along with the other applicants for public money, and politicians often have to make difficult decisions and may occasionally be left with Hobson's choice. But all too often they have sought blandly to suggest that, given a little ingenuity, a quart can be carried in a pint pot.[71] Universities have paid a high price for this sophistry, and it would have been well if the University Grants Committee, which appears these days to be more of a fellow-traveller than an honest broker, had spoken up on occasion rather more forthrightly.

[69] *College Appeal: A Progress Report.* G. Lib. LD. 1158.
[70] *College Reports* (1965), pp. 6–7.
[71] See, for example, Principal Parry's forthright remarks, *Court Minutes* (30 October 1963), pp. 7–10.

In 1965 there was some feeling in College circles that, for all these reasons, the College on the Hill was less aesthetically attractive than had been hoped. Accordingly, I. Dale Owen, a partner in the firm of Sir Percy Thomas & Son, was appointed co-ordinating architect for the site. In a Preliminary Report submitted in June 1966, the co-ordinating architect conceded that the site lacked an 'overall architectural theme'; that the spacing of buildings left something to be desired; and that the variations in size and scale of buildings and the texture and colour of the materials used emphasized 'the lack of unity'. It was believed that the position was not irrecoverable: other new buildings could redress the aesthetic balance, and fine landscaping and tree-planting had already worked a marvellous improvement in the appearance of the site. There is every reason to believe that the co-ordinating architect is right.[72]

At any rate, at long last Aberystwyth had a set of new buildings for its Science departments. During these years there was a considerable change in the professoriate in the Faculty of Science. The headships of the twin departments of Mathematics have changed several times. When V. C. Morton retired in 1961, he was replaced as professor of Pure Mathematics by W. B. Pennington, a Cambridge man then on the staff of the University of London, who was Vice-President of the London Mathematical Society and editor of its *Journal*.[73] Seven years later, however, Professor Pennington died suddenly in the prime of life. A year later A. O. Morris, who had been a member of the staff of the department since 1959 and had a considerable record of published work, was promoted to the chair, which he still occupies.[74] In 1952 the chair of Applied Mathematics was re-established with the appointment of G. J. Kynch, who came to Aberystwyth from Birmingham.[75] When he resigned in 1958, T. V. Davies, an old Aberystwyth student (a notable cricketer in his day), who was then a reader in Mathematics at King's College, London, succeeded to the chair. During his tenure, the two departments of Mathematics moved into their new quarters on Penglais. Conditions there were even more conducive to the traditionally close co-operation between the twin departments, which grew and flourished side by side. In 1968 T. V. Davies resigned and J. Heading, who had an impressive list of publications to his name, was elected to the chair.[76]

Aberystwyth was especially fortunate in the choice of its first professor of Statistics. D. V. Lindley had an outstanding record and was Director of the Statistical Laboratory at Cambridge at the time of his appointment. During the six years he was at Aberystwyth he rapidly built up the new department, and the

[72] *U.C.W. Development Plan. Stage I—Preliminary Report*, p. 8.
[73] *Council Minutes* (8 April 1961), p. 94.
[74] Ibid. (26 March 1969), p. 171. D. S. Meyler, loc. cit.
[75] *Council Minutes* (31 October 1951), p. 2.
[76] Ibid. (22 March 1958, 1 November 1967), pp. 5, 71. D. S. Meyler, loc. cit.

postgraduate diploma and higher degree courses established proved a great attraction for high-quality students from other universities as well as from the Welsh Colleges. The department, which was soon equipped with a computer, was also able to offer a wide range of services to other departments in the College. D. V. Lindley resigned in 1967, and in the following year he was replaced by O. L. Davies, whose first degree had been taken at Swansea and whose extensive list of publications had appeared during the many years he had worked for the I.C.I. corporation. The establishment of the department of Statistics marked a very considerable accession of strength to the work of the College.[77]

The headship of the department of Chemistry also changed several times during the years under review. In 1960 C. W. Davies resigned. There was a large application for the chair, to which A. F. Trotman-Dickenson was elected. The new professor, originally an Oxford man, had had extensive research experience abroad and he was then on the staff of Edinburgh University. He had great energy and a taste for administration which were valuable attributes in the head of a large department that was soon to have considerably increased laboratory facilities at its disposal (an extension was added to the Edward Davies Laboratory in 1966) which enabled a substantial reorganization of the work of the department to be carried out. In 1968 A. F. Trotman-Dickenson resigned on his appointment to the Principalship of the University of Wales Institute of Science and Technology. This time there was an even larger application for the chair, to which J. M. Thomas, a graduate of the University of Wales, whose outstanding contributions to research had been recognized with the award of the Corday-Morgan Prize by the Chemistry Society and the Pettinos Prize by the American Carbon Committee, was elected.[78]

In 1958 R. M. Davies contracted pneumonia and, to the sorrow of his many friends, not least in the United States where his personal and academic qualities were warmly appreciated, died suddenly. The new professor of Physics was W. J. G. Beynon, who had worked for several years in close collaboration with Sir Edward Appleton at the National Physical Laboratories, and had established a considerable reputation for research into the physics of the ionosphere. Professor Beynon was internationally known for his work (he was a founder member of the International Geophysical Year organization) on behalf of co-operation in Science between the countries of the world. These are exciting times for physicists,

---

[77] *Council Minutes* (11 November 1959, 1 November 1967), pp. 2–3, 6. *College Reports* (1962–70), passim. In 1970 a chair in Computer Science was established, to which G. Emery, lecturer in Computer Science at Royal Holloway College, London, was elected. The small new department quickly got into its stride and, as from October 1971, offered joint honours courses in association with several other departments. *College Reports* (1971), p. 54.

[78] *Council Minutes* (25 March 1960, 26 March 1969), pp. 34–5, 169–70. *College Reports* (1960–8), passim. In 1968 Dr. Mansel Davies' fine research record was recognized with the conferment of a personal chair in the department of Chemistry.

and the research work of members of the department (the investigation of the ionosphere by rocket and by radio telescope and the optical tracking of satellites loom large in a typical space-age programme) is particularly varied and interesting. In recent years postgraduate Diploma or M.Sc. courses in electronics and the physics of the atmosphere have also been introduced. Not the least of the strengths of this department is the high quality of the supporting technical staff. In 1970 a second chair in Physics was established to which Norman Twiddy, formerly at York University, was appointed.[79]

There have been fewer changes in the Biology departments. In 1961 T. A. Stephenson, professor of Zoology at the College for twenty-one years, whose researches on sea-shore fauna and flora had given him the status of a recognized authority and led to his election to a Fellowship of the Royal Society in 1951, died suddenly. He was replaced by Bryn M. Jones who had considerable research experience in government service as well as in the academic world, and whose work was currently supported by substantial grants from the British Empire Cancer Campaign. In 1971 Dr. Gwendolen Rees was awarded a personal chair in the department; in the same year, too, she had been elected to a Fellowship of the Royal Society. Dr. Rees joined the department after taking her initial degree at Cardiff; she is the first woman academic in Wales to be elected to the Royal Society.[80] In 1958 Dr. Lily Newton retired after almost thirty years as professor of Botany. Her successor had had an interesting and unusual career: P. F. Wareing had spent nine years in the Inland Revenue department before turning to Botany; he soon more than made up for lost time, for within ten years he was a D.Sc. and had become a professor. The same fine combination of outstanding ability and exceptional energy brought him election to the Royal Society in 1970.[81]

In 1959 R. O. Davies retired from the chair of Agricultural Chemistry after thirty-nine years of service to the College in one capacity or another. T. W. Goodwin, who came from Liverpool with an exceptionally impressive record as a biochemist, was appointed to the professorship. Not long afterwards there was a change of title: the department was renamed under the style Biochemistry and Agricultural Biochemistry and the honours course was largely revised. During the last decade a fine reputation has been built up, and the quality of work done has

---

[79] *Council Minutes* (25 July 1958), pp. 133–4. *College Reports* (1958–71), passim. W. M. Jones (and others), loc. cit., pp. 18–28. In 1965 I. C. Jones, who for many generations of students embodied the Physics department, died suddenly. He exemplified a type of member of staff in which Aberystwyth has always been rich: the long-serving, utterly devoted senior teacher whose concern for students and for the College is never less than total. Over the years, most departments, luckily, have had their equivalents to I. C. Jones.

[80] *Council Minutes* (23 June 1961), pp. 102–3. *College Reports* (1961 and 1971), pp. 56, 65.

[81] *Council Minutes* (27 June 1958), p. 104. Principal's Report, *Court Minutes* (29 October 1958), pp. 10–11. *College Reports* (1971), p. 47. In 1971 J. G. Morris was appointed to a chair in Microbiology, for which there had been a growing demand in the department in recent years.

attracted a steady stream of visitors from overseas. In 1966 T. W. Goodwin returned to Liverpool and in due course he, too, was elected to the Royal Society: Aberystwyth may fairly lay claim to share in the lustre thus earned. H. K. King, who succeeded to the chair, also came to Aberystwyth from Liverpool. In addition to a very long list of published work, he had extensive experience of university administration.[82]

In 1967 the Dairy department, which had made an important contribution to farming in Wales during its years of existence, was finally wound up. For some time the University Grants Committee had increasingly looked askance at the continuation of the Diploma in Dairying, 'sub-university work' for which there was no legitimate place in a university institution, in the judgement of the Committee. During the quinquennial visitation of 1961, Sir Keith Murray bluntly demanded that the College (as it was, Aberystwyth would be the last university or university college to abandon work of this kind) should 'make up its mind to end' an anomaly which was 'becoming increasingly embarrassing' to the University Grants Committee. Thus challenged, the College had no option but to agree. Sir Keith at least conceded that the closure should be accomplished at a civilized *andante* pace. Within six years the department came to an end (in 1965 the College decided to give up degree work in Dairy Science, too) and John Lewis, anchorman and Director since 1940, turned his talents and experience to other good purposes as a Careers Adviser to students in the Faculty of Science.[83]

Five years later, with higher education costs mounting rapidly, the University Grants Committee, not unreasonably, was exhorting universities 'to rationalize their developments, since it no longer made sense for everyone to try to do everything'. In particular, so far as Aberystwyth was concerned, it meant that the departments of Agriculture at the College and at Bangor would have to come to terms of accommodation. Since that time, this enforced assuagement of an old, occasionally bitter, rivalry has gone ahead. In 1970 when J. E. Nichols, one of the two professors of Agriculture appointed at Aberystwyth in 1946, retired, the separate chair of Animal Husbandry lapsed and W. Ellison, who previously had occupied a chair of Crop Husbandry, became professor of Agriculture and sole head of department.[84] At the beginning of the session 1962–3, E. F. Nash, professor of Agricultural Economics, died suddenly. He, too, like A. W. Ashby before him, had made a very substantial contribution to the growth and development of this relatively new university discipline. There was some delay before the chair was was filled. However, in March 1964, H. T. Williams, an old Aberystwyth student

[82] *Council Minutes* (20 March 1959, 25 March 1960, 18 March 1966), pp. 52–3, 58–9, 166–7. *College Reports* (1958–71), passim.

[83] *Council Minutes* (18 May 1961), p. 100. *College Reports* (1962, 1965), pp. 69, 80–1.

[84] *Council Minutes* (10 March 1966), p. 160. Broadly, rationalization meant that Bangor's emphasis would be on animal husbandry, and Aberystwyth would specialize in crop husbandry. Accordingly, the College Animal Health Unit at Peithyll was closed down.

who was then Deputy Principal of Seale-Hayne Agricultural College and had extensive experience of the work of various international agencies concerned with European agriculture, was appointed to replace E. F. Nash.[85]

Geography, which had always had a footing in the two Faculties at Aberystwyth, will serve as a bridge from Science to Arts. The department has borne its share of the expansion of the College in recent years. For a good many years most of the courses in physical geography had been taught in the department of Geology. In 1964, however, it became possible to establish a chair of Physical Geography, to which C. Kidson, who after some years of university teaching had become head of the Coastal Research Section of the Nature Conservancy and had conducted a great deal of experimental work, was appointed. In 1968, when E. G. Bowen retired (his energy and popularity as a lecturer remain undiminished in his Emeritus years), C. Kidson became head of the department, retaining the same title. The College was naturally anxious, if possible, to retain the traditional Aberystwyth connection with Human Geography, with which the Gregynog chair, ever since its foundation, had been associated. Accordingly, Harold Carter, an old student and a member of staff who had specialized in Urban Geography (yet another latter-day development pioneered years before by H. J. Fleure, the 'Father' of the department), was elected to a Gregynog chair of Human Geography. Despite change and growth, the department of Geography retains its strong 'family' tradition and great pride in its pioneering record. Many of its old students occupy eminent positions in the world, and it is worthy of note that, in 1968, sixty-nine former Aberystwyth students were university teachers of Geography, eighteen of them with professorial rank.[86]

There have been slightly fewer professorial changes in the Faculty of Arts in the last twenty years. In 1952 the College lost one of its greatest adornments when T. H. Parry-Williams retired from the chair of Welsh Language and Literature which he had occupied for over thirty years. During that time he had made an immense contribution to Welsh letters and became, as he remains to this day, one of the foremost men in Welsh public life whose name is familiar and whose work has a currency throughout the Celtic world. In the early years of his career, it had been a near thing for Welsh scholarship. In 1919 his prospects were particularly bleak: he then held a temporary lectureship which came up for renewal each year, and it seemed that his hopes of promotion would be permanently blighted by the virulent hostility of the ex-servicemen, who could not forgive him for his con-

---

[85] *College Reports* (1963), p. 79. *Council Minutes* (16 March 1964), pp. 106–7. In 1968 Dr. H. Rees, an old student and senior member of the department, was appointed to a second chair in Agricultural Botany.

[86] Ibid. (20 April 1964, 18 December 1967, 30 April 1968), pp. 140, 163–4, 379. *Geography at Aberystwyth*, pp. xxix–xxxvi. The Geology department, too, had grown considerably in recent years, and in 1970 a chair of Applied Geology was established to which William Davies, who was then Director of Research for a large industrial corporation, was appointed.

scientious objections to the war.[87] Despairing of an academic career, he turned his attention to medicine (in which, no doubt, with his great gifts, he would have achieved an equivalent eminence) and enrolled as a student in Intermediate courses in Science at the College. Happily for the language and literature of Wales, he was restored to professional academic life before his medical career was far advanced. As a matter of fact he broke off his work in a practical class in Intermediate Physics to attend the interview which brought him his chair in Welsh Language and Literature in 1920. This transformation of a first-year student into a professor within the hour must surely be unique in the academic world. T. H. Parry-Williams was the first Aberystwyth student to take first-class honours in Welsh. Subsequently, he had studied at Oxford, at the University of Freiburg, and at the Sorbonne, and he was marvellously equipped for a scholarly career, particularly for original work in Celtic linguistics. His book, *The English Element in Welsh*, published in 1923, was a superb pioneer study in Celtic philology which achieved an authority unchallenged to this day. His list of published work is extensive: even so, it does not fully express the truly brilliant quality (which is admitted on all sides) of the range of his talents. During the years in nominal retirement he has remained vigorously active on most of the important bodies concerned with the cultural life of Wales, and in 1958 his services were fittingly recognized with a knighthood.

There was considerable public interest in the appointment of a successor to T. H. Parry-Williams. And once again the candidates (two of whom were colleagues of long-standing on the staff at Aberystwyth) suffered the embarrassment of a flurry of newspaper comment in the interval before the election was finally made. The controversy, such as it was, centred on the argument that insufficient attention was paid to the claims of modern Welsh literature, and it was suggested that there was a case for two chairs, as there had been years before in the time of T. Gwynn Jones.[88] In the event, Thomas Jones, an old student who had joined the staff in 1933, was appointed to the chair. He had a fine academic record which included a double First, and his many publications were concerned with both the language and the literature of Wales. It was agreed that the question of additional provision for the study of Welsh literature would be considered later. Subsequently, a committee appointed for this purpose recommended that D. Gwenallt Jones should be designated senior lecturer in modern Welsh Literature and that an additional member of staff should be appointed to assist on the literature side.[89] In later years specialists in Irish, Breton, and Cornish were appointed, and in 1965 this valuable extension of the work of the department was considerably strengthened when J. E. Caerwyn Williams, a Welsh scholar who

[87] See above, pp. 204–5.
[88] *Western Mail* (15 and 17 March 1952). *Baner ac Amserau Cymru* (5 March 1952).
[89] *Council Minutes* (19 March 1952, 18 March 1953), pp. 41–2, 62.

had specialized in Irish Studies and had a substantial list of publications in that field to his credit, was elected to a new chair of Irish within the department.[90] Unhappily, in 1969 Thomas Jones (a phenomenally hard worker all his academic life) had to resign because of ill-health. He was given a personal chair for the succeeding session. In 1970 R. G. Gruffydd, a specialist in sixteenth- and seventeenth-century Welsh literature then on the staff at Bangor, was elected professor of Welsh Language and Literature.[91]

On the same day that Thomas Jones was appointed, a new professor of German was elected. C. P. Magill had been educated at Belfast, Cambridge, and the University of Bonn, and he came to Aberystwyth from King's College, London. He occupied the chair until he resigned in 1971, and during his tenure Russian and Swedish studies were developed under the aegis of the German department. C. P. Magill's calm wisdom was much in demand in College matters, and he was a notably successful Vice-Principal during the late 1950s. In 1971 A. R. Robinson, a former member of staff who had accepted a chair in Canada, returned to succeed C. P. Magill.[92] E. R. Briggs remained head of the department of French for twenty-six years until he resigned in 1971. During that time there were important developments: specialists in Spanish and Italian were added to the staff, and recently, so as more accurately to reflect the range of work, the department changed its title to Romance Studies. Aberystwyth was one of the first university institutions in Britain to insist that students reading for degrees in modern languages should spend the penultimate year of their four-year honours courses living and working abroad in the country with which their studies were primarily concerned. The work of all these departments, too, has been powerfully assisted by the extensive use made in recent years of language laboratories.

The department of English remains one of the largest in the College. In 1964 Gwyn Jones, the distinguished authority on the Icelandic saga, who had been Rendel professor since 1940 and had done so much to encourage the work of the Anglo-Welsh school of writers, resigned and accepted a chair at Cardiff. He was replaced by Arthur Johnston, an Oxford man then on the staff of Birkbeck College, London, who was currently chairman of the Boards of Examiners in English for the twenty-five Teachers' Training Colleges attached to the London Institute of Education.[93] During the last decade there has been a strong new emphasis on the literature (American and English) of the twentieth century, and the department has collaborated closely with History to sponsor new courses in American Studies which have proved immensely popular.

In 1969 R. I. Aaron retired after thirty-seven years as professor of Philosophy at Aberystwyth. The authority of his work on John Locke has never been supplanted,

[90] Ibid. (8 April 1965), pp. 153–4. *College Reports* (1952–70), passim.
[91] *Council Minutes* (26 March 1970), pp. 194–5.   [92] Ibid. (30 March 1971).
[93] Ibid. (26 September and 18 December 1964), pp. 47, 240.

and over the years he added to his reputation with other significant contributions to scholarship, notably a volume published in 1952 which included an excellent historical study of the great philosophers. In retirement he continues to publish important work. T. A. Roberts, a senior member of the department, succeeded R. I. Aaron in the chair. The new professor had at one time been head of the department of Historical Theology at the University of Keele, and he has a special interest in eighteenth-century Moral Philosophy.[94] At one time it had been hoped to establish a chair of Psychology within the Philosophy department, but nothing came of this. A most valuable addition to the work of the department within the Faculty of Science in recent years has been the new courses offered in mathematical logic. This may well lead, in due course, to the establishment of a separate chair.

In 1967 R. F. Treharne, who had been professor of History for thirty-seven years, died after a long, painful illness borne with great courage. Under his leadership the work of the department had been steadily deepened and widened: many new special subject options in British and European history were added to the honours scheme, and Aberystwyth was one of the first departments in Britain to offer specialist courses in American and colonial history. Throughout his career R. F. Treharne had been unremittingly active in the Historical Association, of which he was one of the most influential members. He edited *History* for ten years; he founded the Association's immensely valuable summer schools: fittingly, in 1958, he was elected President of the Association. Not long before he died he published a small book on *The Glastonbury Legends*, which won high praise from the reviewers and gave great delight to the discriminating reader. Throughout his long tenure he was a power on the Senate, and it was no accident that on two occasions of especial difficulty for the College, R. F. Treharne was called on to act as Vice-Principal. The new professor of History in succession to R. F. Treharne was S. H. F. Johnston, who had joined the department as a temporary assistant lecturer in 1934, and in the interim had moved through every grade of membership of the staff to the chair. He was a vastly experienced teacher, a first-rate lecturer, and a specialist in military history. During the war he had written regularly on military affairs for *The Spectator*, and, among other things, he had published a fine regimental history of the Cameronians.[95]

In recent years, the department of Welsh History has been beset by misfortune and, indeed, tragedy. In 1964 T. Jones Pierce, professor of Medieval Welsh History, died suddenly after a short illness when he was apparently in the prime of life. This was a heavy blow to Welsh historical scholarship. His chair had been

---

[94] Ibid. (26 March 1969), p. 170.

[95] There is a finely written tribute ('Reginald Francis Treharne (1901–1967): An Appreciation') by Glanmor Williams in the Historical Association publication, *Essays in Thirteenth Century England* (1971). *Council Minutes* (21 June 1967), pp. 236–7.

established in recognition of his personal distinction, and the question of a professorial successor therefore did not arise. Sadly, too, the health of David Williams was steadily deteriorating and, in consequence, the marvellous flow of scholarly works which had distinguished his long tenure as Sir John Williams professor came to an end just before his retirement in 1967. His successor was W. Ogwen Williams, senior lecturer in the department, a specialist in sixteenth-century Welsh History who seemed to have many years of important work before him.[96] Tragically, however, it was not to be: two years later Ogwen Williams lost his life in circumstances that evaded full explanation, and the small band of scholars in Welsh History was reduced still further. A year later I. Gwynedd Jones was appointed to the Sir John Williams chair.[97] The new professor, who was then a senior member of the staff at University College, Swansea, has a fine reputation for meticulous scholarship. A specialist in nineteenth-century Welsh History with a taste for sociological investigation, it may well be that, under his leadership, the work of the department will strike out in new directions.

In the last twenty years or so fewer Aberystwyth students proportionately have entered the teaching profession than formerly. Even so, Wales still produces far more than its share of teachers, and the department of Education at Aberystwyth is now much larger than it was in the years immediately after the war. It is fair to say, too, that the department has never been daunted by the fact that its work has had to be carried on in substandard premises. In 1960 Idwal Jones, 'the most human and humane' of heads of department, as one of his colleagues described him, was forced to retire because of persistent ill health. He was succeeded in the chair by Jac L. Williams, an old Aberystwyth student then on the staff, who had a very wide range of teaching experience and great drive and energy.[98] The work of the department has been developed in several important respects in recent years: courses leading to a Certificate in Biblical Studies and a Diploma in Bilingual Education have been introduced; a new Advanced Course in Education has been established and the honours class in Education (Aberystwyth was one of the first British university institutions to introduce this degree scheme) has grown steadily in size. The department has given a strong lead with its experimental work on the Welsh language as a medium of instruction, and members of the staff have published important work (which has a relevance for many countries other than Wales) on the problems of bilingualism.[99]

Traditionally, professors of Law at Aberystwyth have shown exceptional stamina: T. A. Levi held his chair for thirty-nine years, and in 1970 his successor, D. J. Llewelfryn Davies, retired after three decades as head of the department. During that time he had been the benign father-figure of a department that

---

[96] *Council Minutes* (21 June 1967), pp. 237–8.   [97] Ibid. (16 December 1969), p. 118.
[98] *College Reports* (1960), p. 24. *Council Minutes* (26 October 1960), pp. 2–3.
[99] *College Reports* (1958–71), passim.

continued to send out into the world a steady stream of young men and women destined for distinguished careers in the legal profession. In 1967 J. A. Andrews who, after a fine career at Oxford, had taught at the Universities of Manchester and Birmingham, was appointed to a second chair of Law. And in 1970 T. H. Moseley, a Cambridge man who had formerly been on the staff at Aberystwyth, was elected to the chair vacated by D. J. Llewelfryn Davies.[100] The headship of the department has not hitherto been filled. The curriculum of the LL.B. degree is, naturally, largely governed by the professional requirements of the Law Society. However, one interesting addition (a smart anticipation of the British entry into the Common Market) to the work of the department in the last few years has been the introduction of courses in European Community Law. It is likely that, over the next ten years as additional accommodation becomes available, the Law department will be substantially enlarged.

In 1965 the College at last realized a fifty-year-old ambition when a Faculty of Economic and Social Studies was established. For a short time before the 1914–18 war, W. Jenkyn Jones had been professor of Political Science, but in 1912 soon after he retired, partly for reasons of economy and partly because E. A. Lewis was, to some extent, equipped for the dual responsibility, Political Science was annexed to the chair of Economics. Subsequently, however, Political Science at Aberystwyth withered to nothing, and the double-barrelled title of the chair occupied by R. B. Forrester and Arthur Beecham between 1931 and 1963 did no more for Political Science than formally to express the College's recognition that the subject existed elsewhere as a legitimate academic discipline. An attempt in the years after the 1939–45 war to establish a sub-department of Public Administration did not succeed. However, in 1965, when the new Faculty came into existence, a separate chair in Political Science was re-established. The new professor, I. L. Gowan, is a specialist in local government and, under his leadership, the department is building a reputation for advanced work in this field which, currently, has a new importance, particularly perhaps for Wales at the present time when the virtue of a unitary system of British government is under challenge.[101]

In 1963 Arthur Beecham, who had carried out a considerable moderniza-tion of the work of the department of Economics, resigned his chair to become Vice-Chancellor of the University of Otago. There were now to be two chairs of Economics at Aberystwyth: George Clayton, a Cambridge economist who was currently a senior lecturer at Liverpool, became professor of Economics and head of the department, and E. T. Nevin, a distinguished former Aberystwyth student who had written several good books and had a wide experience as an economic adviser overseas, was appointed to a second chair in Applied Economics.[102]

[100] *Council Minutes* (21 June 1967, 16 June 1970), pp. 238–9, 334–5.
[101] Ibid. (20 April 1964), pp. 164–5. *College Reports* (1965–71), passim.
[102] *Council Minutes* (9 July 1963), pp. 128–9.

During the next four years the two new professors established a notably happy and successful partnership in the department. In 1967, however, George Clayton accepted a chair at Sheffield, and the following year E. T. Nevin, whose investigations of the Welsh economy had attracted a good deal of attention, moved to Swansea. In that same year Graham L. Rees, who had been a student at Aberystwyth for a time, a specialist in monetary problems who was then a senior lecturer at Swansea, was appointed to the chair of Economics. And in April 1970 P. N. Mathur, professor at the University of Poona, a specialist in economic theory with a list of publications almost a yard long to his name, was elected to the second chair.[103]

P. A. Reynolds resigned the Wilson chair in International Politics in 1964. During his fourteen-year tenure the department grew to full stature.[104] L. W. Martin, the new Wilson professor, a Cambridge man who had had a distinguished professional career subsequently at Yale University and the Massachusetts Institute of Technology, united great energy with outstanding ability. He lectured extensively at home and abroad on defence policy, and his services were much in demand by the Institute of Strategic Studies and various government agencies. In recent years the department has conducted a series of war games (role-playing attempts to simulate the conditions in which decisions in international crises are arrived at) which has attracted a great deal of public and official attention. In 1968 L. W. Martin accepted a chair at King's College, London, and in the following year T. E. Evans, a former academic who had subsequently had a long career in the diplomatic service, ultimately serving as British Ambassador at Algiers, Damascus, and Baghdad, was elected to the Wilson chair.[105]

Not the least of the reasons why the growth of the College has proceeded relatively so smoothly in the years since the war has been the quality of the administration. For very many years Aberystwyth has been fortunate to have the assistance of a first-rate hard-core of senior clerical personnel, many of whom have spent thirty years (in some cases even longer) in the service of the College. In December 1966, for example, William Lewis, Estates Officer, who began as an office-boy, retired after completing more than half-a-century of work on behalf of the College.[106] When the growth of the College made it necessary to expand

---

[103] *Council Minutes* (18 March 1968, 21 April 1970), pp. 220–1, 333.

[104] *College Reports* (1964), pp. 46–7. Professor Reynolds paid a handsome tribute to the support he had received in building up the department from I. G. John, his senior (and, for many years, only) colleague.

[105] *Council Minutes* (28 September 1964, 26 March 1969), pp. 168–9, 240–1. *College Reports* (1962–71), passim.

[106] Principal's Report, *Court Minutes* (26 October 1966), p. 7. Although none of his successors quite matched Sergeant Wakeling's colourful personality, all subsequent Head Porters at Aberystwyth have been men to savour. Generations of Aberystwyth students will recall with respect and affection Sergeant Morgan (of whom many delightful stories, unfortunately not recorded in print, are retailed), Chief Petty Officer Brewer (inevitably 'The Admiral'), and W. J. Wintle, who, sadly, died suddenly in January 1972.

rapidly the Registrar's office, the existence of this cadre of devoted, experienced staff guaranteed the maintenance of administrative standards. At a more senior level, it became necessary in October 1955 to appoint a Deputy Registrar. And subsequently several other executive officers, variously ranked as Assistant Registrars or Administrative Assistants, have also been recruited. In 1966 T. Maelgwyn Davies, Registrar since 1944, died after some years of intermittent illness. He had been at the centre of things in times of great stress and unexampled difficulty. T. Maelgwyn Davies was an exacting taskmaster who demanded rather less of others than he was prepared always to give himself to the service of the College, which remains very much in his debt. He was followed in the Registrarship by T. Arfon Owen, who had read modern languages at Oxford and had succeeded the first Deputy Registrar in 1959.[107]

It was perhaps inevitable that, as all the constituent Colleges grew steadily in size (and a large further expansion was in prospect), the continued existence of the federal, national University of Wales would be called into question by some people, chiefly certain members of the Senates of the Colleges. In December 1960 the University Court appointed a Commission to review and report on the functions, powers, structure, and the future status of the University and its constituent Colleges. These matters aroused strong feelings: it soon became evident that the Commission was deeply divided, and a sharp, occasionally fiercely acrimonious, controversy developed. Ultimately, fourteen members of the Commission signed a *Report* that favoured the creation of four unitary universities in Wales, and twelve other members appended their names to a second *Report* that recommended the continuance (with some modifications) of the existing federal University. Principal Thomas Parry of Aberystwyth issued a separate *Statement* which argued that the Commission had exceeded its terms of reference in making recommendations, and offered the opinion that the proper course would have been for the Commission to have presented one Report (in which the opposing cases were set out for the consideration of the Court) signed by all its members.[108] Eventually, in 1964, the second, technically the minority, *Report* was accepted by the University Court, and the survival of the federal University was thereby assured.[109] The corporate opinion of the College at Aberystwyth on the question of the defederation of the University was never expressed. But the evidence suggests that there was less support at Aberystwyth for the proposal to break up the University than at any of the other Colleges. In 1961 Aberystwyth students voted strongly in favour of the retention of the federal University.[110] And it may certainly be

---

[107] *Council Minutes* (13 February 1967), pp. 151–2.

[108] *University of Wales: University Commission. Final Reports* (February 1964).

[109] The controversy did not subside immediately. *The Anvil* (1964, 1965) contains a vigorous defence of the federal University and a number of sharp attacks on opponents. The *Western Mail* during the same period is the best source for critical comment.

[110] *Courier* (26 February 1961).

said that men and women with Aberystwyth affiliations provided the main impetus behind the activities of the 'Friends of the University of Wales', an influential pressure group equipped with a powerfully emotive title organized in defence of the federal University.

Indeed, the most formidable champion of the existing University system was Sir David Hughes Parry, President of the Aberystwyth College. In 1964, however, Sir David, whose health was less robust than formerly, resigned after completing two terms as President. He had been ideally equipped for this office, particularly in a period when the College was expanding rapidly and relations with the University Grants Committee (of which he had an experience unrivalled in Wales) were becoming increasingly important. The President was open-eyed about the competitive world in which universities, whether they liked it or not, now had to exist; and he believed strongly that, if the College were to continue to attract students of quality, amenities must be improved and extended. The retiring President, who was a generous benefactor of his old College, had worked in the closest amity with Principal Parry, and throughout a long and exceptionally distinguished career he had a fine record of service to Aberystwyth. Happily, the new President, like his two predecessors, was an old student of the College. Sir Ben Bowen Thomas (he had been knighted in 1950) had spent the greater part of his professional life in education, and for eighteen years before his retirement in 1963 he had been Permanent Secretary to the Welsh Department of the Ministry of Education. Sir Ben had been active in the public life of Wales (not least in those agencies concerned with social well-being) for forty years or more, and he brought to the Presidency a vast experience of men and affairs in Wales and beyond. The new President was a former member of the College staff; indeed, it appears that on one occasion at least he was privately sounded about the Principalship. At any rate, he had maintained the closest interest in the College throughout his adult life, and in 1964 it was agreed with enthusiasm on all sides that Sir Ben was the natural successor to the Presidency.[111]

Many people at this time were reassured, too, by the fact that the President and the Principal of the College were both thorough Welshmen, deeply concerned to maintain the distinctive traditions of Aberystwyth. For the plain fact was that, as the College grew in size, the number of students drawn from Wales formed a smaller and smaller proportion of the whole (66 per cent in 1960, 47 per cent in 1965, with a further alarming fall in 1969 to 37 per cent, a proportion which, since that time, has gradually been increased to 45 per cent.)[112] In the circumstances there was the very real danger that the Welsh character of the College would be lost; and there were many who echoed the hope expressed by Principal Parry

[111] *Council Minutes* (17 December 1963, 26 June 1964), pp. 103, 236.
[112] *College Reports* (1960, 1965, 1969), pp. 98, 99, 118. *Principal's Address to the Court of Governors* (26 October 1971), p. 6.

in 1959 that the College would 'always be what its official title describes it as being'.[113] There was a feeling, too, that the College could and should do more to foster the Welsh language. In July 1963 the Council approved in principle the recognition of the Welsh language (which was to be given a status equal to English) in the affairs of the College, and a committee was appointed to make recommendations to give effect to the general principle. The committee refused to recommend an official declaration of a fully bilingual policy on the ground that it was impracticable at that stage. However, it was recommended that henceforth, as soon as may be, all College literature and official signs should be in both languages, and College correspondence could be conducted in either Welsh or English, the particular language used to be determined by the circumstances. The academic staff of the College was deeply, in some instances bitterly, divided on this question.[114]

There was also considerable opposition to a proposal in 1967 to establish a Welsh hostel for those students who expressed a desire to live in a hall of that character. Critics of the proposal maintained that it was unwise to abandon the long-standing principle that the body of students in a hall, ideally at least, should be as diverse as possible. On the other hand, those who supported the proposal argued that it was natural and reasonable that students who so desired should be able to live in a hall in which things Welsh (including the language) would be predominant. The Students' Representative Council lodged an official objection, and later organized a march of protest against the scheme.[115] However, in October 1968, Ceredigion became a Welsh hall for men students, and Neuadd Davies Bryan the equivalent for women.

There has been another important innovation in hall accommodation at Aberystwyth in the last few years. In 1968 a new hostel, which differed in several respects from the traditional style hall, was formally opened by Mrs. Enid Parry. Neuadd Cwrt Mawr (the name commemorates Principal J. H. Davies whose family home was so designated) is a mixed hall, restricted to senior students, men and women occupying separate blocks. The hall has no communal dining-room, and residents (most of whom have single study-bedrooms) live in small groups ten strong, each of which has a small, well-equipped kitchen-cum-dining-room at its service. There is an excellent Common Room (which incorporates a licensed club) and a vigorous social life has been established in the hall. Cwrt Mawr has been fortunate in its first Warden, and for a variety of good reasons places are in great demand by students. It was more than ordinarily important that the Cwrt

---

[113] *Court Minutes* (11 November 1959), p. 7.

[114] *Council Minutes* (9 July 1963, 24 June 1964), pp. 192, 229-31. In recent years the College has appointed several members of staff to teach through the medium of Welsh.

[115] Ibid. (18 December 1967), pp. 158-9. *Courier* (14 May 1968). In 1965 Carpenter Hall, the home of generations of women students since 1919, became a hostel for men.

Mawr venture should succeed. Halls of this type are cheaper to build and are more economically administered; indeed, despite relatively low fees, they produce a useful profit. In 1966 Sir John Wolfenden, Chairman of the University Grants Committee, on the occasion of the quinquennial visitation of the College, had stated that, as the lodging accommodation in the town could not be further increased, expansion at Aberystwyth 'would be particularly expensive', because it depended on a costly programme of hostel-building.[116] The College took note of this plain hint to help itself. Cwrt Mawr originally accommodated one hundred and fifty students. Subsequently, other blocks (somewhat less expensively constructed and financed largely by loans with some contribution from the University Grants Committee) have been added, and shortly there will be 500 students in the Cwrt Mawr complex. Without this extraordinarily successful undertaking the expansion of the College would have come to a halt.

More recently still, two other sorely-needed facilities have been provided. The old Students' Union, magnificently as it had served its purpose in its time, was hopelessly inadequate in modern conditions. It was no easy matter to persuade the University Grants Committee, which still, no doubt of necessity, put the provision of additional student places well above social amenities in its list of priorities, to provide the money for a new Students' Union. Eventually, however, the money was forthcoming, and in 1970 the first stage of a fine new Union building was completed and opened. And at the same time a superb new building alongside, the Great Hall, which magnificently answers a need that has been all too miserably evident in the life of the College since the loss by fire of the old College Hall in 1933, was also opened by Lord Morris, Pro-Chancellor of the University of Wales.[117] So far, the College on the Hill has cost £3,935,000, of which almost £300,000 has been contributed by the College from its own resources.[118]

By October 1972 the new College Theatre building adjoining the Great Hall (the focal point of the Penglais site) will also be completed. The total cost of this project is of the order of £300,000. The College has provided £80,000, generous assistance has been forthcoming from the University Grants Committee, the Welsh Arts Council, and various charitable Foundations, and several of the local authorities of Wales have promised substantial donations. This fine addition to the cultural amenities of the area will be available for use by local dramatic groups and visiting professional companies as well as the College Societies.[119] It is fair to say that the various dramatic groups in the College have thoroughly earned the

---

[116] *Council Minutes* (10 March 1966), p. 159. *Court Minutes* (26 October 1966), pp. 8–9.

[117] The Old Students' Association contributed £900 for the Bell of the Great Hall campanile.

[118] To this large total must be added £230,000 spent on buildings on the Buarth, £20,000 for a new Boat House at the harbour, and £26,000 on the Blaendolau Playing Fields.

[119] *College Reports* (1971), p. 9.

right to have a purpose-built Theatre. The strong dramatic tradition at Aberystwyth goes back to the first days of the College. Undeterred by the most daunting difficulties, staff and student drama groups have succeeded year after year, to the delight of audiences who hunger for the theatre, in presenting plays of all kinds, classical and contemporary. Ingenuity has often achieved marvellous victories over the inadequacies of the Examination Hall. The English Society has a long list of superb productions (including a victory in the National Union of Students' drama competition in 1960) to its credit; *Y Gymdeithas Ddrama Gymraeg* (the Welsh Dramatic Society) has continued each year to present full-length and one-act plays; the French Society (since its inauguration in 1909) has regularly presented plays in French (and, latterly, in Spanish and Italian); and in recent years the Staff Drama Group and the College Women's Club have made substantial annual contributions to College theatre.

During the early 1960s, stimulated by the presence of a particularly gifted group of student directors and actors, drama at Aberystwyth achieved new standards. And the inauguration in 1962 of the annual Arts Festival, 'the most ambitious of cultural ventures by students in the post-war period', was a most important addition to the calendar of cultural activities in the College and the town.[120] Other student groups have been equally venturesome in different ways. The Madrigal Singers, who year after year maintain a superb standard, have delighted audiences in the U.S.A. and Canada; student expeditions to Greece, Afghanistan, and elsewhere have been carried out with great success. Each year the organizers of the Rag collections of money for charitable causes have boldly set their sights higher and higher, and Aberystwyth has the proud record of raising a larger *per capita* sum each year for this purpose than any other university or college in Britain. The range of sports activities has been enormously extended in the last few years, and there are now nearly forty clubs affiliated to the Central Athletic Board.[121] In view of the size of the College in relation to many of its university opponents, the successes gained by Aberystwyth teams in U.A.U. competitions are astonishing.[122] Pride of place, inevitably, goes to the rugby team, which has reached the U.A.U. Final on several occasions in the last ten years. But the greatest triumph ever achieved by Aberystwyth rugby came far away in New Zealand in 1971. For the College lays claim to S. J. Dawes, the superb captain of the British Lions team, who demolished so conclusively the absurd diehard notion that brilliant leadership was the prerogative of any one class; and also to Carwyn James, coach to the tourists, whose imaginative tactical ploys gave free rein to the marvellous talents at his disposal.

[120] R. F. Walker, 'Drama in U.C.W. since 1945', pp. 1–7.

[121] In 1964 William Groom, Head Groundsman and unfailing friend of every College team, retired after thirty-six years of service.

[122] These striking successes are detailed in the annual reports of the Director of Physical Education. *College Reports* (1962–71).

Mercifully, Aberystwyth has managed so far to avoid those confrontations between student militancy and governing authority which have so seriously disrupted the life of so many universities in Britain in recent times. Now and then the small Welsh Language Society has resorted to extreme protest action, and there have been occasions when the Students' Representative Council and the general body of students have had to exert pressure on the authorities, whose tradition in social matters is one of caution, for relaxations of the disciplinary code and the introduction of licensed bar facilities in the Union. But all these matters have been satisfactorily resolved at a point well short of serious crisis. The College has drawn a dividend, too, from its willingness for many years (reflected in the early establishment of the College and Students' Joint Committee) to take account of student opinion, at least on certain questions. Helped by the mutual confidence that existed between the authorities and the Union officials, in 1966 Aberystwyth students achieved representation on several College committees. There is no question that this student participation in the government of the College has been a substantial success, and the continuing consultation that has followed partly explains the absence at Aberystwyth of those open antagonisms so apparent elsewhere. It has been said, however, by some critics, that this amity owes something to the current besetting sin of apathy and the lucky chance that extreme radical opinions have not come to dominate the Union at Aberystwyth. Certainly the officers of the Union in recent years have preferred to concentrate their attention on matters of immediate student concern rather than on general political questions, the Vietnam war and the like.[123]

There is no doubt, too, that, despite expansion, the College still draws a large advantage from its relatively small size. The cold impersonality of a very large institution is avoided, and although there are now many more students than formerly, the locale of their daily existence has not been extended unduly. The College is bigger, but the town remains much the same size: everywhere and everyone is within walking distance. Aberystwyth became the object of widespread public attention in the summer term of 1969 when the Prince of Wales, as he was soon to become, spent a term at the College learning Welsh, reading the history of Wales, and continuing certain studies in Modern History. Old students of the College were prominent in the transmission of the news that Prince Charles, son of the Chancellor of the University, was to come to Aberystwyth. The President of the College, an old student, told the Court on 1 November 1967 that the formal message had been

delivered by . . . Dr. Elwyn Davies, as Secretary for Education for Wales, an old student; he received it from the hands of Dr. Goronwy Daniel, Permanent Secretary of the Welsh

---

[123] Arwel Ellis Owen, 'Aberystwyth, 1961–1966', pp. 1–3. B. R. Foster, 'Observations on the Students' Union', pp. 1–3. The President and Treasurer of the Students' Representative Council at the College are now full-time officers, and the Union has a paid Administrator at its service.

Office, another old student, who handed it on behalf of the Rt. Hon. Cledwyn Hughes, Secretary of State for Wales, yet another old student.[124]

During his term at the College Prince Charles lived at Pantycelyn, and every effort was made to make the circumstances of his stay as informal as possible. Beforehand there had been some fears that difficult situations stemming from political protests or hoaxes would arise; and there was some apprehension that the activity of newspapermen (a posse of reporters stayed in the town throughout the term) would disrupt the life of the Hall and the College. In the event, these fears were shown to be idle. A march of protest on Pantycelyn by an ill-assorted gaggle of student anarchists and extreme Welsh nationalists was cheerfully repelled with buckets of water by Pantycelyn students, who objected to this attempted invasion of their home.[125] Thereafter, there was no trouble of any kind. It should be said that the behaviour of the pressmen was impeccable throughout the term.[126] It was unfortunate that Prince Charles was unable to spend a whole session at Aberystwyth. Nevertheless, the Prince certainly made very good use of his time there, and the College may reasonably claim to have helped the Prince of Wales to equip himself for the new responsibilities he was shortly to undertake. In May, at the *Urdd* national *eisteddfod* at Aberystwyth, Prince Charles had a great personal triumph (which was also a fine illustration of the efficacy of Welsh language teaching at the College) when he demonstrated in public his new command of Welsh. In other respects, too, the Prince's stay was a conspicuous success: the general public responded with great enthusiasm to his presence, and large crowds daily lined the route from Pantycelyn to the College. Numbering the Prince of Wales among its old students, Aberystwyth had come a long way since that far-off day almost a hundred years before when the attempt to found a college had been dismissed with scorn and contempt by the powerful.

In September 1969 Dr. Thomas Parry retired after eleven years as Principal of the College. It was not an easy time for the heads of colleges: many of the traditional features of university life (some of which had been carefully nourished over centuries) were under fierce attack by impatient young critics who sometimes showed that they knew not what damage they wrought. Occasionally, a Principal could do no more than grin and bear it: 'A University administrator these days', Dr. Parry wrote ruefully in 1963, 'is far from being the master of his fate (still less the captain of his soul).'[127] Principal Parry was determined to defend 'the

---

[124] *Court Minutes* (1 November 1967), pp. 2–3. This is a neat illustration of the large number (over the years a disproportionate share) of the important offices in Wales, and indeed elsewhere, occupied by old students of Aberystwyth. [125] *Courier* (19 March 1969).

[126] On the other hand, the banality of questions asked at a press conference on 12 March 1969 was astonishing. None of the representatives of the international press who attended seemed to appreciate that here was a situation of very great interest: the arrival at a College with distinctive Welsh and radical traditions of the heir to the throne.

[127] Principal Parry to the Revd. Professor A. H. Curtis, 13 August 1963. C.A. P/Cr/F/2.

age-long concept of a university as a place of rational thought and responsible action'. At the same time, he conceded that there was often a good case for change and adjustment, and where this was so he took action. Goodwill, patience, and common sense were at a premium in these years, and the Principal possessed these qualities in more than ample measure. Throughout his tenure he did his utmost to foster that 'atmosphere of amity and courtesy' which had been a feature of the life of the College for so long.[128] Dr. Parry's easy, democratic manner (the meanest he always treated with the same warm friendliness as the most exalted) was an invaluable attribute in the head of a College which claimed to be peculiarly that of the people. The Principal inherited a difficult situation which he did much to ease. During his time the College almost doubled in size, and the College on the Hill came into being. These were years of difficulty on almost every front when the call for instant wisdom sometimes must have been intolerably demanding, particularly for one who, as he himself said, was 'mentally tortured' by the prospect of the extinction of the Welsh language.[129] Thomas Parry served the College well and faithfully: scholarship and teaching flourished under his encouragement; the immediate welfare and the long-term interests of his students were both his constant concern. He lent great natural dignity to his office.

Twenty-two names were considered for the Principalship. There were some formal applications, and other names were suggested by those empowered to do so. It was decided to proceed by informal methods, and, in the first instance anyway, it was intended to invite some half-dozen or so of those under consideration to meet the members of the selection committee for exploratory discussions over dinner. However, the committee discovered that there was a unanimous choice of the first of those who were to be approached. Dr. Goronwy Daniel met the committee on two occasions. It was unanimously agreed, subject to confirmation by the Council, to invite him to become Principal of the College. On 9 September 1968, after a formal interview, the Council, by acclamation, endorsed this recommendation. Born in Wales and Welsh-speaking, the new Principal (he was knighted before he assumed office) was an old student of the College. He had taken first-class honours in Geology in 1937, and had then gone on to Oxford where he took a doctorate in Economic Statistics. He had a wide variety of professional experience. He had spent a year lecturing at Bristol University, and two more on the staff of the House of Commons. In 1943 he joined the Civil Service and held senior appointments in several ministries before becoming Permanent Under-Secretary at the Welsh Office in 1964. He had published a large number of papers on a variety of subjects, especially energy statistics, local government reorganization and regional planning.[130] The appointment of Sir

[128] *U.C.W. Bulletin and Diary*, No. 18 (1969), pp. 1–3.
[129] Ibid., p. 4.
[130] *Council Minutes* (9 September 1968), pp. 494–7.

PLATE 14

Sir Goronwy Hopkin Daniel
(Principal, 1969–   )

Goronwy Daniel means that, most happily and appropriately in its Centenary year, the offices of President and Principal of the College will be occupied by old students.

The College at Aberystwyth has a great and romantic past, of which it is duly conscious and justifiably proud. For the greater part of its century of existence it had to struggle desperately against the odds. Small, isolated, in the fight to survive it developed an unconquerable spirit and a unique character. In some respects it has always been, as Sir George Stapledon approvingly pointed out, a College 'absolutely and completely unlike any other'.[131] Considering the paucity of financial resources available for most of the time, the achievement of the College is not far short of miraculous. It has more than held its own all along the academic front, and has sometimes given a lead (in more than one instance with international significance) to bigger and much wealthier institutions. To this day it holds a special place in the affections of the people of Wales, not least because its contribution to their well-being has been beyond measure. 'Aber.' (the short form is laden with affection) has always been able to evoke a tremendous loyalty in its students, wheresoever they are derived. Newcomers from the cities sometimes bemoan the absence of some things to which they are accustomed. These laments do not usually long survive: 'the warm social communism' of the life of students and staff at Aberystwyth is, for most people, very much more than ample compensation.[132] And it has always set a special stamp on members of the College never subsequently lost.

It is to be hoped that this will always be so. No doubt growth in size and the provision of fine new buildings have brought definite advantages. But a price of sorts has had to be paid. The College has lost some of its former heart-warming intimacy, its distinctively Welsh character is rather less dominant than it was, and there is a danger that some of its special features will gradually be lost. Herein lies the challenge of the future. The University College of Wales may well continue to grow: but it must never lose its historic identity or barter away its unique character.

[131] *Western Mail* (23 November 1953).

[132] *Courier* (21 May 1960)., 'If when Aber. breathes [the traditional College cry of "Breathe on 'em, Aber.", rearranged], the others fall down, it is under the impact of the wind of fraternity', wrote one departing member of staff. Richard Cobb, 'A Farewell to Aber.', Ibid. (13 May 1961).

Appendix A

PRESIDENTS

The Right Hon. Henry Austin, 1st Baron Aberdare, G.C.B., D.C.L.	1874–1895
The Right Hon. Stuart, Baron Rendel	1895–1913
Sir John Williams, Bt., G.C.V.O., LL.D., M.D., D.SC.	1913–1926
The Right Hon. Lord Davies, M.A., LL.D.	1926–1944
Thomas Jones, C.H., M.A., LL.D.	1944–1954
Sir David Hughes Parry, Q.C., M.A., D.C.L., LL.D.	1955–1964
Sir Ben Bowen Thomas, M.A., LL.D.	1964–

VICE-PRESIDENTS

(Prior to the granting of a Royal Charter in 1889, all Governors who were Members of Parliament or who had contributed £500 or upwards to the College were Vice-Presidents).

To 1889

David Davies, M.P.

David Davis

Lewis Davis

Stephen Evans

Thomas Jones

Morgan Lloyd, Q.C., M.P.

George Osborne Morgan, Q.C., M.P.

Samuel Morley, M.P.

Henry Parnall

Robert Parnall

Eliezer Pugh

John Henry Puleston, M.P.

Henry Richard, M.P.

John Foulkes Roberts

Henry Robertson, M.P.

Thomas Davies

Joseph Evans

John Roberts, M.P.

B. T. Williams, Q.C., M.P.

Sir R. A. Cunliffe, Bt., M.P.

William Davies, M.P.

Sir H. Hussey Vivian, Bt., M.P.

His Grace The Duke of Westminster, K.G.

Sir Love Jones Parry, Bt., M.P.

Lewis Pugh Pugh, M.P.

The Right Hon. Lord Sudeley

Stuart Rendel, M.P.

From 1889

The Right Hon. Stuart, Baron Rendel	1889–1895	John Foulkes Roberts	1889–1902
		Sir Lewis Morris	1896–1907

A. C. Humphreys-Owen, M.P.	1903–1905	Sir George Fossett Roberts	1940–1954
Sir John Williams, Bt.	1906–1913	Ivor Evans	1954–1962
The Right Hon. Lord Davies	1908–1926	Dr. W. Idris Jones	1963–1971
Sir A. Garrod Thomas	1914–1929	The Lady Davies	1964–1966
Sir D. C. Roberts	1927–1940	Sir Graham Sutton, F.R.S.	1967–
The Earl of Lisburne	1929–1964	Dr. William Thomas	1971–

HONORARY TREASURERS

David Davies, M.P.	1875–1887	Sir A. Garrod Thomas	1909–1914
Sir Hugh Owen	1878–1881	Sir D. Lleufer Thomas	1915–1929
Stephen Evans	1881–1888	John Burrell	1929–1932
Stuart Rendel (Lord Rendel)	1887–1889	Major Owen D. Jones	1929–1932
Sir Lewis Morris	1889–1893	The Right Hon. Lord Merthyr	1932–1937
A. C. Humphreys-Owen, M.P.	1889–1903	Sir D. Owen Evans, M.P.	1937–1945
Edward Davies	1893–1898	Ivor Evans	1945–1954
Sir John Williams, Bt.	1899–1906	J. Alban Davies	1954–1968
David Davies (Lord Davies)	1903–1908	The Hon. Islwyn Davies	1968–
Sir D. C. Roberts	1907–1929		

Appendix B

PRINCIPALS

T. C. Edwards 1872–91

T. F. Roberts 1891–1919

J. H. Davies 1919–26

(Sir) H. Stuart-Jones 1927–34

Ifor L. Evans 1934–52

M. Goronwy Rees 1953–7

Thomas Parry 1958–69

Sir Goronwy H. Daniel 1969–

HEADS OF DEPARTMENTS AND OTHER PROFESSORIAL STAFF

AGRICULTURE

T. Parry 1891–1901 (L.)

D. D. Williams 1901–7 (L.)

C. Bryner Jones 1907–19

Abel E. Jones 1919–24

J. Jones Griffith 1924–42

E. J. Roberts 1942–5

J. E. Nichols (Animal Husbandry) 1946–70

W. Ellison (Crop Husbandry) 1946–70, 1970–

AGRICULTURAL BOTANY

R. G. Stapledon 1912–19 (A.), 1919–42

T. J. Jenkin 1942–50

P. T. Thomas 1950–

H. Rees (2nd Chair) 1968–

AGRICULTURAL CHEMISTRY

J. A. Murray 1892–1907 (L.)

J. Jones Griffith 1907–21 (L.), 1921–4 (I.L.)

T. W. Fagan 1925–30 (I.L.), 1930–9

R. O. Davies 1939–54 (I.L.), 1954–9

AGRICULTURAL ECONOMICS

A. W. Ashby 1929–46

E. F. Nash 1946–62

H. T. Williams 1964–

ANIMAL HEALTH

A. N. Worden 1945–8

APPLIED MATHEMATICS

G. A. Schott 1909–10 (L.), 1910–33

Thomas Lewis 1933–50 (I.L.)

G. J. Kynch 1952–8

T. V. Davies 1958–67

J. Heading 1968–

BOTANY

L. Lyell 1874–5

F. W. Rudler 1875–6

W. Keeping 1876–9

T. S. Humpidge 1879–83

J. R. Ainsworth Davis 1883–91 (L.), 1891–4

J. H. Salter 1894–9 (L.), 1899–1903

R. H. Yapp 1903–14

★ For abbreviations see p. 336 below.

J. Lloyd Williams 1914–26
W. Robinson 1926–30
Mrs. Lily Newton 1930–58
P. F. Wareing 1958–
J. G. Morris (Microbiology) 1971–

BIOCHEMISTRY AND AGRICULTURAL
BIOCHEMISTRY
T. W. Goodwin 1959–66
H. K. King 1966–

CHEMISTRY
H. N. Grimley 1872–4
L. Lyell 1874–5
F. W. Rudler 1875–6 and 1877–9
R. D. Roberts 1876–7
T. S. Humpidge 1879–87
H. Lloyd Snape 1888–1901
J. J. Sudborough 1901–11
A. Findlay 1911–19
B. Mouat Jones 1919–21
T. Campbell James 1921–44
C. W. Davies 1944–60
A. F. Trotman-Dickenson 1960–8
Mansel Davies (Personal Chair) 1968–
J. M. Thomas 1969–

COMPARATIVE PHILOLOGY
J. Hoskyns-Abrahall 1872–3
J. M. Angus 1873–1905
Edward Anwyl 1905–14

COMPUTER SCIENCE
G. Emery 1970–

DAIRY DEPARTMENT
Miss B. L. Brown 1901–7 (L.)
Miss M. Fisk 1908–19 (L.)
Miss D. M. Evans 1919–29 (L.)

G. T. Morgan 1930–7 (L.)
John Lewis 1937–40 (L.), 1940–67 (D.)

ECONOMICS
G. Clayton 1963–7
E. T. Nevin (Applied Economics) 1963–8
Graham Rees 1968–
P. N. Mathur (2nd Chair) 1970–

ECONOMICS AND POLITICAL SCIENCE
E. A. Lewis 1912–31
R. B. Forrester 1931–51
A. Beacham 1951–63

EDUCATION
H. Holman 1892–3 (L.), 1893–4
Foster Watson 1894–6 (L.), 1896–1913
C. R. Chapple 1913–39
Idwal Jones 1939–60
Jac L. Williams 1961–

ENGLISH LANGUAGE AND LITERATURE
T. C. Edwards 1872–5
J. R. Buckley 1875–6
W. J. Craig 1876–9
M. W. MacCallum 1879–86
C. H. Herford 1887–1901
G. C. Macaulay 1901–6
J. W. H. Atkins 1906–40
Gwyn Jones 1940–64
A. Johnston 1965–

EXTRA-MURAL STUDIES
Directors
H. Morgan 1920–40
B. B. Thomas 1940–5
Ifan ab Owen Edwards 1946–9
A. D. Rees 1949–

FRENCH LANGUAGE AND LITERATURE

G. Thibaut 1872–5
H. Ethé 1875–94
W. Borsdorf 1894–1903
L. E. Kastner 1903–9
J. L. André Barbier 1909–44
E. R. Briggs 1944–71

GEOGRAPHY

J. Hoskyns-Abrahall 1872–3
L. Lyell 1874–5
F. W. Rudler 1875–6
R. D. Roberts 1876–7
W. Keeping 1877–9
T. S. Humpidge 1879–83
H. J. Fleure 1908–18 (L.)

GEOGRAPHY AND ANTHROPOLOGY

H. J. Fleure 1918–30
C. D. Forde 1930–45
E. G. Bowen 1946–68
C. Kidson (Physical Geography) 1964–
H. Carter (Human Geography) 1968–

GEOLOGY

L. Lyell 1874–5
F. W. Rudler 1875–6
W. Keeping 1876–9
T. S. Humpidge 1879–83
J. R. Ainsworth Davis 1883–91 (L.), 1891–
  1908
O. T. Jones 1909–10 (L.), 1910–19
W. J. Pugh 1919–31
H. P. Lewis 1931–47
A. Wood 1947–
W. Davies (Applied Geology) 1970–

GERMAN

G. Thibaut 1872–5
H. Ethé 1875–1914

M. Brebner 1914–20 (L.)
David Evans 1920–36 (I.L.), 1936–52
C. P. Magill 1952–71
A. R. Robinson 1971–

OLD GERMAN

W. Borsdorf 1894–1903
L. E. Kastner 1903–9

GREEK

T. C. Edwards 1872–91
T. F. Roberts 1891–1909
J. W. Marshall 1909–23
E. D. T. Jenkins 1923–38 (I.L.)

GREEK AND LATIN

E. D. T. Jenkins 1938–47
W. H. Davies 1947–

HEBREW (also ARABIC, SYRIAC,
SANSKRIT, TURKISH, PERSIAN)

G. Thibaut 1872–5
H. Ethé 1875–1914
Norman Jones 1914–16 (L.)

HISTORY

J. Hoskyns-Abrahall 1872–3
J. M. Angus 1873–5
C. J. Cooper 1875–6 (L.)
W. J. Craig 1876–9
M. W. MacCallum 1879–85
J. E. Lloyd 1885–91 (L.), 1891–2
Edward Edwards 1892–5 (L.), 1895–1930
R. F. Treharne 1930–67
S. H. F. Johnston 1967–

COLONIAL HISTORY

T. Stanley Roberts 1915–34
E. Jones Parry 1935–46 (L.)

INTERNATIONAL POLITICS

A. E. Zimmern 1919–21
C. K. Webster 1922–32
Jerome D. Greene 1932–4
E. H. Carr 1936–46
P. A. Reynolds 1950–64
L. W. Martin 1964–8
T. E. Evans 1969–

ITALIAN

G. Thibaut 1872–5
H. Ethé 1875–1900

LATIN

J. Hoskyns-Abrahall 1872–3
J. M. Angus 1873–1905
E. Bensly 1905–19
H. J. Rose 1919–27
J. F. Mountford 1927–32
E. J. Wood 1932–8

LAW

T. A. Levi 1901–40
D. J. Ll. Davies 1940–70
J. A. Andrews 1967–
T. H. Moseley 1970–

CONSTITUTIONAL AND
COMPARATIVE LAW

W. Jethro Brown 1901–6

LIBRARIANS

E. P. Jones 1872–1902
J. D. Williams 1902–32
A. ap Gwynn 1932–68
H. D. Emanuel 1968–70
W. Dieneman 1970–

LOGIC AND PHILOSOPHY

T. C. Edwards 1872–83
J. Brough 1883–5 (L.), 1885–1911

W. Jenkyn Jones 1911–32
R. I. Aaron 1932–69
T. A. Roberts 1969–

MATHEMATICS, NATURAL PHILOSOPHY,
AND ASTRONOMY

H. M. Grimley 1872–9
R. W. Genese 1879–1909

MUSIC

Joseph Parry 1874–80
D. Jenkins 1899–1910 (L.), 1910–15
H. Walford Davies 1919–26
D. J. de Lloyd 1927–48
C. Clements 1948–50 (L.)
H. I. Parrott 1950–

PALAEOGRAPHY AND DIPLOMATICS

E. A. Lewis 1914–42

PHYSICS

F. W. Rudler 1877–9
T. S. Humpidge 1879–84
D. E. Jones 1884–90 (L.), 1891
D. Morgan Lewis 1891–1919
Gwilym Owen 1919–37
E. J. Williams 1938–45
R. M. Davies 1945–6 (Sr.L.), 1946–58
W. J. G. Beynon 1958–
N. D. Twiddy (2nd Chair) 1970–

POLITICAL ECONOMY

C. J. Cooper 1875–6 (L.)
W. J. Craig 1876–9
M. W. MacCallum 1879–85
Edward Edwards 1892–1902 (L.)

POLITICAL SCIENCE

W. Jenkyn Jones 1902–9 (L.), 1909–11
Ivor Gowan 1965–

PURE MATHEMATICS

R. W. Genese 1909–19
W. H. Young 1919–23
G. A. Schott 1923–26
V. C. Morton 1926–33 (I.L.), 1933–61
W. B. Pennington 1961–8
A. O. Morris 1969–

WELSH HISTORY

E. A. Lewis 1931–42
David Williams 1945–67
W. Ogwen Williams 1967–9
I. G. Jones 1970–
T. Jones Pierce (Medieval History) 1945–8
 (S.L.), 1948–64

WELSH LANGUAGE AND LITERATURE

D. Silvan Evans 1875–83
J. E. Lloyd 1885–91 (L.), 1891–2
Edward Anwyl 1892–1914
T. H. Parry-Williams 1920–52
Thomas Jones 1952–69, (Personal Chair)
 1969–70
R. G. Gruffydd 1970–

T. Gwynn Jones (Welsh Liturature) 1913–
 19 (R.), 1919–37
Timothy Lewis (Celtic Philology and
 Palaeography) 1920–42 (R.)
J. E. Caerwyn Williams (Irish) 1965–

WELSH PLANT BREEDING STATION

Directors

R. G. Stapledon 1919–42
T. J. Jenkin 1942–50
E. T. Jones 1950–8
P. T. Thomas 1958–

ZOOLOGY

L. Lyell 1874–5
F. W. Rudler 1875–6
W. Keeping 1876–9
T. S. Humpidge 1879–83
J. R. Ainsworth Davis 1883–91 (L.), 1891–
 1908
H. J. Fleure 1908–10 (L.), 1910–18
R. D. Laurie 1918–22 (I.L.), 1922–40
T. A. Stephenson 1940–61
B. M. Jones 1961–
Miss F. G. Rees (Personal Chair) 1971–

REGISTRARS*

E. P. Jones 1872–92
T. Mortimer Green 1892–1905
J. H. Davies 1905–19

J. Morgan Jones 1936–44
T. Maelgwyn Davies 1944–66
T. Arfon Owen 1967–

*During the years 1919–36, when there was no Registrar, some of the duties of this post
were carried out by:

  (*a*) *a Secretary*
     C. G. Burton 1919–24
     J. L. Newbon 1924–9
     E. B. Hicks 1929–35

  and (*b*) *an Academic Secretary*
     G. J. Walker 1920–36

ABBREVIATIONS

I.L.	Independent Lecturer	R.	Reader
Sr.L.	Senior Lecturer	D.	Director
S.L.	Special Lecturer	A.	Adviser
L.	Lecturer		

Appendix C

PRESIDENTS OF S.R.C.

1900–1	J. R. Johnson	1931–2	I. B. Jones
1901–2	T. J. Rees	1932–3	Jack Moore
1902–3	Towyn Williams	1933–4	Frank R. Lewis
1903–4	D. J. Roberts	1934–5	Lewis Ivor Lewis
1904–5	E. G. Miles	1935–6	R. K. J. Grant
1905–6	O. Arnold Evans	1936–7	W. Lloyd (Mars) Jones
1906–7	C. S. Reed	1937–8	Trevor Lewis
1907–8	Trevor D. Thomas	1938–9	Gwyn Davies
1908–9	R. J. Davies	1939–40	Dyfnallt Morgan
1909–10	D. E. Price	1940–1	Roy Evans
1910–11	W. King	1941–2	Glanmor Williams
1911–12	D. G. Reynolds	1942–3	Miss Agnes Clifford
1912–13	J. F. Powell	1943–4	Tony James
1913–14	Eric Walker	1944–5	Alwyn Williams
1914–15	A. Rowlands	1945–6	K. Protheroe
1915–16	G. R. Lewis (on his enlistment, Glyn Jones)	1946–7	Anthony Cullen
1916–17	B. Rees	1947–8	Dewi Jones (on his resignation, W. J. Anthony-Jones)
1917–18	W. Idris Jones	1948–9	M. Brodie
1918–19	C. Rosebourne	1949–50	Cyril Harris
1919–20	Gethin Williams	1950–1	G. Prys Dafis
1920–1	Tom Hughes Jones	1951–2	John H. Jenkins
1921–2	Tom Jenkins	1952–3	Dewi M. Lloyd
1922–3	Sidney F. Perkins	1953–4	W. R. G. Lewis
1923–4	D. Jeffrey Davies	1954–5	T. Gwynn Jones
1924–5	D. Seaborne Davies	1955–6	Brian Heath
1925–6	A. B. Oldfield Davies	1956–7	J. Derek Pope
1926–7	C. H. Jenkins	1957–8	J. Gwyn Morgan
1927–8	Iwan Morgan	1958–9	John D. Thomas
1928–9	Jack Evans	1959–60	A. G. Hendry
1929–30	C. E. Gittins	1960–1	Aneurin Rhys Hughes
1930–1	T. W. Watkins	1961–2	Hywel Ceri Jones

1962–3	Graham Harrington	1967–8	Roy Widdus
1963–4	Philip Thomas	1968–9	N. Partos
1964–5	Michael Pratley	1969–70	C. R. Loosely
1965–6	Arwel Ellis Owen	1970–1	John Strutte
1966–7	Elgan Edwards	1971–2	Rhys Evans

Appendix D

1892–8 Mr. T. E. Ellis, M.P.	1940 Mr. A. Pinsent
1898–1900 Professor D. E. Jones	1941 Mrs. Myfanwy Ellis
1901 Mr. Edgar Jones	1942 Dr. T. I. Ellis
1902 Mr. D. C. Roberts	1943 Professor T. J. Jenkin
1903 Dr. F. D. Chattaway	1944 Mr. I. C. Jones
1904 Mr. T. R. Dawes	1945 Miss Winifred Hindle
1905 Miss A. M. Dobell	1946 Mr. J. O. Francis
1906 Mr. Austin Keen	1947 Mr. Humphrey D. Roberts
1907 Mr. J. H. Davies	1948 Mr. R. Moelwyn Hughes
1908 Mr. J. Mortimer Angus	1949 Dr. E. Davies-Thomas
1909 Miss C. P. Tremain	1950 Revd. Principal G. A. Edwards
1910 Principal T. F. Roberts	1951 Major Edgar Jones
1911 Dr. T. Campbell James	1952 Professor David Evans
1912 Mrs. T. E. Ellis	1953 Mr. J. W. Fisher
1913 Mr. Thomas Jones	1954 Mr. Tom Owen
1914–19 Professor H. J. Fleure	1955 Dr. Elvet Lewis
1920–2 Mr. H. Howard Humphreys	1956 Dr. T. W. Evans
1923 Professor Olive Wheeler	1957 Professor C. W. Davies
1924 Mr. Jenkin James	1958 Dr. Dilwyn John, C.B.E.
1925 Mr. Jack Edwards	1959 Sir D. Hughes Parry
1926 Professor C. R. Chapple	1960 Mr. Stanley G. Rees
1927 Mrs. E. W. Dobbs	1961 Professor T. Campbell James
1928 Sir E. John Russell, F.R.S.	1962 Sir David L. Evans, O.B.E.
1929 Sir C. Bryner Jones	1963 Professor D. J. Ll. Davies
1930 Dr. William King	1964 Sir W. J. Pugh
1931 Mr. Ernest Evans, M.P.	1965 Dr. W. Idris Jones, C.B.E.
1932 Professor Edward Edwards	1966 Dr. Elwyn Davies
1933 Dr. D. J. Roberts	1967 Dr. William Thomas, C.B.
1934 Dr. J. Davies Bryan	1968 Sir Ben Bowen Thomas
1935 Mr. Howell E. James	1969 Miss R. M. Cohen
1936 Mrs. L. Jameson-Evans	1970 Mr. T. Evans
1937 Major John Edwards	1971 Professor E. G. Bowen
1938 Olive, Baroness Stamp	1972 Miss Mati Rees
1939 Mr. T. Lewis Old	

Appendix E

CÂN COLEG ABERYSTWYTH

English words by J. R. AINSWORTH DAVIS
Welsh version by E. ANWYL
Music by D. JENKINS

1 Yn hy i'r nefoedd wen
   Ein Coleg gŵyd ei ben,
   A'i ieuanc wedd heb arwydd henaint caeth;
   Nid mewn rhyw ddistaw fan,
   Ond draw ar greigiog lan,
   Lle rhua'r don dragwyddol ar y traeth.

   Cytgan
   'Beth yw d'arwyddair di,
   O Goleg ger y lli?'
   'Nid byd byd heb wybodaeth', meddwn ni.
   Rhua, fôr! ei glod yn rhydd,
   Aberystwyth fu a fydd!

2 O lawer gwlad a thref,
   Ei feib a'i ferched ef
   Gaiff aros ennyd wrth dymhestlog fôr.
   Eu gwersi'n gyson wnânt,
   Ond llonder ni chasânt,
   Gan gasglu mwyn atgofion yn ystôr.

3 Ymhell i'r pedwar gwynt,
   Ei blant â ar eu hynt,
   A dysg wasgarant fel y bore wawr.
   O fynydd, rhos, a gwaun,
   A thros y môr ymlaen,
   Eu sanctaidd fflam oleua ddaear lawr.

   Cytgan i'r trydedd pennill
   Boed llon dy oriau di,
   Ein Coleg ger y lli,
   Tra seinia'r stormus don ei chytgan hi.
   Rhua, fôr! ei glod yn rhydd,
   Aberystwyth fu a fydd.

ABERYSTWYTH COLLEGE SONG

1 Some boast their classic stream
Where nymphs and naiads dream,
Their buildings touched by Time till . . ., old and grey;
Our College towers in pride
By the Western waters' side,
Where wild waves vainly beat along the bay.

Chorus

'What may your motto be,
O College by the sea?'
'Nid byd byd heb wybodaeth', answer we.
Rage, ye gales! ye surges, seethe!
Aberystwyth fu a fydd!

2 From near or distant home
Her sons and daughters come,
Awhile to tarry by the wind-swept shore.
Dim midnight oil they burn,
Nor sport and pleasure spurn,
Those days shall dwell in mem'ry evermore.

3 To South, West, East, and North,
Her children travel forth,
Bright kindle learning's torch like morning star,
From mountain, moor, and plain,
Across the purple main,
The *flamma sacra* burns and shines afar.

Chorus for third verse

Fair may your future be,
Our College by the sea,
Where wind and wave make merry minstrelsy.
Rage, ye gales! ye surges, seethe!
Aberystwyth fu a fydd!

Appendix F

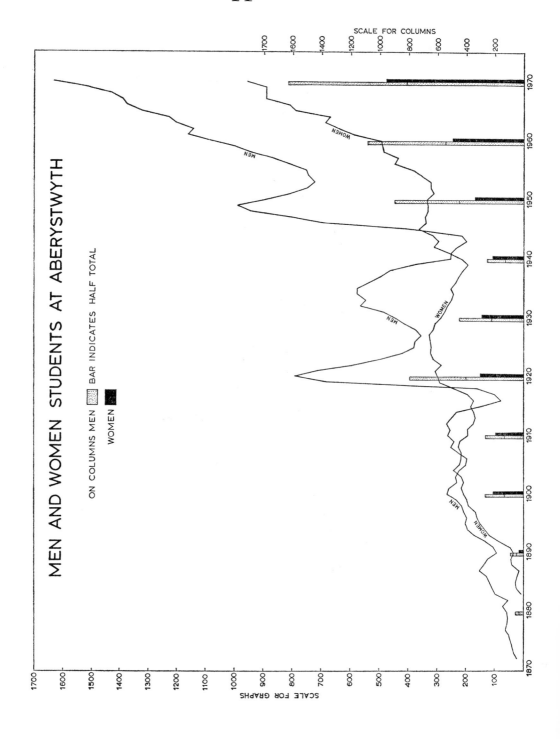

MEN AND WOMEN STUDENTS AT ABERYSTWYTH

Bibliographical Note

THE sources for the history of the University College of Wales are so many and so varied that no one man, no matter how energetic or single-minded he might be, can be certain that he has mastered them all. Who can honestly say that he has plumbed a bottomless pit? One can but tremble for the historian of the College in the future; for with every year that passes, the literature gets dauntingly larger and larger.

The present work would not have been possible had not the College in recent years collected its surviving records in properly organized archives. I am indebted to the heroic labours of Dr. Huw Owen, who collated and arranged the vast mass of papers. There are several hundred large boxes of records, many of them in manuscript, in the College archives, and a hand-list of the papers is available for consultation.

Official papers, however, are not always especially informative; behind the bald statement of the conclusions of a committee there often lies an interesting story or an important difference of opinion over policy. Happily, private collections of papers are usually less cryptic, less discreetly bland, and, therefore, more helpful. Five large collections of manuscripts, all of them deposited in the National Library of Wales, are indispensable for the history of the College. The papers of Lord Rendel provide information about College policy at the highest level over a period of thirty years; and they are supplemented by the Glansevern MSS., the papers of A. C. Humphreys-Owen, which supply valuable corroboration and, occasionally, an alternative opinion on the great issues of much the same time. The manuscripts of J. H. Davies (those so entitled, as well as the Cwrt Mawr collection) are useful, but it is disappointing to find so many *lacunae* in the papers of so renowned a bibliophile and collector of manuscripts. The marvellous richness of the Thomas Jones papers will be evident to the reader. Much of such merit as this book possesses is derived from that source. This collection is still under restriction, and I am deeply indebted to Lady Eirene White and Mr. Tristan Jones for allowing me to see and to use the many volumes of the papers of their father which relate to Wales. The whole collection has been arranged (predictably, a model of its kind) by my friend and former fellow student at Aberystwyth, Professor Gwyn A. Williams. At almost the eleventh hour several large boxes of the papers of Lord Davies (designated the Llandinam MSS.) became available. I am grateful to the Hon. Islwyn Davies, Treasurer of the College, for the opportunity to make use of this important source. Lord Davies' racy letters are a delight and present a fine picture of a fascinating man. I am also grateful to Mrs. K. Idwal Jones for allowing me to see the papers (Penucha MSS.), in her possession, of her father, Sir J. Herbert Lewis, M.P.

One printed source is outstandingly useful: *T. C. Edwards Letters*, the correspondence of the first Principal of the College so ably transcribed by the late Dr. T. I. Ellis, whose pioneering work in this and other aspects of the history of the College lightened my labours. The other sources used are fully detailed in the footnotes: for reasons of space and economy, they are not listed again here. At a later date, it may be possible to publish a comprehensive annotated bibliography.

Index

Numerals followed by the letter 'n' denote references to subject-matter included in the footnotes. Bibliographical citations in the footnotes are not included in the index.